MW01255924

introduction to computing systems

third edition

introduction to computing systems

from bits & gates to C/C++ & beyond

Yale N. Patt
The University of Texas at Austin

Sanjay J. Patel
University of Illinois at Urbana-Champaign

INTRODUCTION TO COMPUTING SYSTEMS
Published by McGraw-Hill Education, 2 Penn Plaza, New York, NY 10121. Copyright ©2020 by McGraw-Hill Education. All rights reserved. Printed in the United States of America. No part of this publication may be reproduced or distributed in any form or by any means, or stored in a database or retrieval system, without the prior written consent of McGraw-Hill Education, including, but not limited to, in any network or other electronic storage or transmission, or broadcast for distance learning.

Some ancillaries, including electronic and print components, may not be available to customers outside the United States.

This book is printed on acid-free paper.

1 2 3 4 5 6 7 8 9 LCR 24 23 22 21 20 19

ISBN 978-1-260-56591-1
MHID 1-260-56591-2

Cover Image: *Front Cover Computing art ©Yale N. Patt; Abstract image in green, orange and yellow ©Design Pics/Tim Antoniuk; Abstract image in orange, green and yellow ©Design Pics/Tim Antoniuk; Computer laptops on a blue abstract background ©loops7/ Getty Images; Illustration of streams of binary code ©Shutterstock/Tavarius*

All credits appearing on page or at the end of the book are considered to be an extension of the copyright page.

The Internet addresses listed in the text were accurate at the time of publication. The inclusion of a website does not indicate an endorsement by the authors or McGraw-Hill Education, and McGraw-Hill Education does not guarantee the accuracy of the information presented at these sites.

mheducation.com/highered

To the memory of my parents,
Abraham Walter Patt A"H and Sarah Clara Patt A"H,
who taught me to value "learning"
even before they taught me to ride a bicycle.

To my loving family,
Amita, Kavi, and Aman.

Contents

Preface

Finally, the third edition! We must first thank all those who have been pushing us to produce a third edition. Since the publication of the second edition was so long ago, clearly the material must be out of date. Wrong! Fundamentals do not change very often, and our intent continues to be to provide a book that explains the fundamentals clearly in the belief that if the fundamentals are mastered, there is no limit to how high one can soar if one's talent and focus are equal to the task.

We must also apologize that it took so long to produce this revision. Please know that the delay in no way reflects any lack of enthusiasm on our part. We are both as passionate about the foundation of computing today as we were 25 years ago when we overhauled the first course in computing that eventually became the first edition of this book. Indeed, we have both continued to teach the course regularly. And, as expected, each time we teach, we develop new insights as to what to teach, new examples to explain things, and new ways to look at things. The result of all this, hopefully, is that we have captured this in the third edition.

It is a pleasure to finally be writing this preface. We have received an enormous number of comments from students who have studied the material in the book and from instructors who have taught from it. It is gratifying to know that a lot of people agree with our approach, and that this agreement is based on real firsthand experience learning from it (in the case of students) and watching students learn from it (in the case of instructors). The excitement displayed in their correspondence continues to motivate us.

Why the Book Happened

This textbook evolved from EECS 100, the first computing course for computer science, computer engineering, and electrical engineering majors at the University of Michigan, Ann Arbor, that Kevin Compton and the first author introduced for the first time in the fall term, 1995.

EECS 100 happened at Michigan because Computer Science and Engineering faculty had been dissatisfied for many years with the lack of student comprehension of some very basic concepts. For example, students had a lot of trouble with pointer variables. Recursion seemed to be "magic," beyond understanding.

We decided in 1993 that the conventional wisdom of starting with a high-level programming language, which was the way we (and most universities) were doing it, had its shortcomings. We decided that the reason students were not getting it was that they were forced to memorize technical details when they did not understand the basic underpinnings.

Our result was the bottom-up approach taken in this book, where we continually build on what the student already knows, only memorizing when absolutely necessary. We did not endorse then and we do not endorse now the popular information hiding approach when it comes to learning. Information hiding is a useful productivity enhancement technique after one understands what is going on. But until one gets to that point, we insist that information hiding gets in the way of understanding. Thus, we continually build on what has gone before so that nothing is magic and everything can be tied to the foundation that has already been laid.

We should point out that we do not disagree with the notion of top-down *design*. On the contrary, we believe strongly that top-down design is correct design. But there is a clear difference between how one approaches a design problem (after one understands the underlying building blocks) and what it takes to get to the point where one does understand the building blocks. In short, we believe in top-down design, but bottom-up learning for understanding.

Major Changes in the Third Edition

The LC-3

A hallmark of our book continues to be the LC-3 ISA, which is small enough to be described in a few pages and hopefully mastered in a very short time, yet rich enough to convey the essence of what an ISA provides. It is the LC "3" because it took us three tries to get it right. Four tries, actually, but the two changes in the LC-3 ISA since the second edition (i.e., changes to the LEA instruction and to the TRAP instruction) are so minor that we decided not to call the slightly modified ISA the LC-4.

The LEA instruction no longer sets condition codes. It used to set condition codes on the mistaken belief that since LEA stands for Load Effective Address, it should set condition codes like LD, LDI, and LDR do. We recognize now that this reason was silly. LD, LDI, and LDR load a register from memory, and so the condition codes provide useful information – whether the value loaded is negative, zero, or positive. LEA loads an address into a register, and for that, the condition codes do not really provide any value. Legacy code written before this change should still run correctly.

The TRAP instruction no longer stores the linkage back to the calling program in R7. Instead, the PC and PSR are pushed onto the system stack and popped by the RTI instruction (renamed Return from Trap or Interrupt) as the last instruction in a trap routine. Trap routines now execute in privileged memory (x0000 to x2FFF). This change allows trap routines to be re-entrant. It does not affect old code provided the starting address of the trap service routines, obtained from the Trap Vector Table, is in privileged memory and the terminating instruction of each trap service routine is changed from RET to RTI.

As before, Appendix A specifies the LC-3 completely.

The Addition of C++

We've had an ongoing debate about how to extend our approach and textbook to C++. One of the concerns about C++ is that many of its language features are too far abstracted from the underlying layers to make for an easy fit to our approach. Another concern is that C++ is such a vast language that any adequate coverage would require an additional thousand pages. We also didn't want to drop C completely, as it serves as a de facto development language for systems and hardware-oriented projects.

We adopted an approach where we cover the common core of C and C++ from Chapters 11 through 19. This common core is similar to what was covered in the second edition, with some minor updates. Chapter 20 serves as a transition, which we aspired to make very smooth, to the core concepts of C++. With this approach, we get to explore the evolution between C and C++, which serves as a key learning opportunity on what changes were essential to boost programmer productivity.

In particular, we focus on classes in C++ as an evolution from structures in C. We discuss classes as a compiler construct, how method calls are made, and the notion of constructors. We touch upon inheritance, too, but leave the details for subsequent treatment in follow-on courses.

An important element of C++ is the introduction of container classes in the Standard Template Library, which is a heavily utilized part of the C++ language. This provides an opportunity to dive deep into the vector class, which serves as a continuation of a running example in the second half around the support for variable-sized arrays in high-level languages, or in particular, C's lack of support for them.

Other Important Updates

Although no chapter in the book has remained untouched, some chapters have been changed more than others. In Chapter 2, we expanded the coverage of the floating point data type and the conversion of fractions between decimal and binary numbers in response to several instructors who wanted them. We moved DeMorgan's Laws from Chapter 3 to Chapter 2 because the concept is really about AND and OR functions and not about digital logic implementation. In Chapter 3, we completely overhauled the description of state, latches, flip-flops, finite state machines, and our example of a danger sign. We felt the explanations in the second edition were not as clear as they needed to be, and the concepts are too important to not get right. We revised Chapter 4 to better introduce the LC-3, including a different set of instructions, leading to our first complete example of a computer program.

Our organization of Chapters 8, 9, and 10 was completely overhauled in order to present essentially the same material in a more understandable way. Although most of our treatment of data structures waits until we have introduced C in the second half of the book, we felt it was important to introduce stacks, queues, and character strings as soon as the students have moved out of programming in machine language so they can write programs dealing with these data structures and see how these structures are actually organized in memory. We moved our discussion of subroutines up to Chapter 8 because of their importance in constructing richer programs.

We also introduced recursion in Chapter 8, although its main treatment is still left for the second half of the book. Both the expressive power of recursion and its misuse are so common in undergraduate curricula that we felt dealing with it twice, first while they are engrossed in the bowels of assembly language and again after moving up to the richness of C, was worthwhile.

Chapter 9 now covers all aspects of I/O in one place, including polling and interrupt-driven I/O. Although the concept of privilege is present in the second edition, we have put greater emphasis on it in the third edition. Our coverage of system calls (the trap routines invoked by the TRAP instruction) appears in Chapter 9. All of the above reduce Chapter 10 to simply a comprehensive example that pulls together a lot of the first half of the book: the simulation of a calculator. Doing so requires 12 subroutines that are laid out in complete detail. Two concepts that are needed to make this happen are stack arithmetic and ASCII/binary conversion, so they are included in Chapter 10.

We reworked all the examples in Chapters 11 through 19 to use the latest ANSI Standard C or C18. We also added more coding examples to further emphasize points and to provide clarity on complex topics such as pointers, arrays, recursion, and pointers to pointers in C. In Chapter 16, we added additional sections on variable-sized arrays in C, and on multidimensional arrays.

Chapter Organization

The book breaks down into two major segments, (a) the underlying structure of a computer, as manifested in the LC-3; and (b) programming in a high-level language, in our case C and C++.

The LC-3

We start with the underpinnings that are needed to understand the workings of a real computer. Chapter 2 introduces the bit and arithmetic and logical operations on bits. Then we begin to build the structure needed to understand the LC-3. Chapter 3 takes the student from an MOS transistor, step by step, to a "real" memory and a finite state machine.

Our real memory consists of four words of three bits each, rather than 16 gigabytes, which is common in most laptops today. Its description fits on a single page (Figure 3.20), making it easy for a student to grasp. By the time students get there, they have been exposed to all the elements needed to construct the memory. The finite state machine is needed to understand how a computer processes instructions, starting in Chapter 4. Chapter 4 introduces the von Neumann execution model and enough LC-3 instructions to allow an LC-3 program to be written. Chapter 5 introduces most of the rest of the LC-3 ISA.

The LC-3 is a 16-bit architecture that includes physical I/O via keyboard and monitor, TRAPs to the operating system for handling service calls, conditional branches on (N, Z, and P) condition codes, a subroutine call/return mechanism, a minimal set of operate instructions (ADD, AND, and NOT), and various addressing modes for loads and stores (direct, indirect, Base+offset).

Chapter 6 is devoted to programming methodology (stepwise refinement) and debugging, and Chapter 7 is an introduction to assembly language programming. We have developed a simulator and an assembler for the LC-3 that runs on Windows, Linux, and MacOS platforms. It can be downloaded from the web at no charge.

Students use the simulator to test and debug programs written in LC-3 machine language and in LC-3 assembly language. The simulator allows online debugging (deposit, examine, single-step, set breakpoint, and so on). The simulator can be used for simple LC-3 machine language and assembly language programming assignments, which are essential for students to master the concepts presented throughout the first ten chapters.

Assembly language is taught, but not to train expert assembly language programmers. Indeed, if the purpose was to train assembly language programmers, the material would be presented in an upper-level course, not in an introductory course for freshmen. Rather, the material is presented in Chapter 7 because it is consistent with the paradigm of the book. In our bottom-up approach, by the time the student reaches Chapter 7, he/she can handle the process of transforming assembly language programs to sequences of 0s and 1s. We go through the process of assembly step by step for a very simple LC-3 Assembler. By hand assembling, the student (at a very small additional cost in time) reinforces the important fundamental concept of translation.

It is also the case that assembly language provides a user-friendly notation to describe machine instructions, something that is particularly useful for writing programs in Chapters 8, 9, and 10, and for providing many of the explanations in the second half of the book. Starting in Chapter 11, when we teach the semantics of C statements, it is far easier for the reader to deal with ADD R1, R2, R3 than to have to struggle with 0001001010000011.

Chapter 8 introduces three important data structures: the stack, the queue, and the character string, and shows how they are stored in memory. The subroutine call/return mechanism of the LC-3 is presented because of its usefulness both in manipulating these data structures and in writing programs. We also introduce recursion, a powerful construct that we revisit much more thoroughly in the second half of the book (in Chapter 17), after the student has acquired a much stronger capability in high-level language programming. We introduce recursion here to show by means of a few examples the execution-time tradeoffs incurred with recursion as a first step in understanding when its use makes sense and when it doesn't.

Chapter 9 deals with input/output and some basic interaction between the processor and the operating system. We introduce the notions of priority and privilege, which are central to a systems environment. Our treatment of I/O is all physical, using keyboard data and status registers for input and display data and status registers for output. We describe both interrupt-driven I/O and I/O under program control. Both are supported by our LC-3 simulator so the student can write interrupt drivers. Finally, we show the actual LC-3 code of the trap service routines that the student has invoked with the TRAP instruction starting in Chapter 4. To handle interrupt-driven I/O and trap service routines, we complete the description of the LC-3 ISA with details of the operation of the Return from Trap or Interrupt (RTI) and TRAP instructions.

The first half of the book concludes with Chapter 10, a comprehensive example of a simple calculator that pulls together a lot of what the students have learned in Chapters 1 through 9.

Programming in C and C++

By the time the student gets to the second part of the textbook, he/she has an understanding of the layers below. In our coverage of programming in C and C++, we leverage this foundation by showing the resulting LC-3 code generated by a compiler with each new concept in C/C++.

We start with the C language because it provides the common, essential core with C++. The C programming language fits very nicely with our bottom-up approach. Its low-level nature allows students to see clearly the connection between software and the underlying hardware. In this book, we focus on basic concepts such as control structures, functions, and arrays. Once basic programming concepts are mastered, it is a short step for students to learn more advanced concepts such as objects and abstraction in C++.

Each time a new high-level construct is introduced, the student is shown the LC-3 code that a compiler would produce. We cover the basic constructs of C (variables, operators, control, and functions), pointers, arrays, recursion, I/O, complex data structures, and dynamic allocation. With C++, we cover some basic improvements over C, classes, and containers.

Chapter 11 is a gentle introduction to high-level programming languages. At this point, students have dealt heavily with assembly language and can understand the motivation behind what high-level programming languages provide. Chapter 11 also contains a simple C program, which we use to kick-start the process of learning C.

Chapter 12 deals with values, variables, constants, and operators. Chapter 13 introduces C control structures. We provide many complete program examples to give students a sample of how each of these concepts is used in practice. LC-3 code is used to demonstrate how each C construct affects the machine at the lower levels.

Chapter 14 introduces functions in C. Students are not merely exposed to the syntax of functions. Rather they learn how functions are actually executed, with argument-passing using a run-time stack. A number of examples are provided.

In Chapter 15, students are exposed to techniques for testing their code, along with debugging high-level source code. The ideas of white-box and black-box testing are discussed.

Chapter 16 teaches pointers and arrays, relying heavily on the student's understanding of how memory is organized. We discuss C's notions of fixed size and variable-length arrays, along with multidimensional array allocation.

Chapter 17 teaches recursion, using the student's newly gained knowledge of functions, stack frames, and the run-time stack. Chapter 18 introduces the details of I/O functions in C, in particular, streams, variable length argument lists, and how C I/O is affected by the various format specifications. This chapter relies on the student's earlier exposure to physical I/O in Chapter 8. Chapter 19 discusses structures in C, dynamic memory allocation, and linked lists.

Chapter 20 provides a jump-start on C++ programming by discussing its roots in C and introducing the idea of classes as a natural evolution from structures. We also cover the idea of containers in the standard template library, to enable students to quickly jump into productive programming with C++.

Along the way, we have tried to emphasize good programming style and coding methodology by means of examples. Novice programmers probably learn at least as much from the programming examples they read as from the rules they are forced to study. Insights that accompany these examples are highlighted by means of lightbulb icons that are included in the margins.

We have found that the concept of pointer variables (Chapter 16) is not at all a problem. By the time students encounter it, they have a good understanding of what memory is all about, since they have analyzed the logic design of a small memory (Chapter 3). They know the difference, for example, between a memory location's address and the data stored there.

Recursion ceases to be magic since, by the time a student gets to that point (Chapter 17), he/she has already encountered all the underpinnings. Students understand how stacks work at the machine level (Chapter 8), and they understand the call/return mechanism from their LC-3 machine language programming experience, and the need for linkages between a called program and the return to the caller (Chapter 8). From this foundation, it is not a large step to explain functions by introducing run-time stack frames (Chapter 14), with a lot of the mystery about argument passing, dynamic declarations, and so on, going away. Since a function can call a function, it is one additional small step (certainly no magic involved) for a function to call itself.

The Simulator/Debugger

The importance of the Simulator/Debugger for testing the programs a student writes cannot be overemphasized. We believe strongly that there is no substitute for hands-on practice testing one's knowledge. It is incredibly fulfilling to a student's education to write a program that does not work, testing it to find out why it does not work, fixing the bugs himself/herself, and then seeing the program run correctly. To that end, the Simulator/Debugger has been completely rewritten. It runs on Windows, Linux, and MacOS while presenting the same user interface (GUI) regardless of which platform the student is using. We have improved our incorporation of interrupt-driven I/O into the Simulator's functionality so students can easily write interrupt drivers and invoke them by interrupting a lower priority executing program. ...in their first course in computing!

Alternate Uses of the Book

We wrote the book as a textbook for a freshman introduction to computing. We strongly believe that our motivated bottom-up approach is the best way for students to learn the fundamentals of computing. We have seen lots of evidence showing that in general, students who understand the fundamentals of how the computer works are better able to grasp the stuff that they encounter later, including the high-level programming languages that they must work in, and that they can learn the rules of these programming languages with far less memorizing because everything makes sense. For us, the best use of the book is a one-semester freshman course for particularly motivated students, or a two-semester sequence where the pace is tempered.

Having said that, we recognize that others see the curriculum differently. Thus, we hasten to add that the book can certainly be used effectively in other ways. In fact, each of the following has been tried, and all have been used successfully:

Two Quarters, Freshman Course

An excellent use of the book. No prerequisites, the entire book can be covered easily in two quarters, the first quarter for Chapters 1–10, the second quarter for Chapters 11–20. The pace is brisk, but the entire book can be covered easily in two academic quarters.

One-Semester, Second Course

Several schools have successfully used the book in their second course, after the students have been exposed to programming with an object-oriented programming language in a milder first course. The rationale is that after exposure to high-level language programming in the first course, the second course should treat at an introductory level digital logic, basic computer organization, and assembly language programming. The first two-thirds of the semester is spent on Chapters 1–10, and the last third on Chapters 11–20, teaching C programming, but also showing how some of the magic from the students' first course can be implemented. Coverage of functions, activation records, recursion, pointer variables, and data structures are examples of topics where getting past the magic is particularly useful. The second half of the book can move more quickly since the student has already taken an introductory programming course. This model also allows students who were introduced to programming with an object-oriented language to pick up C, which they will almost certainly need in some of their advanced software courses.

A Sophomore-Level Computer Organization Course

The book has been used to delve deeply into computer implementation in the sophomore year. The semester is spent in Chapters 1 through 10, often culminating in a thorough study of Appendix C, which provides the complete microarchitecture of a microprogrammed LC-3. We note, however, that some very important ideas in computer architecture are not covered in the book, most notably cache memory, pipelining, and virtual memory. Instructors using the book this way are encouraged to provide extra handouts dealing with those topics. We agree that they are very important to the student's computer architecture education, but we feel they are better suited to a later course in computer architecture and design. This book is not intended for that purpose.

Why LC-3, and Not ARM or RISCV?

We have been asked why we invented the LC-3 ISA, rather than going with ARM, which seems to be the ISA of choice for most mobile devices, or RISCV, which has attracted substantial interest over the last few years.

There are many reasons. First, we knew that the ISA we selected would be the student's first ISA, not his/her last ISA. Between the freshman year and graduation, the student is likely to encounter several ISAs, most of which are in commercial products: ARM, RISCV, x86, and POWER, to name a few.

But all the commercial ISAs have details that have no place in an introductory course but still have to be understood for the student to use them effectively. We could, of course, have subset an existing ISA, but that always ends up in questions of what to take out and what to leave in with a result that is not as clean as one would think at first blush. Certainly not as clean as what one can get when starting from scratch. It also creates an issue whenever the student uses an instruction in an exam or on an assignment that is not in the subset. Not very clean from a pedagogical sense.

We wanted an ISA that was clean with no special cases to deal with, with as few opcodes as necessary so the student could spend almost all his/her time on the fundamental concepts in the course and very little time on the nuances of the instruction set. The formats of all instructions in the LC-3 fit on a single page. Appendix A provides all the details (i.e., the complete data sheet) of the entire LC-3 ISA in 25 pages.

We also wanted an instruction set that in addition to containing only a few instructions was very rich in the breadth of what it embraced. So, we came up with the LC-3, an instruction set with only 15 four-bit opcodes, a small enough number that students can absorb the ISA without even trying. For arithmetic, we have only ADD instead of ADD, SUB, MUL, and DIV. For logical operations, we have AND and NOT, foregoing OR, XOR, etc. We have no shift or rotate instructions. In all these cases, the missing opcodes can be implemented with procedures using the few opcodes that the LC-3 provides. We have loads and stores with three different addressing modes, each addressing mode useful for a different purpose. We have conditional branches, subroutine calls, return from trap or interrupt, and system calls (the TRAP instruction).

In fact, this sparse set of opcodes is a feature! It drives home the need for creating more complex functionality out of simple operations, and the need for abstraction, both of which are core concepts in the book.

Most importantly, we have found from discussions with hundreds of students that starting with the LC-3 does not put them at a disadvantage in later courses. On the contrary: For example, at one campus students were introduced to ARM in the follow-on course, while at another campus, students were introduced to x86.

In both cases, students appreciated starting with the LC-3, and their subsequent introduction to ARM or x86 was much easier as a result of their first learning the fundamental concepts with the LC-3.

A Few Observations

Having now taught the course more than 20 times between us, we note the following:

Understanding, Not Memorizing

Since the course builds from the bottom up, we have found that less memorization of seemingly arbitrary rules is required than in traditional programming courses. Students understand that the rules make sense since by the time a topic is taught, they have an awareness of how that topic is implemented at the levels below it. This approach is good preparation for later courses in design, where understanding of and insights gained from fundamental underpinnings are essential to making the required design tradeoffs.

The Student Debugs the Student's Program

We hear complaints from industry all the time about CS graduates not being able to program. Part of the problem is the helpful teaching assistant, who contributes far too much of the intellectual content of the student's program so the student never has to really master the art. Our approach is to push the student to do the job without the teaching assistant (TA). Part of this comes from the bottom-up approach, where memorizing is minimized and the student builds on what he/she already knows. Part of this is the simulator, which the student uses from the day he/she writes his/her first program. The student is taught debugging from his/her first program and is required from the very beginning to use the debugging tools of the simulator to get his/her programs to work. The combination of the simulator and the order in which the subject material is taught results in students actually debugging their own programs instead of taking their programs to the TA for help ... with the too-frequent result that the TAs end up writing the programs for the students.

Preparation for the Future: Cutting Through Protective Layers

Professionals who use computers in systems today but remain ignorant of what is going on underneath are likely to discover the hard way that the effectiveness of their solutions is impacted adversely by things other than the actual programs they write. This is true for the sophisticated computer programmer as well as the sophisticated engineer.

Serious programmers will write more efficient code if they understand what is going on beyond the statements in their high-level language. Engineers, and not just computer engineers, are having to interact with their computer systems today more and more at the device or pin level. In systems where the computer is being used to sample data from some metering device such as a weather meter or feed-back control system, the engineer needs to know more than just how to program in MATLAB. This is true of mechanical, chemical, and aeronautical engineers today, not just electrical engineers. Consequently, the high-level programming language course, where the compiler protects the student from everything "ugly" underneath, does not serve most engineering students well, and it certainly does not prepare them for the future.

Rippling Effects Through the Curriculum

The material of this text clearly has a rippling effect on what can be taught in subsequent courses. Subsequent programming courses can not only assume the students know the syntax of C/C++ but also understand how it relates to the underlying architecture. Consequently, the focus can be on problem solving and more sophisticated data structures. On the hardware side, a similar effect is seen in courses in digital logic design and in computer organization. Students start the logic design course with an appreciation of what the logic circuits they master are good for. In the computer organization course, the starting point is much further along than when students are seeing the term Program Counter for the first time. Faculty members who have taught the follow-on courses have noticed substantial improvement in students' comprehension compared to what they saw before students took our course.

Acknowledgments

It's been 15 years since the second edition came out, and about 20 years since we first put together a course pack of notes that eventually morphed into the first edition. Through those years, a good number of people have jumped in, volunteered help, adopted the book, read through drafts, suggested improvements, and so on. We could easily fill many pages if we listed all their names. We are indebted to each of them, and we deeply appreciate their contributions.

Still, there are some folks we feel compelled to acknowledge here, and we apologize to all those who have helped immeasurably, but are not mentioned here due to space limitations.

First, Professor Kevin Compton. Kevin believed in the concept of the book since it was first introduced at a curriculum committee meeting that he chaired at Michigan in 1993. Kevin co-taught the course at Michigan the first four times it was offered, in 1995–1997. His insights into programming methodology (independent of the syntax of the particular language) provided a sound foundation for the beginning student. The course at Michigan and this book would be a lot less were it not for Kevin's influence.

Several colleagues and students were our major go-to guys when it came to advice, and insights, on the current version of the book and its future. Wen-mei Hwu, Veynu Narasiman, Steve Lumetta, Matt Frank, Faruk Guvinilir,

Chirag Sakuja, Siavash Zanganeh, Stephen Pruett, Jim Goodman, and Soner Onder have been particularly important to us since the second edition.

McGraw-Hill has been an important partner in this undertaking, starting with Betsy Jones, our first editor. We sent the manuscript of our first edition to several publishers and were delighted with the many positive responses. Nonetheless, one editor stood out. Betsy immediately checked us out, and once she was satisfied, she became a strong believer in what we were trying to accomplish. Throughout the process of the first two editions, her commitment and energy, as well as that of Michelle Flomenhoft, our first development editor, were greatly appreciated. Fifteen years is a long time between editions, and with it have come a whole new collection of folks from McGraw-Hill that we have recently been privileged to work with, especially Dr. Thomas Scaife, Suzy Bainbridge, Heather Ervolino, and Jeni McAtee.

Our book has benefited from extensive comments by faculty members from many universities. Some were in formal reviews of the manuscript, others in e-mails or conversations at technical conferences. We gratefully acknowledge input from Professors Jim Goodman, Wisconsin and Aukland; Soner Onder, Michigan Tech; Vijay Pai, Purdue; Richard Johnson, Western New Mexico; Tore Larsen, Tromso; Greg Byrd, NC State; Walid Najjar, UC Riverside; Sean Joyce, Heidelberg College; James Boettler, South Carolina State; Steven Zeltmann, Arkansas; Mike McGregor, Alberta; David Lilja, Minnesota; Eric Thompson, Colorado, Denver; Brad Hutchings, Brigham Young; Carl D. Crane III, Florida; Nat Davis, Virginia Tech; Renee Elio, University of Alberta; Kelly Flangan, BYU; George Friedman, UIUC; Franco Fummi, Universita di Verona; Dale Grit, Colorado State; Thor Guisrud, Stavanger College; Dave Kaeli, Northeastern; Rasool Kenarangui, UT, Arlington; Joel Kraft, Case Western Reserve; Wei-Ming Lin, UT, San Antonio; Roderick Loss, Montgomery College; Ron Meleshko, Grant MacEwan Community College; Andreas Moshovos, Toronto; Tom Murphy, The Citadel; Murali Narayanan, Kansas State; Carla Purdy, Cincinnati; T. N. Rajashekhara, Camden County College; Nello Scarabottolo, Universita degli Studi di Milano; Robert Schaefer, Daniel Webster College; Tage Stabell-Kuloe, University of Tromsoe; Jean-Pierre Steger, Burgdorf School of Engineering; Bill Sverdlik, Eastern Michigan; John Trono, St. Michael's College; Murali Varansi, University of South Florida; Montanez Wade, Tennessee State; Carl Wick, US Naval Academy; Robert Crisp, Arkansas; Allen Tannenbaum, Georgia Tech; Nickolas Jovanovic, Arkansas–Little Rock; Dean Brock, North Carolina–Asheville; Amar Raheja, Cal State–Pomona; Dayton Clark, Brooklyn College; William Yurcik, Illinois State; Jose Delgado-Frias, Washington State; Peter Drexel, Plymouth State; Mahmoud Manzoul, Jackson State; Dan Connors, Colorado; Massoud Ghyam, USC; John Gray, UMass–Dartmouth; John Hamilton, Auburn; Alan Rosenthal, Toronto; and Ron Taylor, Wright State.

We have continually been blessed with enthusiastic, knowledgeable, and caring TAs who regularly challenge us and provide useful insights into helping us explain things better. Again, the list is too long – more than 100 at this point. Almost all were very good; still, we want to mention a few who were particularly helpful. Stephen Pruett, Siavash Zangeneh, Meiling Tang, Ali Fakhrzadehgan, Sabee Grewal, William Hoenig, Matthew Normyle, Ben Lin, Ameya Chaudhari,

Nikhil Garg, Lauren Guckert, Jack Koenig, Saijel Mokashi, Sruti Nuthalapati, Faruk Guvenilir, Milad Hashemi, Aater Suleman, Chang Joo Lee, Bhargavi Narayanasetty, RJ Harden, Veynu Narasiman, Eiman Ebrahimi, Khubaib, Allison Korczynski, Pratyusha Nidamaluri, Christopher Wiley, Cameron Davison, Lisa de la Fuente, Phillip Duran, Jose Joao, Rustam Miftakhutdinov, Nady Obeid, Linda Bigelow, Jeremy Carillo, Aamir Hasan, Basit Sheik, Erik Johnson, Tsung-Wei Huang, Matthew Potok, Chun-Xun Lin, Jianxiong Gao, Danny Kim, and Iou-Jen Liu.

Several former students, former colleagues, and friends reviewed chapters in the book. We particularly wish to thank Rich Belgard, Alba Cristina de Melo, Chirag Sakhuja, Sabee Grewal, Pradip Bose, and Carlos Villavieja for their help doing this. Their insights have made a much more readable version of the material.

We have been delighted by the enthusiastic response of our colleagues at both The University of Texas at Austin and the University of Illinois, Urbana-Champaign, who have taught from the book and shared their insights with us: Derek Chiou, Jacob Abraham, Ramesh Yerraballi, Nina Telang, and Aater Suleman at Texas, and Yuting Chen, Sayan Mitra, Volodymyr Kindratenko, Yih-Chun Hu, Seth Hutchinson, Steve Lumetta, Juan Jaramillo, Pratik Lahiri, and Wen-mei Hwu at Illinois. Thank you.

Also, there are those who have contributed in many different and often unique ways. Space dictates that we leave out the detail and simply list them and say thank you. Amanda, Bryan, and Carissa Hwu, Mateo Valero, Rich Belgard, Aman Aulakh, Minh Do, Milena Milenkovic, Steve Lumetta, Brian Evans, Jon Valvano, Susan Kornfield, Ed DeFranco, Evan Gsell, Tom Conte, Dave Nagle, Bruce Shriver, Bill Sayle, Dharma Agarwal, David Lilja, Michelle Chapman.

Finally, if you will indulge the first author a bit: This book is about developing a strong foundation in the fundamentals with the fervent belief that once that is accomplished, students can go as far as their talent and energy can take them. This objective was instilled in me by the professor who taught me how to be a professor, Professor William K. Linvill. It has been more than 50 years since I was in his classroom, but I still treasure the example he set.

A Final Word

We are hopeful that you will enjoy teaching or studying from this third edition of our book. However, as we said in the prefaces to both previous editions, we are mindful that the current version of the book will always be a work in progress, and both of us welcome your comments on any aspect of it. You can reach us by email at patt@ece.utexas.edu and sjp@illinois.edu. We hope you will.

Yale N. Patt
Sanjay J. Patel
September, 2019

CHAPTER

1 Welcome Aboard

1.1 What We Will Try to Do

Welcome to *From Bits and Gates to C and Beyond*. Our intent is to introduce you over the next xxx pages to the world of computing. As we do so, we have one objective above all others: to show you very clearly that there is no magic to computing. The computer is a deterministic system—every time we hit it over the head in the same way and in the same place (provided, of course, it was in the same starting condition), we get the same response. The computer is not an electronic genius; on the contrary, if anything, it is an electronic idiot, doing exactly what we tell it to do. It has no mind of its own.

What appears to be a very complex organism is really just a very large, systematically interconnected collection of very simple parts. Our job throughout this book is to introduce you to those very simple parts and, step-by-step, build the interconnected structure that you know by the name *computer*. Like a house, we will start at the bottom, construct the foundation first, and then go on to add layer after layer, as we get closer and closer to what most people know as a full-blown computer. Each time we add a layer, we will explain what we are doing, tying the new ideas to the underlying fabric. Our goal is that when we are done, you will be able to write programs in a computer language such as C using the sophisticated features of that language and to understand what is going on underneath, inside the computer.

1.2 How We Will Get There

We will start (in Chapter 2) by first showing that any information processed by the computer is represented by a sequence of 0s and 1s. That is, we will encode all information as sequences of 0s and 1s. For example, one encoding of the letter *a* that is commonly used is the sequence 01100001. One encoding of the decimal number *35* is the sequence 00100011. We will see how to perform operations on such encoded information.

Once we are comfortable with information represented as codes made up of 0s and 1s and operations (addition, for example) being performed on these representations, we will begin the process of showing how a computer works. Starting in Chapter 3, we will note that the computer is a piece of electronic equipment and, as such, consists of electronic parts operated by voltages and interconnected by wires. Every wire in the computer, at every moment in time, is at either a high voltage or a low voltage. For our representation of 0s and 1s, we do not specify exactly how high. We only care whether there is or is not a large enough voltage relative to 0 volts to identify it as a 1. That is, the absence or presence of a reasonable voltage relative to 0 volts is what determines whether it represents the value 0 or the value 1.

In Chapter 3, we will see how the transistors that make up today's microprocessor (the heart of the modern computer) work. We will further see how those transistors are combined into larger structures that perform operations, such as addition, and into structures that allow us to save information for later use. In Chapter 4, we will combine these larger structures into the von Neumann machine, a basic model that describes how a computer works. We will also begin to study a simple computer, the LC-3. We will continue our study of the LC-3 in Chapter 5. *LC-3* stands for Little Computer 3. We actually started with LC-1 but needed two more shots at it before (we think) we got it right! The LC-3 has all the important characteristics of the microprocessors that you may have already heard of, for example, the Intel 8088, which was used in the first IBM PCs back in 1981. Or the Motorola 68000, which was used in the Macintosh, vintage 1984. Or the Pentium IV, one of the high-performance microprocessors of choice for the PC in the year 2003. Or today's laptop and desktop microprocessors, the Intel Core processors – I3, I5, and I7. Or even the ARM microprocessors that are used in most smartphones today. That is, the LC-3 has all the important characteristics of these "real" microprocessors without being so complicated that it gets in the way of your understanding.

Once we understand how the LC-3 works, the next step is to program it, first in its own language (Chapter 5 and Chapter 6), and then in a language called *assembly language* that is a little bit easier for humans to work with (Chapter 7). Chapter 8 introduces representations of information more complex than a simple number – stacks, queues, and character strings, and shows how to implement them. Chapter 9 deals with the problem of getting information into (input) and out of (output) the LC-3. Chapter 9 also deals with services provided to a computer user by the operating system. We conclude the first half of the book (Chapter 10) with an extensive example, the simulation of a calculator, an app on most smartphones today.

In the second half of the book (Chapters 11–20), we turn our attention to high-level programming concepts, which we introduce via the C and C++ programming languages. High-level languages enable programmers to more effectively develop complex software by abstracting away the details of the underlying hardware. C and C++ in particular offer a rich set of programmer-friendly constructs, but they are close enough to the hardware that we can examine how code is transformed to execute on the layers below. Our goal is to enable you to write short, simple programs using the core parts of these programming languages, all the while being able to comprehend the transformations required for your code to execute on the underlying hardware.

We'll start with basic topics in C such as variables and operators (Chapter 12), control structures (Chapter 13), and functions (Chapter 14). We'll see that these are straightforward extensions of concepts introduced in the first half of the textbook. We then move on to programming concepts in Chapters 15–19 that will enable us to create more powerful pieces of code: Testing and Debugging (Chapter 15), Pointers and Arrays in C (Chapter 16), Recursion (Chapter 17), Input and Output in C (Chapter 18), and Data Structures in C (Chapter 19).

Chapters 20 is devoted to C++, which we present as an evolution of the C programming language. Because the C++ language was initially defined as a superset of C, many of the concepts covered in Chapters 11–19 directly map onto the C++ language. We will introduce some of the core notions in C++ that have helped establish C++ as one of the most popular languages for developing real-world software. Chapter 20 is our Introduction to C++.

In almost all cases, we try to tie high-level C and C++ constructs to the underlying LC-3 so that you will understand what you demand of the computer when you use a particular construct in a C or C++ program.

1.3 Two Recurring Themes

Two themes permeate this book that we as professors previously took for granted, assuming that everyone recognized their value and regularly emphasized them to students of engineering and computer science. However, it has become clear to us that from the git-go, we need to make these points explicit. So, we state them here up front. The two themes are (a) the notion of abstraction and (b) the importance of not separating in your mind the notions of hardware and software. Their value to your development as an effective engineer or computer scientist goes well beyond your understanding of how a computer works and how to program it.

The notion of abstraction is central to all that you will learn and expect to use in practicing your craft, whether it be in mathematics, physics, any aspect of engineering, or business. It is hard to think of any body of knowledge where the notion of abstraction is not critical.

The misguided hardware/software separation is directly related to your continuing study of computers and your work with them.

We will discuss each in turn.

1.3.1 The Notion of Abstraction

The use of abstraction is all around us. When we get in a taxi and tell the driver, "Take me to the airport," we are using abstraction. If we had to, we could probably direct the driver each step of the way: "Go down this street ten blocks, and make a left turn." And, when the driver got there, "Now take this street five blocks and make a right turn." And on and on. You know the details, but it is a lot quicker to just tell the driver to take you to the airport.

Even the statement "Go down this street ten blocks …" can be broken down further with instructions on using the accelerator, the steering wheel, watching out for other vehicles, pedestrians, etc.

More ABSTRACTION = HIGHER LEVEL

Abstraction is a technique for establishing a simpler way for a person to interact with a system, removing the details that are unnecessary for the person to interact effectively with that system. Our ability to abstract is very much a productivity enhancer. It allows us to deal with a situation at a higher level, focusing on the essential aspects, while keeping the component ideas in the background. It allows us to be more efficient in our use of time and brain activity. It allows us to not get bogged down in the detail when everything about the detail is working just fine.

There is an underlying assumption to this, however: *when everything about the detail is just fine.* What if everything about the detail is not just fine? Then, to be successful, our ability to abstract must be combined with our ability to *un*-abstract. Some people use the word *deconstruct*—the ability to go from the abstraction back to its component parts.

Two stories come to mind.

The first involves a trip through Arizona the first author made a long time ago in the hottest part of the summer. At the time he was living in Palo Alto, California, where the temperature tends to be mild almost always. He knew enough to take the car to a mechanic before making the trip and tell him to check the cooling system. That was the abstraction: cooling system. What he had not mastered was that the capability of a cooling system for Palo Alto, California, is not the same as the capability of a cooling system for the summer deserts of Arizona. The result: two days in Deer Lodge, Arizona (population 3), waiting for a head gasket to be shipped in.

The second story (perhaps apocryphal) is supposed to have happened during the infancy of electric power generation. General Electric Co. was having trouble with one of its huge electric power generators and did not know what to do. On the front of the generator were lots of dials containing lots of information, and lots of screws that could be rotated clockwise or counterclockwise as the operator wished. Something on the other side of the wall of dials and screws was malfunctioning and no one knew what to do. As the story goes, they called in one of the early giants in the electric power industry. He looked at the dials and listened to the noises for a minute, then took a small screwdriver from his pocket and rotated one screw 35 degrees counterclockwise. The problem immediately went away. He submitted a bill for $1000 (a lot of money in those days) without any elaboration. The controller found the bill for two minutes' work a little unsettling and asked for further clarification. Back came the new bill:

```
Turning a screw 35 degrees counterclockwise:  $  0.75
Knowing which screw to turn and by how much:    999.25
```

In both stories the message is the same. It is more efficient to think of entities as abstractions. One does not want to get bogged down in details unnecessarily. And as long as nothing untoward happens, we are OK. If there had been no trip to Arizona, the abstraction "cooling system" would have been sufficient. If the electric power generator never malfunctioned, there would have been no need for the power engineering guru's deeper understanding.

As we will see, modern computers are composed of transistors. These transistors are combined to form logic "gates"—an abstraction that lets us think in terms of 0s and 1s instead of the varying voltages on the transistors. A logic circuit is a further abstraction of a combination of gates. When one designs a logic circuit out of gates, it is much more efficient to not have to think about the internals of each gate. To do so would slow down the process of designing the logic circuit. One wants to think of the gate as a component. But if there is a problem with getting the logic circuit to work, it is often helpful to look at the internal structure of the gate and see if something about its functioning is causing the problem.

When one designs a sophisticated computer application program, whether it be a new spreadsheet program, word processing system, or computer game, one wants to think of each of the components one is using as an abstraction. If one spent time thinking about the details of each component when it was not necessary, the distraction could easily prevent the total job from ever getting finished. But when there is a problem putting the components together, it is often useful to examine carefully the details of each component in order to uncover the problem.

The ability to abstract is the most important skill. In our view, one should try to keep the level of abstraction as high as possible, consistent with getting everything to work effectively. Our approach in this book is to continually raise the level of abstraction. We describe logic gates in terms of transistors. Once we understand the abstraction of gates, we no longer think in terms of transistors. Then we build larger structures out of gates. Once we understand these larger abstractions, we no longer think in terms of gates.

The Bottom Line   Abstractions allow us to be much more efficient in dealing with all kinds of situations. It is also true that one can be effective without understanding what is below the abstraction as long as everything behaves nicely. So, one should not pooh-pooh the notion of abstraction. On the contrary, one should celebrate it since it allows us to be more efficient.

In fact, if we never have to combine a component with anything else into a larger system, and if nothing can go wrong with the component, then it is perfectly fine to understand this component only at the level of its abstraction.

But if we have to combine multiple components into a larger system, we should be careful not to allow their abstractions to be the deepest level of our understanding. If we don't know the components below the level of their abstractions, then we are at the mercy of them working together without our intervention. If they don't work together, and we are unable to go below the level of abstraction, we are stuck. And that is the state we should take care not to find ourselves in.

1.3.2 Hardware vs. Software

Many computer scientists and engineers refer to themselves as hardware people or software people. By hardware, they generally mean the physical computer and all the specifications associated with it. By software, they generally mean the programs, whether operating systems like Android, ChromeOS, Linux, or Windows, or database systems like Access, MongoDB, Oracle, or DB-terrific, or application programs like Facebook, Chrome, Excel, or Word. The implication is that the person knows a whole lot about one of these two things and precious little about the other. Usually, there is the further implication that it is OK to be an expert at one of these (hardware OR software) and clueless about the other. It is as if there were a big wall between the hardware (the computer and how it actually works) and the software (the programs that direct the computer to do their bidding), and that one should be content to remain on one side of that wall or the other.

The power of abstraction allows us to "usually" operate at a level where we do not have to think about the underlying layers all the time. This is a good thing. It enables us to be more productive. But if we are clueless about the underlying layers, then we are not able to take advantage of the nuances of those underlying layers when it is very important to be able to.

That is not to say that you must work at the lower level of abstraction and not take advantage of the productivity enhancements that the abstractions provide. On the contrary, you are encouraged to work at the highest level of abstraction available to you. But in doing so, if you are able to, at the same time, keep in mind the underlying levels, you will find yourself able to do a much better job.

As you approach your study and practice of computing, we urge you to take the approach that hardware and software are names for components of two parts of a computing system that work best when they are designed by people who take into account the capabilities and limitations of both.

Microprocessor designers who understand the needs of the programs that will execute on the microprocessor they are designing can design much more effective microprocessors than those who don't. For example, Intel, AMD, ARM, and other major producers of microprocessors recognized a few years ago that a large fraction of future programs would contain video clips as part of e-mail, video games, and full-length movies. They recognized that it would be important for such programs to execute efficiently. The result: most microprocessors today contain special hardware capability to process those video clips. Intel defined additional instructions, initially called their MMX instruction set, and developed special hardware for it. Motorola, IBM, and Apple did essentially the same thing, resulting in the AltiVec instruction set and special hardware to support it.

A similar story can be told about software designers. The designer of a large computer program who understands the capabilities and limitations of the hardware that will carry out the tasks of that program can design the program so it executes more efficiently than the designer who does not understand the nature of the hardware. One important task that almost all large software systems need to carry out is called sorting, where a number of items have to be arranged in some order. The words in a dictionary are arranged in alphabetical order. Students in a class are often graded based on a numerical order, according to their scores on the final exam. There is a large number of fundamentally different programs one can write to arrange a collection of items in order. Donald Knuth, one of the top computer scientists in the world, devoted 391 pages to the task in *The Art of Computer Programming*, vol. 3. Which sorting program works best is often very dependent on how much the software designer is aware of the underlying characteristics of the hardware.

The Bottom Line   We believe that whether your inclinations are in the direction of a computer hardware career or a computer software career, you will be much more capable if you master both. This book is about getting you started on the path to mastering both hardware and software. Although we sometimes ignore making the point explicitly when we are in the trenches of working through a concept, it really is the case that each sheds light on the other. Hard & software

When you study data types, a software concept, in C (Chapter 12), you will understand how the finite word length of the computer, a hardware concept, affects our notion of data types.

When you study functions in C (Chapter 14), you will be able to tie the *rules* of calling a function with the hardware implementation that makes those rules necessary.

When you study recursion, a powerful algorithmic device (initially in Chapter 8 and more extensively in Chapter 17), you will be able to tie it to the hardware. If you take the time to do that, you will better understand when the additional time to execute a procedure recursively is worth it.

When you study pointer variables in C (in Chapter 16), your knowledge of computer memory will provide a deeper understanding of what pointers provide, and very importantly, when they should be used and when they should be avoided.

When you study data structures in C (in Chapter 19), your knowledge of computer memory will help you better understand what must be done to manipulate the actual structures in memory efficiently.

We realize that most of the terms in the preceding five short paragraphs may not be familiar to you *yet*. That is OK; you can reread this page at the end of the semester. What is important to know right now is that there are important topics in the software that are very deeply interwoven with topics in the hardware. Our contention is that mastering either is easier if you pay attention to both.

Most importantly, most computing problems yield better solutions when the problem solver has the capability of both at his or her disposal.

1.4 A Computer System

We have used the word *computer* more than two dozen times in the preceding pages, and although we did not say so explicitly, we used it to mean a system consisting of the software (i.e., computer programs) that directs and specifies the processing of information and the hardware that performs the actual processing of information in response to what the software asks the hardware to do. When we say "performing the actual processing," we mean doing the actual additions, multiplications, and so forth in the hardware that are necessary to get the job done. A more precise term for this hardware is a *central processing unit* (CPU), or simply a *processor* or *microprocessor*. This textbook is primarily about the processor and the programs that are executed by the processor.

1.4.1 A (Very) Little History for a (Lot) Better Perspective

Before we get into the detail of how the processor and the software associated with it work, we should take a moment and note the enormous and unparalleled leaps of performance that the computing industry has made in the relatively short time computers have been around. After all, it wasn't until the 1940s that the first computers showed their faces. One of the first computers was the ENIAC (the Electronic Numerical Integrator and Calculator), a general purpose electronic computer that could be reprogrammed for different tasks. It was designed and built in 1943–1945 at the University of Pennsylvania by Presper Eckert and his colleagues. It contained more than 17,000 vacuum tubes. It was approximately 8 feet high, more than 100 feet wide, and about 3 feet deep (about 300 square feet of floor space). It weighed 30 tons and required 140 kW to operate. Figure 1.1 shows three operators programming the ENIAC by plugging and unplugging cables and switches.

About 40 years and many computer companies and computers later, in the early 1980s, the Burroughs A series was born. One of the dozen or so 18-inch boards that comprise that machine is shown in Figure 1.2. Each board contained 50 or more integrated circuit packages. Instead of 300 square feet, it took up around 50 to 60 square feet; instead of 30 tons, it weighed about 1 ton, and instead of 140 kW, it required approximately 25 kW to operate.

Figure 1.1   The ENIAC, designed and built at University of Pennsylvania, 1943–45.
©Historical/Getty Images

Figure 1.2   A processor board, vintage 1980s. Courtesy of Emilio Salguerio

Fast forward another 30 or so years and we find many of today's computers on desktops (Figure 1.3), in laptops (Figure 1.4), and most recently in smartphones (Figure 1.5). Their relative weights and energy requirements have decreased enormously, and the speed at which they process information has also increased enormously. We estimate that the computing power in a smartphone today (i.e., how fast we can compute with a smartphone) is more than four million times the computing power of the ENIAC!

Figure 1.3
A desktop computer.
©Joby Sessions/
Future/REX/
Shutterstock

Figure 1.4   A laptop. ©Rob
Monk/Future/
REX/Shutterstock

Figure 1.5   A smartphone. ©Oleksiy
Maksymenko/
imageBROKER/REX/Shutterstock

Figure 1.6   A microprocessor. ©Peter Gudella/Shutterstock

The integrated circuit packages that comprise modern digital computers have also seen phenomenal improvement. An example of one of today's microprocessors is shown in Figure 1.6. The first microprocessor, the Intel 4004 in 1971, contained 2300 transistors and operated at 106 KHz. By 1992, those numbers had jumped to 3.1 million transistors at a frequency of 66 MHz on the Intel Pentium microprocessor, an increase in both parameters of a factor of about 1000. Today's microprocessors contain upwards of five billion transistors and can operate at upwards of 4 GHz, another increase in both parameters of about a factor of 1000.

This factor of one million since 1971 in both the number of transistors and the frequency that the microprocessor operates at has had very important implications. The fact that each operation can be performed in one millionth of the time it took in 1971 means the microprocessor can do one million things today in the time it took to do one thing in 1971. The fact that there are more than a million times as many transistors on a chip means we can do a lot more things at the same time today than we could in 1971.

The result of all this is we have today computers that seem able to understand the languages people speak – English, Spanish, Chinese, for example. We have computers that seem able to recognize faces. Many see this as the magic of artificial intelligence. We will see as we get into the details of how a computer works that much of what appears to be magic is really due to how blazingly fast very simple mindless operations (many at the same time) can be carried out.

1.4.2 The Parts of a Computer System

When most people use the word *computer*, they usually mean more than just the processor (i.e., CPU) that is in charge of doing what the software directs.

They usually mean the collection of parts that in combination form their *computer system*. Today that computer system is often a laptop (see Figure 1.4), augmented with many additional devices.

A computer system generally includes, in addition to the processor, a keyboard for typing commands, a mouse or keypad or joystick for positioning on menu entries, a monitor for displaying information that the computer system has produced, memory for temporarily storing information, disks and USB memory sticks of one sort or another for storing information for a very long time, even after the computer has been turned off, connections to other devices such as a printer for obtaining paper copies of that information, and the collection of programs (the software) that the user wishes to execute.

All these items help computer users to do their jobs. Without a printer, for example, the user would have to copy by hand what is displayed on the monitor. Without a mouse, keypad, or joystick, the user would have to type each command, rather than simply position the mouse, keypad, or joystick.

So, as we begin our journey, which focuses on the CPU that occupies a small fraction of 1 square inch of silicon and the software that makes the CPU do our bidding, we note that the computer systems we use contain a lot of additional components.

1.5　Two Very Important Ideas

Before we leave this first chapter, there are two very important ideas that we would like you to understand, ideas that are at the core of what computing is all about.

Idea 1: All computers (the biggest and the smallest, the fastest and the slowest, the most expensive and the cheapest) are capable of computing exactly the same things if they are given enough time and enough memory. That is, anything a fast computer can do, a slow computer can do also. The slow computer just does it more slowly. A more expensive computer cannot figure out something that a cheaper computer is unable to figure out as long as the cheaper computer can access enough memory. (You may have to go to the store to buy more memory whenever it runs out of memory in order to keep increasing memory.) All computers can do exactly the same things. Some computers can do things faster, but none can do more than any other.

Idea 2: We describe our problems in English or some other language spoken by people. Yet the problems are solved by electrons running around inside the computer. It is necessary to transform our problem from the language of humans to the voltages that influence the flow of electrons. This transformation is really a sequence of systematic transformations, developed and improved over the last 70 years, which combine to give the computer the ability to carry out what appear to be some very complicated tasks. In reality, these tasks are simple and straightforward.

The rest of this chapter is devoted to discussing these two ideas.

1.6 Computers as Universal Computational Devices

It may seem strange that an introductory textbook begins by describing how computers work. After all, mechanical engineering students begin by studying physics, not how car engines work. Chemical engineering students begin by studying chemistry, not oil refineries. Why should computing students begin by studying computers?

The answer is that computers are different. To learn the fundamental principles of computing, you must study computers or machines that can do what computers can do. The reason for this has to do with the notion that computers are *universal computational devices*. Let's see what that means.

Before modern computers, there were many kinds of calculating machines. Some were *analog machines*—machines that produced an answer by measuring some physical quantity such as distance or voltage. For example, a slide rule is an analog machine that multiplies numbers by sliding one logarithmically graded ruler next to another. The user can read a logarithmic "distance" on the second ruler. Some early analog adding machines worked by dropping weights on a scale. The difficulty with analog machines is that it is very hard to increase their accuracy.

This is why *digital machines*—machines that perform computations by manipulating a fixed finite set of digits or letters—came to dominate computing. You are familiar with the distinction between analog and digital watches. An analog watch has hour and minute hands, and perhaps a second hand. It gives the time by the positions of its hands, which are really angular measures. Digital watches give the time in digits. You can increase accuracy just by adding more digits. For example, if it is important for you to measure time in hundredths of a second, you can buy a watch that gives a reading like 10:35.16 rather than just 10:35. How would you get an analog watch that would give you an accurate reading to one one-hundredth of a second? You could do it, but it would take a mighty long second hand! When we talk about computers in this book, we will always mean digital machines.

Before modern digital computers, the most common digital machines in the West were adding machines. In other parts of the world another digital machine, the abacus, was common. Digital adding machines were mechanical or electromechanical devices that could perform a specific kind of computation: adding integers. There were also digital machines that could multiply integers. There were digital machines that could put a stack of cards with punched names in alphabetical order. The main limitation of all these machines is that they could do only one specific kind of computation. If you owned only an adding machine and wanted to multiply two integers, you had some pencil-and-paper work to do.

This is why computers are different. You can tell a computer how to add numbers. You can tell it how to multiply. You can tell it how to alphabetize a list or perform any computation you like. When you think of a new kind of computation, you do not have to buy or design a new computer. You just give the old computer a new set of instructions (a program) to carry out the new computation. This is why we say the computer is a *universal computational device*. Computer scientists believe that *anything that can be computed, can be computed by a computer* provided it has enough time and enough memory. When we study computers, we study the fundamentals of all computing. We learn what computation is and what can be computed.

The idea of a universal computational device is due to Alan Turing. Turing proposed in 1937 that all computations could be carried out by a particular kind of machine, which is now called a Turing machine. He gave a mathematical description of this kind of machine, but did not actually build one. Digital computers were not operating until several years later. Turing was more interested in solving a philosophical problem: defining computation. He began by looking at the kinds of actions that people perform when they compute; these include making marks on paper, writing symbols according to certain rules when other symbols are present, and so on. He abstracted these actions and specified a mechanism that could carry them out. He gave some examples of the kinds of things that these machines could do. One Turing machine could add two integers; another could multiply two integers.

Figure 1.7 shows what we call "black box" models of Turing machines that add and multiply. In each case, the operation to be performed is described in the box. The data elements on which to operate are shown as inputs to the box. The result of the operation is shown as output from the box. A black box model provides no information as to exactly how the operation is performed, and indeed, there are many ways to add or multiply two numbers.

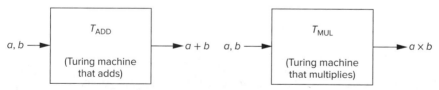

T_{ADD}		T_{MUL}

$a, b \longrightarrow$ (Turing machine that adds) $\longrightarrow a + b$ $\quad a, b \longrightarrow$ (Turing machine that multiplies) $\longrightarrow a \times b$

Figure 1.7   Black box models of Turing machines.

Turing proposed that every computation can be performed by some Turing machine. We call this *Turing's thesis*. Although Turing's thesis has never been proved, there does exist a lot of evidence to suggest it is true. We know, for example, that various enhancements one can make to Turing machines do not result in machines that can compute more.

Perhaps the best argument to support Turing's thesis was provided by Turing himself in his original paper. He said that one way to try to construct a machine more powerful than any particular Turing machine was to make a machine U that could simulate *all* Turing machines. You would simply describe to U the particular Turing machine you wanted it to simulate, say a machine to add two integers, give U the input data, and U would compute the appropriate output, in this case the sum of the inputs. Turing then showed that there was, in fact, a Turing machine that could do this, so even this attempt to find something that could not be computed by Turing machines failed.

Figure 1.8 further illustrates the point. Suppose you wanted to compute $g \cdot (e + f)$. You would simply provide to U descriptions of the Turing machines to add and to multiply, and the three inputs, e, f, and g. U would do the rest.

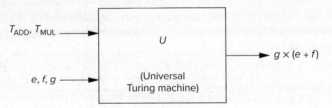

Figure 1.8   Black box model of a universal Turing machine.

In specifying U, Turing had provided us with a deep insight: He had given us the first description of what computers do. In fact, both a computer (with as much memory as it wants) and a universal Turing machine can compute exactly the same things. In both cases, you give the machine a description of a computation and the data it needs, and the machine computes the appropriate answer. Computers and universal Turing machines can compute anything that can be computed because they are *programmable*.

This is the reason that a big or expensive computer cannot do more than a small, cheap computer. More money may buy you a faster computer, a monitor with higher resolution, or a nice sound system. But if you have a small, cheap computer, you already have a universal computational device.

1.7 How Do We Get the Electrons to Do the Work?

Figure 1.9 shows the process we must go through to get the electrons (which actually do the work) to do our bidding. We call the steps of this process the "Levels of Transformation." As we will see, at each level we have choices. If we ignore any of the levels, our ability to make the best use of our computing system can be very adversely affected.

1.7.1 The Statement of the Problem

We describe the problems we wish to solve in a "natural language." Natural languages are languages that people speak, like English, French, Japanese, Italian, and so on. They have evolved over centuries in accordance with their usage. They are fraught with a lot of things unacceptable for providing instructions to a

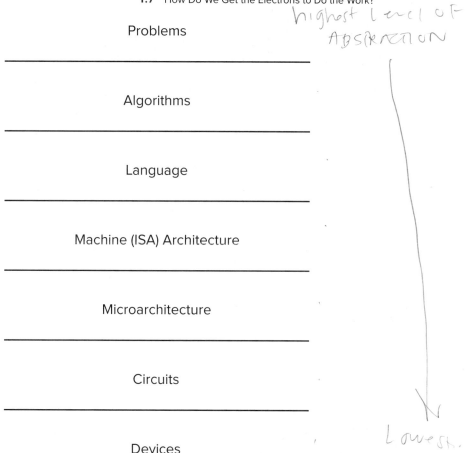

Figure 1.9   Levels of transformation.

computer. Most important of these unacceptable attributes is ambiguity. Natural language is filled with ambiguity. To infer the meaning of a sentence, a listener is often helped by the tone of voice of the speaker, or at the very least, the context of the sentence.

An example of ambiguity in English is the sentence, "Time flies like an arrow." At least three interpretations are possible, depending on whether (1) one is noticing how fast time passes, (2) one is at a track meet for insects, or (3) one is writing a letter to the Dear Abby of Insectville. In the first case, a simile; one is comparing the speed of time passing to the speed of an arrow that has been released. In the second case, one is telling the timekeeper to do his/her job much like an arrow would. In the third case, one is relating that a particular group of flies (time flies, as opposed to fruit flies) are all in love with the same arrow.

Such ambiguity would be unacceptable in instructions provided to a computer. The computer, electronic idiot that it is, can only do as it is told. To tell it to do something where there are multiple interpretations would cause the computer to not know which interpretation to follow.

1.7.2 The Algorithm

The first step in the sequence of transformations is to transform the natural language description of the problem to an algorithm, and in so doing, get rid of the objectionable characteristics of the natural language. An algorithm is a step-by-step procedure that is guaranteed to terminate, such that each step is precisely stated and can be carried out by the computer. There are terms to describe each of these properties.

We use the term *definiteness* to describe the notion that each step is precisely stated. A recipe for excellent pancakes that instructs the preparer to "stir until lumpy" lacks definiteness, since the notion of lumpiness is not precise.

We use the term *effective computability* to describe the notion that each step can be carried out by a computer. A procedure that instructs the computer to "take the largest prime number" lacks effective computability, since there is no largest prime number.

We use the term *finiteness* to describe the notion that the procedure terminates.

For every problem there are usually many different algorithms for solving that problem. One algorithm may require the fewest steps. Another algorithm may allow some steps to be performed concurrently. A computer that allows more than one thing to be done at a time can often solve the problem in less time, even though it is likely that the total number of steps to be performed has increased.

1.7.3 The Program

The next step is to transform the algorithm into a computer program in one of the programming languages that are available. Programming languages are "mechanical languages." That is, unlike natural languages, mechanical languages did not evolve through human discourse. Rather, they were invented for use in specifying a sequence of instructions to a computer. Therefore, mechanical languages do not suffer from failings such as ambiguity that would make them unacceptable for specifying a computer program.

There are more than 1000 programming languages. Some have been designed for use with particular applications, such as Fortran for solving scientific calculations and COBOL for solving business data-processing problems. In the second half of this book, we will use C and C++, languages that were designed for manipulating low-level hardware structures.

Other languages are useful for still other purposes. Prolog is the language of choice for many applications that require the design of an expert system. LISP was for years the language of choice of a substantial number of people working on problems dealing with artificial intelligence. Pascal is a language invented as a vehicle for teaching beginning students how to program.

There are two kinds of programming languages, high-level languages and low-level languages. High-level languages are at a distance (a high level) from the underlying computer. At their best, they are independent of the computer on which the programs will execute. We say the language is "machine independent."

All the languages mentioned thus far are high-level languages. Low-level languages are tied to the computer on which the programs will execute. There is generally one such low-level language for each computer. That language is called the *assembly language* for that computer.

1.7.4 The ISA

The next step is to translate the program into the instruction set of the particular computer that will be used to carry out the work of the program. The instruction set architecture (ISA) is the complete specification of the interface between programs that have been written and the underlying computer hardware that must carry out the work of those programs.

An analogy that may be helpful in understanding the concept of an ISA is provided by the automobile. Corresponding to a computer program, represented as a sequence of 0s and 1s in the case of the computer, is the human sitting in the driver's seat of a car. Corresponding to the microprocessor hardware is the car itself. The "ISA" of the automobile is the specification of everything the human needs to know to tell the automobile what to do, and everything the automobile needs to know to carry out the tasks specified by the human driver. For example, one element of the automobile's "ISA" is the pedal on the floor known as the brake, and its function. The human knows that if he/she steps on the brake, the car will stop. The automobile knows that if it feels pressure from the human on that pedal, the hardware of the automobile must engage those elements necessary to stop the car. The full "ISA" of the car includes the specification of the other pedals, the steering wheel, the ignition key, the gears, windshield wipers, etc. For each, the "ISA" specifies (a) what the human has to do to tell the automobile what he/she wants done, and (b) correspondingly, what the automobile will interpret those actions to mean so it (the automobile) can carry out the specified task.

The ISA of a computer serves the same purpose as the "ISA" of an automobile, except instead of the driver and the car, the ISA of a computer specifies the interface between the computer program directing the computer hardware and the hardware carrying out those directions. For example, consider the set of instructions that the computer can carry out—that is, what operations the computer can perform and where to get the data needed to perform those operations. The term *opcode* is used to describe the operation. The term *operand* is used to describe individual data values. The ISA specifies the acceptable representations for operands. They are called *data types*. A *data type* is a representation of an operand such that the computer can perform operations on that representation. The ISA specifies the mechanisms that the computer can use to figure out where the operands are located. These mechanisms are called *addressing modes*.

The number of opcodes, data types, and addressing modes specified by an ISA vary among different ISAs. Some ISAs have as few as a half dozen opcodes, whereas others have as many as several hundred. Some ISAs have only one data type, while others have more than a dozen. Some ISAs have one or two addressing modes, whereas others have more than 20. The x86, the ISA used in the PC, has more than 200 opcodes, more than a dozen data types, and more than two dozen addressing modes.

The ISA also specifies the number of unique locations that comprise the computer's memory and the number of individual 0s and 1s that are contained in each location.

Many ISAs are in use today. The most widely known example is the x86, introduced by Intel Corporation in 1979 and currently also manufactured by AMD and other companies. Other ISAs and the companies responsible for them include ARM and THUMB (ARM), POWER and z/Architecture (IBM), and SPARC (Oracle).

The translation from a high-level language (such as C) to the ISA of the computer on which the program will execute (such as x86) is usually done by a translating program called a *compiler*. To translate from a program written in C to the x86 ISA, one would need a C to x86 compiler. For each high-level language and each desired target ISA, one must provide a corresponding compiler.

The translation from the unique assembly language of a computer to its ISA is done by an assembler.

1.7.5 The Microarchitecture

The next step is the implementation of the ISA, referred to as its *microarchitecture*. The automobile analogy that we used in our discussion of the ISA is also useful in showing the relationship between an ISA and a microarchitecture that implements that ISA. The automobile's "ISA" describes what the driver needs to know as he/she sits inside the automobile to make the automobile carry out the driver's wishes. All automobiles have the same ISA. If there are three pedals on the floor, it does not matter what manufacturer produced the car, the middle one is always the brake. The one on the right is always the accelerator, and the more it is depressed, the faster the car will move. Because there is only one ISA for automobiles, one does not need one driver's license for Buicks and a different driver's license for Hondas.

The microarchitecture (or implementation) of the automobile's ISA, on the other hand, is about what goes on underneath the hood. Here all automobile makes and models can be different, depending on what cost/performance tradeoffs the automobile designer made before the car was manufactured. Some automobiles come with disc brakes, others (in the past, at least) with drums. Some automobiles have eight cylinders, others run on six cylinders, and still others have only four. Some are turbocharged, some are not. Some automobiles can travel 60 miles on one gallon of gasoline, others are lucky to travel from one gas station to the next without running out of gas. Some automobiles cost 6000 US dollars, others cost 200,000 US dollars. In each case, the "microarchitecture" of the specific automobile is a result of the automobile designers' decisions regarding the tradeoffs of cost and performance. The fact that the "microarchitecture" of every model or make is different is a good reason to take one's Honda, when it is malfunctioning, to a Honda repair person, and not to a Buick repair person.

In the previous section, we identified ISAs of several computer manufacturers, including the x86 (Intel), the PowerPC (IBM and Motorola), and THUMB (ARM). Each has been implemented by many different microarchitectures. For example, the x86's original implementation in 1979 was the 8086, followed by the 80286, 80386, and 80486 in the 1980s. More recently, in 2001, Intel introduced the Pentium IV microprocessor. Even more recently, in 2015, Intel introduced Skylake. Each of these x86 microprocessors has its own microarchitecture.

The story is the same for the PowerPC ISA, with more than a dozen different microprocessors, each having its own microarchitecture.

Each microarchitecture is an opportunity for computer designers to make different tradeoffs between the cost of the microprocessor, the performance that the microprocessor will provide, and the energy that is required to power the microprocessor. Computer design is always an exercise in tradeoffs, as the designer opts for higher (or lower) performance, more (or less) energy required, at greater (or lesser) cost.

1.7.6 The Logic Circuit

The next step is to implement each element of the microarchitecture out of simple logic circuits. Here also there are choices, as the logic designer decides how to best make the tradeoffs between cost and performance. So, for example, even for an operation as simple as addition, there are several choices of logic circuits to perform the operation at differing speeds and corresponding costs.

1.7.7 The Devices

Finally, each basic logic circuit is implemented in accordance with the requirements of the particular device technology used. So, CMOS circuits are different from NMOS circuits, which are different, in turn, from gallium arsenide circuits.

The Bottom Line   In summary, from the natural language description of a problem to the electrons that actually solve the problem by moving from one voltage potential to another, many transformations need to be performed. If we could speak electron, or if the electrons could understand English, perhaps we could just walk up to the computer and get the electrons to do our bidding. Since we can't speak electron and they can't speak English, the best we can do is this systematic sequence of transformations. At each level of transformation, there are choices as to how to proceed. Our handling of those choices determines the resulting cost and performance of our computer.

In this book, we describe each of these transformations. We show how transistors combine to form logic circuits, how logic circuits combine to form the microarchitecture, and how the microarchitecture implements a particular ISA. In our case, the ISA is the LC-3. We complete the process by going from the English-language description of a problem to a C or C++ program that solves the problem, and we show how that C or C++ program is translated (i.e., compiled) to the ISA of the LC-3.

We hope you enjoy the ride.

Exercises

1.1   [1] Explain the first of the two important ideas stated in Section 1.5.

1.2   [1] Can a higher-level programming language instruct a computer to compute more than a lower-level programming language?

1.3   [1] What difficulty with analog computers encourages computer designers to use digital designs?

1.4   [1] Name one characteristic of natural languages that prevents them from being used as programming languages.

1.5   [5] Say we had a "black box," which takes two numbers as input and outputs their sum. See Figure 1.10a. Say we had another box capable of multiplying two numbers together. See Figure 1.10b. We can connect these boxes together to calculate $p \times (m + n)$. See Figure 1.10c. Assume we have an unlimited number of these boxes. Show how to connect them together to calculate:

a. $ax + b$
b. The average of the four input numbers w, x, y, and z
c. $a^2 + 2ab + b^2$ (Can you do it with one add box and one multiply box?)

1.6   [1] Write a statement in a natural language, and offer two different interpretations of that statement.

1.7   [3] The discussion of abstraction in Section 1.3.1 noted that one does not need to understand the makeup of the components as long as "everything about the detail is just fine." The case was made that when everything is not fine, one must be able to deconstruct the components, or be at the mercy of the abstractions. In the taxi example, suppose you did not understand the component, that is, you had no clue how to get to the airport. Using the notion of abstraction, you simply tell the driver, "Take me to the airport." Explain when this is a productivity enhancer, and when it could result in very negative consequences.

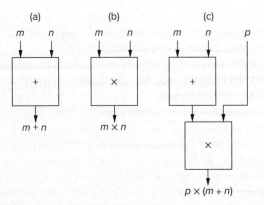

Figure 1.10   "Black boxes" capable of (a) addition, (b) multiplication, and (c) a combination of addition and multiplication.

1.8　[5] John said, "I saw the man in the park with a telescope." What did he mean? How many reasonable interpretations can you provide for this statement? List them. What property does this sentence demonstrate that makes it unacceptable as a statement in a program?

1.9　[1] Are natural languages capable of expressing algorithms?

1.10　[1] Name three characteristics of algorithms. Briefly explain each of these three characteristics.

1.11　[4] For each characteristic of an algorithm, give an example of a procedure that does not have the characteristic and is therefore not an algorithm.

1.12　[5] Are items *a* through *e* in the following list algorithms? If not, what qualities required of algorithms do they lack?

　　　a. Add the first row of the following matrix to another row whose first column contains a non-zero entry. (*Reminder*: Columns run vertically; rows run horizontally.)　(column

$$\begin{bmatrix} 1 & 2 & 0 & 4 \\ 0 & 3 & 2 & 4 \\ 2 & 3 & 10 & 22 \\ 12 & 4 & 3 & 4 \end{bmatrix}$$ row

　　　b. In order to show that there are as many prime numbers as there are natural numbers, match each prime number with a natural number in the following manner. Create pairs of prime and natural numbers by matching the first prime number with 1 (which is the first natural number) and the second prime number with 2, the third with 3, and so forth. If, in the end, it turns out that each prime number can be paired with each natural number, then it is shown that there are as many prime numbers as natural numbers.

　　　c. Suppose you're given two vectors each with 20 elements and asked to perform the following operation: Take the first element of the first vector and multiply it by the first element of the second vector. Do the same to the second elements, and so forth. Add all the individual products together to derive the dot product.

　　　d. Lynne and Calvin are trying to decide who will take the dog for a walk. Lynne suggests that they flip a coin and pulls a quarter out of her pocket. Calvin does not trust Lynne and suspects that the quarter may be weighted (meaning that it might favor a particular outcome when tossed) and suggests the following procedure to fairly determine who will walk the dog.

　　　　1. Flip the quarter twice.
　　　　2. If the outcome is heads on the first flip and tails on the second, then I will walk the dog.
　　　　3. If the outcome is tails on the first flip and heads on the second, then you will walk the dog.

      4. If both outcomes are tails or both outcomes are heads, then we flip twice again.

    Is Calvin's technique an algorithm?

   e. Given a number, perform the following steps in order:

      1. Multiply it by 4
      2. Add 4
      3. Divide by 2
      4. Subtract 2
      5. Divide by 2
      6. Subtract 1
      7. At this point, add 1 to a counter to keep track of the fact that you performed steps 1 through 6. Then test the result you got when you subtracted 1. If 0, write down the number of times you performed steps 1 through 6 and stop. If not 0, starting with the result of subtracting one, perform the seven steps again.

1.13 [4] Two computers, A and B, are identical except for the fact that A has a subtract instruction and B does not. Both have add instructions. Both have instructions that can take a value and produce the negative of that value. Which computer is able to solve more problems, A or B? Prove your result.

1.14 [4] Suppose we wish to put a set of names in alphabetical order. We call the act of doing so *sorting*. One algorithm that can accomplish that is called the bubble sort. We could then program our bubble sort algorithm in C and compile the C program to execute on an x86 ISA. The x86 ISA can be implemented with an Intel Pentium IV microarchitecture. Let us call the sequence "Bubble Sort, C program, x86 ISA, Pentium IV microarchitecture" one *transformation process*.

    Assume we have available four sorting algorithms and can program in C, C++, Pascal, Fortran, and COBOL. We have available compilers that can translate from each of these to either x86 or SPARC, and we have available three different microarchitectures for x86 and three different microarchitectures for SPARC.

   a. How many transformation processes are possible?

   b. Write three examples of transformation processes.

   c. How many transformation processes are possible if instead of three different microarchitectures for x86 and three different microarchitectures for SPARC, there were two for x86 and four for SPARC?

1.15 [7] Identify one advantage of programming in a higher-level language compared to a lower-level language. Identify one disadvantage.

1.16 [1] Name at least three things specified by an ISA.

1.17 [1] Briefly describe the difference between an ISA and a microarchitecture.

1.18 [4] How many ISAs are normally implemented by a single microarchitecture? Conversely, how many microarchitectures could exist for a single ISA?

1.19 [1] List the levels of transformation and name an example for each level.

1.20 [4] The levels of transformation in Figure 1.9 are often referred to as levels of abstraction. Is that a reasonable characterization? If yes, give an example. If no, why not?

1.21 [7] Say you go to the store and buy some word processing software. What form is the software actually in? Is it in a high-level programming language? Is it in assembly language? Is it in the ISA of the computer on which you'll run it? Justify your answer.

1.22 [5] Suppose you were given a task at one of the transformation levels shown in Figure 1.9, and required to transform it to the level just below. At which level would it be most difficult to perform the transformation to the next lower level? Why?

1.23 [5] Why is an ISA unlikely to change between successive generations of microarchitectures that implement it? For example, why would Intel want to make certain that the ISA implemented by the Pentium III is the same as the one implemented by the Pentium II? *Hint:* When you upgrade your computer (or buy one with a newer CPU), do you need to throw out all your old software?

CHAPTER

2

Bits, Data Types, and Operations

2.1 Bits and Data Types

2.1.1 The Bit as the Unit of Information

We noted in Chapter 1 that the computer was organized as a system with several levels of transformation. A problem stated in a natural language such as English is actually solved by the electrons moving around inside the components of the computer.

Inside the computer, millions of very tiny, very fast devices control the movement of those electrons. These devices react to the presence or absence of voltages in electronic circuits. They could react to the actual values of the voltages, rather than simply to the presence or absence of voltages. However, this would make the control and detection circuits more complex than they need to be. It is much easier to detect simply whether or not a voltage exists at a point in a circuit than it is to measure exactly what that voltage is.

To understand this, consider any wall outlet in your home. You could measure the exact voltage it is carrying, whether 120 volts or 115 volts, or 118.6 volts, for example. However, the detection circuitry to determine *only* whether there is a voltage or whether there is no voltage is much simpler. Your finger casually inserted into the wall socket, for example, will suffice.

We symbolically represent the presence of a voltage as "1" and the absence of a voltage as "0." We refer to each 0 and each 1 as a "bit," which is a shortened form of *binary digit*. Recall the digits you have been using since you were a child—0, 1, 2, 3, …, 9. There are ten of them, and they are referred to as decimal digits. In the case of binary digits, there are two of them, 0 and 1.

To be perfectly precise, it is not really the case that the computer differentiates the *absolute* absence of a voltage (i.e., 0) from the *absolute* presence of a voltage (i.e., 1). Actually, the electronic circuits in the computer differentiate voltages *close to* 0 from voltages *far from* 0. So, for example, if the computer expects either a voltage of 1.2 volts or a voltage of 0 volts (1.2 volts signifying 1 and 0 volts signifying 0), then a voltage of 1.0 volts will be taken as a 1 and 0.2 volts will be taken as a 0.

With one wire, one can differentiate only two things. One of them can be assigned the value 0, the other can be assigned the value 1. But to get useful work done by the computer, it is necessary to be able to differentiate a large number of distinct values, and to assign each of them a unique representation. We can accomplish this by combining many wires, that is, many bits. For example, if we use eight bits (corresponding to the voltage present on each of eight wires), we can represent one particular value as 01001110, and another value as 11100111. In fact, if we are limited to eight bits, we can differentiate at most only 256 (i.e., 2^8) different things. In general, with k bits, we can distinguish at most 2^k distinct items. Each pattern of these k bits is a code; that is, it corresponds to a particular item (or value).

2.1.2 Data Types

There are many ways to represent the same value. For example, the number five can be written as a 5. This is the standard decimal notation that you are used to. The value five can also be represented by someone holding up one hand, with all fingers and thumb extended. The person is saying, "The number I wish to communicate can be determined by counting the number of fingers I am showing." A written version of that scheme would be the value 11111. This notation has a name also—*unary*. The Romans had yet another notation for five—the character V. We will see momentarily that a fourth notation for five is the binary representation 00000101.

It is not enough simply to represent values; we must be able to operate on those values. We say a particular representation is a *data type* if there are operations in the computer that can operate on information that is encoded in that representation. Each instruction set architecture (ISA) has its own set of data types and its own set of instructions that can operate on those data types. In this book, we will mainly use two data types: *2's complement integers* for representing positive and negative integers that we wish to perform arithmetic on, and *ASCII codes* for representing characters that we wish to input to a computer via the keyboard or output from the computer via a monitor. Both data types will be explained shortly.

There are other representations of information that could be used, and indeed that are present in most computers. Recall the "scientific notation" from high school chemistry where you were admonished to represent the decimal number 621 as $6.21 \cdot 10^2$. There are computers that represent numbers in that form, and they provide operations that can operate on numbers so represented. That data type is usually called *floating point*. We will examine its representation in Section 2.7.1.

2.2 Integer Data Types

2.2.1 Unsigned Integers

The first representation of information, or data type, that we shall look at is the unsigned integer. As its name suggests, an unsigned integer has no sign (plus or minus) associated with it. An unsigned integer just has a magnitude. Unsigned integers have many uses in a computer. If we wish to perform a task some specific number of times, unsigned integers enable us to keep track of this number easily by simply counting how many times we have performed the task. Unsigned integers also provide a means for identifying different memory locations in the computer in the same way that house numbers differentiate 129 Main Street from 131 Main Street. I don't recall ever seeing a house number with a minus sign in front of it.

We can represent unsigned integers as strings of binary digits. To do this, we use a positional notation much like the decimal system that you have been using since you were three years old.

You are familiar with the decimal number 329, which also uses positional notation. The 3 is worth much more than the 9, even though the absolute value of 3 standing alone is only worth 1/3 the value of 9 standing alone. This is because, as you know, the 3 stands for 300 ($3 \cdot 10^2$) due to its position in the decimal string 329, while the 9 stands for $9 \cdot 10^0$.

Instead of using decimal digits, we can represent unsigned integers using just the binary digits 0 and 1. Here the base is 2, rather than 10. So, for example, if we have five bits (binary digits) available to represent our values, the number 5, which we mentioned earlier, is represented as 00101, corresponding to

$$0 \cdot 2^4 + 0 \cdot 2^3 + 1 \cdot 2^2 + 0 \cdot 2^1 + 1 \cdot 2^0$$

With k bits, we can represent in this positional notation exactly 2^k integers, ranging from 0 to $2^k - 1$. Figure 2.1 shows the five-bit representations for the integers from 0 to 31.

2.2.2 Signed Integers

To do useful arithmetic, however, it is often (although not always) necessary to be able to deal with negative quantities as well as positive. We could take our 2^k distinct patterns of k bits and separate them in half, half for positive integers and half for negative integers. In this way, with five-bit codes, instead of representing integers from 0 to +31, we could choose to represent positive integers from +1 to +15 and negative integers from −1 to −15. There are 30 such integers. Since 2^5 is 32, we still have two 5-bit codes unassigned. One of them, 00000, we would presumably assign to the value 0, giving us the full range of integer values from −15 to +15. That leaves one 5-bit code left over, and there are different ways to assign this code, as we will see momentarily.

We are still left with the problem of determining what codes to assign to what values. That is, we have 32 codes, but which value should go with which code?

Positive integers are represented in the straightforward positional scheme. Since there are k bits, and we wish to use exactly half of the 2^k codes to represent the integers from 0 to $2^{k-1} - 1$, all positive integers will have a leading 0 in their representation. In our example of Figure 2.1 (with $k = 5$), the largest positive integer +15 is represented as 01111.

Note that in all three *signed* data types shown in Figure 2.1 , the representation for 0 and all the positive integers start with a leading 0. What about the representations for the negative integers (in our five-bit example, −1 to −15)?

Representation	Value Represented			
	Unsigned	**Signed Magnitude**	**1's Complement**	**2's Complement**
00000	0	0	0	0
00001	1	1	1	1
00010	2	2	2	2
00011	3	3	3	3
00100	4	4	4	4
00101	5	5	5	5
00110	6	6	6	6
00111	7	7	7	7
01000	8	8	8	8
01001	9	9	9	9
01010	10	10	10	10
01011	11	11	11	11
01100	12	12	12	12
01101	13	13	13	13
01110	14	14	14	14
01111	15	15	15	15
10000	16	−0	−15	−16
10001	17	−1	−14	−15
10010	18	−2	−13	−14
10011	19	−3	−12	−13
10100	20	−4	−11	−12
10101	21	−5	−10	−11
10110	22	−6	−9	−10
10111	23	−7	−8	−9
11000	24	−8	−7	−8
11001	25	−9	−6	−7
11010	26	−10	−5	−6
11011	27	−11	−4	−5
11100	28	−12	−3	−4
11101	29	−13	−2	−3
11110	30	−14	−1	−2
11111	31	−15	−0	−1

Figure 2.1   Four representations of integers.

The first thought that usually comes to mind is: If a leading 0 signifies a *positive* integer, how about letting a leading 1 signify a *negative* integer? The result is the *signed-magnitude* data type shown in Figure 2.1. A second thought (which was actually used on some early computers such as the Control Data Corporation 6600) was the following: Let a negative number be represented by taking the representation of the positive number having the same magnitude, and "flipping" all the bits. That is, if the original representation had a 0, replace it with a 1; if it originally had a 1, replace it with a 0. For example, since +5 is represented as 00101, we designate −5 as 11010. This data type is referred to in the computer engineering community as *1's complement* and is also shown in Figure 2.1.

At this point, you might think that a computer designer could assign any bit pattern to represent any integer he or she wants. And you would be right! Unfortunately, that could complicate matters when we try to build an electronic circuit to add two integers. In fact, the signed-magnitude and 1's complement data types both require unnecessarily cumbersome hardware to do addition. Because computer designers knew what it would take to design a circuit to add two integers, they chose representations that simplified the circuit. The result is the *2's complement* data type, also shown in Figure 2.1. It is used on just about every computer manufactured today.

2.3 2's Complement Integers

We see in Figure 2.1 the representations of the integers from -16 to $+15$ for the 2's complement data type. Why were those representations chosen?

The positive integers, we saw, are represented in the straightforward positional scheme. With five bits, we use exactly half of the 2^5 codes to represent 0 and the positive integers from 1 to $2^4 - 1$.

The choice of representations for the negative integers was based, as we said previously, on the wish to keep the logic circuits as simple as possible. Almost all computers use the same basic mechanism to perform addition. It is called an *arithmetic and logic unit*, usually known by its acronym ALU. We will get into the actual structure of the ALU in Chapters 3 and 4. What is relevant right now is that an ALU has two inputs and one output. It performs addition by adding the binary bit patterns at its inputs, producing a bit pattern at its output that is the sum of the two input bit patterns.

For example, if the ALU processed five-bit input patterns, and the two inputs were 00110 and 00101, the result (output of the ALU) would be 01011. The addition is as follows:

```
 00110
 00101
 01011
```

The addition of two binary strings is performed in the same way the addition of two decimal strings is performed, from right to left, column by column. If the addition in a column generates a carry, the carry is added to the column immediately to its left.

What is particularly relevant is that the binary ALU does not know (and does not care) what the two patterns it is adding represent. It simply adds the two binary patterns. Since the binary ALU only ADDs and does not CARE, it would be nice if our assignment of codes to the integers resulted in the ALU producing correct results when it added two integers.

For starters, it would be nice if, when the ALU adds the representation for an arbitrary integer to the representation of the integer having the same magnitude but opposite sign, the sum would be 0. That is, if the inputs to the ALU are the representations of non-zero integers A and $-A$, the output of the ALU should be 00000.

To accomplish that, the 2's complement data type specifies the representation for each negative integer so that when the ALU adds it to the representation of the positive integer of the same magnitude, the result will be the representation for 0. For example, since 00101 is the representation of +5, 11011 is chosen as the representation for −5.

Moreover, and actually more importantly, as we sequence through representations of −15 to +15, the ALU is adding 00001 to each successive representation. We can express this mathematically as:

$$REPRESENTATION(value + 1) =$$
$$REPRESENTATION(value) + REPRESENTATION(1).$$

This is sufficient to guarantee (as long as we do not get a result larger than +15 or smaller than −15) that the binary ALU will perform addition correctly.

Note in particular the representations for −1 and 0, that is, 11111 and 00000. When we add 00001 to the representation for −1, we do get 00000, but we also generate a carry. That carry, however, does not influence the result. That is, the correct result of adding 00001 to the representation for −1 is 0, not 100000. Therefore, the carry is ignored. In fact, because the carry obtained by adding 00001 to 11111 is ignored, the carry can *always* be ignored when dealing with 2's complement arithmetic.

Note: If we know the representation for A, a shortcut for figuring out the representation for −A(A ≠ 0) is as follows: Flip all the bits of A (the official term for "flip" is *complement*), and add 1 to the complement of A. The sum of A and the complement of A is 11111. If we then add 00001 to 11111, the final result is 00000. Thus, the representation for −A can be easily obtained by adding 1 to the complement of A.

Example 2.1	

What is the 2's complement representation for −13?

1. Let A be +13. Then the representation for A is 01101 since 13 = 8+4+1.
2. The complement of A is 10010.
3. Adding 1 to 10010 gives us 10011, the 2's complement representation for −13.

   We can verify our result by adding the representations for A and −A,

$$\begin{array}{r} 01101 \\ 10011 \\ \hline 00000 \end{array}$$

You may have noticed that the addition of 01101 and 10011, in addition to producing 00000, also produces a carry out of the five-bit ALU. That is, the binary addition of 01101 and 10011 is really 100000. However, as we saw previously, this carry out can be ignored in the case of the 2's complement data type.

At this point, we have identified in our five-bit scheme 15 positive integers. We have constructed 15 negative integers. We also have a representation

LX † n

for 0. With $k = 5$, we can uniquely identify 32 distinct quantities, and we have accounted for only 31 $(15 + 15 + 1)$. The remaining representation is 10000. What value shall we assign to it?

We note that -1 is 11111, -2 is 11110, -3 is 11101, and so on. If we continue this, we note that -15 is 10001. Note that, as in the case of the positive representations, as we sequence backwards from representations of -1 to -15, the ALU is subtracting 00001 from each successive representation. Thus, it is convenient to assign to 10000 the value -16; that is the value one gets by subtracting 00001 from 10001 (the representation for -15).

In Chapter 5 we will specify a computer that we affectionately have named the LC-3 (for Little Computer 3). The LC-3 operates on 16-bit values. Therefore, the 2's complement integers that can be represented in the LC-3 are the integers from $-32,768$ to $+32,767$.

2.4 Conversion Between Binary and Decimal

It is often useful to convert numbers between the 2's complement data type the computer likes and the decimal representation that you have used all your life.

2.4.1 Binary to Decimal Conversion

We convert a 2's complement representation of an integer to a decimal representation as follows: For purposes of illustration, we will assume our number can be represented in eight bits, corresponding to decimal integer values from -128 to $+127$.

Recall that an eight-bit 2's complement integer takes the form

$$b_7 \; b_6 \; b_5 \; b_4 \; b_3 \; b_2 \; b_1 \; b_0$$

where each of the bits b_i is either 0 or 1.

1. Examine the leading bit b_7. If it is a 0, the integer is positive, and we can begin evaluating its magnitude. If it is a 1, the integer is negative. In that case, we need to first obtain the 2's complement representation of the positive number having the same magnitude. We do this by flipping all the bits and adding 1.

2. The magnitude is simply

$$b_6 \cdot 2^6 + b_5 \cdot 2^5 + b_4 \cdot 2^4 + b_3 \cdot 2^3 + b_2 \cdot 2^2 + b_1 \cdot 2^1 + b_0 \cdot 2^0$$

   In either case, we obtain the decimal magnitude by simply adding the powers of 2 that have coefficients of 1.

3. Finally, if the original number is negative, we affix a minus sign in front. Done!

Example 2.2	Convert the 2's complement integer 11000111 to a decimal integer value.

1. Since the leading binary digit is a 1, the number is negative. We must first find the 2's complement representation of the positive number of the same magnitude. This is 00111001.

2. The magnitude can be represented as

$$0 \cdot 2^6 + 1 \cdot 2^5 + 1 \cdot 2^4 + 1 \cdot 2^3 + 0 \cdot 2^2 + 0 \cdot 2^1 + 1 \cdot 2^0$$

or,

$$32 + 16 + 8 + 1.$$

3. The decimal integer value corresponding to 11000111 is −57.

2.4.2 Decimal to Binary Conversion

Converting from decimal to 2's complement is a little more complicated. The crux of the method is to note that a positive binary number is *odd* if the rightmost digit is 1 and *even* if the rightmost digit is 0.

Consider again our generic eight-bit representation:

$$b_7 \cdot 2^7 + b_6 \cdot 2^6 + b_5 \cdot 2^5 + b_4 \cdot 2^4 + b_3 \cdot 2^3 + b_2 \cdot 2^2 + b_1 \cdot 2^1 + b_0 \cdot 2^0$$

We can illustrate the conversion best by first working through an example.

Suppose we wish to convert the value +105 to a 2's complement binary code. We note that +105 is positive. We first find values for b_i, representing the magnitude 105. Since the value is positive, we will then obtain the 2's complement result by simply appending b_7, which we know is 0.

Our first step is to find values for b_i that satisfy the following:

$$105 = b_6 \cdot 2^6 + b_5 \cdot 2^5 + b_4 \cdot 2^4 + b_3 \cdot 2^3 + b_2 \cdot 2^2 + b_1 \cdot 2^1 + b_0 \cdot 2^0$$

Since 105 is odd, we know that b_0 is 1. We subtract 1 from both sides of the equation, yielding

$$104 = b_6 \cdot 2^6 + b_5 \cdot 2^5 + b_4 \cdot 2^4 + b_3 \cdot 2^3 + b_2 \cdot 2^2 + b_1 \cdot 2^1$$

We next divide both sides of the equation by 2, yielding

$$52 = b_6 \cdot 2^5 + b_5 \cdot 2^4 + b_4 \cdot 2^3 + b_3 \cdot 2^2 + b_2 \cdot 2^1 + b_1 \cdot 2^0$$

Since 52 is even, b_1, the only coefficient not multiplied by a power of 2, must be equal to 0.

We iterate this process, each time subtracting the rightmost digit from both sides of the equation, then dividing both sides by 2, and finally noting whether the new decimal number on the left side is odd or even. Continuing where we left off, with

$$52 = b_6 \cdot 2^5 + j_5 \cdot 2^4 + b_4 \cdot 2^3 + b_3 \cdot 2^2 + b_2 \cdot 2^1$$

the process produces, in turn:

$$26 = b_6 \cdot 2^4 + b_5 \cdot 2^3 + b_4 \cdot 2^2 + b_3 \cdot 2^1 + b_2 \cdot 2^0$$

Therefore, $b_2 = 0$.

$$13 = b_6 \cdot 2^3 + b_5 \cdot 2^2 + b_4 \cdot 2^1 + b_3 \cdot 2^0$$

Therefore, $b_3 = 1$.

$$6 = b_6 \cdot 2^2 + b_5 \cdot 2^1 + b_4 \cdot 2^0$$

Therefore, $b_4 = 0$.

$$3 = b_6 \cdot 2^1 + b_5 \cdot 2^0$$

Therefore, $b_5 = 1$.

$$1 = b_6 \cdot 2^0$$

Therefore, $b_6 = 1$, and we are done. The binary representation is 01101001.

Let's summarize the process. If we are given a decimal integer value N, we construct the 2's complement representation as follows:

1. We first obtain the binary representation of the magnitude of N by forming the equation

$$N = b_6 \cdot 2^6 + b_5 \cdot 2^5 + b_4 \cdot 2^4 + b_3 \cdot 2^3 + b_2 \cdot 2^2 + b_1 \cdot 2^1 + b_0 \cdot 2^0$$

and repeating the following, until the left side of the equation is 0:

   a. If N is odd, the rightmost bit is 1. If N is even, the rightmost bit is 0.
   b. Subtract 1 or 0 (according to whether N is odd or even) from N, remove the least significant term from the right side, and divide both sides of the equation by 2.

   Each iteration produces the value of one coefficient b_i.

2. If the original decimal number is positive, append a leading 0 sign bit, and you are done.

3. If the original decimal number is negative, append a leading 0 and then form the negative of this 2's complement representation, and then you are done.

2.4.3 Extending Conversion to Numbers with Fractional Parts

What if the number we wish to convert is not an integer, but instead has a fractional part. How do we handle that wrinkle?

Binary to decimal   The binary to decimal case is straightforward. In a positional notation system, the number

$$0.b_{-1}b_{-2}b_{-3}b_{-4}$$

shows four bits to the right of the binary point, representing (when the corresponding $b_i = 1$) the values 0.5, 0.25, 0.125, and 0.0625. To complete the conversion to decimal, we simply add those values where the corresponding $b_i = 1$. For example, if the fractional part of the binary representation is

$$. 1 \; 0 \; 1 \; 1$$

we would add 0.5 plus 0.125 plus 0.0625, or 0.6875.

Decimal to binary   The decimal to binary case requires a little more work. Suppose we wanted to convert 0.421 to binary. As we did for integer conversion, we first form the equation

$$0.421 = b_{-1} \times 2^{-1} + b_{-2} \times 2^{-2} + b_{-3} \times 2^{-3} + b_{-4} \times 2^{-4} + ...$$

In the case of converting a decimal integer value to binary, we divided by 2 and assigned a 1 or 0 to the coefficient of 2^0 depending on whether the number on the left of the equal sign is odd or even. Here (i.e., in the case of converting a decimal fraction to binary), we multiply both sides of the equation by 2 and assign a 1 or a 0 to the coefficient of 2^0 depending on whether the left side of the equation is greater than or equal to 1 or whether the left side is less than 1. Do you see why?

Since

$$0.842 = b_{-1} \times 2^0 + b_{-2} \times 2^{-1} + b_{-3} \times 2^{-2} + b_{-4} \times 2^{-3} + ...$$

we assign $b_{-1} = 0$. Continuing,

$$1.684 = b_{-2} \times 2^0 + b_{-3} \times 2^{-1} + b_{-4} \times 2^{-2} + ...$$

so we assign $b_{-2} = 1$ and subtract 1 from both sides of the equation, yielding

$$0.684 = b_{-3} \times 2^{-1} + b_{-4} \times 2^{-2} + ...$$

Multiplying by 2, we get

$$1.368 = b_{-3} \times 2^0 + b_{-4} \times 2^{-1} + ...$$

so we assign $b_{-3} = 1$ and subtract 1 from both sides of the equation, yielding

$$0.368 = b_{-4} \times 2^0 + ...$$

which assigns 0 to b_{-4}. We can continue this process indefinitely, until we are simply too tired to go on, or until the left side $= 0$, in which case all bits to the right of where we stop are 0s. In our case, stopping with four bits, we have converted 0.421 decimal to 0.0110 in binary.

2.5 Operations on Bits— Part I: Arithmetic

2.5.1 Addition and Subtraction

Arithmetic on 2's complement numbers is very much like the arithmetic on decimal numbers that you have been doing for a long time.

Addition still proceeds from right to left, one digit at a time. At each point, we generate a sum digit and a carry. Instead of generating a carry after 9 (since 9 is the largest decimal digit), we generate a carry after 1 (since 1 is the largest binary digit).

Example 2.3

Using our five-bit notation, what is $11 + 3$?

```
The decimal value 11 is represented as 01011
The decimal value 3 is represented as  00011
The sum, which is the value 14, is      01110
```

Subtraction is simply addition, preceded by determining the negative of the number to be subtracted. That is, $A - B$ is simply $A + (-B)$.

Example 2.4

What is $14 - 9$?

```
The decimal value 14 is represented as    01110
The decimal value 9 is represented as     01001
```

First we form the negative, that is, -9: 10111   1's Compliment   01001

Adding 14 to -9, we get   01110   -16 + 7
                                           10111
                                          00101

which results in the value 5.   00101

Note again that the carry out is ignored.

Example 2.5

What happens when we add a number to itself (e.g., $x + x$)?

Let's assume for this example eight-bit codes, which would allow us to represent integers from -128 to 127. Consider a value for x, the integer 59, represented as 00111011. If we add 59 to itself, we get the code 01110110. Note that the bits have all shifted to the left by one position. Is that a curiosity, or will that happen all the time as long as the sum $x + x$ is not too large to represent with the available number of bits?

Using our positional notation, the number 59 is

$$0 \cdot 2^6 + 1 \cdot 2^5 + 1 \cdot 2^4 + 1 \cdot 2^3 + 0 \cdot 2^2 + 1 \cdot 2^1 + 1 \cdot 2^0$$

The sum $59 + 59$ is $2 \cdot 59$, which, in our representation, is

$$2 \cdot (0 \cdot 2^6 + 1 \cdot 2^5 + 1 \cdot 2^4 + 1 \cdot 2^3 + 0 \cdot 2^2 + 1 \cdot 2^1 + 1 \cdot 2^0)$$

But that is nothing more than

$$0 \cdot 2^7 + 1 \cdot 2^6 + 1 \cdot 2^5 + 1 \cdot 2^4 + 0 \cdot 2^3 + 1 \cdot 2^2 + 1 \cdot 2^1$$

which shifts each digit one position to the left. Thus, adding a number to itself (provided there are enough bits to represent the result) is equivalent to shifting the representation one bit position to the left.

2.5.2 Sign-Extension

It is often useful to represent a small number with fewer bits. For example, rather than represent the value 5 as 0000000000000101, there are times when it makes more sense to use only six bits to represent the value 5: 000101. There is little confusion, since we are all used to adding leading zeros without affecting the value of a number. A check for $456.78 and a check for $0000456.78 are checks having the same value.

What about negative representations? We obtained the negative representation from its positive counterpart by complementing the positive representation and adding 1. Thus, the representation for −5, given that 5 is represented as 000101, is 111011. If 5 is represented as 0000000000000101, then the representation for −5 is 1111111111111011. In the same way that leading 0s do not affect the value of a positive number, leading 1s do not affect the value of a negative number.

In order to add representations of different lengths, it is first necessary to represent them with the same number of bits. For example, suppose we wish to add the number 13 to −5, where 13 is represented as 0000000000001101 and −5 is represented as 111011. If we do not represent the two values with the same number of bits, we have

$$
\begin{array}{r}
0000000000001101 \\
+ \ 111011 \\ \hline
\end{array}
$$

When we attempt to perform the addition, what shall we do with the missing bits in the representation for −5? If we take the absence of a bit to be a 0, then we are no longer adding −5 to 13. On the contrary, if we take the absence of bits to be 0s, we have changed the −5 to the number represented as 0000000000111011, that is, +59. Not surprisingly, then, our result turns out to be the representation for 72.

However, if we understand that a 6-bit −5 and a 16-bit −5 differ only in the number of meaningless leading 1s, then we first extend the value of −5 to 16 bits before we perform the addition. Thus, we have

$$
\begin{array}{r}
0000000000001101 \\
+ \ 1111111111111011 \\ \hline
0000000000001000
\end{array}
$$

and the result is +8, as we should expect.

The value of a positive number does not change if we extend the sign bit 0 as many bit positions to the left as desired. Similarly, the value of a negative number does not change by extending the sign bit 1 as many bit positions to the left as desired. Since in both cases it is the sign bit that is extended, we refer to the operation as *Sign-EXTension*, often abbreviated SEXT. Sign-extension is performed in order to be able to operate on representations of different lengths. It does not affect the values of the numbers being represented.

2.5.3 Overflow

Up to now, we have always insisted that the sum of two integers be small enough to be represented by the available bits. What happens if such is not the case?

You are undoubtedly familiar with the odometer on the front dashboard of your automobile. It keeps track of how many miles your car has been driven—but only up to a point. In the old days, when the odometer registered 99992 and you drove it 100 miles, its new reading became 00092. A brand new car! The problem, as you know, is that the largest value the odometer could store was 99999, so the value 100092 showed up as 00092. The carry out of the ten-thousands digit was lost. (Of course, if you grew up in Boston, the carry out was not lost at all—it was in full display in the rusted chrome all over the car.)

We say the odometer *overflowed*. Representing 100092 as 00092 is unacceptable. As more and more cars lasted more than 100,000 miles, car makers felt the pressure to add a digit to the odometer. Today, practically all cars overflow at 1,000,000 miles, rather than 100,000 miles.

The odometer provides an example of unsigned arithmetic. The miles you add are always positive miles. The odometer reads 000129 and you drive 50 miles. The odometer now reads 000179. Overflow is a carry out of the leading digit.

In the case of signed arithmetic, or more particularly, 2's complement arithmetic, overflow is a little more subtle.

Let's return to our five-bit 2's complement data type, which allowed us to represent integers from −16 to +15. Suppose we wish to add +9 and +11. Our arithmetic takes the following form:

$$
\begin{array}{r}
01001 \\
01011 \\
\hline
10100
\end{array}
$$

Note that the sum is larger than +15, and therefore too large to represent with our 2's complement scheme. The fact that the number is too large means that the number is larger than 01111, the largest positive number we can represent with a five-bit 2's complement data type. Note that because our positive result was larger than +15, it generated a carry into the leading bit position. But this bit position is used to indicate the sign of a value. Thus, detecting that the result is too large is an easy matter. Since we are adding two positive numbers, the result must be positive. Since the ALU has produced a negative result, something must be wrong. The thing that is wrong is that the sum of the two positive numbers is too large to be represented with the available bits. We say that the result has *overflowed* the capacity of the representation.

Suppose instead, we had started with negative numbers, for example, −12 and −6. In this case, our arithmetic takes the following form:

$$
\begin{array}{r}
10100 \\
11010 \\
\hline
01110
\end{array}
$$

Here, too, the result has overflowed the capacity of the machine, since −12 + −6 equals −18, which is "more negative" than −16, the negative number with the largest allowable magnitude. The ALU obliges by producing a positive result. Again, this is easy to detect since the sum of two negative numbers cannot be positive.

Note that the sum of a negative number and a positive number never presents a problem. Why is that? See Exercise 2.25.

2.6 Operations on Bits— Part II: Logical Operations

We have seen that it is possible to perform arithmetic (e.g., add, subtract) on values represented as binary patterns. Another class of operations useful to perform on binary patterns is the set of *logical* operations.

2.6.1 A Logical Variable

Logical operations operate on logical variables. A logical variable can have one of two values, 0 or 1. The name *logical* is a historical one; it comes from the fact that the two values 0 and 1 can represent the two logical values *false* and *true*, but the use of logical operations has traveled far from this original meaning.

There are several basic logic functions, and most ALUs perform all of them.

2.6.2 The AND Function

AND is a *binary* logical function. This means it requires two pieces of input data. Said another way, AND requires two source operands. Each source is a logical variable, taking the value 0 or 1. The output of AND is 1 only if both sources have the value 1. Otherwise, the output is 0. We can think of the AND operation as the ALL operation; that is, the output is 1 only if ALL two inputs are 1. Otherwise, the output is 0.

A convenient mechanism for representing the behavior of a logical operation is the *truth table*. A truth table consists of $n + 1$ columns and 2^n rows. The first n columns correspond to the n source operands. Since each source operand is a logical variable and can have one of two values, there are 2^n unique values that these source operands can have. Each such set of values (sometimes called an *input combination*) is represented as one row of the truth table. The final column in the truth table shows the output for each input combination.

In the case of a two-input AND function, the truth table has two columns for source operands, and four (2^2) rows for unique input combinations.

A	B	AND
0	0	0
0	1	0
1	0	0
1	1	1

We can apply the logical operation AND to two bit patterns of m bits each. This involves applying the operation individually and independently to each pair of bits in the two source operands. For example, if a and b in Example 2.6 are 16-bit patterns, then c is the AND of a and b. This operation is often called a *bit-wise AND* because the operation is applied to each pair of bits individually and independently.

Example 2.6

If c is the AND of a and b, where $a=0011101001101001$ and $b=0101100100100001$, what is c?

We form the AND of a and b by bit-wise ANDing the two values.

That means individually ANDing each pair of bits a_i and b_i to form c_i. For example, since $a_0=1$ and $b_0=1$, c_0 is the AND of a_0 and b_0, which is 1.

Since $a_6=1$ and $b_6=0$, c_6 is the AND of a_6 and b_6, which is 0.

The complete solution for c is

```
a: 0011101001101001
b: 0101100100100001
c: 0001100000100001
```

Example 2.7

Suppose we have an eight-bit pattern—let's call it A—in which the rightmost two bits have particular significance. The computer could be asked to do one of four tasks depending on the value stored in the two rightmost bits of A. Can we isolate those two bits?

Yes, we can, using a bit mask. A *bit mask* is a binary pattern that enables the bits of A to be separated into two parts—generally the part you care about and the part you wish to ignore. In this case, the bit mask 00000011 ANDed with A produces 0 in bit positions 7 through 2, and the original values of bits 1 and 0 of A in bit positions 1 and 0. The bit mask is said to *mask out* the values in bit positions 7 through 2.

If A is 01010110, the AND of A and the bit mask 00000011 is 00000010. If A is 11111100, the AND of A and the bit mask 00000011 is 00000000.

That is, the result of ANDing any eight-bit pattern with the mask 00000011 is one of the four patterns: 00000000, 00000001, 00000010, or 00000011. The result of ANDing with the mask is to highlight the two bits that are relevant.

2.6.3 The OR Function

OR is also a *binary* logical function. It requires two source operands, both of which are logical variables. The output of OR is 1 if any source has the value 1. Only if both sources are 0 is the output 0. We can think of the OR operation as the ANY operation; that is, the output is 1 if ANY of the two inputs are 1.

The truth table for a two-input OR function is

A	B	OR
0	0	0
0	1	1
1	0	1
1	1	1

In the same way that we applied the logical operation AND to two m-bit patterns, we can apply the OR operation bit-wise to two m-bit patterns.

Example 2.8

If c is the OR of a and b, where $a=0011101001101001$ and $b=0101100100100001$, as before, what is c?

We form the OR of a and b by bit-wise ORing the two values. That means individually ORing each pair of bits a_i and b_i to form c_i. For example, since $a_0=1$ and $b_0=1$, c_0 is the OR of a_0 and b_0, which is 1. Since $a_6=1$ and $b_6=0$, c_6 is the OR of a_6 and b_6, which is also 1.

The complete solution for c is

$$
\begin{array}{ll}
\texttt{a:} & \underline{0011101001101001} \\
\texttt{b:} & \underline{0101100100100001} \\
\texttt{c:} & 0111101101101001
\end{array}
$$

Sometimes this OR operation is referred to as the *inclusive-OR* in order to distinguish it from the exclusive-OR function, which we will discuss momentarily.

2.6.4 The NOT Function

NOT is a *unary* logical function. This means it operates on only one source operand. It is also known as the *complement* operation. The output is formed by complementing the input. We sometimes say the output is formed by *inverting* the input. A 1 input results in a 0 output. A 0 input results in a 1 output.

The truth table for the NOT function is

A	NOT
0	1
1	0

In the same way that we applied the logical operation AND and OR to two m-bit patterns, we can apply the NOT operation bit-wise to one m-bit pattern. If a is as before, then c is the NOT of a.

$$
\begin{array}{ll}
\texttt{a:} & \underline{0011101001101001} \\
\texttt{c:} & 1100010110010110
\end{array}
$$

2.6.5 The Exclusive-OR Function

Exclusive-OR, often abbreviated XOR, is a *binary* logical function. It, too, requires two source operands, both of which are logical variables. The output of XOR is 1 if one (but not both) of the two sources is 1. The output of XOR is 0 if both sources are 1 or if neither source is 1. In other words, the output of XOR is 1 if the two sources are different. The output is 0 if the two sources are the same.

The truth table for the XOR function is

A	B	XOR
0	0	0
0	1	1
1	0	1
1	1	0

In the same way that we applied the logical operation AND to two *m*-bit patterns, we can apply the XOR operation bit-wise to two *m*-bit patterns.

Example 2.9

If *a* and *b* are 16-bit patterns as before, then *c* (shown here) is the XOR of *a* and *b*.

```
a: 0011101001101001
b: 0101100100100001
c: 0110001101001000
```

Note the distinction between the truth table for XOR shown here and the truth table for OR shown earlier. In the case of exclusive-OR, if both source operands are 1, the output is 0. That is, the output is 1 if the first operand is 1 but the second operand is not 1 or if the second operand is 1 but the first operand is not 1. The term *exclusive* is used because the output is 1 if *only* one of the two sources is 1. The OR function, on the other hand, produces an output 1 if only one of the two sources is 1, or if both sources are 1. Ergo, the name *inclusive-OR*.

Example 2.10

Suppose we wish to know if two patterns are identical. Since the XOR function produces a 0 only if the corresponding pair of bits is identical, two patterns are identical if the output of the XOR is all 0s.

2.6.6 DeMorgan's Laws

There are two well-known relationships between AND functions and OR functions, known as DeMorgan's Laws. One of them is illustrated in Figure 2.2. In Figure 2.2a, we complement each of the two inputs *A* and *B* before using them as inputs to the AND function, and we also complement the result produced by

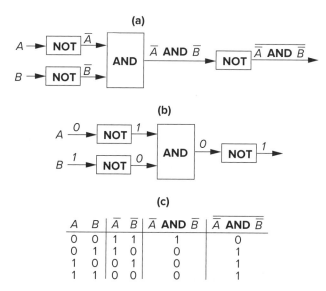

Figure 2.2   DeMorgan's Law.

the AND function. Figure 2.2b shows the output of these functions if $A = 0$ and $B = 1$. Figure 2.2c summarizes by means of a truth table the behavior of the logic functions for all four input combinations of A and B. Note that the NOT of A is represented as $\bar{A}$.

We can describe the behavior of these functions algebraically:

$$\overline{\bar{A} \text{ AND } \bar{B}} = A \text{ OR } B$$

We can also state this behavior in English:

"It is not the case that both A and B are false" is equivalent to saying "At least one of A and B is true."

This equivalence is known as one of two DeMorgan's Laws. Question: Is there a similar result if one inverts both inputs to an OR function, and then inverts the output?

2.6.7 The Bit Vector

We have discussed the AND, OR, and NOT functions performed on m-bit patterns, where each of the m bits is a logical value (0 or 1) and the operations are performed bit-wise (i.e., individually and independently). We have also discussed the use of an m-bit bit mask, where our choice of 0 or 1 for each bit allows us to isolate the bits we are interested in focusing on and ignore the bits that don't matter.

An m-bit pattern where each bit has a logical value (0 or 1) independent of the other bits is called a *bit vector*. It is a convenient mechanism for identifying a property such that some of the bits identify the presence of the property and other bits identify the absence of the property.

There are many uses for bit vectors. The most common use is a bit mask, as we saw in Example 2.7. In that example, we had an eight-bit value, and we wanted to focus on bit 1 and bit 0 of that value. We did not care about the other bits. Performing the AND of that value with the bit mask 00000011 caused bit 7 through bit 2 to be ignored, resulting in the AND function producing 00000000, 00000001, 00000010, or 00000011, depending on the values of bit 1 and bit 0. The bit mask is a bit vector, where the property of each of the bits is whether or not we care about that bit. In Example 2.7, we only cared about bit 1 and bit 0.

Another use of a bit mask could involve a 16-bit 2's complement integer. Suppose the only thing we cared about was whether the integer was odd or even and whether it was positive or negative. The bit vector 1000000000000001 has a 1 in bit 15 that is used to identify a number as positive or negative, and a 1 in bit 0 that is used to identify if the integer is odd or even. If we perform the AND of this bit vector with a 16-bit 2's complement integer, we would get one of four results, depending on whether the integer was positive or negative and odd or even:

```
0000000000000000
0000000000000001
1000000000000000
1000000000000001
```

Another common use of bit vectors involves managing a complex system made up of several units, each of which is individually and independently either *busy* or *available*. The system could be a manufacturing plant where each unit is a particular machine. Or the system could be a taxicab network where each unit is a particular taxicab. In both cases, it is important to identify which units are busy and which are available so that work can be properly assigned.

Say we have *m* such units. We can keep track of these *m* units with a bit vector, where a bit is 1 if the unit is free and 0 if the unit is busy.

Example 2.11

Suppose we have eight machines that we want to monitor with respect to their availability. We can keep track of them with an eight-bit BUSYNESS bit vector, where a bit is 1 if the unit is free and 0 if the unit is busy. The bits are labeled, from right to left, from 0 to 7.

The BUSYNESS bit vector 11000010 corresponds to the situation where only units 7, 6, and 1 are free and therefore available for work assignment.

Suppose work is assigned to unit 7. We update our BUSYNESS bit vector by performing the logical AND, where our two sources are the current bit vector 11000010 and the bit mask 01111111. The purpose of the bit mask is to clear bit 7 of the BUSYNESS bit vector, while leaving alone the values corresponding to all the other units. The result is the bit vector 01000010, indicating that unit 7 is now busy.

Suppose unit 5 finishes its task and becomes idle. We can update the BUSYNESS bit vector by performing the logical OR of it with the bit mask 00100000. The result is 01100010, indicating that unit 5 is now available.

2.7 Other Representations

There are many other representations of information that are used in computers. Two that are among the most useful are the floating point data type and ASCII codes. We will describe both in this section. We will also describe a notation called hexadecimal that, although not a data type, is convenient for humans to use when dealing with long strings of 0s and 1s.

2.7.1 Floating Point Data Type (Greater Range, Less Precision)

Most of the arithmetic in this book uses integer values. The LC-3 computer, which you will start studying in Chapter 4, uses the 16-bit, 2's complement integer data type. That data type provides one bit to identify whether the number is positive or negative and 15 bits to represent the magnitude of the value. With 16 bits used in this way, we can express integer values between $-32,768$ and $+32,767$, that is, between -2^{15} and $+2^{15} - 1$. We say the *precision* of our value is 15 bits, and the *range* is 2^{16}. As you learned in high school chemistry class, sometimes we need to express much larger numbers, but we do not require so many digits of precision. In fact, recall the value $6.022 \cdot 10^{23}$, which you may have been required to memorize back then. The range needed to express the value 10^{23} is far greater than the largest value $2^{15} - 1$ that is available with 16-bit 2's complement integers. On the other hand, the 15 bits of precision available with 16-bit 2's complement integers are overkill. We need only enough bits to express four significant decimal digits (6022).

So we have a problem. We have more bits than we need for precision. But we don't have enough bits to represent the range.

The *floating point* data type solves the problem. Instead of using all the bits to represent the precision of a value, the floating point data type allocates some of the bits to the range of values (i.e., how big or how small) that can be expressed. The rest of the bits (except for the sign bit) are used for precision.

Most ISAs today specify more than one floating point data type. One of them, usually called *float*, consists of 32 bits, allocated as follows:

```
1 bit for the sign (positive or negative)
8 bits for the range (the exponent field)
23 bits for precision (the fraction field)
```

In most computers manufactured today, the format of the 32-bit floating point data type is as shown in Figure 2.3.

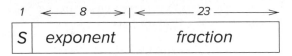

Figure 2.3   The 32-bit floating point data type.

2.7.1.1 Normalized Form

Like Avogadro's number that you learned years ago, the floating point data type represents numbers expressed in scientific notation, and mostly in normalized form:

$$N = (-1)^S \times 1.\,fraction \times 2^{exponent-127},\ 1 \le exponent \le 254$$

where S, *fraction*, and *exponent* are the binary numbers in the fields of Figure 2.3.

We say *mostly* in normalized form because (as noted in the equation) the data type represents a floating point number in normalized form **only** if the eight-bit exponent is restricted to the 254 unsigned integer values, 1 (00000001) through 254 (11111110).

As you know, with eight bits, one can represent 256 values uniquely. For the other two integer values 0 (00000000) and 255 (11111111), the floating point data type does not represent normalized numbers. We will explain what it does represent in Section 2.7.1.2 and Section 2.7.1.3.

Recall again Avogadro's number: (a) an implied + sign (often left out when the value is positive), (b) four decimal digits 6.022 in normalized form (one non-zero decimal digit 6 before the decimal point) times (c) the radix 10 raised to the power 23. The computer's 32-bit floating point data type, on the other hand, consists of (a) a sign bit (positive or negative), (b) 24 binary digits in normalized form (one non-zero binary digit to the left of the binary point) times (c) the radix 2 raised to an exponent expressed in eight bits.

We determine the value of the 32-bit floating point representation shown in Figure 2.3 by examining its three parts.

The sign bit S is just a single binary digit, 0 for positive numbers, 1 for negative numbers. The formula contains the factor -1^S, which evaluates to $+1$ if $S = 0$, and -1 if $S = 1$.

The 23 fraction bits form the 24-bit quantity 1.fraction, where *normalized form* demands exactly one non-zero binary digit to the left of the binary point. Since there exists only one non-zero binary digit (i.e., the value 1), it is unnecessary to explicitly store that bit in our 32-bit floating point format. In fact that is how we get 24 bits of precision, the 1 to the left of the binary point that is always present in normalized numbers and so is unnecessary to store, and the 23 bits of fraction that are actually part of the 32-bit data type.

The eight exponent bits are encoded in what we call an excess code, named for the notion that one can get the *real* exponent by treating the code as an unsigned integer and subtracting the excess (sometimes called the *bias*). In the case of the IEEE Floating Point that almost everyone uses, that excess (or bias) is 127 for 32-bit floating point numbers. Thus, an exponent field containing 10000110 corresponds to the exponent $+7$ (since 10000110 represents the unsigned integer 134, from which we subtract 127, yielding $+7$). An exponent field containing 00000111 corresponds to the exponent -120 (since 00000111 represents the unsigned integer 7, from which we subtract 127, yielding -120). The exponent field gives us numbers as large as 2^{+127} for an exponent field containing 254 (11111110) and as small as 2^{-126} for an exponent field containing 1 (00000001).

Example 2.12

What does the floating point data type

$$00111101100000000000000000000000$$

represent?

The leading bit is a 0. This signifies a positive number. The next eight bits represent the unsigned number 123. If we subtract 127, we get the actual exponent -4. The last 23 bits are all 0. Therefore, the number being represented is $+1.00000000000000000000000 \cdot 2^{-4}$, which is $\frac{1}{16}$.

Example 2.13

How is the number $-6\frac{5}{8}$ represented in the floating point data type?

First, we express $-6\frac{5}{8}$ as a binary number: -110.101.

$$-(1 \cdot 2^2 + 1 \cdot 2^1 + 0 \cdot 2^0 + 1 \cdot 2^{-1} + 0 \cdot 2^{-2} + 1 \cdot 2^{-3})$$

Then we normalize the value, yielding $-1.10101 \cdot 2^2$.

The sign bit is 1, reflecting the fact that $-6\frac{5}{8}$ is a negative number. The exponent field contains 10000001, the unsigned number 129, reflecting the fact that the real exponent is $+2$ ($129 - 127 = +2$). The fraction is the 23 bits of precision, after removing the leading 1. That is, the fraction is 10101000000000000000000. The result is the number $-6\frac{5}{8}$, expressed as a floating point number:

$$1 \quad 10000001 \quad 10101000000000000000000$$

Example 2.14

The following three examples provide further illustrations of the interpretation of the 32-bit floating point data type according to the rules of the IEEE standard.

$$0 \quad 10000011 \quad 00101000000000000000000 \text{ is } 1.00101 \cdot 2^4 = 18.5$$

The exponent field contains the unsigned number 131. Since $131 - 127$ is 4, the exponent is $+4$. Combining a 1 to the left of the binary point with the fraction field to the right of the binary point yields 1.00101. If we move the binary point four positions to the right, we get 10010.1, which is 18.5.

$$1 \quad 10000010 \quad 00101000000000000000000 \text{ is } -1 \cdot 1.00101 \cdot 2^3 = -9.25$$

The sign bit is 1, signifying a negative number. The exponent is 130, signifying an exponent of $130 - 127$, or $+3$. Combining a 1 to the left of the binary point with the fraction field to the right of the binary point yields 1.00101. Moving the binary point three positions to the right, we get 1001.01, which is -9.25.

$$0 \quad 11111110 \quad 11111111111111111111111 \text{ is } \sim 2^{128}$$

The sign is $+$. The exponent is $254 - 127$, or $+127$. Combining a 1 to the left of the binary point with the fraction field to the right of the binary point yields $1.11111111 \ldots 1$, which is approximately 2. Therefore, the result is approximately 2^{128}.

2.7.1.2 Infinities

We noted above that the floating point data type represented numbers expressed in scientific notation in normalized form provided the exponent field does not contain 00000000 or 11111111.

If the exponent field contains 11111111, we use the floating point data type to represent various things, among them the notion of infinity. *Infinity* is represented by the exponent field containing all 1s and the fraction field containing all 0s. We represent positive infinity if the sign bit is 0 and negative infinity if the sign bit is 1.

2.7.1.3 Subnormal Numbers

The smallest number that can be represented in normalized form is

$$N = 1.00000000000000000000000 \times 2^{-126}$$

What about numbers smaller than 2^{-126} but larger than 0? We call such numbers *subnormal numbers* because they cannot be represented in normalized form. The largest subnormal number is

$$N = 0.11111111111111111111111 \times 2^{-126}$$

The smallest subnormal number is

$$N = 0.00000000000000000000001 \times 2^{-126}, \text{ i.e., } 2^{-23} \times 2^{-126} \text{ which is } 2^{-149}.$$

Note that the largest subnormal number is 2^{-126} minus 2^{-149}. Do you see why that is the case?

Subnormal numbers are numbers of the form

$$N = (-1)^S \times 0.\, fraction \times 2^{-126}$$

We represent them with an exponent field of 00000000. The fraction field is represented in the same way as with normalized numbers. That is, if the exponent field contains 00000000, the exponent is -126, and the significant digits are obtained by starting with a leading 0, followed by a binary point, followed by the 23 bits of the fraction field.

Example 2.15

What number corresponds to the following floating point representation?

0   00000000   00001000000000000000000

Answer: The leading 0 means the number is positive. The next eight bits, a zero exponent, means the exponent is -126, and the bit to the left of the binary point is 0. The last 23 bits form the number 0.00001000000000000000000, which equals 2^{-5}. Thus, the number represented is $2^{-5} \cdot 2^{-126}$, which is 2^{-131}.

Including subnormal numbers allows very, very tiny numbers to be represented.

A detailed understanding of IEEE Floating Point Arithmetic is well beyond what should be expected in this first course. Our purpose in including this section in the textbook is to at least let you know that there is, in addition to 2's complement integers, another very important data type available in almost all ISAs, which is called *floating point*; it allows very large and very tiny numbers to be expressed at the cost of reducing the number of binary digits of precision.

2.7.2 ASCII Codes

Another representation of information is the standard code that almost all computer equipment manufacturers have agreed to use for transferring characters between the main computer processing unit and the input and output devices. That code is an eight-bit code referred to as *ASCII*. ASCII stands for American Standard Code for Information Interchange. It (ASCII) greatly simplifies the interface between a keyboard manufactured by one company, a computer made by another company, and a monitor made by a third company.

Each key on the keyboard is identified by its unique ASCII code. So, for example, the digit 3 is represented as 00110011, the digit 2 is 00110010, the lowercase *e* is 01100101, and the ENTER key is 00001101. The entire set of eight-bit ASCII codes is listed in Figure E.2 of Appendix E. When you type a key on the keyboard, the corresponding eight-bit code is stored and made available to the computer. Where it is stored and how it gets into the computer are discussed in Chapter 9.

Most keys are associated with more than one code. For example, the ASCII code for the letter *E* is 01000101, and the ASCII code for the letter *e* is 01100101.

Both are associated with the same key, although in one case the Shift key is also depressed while in the other case, it is not.

In order to display a particular character on the monitor, the computer must transfer the ASCII code for that character to the electronics associated with the monitor. That, too, is discussed in Chapter 9.

2.7.3 Hexadecimal Notation

We have seen that information can be represented as 2's complement integers, as bit vectors, in floating point format, or as an ASCII code. There are other representations also, but we will leave them for another book. However, before we leave this topic, we would like to introduce you to a representation that is used more as a convenience for humans than as a data type to support operations being performed by the computer. This is the *hexadecimal* notation. As we will see, it evolves nicely from the positional binary notation and is useful for dealing with long strings of binary digits without making errors.

It will be particularly useful in dealing with the LC-3 where 16-bit binary strings will be encountered often.

An example of such a binary string is

$$0011110101101110$$

Let's try an experiment. Cover the preceding 16-bit binary string of 0s and 1s with one hand, and try to write it down from memory. How did you do? Hexadecimal notation is about being able to do this without making mistakes. We shall see how.

In general, a 16-bit binary string takes the form

$$a_{15}\, a_{14}\, a_{13}\, a_{12}\, a_{11}\, a_{10}\, a_9\, a_8\, a_7\, a_6\, a_5\, a_4\, a_3\, a_2\, a_1\, a_0$$

where each of the bits a_i is either 0 or 1.

If we think of this binary string as an unsigned integer, its value can be computed as

$$a_{15} \cdot 2^{15} + a_{14} \cdot 2^{14} + a_{13} \cdot 2^{13} + a_{12} \cdot 2^{12} + a_{11} \cdot 2^{11} + a_{10} \cdot 2^{10}$$
$$+\ a_9 \cdot 2^9 + a_8 \cdot 2^8 + a_7 \cdot 2^7 + a_6 \cdot 2^6 + a_5 \cdot 2^5 + a_4 \cdot 2^4 + a_3 \cdot 2^3$$
$$+\ a_2 \cdot 2^2 + a_1 \cdot 2^1 + a_0 \cdot 2^0$$

We can factor 2^{12} from the first four terms, 2^8 from the second four terms, 2^4 from the third set of four terms, and 2^0 from the last four terms, yielding

$$2^{12}(a_{15} \cdot 2^3 + a_{14} \cdot 2^2 + a_{13} \cdot 2^1 + a_{12} \cdot 2^0)$$
$$+\ 2^8(a_{11} \cdot 2^3 + a_{10} \cdot 2^2 + a_9 \cdot 2^1 + a_8 \cdot 2^0)$$
$$+\ 2^4(a_7 \cdot 2^3 + a_6 \cdot 2^2 + a_5 \cdot 2^1 + a_4 \cdot 2^0)$$
$$+\ 2^0(a_3 \cdot 2^3 + a_2 \cdot 2^2 + a_1 \cdot 2^1 + a_0 \cdot 2^0)$$

Note that the largest value inside a set of parentheses is 15, which would be the case if each of the four bits is 1. If we replace what is inside each square bracket with a symbol representing its value (from 0 to 15), and we replace 2^{12} with its equivalent 16^3, 2^8 with 16^2, 2^4 with 16^1, and 2^0 with 16^0, we have

$$h_3 \cdot 16^3 + h_2 \cdot 16^2 + h_1 \cdot 16^1 + h_0 \cdot 16^0$$

where h_3, for example, is a symbol representing

$$a_{15} \cdot 2^3 + a_{14} \cdot 2^2 + a_{13} \cdot 2^1 + a_{12} \cdot 2^0$$

Since the symbols must represent values from 0 to 15, we assign symbols to these values as follows: 0, 1, 2, 3, 4, 5, 6, 7, 8, 9, A, B, C, D, E, F. That is, we represent 0000 with the symbol 0, 0001 with the symbol 1, ... 1001 with 9, 1010 with A, 1011 with B, ... 1111 with F. The resulting notation is called hexadecimal, or base 16.

So, for example, if the hex digits E92F represent a 16-bit 2's complement integer, is the value of that integer positive or negative? How do you know?

Now, then, what is this hexadecimal representation good for, anyway? It seems like just another way to represent a number without adding any benefit. Let's return to the exercise where you tried to write from memory the string

    0011110101101110

If we had first broken the string at four-bit boundaries

    0011 1101 0110 1110

and then converted each four-bit string to its equivalent hex digit

    3   D   6   E

it would have been no problem to jot down (with the string covered) 3D6E.

In summary, although hexadecimal notation can be used to perform base-16 arithmetic, it is mainly used as a convenience for humans. It can be used to represent binary strings that are integers or floating point numbers or sequences of ASCII codes, or bit vectors. It simply reduces the number of digits by a factor of 4, where each digit is in hex (0, 1, 2, ... F) instead of binary (0, 1). The usual result is far fewer copying errors due to too many 0s and 1s.

Exercises

2.1 Given n bits, how many distinct combinations of the n bits exist?

2.2 There are 26 characters in the alphabet we use for writing English. What is the least number of bits needed to give each character a unique bit pattern? How many bits would we need to distinguish between upper- and lowercase versions of all 26 characters?

2.3 *a.* Assume that there are about 400 students in your class. If every student is to be assigned a unique bit pattern, what is the minimum number of bits required to do this?

   b. How many more students can be admitted to the class without requiring additional bits for each student's unique bit pattern?

2.4   Given n bits, how many unsigned integers can be represented with the n bits? What is the range of these integers?

2.5   Using five bits to represent each number, write the representations of 7 and −7 in 1's complement, signed magnitude, and 2's complement integers.

2.6   Write the six-bit 2's complement representation of −32.

2.7   Create a table showing the decimal values of all four-bit 2's complement numbers.

2.8   *a.* What is the largest positive number one can represent in an eight-bit 2's complement code? Write your result in binary and decimal.
   b. What is the greatest magnitude negative number one can represent in an eight-bit 2's complement code? Write your result in binary and decimal.
   c. What is the largest positive number one can represent in n-bit 2's complement code?
   d. What is the greatest magnitude negative number one can represent in n-bit 2's complement code?

2.9   How many bits are needed to represent Avogadro's number ($6.02 \cdot 10^{23}$) in 2's complement binary representation?

2.10   Convert the following 2's complement binary numbers to decimal.
   a. 1010
   b. 01011010
   c. 11111110
   d. 0011100111010011

2.11   Convert these decimal numbers to eight-bit 2's complement binary numbers.
   a. 102
   b. 64
   c. 33
   d. −128
   e. 127

2.12   If the last digit of a 2's complement binary number is 0, then the number is even. If the last two digits of a 2's complement binary number are 00 (e.g., the binary number 01100), what does that tell you about the number?

2.13   Without changing their values, convert the following 2's complement binary numbers into eight-bit 2's complement numbers.
   a. 1010   *c.* 1111111000
   b. 011001   *d.* 01

2.14 Add the following bit patterns. Leave your results in binary form.

  a. 1011 + 0001
  b. 0000 + 1010
  c. 1100 + 0011
  d. 0101 + 0110
  e. 1111 + 0001

2.15 It was demonstrated in Example 2.5 that shifting a binary number one bit to the left is equivalent to multiplying the number by 2. What operation is performed when a binary number is shifted one bit to the right?

2.16 Write the results of the following additions as both eight-bit binary and decimal numbers. For each part, use standard binary addition as described in Section 2.5.1.

  a. Add the 1's complement representation of 7 to the 1's complement representation of −7.
  b. Add the signed magnitude representation of 7 to the signed magnitude representation of −7.
  c. Add the 2's complement representation of 7 to the 2's complement representation of −7.

2.17 Add the following 2's complement binary numbers. Also express the answer in decimal.

  a. 01 + 1011
  b. 11 + 01010101
  c. 0101 + 110
  d. 01 + 10

2.18 Add the following unsigned binary numbers. Also, express the answer in decimal.

  a. 01 + 1011
  b. 11 + 01010101
  c. 0101 + 110
  d. 01 + 10

2.19 Express the negative value −27 as a 2's complement integer, using eight bits. Repeat, using 16 bits. Repeat, using 32 bits. What does this illustrate with respect to the properties of sign-extension as they pertain to 2's complement representation?

2.20 The following binary numbers are four-bit 2's complement binary numbers. Which of the following operations generate overflow? Justify your answer by translating the operands and results into decimal.

  a. 1100 + 0011   *d.* 1000 − 0001
  b. 1100 + 0100   *e.* 0111 + 1001
  c. 0111 + 0001

2.21 Describe what conditions indicate overflow has occurred when two 2's complement numbers are added.

2.22 Create two 16-bit 2's complement integers such that their sum causes an overflow.

2.23 Describe what conditions indicate overflow has occurred when two unsigned numbers are added.

2.24 Create two 16-bit unsigned integers such that their sum causes an overflow.

2.25 Why does the sum of a negative 2's complement number and a positive 2's complement number never generate an overflow?

2.26 You wish to express −64 as a 2's complement number.

    a. How many bits do you need (the minimum number)?

    b. With this number of bits, what is the largest positive number you can represent? (Please give answer in both decimal and binary.)

    c. With this number of bits, what is the largest unsigned number you can represent? (Please give answer in both decimal and binary.)

2.27 The LC-3, a 16-bit machine, adds the two 2's complement numbers 0101010101010101 and 0011100111001111, producing 1000111100100100. Is there a problem here? If yes, what is the problem? If no, why not?

2.28 When is the output of an AND operation equal to 1?

2.29 Fill in the following truth table for a one-bit AND operation.

X	Y	X AND Y
0	0	
0	1	
1	0	
1	1	

2.30 Compute the following. Write your results in binary.

    a. `01010111 AND 11010111`

    b. `101 AND 110`

    c. `11100000 AND 10110100`

    d. `00011111 AND 10110100`

    e. `(0011 AND 0110) AND 1101`

    f. `0011 AND (0110 AND 1101)`

2.31 When is the output of an OR operation equal to 1?

2.32 Fill in the following truth table for a one-bit OR operation.

X	Y	X OR Y
0	0	
0	1	
1	0	
1	1	

2.33   Compute the following:

     a. `01010111 OR 11010111`
     b. `101 OR 110`
     c. `11100000 OR 10110100`
     d. `00011111 OR 10110100`
     e. `(0101 OR 1100) OR 1101`
     f. `0101 OR (1100 OR 1101)`

2.34   Compute the following:

     a. `NOT(1011) OR NOT(1100)`
     b. `NOT(1000 AND (1100 OR 0101))`
     c. `NOT(NOT(1101))`
     d. `(0110 OR 0000) AND 1111`

2.35   In Example 2.11, what are the masks used for?

2.36   Refer to Example 2.11 for the following questions.

     a. What mask value and what operation would one use to indicate that machine 2 is busy?

     b. What mask value and what operation would one use to indicate that machines 2 and 6 are no longer busy? (*Note:* This can be done with only one operation.)

     c. What mask value and what operation would one use to indicate that all machines are busy?

     d. What mask value and what operation would one use to indicate that all machines are idle?

     e. Using the operations discussed in this chapter, develop a procedure to isolate the status bit of machine 2 as the sign bit. For example, if the BUSYNESS pattern is 01011100, then the output of this procedure is 10000000. If the BUSYNESS pattern is 01110011, then the output is 00000000. In general, if the BUSYNESS pattern is:

b7	b6	b5	b4	b3	b2	b1	b0

     the output is:

b2	0	0	0	0	0	0	0

     Hint: What happens when you ADD a bit pattern to itself?

2.37   If n and m are both four-bit 2's complement numbers, and s is the four-bit result of adding them together, how can we determine, using only the logical operations described in Section 2.6, if an overflow occurred during the addition? Develop a "procedure" for doing so. The inputs to the procedure are n, m, and s, and the output will be a bit pattern of all 0s (0000) if no overflow occurred and 1000 if an overflow did occur.

2.38   If n and m are both four-bit unsigned numbers, and s is the four-bit result of adding them together, how can we determine, using only the logical operations described in Section 2.6, if an overflow occurred during the addition? Develop a "procedure" for doing so. The inputs to the procedure are n, m, and s, and the output will be a bit pattern of all 0s (0000) if no overflow occurred and 1000 if an overflow did occur.

2.39 Write IEEE floating point representation of the following decimal numbers.

  a. 3.75
  b. $-55\frac{23}{64}$
  c. 3.1415927
  d. 64,000

2.40 Write the decimal equivalents for these IEEE floating point numbers.

  a. 0 10000000 00000000000000000000000
  b. 1 10000011 00010000000000000000000
  c. 0 11111111 00000000000000000000000
  d. 1 10000000 10010000000000000000000

2.41 *a.* What is the largest exponent the IEEE standard allows for a 32-bit floating point number?
  b. What is the smallest exponent the IEEE standard allows for a 32-bit floating point number?

2.42 A computer programmer wrote a program that adds two numbers. The programmer ran the program and observed that when 5 is added to 8, the result is the character *m*. Explain why this program is behaving erroneously.

2.43 Translate the following ASCII codes into strings of characters by interpreting each group of eight bits as an ASCII character.

  a. x48656c6c6f21
  b. x68454c4c4f21
  c. x436f6d70757465727321
  d. x4c432d32

2.44 What operation(s) can be used to convert the binary representation for 3 (i.e., 0000 0011) into the ASCII representation for 3 (i.e., 0011 0011)? What about the binary 4 into the ASCII 4? What about any digit?

2.45 Convert the following unsigned binary numbers to hexadecimal.

  a. 1101 0001 1010 1111
  b. 001 1111
  c. 1
  d. 1110 1101 1011 0010

2.46 Convert the following hexadecimal numbers to binary.

    a. x10
    b. x801
    c. xF731
    d. x0F1E2D
    e. xBCAD

2.47 Convert the following hexadecimal representations of 2's complement binary numbers to decimal numbers.

    a. xF0 -16   11110000
    b. x7FF
    c. x16
    d. x8000

2.48 Convert the following decimal numbers to hexadecimal representations of 2's complement numbers.

    a. 256
    b. 111
    c. 123,456,789
    d. −44

2.49 Perform the following additions. The corresponding 16-bit binary numbers are in 2's complement notation. Provide your answers in hexadecimal.

    a. x025B + x26DE
    b. x7D96 + xF0A0
    c. xA397 + xA35D
    d. x7D96 + x7412
    e. What else can you say about the answers to parts *c* and *d*?

2.50 Perform the following logical operations. Express your answers in hexadecimal notation.

    a. x5478 AND xFDEA
    b. xABCD OR x1234
    c. NOT((NOT(xDEFA)) AND (NOT(xFFFF)))
    d. x00FF XOR x325C

2.51 What is the hexadecimal representation of the following numbers?

    a. 25,675
    b. 675.625 (i.e., $675\frac{5}{8}$), in the IEEE 754 floating point standard
    c. The ASCII string: Hello

2.52 Consider two hexadecimal numbers: x434F4D50 and x55544552. What values do they represent for each of the five data types shown?

	x434F4D50	x55544552
Unsigned binary		
1's complement		
2's complement		
IEEE 754 floating point		
ASCII string		

2.53 Fill in the truth table for the equations given. The first line is done as an example.

$$Q_1 = \text{NOT(A AND B)}$$
$$Q_2 = \text{NOT(NOT(A) AND NOT(B))}$$

A	B	Q_1	Q_2
0	0	1	0

Express Q_2 another way.

2.54 Fill in the truth table for the equations given. The first line is done as an example.

$$Q_1 = \text{NOT(NOT(X) OR (X AND Y AND Z))}$$
$$Q_2 = \text{NOT((Y OR Z) AND (X AND Y AND Z))}$$

X	Y	Z	Q_1	Q_2
0	0	0	0	1

2.55 We have represented numbers in base-2 (binary) and in base-16 (hex). We are now ready for unsigned base-4, which we will call quad numbers. A quad digit can be 0, 1, 2, or 3.

- *a.* What is the maximum unsigned decimal value that one can represent with 3 quad digits?
- *b.* What is the maximum unsigned decimal value that one can represent with n quad digits? (*Hint:* Your answer should be a function of n.)
- *c.* Add the two unsigned quad numbers: 023 and 221.
- *d.* What is the quad representation of the decimal number 42?
- *e.* What is the binary representation of the unsigned quad number 123.3?
- *f.* Express the unsigned quad number 123.3 in IEEE floating point format.
- *g.* Given a black box that takes m quad digits as input and produces one quad digit for output, what is the maximum number of unique functions this black box can implement?

2.56 Define a new eight-bit floating point format with one sign bit, four bits of exponent, using an excess-7 code (i.e., the bias is 7), and three bits of fraction. If xE5 is the bit pattern for a number in this eight-bit floating point format, what value does it have? (Express as a decimal number.)

3 Digital Logic Structures

In Chapter 1, we stated that computers were built from very large numbers of very simple structures. For example, Intel's Broadwell-E5 microprocessor, introduced in 2016, contained more than seven billion transistors. Similarly, IBM's Power9 microprocessor, introduced in 2017, contained eight billion transistors. In this chapter, we will explain how the MOS transistor works (as a logic element), show how these transistors are connected to form logic gates, and then show how logic gates are interconnected to form larger units that are needed to construct a computer. In Chapter 4, we will connect those larger units and form a computer.

But first, the transistor.

3.1 The Transistor

Most computers today or rather most microprocessors (which form the core of the computer) are constructed out of MOS transistors. MOS stands for *metal-oxide semiconductor*. The electrical properties of metal-oxide semiconductors are well beyond the scope of what we want to understand in this course. They are below our lowest level of abstraction, which means that if somehow transistors start misbehaving, we are at their mercy. However, it is unlikely in this course that we will have any problems from the transistors.

Still, it is useful to know that there are two types of MOS transistors: P-type and N-type. They both operate "logically," very similar to the way wall switches work.

Figure 3.1 shows the most basic of electrical circuits. It consists of (1) a power supply (in this case, the 120 volts that come into your house if you live in the United States, or the 220 volts if you live in most of the rest of the world), (2) a wall switch, and (3) a lamp (plugged into an outlet in the wall). In order for the lamp to glow, electrons must flow; in order for electrons to flow, there must be a closed circuit from the power supply to the lamp and back to the power supply.

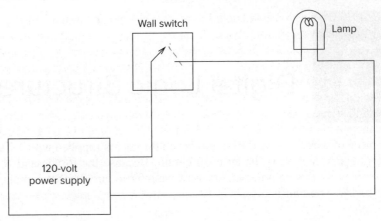

Figure 3.1   A simple electric circuit showing the use of a wall switch.

The lamp can be turned on and off by simply manipulating the wall switch to make or break the closed circuit.

Instead of the wall switch, we could use an N-type or a P-type MOS transistor to make or break the closed circuit. Figure 3.2 shows a schematic rendering of an N-type transistor (a) by itself, and (b) in a circuit. Note (Figure 3.2a) that the transistor has three terminals. They are called the *gate*, the *source*, and the *drain*. The reasons for the names source and drain are not of interest to us in this course. What is of interest is the fact that if the gate of the N-type transistor is supplied with 1.2 volts, the connection from source to drain acts like a piece of wire. We say (in the language of electricity) that we have a *short circuit* between the source and drain. If the gate of the N-type transistor is supplied with 0 volts, the connection between the source and drain is broken. We say that between the source and drain we have an *open circuit*.

Figure 3.2 shows the N-type transistor in a circuit with a battery and a bulb. When the gate is supplied with 1.2 volts, the transistor acts like a piece of wire, completing the circuit and causing the bulb to glow. When the gate is supplied with 0 volts, the transistor acts like an open circuit, breaking the circuit, and causing the bulb to not glow.

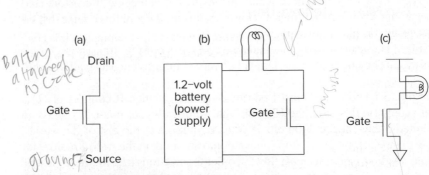

Figure 3.2   The N-type MOS transistor.

Figure 3.2c is a shorthand notation for describing the circuit of Figure 3.2b. Rather than always showing the power supply and the complete circuit, electrical engineers usually show only the terminals of the power supply. The fact that the power supply itself provides the completion of the completed circuit is well understood, and so is not usually shown.

The P-type transistor works in exactly the opposite fashion from the N-type transistor. Figure 3.3 shows the schematic representation of a P-type transistor. When the gate is supplied with 0 volts, the P-type transistor acts (more or less) like a piece of wire, closing the circuit. When the gate is supplied with 1.2 volts, the P-type transistor acts like an open circuit. Because the P-type and N-type transistors act in this complementary way, we refer to circuits that contain both P-type and N-type transistors as CMOS circuits, for *complementary metal-oxide semiconductor*.

Figure 3.3   A P-type MOS transistor.

3.2 Logic Gates

One step up from the transistor is the *logic gate*. That is, we construct basic logic structures out of individual MOS transistors. In Chapter 2, we studied the behavior of the AND, the OR, and the NOT functions. In this chapter, we construct transistor circuits that implement each of these functions. The corresponding circuits are called AND, OR, and NOT *gates*.

3.2.1 The NOT Gate (Inverter)

Figure 3.4 shows the simplest logic structure that exists in a computer. It is constructed from two MOS transistors, one P-type and one N-type. Figure 3.4a is the schematic representation of that circuit. Figure 3.4b shows the behavior of the circuit if the input is supplied with 0 volts. Note that the P-type transistor acts like a short circuit and the N-type transistor acts like an open circuit. The output is, therefore, connected to 1.2 volts. On the other hand, if the input is supplied with 1.2 volts, the P-type transistor acts like an open circuit, but the N-type transistor acts like a short circuit. The output in this case is connected to ground (i.e., 0 volts). The complete behavior of the circuit can be described by means of a table, as shown in Figure 3.4c. If we replace 0 volts with the symbol 0 and 1.2

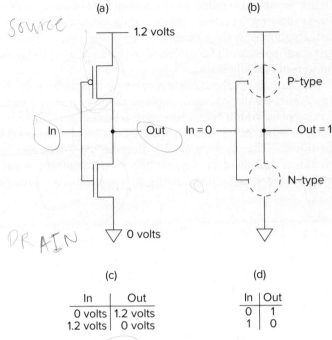

Source

(a)

1.2 volts

In — Out

(b)

P-type

In = 0 — Out = 1

N-type

DRAIN   ▽ 0 volts   ▽

(c)

In	Out
0 volts	1.2 volts
1.2 volts	0 volts

(d)

In	Out
0	1
1	0

Figure 3.4   A CMOS inverter.   AKA Not Gate

volts with the symbol 1, we have the truth table (Figure 3.4d) for the complement or NOT function, which we studied in Chapter 2.

In other words, we have just shown how to construct an electronic circuit that implements the NOT logic function discussed in Chapter 2. We call this circuit a *NOT gate*, or an *inverter*.

3.2.2 OR and NOR Gates

Figure 3.5 illustrates a NOR gate. Figure 3.5a is a schematic of a circuit that implements a NOR gate. It contains two P-type and two N-type transistors.

Figure 3.5b shows the behavior of the circuit if A is supplied with 0 volts and B is supplied with 1.2 volts. In this case, the lower of the two P-type transistors produces an open circuit, and the output C is disconnected from the 1.2-volt power supply. However, the leftmost N-type transistor acts like a piece of wire, connecting the output C to 0 volts.

Note that if both A and B are supplied with 0 volts, the two P-type transistors conduct, and the output C is connected to 1.2 volts. Note further that there is no ambiguity here, since both N-type transistors act as open circuits, and so C is disconnected from ground.

If either A or B is supplied with 1.2 volts, the corresponding P-type transistor results in an open circuit. That is sufficient to break the connection from C to the 1.2-volt source. However, 1.2 volts supplied to the gate of one of the N-type

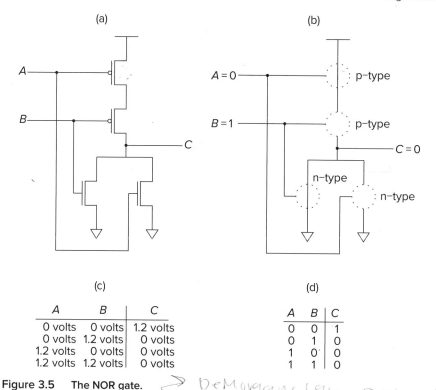

(a) (b) (c) (d)

(c)

A	B	C
0 volts	0 volts	1.2 volts
0 volts	1.2 volts	0 volts
1.2 volts	0 volts	0 volts
1.2 volts	1.2 volts	0 volts

(d)

A	B	C
0	0	1
0	1	0
1	0	0
1	1	0

Figure 3.5   The NOR gate.   → DeMorgans law going on

transistors is sufficient to cause that transistor to conduct, resulting in C being connected to ground (i.e., 0 volts).

Figure 3.5c summarizes the complete behavior of the circuit of Figure 3.5a. It shows the behavior of the circuit for each of the four pairs of voltages that can be supplied to A and B. That is,

$$A = 0 \text{ volts,} \quad B = 0 \text{ volts}$$
$$A = 0 \text{ volts,} \quad B = 1.2 \text{ volts}$$
$$A = 1.2 \text{ volts,} \quad B = 0 \text{ volts}$$
$$A = 1.2 \text{ volts,} \quad B = 1.2 \text{ volts}$$

If we replace the voltages with their logical equivalents, we have the truth table of Figure 3.5d. Note that the output C is exactly the opposite of the logical OR function that we studied in Chapter 2. In fact, it is the NOT-OR function, more typically abbreviated as NOR. We refer to the circuit that implements the NOR function as a NOR gate.

If we augment the circuit of Figure 3.5a by adding an inverter at its output, as shown in Figure 3.6a, we have at the output D the logical function OR. Figure 3.6a is the circuit for an OR gate. Figure 3.6b describes the behavior of this circuit if the input variable A is set to 0 and the input variable B is set to 1. Figure 3.6c shows the circuit's truth table.

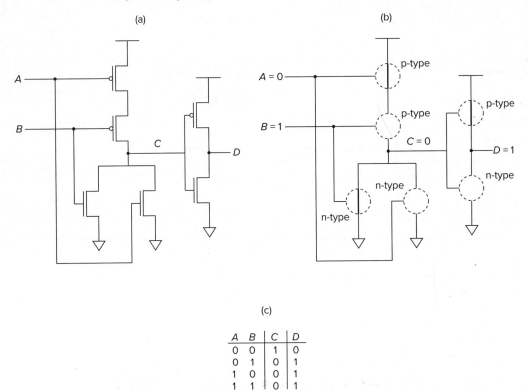

Figure 3.6   The OR gate.

3.2.3 Why We Can't Simply Connect P-Type to Ground

Some bright students have looked at our implementation of the OR gate (a NOR-gate followed by an inverter) and asked the question, why can't we simply connect the transistors as shown in Figure 3.7a?

Logically, it looks very tempting. Four transistors instead of six. Unfortunately, the electrical properties of transistors make this problematic. When we connect a P-type transistor to 1.2 volts or an N-type transistor to ground, there is no voltage across the transistor, resulting in outputs as shown in Figure 3.5, for example, of 0 volts or 1.2 volts, depending on the input voltages to A and B. However, when we connect a P-type transistor to ground or an N-type transistor to 1.2 volts, because of the electrical characteristics of the transistors, we get what is usually referred to as a transmission voltage of approximately 0.5 volts across the transistor. This results in the output of the transistor circuit of Figure 3.7 being 0.5 volts + 0.5 volts, or 1.0 volt if A and B are both 0, and 0.7 volts (1.2 volts minus 0.5 volts) otherwise. Figure 3.7b shows the actual voltages in the resulting truth table, rather than 0s and 1s. That is, even though the transistor circuit looks like it would work, the transmission voltages across the transistors would yield an output voltage of 1 volt for a logical 0 and 0.7 volts for a logical 1. Not what we would like for an OR gate!

(a)

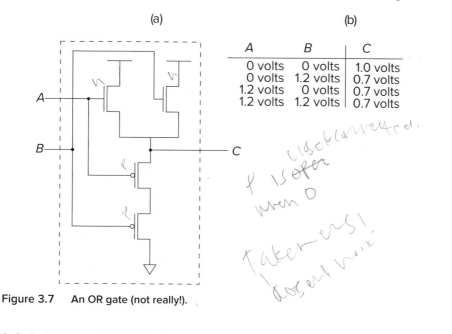

(b)

A	B	C
0 volts	0 volts	1.0 volts
0 volts	1.2 volts	0.7 volts
1.2 volts	0 volts	0.7 volts
1.2 volts	1.2 volts	0.7 volts

closed/connected.
f is open
when 0
Taker-ers!
doesn't work

Figure 3.7   An OR gate (not really!).

3.2.4 AND and NAND Gates

Figure 3.8 shows an AND gate. Note that if either *A* or *B* is supplied with 0 volts, there is a direct connection from *C* to the 1.2-volt power supply. The fact that *C* is at 1.2 volts means the N-type transistor whose gate is connected to *C* provides a path from *D* to ground. Therefore, if either *A* or *B* is supplied with 0 volts, the output *D* of the circuit of Figure 3.8 is 0 volts.   *is (getting relation AB*

(a)

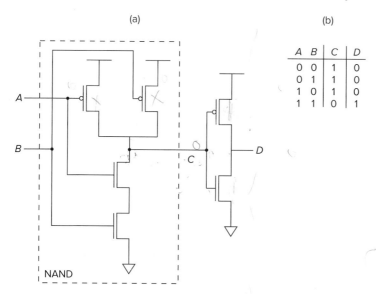

(b)

A	B	C	D
0	0	1	0
0	1	1	0
1	0	1	0
1	1	0	1

NAND

Figure 3.8   The AND gate.

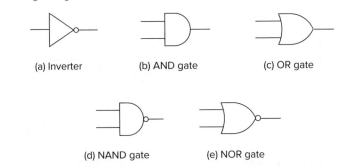

(a) Inverter   (b) AND gate   (c) OR gate

(d) NAND gate   (e) NOR gate

Figure 3.9   Basic logic gates.

Again, we note that there is no ambiguity. The fact that at least one of the two inputs A or B is supplied with 0 volts means that at least one of the two N-type transistors whose gates are connected to A or B is open, and that consequently, C is disconnected from ground. Furthermore, the fact that C is at 1.2 volts means the P-type transistor whose gate is connected to C is open-circuited. Therefore, D is not connected to 1.2 volts.

On the other hand, if both A and B are supplied with 1.2 volts, then both of their corresponding P-type transistors are open. However, their corresponding N-type transistors act like pieces of wire, providing a direct connection from C to ground. Because C is at ground, the rightmost P-type transistor acts like a closed circuit, forcing D to 1.2 volts.

Figure 3.8b is a truth table that summarizes the behavior of the circuit of Figure 3.8a. Note that the circuit is an AND gate. The circuit shown within the dashed lines (i.e., having output C) is a NOT-AND gate, which we generally abbreviate as NAND.

The gates just discussed are very common in digital logic circuits and in digital computers. There are billions of inverters (NOT gates) in Intel's Skylake microprocessor. As a convenience, we can represent each of these gates by standard symbols, as shown in Figure 3.9. The bubble shown in the inverter, NAND, and NOR gates signifies the complement (i.e., NOT) function. From now on, we will not draw circuits showing the individual transistors. Instead, we will raise our level of abstraction and use the symbols shown in Figure 3.9.

3.2.5 Gates with More Than Two Inputs

Before we leave the topic of logic gates, we should note that the notion of AND, OR, NAND, and NOR gates extends to larger numbers of inputs. One could build a three-input AND gate or a four-input OR gate, for example. An n-input AND gate has an output value of 1 only if ALL n input variables have values of 1. If any of the n inputs has a value of 0, the output of the n-input AND gate is 0. An n-input OR gate has an output value of 1 if ANY of the n input variables has a value of 1. That is, an n-input OR gate has an output value of 0 only if ALL n input variables have values of 0.

(a)   (b)

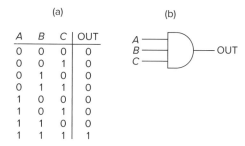

A	B	C	OUT
0	0	0	0
0	0	1	0
0	1	0	0
0	1	1	0
1	0	0	0
1	0	1	0
1	1	0	0
1	1	1	1

Figure 3.10 A three-input AND gate.

Figure 3.10 illustrates a three-input AND gate. Figure 3.10a shows its truth table. Figure 3.10b shows the symbol for a three-input AND gate.

Question: Can you draw a transistor-level circuit for a three-input AND gate? How about a four-input AND gate? How about a four-input OR gate?

3.3 Combinational Logic Circuits

Now that we understand the workings of the basic logic gates, the next step is to build some of the logic structures that are important components of the microarchitecture of a computer.

There are fundamentally two kinds of logic structures, those that include the storage of information and those that do not. In Sections 3.4, 3.5, and 3.6, we will deal with structures that store information. In this section, we will deal with structures that do not store information. These structures are sometimes referred to as *decision elements.* Usually, they are referred to as *combinational logic structures* because their outputs are strictly dependent on the combination of input values that are being applied to the structure *right now*. Their outputs are not at all dependent on any past history of information that is stored internally, since no information can be stored internally in a combinational logic circuit.

We will next examine three useful combinational logic circuits: a decoder, a mux, and a one-bit adder.

3.3.1 Decoder

Figure 3.11 shows a logic gate implementation of a two-input decoder. A decoder has the property that exactly one of its outputs is 1 and all the rest are 0s. The one output that is logically 1 is the output corresponding to the input pattern that it is expected to detect. In general, decoders have n inputs and 2^n outputs. We say the output line that detects the input pattern is *asserted*. That is, that output line has the value 1, rather than 0 as is the case for all the other output lines. In Figure 3.11, note that for each of the four possible combinations of inputs A and B, exactly one output has the value 1 at any one time. In Figure 3.11b, the input to the decoder is 10, resulting in the third output line being asserted.

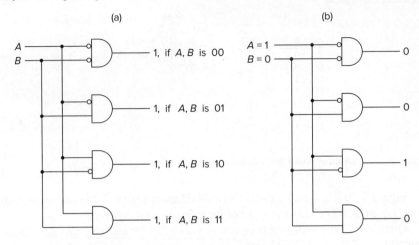

Figure 3.11   A two-input decoder.

The decoder is useful in determining how to interpret a bit pattern. We will see in Chapter 5 that the work to be carried out by each instruction in the LC-3 computer is determined by a four-bit pattern that is the part of the instruction called the *opcode*, A 4-to-16 decoder is a simple combinational logic structure for identifying what work is to be performed by each instruction.

3.3.2 Mux

Figure 3.12a shows a logic gate implementation of a two-input multiplexer, more commonly referred to as a *mux*. The function of a mux is to select one of the inputs (*A* or *B*) and connect it to the output. The select signal (*S* in Figure 3.12) determines which input is connected to the output.

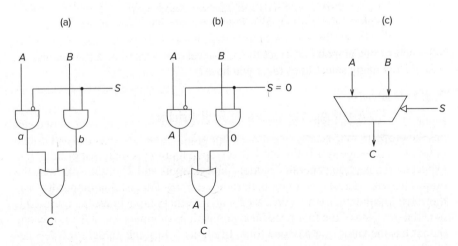

Figure 3.12   A 2-to-1 mux.

(a)   (b)

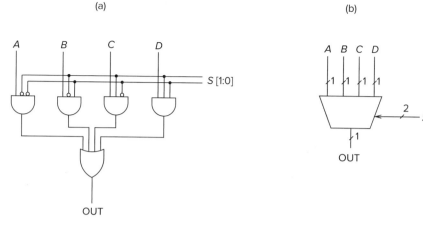

Figure 3.13   A four-input mux.

The mux of Figure 3.12 works as follows: Suppose $S = 0$, as shown in Figure 3.12b. Since the output of an AND gate is 0 unless all inputs are 1, the output of the rightmost AND gate is 0. Also, the output of the leftmost AND gate is whatever the input A is. That is, if $A = 0$, then the output of the leftmost AND gate is 0, and if $A = 1$, then the output of the leftmost AND gate is 1. Since the output of the rightmost AND gate is 0, it has no effect on the OR gate. Consequently, the output at C is exactly the same as the output of the leftmost AND gate. The net result of all this is that if $S = 0$, the output C is identical to the input A.

On the other hand, if $S = 1$, it is B that is ANDed with 1, resulting in the output of the OR gate having the value of B.

In summary, the output C is always connected to either the input A or the input B—which one depends on the value of the select line S. We say S selects the source of the mux (either A or B) to be routed through to the output C. Figure 3.12c shows the standard representation for a mux.

In general, a mux consists of 2^n inputs and n select lines. Figure 3.13a shows a gate-level description of a four-input mux. It requires two select lines. Figure 3.13b shows the standard representation for a four-input mux.

Question: Can you construct the gate-level representation for an eight-input mux? How many select lines must you have?

3.3.3 A One-Bit Adder (a.k.a. a Full Adder)

Recall in Chapter 2, we discussed binary addition. A simple algorithm for binary addition is to proceed as you have always done in the case of decimal addition, from right to left, one column at a time, adding the two digits from the two values plus the carry in, and generating a sum digit and a carry to the next column. The only difference here (with binary addition) is you get a carry after 1, rather than after 9.

Figure 3.14 is a truth table that describes the result of binary addition on **one column** of bits within two n-bit operands. At each column, there are three values

A_i	B_i	C_i	C_{i+1}	S_i
0	0	0	0	0
0	0	1	0	1
0	1	0	0	1
0	1	1	1	0
1	0	0	0	1
1	0	1	1	0
1	1	0	1	0
1	1	1	1	1

Figure 3.14   The truth table for a one-bit adder.

that must be added: one bit from each of the two operands A and B and the carry from the previous column. We designate these three bits as A_i, B_i, and C_i. There are two results, the sum bit (S_i) and the carry over to the next column, C_{i+1}. Note that if only one of the three bits equals 1, we get a sum of 1, and no carry (i.e., $C_{i+1} = 0$). If two of the three bits equal 1, we get a sum of 0, and a carry of 1. If all three bits equal 1, the sum is 3, which in binary corresponds to a sum of 1 and a carry of 1.

Figure 3.15 shows a logic gate implementation of a one-bit adder. Note that each AND gate in Figure 3.15 produces an output 1 for exactly one of the eight input combinations of A_i, B_i, and C_i. The output of the OR gate for C_{i+1} must be 1 in exactly those cases where the corresponding input combinations in Figure 3.14 produce an output 1. Therefore, the inputs to the OR gate that generates C_{i+1}

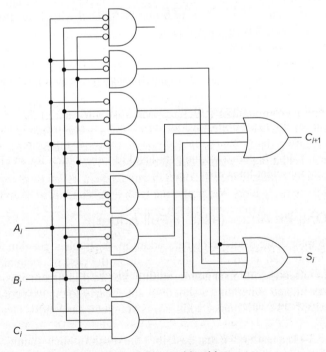

Figure 3.15   Gate-level description of a one-bit adder.

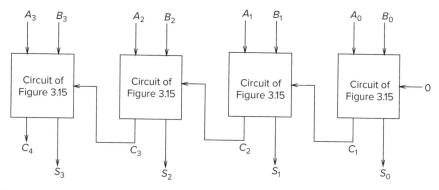

Figure 3.16 A circuit for adding two 4-bit binary numbers.

are the outputs of the AND gates corresponding to those input combinations. Similarly, the inputs to the OR gate that generates S_i are the outputs of the AND gates corresponding to the input combinations that require an output 1 for S_i in the truth table of Figure 3.14.

Note that since the input combination 000 does not result in an output 1 for either C_{i+1} or S_i, its corresponding AND gate is not an input to either of the two OR gates.

Figure 3.16 shows a circuit for adding two 4-bit binary numbers, using four of the one-bit adder circuits of Figure 3.15. Note that the carry out of column i is an input to the addition performed in column $i + 1$.

If we wish to implement a logic circuit that adds two 16-bit numbers, we can do so with a circuit of 16 one-bit adders.

We should point out that historically the logic circuit of Figure 3.15 that provides three inputs (A_i, B_i, and C_i) and two outputs (the sum bit S_i and the carry over to the next column C_{i+1}) has generally been referred to as a *full adder* to differentiate it from another structure, which is called a *half adder*. The distinction between the two is the carry bit. Note that the carry into the rightmost column in Figure 3.16 is 0. That is, in the rightmost circuit, S_0 and C_1 depend only on two inputs, A_0 and B_0. Since that circuit depends on only two inputs, it has been referred to as a half adder. Since the other circuits depend on all three inputs, they are referred to as full adders. We prefer the term one-bit adder as a simpler term for describing what is happening in each column.

3.3.4 The Programmable Logic Array (PLA)

Figure 3.17 illustrates a very common building block for implementing any collection of logic functions one wishes to implement. The building block is called a programmable logic array (PLA). It consists of an array of AND gates (called an AND array) followed by an array of OR gates (called an OR array). The number of AND gates corresponds to the number of input combinations (rows) in the truth table. For n-input logic functions, we need a PLA with 2^n n-input AND

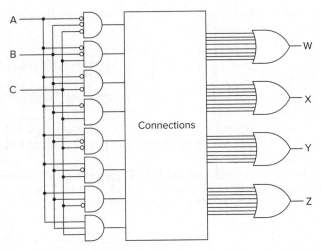

Figure 3.17   **A programmable logic array.**

gates. In Figure 3.17, we have 2^3 three-input AND gates, corresponding to three logical input variables. The number of OR gates corresponds to the number of logic functions we wish to implement, that is, the number of output columns in the truth table. The implementation algorithm is simply to connect the output of an AND gate to the input of an OR gate if the corresponding row of the truth table produces an output 1 for that output column. Hence the notion of programmable. That is, we say we program the connections from AND gate outputs to OR gate inputs to implement our desired logic functions.

     Figure 3.15 shows seven AND gates connected to two OR gates since our requirement was to implement two functions (sum and carry) of three input variables. Figure 3.17 shows a PLA that can implement any four functions of three variables by appropriately connecting AND gate outputs to OR gate inputs. That is, any function of three variables can be implemented by connecting the outputs of all AND gates corresponding to input combinations for which the output is 1 to inputs of one of the OR gates. Thus, we could implement the one-bit adder by *programming* the two OR gates in Figure 3.17 whose outputs are W and X by connecting or not connecting the outputs of the AND gates to the inputs of those two OR gates as specified by the two output columns of Figure 3.14.

3.3.5 Logical Completeness

Before we leave the topic of combinational logic circuits, it is worth noting an important property of building blocks for logic circuits: *logical completeness*. We showed in Section 3.3.4 that any logic function we wished to implement could be accomplished with a PLA. We saw that the PLA consists of only AND gates, OR gates, and inverters. That means that any logic function can be implemented, provided that enough AND, OR, and NOT gates are available. We say that the set of gates {AND, OR, NOT} is *logically complete* because we can build a circuit to carry out the specification of any truth table we wish without using any other kind of gate. That is, the set of gates {AND, OR, and NOT} is logically complete because a barrel of AND gates, a barrel of OR gates, and a barrel of NOT gates are sufficient to build a logic circuit that carries out the specification of any desired truth table. The barrels may have to be big, but the point is, we do not need any other kind of gate to do the job.

Question: Is there any single two-input logic gate that is logically complete? For example, is the NAND gate logically complete? *Hint:* Can I implement a NOT gate with a NAND gate? If yes, can I then implement an AND gate using a NAND gate followed by a NOT gate? If yes, can I implement an OR gate using just AND gates and NOT gates?

If all of the above is true, then the NAND gate is logically complete, and I can implement any desired logic function as described by its truth table with a barrel of NAND gates.

3.4 Basic Storage Elements

Recall our statement at the beginning of Section 3.3 that there are two kinds of logic structures, those that involve the storage of information and those that do not. We have discussed three examples of those that do not: the decoder, the mux, and the full adder. Now we are ready to discuss logic structures that do include the storage of information.

3.4.1 The R-S Latch

A simple example of a storage element is the R-S latch. It can store one bit of information, a 0 or a 1. The R-S latch can be implemented in many ways, the simplest being the one shown in Figure 3.18. Two 2-input NAND gates are connected such that the output of each is connected to one of the inputs of the other. The remaining inputs *S* and *R* are normally held at a logic level 1.

The R-S latch gets its name from the old designations for setting the latch to store a 1 and setting the latch to store a 0. Setting the latch to store a 1 was referred to as *setting* the latch, and setting the latch to store a 0 was referred to as *resetting* the latch. Ergo, R-S.

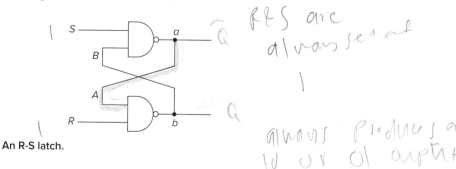

Figure 3.18   An R-S latch.

The Quiescent State   We describe the *quiescent* (or quiet) state of a latch as the state when the latch is storing a value, either 0 or 1, and nothing is trying to change that value. This is the case when inputs S and R both have the logic value 1. In Figure 3.18 the letter a designates the value that is currently stored in the latch, which we also refer to as the output of the latch.

Consider first the case where the value stored and therefore the output a is 1. Since that means the value A is 1 (and since we know the input R is 1 because we are in the quiescent state), the NAND gate's output b must be 0. That, in turn, means B must be 0, which results in the output a equal to 1. As long as the inputs S and R remain 1, the state of the circuit will not change. That is, the R-S latch will continue to store the value 1 (the value of the output a).

If, on the other hand, we assume the output a is 0, then A must be 0, and the output b must be 1. That, in turn, results in B equal to 1, and combined with the input S equal to 1 (again due to quiescence), results in the output a equal to 0. Again, as long as the inputs S and R remain 1, the state of the circuit will not change. In this case, we say the R-S latch stores the value 0.

Setting the Latch to a 1 or a 0   The latch can be set to 1 by momentarily setting S to 0, provided we keep the value of R at 1. Similarly, the latch can be set to 0 by momentarily setting R to 0, provided we keep the value of S at 1. In order for the R-S latch to work properly, both S and R must never be allowed to be set to 0 at the same time.

We use the term *set* to denote setting a variable to 0 or 1, as in "set to 0" or "set to 1." In addition, we often use the term *clear* to denote the act of setting a variable to 0.

If we set S to 0 for a very brief period of time, this causes a to equal 1, which in turn causes A to equal 1. Since R is also 1, the output at b must be 0. This causes B to be 0, which in turn makes a equal to 1. If, after that very brief period of time, we now return S to 1, it does not affect a. Why? Answer: Since B is also 0, and since only one input 0 to a NAND gate is enough to guarantee that the output of the NAND gate is 1, the latch will continue to store a 1 long after S returns to 1.

In the same way, we can clear the latch (set the latch to 0) by setting R to 0 for a very short period of time.

We should point out that if both S and R were allowed to be set to 0 at the same time, the outputs a and b would both be 1, and the final state of the latch would depend on the electrical properties of the transistors making up the gates and not on the logic being performed. How the electrical properties of the transistors would determine the final state in this case is a subject we will have to leave for a later semester. :-(

Finally, we should note that when a digital circuit is powered on, the latch can be in either of its two states, 0 or 1. It does not matter which state since we never use that information until **after** we have set it to 1 or 0.

3.4.2 The Gated D Latch

To be useful, it is necessary to control when a latch is set and when it is cleared. A simple way to accomplish this is with the gated latch.

Figure 3.19 shows a logic circuit that implements a gated D latch. It consists of the R-S latch of Figure 3.18, plus two additional NAND gates that allow the

Assorted Means = 1

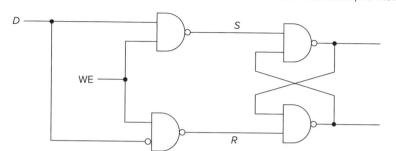

Figure 3.19   A gated D latch.

latch to be set to the value of D, but *only* when WE is asserted (i.e., when WE equals 1). WE stands for *write enable*. When WE is not asserted (i.e., when WE equals 0), the outputs S and R are both equal to 1. Since S and R are inputs to the R-S latch, if they are kept at 1, the value stored in the latch remains unchanged, as we explained in Section 3.4.1. When WE is momentarily set to 1, exactly one of the outputs S or R is set to 0, depending on the value of D. If D equals 1, then S is set to 0. If D equals 0, then both inputs to the lower NAND gate are 1, resulting in R being set to 0. As we saw earlier, if S is set to 0, the R-S latch is set to 1. If R is set to 0, the R-S latch is set to 0. Thus, the R-S latch is set to 1 or 0 according to whether D is 1 or 0. When WE returns to 0, S and R return to 1, and the value stored in the R-S latch persists.

3.5 The Concept of Memory

We now have all the tools we need to describe one of the most important structures in the electronic digital computer, its *memory*. We will see in Chapter 4 how memory fits into the basic scheme of computer processing, and you will see throughout the rest of the book and indeed the rest of your work with computers how important the concept of memory is to computing.

Memory is made up of a (usually large) number of locations, each uniquely identifiable and each having the ability to store a value. We refer to the unique identifier associated with each memory location as its *address*. We refer to the number of bits of information stored in each location as its *addressability*.

For example, an advertisement for a laptop computer might say, "This computer comes with 2 gigabytes of memory." Actually, most ads generally use the abbreviation 2 GB (or, often: 2 Gig). This statement means, as we will explain momentarily, that the laptop includes two billion memory locations, each containing one byte of information.

3.5.1 Address Space

We refer to the total number of uniquely identifiable locations as the memory's *address space*. A 2 GB memory, for example, refers to a memory that consists of two billion uniquely identifiable memory locations.

Actually, the number two billion is only an approximation, due to the way we specify memory locations. Since everything else in the computer is represented by sequences of 0s and 1s, it should not be surprising that memory locations are identified by binary addresses as well. With n bits of address, we can uniquely identify 2^n locations. Ten bits provide 1024 locations, which is approximately 1000. If we have 20 bits to represent each address, we have 2^{20} uniquely identifiable locations, which is approximately one million. With 30 bits, we have 2^{30} locations, which is approximately one billion. In the same way we use the prefixes "kilo" to represent 2^{10} (approximately 1000) and "mega" to represent 2^{20} (approximately one million), we use the prefix "giga" to represent 2^{30} (approximately one billion). Thus, 2 giga really corresponds to the number of uniquely identifiable locations that can be specified with 31 address bits. We say the address space is 2^{31}, which is *exactly* 2,147,483,648 locations, rather than 2,000,000,000, although we colloquially refer to it as two billion.

3.5.2 Addressability

The number of bits stored in each memory location is the memory's addressability. A 2-gigabyte memory (written 2GB) is a memory consisting of 2,147,483,648 memory locations, each containing one byte (i.e., eight bits) of storage. Most memories are byte-addressable. The reason is historical; most computers got their start processing data, and one character stroke on the keyboard corresponds to one 8-bit ASCII code, as we learned in Chapter 2. If the memory is byte-addressable, then each ASCII character occupies one location in memory. Uniquely identifying each byte of memory allows individual bytes of stored information to be changed easily.

Many computers that have been designed specifically to perform large scientific calculations are 64-bit addressable. This is due to the fact that numbers used in scientific calculations are often represented as 64-bit floating-point quantities. Recall that we discussed the floating-point data type in Chapter 2. Since scientific calculations are likely to use numbers that require 64 bits to represent them, it is reasonable to design a memory for such a computer that stores one such number in each uniquely identifiable memory location.

3.5.3 A 2^2-by-3-Bit Memory

Figure 3.20 illustrates a memory of size 2^2 by 3 bits. That is, the memory has an address space of four locations and an addressability of three bits. A memory of size 2^2 requires two bits to specify the address. We describe the two-bit address as A[1:0]. A memory of addressability three stores three bits of information in each memory location. We describe the three bits of data as D[2:0]. In both cases, our notation A[high:low] and D[high:low] reflects the fact that we have numbered the bits of address and data from right to left, in order, starting with the rightmost bit, which is numbered 0. The notation [high:low] means a sequence of $high - low + 1$ bits such that "high" is the bit number of the leftmost (or *high*) bit number in the sequence and "low" is the bit number of the rightmost (or *low*) bit number in the sequence.

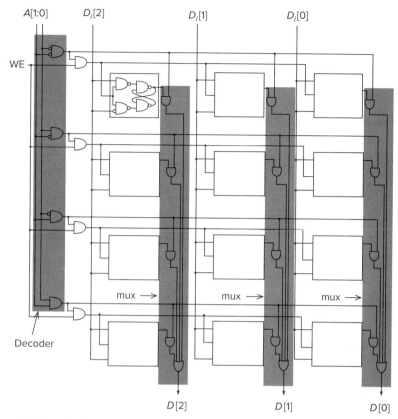

Figure 3.20   A 2^2-by-3-bit memory.

Accesses of memory require decoding the address bits. Note that the address decoder takes as input the address bits $A[1:0]$ and asserts exactly one of its four outputs, corresponding to the *word line* being addressed. In Figure 3.20, each row of the memory corresponds to a unique three-bit word, thus the term *word line*. Memory can be read by applying the address $A[1:0]$, which asserts the word line to be read. Note that each bit of the memory is ANDed with its word line and then ORed with the corresponding bits of the other words. Since only one word line can be asserted at a time, this is effectively a mux with the output of the decoder providing the select function to each bit line. Thus, the appropriate word is read at $D[2:0]$.

Figure 3.21 shows the process of reading location 3. The code for 3 is 11. The address $A[1:0]=11$ is decoded, and the bottom word line is asserted. Note that the three other decoder outputs are not asserted. That is, they have the value 0. The value stored in location 3 is 101. These three bits are each ANDed with their word line producing the bits 101, which are supplied to the three output OR gates. Note that all other inputs to the OR gates are 0, since they have been produced by ANDing with their unasserted word lines. The result is that $D[2:0]$ = 101. That is, the value stored in location 3 is output by the OR gates. Memory

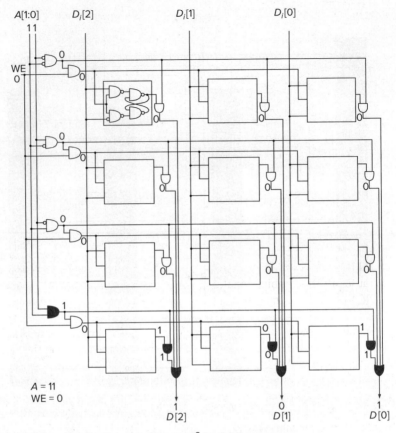

Figure 3.21   Reading location 3 in our 2^2-by-3-bit memory.

can be written in a similar fashion. The address specified by $A[1:0]$ is presented to the address decoder, resulting in the correct word line being asserted. With write enable (WE) also asserted, the three bits $D[2:0]$ can be written into the three gated latches corresponding to that word line.

3.6 Sequential Logic Circuits

In Section 3.3, we discussed digital logic structures that process information (decision structures, we call them) wherein the outputs depend solely on the values that are present on the inputs **now**. Examples are muxes, decoders, and full adders. We call these structures combinational logic circuits. In these circuits, there is no sense of the past. Indeed, there is no capability for storing any information about anything that happened before the present time. In Sections 3.4 and 3.5, we described structures that do store information—in Section 3.4, some basic storage elements, and in Section 3.5, a simple 2^2-by-3-bit memory.

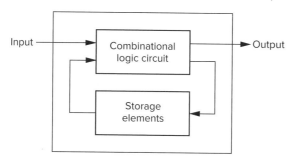

Figure 3.22   Sequential logic circuit block diagram.

In this section, we discuss digital logic structures that can **both** process information (i.e., make decisions) **and** store information. That is, these structures base their decisions not only on the input values now present, but also (and this is very important) on what has happened before. These structures are usually called **sequential logic circuits**. They are distinguishable from combinational logic circuits because, unlike combinational logic circuits, they contain storage elements that allow them to keep track of prior history information. Figure 3.22 shows a block diagram of a sequential logic circuit. Note the storage elements. Note also that the output can be dependent on both the inputs now and the values stored in the storage elements. The values stored in the storage elements reflect the history of what has happened before.

Sequential logic circuits are used to implement a very important class of mechanisms called *finite state machines*. We use finite state machines in essentially all branches of engineering. For example, they are used as controllers of electrical systems, mechanical systems, and aeronautical systems. A traffic light controller that sets the traffic light to red, yellow, or green depends on the light that is currently on (history information) and input information from sensors such as trip wires on the road, a timer keeping track of how long the current light has been on, and perhaps optical devices that are monitoring traffic.

We will see in Chapter 4 when we introduce the von Neumann model of a computer that a finite state machine is at the heart of the computer. It controls the processing of information by the computer.

3.6.1 A Simple Example: The Combination Lock

A simple example shows the difference between combinational logic structures and sequential logic structures. Suppose one wishes to secure a bicycle with a lock, but does not want to carry a key. A common solution is the combination lock. The person memorizes a "combination" and uses it to open the lock. Two common types of locks are shown in Figure 3.23.

In Figure 3.23a, the lock consists of a dial, with the numbers from 0 to 30 equally spaced around its circumference. To open the lock, one needs to know the "combination." One such combination could be: R13-L22-R3. If this were the case, one would open the lock by turning the dial two complete turns to the right (clockwise), and then continuing until the dial points to 13, followed by one

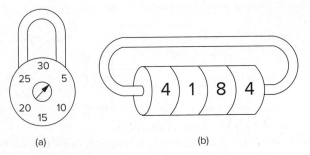

Figure 3.23   Combination locks.

complete turn to the left (counterclockwise), and then continuing until the dial points to 22, followed by turning the dial again to the right (clockwise) until it points to 3. At that point, the lock opens. What is important here is the *sequence* of the turns. The lock will not open, for example if one performed two turns to the right, and then stopped on 22 (instead of 13), followed by one complete turn to the left, ending on 13, followed by one turn to the right, ending on 3. That is, even though the final position of the dial is 3, and even though R22-L13-R3 uses the same three numbers as the combination R13-L22-R3, the lock would not open. Why? Because the lock stores the previous rotations and makes its decision (open or don't open) on the basis of the the history of the past operations, that is, on the correct *sequence* being performed.

Another type of lock is shown in Figure 3.23b. The mechanism consists of (usually) four wheels, each containing the digits 0 through 9. When the digits are lined up properly, the lock will open. In this case, the combination is the set of four digits. Whether or not this lock opens is totally independent of the past rotations of the four wheels. The lock does not care at all about past rotations. The only thing important is the current value of each of the four wheels. This is a simple example of a combinational structure.

It is curious that in our everyday speech, both mechanisms are referred to as "combination locks." In fact, only the lock of Figure 3.23b is a combinational lock. The lock of Figure 3.23a would be better called a sequential lock!

3.6.2 The Concept of State

For the mechanism of Figure 3.23a to work properly, it has to keep track of the sequence of rotations leading up to the opening of the lock. In particular, it has to differentiate the correct sequence R13-L22-R3 from all other sequences. For example, R22-L13-R3 must not be allowed to open the lock. Likewise, R10-L22-R3 must also not be allowed to open the lock.

For the lock of Figure 3.23a to work, it must identify several relevant situations, as follows:

A. The lock is not open, and NO relevant operations have been performed.

B. The lock is not open, but the user has just completed the R13 operation.

C. The lock is not open, but the user has just completed R13, followed by L22.

D. The lock is open, since the user has just completed R13, followed by L22, followed by R3.

We have labeled these four situations A, B, C, and D. We refer to each of these situations as the *state* of the lock.

The notion of **state** is a very important concept in computer engineering, and actually, in just about all branches of engineering. The state of a mechanism—more generally, the state of a system—is a snapshot of that system in which all relevant items are explicitly expressed.

That is: *The state of a system is a snapshot of all the relevant elements of the system at the moment the snapshot is taken.*

In the case of the lock of Figure 3.23a, there are four states A, B, C, and D. Either the lock is open (State D), or if it is not open, we have already performed either zero (State A), one (State B), or two (State C) correct operations. This is the sum total of all possible states that can exist.

Question: Why are there exactly four states needed to describe the combination lock of Figure 3.23a? Can you think of a snapshot of the combination lock after an operation (Rn or Ln) that requires a fifth state because it is not covered by one of the four states A, B, C, or D?

There are many examples of systems that you are familiar with that can be easily described by means of states.

The state of a game of basketball can be described by the scoreboard in the basketball arena. Figure 3.24 shows the state of the basketball game as Texas 73, Oklahoma 68, 7 minutes and 38 seconds left in the second half, 14 seconds left on the shot clock, Texas with the ball, and Texas and Oklahoma each with four team fouls. This is a snapshot of the basketball game. It describes the state of the basketball game at one point in time. If, 12 seconds later, a Texas player were to score

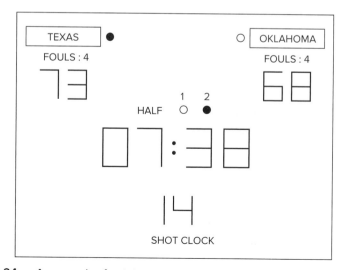

Figure 3.24   An example of a state.

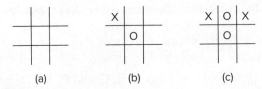

Figure 3.25   Three states in a tic-tac-toe machine.

a two-point shot, the new state would be described by the updated scoreboard. That is, the score would then be Texas 75, Oklahoma 68, the time remaining in the game would be 7 minutes and 26 seconds, the shot clock would be back to 25 seconds, and Oklahoma would have the ball.

The game of tic-tac-toe can also be described in accordance with the notion of state. Recall that the game is played by two people (or, in our case, a person and the computer). The state is a snapshot of the game in progress each time the computer asks the person to make a move. The game is played as follows: There are nine locations on the diagram. The person and then the computer take turns placing an X (the person) and an O (the computer) in an empty location. The person goes first. The winner is the first to place three symbols (three Xs for the person, three Os for the computer) in a straight line, either vertically, horizontally, or diagonally.

The initial state, before either the person or the computer has had a turn, is shown in Figure 3.25a. Figure 3.25b shows a possible state of the game when the person is prompted for a second move, if he/she put an X in the upper left corner as his/her first move, and the computer followed with an O in the middle square as its first move. Figure 3.25c shows a possible state of the game when the person is prompted for a third move if he/she put an X in the upper right corner on the second move, and the computer followed by putting its second O in the upper middle location.

One final example: a very old soft drink machine, when drinks sold for 15 cents, and the machine would only take nickels (5 cents) and dimes (10 cents) and not be able to give change.

The state of the machine can be described as the amount of money inserted, and whether the machine is open (so one can remove a bottle). There are only three possible states:

```
A. The lock is open, so a bottle can be (or has been!) removed.
B. The lock is not open, but 5 cents has been inserted.
C. The lock is not open, but 10 cents has been inserted.
```

3.6.3 The Finite State Machine and Its State Diagram

We have seen that a state is a snapshot of all relevant parts of a system at a particular point in time. At other times, that system can be in other states. We have described four systems: a combination lock, a basketball game, a tic-tac-toe machine, and a very old soft drink machine when a bottle of cola cost only

15 cents. The behavior of each of these systems can be specified by a *finite state machine*, and represented as a *state diagram*.

A finite state machine consists of five elements:

```
1. a finite number of states
2. a finite number of external inputs
3. a finite number of external outputs
4. an explicit specification of all state transitions
5. an explicit specification of what determines each external
   output value.
```

The set of states represents all possible situations (or snapshots) that the system can be in. Each state transition describes what it takes to get from one state to another.

Let's examine the finite state machines for these four systems.

The Combination Lock   A state diagram is a convenient representation of a finite state machine. Figure 3.26 is a state diagram for the combination lock.

Recall, we identified four states A, B, C, and D. Which state we are in depends on the progress we have made in getting from a random initial state to the lock being open. In the state diagram of Figure 3.26, each circle corresponds to one of the four states, A, B, C, or D.

The external inputs are R13, L22, R3, and R-other-than-13, L-other-than-22, and R-other-than-3.

The external output is either the lock is open or the lock is not open. (One logical variable will suffice to describe that!) As shown in the state diagram, in states A, B, and C, the combination lock is locked. In state D, the combination lock is open.

The explicit specifications of all state transitions are shown by the arrows in the state diagram. The more sophisticated term for "arrow" is *arc*. The arrowhead

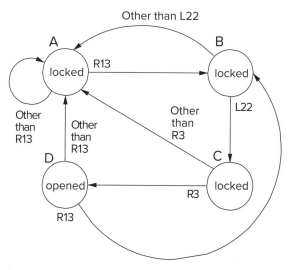

Figure 3.26   State diagram of the combination lock of Figure 3.23a.

on each arc specifics which state the system is coming from and which state it is going to. We refer to the state the system is coming from as the *current state*, and the state it is going to as the *next state*. The combination lock has eight state transitions. Associated with each transition is the input that causes the transition from the current state to the next state. For example, R13 causes the transition from state A to state B.

A couple of things are worth noting. First, it is usually the case that from a current state there are multiple transitions to next states. The state transition that occurs depends on both the current state and the value of the external input. For example, if the combination lock is in state B, and the input is L22, the next state is state C. If the current state is state B and the input is anything other than L22, the next state is state A. In short, the next state is determined by the combination of the current state and the current external input.

The output values of a system can also be determined by the combination of the current state and the value of the current external input. However, as is the case for the combination lock, where states A, B, and C specify the lock is "locked," and state D specifies the lock is "unlocked," the output can also be determined solely by the current state of the system. In all the systems we will study in this book, the output values will be specified solely by the current state of the system.

A Very Old Soft Drink Machine   Figure 3.27 is the state diagram for the soft drink machine.

The soft drink machine has only three states: 5 cents has been inserted, 10 cents has been inserted, and at least 15 cents has been inserted. Transitions are caused by the insertion (the input) of a nickel or a dime. The output is associated only with the states. In states B and C, the machine is locked. Not enough money has been inserted! In state A, the machine is open, so a soft drink can be removed because at least 15 cents has been inserted.

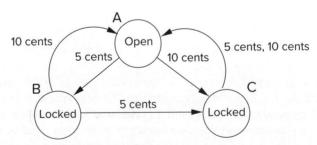

Figure 3.27   State diagram of the soft drink machine.

A Basketball Game   We could similarly draw a state diagram for the basketball game we described earlier, where each state would be one possible configuration of the scoreboard. A transition would occur if either the referee blew a whistle or the other team got the ball. We showed earlier the transition that would be caused by Texas scoring a two-point shot. Clearly, the number of states in the finite state machine describing a basketball game would be huge.

Also clearly, the number of legitimate transitions from one state to another is small, compared to the number of arcs one could draw connecting arbitrary pairs of states. For example, there is no arc from a score of Texas 68, Oklahoma 67 to Texas 75, Oklahoma 91, since no single input can cause that transition. The input is the activity that occurred on the basketball court since the last transition. Some input values are: Texas scored two points, Oklahoma scored three points, Texas stole the ball, Oklahoma successfully rebounded a Texas shot, and so forth.

The output is the final result of the game. The output has three values: Game still in progress, Texas wins, Oklahoma wins.

Question: Can one have an arc from a state where the score is Texas 30, Oklahoma 28 to a state where the score is tied, Texas 30, Oklahoma 30? Is it possible to have two states, one where Texas is ahead 30-28 and the other where the score is tied 30-30, but no arc between the two?

A Tic-Tac-Toe Machine   We could also draw a state diagram for a tic tac toe machine, in our case when a person is playing against a computer. Each state is a representation of the position of the game when the person is asked to put an X into one of the empty cells. Figure 3.25 shows three states. The transition from the state of Figure 3.25a to the state of Figure 3.25b is caused by the person putting an X in the top left cell, followed by the computer putting an O in the center cell. The transition from the state of Figure 3.25b to the state of Figure 3.25c is caused by the person putting an X in the top right cell, followed by the computer putting an O in the top middle cell.

Since there are nine cells, and each state has an X, an O, or nothing in each cell, there must be fewer than 3^9 states in the tic-tac-toe machine. Clearly there are far fewer than that, due to various constraints of the game.

There are nine inputs, corresponding to the nine cells a person can put an X in. There are three outputs: (a) game still in progress, (b) person wins, and (c) computer wins.

3.6.4 The Synchronous Finite State Machine

Up to now a transition from a current state to a next state in our finite state machine happened when it happened. For example, a person could insert a nickel into the soft drink machine and then wait 10 seconds or 10 minutes before inserting the next coin into the machine. And the soft drink machine would not complain. It would not dispense the soft drink until 15 cents was inserted, but it would wait patiently as long as necessary for the 15 cents to be inserted. That is, there is no fixed amount of time between successive inputs to the finite state machine. This is true in the case of all four systems we have discussed. We say these systems are *asynchronous* because there is nothing synchronizing when each state transition must occur.

However, almost no computers work that way. On the contrary, we say that computers are *synchronous* because the state transitions take place, one after the other, at identical fixed units of time. They are controlled by a *synchronous finite state machine*. We will save for Chapter 4 and beyond the state transitions that occur at identical, fixed units of time that control a computer. In this chapter, we will take on a simpler task, the design of a traffic controller, an admittedly simpler structure, but one that is also controlled by a synchronous finite state machine.

It is worth pointing out that both the four asynchronous finite state machines discussed above and the synchronous finite state machine that controls a digital computer share an important characteristic: They carry out work, one state transition at a time, moving closer to a goal. In the case of the combination lock, as long as you make the correct moves, each state transition takes us closer to the lock opening. In the case of the soft drink machine, each state transition takes us closer to enjoying the taste of the soft drink. In the case of a computer, each state transition takes us closer to solving a problem by processing a computer program that someone has written.

3.6.5 The Clock

A synchronous finite state machine transitions from its current state to its next state after an identical fixed interval of time. Control of that synchronous behavior is in part the responsibility of the clock circuit.

A clock circuit produces a signal, commonly referred to as *THE clock*, whose value alternates between 0 volts and some specified fixed voltage. In digital logic terms, the clock is a signal whose value alternates between 0 and 1. Figure 3.28 shows the value of the clock signal as a function of time. Each of the repeated sequence of identical intervals is referred to as a *clock cycle*. A clock cycle starts when the clock signal transitions from 0 to 1 and ends the next time the clock signal transitions from 0 to 1.

We will see in Chapter 5 and beyond that in each clock cycle, a computer can perform a piece of useful work. When people say their laptop computers run at a frequency of 2 gigahertz, they are saying their laptop computers perform two billion pieces of work each second since 2 gigahertz means two billion clock cycles each second, each clock cycle lasting for just one-half of a nanosecond. The synchronous finite state machine makes one state transition each clock cycle.

We will show by means of a traffic signal controller how the clock signal controls the transition, fixed clock cycle after fixed clock cycle, from one state to the next.

In electronic circuit implementations of a synchronous finite state machine, the transition from one state to the next occurs at the start of each clock cycle.

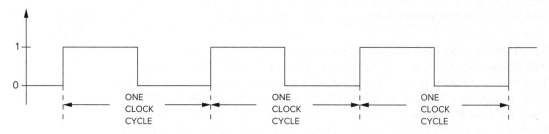

Figure 3.28   A clock signal.

3.6.6 Example: A Danger Sign

Many electrical, mechanical, and aeronautical systems are controlled by a synchronous finite state machine. In this section, we will design the complete logic needed for a synchronous finite state machine to control a traffic danger sign. Figure 3.29 shows the danger sign as it will be placed on the highway. Note the sign says, "Danger, Move Right." The sign contains five lights (labeled 1 through 5 in the figure).

The purpose of our synchronous finite state machine (a.k.a. a controller) is to direct the behavior of our system. In our case, the system is the set of lights on the traffic danger sign. The controller's job is to have the five lights flash on and off to warn automobile drivers to move to the right. The controller is equipped with a switch. When the switch is in the ON position, the controller directs the lights as follows: During one unit of time, all lights will be off. In the next unit of time, lights 1 and 2 will be on. The next unit of time, lights 1, 2, 3, and 4 will be on. Then all five lights will be on. Then the sequence repeats: no lights on, followed by 1 and 2 on, followed by 1, 2, 3, and 4 on, and so forth. Each unit of time lasts one second. To an automobile driver approaching the sign, the five lights clearly direct the driver to move to the right. The lights continue to sequence through these four states as long as the switch is on. If the switch is turned off, all the lights are turned off and remain off.

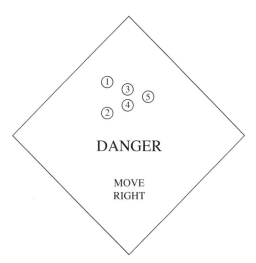

Figure 3.29   A traffic danger sign.

The State Diagram for the Danger Sign Controller   Figure 3.30 is a state diagram for the synchronous finite state machine that controls the lights. There are four states, one for each of the four conditions corresponding to which lights are on. Note that the outputs (whether each light is on or off) are determined by the current state of the system.

If the switch is on (input $= 1$), the transition from each state to the next state happens at one-second intervals, causing the lights to flash in the sequence

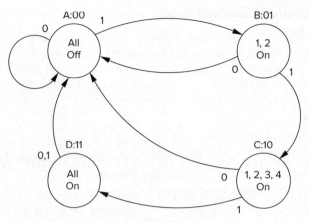

Figure 3.30   State diagram for the danger sign controller.

described. If the switch is turned off (input = 0), the state always transitions to state A, the "all off" state.

The Sequential Logic Circuit for the Danger Sign Controller   Recall that Figure 3.22 shows a generic block diagram for a sequential logic circuit. Figure 3.31 is a block diagram of the specific sequential logic circuit we need to control the lights. Several things are important to note in this figure.

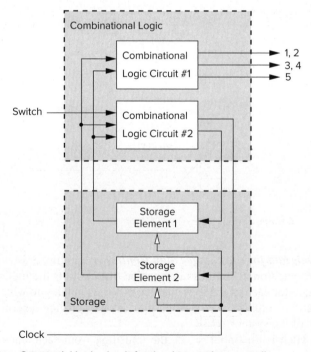

Figure 3.31   Sequential logic circuit for the danger sign controller.

First, the two external inputs: the switch and the clock. The switch determines whether the finite state machine will transition through the four states or whether it will transition to state A, where all lights are off. The other input (the clock) controls the transition from state A to B, B to C, C to D, and D to A by controlling the state of the storage elements. We will see how, momentarily.

Second, there are two storage elements for storing state information. Since there are four states, and since each storage element can store one bit of information, the four states are identified by the contents of the two storage elements: A (00), B (01), C (10), and D (11). Storage element 2 contains the high bit; storage element 1 contains the low bit. For example, the danger sign controller is in state B when storage element 2 is 0 and storage element 1 is 1.

Third, combinational logic circuit 1 shows that the on/off behavior of the lights is controlled by the storage elements. That is, the input to the combinational logic circuit is from the two storage elements, that is, the current state of the finite state machine.

Finally, combinational logic circuit 2 shows that the transition from the current state to the next state depends on the two storage elements and the switch. If the switch is on, the output of combinational logic circuit 2 depends on the state of the two storage elements.

The Combinational Logic   Figure 3.32 shows the logic that implements combinational logic circuits 1 and 2.

Two sets of outputs are required for the controller to work properly: a set of external outputs for the lights and a set of internal outputs for the inputs to the two storage elements that keep track of the state.

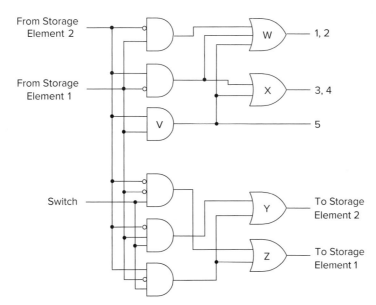

Figure 3.32   Combinational logic circuits 1 and 2.

First, let us look at the outputs that control the lights. As we have said, there are only three outputs necessary to control the lights. Light 5 is controlled by the output of the AND gate labeled V, since the only time light 5 is on is when the controller is in state 11. Lights 3 and 4 are controlled by the output of the OR gate labeled X, since there are two states in which those lights are on, those labeled 10 and 11. Why are lights 1 and 2 controlled by the output of the OR gate labeled W? See Exercise 3.42.

Next, let us look at the internal outputs that control the storage elements, which specify the next state of the controller. Storage element 2 should be set to 1 for the next clock cycle if the next state is 10 or 11. This is true only if the switch is on and the current state is either 01 or 10. Therefore, the output signal that will make storage element 2 be 1 in the next clock cycle is the output of the OR gate labeled Y. Why is the next state of storage element 1 controlled by the output of the OR gate labeled Z? See Exercise 3.42.

The Two Storage Elements   In order for the danger sign controller to work, the state transitions must occur once per second when the switch is on.

A Problem with Gated Latches as Storage Elements   What would happen if the storage elements were gated D latches? If the two storage elements were gated D latches, when the write enable signal (the clock) is 1, the output of OR gates Y and Z would immediately change the bits stored in the two gated D latches. This would produce new input values to the three AND gates that are input to OR gates Y and Z, producing new outputs that would be applied to the inputs of the gated latches, which would in turn change the bits stored in the gated latches, which would in turn mean new inputs to the three AND gates and new outputs of OR gates Y and Z. This would happen again and again, continually changing the bits stored in the two storage elements as long as the Write Enable signal to the gated D latches was asserted. The result: We have no idea what the state of the finite state machine would be for the next clock cycle. And, even in the current clock cycle, the state of the storage elements would change so fast that the five lights would behave erratically.

The problem is the gated D latch. We want the output of OR gates Y and Z to transition to the next state at the end of the current clock cycle and allow the current state to remain unchanged until then. That is, we do not want the input to the storage elements to take effect until the end of the current clock cycle. Since the output of a gated D latch changes immediately in response to its input if the Write Enable signal is asserted, it cannot be the storage element for our synchronous finite state machine. We need storage elements that allow us to read the current state throughout the current clock cycle, and not write the next state values into the storage elements until the beginning of the next clock cycle.

The Flip-Flop to the Rescue   It is worth repeating: To prevent the above from happening, we need storage elements that allow us to read the current state throughout the current clock cycle, and not write the next state values into the storage elements until the beginning of the next clock cycle. That is, the function

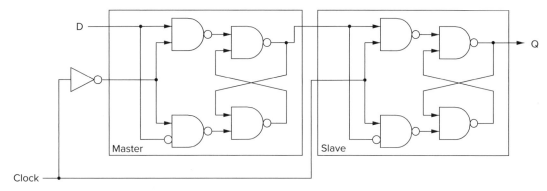

Figure 3.33   A master/slave flip-flop.

to be performed during a single clock cycle involves reading and writing a particular variable. Reading must be allowed throughout the clock cycle, and writing must occur at the end of the clock cycle.

A flip-flop can accomplish that. One example of a flip-flop is the master/slave flip-flop shown in Figure 3.33. The master/slave flip-flop can be constructed out of two gated *D* latches, one referred to as the master, the other referred to as the slave. Note that the write enable signal of the master is 1 when the clock is 0, and the write enable signal of the slave is 1 when the clock is 1.

Figure 3.34 is a timing diagram for the master/slave flip-flop, which shows how and why the master/slave flip-flop solves the problem. A timing diagram shows time passing from left to right. Note that clock cycle n starts at the time labeled 1 and ends at the time labeled 4. Clock cycle n+1 starts at the time labeled 4.

Consider clock cycle n, which we will discuss in terms of its first half A, its second half B, and the four time points labeled 1, 2, 3, and 4.

At the start of each clock cycle, the outputs of the storage elements are the outputs of the two slave latches. These outputs (starting at time 1) are input to the AND gates, resulting in OR gates Y and Z producing the next state values for the storage elements (at time 2). The timing diagram shows the propagation delay of the combinational logic, that is, the time it takes for the combinational logic to produce outputs of OR gates Y and Z. Although OR gates Y and Z produce the Next State value sometime during half-cycle A, the write enable signal to the master latches is 0, so the next state cannot be written into the master latches.

At the start of half-cycle B (at time 3), the clock signal is 0, which means the write enable signal to the master latches is 1, and the master latches can be written. However, during the half-cycle B, the write enable to the slave latches is 0, so the slave latches cannot write the new information now stored in the master latches.

At the start of clock cycle n+1 (at time 4), the write enable signal to the slave latches is 1, so the slave latches can store the next state value that was created by the combinational logic during clock cycle n. This becomes the current state for clock cycle n+1.

92

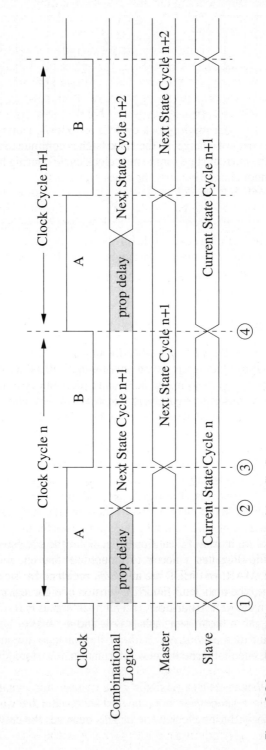

Figure 3.34   Timing diagram for a master/slave flip-flop.

Since the write enable signal to the master latches is now 0, the state of the master latches cannot change. Thus, although the write enable signal to the slave latches is 1, those latches do not change because the master latches cannot change.

In short, the output of the slave latches contains the current state of the system for the duration of the clock cycle and produces the inputs to the six AND gates in the combinational logic circuits. Their state changes at the start of the clock cycle by storing the next state information created by the combinational logic during the previous cycle but does not change again during the clock cycle. The reason they do not change again during the clock cycle is as follows: During half-cycle A, the master latches cannot change, so the slave latches continue to see the state information that is the current state for the new clock cycle. During half-cycle B, the slave latches cannot change because the clock signal is 0.

Meanwhile, during half-cycle B, the master latches can store the next state information produced by the combinational logic, but they cannot write it into the slave latches until the start of the next clock cycle, when it becomes the state information for the next clock cycle.

3.7 Preview of Coming Attractions: The Data Path of the LC-3

In Chapter 5, we will specify a computer, which we call the LC-3, and you will have the opportunity to write computer programs to execute on it. We close out Chapter 3 with a discussion of Figure 3.35, the *data path* of the LC-3 computer.

The data path consists of all the logic structures that combine to process information in the core of the computer. Right now, Figure 3.35 is undoubtedly more than a little intimidating, but you should not be concerned by that. You are not ready to analyze it yet. That will come in Chapter 5. We have included it here, however, to show you that you are already familiar with many of the basic structures that make up a computer. For example, you see five MUXes in the data path, and you already know how they work. Also, an adder (shown as the ALU symbol with a + sign inside) and an ALU. You know how those elements are constructed from gates.

One element that we have not identified explicitly yet is a register. A register is simply a set of *n* flip-flops that collectively are used to store one *n*-bit value. In Figure 3.35, PC, IR, MAR, and MDR are all 16-bit registers that store 16 bits of information each. The block labeled REG FILE consists of eight registers that each store 16 bits of information. As you know, one bit of information can be stored in one flip-flop. Therefore, each of these registers consists of 16 flip-flops. The data path also shows three 1-bit registers, *N*, *Z*, and *P*. Those registers require only one flip-flop each. In fact, a register can be any size that we need. The size depends only on the number of bits we need to represent the value we wish to store.

One way to implement registers is with master/slave flip-flops. Figure 3.36 shows a four-bit register made up of four master/slave flip-flops. We usually need flip-flops, rather than latches, because it is usually important to be able to both read the contents of a register throughout a clock cycle and also store a new value

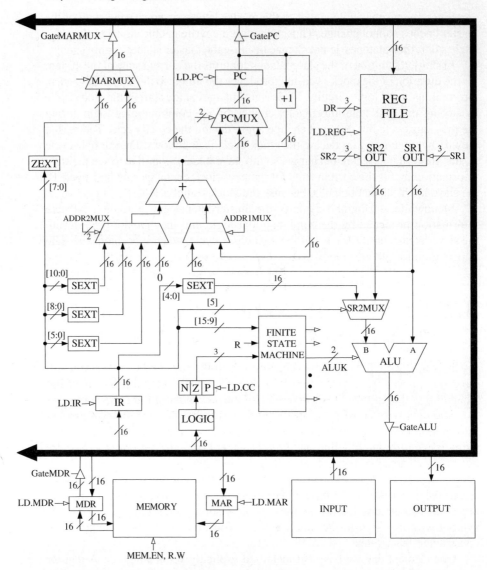

Figure 3.35   **The data path of the LC-3 computer.**

in the register at the end of that same clock cycle. As shown in Figure 3.36, the four-bit value stored in the register during a clock cycle is Q_3, Q_2, Q_1, Q_0. At the end of that clock cycle, the value D_3, D_2, D_1, D_0 is written into the register.

The arrows in Figure 3.35 represent wires that transmit values from one structure to another. Most of the arrows include a cross-hatch with a number next to it. The number represents the number of wires, corresponding to the number of bits being transmitted. Thus, for example, the arrow from the register labeled PC to one of the inputs of the MUX labeled ADDR1MUX indicates that 16 bits are transmitted from PC to an input of ADDR1MUX.

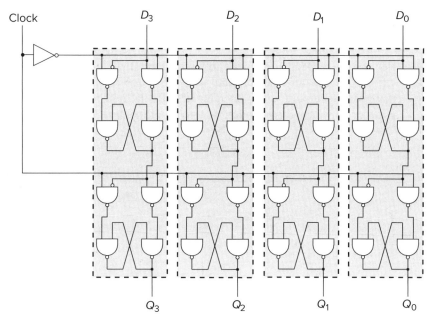

Figure 3.36   A four-bit register.

In Chapter 5, we will see why these elements must be connected as shown in order to execute programs written for the LC-3 computer. For now, just enjoy the fact that the components look familiar. In Chapters 4 and 5, we will raise the level of abstraction again and put these components together into a working computer.

Exercises

3.1   In the following table, write whether each type of transistor will act as an open circuit or a closed circuit.

	N-type	P-type
Gate = 1		
Gate = 0		

3.2   Replace the missing parts in the following circuit with either a wire or no wire to give the output OUT a logical value of 0 when the input IN is a logical 1.

IN = 1 ⎯⎯⎯   ⎯⎯⎯ OUT = 0

3.3   A two-input AND and a two-input OR are both examples of two-input logic functions. How many different two-input logic functions are possible?

3.4   Replace the missing parts in the following circuit with either a wire or no wire to give the output C a logical value of 1. Describe a set of inputs that give the output C a logical value of 0. Replace the missing parts with wires or no wires corresponding to that set of inputs.

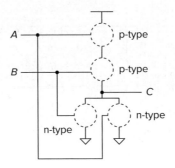

3.5   Complete a truth table for the transistor-level circuit in Figure 3.37.

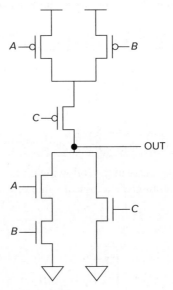

Figure 3.37   Diagram for Exercise 3.5.

3.6   For the transistor-level circuit in Figure 3.38, fill in the truth table. What is Z in terms of A and B?

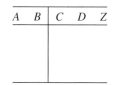

A	B	C	D	Z

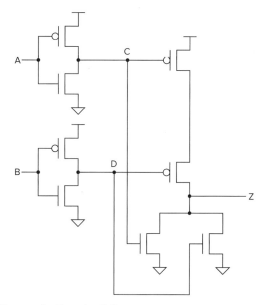

Figure 3.38   Diagram for Exercise 3.6.

3.7   The following circuit has a major flaw. Can you identify it?
Hint: Evaluate the circuit for all sets of inputs.

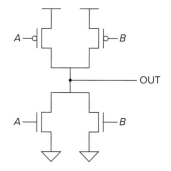

3.8   The transistor-level circuit below implements the logic equation given below. Label the inputs to all the transistors.

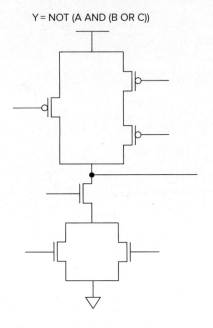

Y = NOT (A AND (B OR C))

3.9   What does the following transistor circuit do?

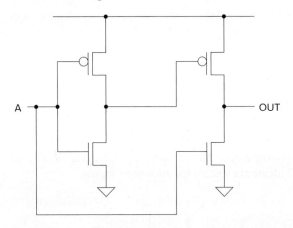

A

OUT

3.10 For what values of A, B, C, D, E, and F will the output of the six-input AND gate be 1?

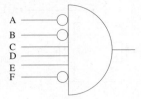

A
B
C
D
E
F

3.11 A student knew that an inverter contained one P-type transistor and one N-type transistor, but he wired them up wrong, as shown below.

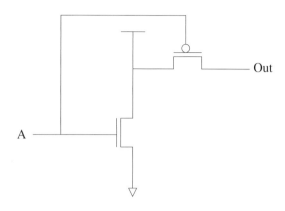

What is the value of Out when A = 0?
What is the value of Out when A = 1?

3.12 A function is described by the truth table shown on the left. Your job: Complete the logic implementation shown on the right by adding the appropriate connections.

A   B   C

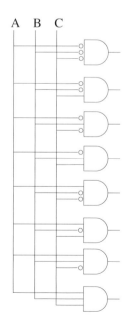
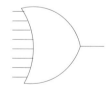

A	B	C	Out
0	0	0	1
0	0	1	1
0	1	0	0
0	1	1	0
1	0	0	1
1	0	1	0
1	1	0	0
1	1	1	1

3.13 The following logic diagram produces the logical value OUT.

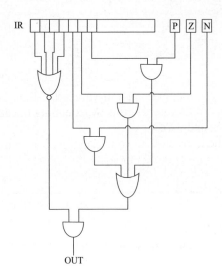

What does the value 0 or 1 for OUT signify?

3.14 The following logic circuits consist of two exclusive-OR gates. Construct the output truth table.

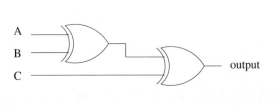

A	B	C	output
0	0	0	
0	0	1	
0	1	0	
0	1	1	
1	0	0	
1	0	1	
1	1	0	
1	1	1	

3.15 Fill in the truth table for the logical expression NOT(NOT(A) OR NOT(B)). What single logic gate has the same truth table?

A	B	NOT(NOT(A) OR NOT(B))
0	0	
0	1	
1	0	
1	1	

3.16 Fill in the truth table for a two-input NOR gate.

A	B	A NOR B
0	0	
0	1	
1	0	
1	1	

3.17 *a.* Draw a transistor-level diagram for a three-input AND gate and a three-input OR gate. Do this by extending the designs from Figure 3.6a and 3.7a.

   b. Replace the transistors in your diagrams from part *a* with either a wire or no wire to reflect the circuit's operation when the following inputs are applied.
   (1) $A = 1, B = 0, C = 0$
   (2) $A = 0, B = 0, C = 0$
   (3) $A = 1, B = 1, C = 1$

3.18 Following the example of Figure 3.11a, draw the gate-level schematic of a three-input decoder. For each output of this decoder, write the input conditions under which that output will be 1.

3.19 How many output lines will a five-input decoder have?

3.20 How many output lines will a 16-input multiplexer have? How many select lines will this multiplexer have?

3.21 If A and B are four-bit unsigned binary numbers, 0111 and 1011, complete the table obtained when using a two-bit full adder from Figure 3.15 to calculate each bit of the sum, S, of A and B. Check your answer by adding the decimal value of A and B and comparing the sum with S. Are the answers the same? Why or why not?

C_{in}				0
A	0	1	1	1
B	1	0	1	1
S				
C_{out}				

3.22 Given the following truth table, generate the gate-level logic circuit, using the implementation algorithm referred to in Section 3.3.4.

A	B	C	Z
0	0	0	1
0	0	1	0
0	1	0	0
0	1	1	1
1	0	0	0
1	0	1	1
1	1	0	1
1	1	1	0

3.23 *a.* Given four inputs *A*, *B*, *C*, and *D* and one output *Z*, create a truth table for a circuit with at least seven input combinations generating 1s at the output. (How many rows will this truth table have?)

   b. Now that you have a truth table, generate the gate-level logic circuit that implements this truth table. Use the implementation algorithm referred to in Section 3.3.4.

3.24 Implement the following functions using AND, OR, and NOT logic gates. The inputs are *A*, *B*, and the output is *F*.

   a. *F* has the value 1 only if *A* has the value 0 and *B* has the value 1.

   b. *F* has the value 1 only if *A* has the value 1 and *B* has the value 0.

   c. Use your answers from parts *a* and *b* to implement a one-bit adder. The truth table for the one-bit adder is given below.

A	*B*	Sum
0	0	0
0	1	1
1	0	1
1	1	0

   d. Is it possible to create a four-bit adder (a circuit that will correctly add two 4-bit quantities) using only four copies of the logic diagram from part *c*? If not, what information is missing? *Hint*: When $A = 1$ and $B = 1$, a sum of 0 is produced. What information is lost?

3.25 Logic circuit 1 in Figure 3.39 has inputs *A*, *B*, *C*. Logic circuit 2 in Figure 3.40 has inputs *A* and *B*. Both logic circuits have an output *D*. There is a fundamental difference between the behavioral characteristics of these two circuits. What is it? *Hint*: What happens when the voltage at input *A* goes from 0 to 1 in both circuits?

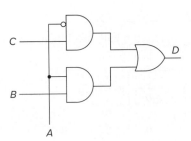

Figure 3.39   Logic circuit 1 for Exercise 3.25.

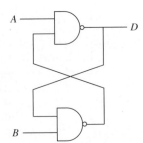

Figure 3.40   Logic circuit 2 for Exercise 3.25.

3.26 Generate the gate-level logic that implements the following truth table.
From the gate-level structure, generate a transistor diagram that
implements the logic structure. Verify that the transistor
diagram implements the truth table.

in_0	in_1	$f(in_0, in_1)$
0	0	1
0	1	0
1	0	1
1	1	1

3.27 You know a byte is eight bits. We call a four-bit quantity a *nibble*. If a
byte-addressable memory has a 14-bit address, how many nibbles of
storage are in this memory?

3.28 Implement a 4-to-1 mux using only 2-to-1 muxes making sure to
properly connect all of the terminals. Remember that you will have
four inputs, two control signals, and one output. Write out the truth table
for this circuit.

3.29 Given the logic circuit in Figure 3.41, fill in the truth table for the output
value Z.

A	B	C	Z
0	0	0	
0	0	1	
0	1	0	
0	1	1	
1	0	0	
1	0	1	
1	1	0	
1	1	1	

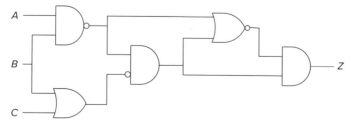

Figure 3.41   Diagram for Exercise 3.29.

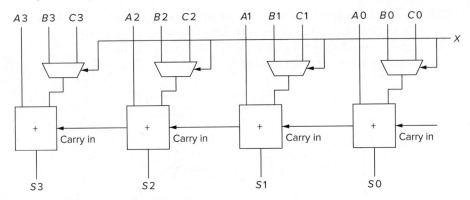

Figure 3.42   Diagram for Exercise 3.30.

3.30 *a.* Figure 3.42 shows a logic circuit that appears in many of today's
processors. Each of the boxes is a full-adder circuit. What does the
value on the wire X do? That is, what is the difference in the output
of this circuit if $X = 0$ vs. if $X = 1$?

b. Construct a logic diagram that implements an adder/subtractor. That
is, the logic circuit will compute $A + B$ or $A - B$ depending on
the value of X. *Hint*: Use the logic diagram of Figure 3.42 as a
building block.

3.31 Say the speed of a logic structure depends on the largest number of logic
gates through which any of the inputs must propagate to reach an output.
Assume that a NOT, an AND, and an OR gate all count as one gate
delay. For example, the propagation delay for a two-input decoder
shown in Figure 3.11 is 2 because some inputs propagate through
two gates.

a. What is the propagation delay for the two-input mux shown in
Figure 3.12?

b. What is the propagation delay for the one-bit full adder in
Figure 3.15?

c. What is the propagation delay for the four-bit adder shown in
Figure 3.16?

d. What if the four-bit adder were extended to 32 bits?

3.32 Recall that the adder was built with individual "**slices**" that produced
a sum bit and a carry-out bit based on the two operand bits A and B
and the carry-in bit. We called such an element a full adder. Suppose
we have a 3-to-8 decoder and two 6-input OR gates, as shown below.
Can we connect them so that we have a full adder? If so, please do.
(*Hint*: If an input to an OR gate is not needed, we can simply put an
input 0 on it and it will have no effect on anything. For example, see the
following figure.)

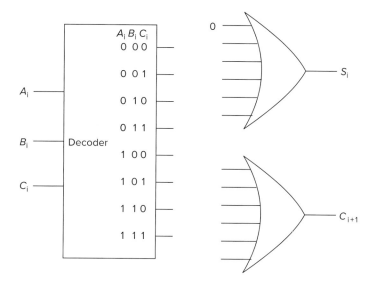

3.33 For this question, refer to the figure that follows.

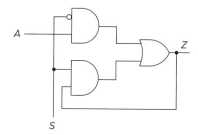

    a. Describe the output of this logic circuit when the select line *S* is a logical 0. That is, what is the output *Z* for each value of *A*?

    b. If the select line *S* is switched from a logical 0 to 1, what will the output be?

    c. Is this logic circuit a storage element?

3.34 Having designed a binary adder, you are now ready to design a 2-bit by 2-bit unsigned binary multiplier. The multiplier takes two 2-bit inputs A[1:0] and B[1:0] and produces an output *Y*, which is the product of A[1:0] and B[1:0]. The standard notation for this is:

$$Y = A10 \cdot B10$$

    a. What is the maximum value that can be represented in two bits for *A*(A[1:0])?

    b. What is the maximum value that can be represented in two bits for *B*(B[1:0])?

    c. What is the maximum possible value of Y?

    d. What is the number of required bits to represent the maximum value of Y?

    e. Write a truth table for the multiplier described above. You will have a four-input truth table with the inputs being A[1], A[0], B[1], and B[0].

    f. Implement the third bit of output, Y[2] from the truth table using only AND, OR, and NOT gates.

3.35 A 16-bit register contains a value. The value x75A2 is written into it. Can the original value be recovered?

3.36 A comparator circuit has two 1-bit inputs A and B and three 1-bit outputs G (greater), E (Equal), and L (less than). Refer to Figures 3.43 and 3.44 for this problem.

G is 1 if $A > B$ E is 1 if $A = B$ L is 1 if $A < B$
0 otherwise   0 otherwise   0 otherwise

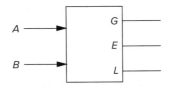

Figure 3.43   Diagram for Exercise 3.36.

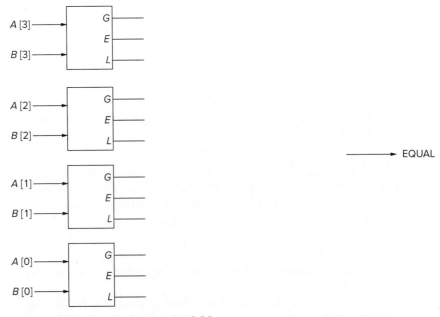

Figure 3.44   Diagram for Exercise 3.36.

a. Draw the truth table for a one-bit comparator.

A	B	G	E	L
0	0			
0	1			
1	0			
1	1			

b. Implement *G*, *E*, and *L* using AND, OR, and NOT gates.
c. Using the one-bit comparator as a basic building block, construct a four-bit equality checker such that output EQUAL is 1 if A30 = B30, 0 otherwise.

3.37 If a computer has eight-byte addressability and needs three bits to access a location in memory, what is the total size of memory in bytes?

3.38 Distinguish between a memory address and the memory's addressability.

3.39 Refer to Figure 3.21, the diagram of the four-entry, 2^2-by-3-bit memory.

a. To read from the fourth memory location, what must the values of A10 and WE be?
b. To change the number of entries in the memory from 4 to 60, how many address lines would be needed? What would the addressability of the memory be after this change was made?
c. Suppose the minimum width (in bits) of the program counter (the program counter is a special register within a CPU, and we will discuss it in detail in Chapter 4) is the minimum number of bits needed to address all 60 locations in our memory from part *b*. How many additional memory locations could be added to this memory without having to alter the width of the program counter?

3.40 For the memory shown in Figure 3.45:

a. What is the address space?
b. What is the addressability?
c. What is the data at address 2?

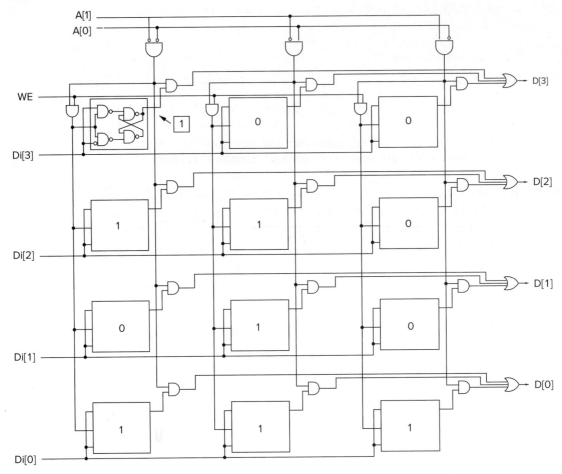

Figure 3.45   Diagram for Exercise 3.40.

3.41 Given a memory that is addressed by 22 bits and is 3-bit addressable, how many bits of storage does the memory contain?

3.42 A combinational logic circuit has two inputs. The values of those two inputs during the past ten cycles were 01, 10, 11, 01, 10, 11, 01, 10, 11, and 01. The values of these two inputs during the current cycle are 10. Explain the effect on the current output due to the values of the inputs during the previous ten cycles.

3.43 In the case of the lock of Figure 3.23a, there are four states A, B, C, and D, as described in Section 3.6.2. Either the lock is open (State D), or if it is not open, we have already performed either zero (State A), one (State B), or two (State C) correct operations. This is the sum total of all possible states that can exist. Exercise: Why is that the case? That is, what would be the snapshot of a fifth state that describes a possible situation for the combination lock?

3.44 Recall Section 3.6.2. Can one have an arc from a state where the score is Texas 30, Oklahoma 28 to a state where the score is tied, Texas 30, Oklahoma 30? Draw an example of the scoreboards (like the one in Figure 3.24) for the two states.

3.45 Recall again Section 3.6.2. Is it possible to have two states, one where Texas is ahead 30-28 and the other where the score is tied 30-30, but no arc between the two? Draw an example of two scoreboards, one where the score is 30-28 and the other where the score is 30-30, but there can be no arc between the two. For each of the three output values, game in progress, Texas wins, Oklahoma wins, draw an example of a scoreboard that corresponds to a state that would produce that output.

3.46 Refer to Section 3.6.2. Draw a partial finite state machine for the game of tic-tac-toe.

3.47 The IEEE campus society office sells sodas for 35 cents. Suppose they install a soda controller that only takes the following three inputs: nickel, dime, and quarter. After you put in each coin, you push a pushbutton to register the coin. If at least 35 cents has been put in the controller, it will output a soda and proper change (if applicable). Draw a finite state machine that describes the behavior of the soda controller. Each state will represent how much money has been put in (*Hint*: There will be seven of these states). Once enough money has been put in, the controller will go to a final state where the person will receive a soda and proper change (*Hint*: There are five such final states). From the final state, the next coin that is put in will start the process again.

3.48 Refer to Figure 3.32. Why are lights 1 and 2 controlled by the output of the OR gate labeled *W*? Why is the next state of storage element 2 controlled by the output of the OR gate labeled *Y*?

3.49 The following figure shows an implementation of a finite state machine with an input *X* and output *Z*. S1, S0 specifies the present state. D1, D0 specifies the next state.

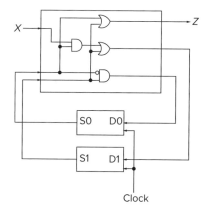

a. Complete the rest of the following table.

S1	S0	X	D1	D0	Z
0	0	0			
0	0	1			
0	1	0			
0	1	1	1	0	1
1	0	0			
1	0	1			
1	1	0			
1	1	1			

b. Draw the state diagram for the truth table of part *a.*

3.50 Prove that the NAND gate, by itself, is logically complete (see Section 3.3.5) by constructing a logic circuit that performs the AND function, a logic circuit that performs the NOT function, and a logic circuit that performs the OR function. Use only NAND gates in these three logic circuits.

3.51 We have learned that we can write one bit of information with a logic circuit called a transparent latch and that the bit written is available to be read almost immediately after being written.

Sometimes it is useful to be able to store a bit but not be able to read the value of that bit until the next cycle. An example of a logic circuit that has this property is a _____.

3.52 A student decided to design a latch as shown below. For what values of A and B will the latch remain in the quiescent state (i.e., its output will not change)?

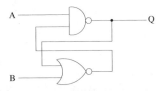

★**3.53** The master/slave flip-flop we introduced in the chapter is shown below. Note that the input value is visible at the output after the clock transitions from 0 to 1.

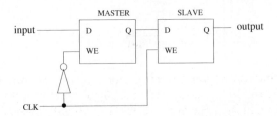

Shown below is a circuit constructed with three of these flip-flops.

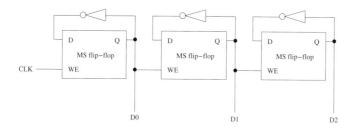

Fill in the entries for D2, D1, D0 for each of clock cycles shown

	cycle 0	cycle 1	cycle 2	cycle 3	cycle 4	cycle 5	cycle 6	cycle 7
D2	0							
D1	0							
D0	0							

In ten words or less, what is this circuit doing?

★**3.54** An 8-to-1 mux (shown below) outputs one of the eight sources, A, B, C, D, E, F, G, H depending on S[2:0], as shown. Note the value of S[2:0] corresponding to each source is shown just below the input to the mux. For example, when S[2:0] = 001, B is provided to the output.

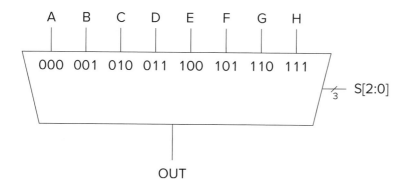

We can implement an 8-to-1 mux with a logic circuit of 2-to-1 muxes, as shown below. In this case, the 0 and 1 below the two inputs to each mux correspond to the value of the select line that will cause that input to be provided to the output of that mux.

Note that only two of the sources are shown. Note also that none of the select bits are labeled. Your task: Finish the job.

a. Label the select line of each mux, according to whether it is S[2], S[1], or S[0].

b. Label the remaining six sources to the 2-to-1 mux circuit, so the circuit behaves exactly like the 8-to-1 mux shown above.

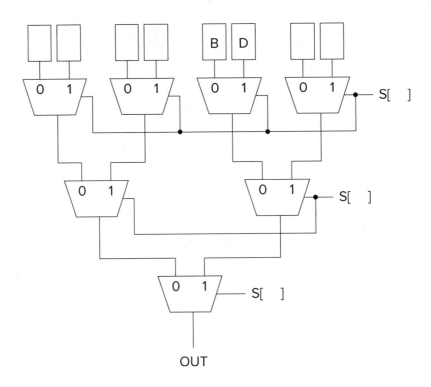

OUT

★3.55 We wish to implement two logic functions Y(a,b,c) and Z(a,b). Y is 1 in exactly those cases where an odd number of a, b, and c equal 1. Z is the exclusive-OR of a and b.

a. Construct the truth tables for Y and Z.

a	b	c	Y	Z
0	0	0		
0	0	1		
0	1	0		
0	1	1		
1	0	0		
1	0	1		
1	1	0		
1	1	1		

b. Implement the two logic functions Y and Z described above using ONLY the logic circuits provided below: a 3-to-8 decoder and two OR gates. That is, draw the wires from the outputs of the decoder to the inputs of the OR gates as necessary to do the job. You can assume you have as many inputs to each OR gate as you find necessary.

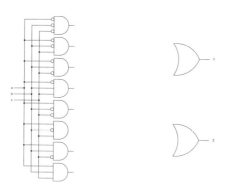

★3.56 Shown below is the partially completed state diagram of a finite state machine that takes an input string of H (heads) and T (tails) and produces an output of 1 every time the string HTHH occurs.

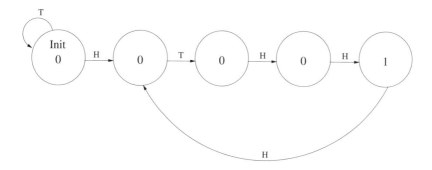

For example,
    if the input string is: H   H   H   H   H   T   H   H   T   H   H
H   H   H   T   H   H   T,
    the output would be: 0   0   0   0   0   0   0   1   0   0   1
0   0   0   0   0   1   0.
Note that the eighth coin toss (H) is part of two HTHH sequences.

a. Complete the state diagram of the finite state machine that will do this for any input sequence of any length.
b. If we decide to implement this finite state machine with a sequential logic circuit (similar to the danger sign we designed in class), how many state variables would we need?

★3.57 Shown below is a state diagram for a four-state machine and the truth
table showing the behavior of this state machine. Some of the entries in
both are missing.

Note that the states are labeled 00, 01, 10, and 11 and the output of each
state Z (0 or 1) is shown in each state. The input is shown as X.

Your job is to complete both the truth table and the state machine.

S[1]	S[0]	X	S'[1]	S'[0]	Z
0	0	0			
0	0	1	1	1	
0	1	0			
0	1	1			1
1	0	0			0
1	0	1	0	1	
1	1	0	0	0	
1	1	1			

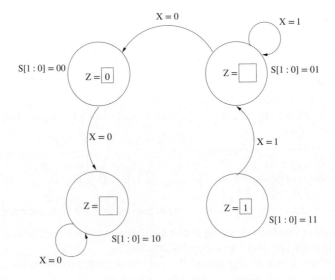

★3.58 The following transistor circuit produces the accompanying truth table. The inputs to some of the gates of the transistors are not specified. Also, the outputs for some of the input combinations of the truth table are not specified.

Your job: Complete both specifications. That is, all transistors will have their gates properly labeled with either A, B, or C, and all rows of the truth table will have a 0 or 1 specified as the output.

Note that this is not a problematic circuit. For every input combination, the output is either connected to ground (i.e., OUT=0) or to the positive end of the battery (i.e., OUT=1).

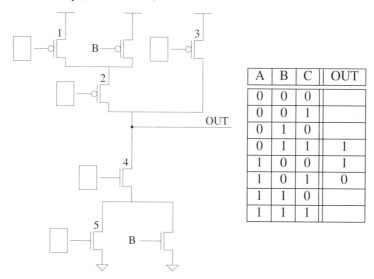

A	B	C	OUT
0	0	0	
0	0	1	
0	1	0	
0	1	1	1
1	0	0	1
1	0	1	0
1	1	0	
1	1	1	

★3.59 Most word processors will correct simple errors in spelling and grammar. Your job is to specify a finite state machine that will capitalize the personal pronoun I in certain instances if it is entered as a lowercase i. For example,

i think i'm in love will be corrected to **I think I'm in love**.

Input to your finite state machine will be any sequence of characters from a standard keyboard. Your job is to replace the **i** with an **I** if
    the i is the first character input or is preceded by a *space*, and
    the i is followed by a *space* or by an *apostrophe*.

Shown below is a finite state machine with some of the inputs and some of the outputs unspecified. Your job is to complete the specification.

Inputs are from the set $\{i, A, S, O\}$, where
> A represents an apostrophe,
> S represents a space,
> O represents any character other than i, apostrophe, or *space*.

The output Z corresponding to each state is 0 or 1, where 0 means "do nothing," 1 means "change the most recent **i** to an **I**."

Note: This exercise in developing a finite state machine word processor is only a first step since a lot of "i to I" will not fix the problem. For example,
> i' am —> I' am, i'abcd —> I'abcd, and i'i —> I'i are all bad!

But it is a first step!

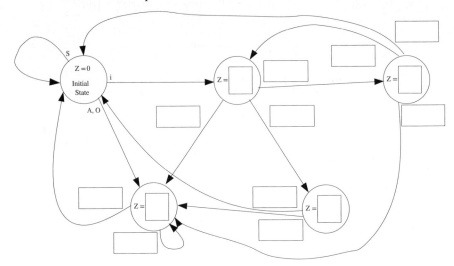

★**3.60** A finite state machine is connected to a 2^3-by-2-bit memory as shown below:

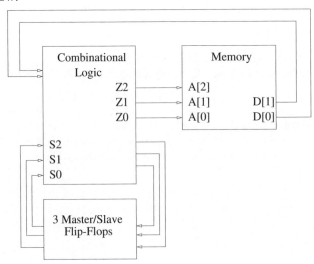

The contents of the memory is shown below to the left. The next state transition table is shown below to the right.

Address A[2:0]	Content D[1:0]		Current State S[2:0]	Next State D[1:0] 00	D[1:0] 01	D[1:0] 10	D[1:0] 11
000	11						
001	10		000	001	010	110	100
010	01		001	100	000	011	110
011	10		010	010	100	111	010
100	01		011	001	100	100	010
101	00		100	110	011	011	111
110	00		101	100	010	100	110
111	01		110	001	110	100	010
			111	000	101	111	101

The output Z0, Z1, Z2 is the current state of the finite state machine. That is, Z0=S0, Z1=S1, Z2=S2. The cycle time of the finite state machine is long enough so that during a single cycle, the following happens: The output of the finite state machine accesses the memory, and the values supplied by the memory are input to the combinational logic, which determines the next state of the machine.

a. Complete the following table.

Cycles	State	Data
Cycle 0	000	11
Cycle 1		
Cycle 2		
Cycle 3		

b. What will the state of the FSM be just before the end of cycle 100? Why?

★**3.61**   The logic diagram shown below is a finite state machine.

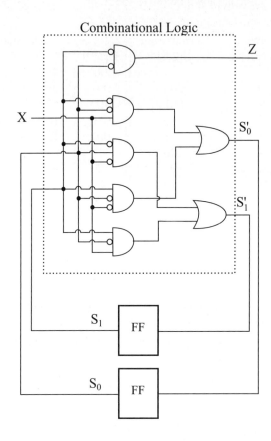

a. Construct the truth table for the combinational logic:

S1	S0	X	Z	S1'	S0'
0	0	0			
0	0	1			
0	1	0			
0	1	1			
1	0	0			
1	0	1			
1	1	0			
1	1	1			

b. Complete the state machine.
(We have provided nine states. You will not need all of them. Use only as many as you need):

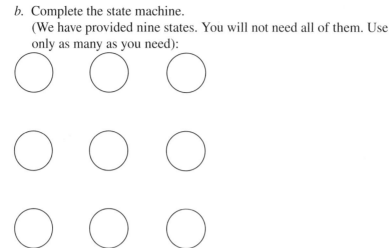

★3.62   You are taking three courses, one each in computing (C), engineering (E), and math (M). In each course, you periodically receive assignments. You never receive more than one assignment at a time. You also never receive another assignment in a course if you currently have an assignment in that course that has not been completed. You must procrastinate (i.e., do nothing) unless you have unfinished assignments in both computing and engineering.

Design a finite state machine to describe the state of the work you have to do and whether you are working or procrastinating.

a. Label each state with the unfinished assignments (with letters C,E,M) for when you are in that state. There are far more states provided than you actually need. Use only what you need.

b. There are six inputs: c, e, m, $\bar{c}$, $\bar{e}$, $\bar{m}$. c, e, m refer to you receiving an assignment. $\bar{c}$, $\bar{e}$, $\bar{m}$ refer to you completing an assignment. Draw the transition arc for each state/input pair. For example, if you had previously only had an unfinished assignment in math and you received an assignment in computing, you would transition from state M to state CM, as shown below.

c. The output of each state is your behavior, 1 if you are working on an assignment, 0 if you are procrastinating. Label the outputs of each state.

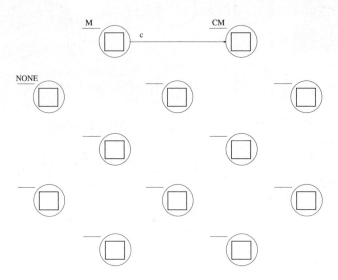

CHAPTER

The von Neumann Model

We are now ready to raise our level of abstraction another notch. We will build on the logic structures that we studied in Chapter 3, both decision elements and storage elements, to construct the basic computer model first proposed in the 1940s, usually referred to as the von Neumann machine. ...and, we will write our first computer program in the ISA of the LC-3.

4.1 Basic Components

To get a task done by a computer, we need two things: (a) a **computer program** that specifies what the computer must do to perform the task, and (b) the **computer** that is to carry out the task.

A computer program consists of a set of instructions, each specifying a well-defined piece of work for the computer to carry out. The *instruction* is the smallest piece of work specified in a computer program. That is, the computer either carries out the work specified by an instruction or it does not. The computer does not have the luxury of carrying out only a piece of an instruction.

John von Neumann proposed a fundamental model of a computer for processing computer programs in 1946. Figure 4.1 shows its basic components. We have taken a little poetic license and added a few of our own minor embellishments to von Neumann's original diagram. The von Neumann model consists of five parts: *memory, a processing unit, input, output*, and *a control unit*. The computer program is contained in the computer's memory. The data the program needs to carry out the work of the program is either contained in the program's memory or is obtained from the input devices. The results of the program's execution are provided by the output devices. The order in which the instructions are carried out is performed by the control unit.

We will describe each of the five parts of the von Neumann model in greater detail.

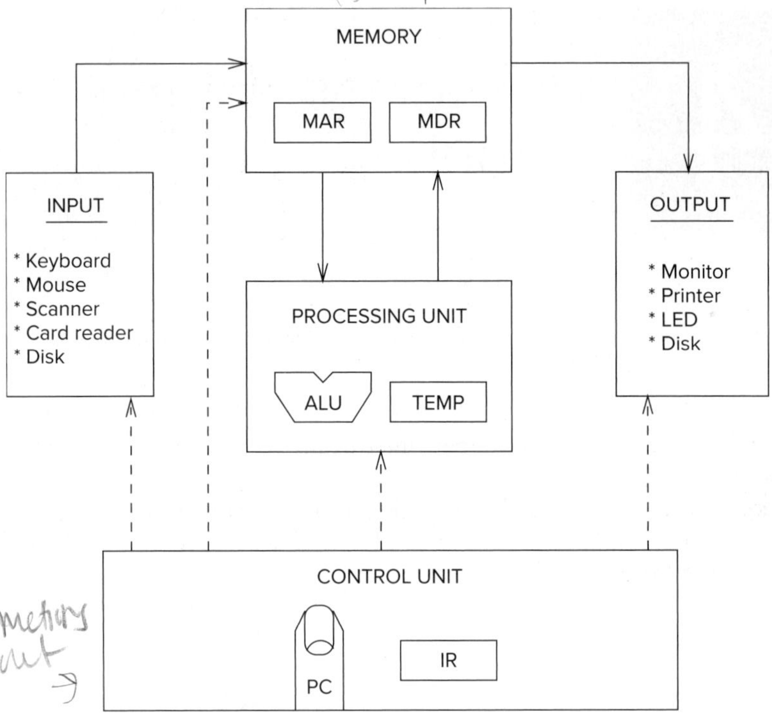

[handwritten: · A (known Register in 4 of Itself)]
[handwritten: location is a ↑]

Figure 4.1   The von Neumann model, overall block diagram.

[handwritten in left margin: order of which Instructions are carried out →]

4.1.1 Memory

Recall that in Chapter 3 we examined a simple 2^2-by-3-bit memory that was constructed out of gates and latches. A more realistic memory for one of today's computer systems is 2^{34} by 8 bits. That is, a typical memory in today's world of computers consists of 2^{34} distinct memory locations, each of which is capable of storing eight bits of information. We say that such a memory has an *address space* of 2^{34} uniquely identifiable locations, and an *addressability* of eight bits. We refer to such a memory as a 16-gigabyte memory (abbreviated, 16 GB). The "16 giga" refers to the 2^{34} locations, and the "byte" refers to the eight bits stored in each location. The term is 16 giga because 16 is 2^4 and *giga* is the term we use to represent 2^{30}, which is approximately one billion; 2^4 times $2^{30} = 2^{34}$. A *byte* is the word we use to describe eight bits, much the way we use the word *gallon* to describe four quarts.

We note (as we will note again and again) that with k bits, we can represent uniquely 2^k items. Thus, to uniquely identify 2^{34} memory locations, each location must have its own 34-bit address. In Chapter 5, we will begin the complete definition of the LC-3 computer. We will see that the memory address space of the LC-3 is 2^{16}, and the addressability is 16 bits.

Recall from Chapter 3 that we access memory by providing the address from which we wish to read, or to which we wish to write. To read the contents of a

000	
001	
010	
011	
100	00000110
101	
110	00000100
111	

Figure 4.2   Location 6 contains the value 4; location 4 contains the value 6.

memory location, we first place the address of that location in the memory's address register (**MAR**) and then interrogate the computer's memory. The information stored in the location having that address will be placed in the memory's data register (**MDR**). To write (or store) a value in a memory location, we first write the address of the memory location in the MAR, and the value to be stored in the MDR. We then interrogate the computer's memory with the write enable signal asserted. The information contained in the MDR will be written into the memory location whose address is in the MAR.

Before we leave the notion of memory for the moment, let us again emphasize the two characteristics of a memory location: its address and what is stored there. Figure 4.2 shows a representation of a memory consisting of eight locations. Its addresses are shown at the left, numbered in binary from 0 to 7. Each location contains eight bits of information. Note that the value 6 is stored in the memory location whose address is 4, and the value 4 is stored in the memory location whose address is 6. These represent two very different situations.

Finally, an analogy: the post office boxes in your local post office. The box number is like the memory location's address. Each box number is unique. The information stored in the memory location is like the letters contained in the post office box. As time goes by, what is contained in the post office box at any particular moment can change. But the box number remains the same. So, too, with each memory location. The value stored in that location can be changed, but the location's memory address remains unchanged.

4.1.2 Processing Unit

The actual processing of information in the computer is carried out by the *processing unit*. The processing unit in a modern computer can consist of many sophisticated complex functional units, each performing one particular operation (divide, square root, etc.). The simplest processing unit, and the one normally thought of when discussing the basic von Neumann model, is the **ALU**. *ALU* is the abbreviation for Arithmetic and Logic Unit, so called because it is usually capable of performing basic arithmetic functions (like ADD and SUBTRACT) and basic logic operations (like bit-wise AND, OR, and NOT) that we have already studied in Chapter 2. We will see in Chapter 5 that the LC-3 has an ALU, which can perform ADD, AND, and NOT operations. Two of these (ADD and AND) we will discuss in this chapter.

The ALU normally processes data elements of a fixed size referred to as the *word length* of the computer. The data elements are called *words*. For example, to perform ADD, the ALU receives two words as inputs and produces a single word (the sum) as output. Each ISA has its own word length, depending on the intended use of the computer.

Most microprocessors today that are used in PCs or workstations have a word length of 64 bits (as is the case with Intel's "Core" processors) or 32 bits (as is the case with Intel's "Atom" processors). Even most microprocessors now used in cell phones have 64-bit word lengths, such as Apple's A7 through A11 processors, and Qualcomm's SnapDragon processors. However, the microprocessors used in very inexpensive applications often have word lengths of as little as 16 or even 8 bits.

In the LC-3, the ALU processes 16-bit words. We say the LC-3 has a word length of 16 bits.

It is almost always the case that a computer provides some small amount of storage very close to the ALU to allow results to be temporarily stored if they will be needed to produce additional results in the near future. For example, if a computer is to calculate $(A+B) \cdot C$, it could store the result of $A+B$ in memory, and then subsequently read it in order to multiply that result by C. However, the time it takes to access memory is long compared to the time it takes to perform the ADD or MULTIPLY. Almost all computers, therefore, have temporary storage for storing the result of $A + B$ in order to avoid the much longer access time that would be necessary when it came time to multiply. The most common form of temporary storage is a set of registers, like the register described in Section 3.7. Typically, the size of each register is identical to the size of values processed by the ALU; that is, they each contain one word. The LC-3 has eight registers (R0, R1, ... R7), each containing 16 bits.

Current microprocessors typically contain 32 registers, each consisting of 32 or 64 bits, depending on the architecture. These serve the same purpose as the eight 16-bit registers in the LC-3. However, the importance of temporary storage for values that most modern computers will need shortly means many computers today have an additional set of special-purpose registers consisting of 128 bits of information to handle special needs. Those special needs we will have to save for later in your studies.

4.1.3 Input and Output

In order for a computer to process information, the information must get into the computer. In order to use the results of that processing, those results must be displayed in some fashion outside the computer. Many devices exist for the purposes of input and output. They are generically referred to in computer jargon as *peripherals* because they are in some sense accessories to the processing function. Nonetheless, they are no less important.

In the LC-3 we will have the two most basic input and output devices. For input, we will use the keyboard; for output, we will use the monitor.

There are, of course, many other input and output devices in computer systems today. For input we have among other things the mouse, digital scanners, and shopping mall kiosks to help you navigate the shopping mall. For output we have among other things printers, LED displays, disks, and shopping mall kiosks to help you navigate the shopping mall. :-) In the old days, a lot of input and output was carried out by punched cards. Fortunately, for those who would have to lug around boxes of cards, the use of punched cards has largely disappeared.

4.1.4 Control Unit

The control unit is like the conductor of an orchestra; it is in charge of making all the other parts of the computer play together. As we will see when we describe the step-by-step process of executing a computer program, it is the control unit that keeps track of both where we are within the process of executing the program and where we are in the process of executing each instruction.

To keep track of which instruction is being executed, the control unit has an *instruction register* to contain that instruction. To keep track of which instruction is to be processed next, the control unit has a register that contains the next instruction's address. For historical reasons, that register is called the *program counter* (abbreviated PC), although a better name for it would be the *instruction pointer*, since the contents of this register is, in some sense, "pointing" to the next instruction to be processed. Curiously, Intel does in fact call that register the instruction pointer, but the simple elegance of that name has not caught on.

4.2 The LC-3: An Example von Neumann Machine

In Chapter 5, we will specify in detail the LC-3, a simple computer that we will study extensively. We have already shown you its data path in Chapter 3 (Figure 3.35) and identified several of its structures in Section 4.1. In this section, we will pull together all the parts of the LC-3 we need to describe it as a von Neumann computer (see Figure 4.3).

We constructed Figure 4.3 by starting with the LC-3's full data path (Figure 3.35) and removing all elements that are not essential to pointing out the five basic components of the von Neumann model.

Note that there are two kinds of arrowheads in Figure 4.3: filled-in and not-filled-in. Filled-in arrowheads denote data elements that flow along the corresponding paths. Not-filled-in arrowheads denote control signals that control the processing of the data elements. For example, the box labeled ALU in the processing unit processes two 16-bit values and produces a 16-bit result. The two sources and the result are all data, and are designated by filled-in arrowheads. The operation performed on those two 16-bit data elements (it is labeled ALUK) is part of the control—therefore, a not-filled-in arrowhead.

MEMORY consists of the storage elements, along with the Memory Address Register (MAR) for addressing individual locations and the

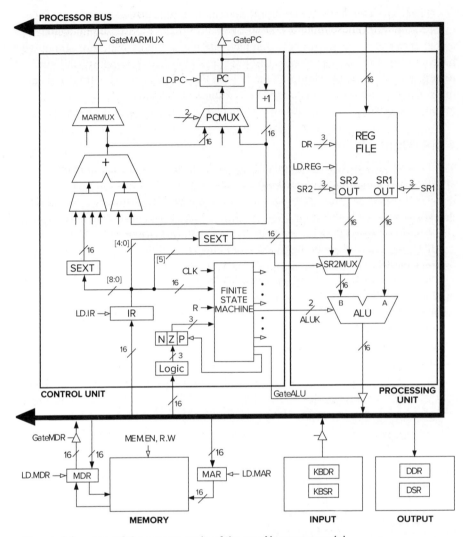

Figure 4.3 The LC-3 as an example of the von Neumann model.

Memory Data Register (MDR) for holding the contents of a memory location on its way to/from the storage. Note that the MAR contains 16 bits, reflecting the fact that the memory address space of the LC-3 is 2^{16} memory locations. The MDR contains 16 bits, reflecting the fact that each memory location contains 16 bits—that is, the LC-3 is 16-bit addressable.

INPUT/OUTPUT consists of a keyboard and a monitor. The simplest keyboard requires two registers: a keyboard data register (KBDR) for holding the ASCII codes of keys struck and a keyboard status register (KBSR) for maintaining status information about the keys struck. The simplest monitor also requires two registers: a display data register (DDR) for holding the ASCII code of something to be displayed on the screen and a display status register (DSR) for maintaining associated status information. These input and output registers will be discussed in detail in Chapter 9.

THE PROCESSING UNIT consists of a functional unit (ALU) that performs arithmetic and logic operations and eight registers (R0, ... R7) for storing temporary values that will be needed in the near future as operands for subsequent instructions. The LC-3 ALU can perform one arithmetic operation (addition) and two logical operations (bitwise AND and bitwise NOT).

THE CONTROL UNIT consists of all the structures needed to manage the processing that is carried out by the computer. Its most important structure is the finite state machine, which directs all the activity. Recall the finite state machines in Section 3.6. Processing is carried out step by step, or rather, clock cycle by clock cycle. Note the CLK input to the finite state machine in Figure 4.3. It specifies how long each clock cycle lasts. The instruction register (IR) is also an input to the finite state machine since the LC-3 instruction being processed determines what activities must be carried out. The program counter (PC) is also a part of the control unit; it keeps track of the next instruction to be executed after the current instruction finishes.

Note that all the external outputs of the finite state machine in Figure 4.3 have arrowheads that are not filled in. These outputs control the processing throughout the computer. For example, one of these outputs (two bits) is ALUK, which controls the operation performed in the ALU (ADD, AND, or NOT) during the current clock cycle. Another output is GateALU, which determines whether or not the output of the ALU is provided to the processor bus during the current clock cycle.

The complete description of the data path, control, and finite state machine for one implementation of the LC-3 is the subject of Appendix C.

4.3 Instruction Processing

The central idea in the von Neumann model of computer processing is that the program and data are both stored as sequences of bits in the computer's memory, and the program is executed one instruction at a time under the direction of the control unit.

4.3.1 The Instruction

The most basic unit of computer processing is the instruction. It is made up of two parts, the *opcode* (what the instruction does) and the *operands* (who it does it to!).

There are fundamentally three kinds of instructions: *operates*, *data movement*, and *control*, although many ISAs have some special instructions that are necessary for those ISAs. **Operate** instructions operate on data. The LC-3 has three operate instructions: one arithmetic (ADD) and two logicals (AND and

NOT). **Data movement** instructions move information from the processing unit to and from memory and to and from input/output devices. The LC-3 has six data movement instructions.

Control instructions are necessary for altering the sequential processing of instructions. That is, normally the next instruction executed is the instruction contained in the next memory location. If a program consists of instructions 1,2,3,4...10 located in memory locations A, A+1, A+2, ...A+9, normally the instructions would be executed in the sequence 1,2,3...10. We will see before we leave Chapter 4, however, that sometimes we will want to change the sequence. Control instructions enable us to do that.

An LC-3 instruction consists of 16 bits (one word), numbered from left to right, bit [15] to bit [0]. Bits [15:12] contain the opcode. This means there are at most 2^4 distinct opcodes. Actually, we use only 15 of the possible four-bit codes. One is reserved for some future use. Bits [11:0] are used to figure out where the operands are.

In this chapter, we will introduce five of the LC-3's 15 instructions: two operates (ADD and AND), one data movement (LD), and two control (BR and TRAP). We will save for Chapters 5, 8, and 9 the other ten instructions.

Example 4.1	

The ADD Instruction The ADD instruction is an operate instruction that requires three operands: two source operands (the numbers to be added) and one destination operand (where the sum is to be stored after the addition is performed). We said that the processing unit of the LC-3 contained eight registers for purposes of storing data that may be needed later. In fact, the ADD instruction **requires** that at least one of the two source operands is contained in one of these registers, and that the result of the ADD is put into one of these eight registers. Since there are eight registers, three bits are necessary to identify each register. The 16-bit LC-3 ADD instruction has one of the following two forms (we say *formats*):

15	14	13	12	11	10	9	8	7	6	5	4	3	2	1	0
0	0	0	1	1	1	0	0	1	0	0	0	0	1	1	0
ADD				R6			R2						R6		

15	14	13	12	11	10	9	8	7	6	5	4	3	2	1	0
0	0	0	1	1	1	0	0	1	0	1	0	0	1	1	0
ADD				R6			R2					imm			

Both formats show the four-bit opcode for ADD, contained in bits [15:12]: 0001. Bits [11:9] identify the location to be used for storing the result, in this case register 6 (R6). Bits [8:6] identify the register that contains one of the two source operands, in this case R2. The only difference in the two formats is the 1 or 0 stored in bit 5, and what that means. In the first case, bit 5 is 0, signifying that the second source operand is in the register specified by bits [2:0], in this case R6. In the second case, bit 5 is 1, signifying that the second source operand is formed by sign-extending the integer in bits [4:0] to 16 bits. In this case, the second source operand is the positive integer 6.

Thus, the instruction we have just encoded is interpreted, depending on whether bit 5 is a 0 or a 1 as either "Add the contents of register 2 (R2) to the contents of register 6 (R6) and store the result back into register 6 (R6)," or "Add the contents of register 2 (R2) to the positive integer 6 and store the result into register 6." We will use both formats in a program we will write before we leave Chapter 4.

Example 4.2

The AND Instruction   The AND instruction is also an operate instruction, and its behavior is essentially identical to the ADD instruction, except for one thing. Instead of ADDing the two source operands, the AND instruction performs a bit-wise AND of the corresponding bits of the two source operands. For example, the instruction shown below

15	14	13	12	11	10	9	8	7	6	5	4	3	2	1	0
0	1	0	1	0	1	0	0	1	1	1	0	0	0	0	0

| AND | R2 | R3 | imm |

is an AND instruction since bits [15:12] = 0101. The two sources are R3 and the immediate value 0. The instruction loads R2 with the value 0 since the AND instruction performs a bit-wise AND where the bit of the second operand is always 0. As we shall see, this instruction is a convenient technique for making sure a particular register contains 0 at the start of processing. We refer to this technique as *initializing R2 to 0.*

Example 4.3

The LD Instruction   The LD instruction requires two operands. *LD* stands for load, which is computerese for "go to a particular memory location, read the value that is contained there, and store that value in one of the registers." The two operands that are required are the value to be read from memory and the destination register that will contain that value after the instruction has completed processing. There are many formulas that can be used for calculating the address of the memory location to be read. Each formula is called an *addressing mode*. The particular addressing mode identified by the use of the opcode LD is called **PC+offset**. We will see in Chapter 5 that there are other addressing modes in the LC-3 ISA corresponding to other formulas for calculating the address of a memory location.

The 16-bit LC-3 LD instruction has the following format:

15	14	13	12	11	10	9	8	7	6	5	4	3	2	1	0
0	0	1	0	0	1	0	0	1	1	0	0	0	1	1	0

| LD | R2 | 198 |

The four-bit opcode for LD is 0010. Bits [11:9] identify the register that will contain the value read from memory after the instruction is executed. Bits [8:0] are used to calculate the address of the location to be read. Since the addressing mode for LD is PC+offset, this address is computed by sign-extending the 2's complement integer contained in bits [8:0] to 16 bits and adding it to the current contents of the program counter. In summary, the instruction tells the computer to add 198 to the contents of the PC to form the address of a memory location and to load the contents of that memory location into R2.

If bits [8:0] had been 111111001, the instruction would have been interpreted: "Add −7 to the contents of the PC to form the address of a memory location."

4.3.2 The Instruction Cycle (NOT the Clock Cycle!)

Instructions are processed under the direction of the control unit in a very systematic, step-by-step manner. The entire sequence of steps needed to process an instruction is called the *instruction cycle*. The instruction cycle consists of six sequential *phases*, each phase requiring zero or more steps. We say zero steps to indicate that most computers have been designed such that not all instructions require all six phases. We will discuss this momentarily. But first, we will examine the six phases of the instruction cycle:

```
FETCH
DECODE
EVALUATE ADDRESS
FETCH OPERANDS
EXECUTE
STORE RESULT
```

The process is as follows (again refer to Figure 4.3, our simplified version of the LC-3 data path):

4.3.2.1 FETCH

The FETCH phase obtains the next instruction from memory and loads it into the instruction register (IR) of the control unit. Recall that a computer program consists of a number of instructions, that each instruction is represented by a sequence of bits, and that the entire program (in the von Neumann model) is stored in the computer's memory. In order to carry out the work of an instruction, we must first identify where it is. The program counter (PC) contains the address of the next instruction to be processed. Thus, the FETCH phase takes the following steps:

```
First the MAR is loaded with the contents of the PC.
Next, the memory is interrogated, which results
in the next instruction being placed by the memory
into the MDR.
Finally, the IR is loaded with the contents
of the MDR.
```

We are now ready for the next phase, decoding the instruction. However, when the instruction finishes execution, and we wish to fetch the next instruction, we would like the PC to contain the address of the next instruction. This is accomplished by having the FETCH phase perform one more task: incrementing the PC. In that way, after the current instruction finishes, the FETCH phase of the next instruction will load into the IR the contents of the next memory location, provided the execution of the current instruction does not involve changing the value in the PC.

The complete description of the FETCH phase is as follows:

```
Step 1:  Load the MAR with the contents of the PC, and
         simultaneously increment the PC.
```

```
Step 2:    Interrogate memory, resulting in the instruction
           being placed in the MDR.
Step 3:    Load the IR with the contents of the MDR.
```

Each of these steps is under the direction of the control unit, much like, as we said previously, the instruments in an orchestra are under the control of a conductor's baton. Each stroke of the conductor's baton corresponds to one *machine cycle*. We will see in Section 4.3.5 that the amount of time taken by each machine cycle is one clock cycle. In fact, we often use the two terms interchangeably. Step 1 takes one clock cycle. Step 2 could take one clock cycle or many clock cycles, depending on how long it takes to access the computer's memory. Step 3 takes one clock cycle. In a modern digital computer, a clock cycle takes a very small fraction of a second.

Indeed, a 3.1 GHz Intel Core i7 completes 3.1 billion clock cycles in one second. Said another way, one clock cycle takes 0.322 billionths of a second (0.322 nanoseconds). Recall that the light bulb that is helping you read this text is switching on and off at the rate of 60 times a second. Thus, in the time it takes a light bulb to switch on and off once, today's computers can complete more than 51 million clock cycles!

4.3.2.2 DECODE

The DECODE phase examines the instruction in order to figure out what the microarchitecture is being asked to do. Recall the decoders we studied in Chapter 3. In the LC-3, a 4-to-16 decoder identifies which of the 16 opcodes is to be processed (even though one of the 16 is not used!). Input is the four-bit opcode IR [15:12]. The output line asserted is the one corresponding to the opcode at the input. Depending on which output of the decoder is asserted, the remaining 12 bits identify what else is needed to process that instruction.

4.3.2.3 EVALUATE ADDRESS

This phase computes the address of the memory location that is needed to process the instruction. Recall the example of the LD instruction: The LD instruction causes a value stored in memory to be loaded into a register. In that example, the address was obtained by sign-extending bits [8:0] of the instruction to 16 bits and adding that value to the current contents of the PC. This calculation was performed during the EVALUATE ADDRESS phase. It is worth noting that not all instructions access memory to load or store data. For example, we have already seen that the ADD and AND instructions in the LC-3 obtain their source operands from registers or from the instruction itself and store the result of the ADD or AND instruction in a register. For those instructions, the EVALUATE ADDRESS phase is not needed.

4.3.2.4 FETCH OPERANDS

This phase obtains the source operands needed to process the instruction. In the LD example, this phase took two steps: loading MAR with the address calculated in the EVALUATE ADDRESS phase and reading memory that resulted in the source operand being placed in MDR.

In the ADD example, this phase consisted of obtaining the source operands from R2 and R6. In most current microprocessors, this phase (for the ADD instruction) can be done at the same time the instruction is being executed (the fifth phase of the instruction cycle). Exactly how we can speed up the processing of an instruction in this way is a fascinating subject, but it is one we are forced to leave for later in your education.

4.3.2.5 EXECUTE

This phase carries out the execution of the instruction. In the ADD example, this phase consisted of the step of performing the addition in the ALU.

4.3.2.6 STORE RESULT

The final phase of an instruction's execution. The result is written to its designated destination. In the case of the ADD instruction, in many computers this action is performed during the EXECUTE phase. That is, in many computers, including the LC-3, an ADD instruction can fetch its source operands, perform the ADD in the ALU, and store the result in the destination register all in a single clock cycle. A separate STORE RESULT phase is not needed.

Once the instruction cycle has been completed, the control unit begins the instruction cycle for the next instruction, starting from the top with the FETCH phase. Since the PC was updated during the previous instruction cycle, it contains at this point the address of the instruction stored in the next sequential memory location. Thus, the next sequential instruction is fetched next. Processing continues in this way until something breaks this sequential flow, or the program finishes execution.

It is worth noting again that although the instruction cycle consists of six phases, not all instructions require all six phases. As already pointed out, the LC-3 ADD instruction does not require a separate EVALUATE ADDRESS phase or a separate STORE RESULT phase. The LC-3 LD instruction does not require an EXECUTE phase. On the other hand, there are instructions in other ISAs that require all six phases.

Example 4.4

ADD [eax], edx   This is an example of an Intel x86 instruction that requires all six phases of the instruction cycle. All instructions require the first two phases, FETCH and DECODE. This instruction uses the eax register to calculate the address of a memory location (EVALUATE ADDRESS). The contents of that memory location is then read (FETCH OPERAND), added to the contents of the edx register (EXECUTE), and the result written into the memory location that originally contained the first source operand (STORE RESULT).

4.3.3 Changing the Sequence of Execution

Everything we have said thus far happens when a computer program is executed in sequence. That is, the first instruction is executed, then the second instruction is executed, followed by the third instruction, and so on.

We have identified two types of instructions, the ADD and AND, which are examples of *operate instructions* in that they operate on data, and the LD, which is an example of a *data movement instruction* in that it moves data from one place to another. There are other examples of both operate instructions and data movement instructions, as we will discover in Chapter 5 when we study the LC-3 in greater detail.

There is a third type of instruction, the *control instruction*, whose purpose is to change the sequence of instruction execution. For example, there are times, as we shall see very soon, when it is desirable to first execute the first instruction, then the second, then the third, then the first again, the second again, then the third again, then the first for the third time, the second for the third time, and so on. As we know, each instruction cycle starts with loading the MAR with the PC. Thus, if we wish to change the sequence of instructions executed, we must change the contents of the PC between the time it is incremented (during the FETCH phase of one instruction) and the start of the FETCH phase of the next instruction.

Control instructions perform that function by loading the PC during the EXECUTE phase, which wipes out the incremented PC that was loaded during the FETCH phase. The result is that, at the start of the next instruction cycle, when the computer accesses the PC to obtain the address of an instruction to fetch, it will get the address loaded during the previous instruction's EXECUTE phase, rather than the next sequential instruction in the computer's program.

The most common control instruction is the *conditional branch* (BR), which either changes the contents of the PC or does not change the contents of the PC, depending on the result of a previous instruction (usually the instruction that is executed immediately before the conditional branch instruction).

The BR Instruction   The BR instruction consists of three parts, the opcode (bits [15:12] = 0000), the condition to be tested (bits [11:9]), and the addressing mode bits (bits [8:0]) that are used to form the address to be loaded into the PC if the result of the previous instruction agrees with the test specified by bits [11:9]. The addressing mode, i.e., the mechanism used to determine the actual address, is the same one we used in the LD instruction. Bits [8:0] are sign-extended to 16 bits and then added to the current contents of the PC.

Example 4.5

Suppose the BR instruction shown below is located in memory location x36C9.

15	14	13	12	11	10	9	8	7	6	5	4	3	2	1	0
0	0	0	0	1	0	1	1	1	1	1	1	1	0	1	0

BR   condition   −6

The opcode 0000 identifies the instruction as a conditional branch. Bits [11:9] = 101 specifies that the test to be performed on the most recent result is whether or not that result is something other than 0. In Chapter 5 we will describe in detail all the tests that can be performed on the most recent result. For now, we will just use one test: Is the result not zero? Bits [8:0] is the value −6.

Assume the previous instruction executed (in memory location x36C8) was an ADD instruction and the result of the ADD was 0. Since the test "not-zero" failed, the BR instruction would do nothing during its EXECUTE phase, and so the next
(*continued on next page*)

instruction executed would be the instruction at M[x36CA], the address formed by
incrementing the PC during the FETCH phase of the BR instruction's instruction
cycle.

On the other hand, if the result of the ADD instruction is not 0, then the test
succeeds, causing the BR instruction to load PC with x36C4, the address formed by
sign-extending bits [8:0] to 16 bits and adding that value (-6) to the incremented PC
(x36CA).

Thus, the next instruction executed after the BR instruction at x36C9 is either
the instruction at x36CA or the one at x36C4, depending on whether the result of the
ADD instruction was zero or not zero.

4.3.4 Control of the Instruction Cycle

The instruction cycle is controlled by a synchronous finite state machine. An
abbreviated version of its state diagram, highlighting a few of the LC-3 instructions discussed in this chapter, is shown in Figure 4.4. As is the case with the
finite state machines studied in Section 3.6, each state corresponds to one machine
cycle of activity that takes one clock cycle to perform. The processing controlled
by each state is described within the node representing that state. The arcs show
the next state transitions.

Processing starts with State 1. The FETCH phase takes three clock cycles,
corresponding to the three steps described earlier. In the first clock cycle, the
MAR is loaded with the contents of the PC, and the PC is incremented. In order
for the contents of the PC to be loaded into the MAR (see Figure 4.3), the finite
state machine must assert GatePC and LD.MAR. GatePC connects the PC to the
processor bus. LD.MAR, the write enable signal of the MAR register, loads the
contents of the bus into the MAR at the end of the current clock cycle. (Registers
are loaded at the end of the clock cycle if the corresponding control signal is
asserted.)

In order for the PC to be incremented (again, see Figure 4.3), the finite
state machine must assert the PCMUX select lines to choose the output of the
box labeled +1 and must also assert the LD.PC signal to load the output of the
PCMUX into the PC at the end of the current cycle.

The finite state machine then goes to State 2. Here, the MDR is loaded with
the instruction, which is read from memory.

In State 3, the instruction is transferred from the MDR to the instruction
register (IR). This requires the finite state machine to assert GateMDR and LD.IR,
which causes the IR to be loaded at the end of the clock cycle, concluding the
FETCH phase of the instruction cycle.

The DECODE phase takes one clock cycle. In State 4, using the external
input IR, and in particular the opcode bits of the instruction, the finite state
machine can go to the appropriate next state for processing instructions depending on the particular opcode in IR [15:12]. Three of the 15 paths out of State 4
are shown. Processing continues clock cycle by clock cycle until the instruction
completes execution, and the next state logic returns the finite state machine to
State 1.

As has already been discussed, it is sometimes necessary not to execute the next sequential instruction but rather to access another location to find the next instruction to execute. As we have said, instructions that change the flow of instruction processing in this way are called control instructions. In the case of the conditional branch instruction (BR), at the end of its instruction cycle, the PC contains one of two addresses: either the incremented PC that was loaded in State 1 or the new address computed from sign-extending bits [8:0] of the BR instruction and adding it to the PC, which was loaded in State 63. Which address gets loaded into the PC depends on the test of the most recent result.

Appendix C contains a full description of the implementation of the LC-3, including its full state diagram and data path. We will not go into that level of detail in this chapter. Our objective here is to show you that there is nothing magic about the processing of the instruction cycle, and that a properly completed

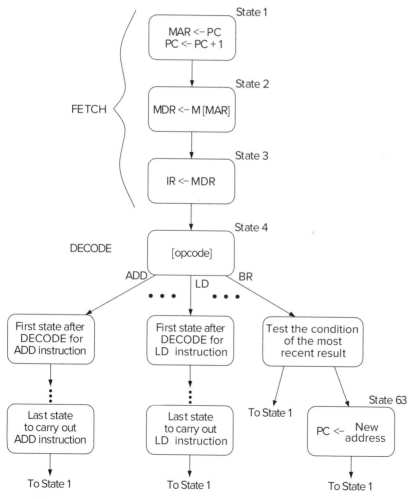

Figure 4.4   An abbreviated state diagram of the LC-3.

state diagram would be able to control, clock cycle by clock cycle, all the steps required to execute all the phases of every instruction cycle. Since each instruction cycle ends by returning to State 1, the finite state machine can process, clock cycle by clock cycle, a complete computer program.

4.3.5 Halting the Computer (the TRAP Instruction)

From everything we have said, it appears that the computer will continue processing instructions, carrying out the instruction cycle again and again, *ad nauseum*. Since the computer does not have the capacity to be bored, must this continue until someone pulls the plug and disconnects power to the computer?

Usually, user programs execute under the control of an operating system. Linux, DOS, MacOS, and Windows are all examples of operating systems. Operating systems are just computer programs themselves. As far as the computer is concerned, the instruction cycle continues whether a user program is being processed or the operating system is being processed. This is fine as far as user programs are concerned since each user program terminates with a control instruction that changes the PC to again start processing the operating system—often to initiate the execution of another user program.

But what if we actually want to stop this potentially infinite sequence of instruction cycles? Recall our analogy to the conductor's baton, beating at the rate of billions of clock cycles per second. Stopping the instruction sequencing requires stopping the conductor's baton. We have pointed out many times that there is inside the computer a component that corresponds very closely to the conductor's baton. It is called the **clock**, and it defines the amount of time each machine cycle takes. We saw in Chapter 3 that the clock enables the synchronous finite state machine to continue on to the next clock cycle. In Chapter 3 the next clock cycle corresponded to the next state of the danger sign we designed. Here the next clock cycle corresponds to the next state of the instruction cycle, which is either the next state of the current phase of the instruction cycle or the first state of the next phase of the instruction cycle. Stopping the instruction cycle requires stopping the clock.

Figure 4.5a shows a block diagram of the clock circuit, consisting primarily of a clock generator and a RUN latch. The clock generator is a crystal oscillator, a piezoelectric device that you may have studied in your physics or chemistry class. For our purposes, the crystal oscillator is a black box (recall our definition of black box in Section 1.4) that produces the oscillating voltage shown in Figure 4.5b. Note the resemblance of that voltage to the conductor's baton. Every clock cycle, the voltage rises to 1.2 volts and then drops back to 0 volts.

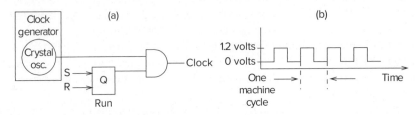

Figure 4.5   The clock circuit and its control.

If the RUN latch is in the 1 state (i.e., $Q = 1$), the output of the clock circuit is the same as the output of the clock generator. If the RUN latch is in the 0 state (i.e., $Q = 0$), the output of the clock circuit is 0.

Thus, stopping the instruction cycle requires only clearing the RUN latch. Every computer has some mechanism for doing that. In some older machines, it is done by executing a HALT instruction. In the LC-3, as in many other machines, it is done under control of the operating system, as we will see in Chapter 9. For now it is enough to know that if a user program requires help from the operating system, it requests that help with the TRAP instruction (opcode = 1111) and an eight-bit code called a *trap vector*, which identifies the help that the user program needs. The eight-bit code x25 tells the operating system that the program has finished executing and the computer can stop processing instructions.

Question: If a HALT instruction can clear the RUN latch, thereby stopping the instruction cycle, what instruction is needed to set the RUN latch, thereby reinitiating the instruction cycle? *Hint:* This is a trick question!

4.4 Our First Program: A Multiplication Algorithm

We now have all that we need to write our first program. We have a data movement instruction LD to load data from memory into a register, and we have two operate instructions, ADD for performing arithmetic and AND for performing a bit-wise logical operation. We have a control instruction BR for loading the PC with an address different from the incremented PC so the instruction to be executed next will NOT be the instruction in the next sequential location in memory. And we have the TRAP instruction (a.k.a. system call) that allows us to ask the operating system for help, in this case to stop the computer. With all that under our belt, we can write our first program.

Suppose the computer does not know how to multiply two positive integers. In the old days, that was true for a lot of computers! They had ADD instructions, but they did not have multiply instructions. What to do? Suppose we wanted to multiply 5 times 4. Even if we do not know how to multiply, if we know that 5 times 4 is 5+5+5+5, and the computer has an ADD instruction, we can write a program that can multiply. All we have to do is add 5 to itself four times.

Figure 4.6 illustrates the process.

Let us assume that memory location x3007, abbreviated M[x3007], contains the value 5, and M[x3008] contains the value 4. We start by copying the two values from memory to the two registers R1 and R2. We are going to accumulate the results of the additions in R3, so we initialize R3 to 0. Then we add 5 to R3, and subtract 1 from R2 so we will know how many more times we will need to add 5 to R3. We keep doing this (adding 5 to R3 and subtracting 1 from R2) until R2 contains the value 0. That tells us that we have added 5 to R3 four times and we are done, so we HALT the computer. R3 contains the value 20, the result of our multiplication.

Figure 4.7 shows the actual LC-3 program, stored in memory locations x3000 to x3008.

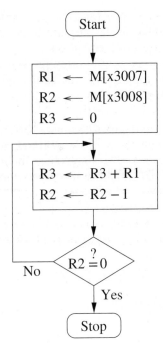

Figure 4.6   Flowchart for an algorithm that multiplies two positive integers.

The program counter, which keeps track of the next instruction to be executed, initially contains the address x3000.

To move the data from memory locations M[x3007] and M[x3008] to R1 and R2, we use the data movement instruction LD. The LC-3 computer executes the LD instruction in M[x3000] by sign-extending the offset (in this case 6) to 16 bits, adding it to the incremented PC (in this case x3001 since we incremented the PC during the FETCH phase of this instruction), fetching the data from M[x3007], and loading it in R1. The LD instruction in M[x3001] is executed in the same way.

Address	15	14	13	12	11	10	9	8	7	6	5	4	3	2	1	0	
x3000	0	0	1	0	0	0	1	0	0	0	0	0	0	1	1	0	R1 <- M[x3007]
x3001	0	0	1	0	0	1	0	0	0	0	0	0	0	1	1	0	R2 <- M[x3008]
x3002	0	1	0	1	0	1	1	0	1	1	1	0	0	0	0	0	R3 <- 0
x3003	0	0	0	1	0	1	1	0	1	1	0	0	0	0	0	1	R3 <- R3+R1
x3004	0	0	0	1	0	1	0	0	1	0	1	1	1	1	1	1	R2 <- R2-1
x3005	0	0	0	0	1	0	1	1	1	1	1	1	1	1	0	1	BR not-zero M[x3003]
x3006	1	1	1	1	0	0	0	0	0	0	1	0	0	1	0	1	HALT
x3007	0	0	0	0	0	0	0	0	0	0	0	0	0	1	0	1	The value 5
x3008	0	0	0	0	0	0	0	0	0	0	0	0	0	1	0	0	The value 4

Figure 4.7   A program that multiplies without a multiply instruction.

R3 is initialized to 0 by performing a bit-wise AND of the contents of R3 with the sign-extended immediate value 0 and loading the result into R3.

Next the computer executes the ADD instructions at M[x3003] and M[x3004]. The ADD instruction at M[x3003] adds the contents of R1 to the contents of R3 and loads the result into R3. The ADD instruction at M[x3004] adds −1 to the contents of R2, which keeps track of how many times the value 5 has been added to R3.

At this point, the PC contains the address x3005. The BR instruction in M[x3005] loads the PC with the address x3003 if the result of the previous instruction (the one in M[x3004]) is not 0. If the result of the previous instruction is 0, the BR instruction does nothing, and so the next instruction to be executed is the instruction at M[x3006], i.e., the incremented PC is x3006.

Thus, the two ADD instructions execute again and again, until the result of executing the instruction in M[x3004] produces the value 0, indicating that the value 5 has been added four times. Finally, the TRAP instruction in M[x3006] is executed, which is a call to the operating system to halt the computer.

Exercises

4.1 Name the five components of the von Neumann model. For each component, state its purpose.

4.2 Briefly describe the interface between the memory and the processing unit. That is, describe the method by which the memory and the processing unit communicate.

4.3 What is misleading about the name *program counter*? Why is the name *instruction pointer* more insightful?

4.4 What is the word length of a computer? How does the word length of a computer affect what the computer is able to compute? That is, is it a valid argument, in light of what you learned in Chapter 1, to say that a computer with a larger word size can process more information and therefore is capable of computing more than a computer with a smaller word size?

4.5 The following table represents a small memory. Refer to this table for the following questions.

Address	Data
0000	0001 1110 0100 0011
0001	1111 0000 0010 0101
0010	0110 1111 0000 0001
0011	0000 0000 0000 0000
0100	0000 0000 0110 0101
0101	0000 0000 0000 0110
0110	1111 1110 1101 0011
0111	0000 0110 1101 1001

    a. What binary value does location 3 contain? Location 6?

    b. The binary value within each location can be interpreted in many ways. We have seen that binary values can represent unsigned numbers, 2's complement signed numbers, floating point numbers, and so forth.

       (1) Interpret location 0 and location 1 as 2's complement integers.

       (2) Interpret location 4 as an ASCII value.

       (3) Interpret locations 6 and 7 as an IEEE floating point number. Location 6 contains number[15:0]. Location 7 contains number[31:16].

       (4) Interpret location 0 and location 1 as unsigned integers.

    c. In the von Neumann model, the contents of a memory location can also be an instruction. If the binary pattern in location 0 were interpreted as an instruction, what instruction would it represent?

    d. A binary value can also be interpreted as a memory address. Say the value stored in location 5 is a memory address. To which location does it refer? What binary value does that location contain?

4.6 What are the two components of an instruction? What information do these two components contain?

4.7 Suppose a 32-bit instruction takes the following format:

OPCODE	SR	DR	IMM

If there are 60 opcodes and 32 registers, what is the range of values that can be represented by the immediate (IMM)? Assume IMM is a 2's complement value.

4.8 Suppose a 32-bit instruction takes the following format:

OPCODE	DR	SR1	SR2	UNUSED

If there are 225 opcodes and 120 registers,

    a. What is the minimum number of bits required to represent the OPCODE?

    b. What is the minimum number of bits required to represent the destination register (DR)?

    c. What is the maximum number of UNUSED bits in the instruction encoding?

4.9 The FETCH phase of the instruction cycle does two important things. One is that it loads the instruction to be processed next into the IR. What is the other important thing?

4.10 Examples 4.1, 4.2, and 4.5 illustrate the processing of the ADD, LDR, and JMP instructions. The PC, IR, MAR, and MDR are written in various phases of the instruction cycle, depending on the opcode of the particular instruction. In each location in the following table, enter the opcodes that write to the corresponding register (row) during the corresponding phase (column) of the instruction cycle.

	Fetch Instruction	Decode	Evaluate Address	Fetch Data	Execute	Store Result
PC						
IR						
MAR						
MDR						

4.11 State the phases of the instruction cycle, and briefly describe what operations occur in each phase.

4.12 For the instructions ADD, LDR, and JMP, write the operations that occur in each phase of the instruction cycle.

4.13 Say it takes 100 cycles to read from or write to memory and only one cycle to read from or write to a register. Calculate the number of cycles it takes for each phase of the instruction cycle for both the IA-32 instruction "ADD [eax], edx" (refer to) and the LC-3 instruction "ADD R6, R2, R6." Assume each phase (if required) takes one cycle, unless a memory access is required.

4.14 Describe the execution of the JMP instruction if R3 contains x369C (refer to Example 4.5).

4.15 If a HALT instruction can clear the RUN latch, thereby stopping the instruction cycle, what instruction is needed to set the RUN latch, thereby reinitiating the instruction cycle?

4.16 *a.* If a machine cycle is 2 nanoseconds (i.e., $2 \cdot 10^{-9}$ seconds), how many machine cycles occur each second?

    b. If the computer requires on the average eight cycles to process each instruction, and the computer processes instructions one at a time from beginning to end, how many instructions can the computer process in 1 second?

    c. Preview of future courses: In today's microprocessors, many features are added to increase the number of instructions processed each second. One such feature is the computer's equivalent of an assembly line. Each phase of the instruction cycle is implemented as one or more separate pieces of logic. Each step in the processing of an instruction picks up where the previous step left off in the previous machine cycle. Using this feature, an instruction can be fetched from memory every machine cycle and handed off at the end of the machine cycle to the decoder, which performs the decoding function during the next machine cycle while the next instruction is being fetched. Ergo, the assembly line. Assuming instructions are located at sequential addresses in memory, and nothing breaks the sequential flow, how many instructions can the microprocessor execute each second if the assembly line is present? (The assembly line is called a pipeline, which you will encounter in your advanced courses. There are many reasons why the assembly line cannot operate at its maximum rate, a topic you will consider at length in some of these courses.)

★4.17   In this problem we perform five successive accesses to memory. The following table shows for each access whether it is a read (load) or write (store), and the contents of the MAR and MDR at the completion of the access. Some entries are not shown. Note that we have shortened the addressability to 5 bits, rather than the 16 bits that we are used to in the LC-3, in order to decrease the excess writing you would have to do.

Operations on Memory

	R/W	MAR	MDR				
Operation 1	W		1	1	1	1	0
Operation 2							
Operation 3	W		1	0			
Operation 4							
Operation 5							

The following three tables show the contents of memory locations x4000 to x4004 before the first access, after the third access, and after the fifth access. Again, not all entries are shown. We have added an unusual constraint to this problem in order to get one correct answer. The MDR can ONLY be loaded from memory as a result of a load (read) access.

Memory before Access 1

x4000	0	1	1	0	1
x4001	1	1	0	1	0
x4002		1			
x4003	1	0	1	1	0
x4004	1	1	1	1	0

Memory after Access 3

x4000				0	
x4001		0			0
x4002					
x4003					
x4004	1	1	1	1	0

Memory after Access 5

x4000					
x4001					
x4002					
x4003	0	1	1	0	1
x4004	1	1	1	1	0

Your job: Fill in the missing entries.
Hint: As you know, writes to memory require MAR to be loaded with the memory address and MDR to loaded with the data to be written (stored). The data in the MDR must come from a previous read (load).

★4.18   The 2^2-by-3 bit memory discussed in class is accessed during five consecutive clock cycles. The table below shows the values of the two-bit address, one-bit write enable, and three-bit data-in signals during each access.

	A[1:0]	WE	$D_{in}[2:0]$
cycle 1	0 1	1	1 0 1
cycle 2	1 1	0	1 1 0
cycle 3	1 0	1	0 1 0
cycle 4	0 1	1	0 1 1
cycle 5	0 0	0	0 0 0

Your job: Fill in the value stored in each memory cell and the three data-out lines just before the end of the fifth cycle. Assume initially that all 12 memory cells store the value 1. In the figure below, each question mark (?) indicates a value that you need to fill in.

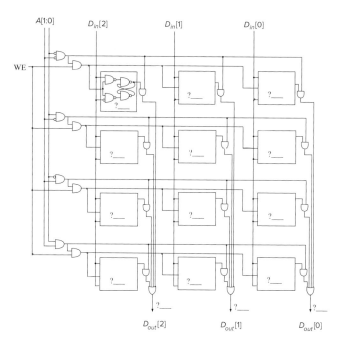

★4.19 Shown below is a byte-addressable memory consisting of eight locations, and its associated MAR and MDR. Both MAR and MDR consist of flip-flops that are latched at the start of each clock cycle based on the values on their corresponding input lines. A memory read is initiated every cycle, and the data is available by the end of that cycle.

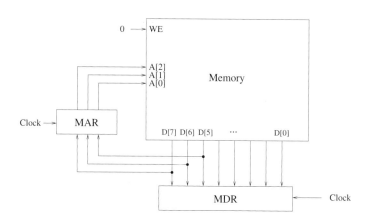

Just before the start of cycle 1, MAR contains 000, MDR contains 00010101, and the contents of each memory location is as shown.

Memory Location	Value
x0	01010000
x1	11110001
x2	10000011
x3	00010101
x4	11000110
x5	10101011
x6	00111001
x7	01100010

a. What do MAR and MDR contain just before the end of cycle 1?

MAR: [ ]   MDR: [ ]

b. What does MDR contain just before the end of cycle 4?

MDR: [ ]

CHAPTER

5

The LC-3

In Chapter 4, we discussed the basic components of a computer—its memory, its processing unit, including the associated temporary storage (usually a set of registers), input and output devices, and the control unit that directs the activity of all the units (including itself!). We also studied the six phases of the instruction cycle—FETCH, DECODE, ADDRESS EVALUATION, OPERAND FETCH, EXECUTE, and STORE RESULT. We used elements of the LC-3 to illustrate some of the concepts. In fact, we introduced five opcodes: two operate instructions (ADD and AND), one data movement instruction (LD), and two control instructions (BR and TRAP). We are now ready to study the LC-3 in much greater detail.

Recall from Chapter 1 that the ISA is the interface between what the software commands and what the hardware actually carries out. In this chapter, we will point out most of the important features of the ISA of the LC-3. (A few elements we will leave for Chapter 8 and Chapter 9.) You will need these features to write programs in the LC-3's own language, that is, in the LC-3's *machine language*.

A complete description of the ISA of the LC-3 is contained in Appendix A.

5.1 The ISA: Overview

The ISA specifies all the information about the computer that the software has to be aware of. In other words, the ISA specifies everything in the computer that is available to a programmer when he/she writes programs in the computer's own machine language. Most people, however, do not write programs in the computer's own machine language, but rather opt for writing programs in a high-level language like C++ or Python (or Fortran or COBOL, which have been around for more than 50 years). Thus, the ISA also specifies everything in the computer that is needed by someone (a compiler writer) who wishes to translate programs written in a high-level language into the machine language of the computer.

The ISA specifies the memory organization, register set, and instruction set, including the opcodes, data types, and addressing modes of the instructions in the instruction set.

5.1.1 Memory Organization

The LC-3 memory has an address space of 2^{16} (i.e., 65,536) locations, and an addressability of 16 bits. Not all 65,536 addresses are actually used for memory locations, but we will leave that discussion for Chapter 9. Since the normal unit of data that is processed in the LC-3 is 16 bits, we refer to 16 bits as one *word*, and we say the LC-3 is *word-addressable*.

5.1.2 Registers

Since it usually takes far more than one clock cycle to obtain data from memory, the LC-3 provides (like almost all computers) additional temporary storage locations that can be accessed in a single clock cycle.

The most common type of temporary storage locations, and the one used in the LC-3, is a set of registers. Each register in the set is called a *general purpose register* (GPR). Like memory locations, registers store information that can be operated on later. The number of bits stored in each register is usually one word. In the LC-3, this means 16 bits.

Registers must be uniquely identifiable. The LC-3 specifies eight GPRs, each identified by a three-bit register number. They are referred to as R0, R1, ... R7. Figure 5.1 shows a snapshot of the LC-3's register set, sometimes called a *register file*, with the eight values 1, 3, 5, 7, −2, −4, −6, and −8 stored in R0, ... R7, respectively.

Recall from Chapter 4 that the instruction to ADD the contents of R0 to R1 and store the result in R2 is specified as

Register 0	(R0)	0000000000000001
Register 1	(R1)	0000000000000011
Register 2	(R2)	0000000000000101
Register 3	(R3)	0000000000000111
Register 4	(R4)	1111111111111110
Register 5	(R5)	1111111111111100
Register 6	(R6)	1111111111111010
Register 7	(R7)	1111111111111000

Figure 5.1   A snapshot of the LC-3's register file.

Register 0	(R0)	0000000000000001
Register 1	(R1)	0000000000000011
Register 2	(R2)	0000000000000100
Register 3	(R3)	0000000000000111
Register 4	(R4)	1111111111111110
Register 5	(R5)	1111111111111100
Register 6	(R6)	1111111111111010
Register 7	(R7)	1111111111111000

Figure 5.2   The register file of Figure 5.1 after the ADD instruction.

15	14	13	12	11	10	9	8	7	6	5	4	3	2	1	0
0	0	0	1	0	1	0	0	0	0	0	0	0	0	0	1

        ADD   R2   R0   R1

where the two *sources* of the ADD instruction are specified in bits [8:6] and bits [2:0]. The *destination* of the ADD result is specified in bits [11:9]. Figure 5.2 shows the contents of the register file of Figure 5.1 AFTER the instruction

                    ADD R2, R1, R0.

is executed.

5.1.3 The Instruction Set

Recall from Chapter 4 that an instruction is made up of two things, its *opcode* (what the instruction is asking the computer to do) and its *operands* (who the computer is expected to do it to!). The instruction set is defined by its set of opcodes, *data types*, and *addressing modes*. The addressing modes determine where the operands are located. The data type is the representation of the operands in 0s and 1s.

The instruction ADD R2, R0, R1 has an opcode ADD, one addressing mode (*register mode*), and one data type (2's complement integer). The instruction directs the computer to perform a 2's complement integer addition and specifies the locations (GPRs) where the computer is expected to find the operands and the location (a GPR) where the computer is to write the result.

We saw in Chapter 4 that the ADD instruction can also have two addressing modes (register mode and immediate mode), where one of the two operands is literally contained in bits [4:0] of the instruction.

Figure 5.3 lists all the instructions of the LC-3, the bit encoding [15:12] for each opcode, and the format of each instruction. Some of them you will recognize from Chapter 4. Many others will be explained in Sections 5.2, 5.3, and 5.4.

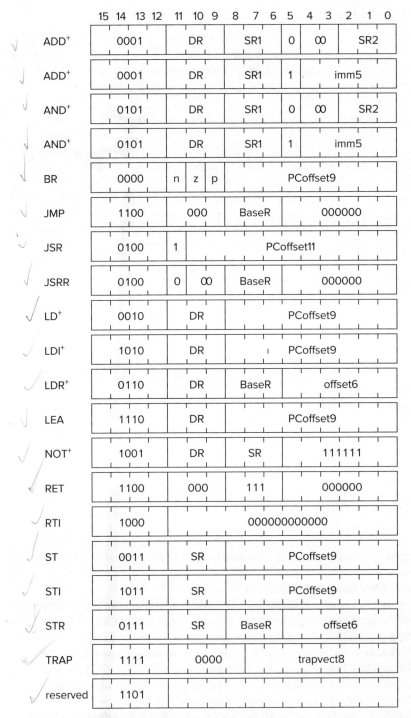

Figure 5.3 Formats of the entire LC-3 instruction set. *Note*: + indicates instructions that modify condition codes.

5.1.4 Opcodes

Some ISAs have a very large number of opcodes, one for each of a very large number of tasks that a program may wish to carry out. The x86 ISA has more than 200 opcodes. Other ISAs have a very small set of opcodes. Some ISAs have specific opcodes to help with processing scientific calculations. For example, the Hewlett Packard *Precision Architecture* can specify the compound operation $(A \cdot B) + C$ with one opcode; that is, a multiply, followed by an add on three source operands A, B, and C. Other ISAs have instructions that process video images obtained from the World Wide Web. The Intel x86 ISA added a number of instructions which they originally called *MMX instructions* because they e**X**tended the ISA to assist with **M**ulti**M**edia applications that use the web. Still other ISAs have specific opcodes to help with handling the tasks of the operating system. For example, the VAX ISA, popular in the 1980s, used a single opcode instead of a long sequence of instructions that other computers used to save the information associated with a program that was in the middle of executing prior to switching to another program. The decision as to which instructions to include or leave out of an ISA is usually a hotly debated topic in a company when a new ISA is being specified.

The LC-3 ISA has 15 instructions, each identified by its unique opcode. The opcode is specified in bits [15:12] of the instruction. Since four bits are used to specify the opcode, 16 distinct opcodes are possible. However, the LC-3 ISA specifies only 15 opcodes. The code 1101 has been left unspecified, reserved for some future need that we are not able to anticipate today.

As we already discussed briefly in Chapter 4, there are three different types of instructions, which means three different types of opcodes: *operates*, *data movement*, and *control*. Operate instructions process information. Data movement instructions move information between memory and the registers and between registers/memory and input/output devices. Control instructions change the sequence of instructions that will be executed. That is, they enable the execution of an instruction other than the one that is stored in the next sequential location in memory.

5.1.5 Data Types

As we first pointed out in Section 2.1.2, a *data type* is a representation of information such that the ISA has opcodes that operate on that representation. There are many ways to represent the same information in a computer. That should not surprise us, since in our daily lives, we regularly represent the same information in many different ways. For example, a child, when asked how old he is, might hold up three fingers, signifying that he is 3 years old. If the child is particularly precocious, he might write the decimal digit *3* to indicate his age. Or, if the child is a CS or CE major at the university, he might write 0000000000000011, the 16-bit binary representation for 3. If he is a chemistry major, he might write $3.0 \cdot 10^0$. All four represent the same value: 3.

In addition to the representation of a single number by different bit patterns in different data types, it is also the case that the same bit pattern can correspond to different numbers, depending on the data type. For example, the 16

bits 0011000100110000 represent the 2's complement integer 12,592, the ASCII code for 10, and a bit vector such that b_13, b_12, b_7, b_4, and b_3 have the relevant property of the bit vector.

That should also not surprise us, since in our daily lives, the same representation can correspond to multiple interpretations, as is the case with a red light. When you see it on the roadway while you are driving, it means you should stop. When you see it at Centre Bell where the Montreal Canadiens play hockey, it means someone has just scored a goal.

Every opcode will interpret the bit patterns of its operands according to the data type it is designed to support. In the case of the ADD opcode, for example, the hardware will interpret the bit patterns of its operands as 2's complement integers. Therefore, if a programmer stored the bit pattern 0011000100110000 in R3, thinking that the bit pattern represented the integer 10, the instruction ADD R4, R3, #10 would write the integer 12,602 into R4, and not the ASCII code for the integer 20. Why? Because the opcode ADD interprets the bit patterns of its operands as 2's complement integers, and not ASCII codes, regardless what the person creating those numbers intended.

5.1.6 Addressing Modes

An addressing mode is a mechanism for specifying where the operand is located. An operand can generally be found in one of three places: in memory, in a register, or as a part of the instruction. If the operand is a part of the instruction, we refer to it as a *literal* or as an *immediate* operand. The term *literal* comes from the fact that the bits of the instruction **literally** form the operand. The term *immediate* comes from the fact that we can obtain the operand immediately from the instruction, that is, we don't have to look elsewhere for it.

The LC-3 supports five addressing modes: immediate (or literal), register, and three memory addressing modes: *PC-relative*, *indirect*, and *Base+offset*. We will see in Section 5.2 that operate instructions use two addressing modes: register and immediate. We will see in Section 5.3 that data movement instructions use four of the five addressing modes.

5.1.7 Condition Codes

One final item will complete our overview of the ISA of the LC-3: condition codes. The LC-3 has three single-bit registers that are individually set (set to 1) or cleared (set to 0) each time one of the eight general purpose registers is written into as a result of execution of one of the operate instructions or one of the load instructions. Each operate instruction performs a computation and writes the result into a general purpose register. Each load instruction reads the contents of a memory location and writes the value found there into a general purpose register. We will discuss all the operate instructions in Section 5.2 and all the load instructions in Section 5.3.

The three single-bit registers are called *N*, *Z*, and *P*, corresponding to their meaning: negative, zero, and positive. Each time a GPR is written by an operate or a load instruction, the N, Z, and P one-bit registers are individually set to 0 or 1, corresponding to whether the result written to the GPR is negative, zero, or positive. That is, if the result is negative, the N register is set, and Z and P are cleared. If the result is zero, Z is set and N and P are cleared. If the result is positive, P is set and N and Z are cleared.

The set of three single-bit registers are referred to as *condition codes* because the condition of those bits are used to change the sequence of execution of the instructions in a computer program. Many ISAs use condition codes to change the execution sequence. SPARC and x86 are two examples. We will show how the LC-3 does it in Section 5.4.

5.2 Operate Instructions

5.2.1 ADD, AND, and NOT

Operate instructions process data. Arithmetic operations (like ADD, SUB, MUL, and DIV) and logical operations (like AND, OR, NOT, XOR) are common examples. The LC-3 has three operate instructions: ADD, AND, and NOT.

The **NOT** (opcode = 1001) instruction is the only operate instruction that performs a *unary* operation, that is, the operation requires one source operand. The NOT instruction bit-wise complements a 16-bit source operand and stores the result in a destination register. NOT uses the register addressing mode for both its source and destination. Bits [8:6] specify the source register and bits [11:9] specify the destination register. Bits [5:0] must contain all 1s.

If R5 initially contains 0101000011110000, after executing the following instruction:

15	14	13	12	11	10	9	8	7	6	5	4	3	2	1	0
1	0	0	1	0	1	1	1	0	1	1	1	1	1	1	1
NOT				R3			R5								

R3 will contain 1010111100001111.

Figure 5.4 shows the key parts of the data path that are used to perform the NOT instruction shown here. Since NOT is a unary operation, only the A input of the ALU is relevant. It is sourced from R5. The control signal to the ALU directs the ALU to perform the bit-wise complement operation. The output of the ALU (the result of the operation) is stored in R3 and the condition codes are set, completing the execution of the NOT instruction.

Recall from Chapter 4 that the **ADD** (opcode = 0001) and **AND** (opcode = 0101) instructions both perform *binary* operations; they require two 16-bit source operands. The ADD instruction performs a 2's complement addition of its two source operands. The AND instruction performs a bit-wise AND of each pair of bits of its two 16-bit operands. Like the NOT, the ADD and AND use the register addressing mode for one of the source operands and for the destination operand. Bits [8:6] specify the source register, and bits [11:9] specify the destination register (where the result will be written).

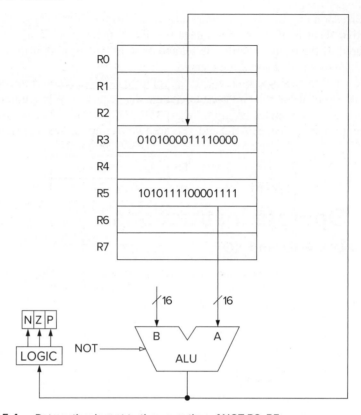

Figure 5.4   Data path relevant to the execution of NOT R3, R5.

5.2.2 Immediates

The second source operand for both ADD and AND instructions (as also discussed in Chapter 4) can be specified by either register mode or as an immediate operand. Bit [5] determines which. If bit [5] is 0, then the second source operand uses a register, and bits [2:0] specify which register. In that case, bits [4:3] are set to 0 to complete the specification of the instruction.

In the ADD instruction shown below, if R4 contains the value 6 and R5 contains the value -18, then R1 will contain the value -12 after the instruction is executed.

15	14	13	12	11	10	9	8	7	6	5	4	3	2	1	0
0	0	0	1	0	0	1	1	0	0	0	0	0	1	0	1

ADD   R1   R4   R5

If bit [5] is 1, the second source operand is contained within the instruction. In that case the second source operand is obtained by sign-extending bits [4:0] to 16 bits before performing the ADD or AND. The result of the ADD (or AND) instruction is written to the destination register and the condition codes are set,

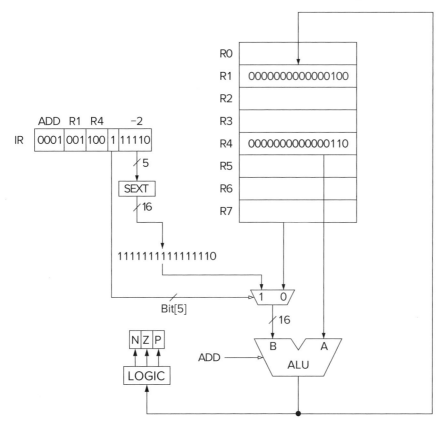

Figure 5.5   Data path relevant to the execution of ADD R1, R4, #−2.

completing the execution of the ADD (or AND) instruction. Figure 5.5 shows the key parts of the data path that are used to perform the instruction

    ADD R1, R4, #-2.

Since the immediate operand in an ADD or AND instruction must fit in bits [4:0] of the instruction, not all 2's complement integers can be immediate operands. Question: Which integers are OK (i.e., which integers can be used as immediate operands)?

<table>
<tr><td colspan="16">**Example 5.1**</td></tr>
</table>

What does the following instruction do?

15	14	13	12	11	10	9	8	7	6	5	4	3	2	1	0
0	1	0	1	0	1	0	0	1	0	1	0	0	0	0	0

ANSWER: Register 2 is cleared (i.e., set to all 0s).

Example 5.2

What does the following instruction do?

15	14	13	12	11	10	9	8	7	6	5	4	3	2	1	0
0	0	0	1	1	1	0	1	1	0	1	0	0	0	0	1

ANSWER: Register 6 is incremented (i.e., R6 ← R6 + 1).
     Note that a register can be used as a source and also as a destination in the same instruction. This is true for all instructions in the LC-3.

Example 5.3

Recall that the negative of an integer represented in 2's complement can be obtained by complementing the number and adding 1. Therefore, assuming the values A and B are in R0 and R1, what sequence of three instructions performs "A minus B" and writes the result into R2?

ANSWER:

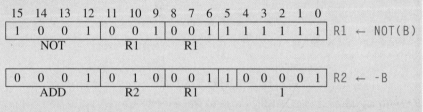

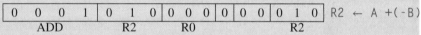

 Question: What distasteful result is also produced by this sequence? How can it easily be avoided?

5.2.3 The LEA Instruction (Although Not Really an Operate)

Where to put the LEA instruction is a matter for debate (when you have nothing more important to do!). It does not really operate on data, it simply loads a register with an address. It clearly does not move data from memory to a register, nor is it a control instruction. We had to put it somewhere, so we chose to discuss it here!

   LEA (opcode = 1110) loads the register specified by bits [11:9] of the instruction with the value formed by adding the incremented program counter to the sign-extended bits [8:0] of the instruction. We saw this method of constructing an address in Chapter 4 with the LD instruction. However, in this case, the instruction does not access memory, it simply loads the computed address into a register. Perhaps a better name for this opcode would be CEA (for Compute Effective Address). However, since many microprocessors in industry that have this instruction in their ISAs call it LEA (for Load Effective Address), we have chosen to use the same acronym.

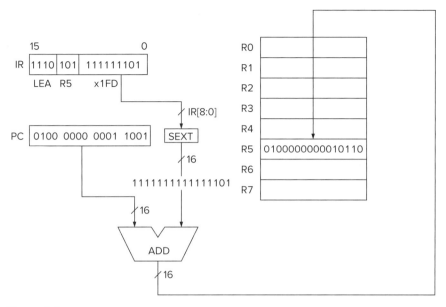

Figure 5.6   Data path relevant to the execution of LEA R5, #−3.

We shall see shortly that the LEA instruction is useful to initialize a register with an address that is very close to the address of the instruction doing the initializing.

If memory location x4018 contains the instruction LEA R5, #−3, and the PC contains x4018,

$x\,4018$

15	14	13	12	11	10	9	8	7	6	5	4	3	2	1	0
1	1	1	0	1	0	1	1	1	1	1	1	1	1	0	1

       LEA   R5   −3

PC = 4019

R5 = 4016

R5 will contain x4016 after the instruction at x4018 is executed. Question: Why will R5 not contain the address x4015? *P C Counter*.

Figure 5.6 shows the relevant parts of the data path required to execute the LEA instruction. Note that the value to be loaded into the register does **not** involve any access to memory. ...nor does it have any effect on the condition codes.

5.3 Data Movement Instructions

Data movement instructions move information between the general purpose registers and memory and between the registers and the input/output devices. We will ignore for now the business of moving information from input devices to registers and from registers to output devices. This will be an important part of Chapter 9. In this chapter, we will confine ourselves to moving information between memory and the general purpose registers.

[handwritten margin notes: MEMORY → Reg = LOAD; Reg → MEM = STORE]

The process of moving information from memory to a register is called a *load*, and the process of moving information from a register to memory is called a *store*. In both cases, the information in the location containing the source operand remains unchanged. In both cases, the location of the destination operand is overwritten with the source operand, destroying in the process the previous value that was in the destination location.

The LC-3 contains six instructions that move information: LD, LDR, LDI, ST, STR, and STI.

The format of the load and store instructions is as follows:

15	14	13	12	11	10	9	8	7	6	5	4	3	2	1	0
opcode				DR or SR			Addr Gen bits								

Data movement instructions require two operands, a source and a destination. The source is the data to be moved; the destination is the location where it is moved to. One of these locations is a register, the other is a memory location or an input/output device. In this chapter we will assume the second operand is in memory. In Chapter 9 we will study the cases where the second operand is an input or output device.

Bits [11:9] specify one of these operands, the register. If the instruction is a load, *DR* refers to the destination general purpose register that will contain the value after it is read from memory (at the completion of the instruction cycle). If the instruction is a store, *SR* refers to the register that contains the value that will be written to memory.

Bits [8:0] contain the *address generation bits*. That is, bits [8:0] contain information that is used to compute the 16-bit address of the second operand. In the case of the LC-3's data movement instructions, there are three ways to interpret bits [8:0]. They are collectively called *addressing modes*. The opcode specifies how to interpret bits [8:0]. That is, the LC-3's opcode specifies which of the three addressing modes should be used to obtain the address of the operand from bits [8:0] of the instruction.

5.3.1 PC-Relative Mode

LD (opcode = 0010) and **ST** (opcode = 0011) specify the *PC-relative* addressing mode. We have already discussed this addressing mode in Chapter 4. It is so named because bits [8:0] of the instruction specify an offset relative to the PC. The memory address is computed by sign-extending bits [8:0] to 16 bits and adding the result to the incremented PC. The incremented PC is the contents of the program counter after the FETCH phase, that is, after the PC has been incremented. If the instruction is LD, the computed address (PC + offset) specifies the memory location to be accessed. Its contents is loaded into the register specified by bits [11:9] of the instruction. If the instruction is ST, the contents of the register specified by bits [11:9] of the instruction is written into the memory location whose address is PC + offset. ...and the N, Z, and P one-bit condition codes are set depending on whether the value loaded is negative, positive, or zero.

If the following instruction is located at x4018, it will cause the contents of x3FC8 to be loaded into R2.

15	14	13	12	11	10	9	8	7	6	5	4	3	2	1	0
0	0	1	0	0	1	0	1	1	0	1	0	1	1	1	1

LD   R2   x1AF

Figure 5.7 shows the relevant parts of the data path required to execute this instruction. The three steps of the LD instruction are identified. In step 1, the incremented PC (x4019) is added to the sign-extended value contained in IR [8:0] (xFFAF), and the result (x3FC8) is loaded into the MAR. In step 2, memory is read and the contents of x3FC8 is loaded into the MDR. Suppose the value stored in x3FC8 is 5. In step 3, the value 5 is loaded into R2, and the NZP condition codes are set, completing the instruction cycle.

Note that the address of the memory operand is limited to a small range of the total memory. That is, the address can only be within +256 or −255 locations of the LD or ST instruction. This is the range provided by the sign-extended value contained in bits [8:0] of the instruction. If a load instruction needs to access a memory location further away from the load instruction, one of the other two addressing modes must be used.

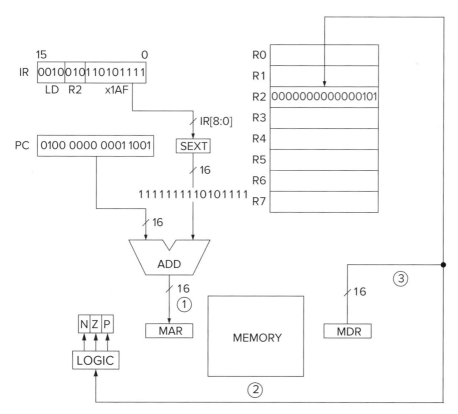

Figure 5.7   Data path relevant to execution of LD R2, x1AF.

5.3.2 Indirect Mode

LDI (opcode = 1010) and **STI** (opcode = 1011) specify the *indirect* addressing mode. An address is first formed exactly the same way as with LD and ST.
However, instead of this address being the **address of the operand** to be loaded
or stored, it is **the address** of the address of the operand to be loaded or stored.
Hence the name *indirect*. Note that the address of the operand can be anywhere
in the computer's memory, not just within the range provided by bits [8:0] of the
instruction as is the case for LD and ST. The destination register for the LDI and
the source register for STI, like all the other loads and stores, are specified in bits
[11:9] of the instruction.

If the instruction

15	14	13	12	11	10	9	8	7	6	5	4	3	2	1	0
1	0	1	0	0	1	1	1	1	1	0	0	1	1	0	0
	LDI				R3					x1CC					

is in x4A1B, and the contents of x49E8 is x2110, execution of this instruction
results in the contents of x2110 being loaded into R3.

Figure 5.8 shows the relevant parts of the data path required to execute this
instruction. As is the case with the LD and ST instructions, the first step consists
of adding the incremented PC (x4A1C) to the sign-extended value contained in
IR [8:0] (xFFCC), and the result (x49E8) loaded into the MAR. In step 2, memory
is in x4A1B and x2110 is in x49E8, and execution of this instruction results in the

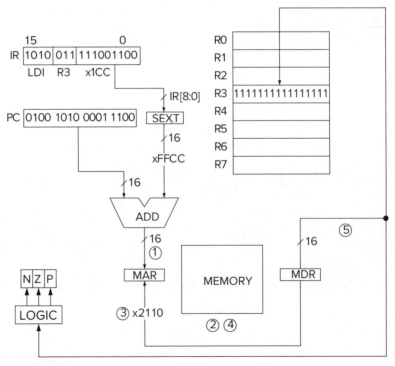

Figure 5.8   Data path relevant to the execution of LDI R3, x1CC.

contents of x2110 being loaded into R3. In step 3, since x2110 is not the operand, but the address of the operand, it is loaded into the MAR. In step 4, memory is again read, and the MDR again loaded. This time the MDR is loaded with the contents of x2110. Suppose the value -1 is stored in memory location x2110. In step 5, the contents of the MDR (i.e., -1) is loaded into R3 and the NZP condition codes are set, completing the instruction cycle.

5.3.3 Base+offset Mode

LDR (opcode = 0110) and **STR** (opcode = 0111) specify the *Base+offset* addressing mode. The Base+offset mode is so named because the address of the operand is obtained by adding a sign-extended six-bit offset to a base register. The six-bit offset is obtained from the instruction, bits [5:0]. The base register is specified by bits [8:6] of the instruction.

If R2 contains the 16-bit quantity x2345, the following instruction loads R1 with the contents of x2362.

15	14	13	12	11	10	9	8	7	6	5	4	3	2	1	0
0	1	1	0	0	0	1	0	1	0	0	1	1	1	0	1

LDR   R1   R2   x1D

Figure 5.9 shows the relevant parts of the data path required to execute this instruction. First the contents of R2 (x2345) is added to the sign-extended value

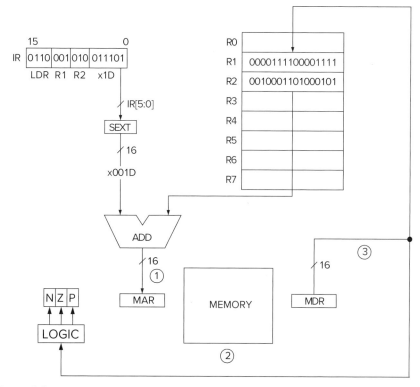

Figure 5.9 Data path relevant to the execution of LDR R1, R2, x1D.

contained in IR [5:0] (x001D), and the result (x2362) is loaded into the MAR. Second, memory is read, and the contents of x2362 is loaded into the MDR. Suppose the value stored in memory location x2362 is x0F0F. Third, and finally, the contents of the MDR (in this case, x0F0F) is loaded into R1 and the NZP condition codes are set, completing the execution of the LDR instruction.

Note that the Base+offset addressing mode also allows the address of the operand to be anywhere in the computer's memory.

5.3.4 An Example

We conclude our study of addressing modes with a comprehensive example. Assume the contents of memory locations x30F6 through x30FC are as shown in Figure 5.10, and the PC contains x30F6. We will examine the effects of carrying out the seven instructions starting at location x30FC.

Since the PC points initially to location x30F6, the first instruction to be executed is the one stored in location x30F6. The opcode of that instruction is 1110, load effective address (LEA). LEA loads the register specified by bits [11:9] with the address formed by sign-extending bits [8:0] of the instruction and adding the result to the incremented PC. The 16-bit value obtained by sign-extending bits [8:0] of the instruction is xFFFD. The incremented PC is x30F7. Therefore, at the end of execution of the LEA instruction, R1 contains x30F4, and the PC contains x30F7.

Next, the instruction stored in location x30F7 is executed. Since the opcode 0001 specifies ADD, the sign-extended immediate in bits [4:0] (since bit [5] is 1) is added to the contents of the register specified in bits [8:6], and the result is written to the register specified by bits [11:9]. Since the previous instruction wrote x30F4 into R1, and the sign-extended immediate value is x000E, the sum is x3102. At the end of execution of this instruction, R2 contains x3102, and the PC contains x30F8. R1 still contains x30F4.

Next, the instruction stored in x30F8. The opcode 0011 specifies the ST instruction, which stores the contents of the register specified by bits [11:9] (R2) into the memory location whose address is computed using the PC-relative addressing mode. That is, the address is computed by adding the incremented PC (x30F9) to the 16-bit value obtained by sign-extending bits [8:0] of the instruction

Address	15	14	13	12	11	10	9	8	7	6	5	4	3	2	1	0
x30F6	1	1	1	0	0	0	1	1	1	1	1	1	1	1	0	1
x30F7	0	0	0	1	0	1	0	0	0	1	1	0	1	1	1	0
x30F8	0	0	1	1	0	1	0	1	1	1	1	1	1	0	1	1
x30F9	0	1	0	1	0	1	0	0	1	0	1	0	0	0	0	0
x30FA	0	0	0	1	0	1	0	0	1	0	1	0	0	1	0	1
x30FB	0	1	1	1	0	1	0	0	0	1	0	0	1	1	1	0
x30FC	1	0	1	0	0	1	1	1	1	1	1	0	1	1	1

Figure 5.10   A code fragment illustrating the three addressing modes.

(xFFFB). Therefore, at the end of execution of the ST instruction, memory location x30F4 (i.e., x30F9 + xFFFB) contains the value stored in R2 (x3102) and the PC contains x30F9.

Next the instruction at x30F9. The AND instruction, with an immediate operand x0000. At the end of execution, R2 contains the value 0, and the PC contains x30FA.

At x30FA, the opcode 0001 specifies the ADD instruction. After execution, R2 contains the value 5, and the PC contains x30FB.

At x30FB, the opcode 0111 signifies the STR instruction. STR (like LDR) uses the Base+offset addressing mode. The memory address is obtained by adding the contents of the BASE register (specified by bits [8:6]) to the sign-extended offset contained in bits [5:0]. In this case, bits [8:6] specify R1, which contains x30F4. The 16-bit sign-extended offset is x000E. Since x30F4 + x000E is x3102, the memory address is x3102. The STR instruction stores into x3102 the contents of the register specified by bits [11:9], in this case R2. Since R2 contains the value 5, at the end of execution of this instruction, M[x3102] contains the value 5, and the PC contains x30FC.

Finally the instruction at x30FC. The opcode 1010 specifies LDI. LDI (like STI) uses the indirect addressing mode. The memory address is obtained by first forming an address as is done in the PC-relative addressing mode. Bits [8:0] are sign-extended to 16 bits (xFFF7) and added to the incremented PC (x30FD). Their sum (x30F4) is the **address** of the operand address. Since M[x30F4] contains x3102, x3102 is the operand address. The LDI instruction loads the value found at this address (in this case 5) into the register identified by bits [11:9] of the instruction (in this case R3). At the end of execution of this instruction, R3 contains the value 5 and the PC contains x30FD.

5.4 Control Instructions

Control instructions change the sequence of instructions to be executed. If there were no control instructions, the next instruction fetched after the current instruction finishes would always be the instruction located in the next sequential memory location. As you know, this is because the PC is incremented in the FETCH phase of each instruction cycle. We have already seen in the program of Section 4.4 that it is often useful to be able to break that sequence.

The LC-3 has five opcodes that enable the sequential execution flow to be broken: conditional branch, unconditional jump, subroutine call (sometimes called *function*), TRAP, and RTI (Return from Trap or Interrupt). In this section, we will deal almost entirely with the most common control instruction, the *conditional branch*. We will also discuss the unconditional jump and the TRAP instruction. The TRAP instruction, often called *service call*, is useful because it allows a programmer to get help from the operating system to do things that the typical programmer does not fully understand how to do. Typical examples: getting information into the computer from input devices, displaying information to output devices, and stopping the computer. The TRAP instruction breaks the sequential execution of a user program to start a sequence of instructions in the operating system. How the TRAP instruction does this, and in fact, most of the discussion of the TRAP instruction and all of the discussion of the subroutine call and the return from interrupt we will leave for Chapters 8 and 9.

5.4.1 Conditional Branches

Of the five instructions which change the execution flow from the next sequential instruction to an instruction located someplace else in the program, only one of them decides each time it is executed whether to execute the next instruction in sequence or whether to execute an instruction from outside that sequence. The instruction that makes that decision each time it is executed is the conditional branch instruction **BR** (opcode = 0000).

Like all instructions in the LC-3, the PC is incremented during the FETCH phase of its instruction cycle. Based on the execution of previous instructions in the program, the conditional branch's EXECUTE phase either does nothing or it loads the PC with the address of the instruction it wishes to execute next. If the conditional branch instruction does nothing during the EXECUTE phase, then the incremented PC will remain unchanged, and the next instruction executed will be the next instruction in sequence.

That decision, whether to do nothing to the incremented PC or whether to change it, is based on previous results computed by the program, which are reflected in the condition codes discussed in Section 5.1.7. We will explain.

The format of the conditional branch instruction is as follows:

15	14	13	12	11	10	9	8	7	6	5	4	3	2	1	0
0	0	0	0	n	z	p				PCoffset					

Bits [11], [10], and [9] are associated with the three condition codes, N, Z, and P.

As you know, the three operate instructions (ADD, AND, and NOT) and the three load instructions (LD, LDI, and LDR) in the LC-3 write values into general purpose registers, and also set the three condition codes in accordance with whether the value written is negative, zero, or positive.

The conditional branch instruction uses that information to determine whether or not to depart from the usual sequential execution of instructions that we get as a result of incrementing the PC during the FETCH phase of each instruction.

We said (without explanation) in the computer program we studied in Section 4.4 that if bits [11:9] of the conditional branch instruction are 101, we will depart from the usual sequential execution if the last value written into a register by one of the six instructions listed above is not 0. We are now ready to see exactly what causes that to happen.

During the EXECUTE phase of the BR instruction cycle, the processor examines the condition codes whose associated bits in the instruction, bits [11:9], are 1. Note the lower case **n**, **z**, and **p** in bits [11:9] of the BR instruction format shown above. If bit [11] is 1, condition code N is examined. If bit [10] is 1, condition code Z is examined. If bit [9] is 1, condition code P is examined. If any of bits [11:9] are 0, the associated condition codes are not examined. If any of the condition codes that are examined are set (i.e., equal to 1), then the PC is loaded with the address obtained in the EVALUATE ADDRESS phase. If none of the condition codes that are examined are set, the incremented PC is left unchanged, and the next sequential instruction will be fetched at the start of the next instruction cycle.

The address obtained during the EVALUATE ADDRESS phase of the instruction cycle is generated using the PC-relative addressing mode.

In our example in Section 4.4, the ADD instruction in memory location x3004 subtracted 1 from R2, wrote the result to R2, and set the condition codes. The BR instruction in memory location x3005 shows bits [11:9] = 101. Since bit [11] is 1, if the N bit is set, the result of the ADD must have been negative. Since bit [9] is also 1, if the P bit is set, the result must have been positive. Since bit [10] is 0, we do not examine the Z bit. Thus if the previous result is positive or negative (i.e., not 0), the PC is loaded with x3003, the address calculated in the EVALUATE ADDRESS phase of the branch instruction.

Recall that the program of Figure 4.7 used R2 to keep track of the number of times the number 5 was added to R3. As long as we were not done with all our additions, the result of subtracting 1 from R2 was not zero. When we were done with our additions, subtracting 1 from R2 produced the result 0, so Z was set to 1, N and P were set to 0. At that point, bits [11:9] checked the N and P condition codes which were 0, so the incremented PC was not changed, and the instruction at location x3006, a trap to the operating system to halt the computer, was executed next.

Let's Look at Another Example.   Suppose the following instruction is located at x4027, and the last value loaded into a general purpose register was 0.

15	14	13	12	11	10	9	8	7	6	5	4	3	2	1	0
0	0	0	0	0	1	0	0	1	1	0	1	1	0	0	1
	BR			n	z	p					x0D9				

Figure 5.11 shows the data path elements that are required to execute this instruction. Note the logic required to determine whether the sequential instruction flow should be broken. Each of the three AND gates corresponds to one of the three condition codes. The output of the AND gate is 1 if the corresponding condition code is 1 and if the associated bit in the instruction directs the hardware to check that condition code. If any of the three AND gates have an output 1, the OR gate has an output 1, indicating that the sequential instruction flow should be broken, and the PC should be loaded with the address evaluated during the EVALUATE ADDRESS phase of the instruction cycle.

In the case of the conditional branch instruction at x4027, the answer is yes, and the PC is loaded with x4101, replacing x4028, which had been loaded into the PC during the FETCH phase of the BR instruction.

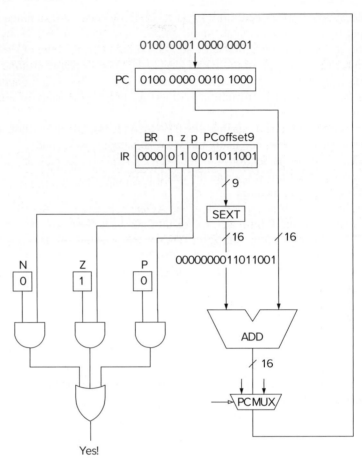

Figure 5.11   Data path relevant to the execution of BRz x0D9.

Another Example.   If all three bits [11:9] are 1, then all three condition codes
are examined. In this case, since the last result stored into a register had to be
either negative, zero, or positive (there are no other choices!), one of the three
condition codes must be in state 1. Since all three are examined, the PC is loaded
with the address obtained in the EVALUATE ADDRESS phase. We call this an
*un*conditional branch since the instruction flow is changed unconditionally, that
is, independent of the data.

For example, if the following instruction, located at x507B, is executed, the
PC is loaded with x5001.

15	14	13	12	11	10	9	8	7	6	5	4	3	2	1	0
0	0	0	0	1	1	1	1	1	0	0	0	0	1	0	1

BR   n z p   x185

Question: What happens if all three bits [11:9] in the BR instruction are 0?

5.4.2 Two Methods of Loop Control

We saw in Section 4.4 in our multiplication program that we repeatedly executed a sequence of instructions until the value in a register was zero. We call that sequence a *loop body*, and each time the loop body is executed we call it one *iteration* of the loop body. The BR instruction at the end of the sequence controls the number of times the loop body is executed. There are two common ways to control the number of iterations.

Loop Control with a Counter   Suppose we know that the 12 locations x3100 to x310B contain integers, and we wish to compute the sum of these 12 integers.

A flowchart for an algorithm to solve the problem is shown in Figure 5.12.

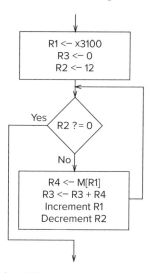

Figure 5.12   An algorithm for adding integers using a counter for loop control.

First, as in all algorithms, we must *initialize our variables*. That is, we must set up the initial values of the variables that the computer will use in executing the program that solves the problem. There are three such variables: the address of the next integer to be added (assigned to R1), the running sum (assigned to R3), and the number of integers left to be added (assigned to R2). The three variables are initialized as follows: The address of the first integer to be added is put in R1. R3, which will keep track of the running sum, is initialized to 0. R2, which will keep track of the number of integers left to be added, is initialized to 12. Then the process of adding begins.

The program repeats the process of loading into R4 one of the 12 integers and adding it to R3. Each time we perform the ADD, we increment R1 so it will point to (i.e., contain the address of) the next number to be added and decrement R2 so we will know how many numbers still need to be added. When R2 becomes zero, the Z condition code is set, and we can detect that we are done.

The 10-instruction program shown in Figure 5.13 accomplishes the task.

The details of the program execution are as follows: The program starts with PC = x3000. The first instruction (at location x3000) initializes R1 with

Address	15	14	13	12	11	10	9	8	7	6	5	4	3	2	1	0	
x3000	1	1	1	0	0	0	1	0	1	1	1	1	1	1	1	1	R1<- 3100
x3001	0	1	0	1	0	1	1	0	1	1	1	0	0	0	0	0	R3 <- 0
x3002	0	1	0	1	0	1	0	0	1	0	1	0	0	0	0	0	R2 <- 0
x3003	0	0	0	1	0	1	0	0	1	0	1	0	1	1	0	0	R2 <- 12
x3004	0	0	0	0	0	1	0	0	0	0	0	0	0	1	0	1	BRz x300A
x3005	0	1	1	0	1	0	0	0	1	0	0	0	0	0	0	0	R4 <- M[R1]
x3006	0	0	0	1	0	1	1	0	1	1	0	0	0	1	0	0	R3 <- R3+R4
x3007	0	0	0	1	0	0	1	0	0	1	1	0	0	0	0	1	R1 <- R1+1
x3008	0	0	0	1	0	1	0	0	1	0	1	1	1	1	1	1	R2 <- R2-1
x3009	0	0	0	0	1	1	1	1	1	1	1	1	1	0	1	0	BRnzp x3004

Figure 5.13   A program that implements the algorithm of Figure 5.12.

the address x3100. (The incremented PC is x3001; the sign-extended PCoffset is x00FF.)

The instruction at x3001 clears R3. R3 will keep track of the running sum, so it must start with the value 0. As we said previously, this is called *initializing* the SUM to zero.

The instructions at x3002 and x3003 initialize R2 to 12, the number of integers to be added. R2 will keep track of how many numbers have already been added. This will be done (by the instruction in x3008) by decrementing R2 after each addition takes place.

The instruction at x3004 is a conditional branch instruction. Note that bit [10] is a 1. That means that the Z condition code will be examined. If it is set, we know R2 must have just been decremented to 0. That means there are no more numbers to be added, and we are done. If it is clear, we know we still have work to do, and we continue with another iteration of the loop body.

The instruction at x3005 loads the next integer into R4, and the instruction at x3006 adds it to R3.

The instructions at x3007 and x3008 perform the necessary bookkeeping. The instruction at x3007 increments R1, so R1 will point to the next location in memory containing an integer to be added. The instruction at x3008 decrements R2, which is keeping track of the number of integers still to be added, and sets the condition codes.

The instruction at x3009 is an unconditional branch, since bits [11:9] are all 1. It loads the PC with x3004. It also does not affect the condition codes, so the next instruction to be executed (the conditional branch at x3004) will be based on the instruction executed at x3008.

This is worth saying again. The conditional branch instruction at x3004 follows the instruction at x3009, which does not affect condition codes, which in turn follows the instruction at x3008. Thus, the conditional branch instruction at x3004 will be based on the condition codes set by the instruction at x3008. The instruction at x3008 sets the condition codes based on the value produced by decrementing R2. As long as there are still integers to be added, the ADD instruction at x3008 will produce a value greater than zero and therefore clear the Z condition code. The conditional branch instruction at x3004 examines the

Z condition code. As long as Z is clear, the PC will not be affected, and the next iteration of the loop body will begin. That is, the next instruction cycle will start with an instruction fetch from x3005.

The conditional branch instruction causes the execution sequence to follow: x3000, x3001, x3002, x3003, x3004, x3005, x3006, x3007, x3008, x3009, x3004, x3005, x3006, x3007, x3008, x3009, x3004, x3005, and so on. The loop body consists of the instructions at x3005 to x3009. When the value in R2 becomes 0, the PC is loaded with x300A, and the program continues at x300A with its next activity.

You may have noticed that we can remove the branch instruction at x3004 if we replace the unconditional branch instruction at x3009 with a conditional branch that tests for not 0 (i.e., bits [11:9]=101), and branches to the instruction currently located in x3005. It is tempting to do that since it decreases the loop body by one instruction. BUT, we admonish you not to do that! The program as shown obeys the rules of structured programming that we will discuss in Chapter 6. The shortcut does work for this simple example, but it breaks the methodology of structured programming. You do not want to get in the habit of taking such shortcuts, since for larger programs it is a clear invitation to disaster. More on this in Chapter 6.

Finally, it is worth noting that we could have written a program to add these 12 integers **without** any control instructions. We still would have needed the LEA instruction in x3000 to initialize R1. We would not have needed the instruction at x3001 to initialize the running sum, nor the instructions at x3002 and x3003 to initialize the number of integers left to be added. We could have loaded the contents of x3100 directly into R3, and then repeatedly (by incrementing R1), loaded subsequent integers into R4 and adding R4 to the running sum in R3 11 more times! After the addition of the twelfth integer, we would go on to the next task, as does the example of Figure 5.13 with the branch instruction in x3004.

Unfortunately, instead of a 10-instruction program, we would have a 35-instruction program. Moreover, if we had wished to add 100 integers without any control instructions instead of 12, we would have had a 299-instruction program instead of 10. The control instructions in the example of Figure 5.13 permit the reuse of sequences of code (the loop body) by breaking the sequential instruction execution flow.

Loop Control with a Sentinel   The example above controls the number of times the loop body executes by means of a counter. We knew we wanted to execute the loop 12 times, so we simply set a counter to 12, and then after each execution of the loop, we decremented the counter and checked to see if it was zero. If it was not zero, we set the PC to the start of the loop and continued with another iteration.

A second method for controlling the number of executions of a loop is to use a *sentinel*. This method is particularly effective if we do not know ahead of time how many iterations we will want to perform. Each iteration is usually based on processing a value. We append to our sequence of values to be processed a value that we know ahead of time can never occur (i.e., the sentinel). For example, if we are adding a sequence of numbers, a sentinel could be a letter A or a *, that is, something that is not a number. Our loop test is simply a test for the occurrence of the sentinel. When we find it, we know we are done.

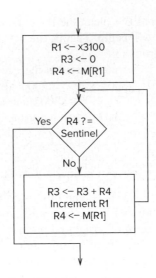

Figure 5.14   An algorithm for adding integers using a sentinel for loop control.

Address	15	14	13	12	11	10	9	8	7	6	5	4	3	2	1	0	
x3000	1	1	1	0	0	0	1	0	1	1	1	1	1	1	1	1	R1<- x3100
x3001	0	1	0	1	0	1	1	0	1	1	1	0	0	0	0	0	R3 <- 0
x3002	0	1	1	0	1	0	0	0	1	0	0	0	0	0	0	0	R4 <- M[R1]
x3003	0	0	0	0	1	0	0	0	0	0	0	0	1	0	0	BRn x3008
x3004	0	0	0	1	0	1	1	0	1	1	0	0	0	1	0	0	R3 <- R3+R4
x3005	0	0	0	1	0	0	1	0	0	1	1	0	0	0	0	1	R1 <- R1+1
x3006	0	1	1	0	1	0	0	0	1	0	0	0	0	0	0	0	R4 <- M[R1]
x3007	0	0	0	0	1	1	1	1	1	1	1	1	1	0	1	1	BRnzp x3003

Figure 5.15   A program that implements the algorithm of Figure 5.14.

Suppose we know the values stored in locations x3100 to x310B are all positive. Then we could use any negative number as a sentinel. Let's say the sentinel stored at memory address x310C is −1. The resulting flowchart for this solution is shown in Figure 5.14, and the resulting program is shown in Figure 5.15.

As before, the instruction at x3000 loads R1 with the address of the first value to be added, and the instruction at x3001 initializes R3 (which keeps track of the sum) to 0.

At x3002, we load the contents of the next memory location into R4. If the sentinel is loaded, the N condition code is set.

The conditional branch at x3003 examines the N condition code. If N=1, PC is loaded with x3008 and onto the next task. If N=0, R4 must contain a valid number to be added. In this case, the number is added to R3 (x3004), R1 is incremented to point to the next memory location (x3005), R4 is loaded with the contents of the next memory location (x3006), and the PC is loaded with x3003 to begin the next iteration (x3007).

5.4.3 The JMP Instruction

The conditional branch instruction, for all its capability, does have one unfortunate limitation. The next instruction executed must be within the range of addresses that can be computed by adding the incremented PC to the sign-extended offset obtained from bits [8:0] of the instruction. Since bits [8:0] specify a 2's complement integer, the next instruction executed after the conditional branch can be at most +256 or −255 locations from the branch instruction itself.

What if we would like to execute next an instruction that is 2000 locations from the current instruction? We cannot fit the value 2000 into the nine-bit field; ergo, the conditional branch instruction does not work.

The LC-3 ISA does provide an instruction **JMP** (opcode = 1100) that can do the job.

The JMP instruction loads the PC with the contents of the register specified by bits [8:6] of the instruction. If the following JMP instruction is located at address x4000,

x4000

15	14	13	12	11	10	9	8	7	6	5	4	3	2	1	0
1	1	0	0	0	0	0	0	1	0	0	0	0	0	0	0

JMP   BaseR

R2 contains the value x6600, and the PC contains x4000, then the instruction at x4000 (the JMP instruction) will be executed, followed by the instruction located at x6600. Since registers contain 16 bits (the full address space of memory), the JMP instruction has no limitation on where the next instruction to be executed must reside.

5.4.4 The TRAP Instruction

We will discuss the details of how the TRAP instruction works in Chapter 9. However, because it will be useful long before that to get data into and out of the computer, we discuss the TRAP instruction here. The **TRAP** (opcode = 1111) instruction changes the PC to a memory address that is part of the operating system so that the operating system will perform some task on behalf of the program that is executing. In the language of operating system jargon, we say the TRAP instruction invokes an operating system *service call*. Bits [7:0] of the TRAP instruction form the *trapvector*, an eight-bit code that identifies the service call that the program wishes the operating system to perform on its behalf. Table A.2 contains the trapvectors for all the service calls that we will use with the LC-3 in this book.

15	14	13	12	11	10	9	8	7	6	5	4	3	2	1	0
1	1	1	1	0	0	0	0				trapvector				

Once the operating system is finished performing the service call, the program counter is set to the address of the instruction following the TRAP instruction, and the program continues. In this way, a program can, during its execution, request services from the operating system and continue processing after each such service is performed. The services we will require for now are

```
* Input a character from the keyboard (trapvector = x23).
* Output a character to the monitor (trapvector = x21).
* Halt the program (trapvector = x25).
```

5.5 Another Example: Counting Occurrences of a Character

We will finish our introduction to the ISA of the LC-3 with another example program. Suppose we would like to be able to input a character from the keyboard, then count the number of occurrences of that character in a file, and finally display that count on the monitor. We will simplify the problem by assuming that the number of occurrences of any character that we would be interested in is small enough that it can be expressed with a single decimal digit. That is, there will be at most nine occurrences. This simplification allows us to not have to worry about complex conversion routines between the binary count and the ASCII display on the monitor—a subject we will get into in Chapter 10, but not today.

Figure 5.16 is a flowchart of the algorithm that solves this problem. Note that each step is expressed both in English and also (in parentheses) in terms of an LC-3 implementation.

The first step is (as always) to initialize all the variables. This means providing starting values (called *initial values*) for R0, R1, R2, and R3, the four registers the computer will use to execute the program that will solve the problem. R2 will keep track of the number of occurrences; in Figure 5.16, it is referred to as *Count*. It is initialized to zero. R3 will point to the next character in the file that is being examined. We refer to it as a *pointer* since it points to (i.e., contains the **address** of) the location where the next character of the file that we wish to examine resides. The pointer is initialized with the address of the **first** character in the file. R0 will hold the character that is being counted; we will input that character from the keyboard and put it in R0. R1 will hold, in turn, each character that we get from the file being examined.

We should also note that there is no requirement that the file we are examining be close to or far away from the program we are developing. For example, it is perfectly reasonable for the program we are developing to start at x3000 and the file we are examining to start at x9000. If that were the case, in the initialization process, R3 would be initialized to x9000.

The next step is to count the number of occurrences of the input character. This is done by processing, in turn, each character in the file being examined, until the file is exhausted. Processing each character requires one iteration of a loop. Recall from Section 5.4.3 that there are two common methods for keeping track of iterations of a loop. We will use the sentinel method, using the ASCII code for EOT (End of Transmission) (00000100) as the sentinel. A table of ASCII codes is in Appendix E.

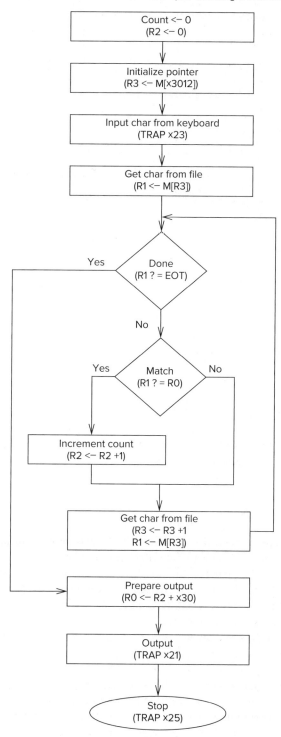

Figure 5.16   An algorithm to count occurrences of a character.

Address	15	14	13	12	11	10	9	8	7	6	5	4	3	2	1	0	
x3000	0	1	0	1	0	1	0	0	1	0	1	0	0	0	0	0	R2 <- 0
x3001	0	0	1	0	0	1	1	0	0	0	0	1	0	0	0	0	R3 <- M[x3012]
x3002	1	1	1	1	0	0	0	0	0	0	1	0	0	0	1	1	TRAP x23
x3003	0	1	1	0	0	0	1	0	1	1	0	0	0	0	0	0	R1 <- M[R3]
x3004	0	0	0	1	1	0	0	0	0	1	1	1	1	1	0	0	R4 <- R1-4
x3005	0	0	0	0	0	1	0	0	0	0	0	0	1	0	0	0	BRz x300E
x3006	1	0	0	1	0	0	1	0	0	1	1	1	1	1	1	1	R1 <- NOT R1
x3007	0	0	0	1	0	0	1	0	0	1	1	0	0	0	0	1	R1 <- R1 + 1
x3008	0	0	0	1	0	0	1	0	0	1	0	0	0	0	0	0	R1 <- R1 + R0
x3009	0	0	0	0	1	0	1	0	0	0	0	0	0	0	0	1	BRnp x300B
x300A	0	0	0	1	0	1	0	0	1	0	1	0	0	0	0	1	R2 <- R2 + 1
x300B	0	0	0	1	0	1	1	0	1	1	1	0	0	0	0	1	R3 <- R3 + 1
x300C	0	1	1	0	0	0	1	0	1	1	0	0	0	0	0	0	R1 <- M[R3]
x300D	0	0	0	0	1	1	1	1	1	1	1	1	0	1	1	0	BRnzp x3004
x300E	0	0	1	0	0	0	0	0	0	0	0	0	0	1	0	0	R0 <- M[x3013]
x300F	0	0	0	1	0	0	0	0	0	0	0	0	0	0	1	0	R0 <- R0 + R2
x3010	1	1	1	1	0	0	0	0	0	0	1	0	0	0	0	1	TRAP x21
x3011	1	1	1	1	0	0	0	0	0	0	1	0	0	1	0	1	TRAP x25
x3012							Starting address of file										
x3013	0	0	0	0	0	0	0	0	0	0	1	1	0	0	0	0	ASCII TEMPLATE

Figure 5.17   A machine language program that implements the algorithm of Figure 5.16.

In each iteration of the loop, the contents of R1 is first compared to the ASCII code for EOT. If they are equal, the loop is exited, and the program moves on to the final step, displaying on the screen the number of occurrences. If not, there is work to do. R1 (the current character under examination) is compared to R0 (the character input from the keyboard). If they match, R2 is incremented. In either case, we move on to getting the next character. The pointer R3 is incremented, the next character is loaded into R1, and the program returns to the test that checks for the sentinel at the end of the file.

When the end of the file is reached, all the characters have been examined, and the count is contained as a binary number in R2. In order to display the count on the monitor, it is first converted to an ASCII code. Since we have assumed the count is less than 10, we can do this by putting a leading 0011 in front of the four-bit binary representation of the count. Note in Figure E.2 the relationship between the binary value of each decimal digit between 0 and 9 and its corresponding ASCII code. Finally, the count is output to the monitor, and the program terminates.

Figure 5.17 is a machine language program that implements the flowchart of Figure 5.16.

First the initialization steps. The instruction at x3000 clears R2 by ANDing it with x0000. The instruction at x3001 loads the starting address of the file to be examined into R3. Again, we note that this file can be anywhere in memory. Prior to starting execution at x3000, some sequence of instructions must have stored the first address of this file in x3012. Location x3002 contains the TRAP instruction, which requests the operating system to perform a service call on behalf of this program. The function requested, as identified by the eight-bit trapvector 00100011 (i.e., x23), is to load into R0 the ASCII code of the next character typed on the keyboard. Table A.2 lists trapvectors for all operating system service calls that can be performed on behalf of a user program. The instruction at x3003 loads the character pointed to by R3 into R1.

Then the process of examining characters begins. We start (x3004) by subtracting 4 (the ASCII code for EOT) from R1 and storing it in R4. If the result is zero, the end of the file has been reached, and it is time to output the count. The instruction at x3005 conditionally branches to x300E, where the process of outputting the count begins.

If R4 is not equal to zero, the character in R1 is legitimate and must be examined. The sequence of instructions at locations x3006, x3007, and x3008 determines whether the contents of R1 and R0 are identical. Taken together, the three instructions compute

$$R0 - R1$$

This produces all zeros only if the bit patterns of R1 and R0 are identical. If the bit patterns are not identical, the conditional branch at x3009 branches to x300B; that is, it skips the instruction at x300A, which increments the counter (R2).

The instruction at x300B increments R3, so it will point to the next character in the file being examined, the instruction at x300C loads that character into R1, and the instruction at x300D unconditionally takes us back to x3004 to start processing that character.

When the sentinel (EOT) is finally detected, the process of outputting the count begins (at x300E). The instruction at x300E loads 00110000 into R0, and the instruction at x300F adds the count to R0. This converts the binary representation of the count (in R2) to the ASCII representation of the count (in R0). The instruction at x3010 invokes a TRAP to the operating system to output the contents of R0 to the monitor. When that is done and the program resumes execution, the instruction at x3011 invokes a TRAP instruction to terminate the program.

Question: Can you improve the execution of the above program? *Hint:* How many times are the instructions at x3006 and x3007 executed. What small change will decrease the total number of instructions that have to be executed.

5.6 The Data Path Revisited

Before we leave Chapter 5, let us revisit the data path diagram that we first encountered in Chapter 3 (Figure 3.35). Many of the structures we have seen earlier in this chapter in Figures 5.4, 5.5, 5.6, 5.7, 5.8, 5.9, and 5.11. We reproduce the data path diagram as Figure 5.18. Note at the outset that there are two kinds of arrows in the data path, those with arrowheads filled in and those with arrowheads not filled in. Filled-in arrowheads designate information that is processed. Unfilled-in arrowheads designate control signals. Control signals emanate from the block labeled "Finite State Machine." The connections from the finite state machine to most control signals have been left off Figure 5.18 to reduce unnecessary clutter in the diagram.

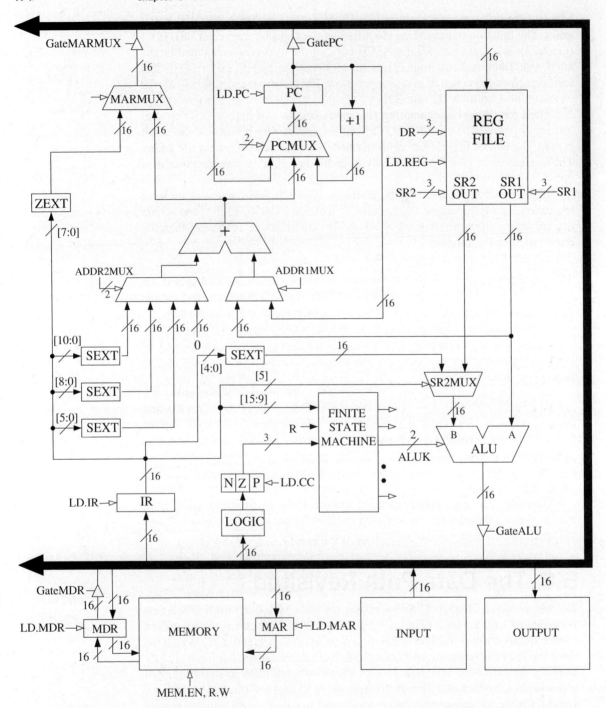

Figure 5.18   The data path of the LC-3.

5.6.1 Basic Components of the Data Path

5.6.1.1 The Global Bus

The most obvious item on the data path diagram is the heavy black structure with arrowheads at both ends. This represents the data path's global bus. The LC-3 global bus consists of 16 wires and associated electronics. It allows one structure to transfer up to 16 bits of information to another structure by making the necessary electronic connections on the bus. Exactly one value can be transferred on the bus at one time. Note that each structure that supplies values to the bus has a triangle just behind its input arrow to the bus. This triangle (called a *tri-state device*) allows the computer's control logic to enable exactly one supplier to provide information to the bus at any one time. The structure wishing to obtain the value being supplied can do so by asserting its LD.x (load enable) signal (recall our discussion of gated latches in Section 3.4.2). Not all computers have a single global bus. The pros and cons of a single global bus is yet another topic that will have to wait for later in your education.

5.6.1.2 Memory

One of the most important parts of any computer is the memory that contains both instructions and data. Memory is accessed by loading the memory address register (MAR) with the address of the location to be accessed. To perform a load, control signals then read the contents of that memory location, and the result of that read is delivered by the memory to the memory data register (MDR). On the other hand, to perform a store, what is to be stored is loaded into the MDR. Then the control signals assert a write enable (WE) signal in order to store the value contained in MDR in the memory location specified by MAR.

5.6.1.3 The ALU and the Register File

The ALU is the processing element. It has two inputs, source 1 from a register and source 2 from either a register or the sign-extended immediate value provided by the instruction. The registers (R0 through R7) can provide two values: source 1, which is controlled by the three-bit register number SR1, and source 2, which is controlled by the three-bit register number SR2. SR1 and SR2 are fields in the LC-3 operate instructions. The selection of a second register operand or a sign-extended immediate operand is determined by bit [5] of the LC-3 instruction. Note the mux that provides source 2 to the ALU. The select line of that mux is bit [5] of the LC-3 operate instruction.

The results of an ALU operation are (a) a result that is stored in one of the registers, and (b) the three single-bit condition codes. Note that the ALU can supply 16 bits to the bus, and that value can then be written into the register specified by the three-bit register number DR. Also, note that the 16 bits supplied to the bus are also input to logic that determines whether that 16-bit value is negative, zero, or positive. The three one-bit condition code registers N, Z, and P are set accordingly.

5.6.1.4 The PC and the PCMUX

At the start of each instruction cycle, the PC supplies to the MAR over the global bus the address of the instruction to be fetched. In addition, the PC, in turn, is supplied via the three-to-one PCMUX. During the FETCH phase of the instruction cycle, the PC is incremented and written into the PC. That is shown as the rightmost input to the PCMUX.

If the current instruction is a control instruction, then the relevant source of the PCMUX depends on which control instruction is currently being processed. If the current instruction is a conditional branch and the branch is taken, then the PC is loaded with the incremented PC + PCoffset (the 16-bit value obtained by sign-extending IR [8:0]). Note that this addition takes place in the special adder and not in the ALU. The output of the adder is the middle input to PCMUX. The third input to PCMUX is obtained from the global bus. Its use will become clear after we discuss other control instructions in Chapters 9.

5.6.1.5 The MARMUX

As you know, memory is accessed by supplying the address to the MAR. The MARMUX controls which of two sources will supply the MAR with the appropriate address during the execution of a load, a store, or a TRAP instruction. The right input to the MARMUX is obtained by adding either the incremented PC or a base register to zero or a literal value supplied by the IR. Whether the PC or a base register and what literal value depends on which opcode is being processed. The control signal ADDR1MUX specifies the PC or base register. The control signal ADDR2MUX specifies which of four values is to be added. The left input to MARMUX provides the zero-extended trapvector, which is needed to invoke service calls, and will be discussed in detail in Chapter 9.

5.6.2 The Instruction Cycle Specific to the LC-3

We complete our tour of the LC-3 data path by following the flow through an instruction cycle. Suppose the content of the PC is x3456 and the content of location x3456 is

15	14	13	12	11	10	9	8	7	6	5	4	3	2	1	0
0	1	1	0	0	1	1	0	1	0	0	0	0	1	0	0

LDR   R3   R2   4

Suppose the LC-3 has just completed processing the instruction at x3455, which happened to be an ADD instruction.

5.6.2.1 FETCH

As you know, the instruction cycle starts with the FETCH phase. That is, the instruction is obtained by accessing memory with the address contained in the PC. In the first cycle, the contents of the PC is loaded via the global bus into the MAR, and the PC is incremented and loaded into the PC. At the end of this cycle, the PC contains x3457. In the next cycle (if memory can provide information in one cycle), the memory is read, and the instruction 0110011010000100 is loaded into the MDR. In the next cycle, the contents of the MDR is loaded into the instruction register (IR), completing the FETCH phase.

5.6.2.2 DECODE

In the next cycle, the contents of the IR is decoded, resulting in the control logic providing the correct control signals (unfilled arrowheads) to control the processing of the rest of this instruction. The opcode is 0110, identifying the LDR instruction. This means that the Base+offset addressing mode is to be used to determine the address of data to be loaded into the destination register R3.

5.6.2.3 EVALUATE ADDRESS

In the next cycle, the contents of R2 (the base register) and the sign-extended bits [5:0] of the IR are added and supplied via the MARMUX to the MAR. The SR1 field specifies 010, the register to be read to obtain the base address. ADDR1MUX selects SR1OUT, and ADDR2MUX selects the second from the right source.

5.6.2.4 OPERAND FETCH

In the next cycle (or more than one, if memory access takes more than one cycle), the value at that address is loaded into the MDR.

5.6.2.5 EXECUTE

The LDR instruction does not require an EXECUTE phase, so this phase takes zero cycles.

5.6.2.6 STORE RESULT

In the last cycle, the contents of the MDR is gated onto the global bus, from which it is loaded into R3 and supplied to the condition code logic in order to set the NZP condition codes.

Exercises

5.1   Given instructions ADD, JMP, LEA, and NOT, identify whether the instructions are operate instructions, data movement instructions, or control instructions. For each instruction, list the addressing modes that can be used with the instruction.

5.2   A memory's addressability is 64 bits. What does that tell you about the size of the MAR and MDR?

5.3   There are two common ways to terminate a loop. One way uses a counter to keep track of the number of iterations. The other way uses an element called a _____. What is the distinguishing characteristic of this element?

5.4   Say we have a memory consisting of 256 locations, and each location contains 16 bits.

  a. How many bits are required for the address?

  b. If we use the PC-relative addressing mode, and want to allow control transfer between instructions 20 locations away, how many bits of a branch instruction are needed to specify the PC-relative offset?

  c. If a control instruction is in location 3, what is the PC-relative offset of address 10? Assume that the control transfer instructions work the same way as in the LC-3.

5.5   *a.* What is an addressing mode?
   b. Name three places an instruction's operands might be located.
   c. List the five addressing modes of the LC-3, and for each one state
        where the operand is located (from part *b*).
   d. What addressing mode is used by the ADD instruction shown in
        Section 5.1.2?

5.6   Recall the machine busy example from Section 2.6.7. Assuming the
        BUSYNESS bit vector is stored in R2, we can use the LC-3 instruction
        0101 011 010 1 00001 (AND R3, R2, #1) to determine whether machine 0
        is busy or not. If the result of this instruction is 0, then machine 0 is busy.

   a. Write an LC-3 instruction that determines whether machine 2 is busy.
   b. Write an LC-3 instruction that determines whether both machines 2
        and 3 are busy.
   c. Write an LC-3 instruction that indicates none of the machines are
        busy.
   d. Can you write an LC-3 instruction that determines whether machine 6
        is busy? Is there a problem here?

5.7   What is the largest positive number we can represent literally (i.e., as an
        immediate value) within an LC-3 ADD instruction?

5.8   We want to increase the number of registers that we can specify in the
        LC-3 ADD instruction to 32. Do you see any problem with that? Explain.

5.9   We would like to have an instruction that does nothing. Many ISAs
        actually have an opcode devoted to doing nothing. It is usually called
        NOP, for NO OPERATION. The instruction is fetched, decoded, and
        executed. The execution phase is to do nothing! Which of the following
        three instructions could be used for NOP and have the program still work
        correctly?

   a. 0001 001 001 1 00000
   b. 0000 111 000000001
   c. 0000 000 000000000

        What does the ADD instruction do that the others do not do?

5.10 What is the difference between the following LC-3 instructions A and B?
        How are they similar? How are they different?

   A: 0000111101010101
   B: 0100111101010101

5.11 We wish to execute a single LC-3 instruction that will subtract the
        decimal number 20 from register 1 and put the result into register 2. Can
        we do it? If yes, do it. If not, explain why not.

5.12 After executing the following LC-3 instruction: ADD R2, R0, R1, we
        notice that R0[15] equals R1[15], but is different from R2[15]. We are
        told that R0 and R1 contain UNSIGNED integers (that is, nonnegative
        integers between 0 and 65,535). Under what conditions can we trust the
        result in R2?

5.13 *a.* How might one use a single LC-3 instruction to move the value in R2 into R3?

b. The LC-3 has no subtract instruction. How could one perform the following operation using only three LC-3 instructions:

$$R1 \leftarrow R2 - R3$$

c. Using only one LC-3 instruction and without changing the contents of any register, how might one set the condition codes based on the value that resides in R1?

d. Is there a sequence of LC-3 instructions that will cause the condition codes at the end of the sequence to be N = 1, Z = 1, and P = 0? Explain.

e. Write an LC-3 instruction that clears the contents of R2.

5.14 The LC-3 does not have an opcode for the logical function OR. That is, there is no instruction in the LC-3 ISA that performs the OR operation. However, we can write a sequence of instructions to implement the OR operation. The following four-instruction sequence performs the OR of the contents of register 1 and register 2 and puts the result in register 3. Fill in the two missing instructions so that the four-instruction sequence will do the job.

```
(1): 1001 100 001 111111
(2):
(3): 0101 110 100 000 101
(4):
```

5.15 State the contents of R1, R2, R3, and R4 after the program starting at location x3100 halts.

Address	Data
0011 0001 0000 0000	1110 001 000100000
0011 0001 0000 0001	0010 010 000100000
0011 0001 0000 0010	1010 011 000100000
0011 0001 0000 0011	0110 100 010 000001
0011 0001 0000 0100	1111 0000 0010 0101
⋮	⋮
⋮	⋮
0011 0001 0010 0010	0100 0101 0110 0110
0011 0001 0010 0011	0100 0101 0110 0111
⋮	⋮
⋮	⋮
0100 0101 0110 0111	1010 1011 1100 1101
0100 0101 0110 1000	1111 1110 1101 0011

5.16 Which LC-3 addressing mode makes the most sense to use under the following conditions? (There may be more than one correct answer to each of these; therefore, justify your answers with some explanation.)

    a. You want to load one value from an address that is less than $\pm 2^8$ locations away.

    b. You want to load one value from an address that is more than 2^8 locations away.

    c. You want to load an array of sequential addresses.

5.17 How many times does the LC-3 make a read or write request to memory during the processing of the LD instruction? How many times during the processing of the LDI instruction? How many times during the processing of the LEA instruction? Processing includes all phases of the instruction cycle.

5.18 The program counter contains the address of an LDR instruction. In order for the LC-3 to process that instruction, how many memory accesses must be made? Repeat this task for STI and TRAP.

5.19 The LC-3 Instruction Register (IR) is made up of 16 bits, of which the least significant nine bits [8:0] represent the PC-relative offset for the LD instruction. If we change the ISA so that bits [6:0] represent the PC-relative offset, what is the new range of addresses we can load data from using the LD instruction?

5.20 If we made the LC-3 ISA such that we allow the LD instruction to load data only ± 32 locations away from the incremented PC value, how many bits would be required for the PC-relative offset in the LD instruction?

5.21 What is the maximum number of TRAP service routines that the LC-3 ISA can support? Explain.

5.22 The PC contains x3010. The following memory locations contain values as shown:

x3050:	x70A4
x70A2:	x70A3
x70A3:	xFFFF
x70A4:	x123B

The following three LC-3 instructions are then executed, causing a value to be loaded into R6. What is that value?

x3010	1110 0110 0011 1111
x3011	0110 1000 1100 0000
x3012	0110 1101 0000 0000

We could replace the three-instruction sequence with a single instruction. What is it?

5.23 Suppose the following LC-3 program is loaded into memory starting at location x30FF:

```
x30FF    1110 0010 0000 0001
x3100    0110 0100 0100 0010
x3101    1111 0000 0010 0101
x3102    0001 0100 0100 0001
x3103    0001 0100 1000 0010
```

If the program is executed, what is the value in R2 at the end of execution?

5.24 An LDR instruction, located at x3200, uses R4 as its base register. The value currently in R4 is x4011. What is the largest address that this instruction can load from? Suppose we redefine the LDR offset to be zero-extended, rather than sign-extended. Then what would be the largest address that this instruction could load from? With the new definition, what would be the smallest address that this instruction could load from?

5.25 Write an LC-3 program that compares two numbers in R2 and R3 and puts the larger number in R1. If the numbers are equal, then R1 is set equal to 0.

5.26 Your task is to consider the successor to the LC-3. We will add ten additional opcodes to the ISA and expand the register set from 8 to 16. We will change the memory to byte-addressable, with total address space of 64K bytes. Instructions will remain 16 bits wide. Also, we will encode all instructions, both old and new, with the same fields as the original 15 instructions, although we may need to change the size of some of the fields.

    a. Is there any problem completing the detailed specification of the successor to the LC-3, as described above? Explain.

    b. How many bits do we need in the PC to be able to address all of memory?

    c. If we want 128 different operating system routines to be able to be accessed with a trap instruction and we form the address of each of these routines by shifting the trap vector to the left by five bits, what is the minimum amount of memory required by the trap service routines?

    d. If, in the new version of the LC-3, we reduced the number of registers from eight to four and kept the number of opcodes at 16, what is the largest immediate value we could represent in an ADD instruction on this new machine?

5.27 Before the seven instructions are executed in the example of Section 5.3.4, R2 contains the value xAAAA. How many different values are contained in R2 during the execution of the seven instructions? What are they?

5.28 It is the case that we REALLY don't need to have load indirect (1010) and store indirect (1011) instructions. We can accomplish the same results using other instruction sequences instead of using these instructions. Replace the store indirect (1011) instruction in the code below with whatever instructions are necessary to perform the same function.

```
x3000     0010 0000 0000 0010
x3001     1011 0000 0000 0010
x3002     1111 0000 0010 0101
x3003     0000 0000 0100 1000
x3004     1111 0011 1111 1111
```

5.29 The LC-3 ISA contains the instruction LDR DR, BaseR, offset. After the instruction is decoded, the following operations (called microinstructions) are carried out to complete the processing of the LDR instruction:

```
MAR ← BaseR + SEXT(Offset6) ; set up the memory address
MDR ← Memory[MAR] ; read mem at BaseR + offset
DR  ← MDR ; load DR
```

Suppose that the architect of the LC-3 wanted to include an instruction MOVE DR, SR that would copy the memory location with address given by SR and store it into the memory location whose address is in DR.

a. The MOVE instruction is not really necessary since it can be accomplished with a sequence of existing LC-3 instructions. What sequence of existing LC-3 instructions implements (also called "emulates") MOVE R0,R1?

b. If the MOVE instruction were added to the LC-3 ISA, what sequence of microinstructions, following the decode operation, would emulate MOVE DR,SR?

5.30 The following table shows a part of the LC-3's memory:

Address	Data
0011 0001 0000 0000	1001 001 001 111111
0011 0001 0000 0001	0001 010 000 000 001
0011 0001 0000 0010	1001 010 010 111111
0011 0001 0000 0011	0000 010 111111100

State what is known about R1 and R0 if the conditional branch redirects control to location x3100.

5.31 The figure below shows a snapshot of the eight registers of the LC-3 before and after the instruction at location x1000 is executed. Fill in the bits of the instruction at location x1000.

	BEFORE		AFTER
R0	x0000	R0	x0000
R1	x1111	R1	x1111
R2	x2222	R2	x2222
R3	x3333	R3	x3333
R4	x4444	R4	x4444
R5	x5555	R5	xFFF8
R6	x6666	R6	x6666
R7	x7777	R7	x7777

0x1000 : | 0 | 0 | 0 | 1 | | | | | | | | | | | | |

5.32 If the condition codes have values N = 0, Z = 0, P = 1 at the beginning of the execution of the following sequence of LC-3 instructions, what will their values be at the end of the execution of the following sequence of LC-3 instructions?

x3050	0000 0010 0000 0010
x3051	0101 0000 0010 0000
x3052	0000 1110 0000 0010
x3053	0101 0000 0010 0000
x3054	0001 0000 0011 1111

5.33 If the value stored in R0 is 5 at the end of the execution of the following instructions, what can be inferred about R5?

x2FFF	0101 0000 0010 0000
x3000	0101 1111 1110 0000
x3001	0001 1101 1110 0001
x3002	0101 1001 0100 0110
x3003	0000 0100 0000 0001
x3004	0001 0000 0010 0001
x3005	0001 1101 1000 0110
x3006	0001 1111 1110 0001
x3007	0001 0011 1111 1000
x3008	0000 1001 1111 1001
x3009	0101 1111 1110 0000

5.34   Using the overall data path in Figure 5.18, identify the elements that implement the NOT instruction of Figure 5.4.

5.35   Using the overall data path in Figure 5.18, identify the elements that implement the ADD instruction of Figure 5.5.

5.36   Using the overall data path in Figure 5.18, identify the elements that implement the LD instruction of Figure 5.7.

5.37   Using the overall data path in Figure 5.18, identify the elements that implement the LDI instruction of Figure 5.8.

5.38   Using the overall data path in Figure 5.18, identify the elements that implement the LDR instruction of Figure 5.9.

5.39   Using the overall data path in Figure 5.18, identify the elements that implement the LEA instruction of Figure 5.6.

5.40   The following logic diagram shows part of the control structure of the LC-3 machine. What is the purpose of the signal labeled A?

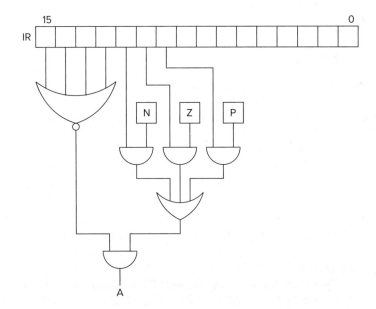

5.41   A part of the implementation of the LC-3 architecture is shown in the following diagram.

   a. What information does Y provide?
   b. The signal X is the control signal that gates the gated D latch. Is there an error in the logic that produces X?

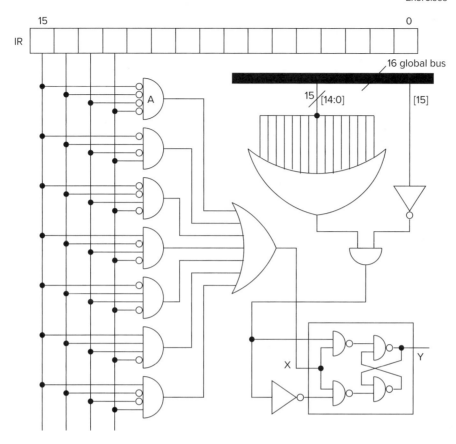

5.42 The LC-3 macho-company has decided to use opcode 1101 to implement a new instruction. They need your help to pick the most useful one from the following:

   a. MOVE Ri, Rj; The contents of Rj are copied into Ri.
   b. NAND Ri, Rj, Rk; Ri is the bit-wise NAND of Rj, Rk
   c. SHFL Ri, Rj, #2; The contents of Rj are shifted left 2 bits and stored into Ri.
   d. MUL Ri, Rj, Rk; Ri is the product of 2's complement integers in Rj, Rk.

   Justify your answer.

5.43 When a computer executes an instruction, the state of the computer is changed as a result of that execution. Is there any difference in the state of the LC-3 computer as a result of executing instruction 1 below vs. executing instruction 2 below? Explain. We can assume the state of the LC-3 computer before execution is the same in both cases.

```
instruction 1: 0001 000 000 1 00000   register 0 <-- register 0 + \#0

instruction 2: 0000 111 000000000   branch to PC' + \#0 if any of N,Z,orP is set
```

5.44 A program wishes to load a value from memory into register 1, and on the basis of the value loaded, execute code starting at x3040 if the value loaded is positive, execute code starting at x3080 if the value loaded is negative, or execute code starting at location x3003 if the value loaded is zero. The first instruction of this program (load a value into register R1) is shown in x3000.

a. Write the instructions for locations x3001 and x3002.

x3000:	0010 001 011111111

x3001:	

x3002:	

b. The program segment below starts execution at x3000. When the program halts, what is contained in register 0?

```
x3000: 0101 000 000 1 00000    ;register 0 <-- 0
x3001: 0001 000 000 1 00001    ;register 0 <-- register 0 + 1
x3002: 0000 001 111111110      ;branch p -2
x3003: 1111 0000 0010 0101     ;TRAP x25
```

c. Two of the outputs of a 3-to-8 decoder are used as inputs to an AND gate as shown below.

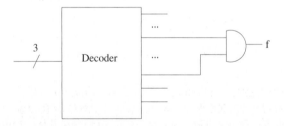

5.45 In class we showed the first few states of the finite state machine that is required for processing instructions of a computer program written for LC-3. In the first state, the computer does two things, represented as:

```
MAR <-- PC
PC <-- PC+1
```

Why does the microarchitecture put the contents of the PC into the MAR? Why does the microarchitecture increment the PC?

5.46 R0 contains the ASCII code of a capital letter in the English alphabet. If the instruction

        0001000000000001

is executed, we wish to end up with the lowercase version of that letter in R0. What must be true of the values in the other registers before this instruction executes for this to happen?

5.47 The following diagram describes a 2^2 by 16-bit memory. Each of the four muxes has four-bit input sources and a four-bit output, and each four-bit source is the output of a single four-bit memory cell.

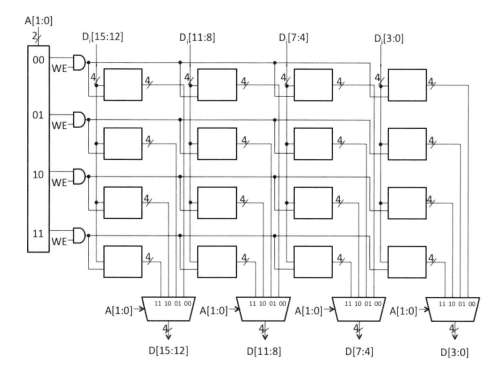

 a. Unfortunately, the memory was wired by a student, and he got the inputs to some of the muxes mixed up. That is, instead of the four bits from a memory cell going to the correct four-bit input of the mux, the four bits all went to one of the other four-bit sources of that mux. The result was, as you can imagine, a mess. To figure out the mix-up in the wiring, the following sequence of memory accesses was performed:

Read/Write	MDR	MAR
Write	x134B	01
Write	xFCA2	10
Write	xBEEF	11
Write	x072A	00
Read	xF34F	10
Read	x1CAB	01
Read	x0E2A	00

Note: On a write, MDR is loaded before the access. On a read, MDR is loaded as a result of the access. Your job is to identify the mix-up in the wiring. Show which memory cells were wired to which mux inputs by filling in their corresponding addresses in the blanks provided. Note that one address has already been supplied for you.

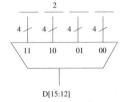

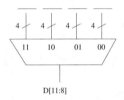

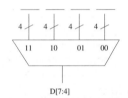

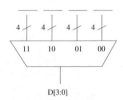

b. After rewiring the muxes correctly and initializing all memory cells to **xF**, the following sequence of accesses was performed. Note that some of the information about each access has been left out.
Your job: Fill in the blanks.

Read/Write	MDR	MAR
Write	x72____	0__
Write	x8FAF	11
Read	x72A3	__0
Read	xFFFF	1__
Write	x732D	__1
Read	xFFFF	0__
Write	x__7____	0__
Read	x37A3	__1
Read	x_____D	__1

Show the contents of the memory cells by putting the hex digit that is stored in each after all the accesses have been performed.

	D[15:12]	D[11:8]	D[7:4]	D[3:0]
Address				
00				
01				
10				
11				

5.48 After these two instructions execute:

```
x3030   0001 000 001 0 00 010
x3031   0000 011 000000111
```

the next instruction to execute will be the instruction at x3039 if what condition is met?

5.49 We wish to know if R0 is being used as the Base Register for computing the address in an LDR instruction. Since the instruction is in memory, we can load it into R4. And, since the Base Register is identified in bits 8:6 of the instruction, we can load R5 with 0000000111000000 and then execute AND R6,R5,R4. We would know that R0 is the base register if what condition is met?

★**5.50** Three instructions all construct an address by sign-extending the low nine bits of the instruction and adding it to the incremented PC.

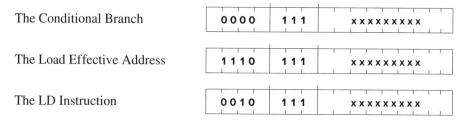

The Conditional Branch

The Load Effective Address

The LD Instruction

The xxxxxxxx represents the nine-bit offset that is sign-extended.

Where does the LC-3 microarchitecture put the result of adding the nine-bit sign-extended offset to the incremented PC?

★5.51   An aggressive young engineer decides to build and sell the LC-3 but
is told that if he wants to succeed, he really needs a SUBTRACT
instruction. Given the unused opcode 1101, he decides to specify the
SUBTRACT instruction as follows:

15	12	11	9	8	6	5	3	2	0
1101		DR		SR1		000		SR2	

The instruction is defined as: DR ← SR2 - SR1, and the condition codes
are set. **Assume DR, SR1, and SR2 are all different registers**.
To accomplish this, the engineer needs to add three states to the state
machine and a mux and register A to the data path. The modified state
machine is shown below, and the modified data path is shown on the next
page. The mux is controlled by a new control signal SR2SEL, which
selects one of its two sources.

    SR2SEL/1: SR2OUT, REGISTER_A

Your job:

For the state machine shown below, fill in the empty boxes with the
control signals that are needed in order to implement the SUBTRACT
instruction.

For the data path, fill in the value in register A.

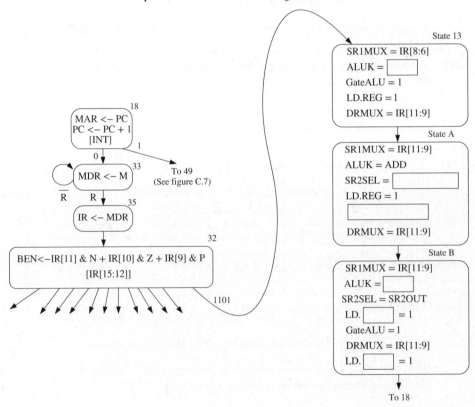

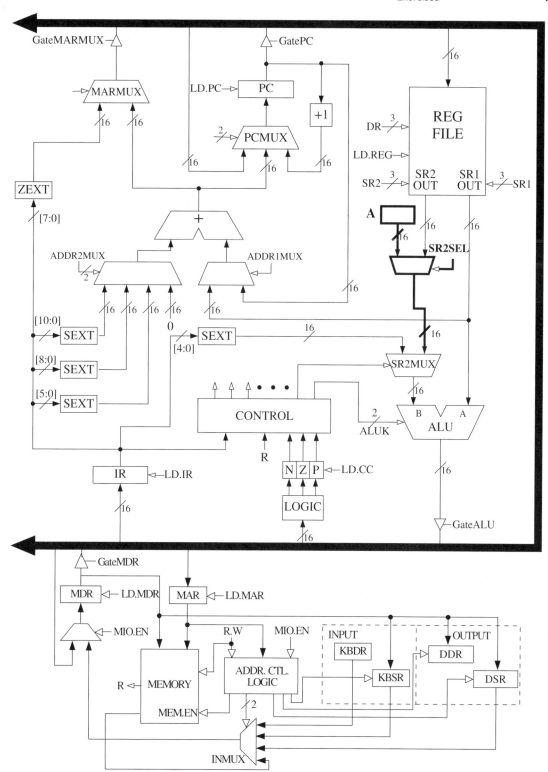

5.52 Here is a list of the 16 opcodes. Circle the ones that write to a general purpose register (R0 to R7) at some point during the instruction cycle.

ADD	AND	BR	JMP	JSR	LD	LEA	LDI
LDR	NOT	RTI	ST	STI	STR	TRAP	reserved

5.53 The eight general purpose registers of the LC-3 (R0 to R7) make up the register file. To write a value to a register, the LC-3 control unit must supply 16 bits of data (BUS[15:0]), a destination register (DR[2:0]), and a write enable signal (LD.REG) to load a register. The combinational logic block shows inputs BUS[15:0], DR[2:0], and LD.REG and outputs DinR0[15:0], DinR1[15:0], DinR2[15:0], ... DinR7[15:0], LD.R0, LD.R1, LD.R2, ... LD.R7.

Your job: Add wires, logic gates, and standard logic blocks as necessary to complete the combinational logic block. *Note:* If you use a standard logic block, it is not necessary to show the individual gates. However, it is necessary to identify the logic block specifically (e.g., "16-to-1 mux"), along with labels for each relevant input or output, according to its function.

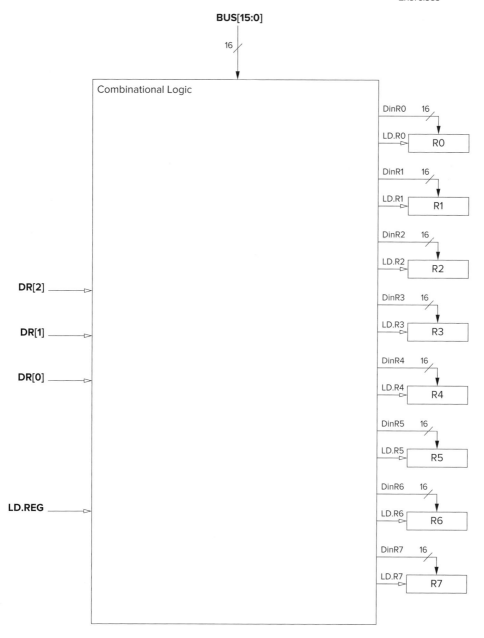

BUS[15:0]

5.54 All instructions load the MDR during the fetch phase of the instruction cycle to fetch the instruction from memory on its way to the IR. After decode has completed, some instructions load the MDR again, using the source 0 input to the mux labeled A on the data path. Other instructions load the MDR, using the source 1 input to mux A. Only one of the 15 LC-3 instructions loads the MDR after decode, using both source 0 and source 1 at different times during the processing of that instruction. What is the opcode of that instruction?

★5.55 An LC-3 program starts execution at x3000. During the execution of the program, snapshots of all eight registers were taken at six different times as shown below: before the program executes, after execution of instruction 1, after execution of instruction 2, after execution of instruction 3, after execution of instruction 4, after execution of instruction 5, and after execution of instruction 6.

Registers	Initial Value	After 1st Instruction	After 2nd Instruction	After 3rd Instruction	After 4th Instruction	After 5th Instruction	After 6th Instruction
R0	x4006	x4050	x4050	x4050	x4050	x4050	x4050
R1	x5009	x5009	x5009	x5009	x5009	x5009	x5009
R2	x4008	x4008	x4008	x4008	x4008	x4008	xC055
R3	x4002			x8005	x8005	x8005	x8005
R4	x4003	x4003	x4003	x4003			x4003
R5	x400D	x400D			x400D	x400D	x400D
R6	x400C	x400C	x400C	x400C	x400C	x400C	x400C
R7	x6001	x6001	x6001	x6001			x400E

Also, during the execution of the program, the PC trace, the MAR trace, and the MDR trace were also recorded as shown below. Note that a PC trace records the addresses of the instructions executed in sequence by the program.

PC Trace
x400D
x400E

MAR Trace	MDR Trace
	xA009
x3025	
	x1703
	x4040
x400E	x1403

Your job: Fill in the missing entries in the three tables above.

5.56   This problem tests your knowledge of the instruction cycle for processing the NOT instruction. You are asked to show the values of several control signals in every clock cycle of the sequence that is used to process the NOT instruction.

The instruction cycle starts with state 18 as shown in the following table. Your job: Identify each state in the sequence, and show the values of the control signals listed during each state in the sequence. Use the convention specified below. For a particular state, if the value of a control signal does not matter, fill it with an X. You may not have to use all the rows.

Note: Assume a memory access takes one clock cycle.

Cycle	State	LD.PC	LD.MAR	LD.MDR	LD.REG	LD.CC	GateALU	GatePC	ALUK	PCMUX
1	18									
2										
3										
4										
5										
6										
7										
8										
9										
10										

```
LD.PC    0: load not enabled          GateALU  0: do not pass signal
         1: load enabled                       1: pass signal

LD.MAR   0: load not enabled          GatePC   0: do not pass signal
         1: load enabled                       1: pass signal

LD.MDR   0: load not enabled          ALUK     00: ADD
         1: load enabled                       01: AND
                                               10: NOT
LD.REG   0: load not enabled                   11: Pass input A
         1: load enabled
                                      PCMUX    00: PC+1
LD.CC    0: load not enabled                   01: BUS
         1: load enabled                       10: from adder
```

5.57   Note boldface signal lines on the following data path.

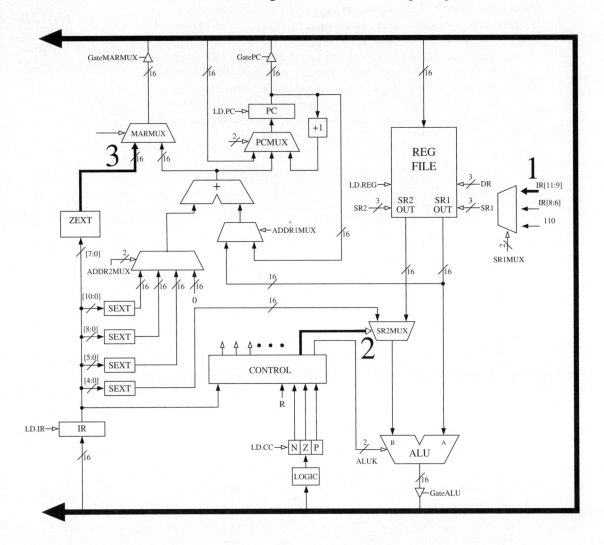

1. What opcodes use IR [11:9] as inputs to SR1?

2. Where does the control signal of this mux come from? Be specific!

3. What opcodes use this input to the MARMUX?

5.58   Let's use the unused opcode to implement a new instruction, as shown below:

15	12	11	9	8	6	5	3	2	0
1101		Reg1		Reg2		000		Reg3	

To accomplish this, we will need a small addition to the data path, shown below in boldface:

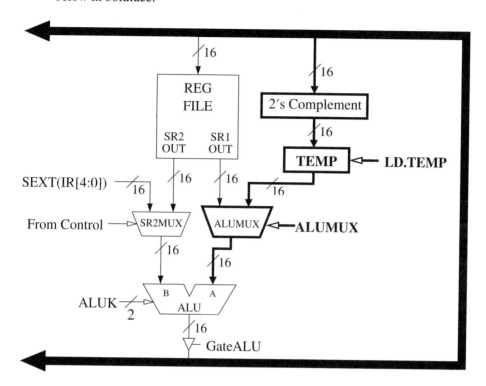

The following five additional states are needed to control the data path to carry out the work of this instruction.

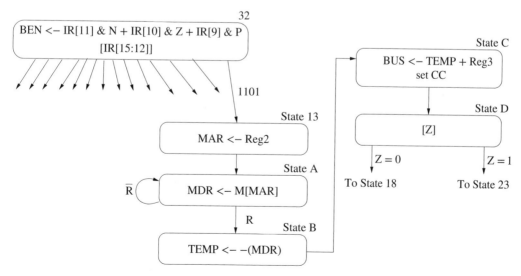

Note: State B loads the negative of the contents of MDR into TEMP.

a. Complete the following table by identifying the values of the control signals needed to carry out the work of each state.

	LD.PC	LD.MAR	LD.MDR	LD.CC	LD.TEMP	GatePC	GateMDR	GateALU	SR1MUX[1:0]	ALUMUX	ALUK[1:0]	MIO.EN	R.W
State 13													
State A													
State B													
State C													
State D													

LD.PC   0: load not enabled
         1: load enabled

LD.MAR   0: load not enabled
         1: load enabled

LD.MDR   0: load not enabled
         1: load enabled

LD.CC   0: load not enabled
         1: load enabled

LD.TEMP 0: load not enabled
         1: load enabled

GatePC   0: do not pass signal
         1: pass signal

GateMDR 0: do not pass signal
         1: pass signal

GateALU 0: do not pass signal
         1: pass signal

SR1MUX   00: Source IR [11:9]
         01: Source IR [8:6]
         10: Source R6

ALUMUX   0: Choose SR1
         1: Choose TEMP

ALUK   00: ADD
         01: AND
         10: NOT
         11: Pass input A

MIO.EN   0: MIO not enabled
         1: MIO enabled

R.W   0: Read
         1: Write

b. What does the new instruction do?

5.59 Every LC-3 instruction takes eight cycles to be fetched and decoded, if we assume every memory access takes five cycles. The total number of cycles an LC-3 instruction takes to be completely processed, however, depends on what has to be done for that instruction.

Assuming every memory access takes five cycles, and assuming the LC-3 processes one instruction at a time, from beginning to end, how many clock cycles does each instruction take? For each instruction, how many cycles are required to process it?

Instruction	Number of cycles
ADD	
AND	
LD	
LEA	
LDI	
NOT	
BRnzp	
TRAP	

5.60

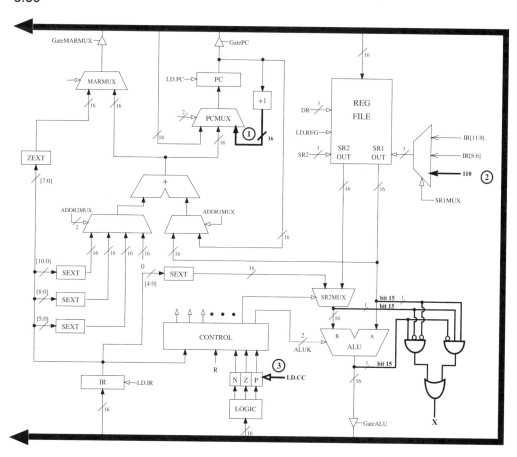

Note that several of the lines (i.e., signals) in the LC-3 data path have been drawn in boldface. Each line is designated by a boldface number 1, 2, or 3. Not all instructions use all three lines. That is, some instructions would not function correctly if the line (i.e., signal) were removed.

List the opcodes that utilize line 1 during their processing of an instruction.

List the opcodes that utilize line 2 during their processing of an instruction.

List the opcodes that require LD.CC=1 on line 3 during their processing of an instruction.

Note the logic (in boldface) added to the data path. The output of that logic is labeled X. What does X=1 indicate if ALUK is ADD?

★5.61   During the execution of an LC-3 program, the processor data path was monitored for four instructions in the program that were processed consecutively. The table shows all clock cycles during which the bus was utilized. It shows the clock cycle number, the value on the bus, and the state (from the state machine diagram) for some of these clock cycles. Processing of the first instruction starts at clock cycle T. Each memory access in this LC-3 machine takes five clock cycles.

Your job: Fill in the missing entries in the table. You only need to fill in the cells not marked with x.

Note: There are five clock cycles for which you need to provide the control signals. Not all LC-3 control signals are shown in the table. However, all control signals that are required for those five clock cycles have been included.

Note: For the DRMUX signal, write '11.9', 'R7', or 'SP'; for the R.W signal, write an 'R' or a 'W'; for the PCMUX signal, write 'PC+1', 'BUS', or 'ADDER'; for all other control signals, write down the actual bit. If a control signal is not relevant in a given cycle, mark it with a dash (i.e., -).

Inst. #	Clock Cycle	Bus	State	Gate PC	Gate MDR	Gate ALU	Gate MARMUX	LD. PC	LD. MDR	LD. MAR	LD. CC	LD. Reg	DR MUX	MIO. EN	R.W	PC MUX
Inst. 1	T + 0	x3010														
	T + 6			x	x	x	x	x	x	x	x	x	x	x	x	x
	T + 8	x00AB		x	x	x	x	x	x	x	x	x	x	x	x	x
	T + 9		28													
	T + 10		28													
	T + 11		28													
	T + 12	x	28	x	x	x	x	x	x	x	x	x	x	x	x	x
	T + 13	x	28	x	x	x	x	x	x	x	x	x	x	x	x	x
	T + 14			x	x	x	x	x	x	x	x	x	x	x	x	x
Inst. 2	T + 15	x1510	18	x	x	x	x	x	x	x	x	x	x	x	x	x
		x2219		x	x	x	x	x	x	x	x	x	x	x	x	x
				x	x	x	x	x	x	x	x	x	x	x	x	x
	T + 29	x8001														
Inst. 3	T + 30			x	x	x	x	x	x	x	x	x	x	x	x	
	T + 36	x0804		x	x	x	x	x	x	x	x	x	x	x	x	
Inst. 4			18	x	x	x	x	x	x	x	x	x	x	x	x	x
	x	x1200	x	x	x	x	x	x	x	x	x	x	x	x	x	x
	x	x0000	x	x	x	x	x	x	x	x	x	x	x	x	x	x

CHAPTER

6 Programming

We are now ready to develop programs to solve problems with the computer. In this chapter we attempt to do two things: first, we develop a methodology for constructing programs to solve problems (Section 6.1, Problem Solving), and second, we develop a methodology for fixing those programs (Section 6.2, Debugging) under the likely condition that we did not get everything right the first time.

There is a long tradition that the errors present in programs are referred to as *bugs*, and the process of removing those errors is called *debugging*. The opportunities for introducing bugs into a complicated program are so great that it usually takes much more time to get the program to work correctly (debugging) than it does to create the program in the first place.

6.1 Problem Solving

6.1.1 Systematic Decomposition

Recall from Chapter 1 that in order for electrons to solve a problem, we need to go through several levels of transformation to get from a natural language description of the problem (in our case English, although many of you might prefer Italian, Mandarin, Hindi, or something else) to something electrons can deal with. Once we have a natural language description of the problem, the next step is to transform the problem statement into an algorithm. That is, the next step is to transform the problem statement into a step-by-step procedure that has the properties of definiteness (each step is precisely stated), effective computability (each step can be carried out by a computer), and finiteness (the procedure terminates).

In the late 1960s, the concept of *structured programming* emerged as a way to dramatically improve the ability of average programmers to take a complex description of a problem and systematically decompose it into smaller and smaller manageable units so that they could ultimately write a program that executed correctly. The methodology has also been called *systematic decomposition* because the larger tasks are systematically broken down into smaller ones.

We will find the systematic decomposition model a useful technique for designing computer programs to carry out complex tasks.

6.1.2 The Three Constructs: Sequential, Conditional, Iterative

Systematic decomposition is the process of taking a task, that is, a unit of work (see Figure 6.1a), and breaking it into smaller units of work such that the collection of smaller units carries out the same task as the one larger unit. The idea is that if one starts with a large, complex task and applies this process again and again, one will end up with very small units of work and consequently be able to easily write a program to carry out each of these small units of work. The process is also referred to as *stepwise refinement,* because the process is applied one step at a time, and each step refines one of the tasks that is still too complex into a collection of simpler subtasks.

The idea is to replace each larger unit of work with a construct that correctly decomposes it. There are basically three constructs for doing this: *sequential, conditional,* and *iterative.*

The **sequential** construct (Figure 6.1b) is the one to use if the designated task can be broken down into two subtasks, one following the other. That is, the computer is to carry out the first subtask completely, *then* go on and carry out the second subtask completely— *never* going back to the first subtask after starting the second subtask.

The **conditional** construct (Figure 6.1c) is the one to use if the task consists of doing one of two subtasks but not both, depending on some condition. If the

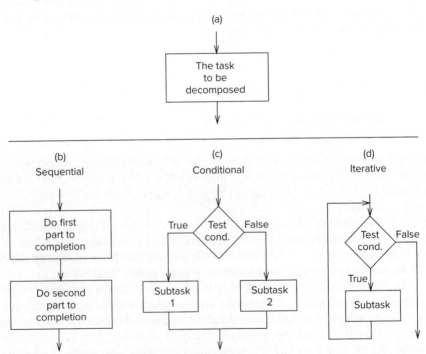

Figure 6.1   **The basic constructs of structured programming.**

condition is true, the computer is to carry out one subtask. If the condition is not true, the computer is to carry out a different subtask. Either subtask may be vacuous; that is, it may *do nothing*. Regardless, after the correct subtask is completed, the program moves onward. The program never goes back and retests the condition.

The **iterative** construct (Figure 6.1d) is the one to use if the task consists of doing a subtask a number of times, but only as long as some condition is true. If the condition is true, do the subtask. After the subtask is finished, go back and test the condition again. As long as the result of the condition tested is true, the program continues to carry out the same subtask again and again. The first time the test is not true, the program proceeds onward.

Note in Figure 6.1 that whatever the task of Figure 6.1a, work starts with the arrow into the top of the "box" representing the task and finishes with the arrow out of the bottom of the box. There is no mention of what goes on *inside* the box. In each of the three possible decompositions of Figure 6.1a (i.e., Figure 6.1b, c, and d), there is exactly *one entrance into the construct* and exactly *one exit out of the construct*. Thus, it is easy to replace any task of the form of Figure 6.1a with whichever of its three decompositions apply. We will see how with several examples.

6.1.3 LC-3 Control Instructions to Implement the Three Constructs

Before we move on to an example, we illustrate in Figure 6.2 the use of LC-3 control instructions to direct the program counter to carry out each of the three

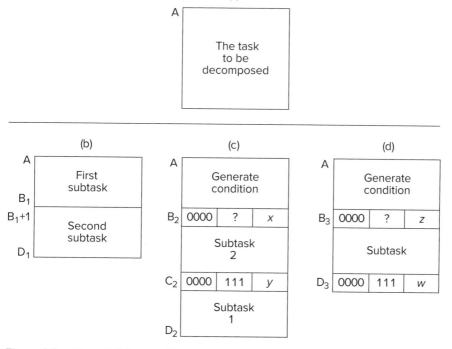

Figure 6.2   Use of LC-3 control instructions to implement structured programming.

decomposition constructs. That is, Figure 6.2b, c, and d corresponds respectively to the three constructs shown in Figure 6.1b, c, and d.

We use the letters A, B, C, and D to represent addresses in memory containing LC-3 instructions. The letter A, for example, represents the address of the first LC-3 instruction to be executed in all three cases, since it is the starting address of the task to be decomposed (shown in Figure 6.2a).

Figure 6.2b illustrates the control flow of the sequential decomposition. Note that no control instructions are needed since the PC is incremented from Address B_1 to Address B_1+1. The program continues to execute instructions through address D_1. It does not return to the first subtask.

Figure 6.2c illustrates the control flow of the conditional decomposition. First, a condition is generated, resulting in the setting of one of the condition codes. This condition is tested by the conditional branch instruction at Address B_2. If the condition is true, the PC is set to Address C_2+1, and subtask 1 is executed. (*Note: x* equals 1 + the number of instructions in subtask 2.) If the condition is false, the PC (which had been incremented during the FETCH phase of the branch instruction) fetches the instruction at Address B_2+1, and subtask 2 is executed. Subtask 2 terminates in a branch instruction that at address C_2 unconditionally branches to D_2+1. (*Note: y* equals the number of instructions in subtask 1.)

Figure 6.2d illustrates the control flow of the iterative decomposition. As in the case of the conditional construct, first a condition is generated, a condition code is set, and a conditional branch instruction is executed. In this case, the condition bits of the instruction at address B_3 are set to cause a conditional branch if the condition generated is false. If the condition is false, the PC is set to address D_3+1. (*Note: z* equals 1 + the number of instructions in the subtask in Figure 6.2d.) On the other hand, as long as the condition is true, the PC will be incremented to B_3+1, and the subtask will be executed. The subtask terminates in an unconditional branch instruction at address D_3, which sets the PC to A to again generate and test the condition. (*Note: w* equals the total number of instructions in the decomposition shown as Figure 6.2d.)

Now, we are ready to move on to an example.

6.1.4 The Character Count Example from Chapter 5, Revisited

Recall the example of Section 5.5. The statement of the problem is as follows: "We wish to input a character from the keyboard, count the number of occurrences of that character in a file, and display that count on the monitor."

The systematic decomposition of this English language statement of the problem to the final LC-3 implementation is shown in Figure 6.3. Figure 6.3a is a brief statement of the problem.

In order to solve the problem, it is always a good idea first to examine exactly what is being asked for, and what is available to help solve the problem. In this case, the statement of the problem says that we will get the character of interest from the keyboard, and that we must examine all the characters in a file and determine how many are identical to the character obtained from the keyboard. Finally, we must output the result.

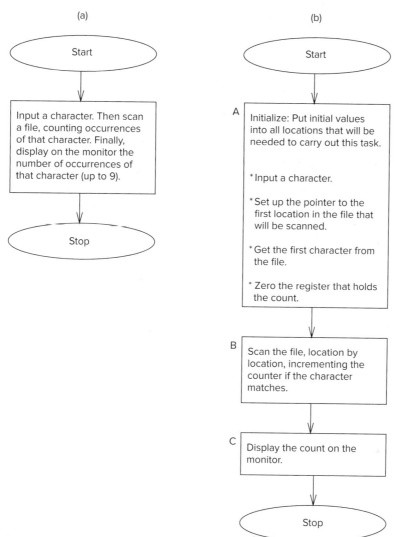

Figure 6.3 Stepwise refinement of the character count program (Fig. 6.3 continued on next page.)

To do this, we will need to examine in turn all the characters in a file, we will need to compare each to the character we input from the keyboard, and we will need a counter to increment each time we get a match.

We will need registers to hold all these pieces of information:

1. The character input from the keyboard.
2. Where we are (a pointer) in our scan of the file.
3. The character in the file that is currently being examined.
4. The count of the number of occurrences.

We will also need to know when we have reached the end of the file.

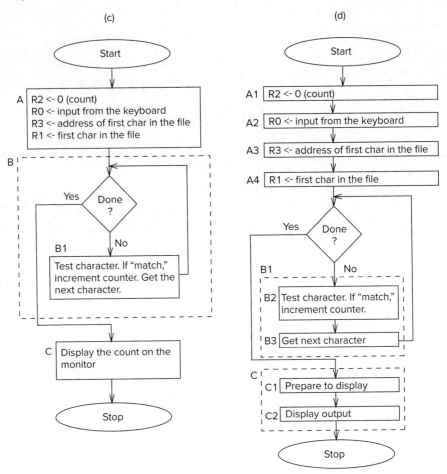

Figure 6.3   Stepwise refinement of the character count program (Fig. 6.3 continued on next page.)

The problem decomposes naturally (using the sequential construct) into three parts as shown in Figure 6.3b: (A) initialization, which includes keyboard input of the character to be "counted," (B) the process of determining how many occurrences of the character are present in the file, and (C) displaying the count on the monitor.

We have seen the importance of proper initialization in several examples already. Before a computer program can get to the crux of the problem, it must have the correct initial values. These initial values do not just show up in the GPRs by magic. They get there as a result of the first set of steps in every algorithm: the initialization of its variables.

In this particular algorithm, initialization (as we said in Chapter 5) consists of starting the counter at 0, setting the pointer to the address of the first character in the file to be examined, getting an input character from the keyboard, and getting the first character from the file. Collectively, these four steps comprise the initialization of the algorithm shown in Figure 6.3b as A.

(e)

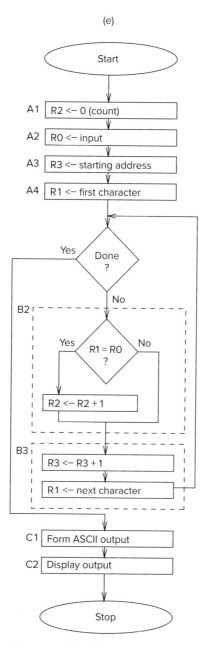

Figure 6.3 Stepwise refinement of the character count program (continued Fig. 6.3 from previous page.)

Figure 6.3c decomposes B into an iteration construct, such that as long as there are characters in the file to examine, the loop iterates. B1 shows what gets accomplished in each iteration. The character is tested and the count incremented if there is a match. Then the next character is prepared for examination. Recall from Chapter 5 that there are two basic techniques for controlling the number of iterations of a loop: the sentinel method and the use of a counter. Since we are unlikely to know how many characters there are in a random file, and since each file ends with an end of text (EOT) character, our choice is obvious. We use the sentinel method, that is, testing each character to see if we are examining a character in the file or the EOT character.

Figure 6.3c also shows the initialization step in greater detail. Four LC-3 registers (R0, R1, R2, and R3) have been specified to handle the four requirements of the algorithm: the input character from the keyboard, the current character being tested, the counter, and the pointer to the next character to be tested.

Figure 6.3d decomposes both B1 and C using the sequential construct in both cases. In the case of B1, first the current character is tested (B2), and the counter incremented if we have a match, and then the next character is fetched (B3). In the case of C, first the count is prepared for display by converting it from a 2's complement integer to an ASCII code (C1), and then the actual character output is performed (C2).

Finally, Figure 6.3e completes the decomposition, replacing B2 with the elements of the condition construct and B3 with the sequential construct (first the pointer is incremented, and then the next character to be scanned is loaded).

The last step (and usually the easiest part) is to write the LC-3 code corresponding to each box in Figure 6.3e. Note that Figure 6.3e is essentially identical to Figure 5.16 of Chapter 5 (except now you know where it all came from!).

Before leaving this topic, it is worth pointing out that it is not always possible to understand everything at the outset. When you find that to be the case, it is not a signal simply to throw up your hands and quit. In such cases (which realistically are most cases), you should see if you can make sense of a piece of the problem and expand from there. Problems are like puzzles; initially they can be opaque, but the more you work at it, the more they yield under your attack. Once you do understand what is given, what is being asked for, and how to proceed, you are ready to return to square one (Figure 6.3a) and restart the process of systematically decomposing the problem.

6.2 Debugging

Debugging a program is pretty much applied common sense. A simple example comes to mind: You are driving to a place you have never visited, and somewhere along the way you made a wrong turn. What do you do now? One common "driving debugging" technique is to wander aimlessly, hoping to find your way back. When that does not work, and you are finally willing to listen to the person sitting next to you, you turn around and return to some "known" position on the route. Then, using a map (very difficult for some people), you follow the directions provided, periodically comparing where you are (from landmarks you see out the window) with where the map says you should be, until you reach your desired destination.

Debugging is somewhat like that. A logical error in a program can make you take a wrong turn. The simplest way to keep track of where you are as compared to where you want to be is to *trace* the program. This consists of keeping track of the **sequence** of instructions that have been executed and the **results** produced by each instruction executed. When you examine the sequence of instructions executed, you can detect errors in the flow of the program. When you compare what each instruction has done to what it is supposed to do, you can detect logical errors in the program. In short, when the behavior of the program as it is executing is different from what it should be doing, you know there is a bug.

A useful technique is to partition the program into parts, often referred to as *modules*, and examine the results that have been computed at the end of execution of each module. In fact, the structured programming approach discussed in Section 6.1 can help you determine where in the program's execution you should examine results. This allows you to systematically get to the point where you are focusing your attention on the instruction or instructions that are causing the problem.

6.2.1 Debugging Operations

Many sophisticated debugging tools are offered in the marketplace, and undoubtedly you will use many of them in the years ahead. In Chapter 15, for example, we will examine debugging techniques using a source-level debugger for C.

Right now, however, we wish to stay at the level of the machine architecture, so we will see what we can accomplish with a few very elementary interactive debugging operations. We will set breakpoints, single-step, and examine the state of a program written in the LC-3 ISA.

In Chapter 15, we will see these same concepts again: breakpoints, single-stepping, and examining program state that we are introducing here, but applied to a C program, instead of the 0s and 1s of a program written in the LC-3 ISA.

When debugging interactively, the user sits in front of the keyboard and monitor and issues commands to the computer. In our case, this means operating an LC-3 simulator, using the menu available with the simulator. It is important to be able to:

1. Write values into memory locations and into registers.
2. Execute instruction sequences in a program.
3. Stop execution when desired.
4. Examine what is in memory and registers at any point in the program.

   These few simple operations will go a long way toward debugging programs.

6.2.1.1 Set Values

In order to test the execution of a part of a program in isolation without having to worry about parts of the program that come before it, it is useful to first write values in memory and in registers that would have been written by earlier parts of the program. For example, suppose one module in your program supplies input from a keyboard, and a subsequent module operates on that input. Suppose you want to test the second module before you have finished debugging the first module. If you know that the keyboard input module ends up with an ASCII code in R0, you can test the module that operates on that input by first writing an ASCII code into R0.

6.2.1.2 Execute Sequences

It is important to be able to execute a sequence of instructions and then stop execution in order to examine the values that the program has computed as a result of executing that sequence. Three simple mechanisms are usually available for doing this: run, step, and set breakpoints.

The **Run** command causes the program to execute until something makes it stop. This can be either a HALT instruction or a breakpoint.

The **Step** command causes the program to execute a fixed number of instructions and then stop. The interactive user enters the number of instructions he/she wishes the simulator to execute before it stops. When that number is 1, the computer executes one instruction, then stops. Executing one instruction and then stopping is called *single-stepping*. It allows the person debugging the program to examine the individual results of each instruction executed.

The **Set Breakpoint** command causes the program to stop execution at a specific instruction in a program. Executing the debugging command Set Breakpoint consists of adding an address to a list maintained by the simulator. During the FETCH phase of each instruction, the simulator compares the PC with the addresses in that list. If there is a match, execution stops. Thus, the effect of setting a breakpoint is to allow execution to proceed until the PC contains an address that has been set as a breakpoint. This is useful if one wishes to know what has been computed up to a particular point in the program. One sets a breakpoint at that address in the program and executes the Run command. The program executes until that point and then stops so the user can examine what has been computed up to that point. (When one no longer wishes to have the program stop execution at that point, the breakpoint can be removed by executing the Clear Breakpoint command.)

6.2.1.3 Display Values

Finally, it is useful to examine the results of execution when the simulator has stopped execution. The Display command allows the user to examine the contents of any memory location or any register.

6.2.2 Use of an Interactive Debugger

We conclude this chapter with four examples, showing how the use of interactive debugging operations can help us find errors in a program. We have chosen the following four errors: (1) incorrectly setting the loop control so that the loop executes an incorrect number of times, (2) confusing the load instruction 0010, which loads a register with the *contents* of a memory location, with the load effective address instruction 1110, which loads a register with the *address* of a memory location, (3) forgetting which instructions set the condition codes, resulting in a branch instruction testing the wrong condition, and (4) not covering all possible cases of input values.

6.2.2.1 Example 1: Multiplying Without a Multiply Instruction

Let's start with an example we have seen before, multiplying two positive integers when the computer (such as the LC-3) does not have a multiply instruction. This time we will assume the two integers to be multiplied are in R4 and R5, and the result of execution (the product of those two integers) will be put in R2. Figure 6.4 shows the program we have written to do the job.

Address	15	14	13	12	11	10	9	8	7	6	5	4	3	2	1	0	
x3200	0	1	0	1	0	1	0	0	1	0	1	0	0	0	0	0	R2 <- 0
x3201	0	0	0	1	0	1	0	0	1	0	0	0	0	1	0	0	R2 <- R2 + R4
x3202	0	0	0	1	1	0	1	1	0	1	1	1	1	1	1	1	R5 <- R5 - 1
x3203	0	0	0	0	0	1	1	1	1	1	1	1	1	1	0	1	BRzp x3201
x3204	1	1	1	1	0	0	0	0	0	0	1	0	0	1	0	1	HALT

Figure 6.4   Debugging Example 1. An LC-3 program to multiply (without a Multiply instruction).

If we examine the program instruction by instruction, we note that the program first clears R2 (i.e., initializes R2 to 0) and then attempts to perform the multiplication by adding R4 to itself a number of times equal to the initial value in R5. Each time an add is performed, R5 is decremented. When R5 = 0, the program terminates.

It looks like the program should work! Upon execution, however, we find that if R4 initially contains the integer 10 and R5 initially contains the integer 3, the program produces the result 40. What went wrong?

Our first thought is to trace the program. Before we do that, we note that the program assumes positive integers in R4 and R5. Using the Set Values command, we put the value 10 in R4 and the value 3 in R5.

It is also useful to annotate each instruction with some algorithmic description of **exactly** what each instruction is doing. While this can be very tedious and not very helpful in a 10,000-instruction program, it often can be very helpful after one has isolated a bug to within a few instructions. There is a big difference between quickly eyeballing a sequence of instructions and stating precisely what each instruction is doing. Quickly eyeballing often results in mistaking what one eyeballs! Stating precisely usually does not. We have included in Figure 6.4, next to each instruction, such an annotation.

Figure 6.5a shows a trace of the program, which we can obtain by single-stepping. The column labeled *PC* shows the contents of the PC at the start of each instruction. R2, R4, and R5 show the values in those three registers at the start of each instruction.

A quick look at the trace shows that the loop body was executed four times, rather than three. That suggests that the condition codes for our branch instruction could have been set incorrectly. From there it is a short step to noting that the branch should have been taken only when R5 was positive, and not when R5 is 0. That is, bit [10]=1 in the branch instruction caused the extra iteration of the loop.

(a)

PC	R2	R4	R5
x3201	0	10	3
x3202	10	10	3
x3203	10	10	2
x3201	10	10	2
x3202	20	10	2
x3203	20	10	1
x3201	20	10	1
x3202	30	10	1
x3203	30	10	0
x3201	30	10	0
x3202	40	10	0
x3203	40	10	−1
x3204	40	10	−1
	40	10	−1

(b)

PC	R2	R4	R5
x3203	10	10	2
x3203	20	10	1
x3203	30	10	0
x3203	40	10	−1

Figure 6.5   Debugging Example 1. (a) A trace of the Multiply program. (b) Tracing with breakpoints.

The program can be corrected by simply replacing the instruction at x3203 with

15	14	13	12	11	10	9	8	7	6	5	4	3	2	1	0
0	0	0	0	0	0	1	1	1	1	1	1	1	1	0	1

BR   n   z   p   −3

We should also note that we could have saved a lot of the work of tracing the program by using a breakpoint. That is, instead of examining the results of **each instruction,** if we set a breakpoint at x3203, we would examine the results of **each iteration** of the loop. Setting a breakpoint to stop the program after each iteration of the loop is often enough to have us see the problem (and debug the program) without the tedium of single-stepping each iteration of the loop. Figure 6.5b shows the results of tracing the program, where each step is one iteration of the loop. We see that the loop executed four times instead of three, immediately identifying the bug.

One last comment before we leave this example. Before we started tracing the program, we initialized R4 and R5 with values 10 and 3. When testing a program, it is important to judiciously choose the initial values for the test. Here, the program stated that the program had to work only for positive integers. So, 10 and 3 are probably OK. What if a (different) multiply program had been written to work for all integers? Then we could have tried initial values of −6 and 3, 4 and −12, and perhaps −5 and −7. The problem with this set of tests is that we have left out one of the most important initial values of all: 0. For the program to work for "all" integers, it has to work for 0 as well. The point is that, for a program to work, it must work for all valid source operands, and a good test of such a program is to set source operands to the unusual values, the ones the programmer may have failed to consider. These values are often referred to colloquially as *corner*

cases, and more often that not, they are the values for which the program does not operate correctly.

6.2.2.2 Example 2: Adding a Column of Numbers

The program of Figure 6.6 is supposed to add the numbers stored in the ten locations starting with x3100, and leave the result in R1.

Address	15	14	13	12	11	10	9	8	7	6	5	4	3	2	1	0	
x3000	0	1	0	1	0	0	1	0	0	1	1	0	0	0	0	0	R1 <- 0
x3001	0	1	0	1	1	0	0	1	0	0	1	0	0	0	0	0	R4 <- 0
x3002	0	0	0	1	1	0	0	1	0	0	1	0	1	0	1	0	R4 <- R4 + 10
x3003	0	0	1	0	0	1	0	0	1	1	1	1	1	1	0	0	R2 <- M[x3100]
x3004	0	1	1	0	0	1	1	0	1	0	0	0	0	0	0	0	R3 <- M[R2]
x3005	0	0	0	1	0	1	0	0	1	0	1	0	0	0	0	1	R2 <- R2 + 1
x3006	0	0	0	1	0	0	1	0	0	1	0	0	0	0	1	1	R1 <- R1 + R3
x3007	0	0	0	1	1	0	0	1	0	0	1	1	1	1	1	1	R4 <- R4 - 1
x3008	0	0	0	0	0	0	1	1	1	1	1	1	1	0	1	1	BRp x3004
x3009	1	1	1	1	0	0	0	0	0	0	1	0	0	1	0	1	HALT

Figure 6.6   Debugging Example 2. An LC-3 program to add 10 integers.

The contents of the 20 memory locations starting at location x3100 are shown in Figure 6.7.

The program should work as follows: The instructions in x3000 to x3003 initialize the variables. In x3000, the sum (R1) is initialized to 0. In x3001 and

Address	Contents
x3100	x3107
x3101	x2819
x3102	x0110
x3103	x0310
x3104	x0110
x3105	x1110
x3106	x11B1
x3107	x0019
x3108	x0007
x3109	x0004
x310A	x0000
x310B	x0000
x310C	x0000
x310D	x0000
x310E	x0000
x310F	x0000
x3110	x0000
x3111	x0000
x3112	x0000
x3113	x0000

Figure 6.7   Contents of memory locations x3100 to x3113 for debugging Example 2.

PC	R1	R2	R4
x3001	0	x	x
x3002	0	x	0
x3003	0	x	#10
x3004	0	x3107	#10

Figure 6.8   Debugging Example 2. A trace of the first four instructions of the Add program.

x3002, the loop control (R4), which counts the number of values added to R1, is initialized to #10. The program subtracts 1 each time through the loop and repeats until R4 contains 0. In x3003, the base register (R2) is initialized to the starting location of the values to be added: x3100.

From there, each time through the loop, one value is loaded into R3 (in x3004), the base register is incremented to get ready for the next iteration (x3005), the value in R3 is added to R1, which contains the running sum (x3006), the counter is decremented (x3007), the P bit is tested, and if true, the PC is set to x3004 to begin the next iteration of the loop body (x3008). After ten times through the loop, R4 contains 0, the P bit is 0, the branch is not taken, and the program terminates (x3009).

It looks like the program should work. However, when we execute the program and then check the value in R1, we find the number x0024, which is not x8135, the sum of the numbers stored in locations x3100 to x3109. What went wrong?

We turn to the debugger and trace the program. Figure 6.8 shows a trace of the first four instructions executed. Note that after the instruction at x3003 has executed, R2 contains x3107, not x3100 as we had expected. The problem is that the opcode 0010 loaded the **contents** of M[x3100] (i.e., x3107) into R2, not the **address** x3100. The result was to add the ten numbers starting at M[x3107] instead of the ten numbers starting at M[x3100].

Our mistake: We used the wrong opcode. We should have used the opcode 1110, which would have loaded R2 with the address x3100. We correct the bug by replacing the opcode 0010 with 1110, and the program runs correctly.

6.2.2.3 Example 3: Does a Sequence of Memory Locations Contain a 5?

The program of Figure 6.9 has been written to examine the contents of the ten memory locations starting at address x3100 and to store a 1 in R0 if any of them contains a 5 and a 0 in R0 if none of them contains a 5.

The program is supposed to do the following: The first six instructions (at x3000 to x3005) initialize R0 to 1, R1 to −5, and R3 to 10. The instruction at x3006 initializes R4 to the address (x3100) of the first location to be tested, and x3007 loads the contents of x3100 into R2.

The instructions at x3008 and x3009 determine if R2 contains the value 5 by adding −5 to R2 and branching to x300F if the result is 0. Since R0 is initialized to 1, the program terminates with R0 reporting the presence of a 5 among the locations tested.

Address	15	14	13	12	11	10	9	8	7	6	5	4	3	2	1	0	
x3000	0	1	0	1	0	0	0	0	0	0	1	0	0	0	0	0	R0 <- 0
x3001	0	0	0	1	0	0	0	0	0	0	1	0	0	0	0	1	R0 <- R0 + 1
x3002	0	1	0	1	0	0	1	0	0	1	1	0	0	0	0	0	R1 <- 0
x3003	0	0	0	1	0	0	1	0	0	1	1	1	1	0	1	1	R1 <- R1 - 5
x3004	0	1	0	1	0	1	1	0	1	1	1	0	0	0	0	0	R3 <- 0
x3005	0	0	0	1	0	1	1	0	1	1	1	0	1	0	1	0	R3 <- R3 + 10
x3006	0	0	1	0	1	0	0	0	0	0	0	0	1	0	0	1	R4 <- M[x3010]
x3007	0	1	1	0	0	1	0	1	0	0	0	0	0	0	0	0	R2 <- M[R4]
x3008	0	0	0	1	0	1	0	0	1	0	0	0	0	0	0	1	R2 <- R2 + R1
x3009	0	0	0	0	0	1	0	0	0	0	0	0	0	1	0	1	BRz x300F
x300A	0	0	0	1	1	0	0	1	0	0	1	0	0	0	0	1	R4 <- R4 + 1
x300B	0	0	0	1	0	1	1	0	1	1	1	1	1	1	1	1	R3 <- R3 - 1
x300C	0	1	1	0	0	1	0	1	0	0	0	0	0	0	0	0	R2 <- M[R4]
x300D	0	0	0	0	0	0	1	1	1	1	1	1	1	0	1	0	BRp x3008
x300E	0	1	0	1	0	0	0	0	0	0	1	0	0	0	0	0	R0 <- 0
x300F	1	1	1	1	0	0	0	0	0	0	1	0	0	1	0	1	HALT
x3010	0	0	1	1	0	0	0	1	0	0	0	0	0	0	0	0	x3100

Figure 6.9   Debugging Example 3. An LC-3 program to detect the presence of a 5.

x300A increments R4, preparing to load the next value. x300B decrements R3, indicating the number of values remaining to be tested. x300C loads the next value into R2. x300D branches back to x3008 to repeat the process if R3 still indicates more values to be tested. If R3 = 0, we have exhausted our tests, so R0 is set to 0 (x300E), and the program terminates (x300F).

When we run the program for some sample data that contains a 5 in one of the memory locations, the program terminates with R0 = 0, indicating there were no 5s in locations x3100 to x310A.

What went wrong? We examine a trace of the program, with a breakpoint set at x300D. The results are shown in Figure 6.10.

The first time the PC is at x300D, we have already tested the value stored in x3100, we have loaded 7 (the contents of x3101) into R2, and R3 indicates there are still nine values to be tested. R4 contains the address from which we most recently loaded R2.

The second time the PC is at x300D, we have loaded 32 (the contents of x3102) into R2, and R3 indicates there are eight values still to be tested. The third time the PC is at x300D, we have loaded 0 (the contents of x3103) into R2, and R3 indicates seven values still to be tested. The value 0 loaded into R2 causes the branch instruction at x300D to be not taken, R0 is set to 0 (x300E), and the program terminates (x300F) before the locations containing a 5 are tested.

PC	R1	R2	R3	R4
x300D	-5	7	9	3101
x300D	-5	32	8	3102
x300D	-5	0	7	3013

Figure 6.10   Debugging Example 3. Tracing Example 3 with a breakpoint at x300D.

The error in the program occurred because the branch instruction immediately followed the load instruction that set the condition codes based on what was loaded. That wiped out the condition codes set by the iteration control instruction at x300B, which was keeping track of the number of iterations left to do. Since the branch instruction should branch if there are still more memory locations to examine, the branch instruction should have immediately followed the iteration control instruction and NOT the load instruction which also sets condition codes.

A conditional branch instruction should be considered the second instruction in a pair of instructions.

```
Instruction A  ; sets the condition codes
BR instruction ; branches based on the condition codes
```

The first instruction in the pair (Instruction A) sets the condition codes. The second instruction (BR) branches or not, depending on the condition codes set by instruction A. It is important to never insert any instruction that sets condition codes between instruction A and the branch instruction, since doing so will wipe out the condition codes set by instruction A that are needed by the branch instruction.

Since the branch at x300D was based on the value loaded into R2, instead of how many values remained to be tested, the third time the branch instruction was executed, it was not taken when it should have been. If we interchange the instructions at x300B and x300C, the branch instruction at x300D immediately follows the iteration control instruction, and the program executes correctly.

It is also worth noting that the branch at x300D *coincidentally* behaved correctly the first two times it executed because the load instruction at x300C loaded positive values into R2. The bug did not produce incorrect behavior until the third iteration. It would be nice if bugs would manifest themselves the first time they are encountered, but that is often not the case. Coincidences do occur, which adds to the challenges of debugging.

6.2.2.4 Example 4: Finding the First 1 in a Word

Our last example contains an error that is usually one of the hardest to find, as we will see. The program of Figure 6.11 has been written to examine the contents of a memory location, find the first bit (reading from left to right) that is set, and store its bit position into R1. If no bit is set, the program is to store −1 in R1. For

Address	15	14	13	12	11	10	9	8	7	6	5	4	3	2	1	0	
x3000	0	1	0	1	0	0	1	0	0	1	1	0	0	0	0	0	R1 <- 0
x3001	0	0	0	1	0	0	1	0	0	1	1	0	1	1	1	1	R1 <- R1 + 15
x3002	1	0	1	0	0	1	0	0	0	0	0	0	0	1	1	0	R2 <- M[M[x3009]]
x3003	0	0	0	0	1	0	0	0	0	0	0	0	0	1	0	0	BRn x3008
x3004	0	0	0	1	0	0	1	0	0	1	1	1	1	1	1	1	R1 <- R1 - 1
x3005	0	0	0	1	0	1	0	0	1	0	0	0	0	0	1	0	R2 <- R2 + R2
x3006	0	0	0	0	1	0	0	0	0	0	0	0	0	0	0	1	BRn x3008
x3007	0	0	0	0	1	1	1	1	1	1	1	1	1	1	0	0	BRnzp x3004
x3008	1	1	1	1	0	0	0	0	0	0	1	0	0	1	0	1	HALT
x3009	0	0	1	1	0	1	0	0	0	0	0	0	0	0	0	0	x3400

Figure 6.11   Debugging Example 4. An LC-3 program to find the first 1 in a word.

example, if the location examined contained 0010000110000000, the program would terminate with R1 = 13. If the location contained 0000000000000110, the program would terminate with R1 = 2.

The program Figure 6.11 is supposed to work as follows (and it usually does): x3000 and x3001 initialize R1 to 15, the bit number of the leftmost bit.

x3002 loads R2 with the contents of x3400, the bit pattern to be examined. Since x3400 is too far from x3000 for a LD instruction, the load indirect instruction is used, obtaining the location of the bit pattern in x3009.

x3003 tests the most significant bit of the bit pattern (bit [15]), and if it is a 1, branches to x3008, where the program terminates with R1=15. If the most significant bit is 0, the branch is not taken, and processing continues at x3004.

The loop body, locations x3004 to x3007, does two things. First (x3004), it subtracts 1 from R1, yielding the bit number of the next bit to the right. Second (x3005), it adds R2 to itself, resulting in the contents of R2 shifting left one bit, resulting in the next bit to the right being shifted into the bit [15] position. Third (x3006), the BR instruction tests the "new" bit [15], and if it is a 1, branches to x3008, where the program halts with R1 containing the actual bit number of the current leftmost bit. If the new bit [15] is 0, x3007 is an unconditional branch to x3004 for the next iteration of the loop body.

The process continues until the first 1 is found. The program works correctly almost all the time. However, when we ran the program on our data, the program failed to terminate. What went wrong?

A trace of the program, with a breakpoint set at x3007, is shown in Figure 6.12.

PC	R1
x3007	14
x3007	13
x3007	12
x3007	11
x3007	10
x3007	9
x3007	8
x3007	7
x3007	6
x3007	5
x3007	4
x3007	3
x3007	2
x3007	1
x3007	0
x3007	−1
x3007	−2
x3007	−3
x3007	−4

Figure 6.12   Debugging Example 4. A Trace of Debugging Example 4 with a breakpoint at x3007.

Each time the PC contained the address x3007, R1 contained a value smaller by 1 than the previous time. The reason is as follows: After R1 was decremented and the value in R2 shifted left, the bit tested was a 0, and so the program did not terminate. This continued for values in R1 equal to 14, 13, 12, 11, 10, 9, 8, 7, 6, 5, 4, 3, 2, 1, 0, −1, −2, −3, −4, and so forth.

The problem was that the initial value in x3400 was x0000. The program worked fine as long as there was at least one 1 present. For the case where x3400 contained all zeros, the conditional branch at x3006 was never taken, and so the program continued with execution of x3007, then x3004, x3005, x3006, x3007, and then back again to x3004. There was no way to break out of the sequence x3004, x3005, x3006, x3007, and back again to x3004. We call the sequence x3004 to x3007 a loop. Because there is no way for the program execution to break out of this loop, we call it an *infinite loop*. Thus, the program never terminates, and so we can never get the correct answer.

Again, we emphasize that this is often the hardest error to detect because it is as we said earlier a corner case. The programmer assumed that at least one bit was set. What if no bits are set? That is, it is not enough for a program to execute correctly most of the time; it must execute correctly all the time, independent of the data that the program is asked to process.

Exercises

6.1 Can a procedure that is *not* an algorithm be constructed from the three basic constructs of structured programming? If so, demonstrate through an example.

6.2 The LC-3 has no Subtract instruction. If a programmer needed to subtract two numbers, he/she would have to write a routine to handle it. Show the systematic decomposition of the process of subtracting two integers.

6.3 Recall the machine busy example from previous chapters. Suppose memory location x4000 contains an integer between 0 and 15 identifying a particular machine that has just become busy. Suppose further that the value in memory location x4001 tells which machines are busy and which machines are idle. Write an LC-3 machine language program that sets the appropriate bit in x4001 indicating that the machine in x4000 is busy.

For example, if x4000 contains x0005 and x4001 contains x3101 at the start of execution, x4001 should contain x3121 after your program terminates.

6.4 Write a short LC-3 program that compares the two numbers in R1 and R2 and puts the value 0 in R0 if R1 = R2, 1 if R1 > R2, and −1 if R1 < R2.

6.5 Which of the two algorithms for multiplying two numbers is preferable and why? $88 \cdot 3 = 88 + 88 + 88$ OR $3 + 3 + 3 + 3 + \ldots + 3$?

6.6 Use your answers from Exercises 6.4 and 6.5 to develop a program that efficiently multiplies two integers and places the result in R3. Show the complete systematic decomposition, from the problem statement to the final program.

6.7 What does the following LC-3 program do?

x3001	1110	0000	0000	1100
x3002	1110	0010	0001	0000
x3003	0101	0100	1010	0000
x3004	0010	0100	0001	0011
x3005	0110	0110	0000	0000
x3006	0110	1000	0100	0000
x3007	0001	0110	1100	0100
x3008	0111	0110	0000	0000
x3009	0001	0000	0010	0001
x300A	0001	0010	0110	0001
x300B	0001	0100	1011	1111
x300C	0000	0011	1111	1000
x300D	1111	0000	0010	0101
x300E	0000	0000	0000	0101
x300F	0000	0000	0000	0100
x3010	0000	0000	0000	0011
x3011	0000	0000	0000	0110
x3012	0000	0000	0000	0010
x3013	0000	0000	0000	0100
x3014	0000	0000	0000	0111
x3015	0000	0000	0000	0110
x3016	0000	0000	0000	1000
x3017	0000	0000	0000	0111
x3018	0000	0000	0000	0101

6.8 Why is it necessary to initialize R2 in the character counting example in Section 6.1.4? In other words, in what manner might the program behave incorrectly if the R2 ← 0 step were removed from the routine?

6.9 Using the iteration construct, write an LC-3 machine language routine that displays exactly 100 Zs on the screen.

6.10 Using the conditional construct, write an LC-3 machine language routine that determines if a number stored in R2 is odd.

6.11 Write an LC-3 machine language routine to increment each of the numbers stored in memory location A through memory location B. Assume these locations have already been initialized with meaningful numbers. The addresses A and B can be found in memory locations x3100 and x3101.

6.12 *a.* Write an LC-3 machine language routine that echoes the last character typed at the keyboard. If the user types an *R,* the program then immediately outputs an *R* on the screen.

b. Expand the routine from part *a* such that it echoes a line at a time. For example, if the user types:

The quick brown fox jumps over the lazy dog.

then the program waits for the user to press the Enter key (the ASCII code for which is x0A) and then outputs the same line.

6.13   Notice that we can shift a number to the left by one bit position by adding it to itself. For example, when the binary number 0011 is added to itself, the result is 0110. Shifting a number one bit pattern to the right is not as easy. Devise a routine in LC-3 machine code to shift the contents of memory location x3100 to the right by one bit.

6.14   Consider the following machine language program:

x3000	0101	0100	1010	0000
x3001	0001	0010	0111	1111
x3002	0001	0010	0111	1111
x3003	0001	0010	0111	1111
x3004	0000	1000	0000	0010
x3005	0001	0100	1010	0001
x3006	0000	1111	1111	1010
x3007	1111	0000	0010	0101

What are the possible initial values of R1 that cause the final value in R2 to be 3?

6.15   Shown below are the contents of memory and registers **before** and **after** the LC-3 instruction at location x3010 is executed. Your job: Identify the instruction stored in x3010. *Note:* There is enough information below to uniquely specify the instruction at x3010.

	Before	After
R0:	x3208	x3208
R1:	x2d7c	x2d7c
R2:	xe373	xe373
R3:	x2053	x2053
R4:	x33ff	x33ff
R5:	x3f1f	x3f1f
R6:	xf4a2	xf4a2
R7:	x5220	x5220
...		
x3400:	x3001	x3001
x3401:	x7a00	x7a00
x3402:	x7a2b	x7a2b
x3403:	xa700	xa700
x3404:	xf011	xf011
x3405:	x2003	x2003
x3406:	x31ba	xe373
x3407:	xc100	xc100
x3408:	xefef	xefef
...		

6.16 An LC-3 program is located in memory locations x3000 to x3006. It starts executing at x3000. If we keep track of all values loaded into the MAR as the program executes, we will get a sequence that starts as follows. Such a sequence of values is referred to as a trace.

MAR Trace
---
x3000
x3005
x3001
x3002
x3006
x4001
x3003
x0021

We have shown below some of the bits stored in locations x3000 to x3006. Your job is to fill in each blank space with a 0 or a 1, as appropriate.

x3000	0	0	1	0	0	0	0									
x3001	0	0	0	1	0	0	0	0	0	0	1	0	0	0	0	1
x3002	1	0	1	1	0	0	0									
x3003																
x3004	1	1	1	1	0	0	0	0	0	0	1	0	0	1	0	1
x3005	0	0	0	0	0	0	0	0	0	0	1	1	0	0	0	0
x3006																

6.17 Shown below are the contents of registers before and after the LC-3 instruction at location x3210 is executed. Your job: Identify the instruction stored in x3210. *Note:* There is enough information below to uniquely specify the instruction at x3210.

	Before	After
R0:	xFF1D	xFF1D
R1:	x301C	x301C
R2:	x2F11	x2F11
R3:	x5321	x5321
R4:	x331F	x331F
R5:	x1F22	x1F22
R6:	x01FF	x01FF
R7:	x341F	x3211
PC:	x3210	x3220
N:	0	0
Z:	1	1
P:	0	0

6.18 The LC-3 has no Divide instruction. A programmer needing to divide two numbers would have to write a routine to handle it. Show the systematic decomposition of the process of dividing two positive integers. Write an LC-3 machine language program starting at location x3000 that divides the number in memory location x4000 by the number in memory location x4001 and stores the quotient at x5000 and the remainder at x500l.

6.19 It is often necessary to encrypt messages to keep them away from prying eyes. A message can be represented as a string of ASCII characters, one per memory location, in consecutive memory locations. Bits [15:8] of each location contain 0, and the location immediately following the string contains x0000.

A student who has not taken this course has written the following LC-3 machine language program to encrypt the message starting at location x4000 by adding 4 to each character and storing the resulting message at x5000. For example, if the message at x4000 is "Matt," then the encrypted message at x5000 is "Qeyy." However, there are four bugs in his code. Find and correct these errors so that the program works correctly.

x3000	1110	0000	0000	1010
x3001	0010	0010	0000	1010
x3002	0110	0100	0000	0000
x3003	0000	0100	0000	0101
x3004	0001	0100	1010	0101
x3005	0111	0100	0100	0000
x3006	0001	0000	0010	0001
x3007	0001	0010	0110	0001
x3008	0000	1001	1111	1001
x3009	0110	0100	0100	0000
x300A	1111	0000	0010	0101
x300B	0100	0000	0000	0000
x300C	0101	0000	0000	0000

6.20 Redo Exercise 6.18 for all integers, not just positive integers.

6.21 You have been asked to design the volume control system in a stereo. The user controls the volume by using Volume Up and Volume Down buttons on the stereo. When the user presses the Volume Up button, the volume should increase by 1; when the user presses the Volume Down button, the volume should decrease by 1. The volume level is represented as a four-bit unsigned value, ranging from 0 to 15. If the user presses Volume Up when the volume is already at the maximum level of 15, the volume should remain at 15; similarly, if the user presses Volume Down when the volume is already at the minimum level of 0, the volume should remain at 0. The memory location x3100 has been directly hooked up to the speakers so that reading bits 3 through 0 from that memory location will give the current speaker volume, while writing bits [3:0] of that memory location will set the new speaker volume.

When the user presses one of the volume buttons, the stereo hardware will reset the PC of the processor to x3000 and begin execution. If the user presses Volume Up, then memory location x3101 will be set to 1; otherwise, if the user presses Volume Down, then the memory location x3101 will be set to 0.

Below is the program that controls the volume on the stereo. Two of the instructions in the program have been left out. Your job: Fill in the missing instructions so that the program controls the volume correctly as specified.

Address	Contents	Description
x3000	0010000011111111	R0 ← M[x3100]
x3001	0010001011111111	R1 ← M[x3101]
x3002	0000010000000100	Branch to x3007 if Z is set
x3003		
x3004	0000010000000101	Branch to x300A if Z is set
x3005	0001000000100001	R0 ← R0 + x0001
x3006	0000111000000011	Branch always to x300A
x3007	0001001000100000	R1 ← R0 + x0000
x3008	0000010000000001	Branch to x300A if Z is set
x3009		
x300A	0011000011110101	M[x3100] ← R0
x300B	1111000000100101	TRAP x25

★6.22 A warehouse is controlled by an electronic lock having an n-digit combination. The electronic lock has ten buttons labeled 0 to 9 on its face. To open the lock, a user presses a sequence of n buttons. The corresponding ASCII characters get loaded into sequential locations of memory, starting at location x3150. After n buttons have been pressed, the null character x00 is loaded into the next sequential memory location. The following program determines whether or not the lock should open, depending on whether the combination entered agrees with the combination stored in the n memory locations starting at x3100. If the lock should open, the program stores a 1 in location x3050. If the lock should not open, the program stores a 0 in location x3050.

Note that some of the instructions are missing.

Complete the program by filling in the missing instructions.

x3000	0101 101 101 1 00000	; R5 <– x0000
x3001	0010 000 000001111	; R0 <– M[x3011]
x3002	0010 001 000001101	; R1 <– M[x3010]
x3003	0110 010 000 000000	; R2 <– M[R0]
x3004		
x3005	0110 011 001 000000	; R3 <– M[R1]
x3006	1001 011 011 111111	; NOT R3
x3007	0001 011 011 1 00001	; R3 <– R3 + 1
x3008		
x3009	0000 101 000000100	; Branch to x300E if N or P is set
x300A		
x300B		
x300C	0000 111 111110110	; Branch always to x3003
x300D		
x300E	0011 101 001000001	; Store R5 in x3050
x300F	1111 0000 0010 0101	; HALT
x3010	0011 0001 0000 0000	; x3100
x3011	0011 0001 0101 0000	; x3150

A simple change to the contents of memory will allow us to eliminate the instructions at memory locations x3006 and x3007 in our program. What is the change?

★6.23   The PC is loaded with x3000, and the instruction at address x3000 is executed. In fact, execution continues and four more instructions are executed. The table below contains the contents of various registers at the end of execution for each of the five (total) instructions.
Your job: Complete the table.

	PC	MAR	MDR	IR	R0	R1
Before execution starts	x3000	——	——	——	x0000	x0000
After the first finishes			xB333	x2005		
After the 2nd finishes				x0601		
After the 3rd finishes			x1___			x0001
After the 4th finishes			x1___		x6666	
After the 5th finishes				x0BFC		

Let's start execution again, starting with PC = x3000. First, we re-initialize R0 and R1 to 0, and set a breakpoint at x3004. We press RUN eleven times, and each time the program executes until the breakpoint. What are the final values of R0 and R1?

6.24   A student is debugging his program. His program does not have access to memory locations x0000 to x2FFF. Why that is the case we will discuss before the end of the book. The term is "privileged memory" but not something for you to worry about today.

He sets a breakpoint at x3050, and then starts executing the program. When the program stops, he examines the contents of several memory locations and registers, then hits single step. The simulator executes one instruction and then stops. He again examines the contents of the memory locations and registers. They are as follows:

	Before	After
PC	x3050	x3051
R0	x2F5F	xFFFF
R1	x4200	x4200
R2	x0123	x0123
R3	x2323	x2323
R4	x0010	x0010
R5	x0000	x0000
R6	x1000	x1000
R7	x0522	x0522
M[x3050]	**x6???**	**x6???**
M[x4200]	x5555	x5555
M[x4201]	xFFFF	xFFFF

Complete the contents of location x3050

| 0 | 1 | 1 | 0 | | | | | | | | | | | | |

6.25 A student is writing a program and needs to subtract the contents of R1 from the contents of R2 and put the result in R3. Instead of writing:

```
NOT    R3,R1
ADD    R3,R3,#1
ADD    R3,R3,R2
```

she writes:

```
NOT    R3,R1
.FILL  x16E1
ADD    R3,R3,R2
```

She assembles the program and attempts to execute it. Does the subtract execute correctly? Why or why not?

★**6.26** During the execution of an LC-3 program, an instruction in the program starts executing at clock cycle T and requires 15 cycles to complete. The table lists **ALL** five clock cycles during the processing of this instruction, which require use of the bus. The table shows for each of those clock cycles: which clock cycle, the state of the state machine, the value on the bus, and the important control signals that are active during that clock cycle.

Cycle	State	Bus	Important Control Signals for This Cycle
T	18	x3010	LD.MAR = 1, LD.PC =1, PCMux = PC + 1, GatePC = 1
T + 4			
T + 6		x3013	
T + 10		x4567	
T + 14		x0000	LD.REG = 1, LD.CC = 1, GateMDR = 1, DR = 001

    a. Fill in the missing entries in the table.
    b. What is the instruction being processed?
    c. Where in memory is that instruction?
    d. How many clock cycles does it take memory to read or write?
    e. There is enough information above for you to know the contents of three memory locations. What are they, and what are their contents?

★6.27   An LC-3 program starts execution at x3000. During the execution of the program, a snapshot of all eight registers was taken at six different times as shown below: before the program executes, after execution of instruction 1, after execution of instruction 2, after execution of instruction 3, after execution of instruction 4, after execution of instruction 5, and after execution of instruction 6.

Registers	Initial Value	After 1st Instruction	After 2nd Instruction	After 3rd Instruction	After 4th Instruction	After 5th Instruction	After 6th Instruction
R0	x4006	x4050	x4050	x4050	x4050	x4050	x4050
R1	x5009	x5009	x5009	x5009	x5009	x5009	x5009
R2	x4008	x4008	x4008	x4008	x4008	x4008	xC055
R3	x4002			x8005	x8005	x8005	x8005
R4	x4003	x4003	x4003	x4003			x4003
R5	x400D	x400D			x400D	x400D	x400D
R6	x400C	x400C	x400C	x400C	x400C	x400C	x400C
R7	x6001	x6001	x6001	x6001			x400E

    Also, during the execution of the program, the PC trace, the MAR trace, and the MDR trace were recorded as shown below. Note that a PC trace records the addresses of the instructions executed in sequence by the program.

PC Trace
x400D
x400E

MAR Trace	MDR Trace
	xA009
x3025	
	x1703
	x4040
x400E	x1403

Your job: Fill in the missing entries in the three tables above.

CHAPTER

7 Assembly Language

By now, you are probably a little tired of 1s and 0s and keeping track of 0001 meaning ADD and 1001 meaning NOT. Also, wouldn't it be nice if we could refer to a memory location by some meaningful symbolic name instead of memorizing its 16-bit address? And wouldn't it be nice if we could represent each instruction in some more easily comprehensible way, instead of having to keep track of which bit of an instruction conveys which individual piece of information about that instruction? It turns out that help is on the way.

In this chapter, we introduce assembly language, a mechanism that does all of the above, and more.

7.1 Assembly Language Programming— Moving Up a Level

Recall the levels of transformation identified in Figure 1.9 of Chapter 1. Algorithms are transformed into programs described in some mechanical language. This mechanical language can be, as it is in Chapter 5, the machine language of a particular computer. Recall that a program is in a computer's machine language if every instruction in the program is from the ISA of that computer.

On the other hand, the mechanical language can be more user-friendly. We generally partition mechanical languages into two classes, high-level and low-level. Of the two, high-level languages are much more user-friendly. Examples are C, C++, Java, Fortran, COBOL, Python, plus more than a thousand others. Instructions in a high-level language almost (but not quite) resemble statements in a natural language such as English. High-level languages tend to be ISA independent. That is, once you learn how to program in C (or Fortran or Python) for one ISA, it is a small step to write programs in C (or Fortran or Python) for another ISA.

Before a program written in a high-level language can be executed, it must be translated into a program in the ISA of the computer on which it is expected to execute. It is often the case that each statement in the high-level language specifies several instructions in the ISA of the computer. In Chapter 11, we will introduce the high-level language C, and in Chapters 12 through 19, we will show the relationship between various statements in C and their corresponding translations to LC-3 code. In this chapter, however, we will only move up a small step from the ISA we dealt with in Chapter 5.

A small step up from the ISA of a machine is that ISA's assembly language. Assembly language is a low-level language. There is no confusing an instruction in a low-level language with a statement in English. Each assembly language instruction usually specifies a single instruction in the ISA. Unlike high-level languages, which are usually ISA independent, low-level languages are very much ISA dependent. In fact, it is usually the case that each ISA has only one assembly language.

The purpose of assembly language is to make the programming process more user-friendly than programming in machine language (i.e., in the ISA of the computer with which we are dealing), while still providing the programmer with detailed control over the instructions that the computer can execute. So, for example, while still retaining control over the detailed instructions the computer is to carry out, we are freed from having to remember what opcode is 0001 and what opcode is 1001, or what is being stored in memory location 0011111100001010 and what is being stored in location 0011111100000101. Assembly languages let us use mnemonic devices for opcodes, such as ADD for 0001 and NOT for 1001, and they let us give meaningful symbolic names to memory locations, such as SUM or PRODUCT, rather than use the memory locations' 16-bit addresses. This makes it easier to differentiate which memory location is keeping track of a SUM and which memory location is keeping track of a PRODUCT. We call these names *symbolic addresses*.

We will see, starting in Chapter 11, that when we take the larger step of moving up to a higher-level language (such as C), programming will be even more user-friendly, but in doing so, we will relinquish some control over exactly which detailed ISA instructions are to be carried out to accomplish the work specified by a high-level language statement.

7.2 An Assembly Language Program

We will begin our study of the LC-3 assembly language by means of an example. The program in Figure 7.1 multiplies the integer initially stored in NUMBER by 6 by adding the integer to itself six times. For example, if the integer is 123, the program computes the product by adding $123 + 123 + 123 + 123 + 123 + 123$. Where have you seen that before? :-)

The program consists of 21 lines of code. We have added a *line number* to each line of the program in order to be able to refer to individual lines easily. This is a common practice. These line numbers are not part of the program. Ten lines start with a semicolon, designating that they are strictly for the benefit of

```
01  ;
02  ; Program to multiply an integer by the constant 6.
03  ; Before execution, an integer must be stored in NUMBER.
04  ;
05          .ORIG    x3050
06          LD       R1,SIX
07          LD       R2,NUMBER
08          AND      R3,R3,#0      ; Clear R3. It will
09                                 ; contain the product.
0A  ; The inner loop
0B  ;
0C  AGAIN   ADD      R3,R3,R2
0D          ADD      R1,R1,#-1     ; R1 keeps track of
0E          BRp      AGAIN         ; the iterations
0F  ;
10          HALT
11  ;
12  NUMBER  .BLKW    1
13  SIX     .FILL    x0006
14  ;
15          .END
```

Figure 7.1   An assembly language program.

the human reader. More on this momentarily. Seven lines (06, 07, 08, 0C, 0D, 0E, and 10) specify assembly language instructions to be translated into machine language instructions of the LC-3, which will be executed when the program runs. The remaining four lines (05, 12, 13, and 15) contain pseudo-ops, which are messages from the programmer to the translation program to help in the translation process. The translation program is called an *assembler* (in this case the LC-3 assembler), and the translation process is called *assembly*.

7.2.1 Instructions

Instead of an instruction being 16 0s and 1s, as is the case in the LC-3 ISA, an instruction in assembly language consists of four parts, as follows:

```
Label   Opcode   Operands   ; Comment
```

Two of the parts (Label and Comment) are optional. More on that momentarily.

7.2.1.1 Opcodes and Operands

Two of the parts (Opcode and Operands) are **mandatory**. For an assembly language instruction to correspond to an instruction in the LC-3 ISA, it must have an Opcode (the thing the instruction is to do), and the appropriate number of Operands (the things it is supposed to do it to). Not surprisingly, this was exactly what we encountered in Chapter 5 when we studied the LC-3 ISA.

The Opcode is a symbolic name for the opcode of the corresponding LC-3 instruction. The idea is that it is easier to remember an operation by the symbolic name ADD, AND, or LDR than by the four-bit quantity 0001, 0101, or 0110. Figure 5.3 (also Figure A.2) lists the Opcodes of the 15 LC-3 instructions. Pages 658 through 673 show the assembly language representations for the 15 LC-3 instructions.

The number of operands depends on the operation being performed. For example, the ADD instruction (line 0C in the program of Figure 7.1) requires three operands (two sources to obtain the numbers to be added, and one destination to designate where the result is to be stored). All three operands must be explicitly identified in the instruction.

```
AGAIN    ADD    R3,R3,R2
```

In this case the operands to be added are obtained from register 2 and from register 3. The result is to be placed in register 3. We represent each of the registers 0 through 7 as R0, R1, R2, ... , R7, rather than 000, 001, 010, ... , 111.

The LD instruction (line 07 of the program in Figure 7.1) requires two operands (the memory location from which the value is to be read and the destination register that is to contain the value after the instruction finishes execution). In LC-3 assembly language, we assign symbolic names called *labels* to the memory locations so we will not have to remember their explicit 16-bit addresses. In this case, the location from which the value is to be read is given the label *NUMBER*. The destination (i.e., where the value is to be loaded) is register 2.

```
LD    R2, NUMBER
```

As we discussed in Section 5.1.6, operands can be obtained from registers, from memory, or they may be literal (i.e., immediate) values in the instruction. In the case of register operands, the registers are explicitly represented (such as R2 and R3 in line 0C). In the case of memory operands, the symbolic name of the memory location is explicitly represented (such as NUMBER in line 07 and SIX in line 06). In the case of immediate operands, the actual value is explicitly represented (such as the value 0 in line 08).

```
AND  R3, R3, #0 ; Clear R3. It will contain the product.
```

A literal value must contain a symbol identifying the representation base of the number. We use # for decimal, x for hexadecimal, and b for binary. Sometimes there is no ambiguity, such as in the case 3F0A, which is a hex number. Nonetheless, we write it as x3F0A. Sometimes there is ambiguity, such as in the case 1000. x1000 represents the decimal number 4096, b1000 represents the decimal number 8, and #1000 represents the decimal number 1000.

7.2.1.2 Labels

Labels are symbolic names that are used to identify memory locations that are referred to explicitly in the program. In LC-3 assembly language, a label consists of from 1 to 20 alphanumeric characters (i.e., each character is a capital or lowercase letter of the English alphabet, or a decimal digit), starting with a letter of the alphabet.

However, not all sequences of characters that follow these rules can be used as labels. You know that computer programs cannot tolerate ambiguity. So ADD,

NOT, x1000, R4, and other character strings that have specific meanings in an LC-3 program cannot be used as labels. They could confuse the LC-3 assembler as it tries to translate the LC-3 assembly language program into a program in the LC-3 ISA. Such not-allowed character strings are often referred to as *reserved words*.

NOW, Under21, R2D2, R785, and C3PO are all examples of legitimate LC-3 assembly language labels.

We said we give a label (i.e., a symbolic name) to a memory location if we explicitly refer to it in the program. There are two reasons for explicitly referring to a memory location.

1. The location is the target of a branch instruction (e.g., AGAIN in line 0C). That is, the label AGAIN identifies the location of the instruction that will be executed next if the branch is taken.

2. The location contains a value that is loaded or stored (e.g., NUMBER in line 12, and SIX in line 13).

Note the location AGAIN (identified in line 0C) is specifically referenced by the branch instruction in line 0E.

```
BRp    AGAIN
```

If the result of ADD R1,R1,#–1 is positive (which results in the P bit being set), then the program branches to the location explicitly referenced as AGAIN to perform another iteration.

The location NUMBER is specifically referenced by the load instruction in line 07. The value stored in the memory location explicitly referenced as NUMBER is loaded into R2.

If a location in the program is not explicitly referenced, then there is no need to give it a label.

7.2.1.3 Comments

Comments are messages intended only for human consumption. They have no effect on the translation process and indeed are not acted on by the LC-3 assembler. They are identified in the program by semicolons. A semicolon signifies that the rest of the line is a comment and is to be ignored by the assembler. If the semicolon is the first nonblank character on the line, the entire line is ignored. If the semicolon follows the operands of an instruction, then only the comment is ignored by the assembler.

The purpose of comments is to make the program more comprehensible to the human reader. Comments help explain a nonintuitive aspect of an instruction or a set of instructions. In lines 08 and 09, the comment "Clear R3; it will contain the product" lets the reader know that the instruction on line 08 is initializing R3 prior to accumulating the product of the two numbers. While the purpose of line 08 may be obvious to the programmer today, it may not be the case two years from now, after the programmer has written an additional 30,000 instructions and cannot remember why he/she wrote AND R3,R3,#0. It may also be the case that two years from now, the programmer no longer works for the company, and the company needs to modify the program in response to a product update. If the task is assigned to someone who has never seen the program before, comments go a long way toward helping that person understand the program.

It is important to make comments that provide additional insight and do not just restate the obvious. There are two reasons for this. First, comments that restate the obvious are a waste of everyone's time. Second, they tend to obscure the comments that say something important because they add clutter to the program. For example, in line 0D, the comment "Decrement R1" would be a bad idea. It would provide no additional insight to the instruction, and it would add clutter to the page.

Another purpose of comments is to make the visual presentation of a program easier to understand. That is, comments are used to separate pieces of a program from each other to make the program more readable. Lines of code that work together to compute a single result are placed on successive lines, but they are separated from the rest of the program by blank lines. For example, note that lines 0C through 0E, which together form the loop body that is the crux of this computer program, are separated from the rest of the code by lines 0B and 0F. There is nothing on lines 0B and 0F other than the semicolons in the first column.

Incidentally, another opportunity to make a program easier to read is the judicious use of white space, accomplished by adding extra spaces to a line that are ignored by the assembler—for example, having all the opcodes start in the same column on the page, whether or not the instruction has a label.

7.2.2 Pseudo-Ops (Assembler Directives)

The LC-3 assembler is a program that takes as input a string of characters representing a computer program written in LC-3 assembly language and translates it into a program in the ISA of the LC-3. Pseudo-ops help the assembler perform that task.

The more formal name for a pseudo-op is *assembler directive*. It is called a pseudo-op because, like its Greek root "pseudes" (which means "false"), it does not refer to an operation that will be performed by the program during execution. Rather, the pseudo-op is strictly a message from the assembly language programmer to the assembler to help the assembler in the assembly process. Once the assembler handles the message, the pseudo-op is discarded. The LC-3 assembly language contains five pseudo-ops that we will find useful in our assembly language programming: .ORIG, .FILL, .BLKW, .STRINGZ, and .END. All are easily recognizable by the dot as their first character.

7.2.2.1 .ORIG

.ORIG tells the assembler where in memory to place the LC-3 program. In line 05, .ORIG x3050 says, place the first LC-3 ISA instruction in location x3050. As a result, 0010001000001100 (the translated LD R1,SIX instruction) is put in location x3050, and the rest of the translated LC-3 program is placed in the subsequent sequential locations in memory. For example, if the program consists of x100 LC-3 instructions, and .ORIG says to put the first instruction in x3050, the remaining xFF instructions are placed in locations x3051 to x314F.

7.2.2.2 .FILL

.FILL tells the assembler to set aside the next location in the program and initialize it with the value of the operand. The value can be either a number or a label. In line 13, the ninth location in the resulting LC-3 program is initialized to the value x0006.

7.2.2.3 .BLKW

.BLKW tells the assembler to set aside some number of sequential memory locations (i.e., a **BL**oc**K** of **W**ords) in the program. The actual number is the operand of the .BLKW pseudo-op. In line 12, the pseudo-op instructs the assembler to set aside one location in memory (and, incidentally, to label it NUMBER).

The pseudo-op .BLKW is particularly useful when the actual value of the operand is not yet known. In our example we assumed the number in location NUMBER was 123. How did it get there? A common use of .BLKW is to set aside a location in the program, as we did here, and have another section of code produce the number, perhaps from input from a keyboard (which we cannot know at the time we write the program), and store that value into NUMBER before we execute the code in Figure 7.1.

7.2.2.4 .STRINGZ

.STRINGZ tells the assembler to initialize a sequence of $n+1$ memory locations. The argument is a sequence of n characters inside double quotation marks. The first n words of memory are initialized with the zero-extended ASCII codes of the corresponding characters in the string. The final word of memory is initialized to 0. The last word, containing x0000, provides a convenient sentinel for processing the string of ASCII codes.

For example, the code fragment

```
        .ORIG      x3010
HELLO   .STRINGZ   "Hello, World!"
```

would result in the assembler initializing locations x3010 through x301D to the following values:

```
x3010: x0048
x3011: x0065
x3012: x006C
x3013: x006C
x3014: x006F
x3015: x002C
x3016: x0020
x3017: x0057
x3018: x006F
x3019: x0072
x301A: x006C
x301B: x0064
x301C: x0021
x301D: x0000
```

7.2.2.5 .END

.END tells the assembler it has reached the end of the program and need not even look at anything after it. That is, any characters that come after .END will not be processed by the assembler. *Note:* .END does not stop the program during execution. In fact, .END does not even **exist** at the time of execution. It is simply a delimiter—it marks the end of the program. It is a message from the programmer, telling the assembler where the assembly language program ends.

7.2.3 Example: The Character Count Example of Section 5.5, Revisited Again!

Now we are ready for a complete example. Let's consider again the problem of Section 5.5. We wish to write a program that will take a character that is input from the keyboard and count the number of occurrences of that character in a file. As before, we first develop the algorithm by constructing the flowchart. Recall that in Section 6.1, we showed how to decompose the problem systematically so as to generate the flowchart of Figure 5.16. In fact, the final step of that process in Chapter 6 is the flowchart of Figure 6.3e, which is essentially identical to Figure 5.16. Next, we use the flowchart to write the actual program. This time, however, we enjoy the luxury of not worrying about 0s and 1s and instead write the program in LC-3 assembly language. The program is shown in Figure 7.2.

A few comments about this program: Three times during this program, assistance in the form of a service call is required of the operating system. In each case, a TRAP instruction is used. TRAP x23 causes a character to be input from the keyboard and placed in R0 (line 0D). TRAP x21 causes the ASCII code in R0 to be displayed on the monitor (line 28). TRAP x25 causes the machine to be halted (line 29). As we said before, we will leave the details of how the TRAP instruction is carried out until Chapter 9.

The ASCII codes for the decimal digits 0 to 9 (0000 to 1001) are x30 to x39. The conversion from binary to ASCII is done simply by adding x30 to the binary value of the decimal digit. Line 2D shows the label ASCII used to identify the memory location containing x0030. The LD instruction in line 26 uses it to load x30 into R0, so it can convert the count that is in R2 from a binary value to an ASCII code. That is done by the ADD instruction in line 27. TRAP x21 in line 28 prints the ASCII code to the monitor.

The file that is to be examined starts at address x4000 (see line 2E). Usually, this starting address would not be known to the programmer who is writing this program since we would want the program to work on many files, not just the one starting at x4000. To accomplish that, line 2E would be replaced with .BLKW 1 and be filled in by some other piece of code that knew the starting address of the desired file before executing the program of Figure 7.2. That situation will be discussed in Section 7.4.

```
01    ;
02    ; Program to count occurrences of a character in a file.
03    ; Character to be input from the keyboard.
04    ; Result to be displayed on the monitor.
05    ; Program works only if no more than 9 occurrences are found.
06    ;
07    ;
08    ; Initialization
09    ;
0A            .ORIG    x3000
0B            AND      R2,R2,#0      ; R2 is counter, initialize to 0
0C            LD       R3,PTR        ; R3 is pointer to characters
0D            TRAP     x23           ; R0 gets character input
0E            LDR      R1,R3,#0      ; R1 gets the next character
0F    ;
10    ; Test character for end of file
11    ;
12    ;
13    TEST    ADD      R4,R1,#-4     ; Test for EOT
14            BRz      OUTPUT        ; If done, prepare the output
15    ;
16    ; Test character for match.  If a match, increment count.
17    ;
18            NOT      R1,R1
19            ADD      R1,R1,#1      ; R1 <-- -R1
1A            ADD      R1,R1,R0      ; R1 <-- R0-R1. If R1=0, a match!
1B            BRnp     GETCHAR       ; If no match, do not increment
1C            ADD      R2,R2,#1
1D    ;
1E    ; Get next character from the file
1F    ;
20    GETCHAR ADD      R3,R3,#1      ; Increment the pointer
21            LDR      R1,R3,#0      ; R1 gets the next character to test
22            BRnzp    TEST
23    ;
24    ; Output the count.
25    ;
26    OUTPUT  LD       R0,ASCII      ; Load the ASCII template
27            ADD      R0,R0,R2      ; Convert binary to ASCII
28            TRAP     x21           ; ASCII code in R0 is displayed
29            TRAP     x25           ; Halt machine
2A    ;
2B    ; Storage for pointer and ASCII template
2C    ;
2D    ASCII   .FILL    x0030
2E    PTR     .FILL    x4000
2F            .END
```

Figure 7.2   The assembly language program to count occurrences of a character.

7.3 The Assembly Process

7.3.1 Introduction

Before an LC-3 assembly language program can be executed, it must first be translated into a machine language program, that is, one in which each instruction is in the LC-3 ISA. It is the job of the LC-3 assembler to perform that translation.

If you have available an LC-3 assembler, you can cause it to translate your assembly language program into a machine language program by executing an appropriate command. In the LC-3 assembler that is generally available via the web, that command is *assemble*, and it requires as an argument the filename of your assembly language program. For example, if the filename is solution1.asm, then

```
assemble solution1.asm outfile
```

produces the file outfile, which is in the ISA of the LC-3. It is necessary to check with your instructor for the correct command line to cause the LC-3 assembler to produce a file of 0s and 1s in the ISA of the LC-3.

7.3.2 A Two-Pass Process

In this section, we will see how the assembler goes through the process of translating an assembly language program into a machine language program. We will use as our input to the process the assembly language program of Figure 7.2.

You remember that there is in general a one-to-one correspondence between instructions in an assembly language program and instructions in the final machine language program. We could try to perform this translation in one pass through the assembly language program. Starting from the top of Figure 7.2, the assembler discards lines 01 to 09, since they contain only comments. Comments are strictly for human consumption; they have no bearing on the translation process. The assembler then moves on to line 0A. Line 0A is a pseudo-op; it tells the assembler that the machine language program is to start at location x3000. The assembler then moves on to line 0B, which it can easily translate into LC-3 machine code. At this point, we have

```
x3000:   0101010010100000
```

The LC-3 assembler moves on to translate the next instruction (line 0C). Unfortunately, it is unable to do so since it does not know the meaning of the symbolic address PTR. At this point the assembler is stuck, and the assembly process fails.

To prevent this from occurring, the assembly process is done in two complete passes (from beginning to .END) through the entire assembly language program. The objective of the first pass is to identify the actual binary addresses corresponding to the symbolic names (or labels). This set of correspondences is known as the *symbol table*. In pass 1, we construct the symbol table. In pass 2, we translate the individual assembly language instructions into their corresponding machine language instructions.

Thus, when the assembler examines line 0C for the purpose of translating

```
LD R3,PTR
```

during the second pass, it already knows that PTR is the symbolic address of memory location x3013 (from the first pass). Thus, it can easily translate line 0C to

$$\text{x3001:} \quad \text{0010011000010001}$$

The problem of not knowing the 16-bit address corresponding to PTR no longer exists.

7.3.3 The First Pass: Creating the Symbol Table

For our purposes, the symbol table is simply a correspondence of symbolic names with their 16-bit memory addresses. We obtain these correspondences by passing through the assembly language program once, noting which instruction is assigned to which memory location, and identifying each label with the memory address of its assigned entry.

Recall that we provide labels in those cases where we have to refer to a location, either because it is the target of a branch instruction or because it contains data that must be loaded or stored. Consequently, if we have not made any programming mistakes, and if we identify all the labels, we will have identified all the symbolic addresses used in the program.

The preceding paragraph assumes that our entire program exists between our .ORIG and .END pseudo-ops. This is true for the assembly language program of Figure 7.2. In Section 7.4, we will consider programs that consist of multiple parts, each with its own .ORIG and .END, wherein each part is assembled separately.

The first pass starts, after discarding the comments on lines 01 to 09, by noting (line 0A) that the first instruction will be assigned to address x3000. We keep track of the location assigned to each instruction by means of a location counter (LC). The LC is initialized to the address specified in .ORIG, that is, x3000.

The assembler examines each instruction in sequence and increments the LC once for each assembly language instruction. If the instruction examined contains a label, a symbol table entry is made for that label, specifying the current contents of LC as its address. The first pass terminates when the .END pseudo-op is reached.

The first instruction that has a label is at line 13. Since it is the fifth instruction in the program and since the LC at that point contains x3004, a symbol table entry is constructed thus:

Symbol	Address
TEST	x3004

The second instruction that has a label is at line 20. At this point, the LC has been incremented to x300B. Thus, a symbol table entry is constructed, as follows:

Symbol	Address
GETCHAR	x300B

At the conclusion of the first pass, the symbol table has the following entries:

Symbol	Address
TEST	x3004
GETCHAR	x300B
OUTPUT	x300E
ASCII	x3012
PTR	x3013

7.3.4 The Second Pass: Generating the Machine Language Program

The second pass consists of going through the assembly language program a second time, line by line, this time with the help of the symbol table. At each line, the assembly language instruction is translated into an LC-3 machine language instruction.

Starting again at the top, the assembler again discards lines 01 through 09 because they contain only comments. Line 0A is the .ORIG pseudo-op, which the assembler uses to initialize LC to x3000. The assembler moves on to line 0B and produces the machine language instruction 0101010010100000. Then the assembler moves on to line 0C.

This time, when the assembler gets to line 0C, it can completely assemble the instruction since it knows that PTR corresponds to x3013. The instruction is LD, which has an opcode encoding of 0010. The destination register (DR) is R3, that is, 011.

The only part of the LD instruction left to do is the PCoffset. It is computed as follows: The assembler knows that PTR is the label for address x3013 and that the incremented PC is LC+1, in this case x3002. Since PTR (x3013) must be the sum of the incremented PC (x3002) and the sign-extended PCoffset, PCoffset must be x0011. Putting this all together, the assembler sets x3001 to 0010011000010001 and increments the LC to x3002.

Note: In order to use the LD instruction, it is necessary that the source of the load, in this case the address whose label is PTR, is not more than +256 or −255 memory locations from the LD instruction itself. If the address of PTR had been greater than LC+1+255 or less than LC+1−256, then the offset would not fit in bits [8:0] of the instruction. In such a case, an assembly error would have occurred, preventing the assembly process from finishing successfully. Fortunately, PTR is close enough to the LD instruction, so the instruction assembled correctly.

The second pass continues. At each step, the LC is incremented and the location specified by LC is assigned the translated LC-3 instruction or, in the case of .FILL, the value specified. When the second pass encounters the .END pseudo-op, assembly terminates.

The resulting translated program is shown in Figure 7.3.

That process was, on a good day, merely tedious. Fortunately, you do not have to do it for a living—the LC-3 assembler does that. And, since you now know the

Address	Binary
	0011000000000000
x3000	0101010010100000
x3001	0010011000010001
x3002	1111000000100011
x3003	0110001011000000
x3004	0001100001111100
x3005	0000010000001000
x3006	1001001001111111
x3007	0001001001000000
x3008	1001001001111111
x3009	0000101000000001
x300A	0001010010100001
x300B	0001011011100001
x300C	0110001011000000
x300D	0000111111110110
x300E	0010000000000011
x300F	0001000000000010
x3010	1111000000100001
x3011	1111000000100101
x3012	0000000000110000
x3013	0100000000000000

Figure 7.3 The machine language program for the assembly language program of Figure 7.2.

LC-3 assembly language, there is no need to program in machine language. Now we can write our programs symbolically in LC-3 assembly language and invoke the LC-3 assembler to create the machine language versions that can execute on an LC-3 computer.

7.4 Beyond the Assembly of a Single Assembly Language Program

Our purpose in this chapter has been to take you up one more step from the ISA of the computer and introduce assembly language. Although it is still quite a large step from C or C++, assembly language does, in fact, save us a good deal of pain. We have also shown how a rudimentary two-pass assembler actually works to translate an assembly language program into the machine language of the LC-3 ISA.

There are many more aspects to sophisticated assembly language programming that go well beyond an introductory course. However, our reason for teaching assembly language is not to deal with its sophistication, but rather to show its innate simplicity. Before we leave this chapter, however, there are a few additional highlights we should explore.

7.4.1 The Executable Image

When a computer begins execution of a program, the entity being executed is called an *executable image*. The executable image is created from modules often created independently by several different programmers. Each module is translated separately into an object file. We have just gone through the process of performing that translation ourselves by mimicking the LC-3 assembler. Other modules, some written in C perhaps, are translated by the C compiler. Some modules are written by users, and some modules are supplied as library routines by the operating system. Each object file consists of instructions in the ISA of the computer being used, along with its associated data. The final step is to combine (i.e., *link*) all the object modules together into one executable image. During execution of the program, the FETCH, DECODE, ... instruction cycle is applied to instructions in the executable image.

7.4.2 More than One Object File

It is very common to form an executable image from more than one object file. In fact, in the real world, where most programs invoke libraries provided by the operating system as well as modules generated by other programmers, it is much more common to have multiple object files than a single one.

A case in point is our example character count program. The program counts the number of occurrences of a character in a file. A typical application could easily have the program as one module and the input data file as another. If this were the case, then the starting address of the file, shown as x4000 in line 2E of Figure 7.2, would not be known when the program was written. If we replace line 2E with

```
PTR  .FILL  STARTofFILE
```

then the program of Figure 7.2 will not assemble because there will be no symbol table entry for STARTofFILE. What can we do?

If the LC-3 assembly language, on the other hand, contained the pseudo-op .EXTERNAL, we could identify STARTofFILE as the symbolic name of an address that is not known at the time the program of Figure 7.2 is assembled. This would be done by the following line

```
.EXTERNAL  STARTofFILE,
```

which would send a message to the LC-3 assembler that the absence of label STARTofFILE is not an error in the program. Rather, STARTofFILE is a label in some other module that will be translated independently. In fact, in our case, it will be the label of the location of the first character in the file to be examined by our character count program.

If the LC-3 assembly language had the pseudo-op .EXTERNAL, and if we had designated STARTofFILE as .EXTERNAL, the LC-3 assembler would be able to create a symbol table entry for STARTofFILE, and instead of assigning it an address, it would mark the symbol as belonging to another module. At *link time,* when all the modules are combined, the linker (the program that manages the "combining" process) would use the symbol table entry for STARTofFILE in another module to complete the translation of our revised line 2E.

In this way, the .EXTERNAL pseudo-op allows references by one module to symbolic locations in another module without a problem. The proper translations are resolved by the linker.

Exercises

7.1 An assembly language program contains the following two instructions. The assembler puts the translated version of the LDI instruction that follows into location x3025 of the object module. After assembly is complete, what is in location x3025?

```
PLACE   .FILL   x45A7
        LDI     R3, PLACE
```

7.2 An LC-3 assembly language program contains the instruction:

```
ASCII   LD R1, ASCII
```

The symbol table entry for ASCII is x4F08. If this instruction is executed during the running of the program, what will be contained in R1 immediately after the instruction is executed?

7.3 What is the problem with using the string AND as a label?

7.4 Create the symbol table entries generated by the assembler when translating the following routine into machine code:

```
             .ORIG   x301C
             ST      R3, SAVE3
             ST      R2, SAVE2
             AND     R2, R2, #0
TEST         IN
             BRz     TEST
             ADD     R1, R0, #-10
             BRn     FINISH
             ADD     R1, R0, #-15
             NOT     R1, R1
             BRn     FINISH
             HALT
FINISH       ADD     R2, R2, #1
             HALT
SAVE3        .FILL   X0000
SAVE2        .FILL   X0000
             .END
```

7.5   *a.* What does the following program do?

```
          .ORIG   x3000
          LD      R2, ZERO
          LD      R0, M0
          LD      R1, M1
LOOP      BRz     DONE
          ADD     R2, R2, R0
          ADD     R1, R1, -1
          BR      LOOP
DONE      ST      R2, RESULT
          HALT
RESULT    .FILL   x0000
ZERO      .FILL   x0000
M0        .FILL   x0004
M1        .FILL   x0803
          .END
```

b. What value will be contained in RESULT after the program runs to completion?

7.6   Our assembler has crashed, and we need your help! Create a symbol table for the following program, and assemble the instructions at labels A, B, and D.

```
          .ORIG   x3000
          AND     R0, R0, #0
A         LD      R1, E
          AND     R2, R1, #1
          BRp     C
B         ADD     R1, R1, #-1
C         ADD     R0, R0, R1
          ADD     R1, R1, #-2
D         BRp     C
          ST      R0, F
          TRAP    x25
E         .BLKW   1
F         .BLKW   1
          .END
```

You may assume another module deposits a positive value into E before the module executes. In 15 words or fewer, what does this program do?

7.7   Write an LC-3 assembly language program that counts the number of 1s in the value stored in R0 and stores the result into R1. For example, if R0 contains 0001001101110000, then after the program executes, the result stored in R1 would be 0000 0000 0000 0110.

7.8   An engineer is in the process of debugging a program she has written. She is looking at the following segment of the program and decides to place a breakpoint in memory at location 0xA404. Starting with the PC = 0xA400, she initializes all the registers to zero and runs the program until the breakpoint is encountered.

```
Code Segment:
...
0xA400  THIS1  LEA   R0, THIS1
0xA401  THIS2  LD    R1, THIS2
0xA402  THIS3  LDI   R2, THIS5
0xA403  THIS4  LDR   R3, R0, #2
0xA404  THIS5  .FILL xA400
...
```

Show the contents of the register file (in hexadecimal) when the breakpoint is encountered.

7.9   What is the purpose of the .END pseudo-op? How does it differ from the HALT instruction?

7.10   The following program fragment has an error in it. Identify the error and explain how to fix it.

```
          ADD    R3, R3, #30
          ST     R3, A
          HALT
  A       .FILL  #0
```

Will this error be detected when this code is assembled or when this code is run on the LC-3?

7.11   The LC-3 assembler must be able to convert constants represented in ASCII into their appropriate binary values. For instance, x2A translates into 00101010 and #12 translates into 00001100. Write an LC-3 assembly language program that reads a decimal or hexadecimal constant from the keyboard (i.e., it is preceded by a # character signifying it is a decimal, or x signifying it is hex) and prints out the binary representation. Assume the constants can be expressed with no more than two decimal or hex digits.

7.12   What does the following LC-3 program do?

```
                        .ORIG   x3000
                        AND     R5, R5, #0
                        AND     R3, R3, #0
                        ADD     R3, R3, #8
                        LDI     R1, A
                        ADD     R2, R1, #0
                AG      ADD     R2, R2, R2
                        ADD     R3, R3, #-1
                        BRnp    AG
                        LD      R4, B
                        AND     R1, R1, R4
                        NOT     R1, R1
                        ADD     R1, R1, #1
                        ADD     R2, R2, R1
                        BRnp    NO
                        ADD     R5, R5, #1
        NO      HALT
        B       .FILL   xFF00
        A       .FILL   x4000
                .END
```

7.13   The following program adds the values stored in memory locations A, B, and C and stores the result into memory. There are two errors in the code. For each, describe the error and indicate whether it will be detected at assembly time or at run time.

```
Line No.
1                   .ORIG x3000
2       ONE     LD  R0, A
3               ADD R1, R1, R0
4       TWO     LD  R0, B
5               ADD R1, R1, R0
6       THREE   LD  R0, C
7               ADD R1, R1, R0
8               ST  R1, SUM
9               TRAP x25
10      A       .FILL x0001
11      B       .FILL x0002
12      C       .FILL x0003
13      D       .FILL x0004
14              .END
```

7.14   *a.* Assemble the following program:

```
                    .ORIG   x3000
                    STI     R0, LABEL
                    OUT
                    HALT
            LABEL   .STRINGZ "%"
                    .END
```

    b. The programmer intended the program to output a % to the monitor and then halt. Unfortunately, the programmer got confused about the semantics of each of the opcodes (i.e., exactly what function is carried out by the LC-3 in response to each opcode). Replace exactly **one** opcode in this program with the correct opcode to make the program work as intended.

    c. The original program from part *a* was executed. However, execution exhibited some very strange behavior. The strange behavior was in part due to the programming error and in part due to the fact that the value in R0 when the program started executing was x3000. Explain what the strange behavior was and why the program behaved that way.

7.15 The following is an LC-3 program that performs a function. Assume a sequence of integers is stored in consecutive memory locations, one integer per memory location, starting at the location x4000. The sequence terminates with the value x0000. What does the following program do?

```
                .ORIG   x3000
                LD      R0, NUMBERS
                LD      R2, MASK
        LOOP    LDR     R1, R0, #0
                BRz     DONE
                AND     R5, R1, R2
                BRz     L1
                BRnzp   NEXT
        L1      ADD     R1, R1, R1
                STR     R1, R0, #0
        NEXT    ADD     R0, R0, #1
                BRnzp   LOOP
        DONE    HALT
        NUMBERS .FILL   x4000
        MASK    .FILL   x8000
                .END
```

7.16 Assume a sequence of nonnegative integers is stored in consecutive memory locations, one integer per memory location, starting at location x4000. Each integer has a value between 0 and 30,000 (decimal). The sequence terminates with the value −1 (i.e., xFFFF).

What does the following program do?

```
                .ORIG     x3000
                AND       R4, R4, #0
                AND       R3, R3, #0
                LD        R0, NUMBERS
        LOOP    LDR       R1, R0, #0
                NOT       R2, R1
                BRz       DONE
                AND       R2, R1, #1
                BRz       L1
                ADD       R4, R4, #1
                BRnzp     NEXT
        L1      ADD       R3, R3, #1
        NEXT    ADD       R0, R0, #1
                BRnzp     LOOP
        DONE    TRAP      x25
        NUMBERS .FILL     x4000
                .END
```

7.17 Suppose you write two separate assembly language modules that you expect to be combined by the linker. Each module uses the label AGAIN, and neither module contains the pseudo-op .EXTERNAL AGAIN. Is there a problem using the label AGAIN in both modules? Why or why not?

7.18 The following LC-3 program compares two character strings of the same length. The source strings are in the .STRINGZ form. The first string starts at memory location x4000, and the second string starts at memory location x4100. If the strings are the same, the program terminates with the value 1 in R5. Insert instructions at (a), (b), and (c) that will complete the program.

```
                .ORIG     x3000
                LD        R1, FIRST
                LD        R2, SECOND
                AND       R0, R0, #0
        LOOP    -------------- (a)
                LDR       R4, R2, #0
                BRz       NEXT
                ADD       R1, R1, #1
                ADD       R2, R2, #1
                -------------- (b)
                -------------- (c)
                ADD       R3, R3, R4
                BRz       LOOP
                AND       R5, R5, #0
                BRnzp     DONE
        NEXT    AND       R5, R5, #0
                ADD       R5, R5, #1
        DONE    TRAP      x25
        FIRST   .FILL     x4000
        SECOND  .FILL     x4100
                .END
```

7.19 When the following LC-3 program is executed, how many times will the instruction at the memory address labeled LOOP execute?

```
        .ORIG   x3005
        LEA     R2, DATA
        LDR     R4, R2, #0
LOOP    ADD     R4, R4, #-3
        BRzp    LOOP
        TRAP    x25
DATA    .FILL   x000B
        .END
```

7.20 LC-3 assembly language modules (a) and (b) have been written by different programmers to store x0015 into memory location x4000. What is fundamentally different about their approaches?

a.
```
        .ORIG   x5000
        AND     R0, R0, #0
        ADD     R0, R0, #15
        ADD     R0, R0, #6
        STI     R0, PTR
        HALT
PTR     .FILL   x4000
        .END
```

b.
```
        .ORIG   x4000
        .FILL   x0015
        .END
```

7.21 Assemble the following LC-3 assembly language program.

```
        .ORIG   x3000
        AND     R0, R0, #0
        ADD     R2, R0, #10
        LD      R1, MASK
        LD      R3, PTR1
LOOP    LDR     R4, R3, #0
        AND     R4, R4, R1
        BRz     NEXT
        ADD     R0, R0, #1
NEXT    ADD     R3, R3, #1
        ADD     R2, R2, #-1
        BRp     LOOP
        STI     R0, PTR2
        HALT
MASK    .FILL   x8000
PTR1    .FILL   x4000
PTR2    .FILL   x5000
        .END
```

What does the program do (in no more than 20 words)?

7.22 The LC-3 assembler must be able to map an instruction's mnemonic opcode into its binary opcode. For instance, given an ADD, it must generate the binary pattern 0001. Write an LC-3 assembly language program that prompts the user to type in an LC-3 assembly language opcode and then displays its binary opcode. If the assembly language opcode is invalid, it displays an error message.

7.23 The following LC-3 program determines whether a character string is a palindrome or not. A palindrome is a string that reads the same backwards as forwards. For example, the string "racecar" is a palindrome. Suppose a string starts at memory location x4000 and is in the .STRINGZ format. If the string is a palindrome, the program terminates with the value 1 in R5. If not, the program terminates with the value 0 in R5. Insert instructions at (a)–(e) that will complete the program.

```
              .ORIG  x3000
              LD     R0, PTR
              ADD    R1, R0, #0
       AGAIN  LDR    R2, R1, #0
              BRz    CONT
              ADD    R1, R1, #1
              BRnzp  AGAIN
       CONT   --------------(a)
       LOOP   LDR    R3, R0, #0
              --------------(b)
              NOT    R4, R4
              ADD    R4, R4, #1
              ADD    R3, R3, R4
              BRnp   NO
              --------------(c)
              --------------(d)
              NOT    R2, R0
              ADD    R2, R2, #1
              ADD    R2, R1, R2
              BRnz   YES
              --------------(e)
       YES    AND    R5, R5, #0
              ADD    R5, R5, #1
              BRnzp  DONE
       NO     AND    R5, R5, #0
       DONE   HALT
       PTR    .FILL  x4000
              .END
```

7.24 We want the following program fragment to shift R3 to the left by four bits, but it has an error in it. Identify the error and explain how to fix it.

```
              .ORIG  x3000
              AND    R2, R2, #0
              ADD    R2, R2, #4
       LOOP   BRz    DONE
              ADD    R2, R2, #-1
              ADD    R3, R3, R3
              BR     LOOP
       DONE   HALT
              .END
```

7.25 What does the pseudo-op .FILL xFF004 do? Why?

7.26 Recall the assembly language program of Exercise 7.6. Consider the following program:

```
          .ORIG     x3000
          AND       R0, R0, #0
   D      LD        R1, A
          AND       R2, R1, #1
          BRp       B
   E      ADD       R1, R1, #-1
   B      ADD       R0, R0, R1
          ADD       R1, R1, #-2
   F      BRp       B
          ST        R0, C
          TRAP      x25
   A      .BLKW     1
   C      .BLKW     1
          .END
```

The assembler translates both assembly language programs into machine language programs. What can you say about the two resulting machine language programs?

7.27 Consider the following LC-3 assembly language program:

```
          .ORIG x3000
          AND R2, R2, #0
          AND R6, R6, #0
          ADD R2, R2, #1
   TOP    ADD R3, R2, #0
          ADD R4, R1, #0
   SEARCH ADD R3, R3, R3
          ADD R4, R4, #-1
          BRp SEARCH
          AND R5, R3, R0
          BRz NEXT
          ADD R6, R6, R2
   NEXT   ADD R2, R2, R2
          BRzp TOP
   END    ST R6, RESULT
          HALT
   RESULT .BLKW 1
          .END
```

What does it do (in 20 words or fewer)? Please be BRIEF but PRECISE. You can assume that some of the registers will already contain numbers that are relevant to the program.

What is the function of R0? For what range of input values does the program function as you've described above?

What is the function of R1? For what range of input values does the program function as you've described above?

What is the function of R6? For what range of input values does the program function as you've described above?

★7.28   Consider the following program:

```
            .ORIG x3000
            LD  R0, A
            LD  R1, B
            BRz DONE
            --------- (a)
            --------- (b)
            BRnzp AGAIN
    DONE    ST  R0, A
            HALT
    A       .FILL x0--- (c)
    B       .FILL x0001
            .END
```

The program uses only R0 and R1. Note lines (a) and (b) indicate two missing instructions. Complete line (c). Note also that one of the instructions in the program must be labeled AGAIN, and that label is missing.

After execution of the program, the contents of A is x1800.

During execution, we examined the computer during each clock cycle and recorded some information for certain clock cycles, producing the table shown below. The table is ordered by the cycle number in which the information was collected. Note that each memory access takes five clock cycles.

Cycle Number	State Number	Control Signals					
1	18	LD.MAR: ☐		LD.REG: ☐		GateMDR: ☐	
		LD.PC: ☐		PCMUX: ☐		GatePC: ☐	
☐	0	LD.MAR: ☐		LD.REG: ☐		BEN ☐	
		LD.PC: ☐		LD.CC: ☐			
☐	☐	LD.REG: 1		DR: 000		GateMDR: ☐	
		GateALU: ☐		GateMARMUX: ☐			
57	1	LD.MAR: ☐		ALUK: ☐		GateALU: ☐	
		LD.REG: ☐		DR: ☐		GatePC: ☐	
77	22	ADDR1MUX: ☐		ADDR2MUX: ☐			
		LD.PC: ☐		LD.MAR ☐		PCMUX: ☐	
101	15						

Fill in the missing instructions in the program, and complete the program by labeling the appropriate instruction AGAIN. Also, fill in the missing information in the table.

Given values for A and B, what does the program do?

★7.29   An LC-3 program is executing on the LC-3 simulator when a breakpoint is encountered, and the simulator stops. At that point, **the contents of several registers are as shown in the first row of the table.** After the run button is subsequently pushed, the next four instructions that are executed, none of which are an STI or LDI, produce the values shown in the table, **two rows of the table per instruction executed.** The first row of each pair shows the contents after the fetch phase of the corresponding instruction, and the second row of each pair after that instruction completes.

Note that some values are missing and are presented by letters A, B, C, D, E, F, G, H, I, and J.

PC	MAR	MDR	IR	R0	R1	R2	R3	R4	R5	R6	R7
x1800	x7FFF	x2211	xBFFE	x31FF	x2233	x5177	x3211	x21FF	x5233	x3177	x2211
A	x1800	B	B	x31FF	x2233	x5177	x3211	x21FF	x5233	x3177	x2211
A	x1800	B	B	x31FF	x2233	x5177	x3211	x21FF	C	x3177	x2211
D	A	E	E	x31FF	x2233	x5177	x3211	x21FF	C	x3177	x2211
D	F	G	E	x31FF	x2233	x5177	x3211	x21FF	C	x3177	x2211
H	D	I	I	x31FF	x2233	x5177	x3211	x21FF	C	x3177	x2211
F	D	I	I	x31FF	x2233	x5177	x3211	x21FF	C	x3177	x2211
A	F	J	J	x31FF	x2233	x5177	x3211	x21FF	C	x3177	x2211
A	F	J	J	x31FF	x2233	x5177	x3211	x223A	C	x3177	x2211

Your job: Determine the values of A, B, C, D, E, F, G, H, I, and J. Note that some of the values may be identical.

A	B	C	D	E

F	G	H	I	J
			x ˙F˙	

★7.30   There are times when one wants to implement a stack in memory, but cannot provide enough memory to be sure there will always be plenty of space to push values on the stack. Furthermore, there are times (beyond EE 306) when it is OK to lose some of the oldest values pushed on the stack. We can save that discussion for the last class if you like.

In such situations, a reasonable technique is to specify a circular stack as shown below. In this case, the stack occupies five locations x3FFB to x3FFF. Initially, the stack is empty, with R6 = x4000. The figure shows the result of successively pushing the values 1, 2, 3, 4, 5, 6, 7, 8 on the stack.

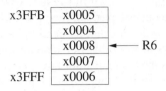

That is, the 1 was written into x3FFF, the 2 was written into x3FFE, etc. When the time came to push the 6, the stack was full, so R6 was set to x3FFF, and the 6 was written into x3FFF, clobbering the 1 which was originally pushed.

If we now pop five elements off the stack, we get 8, 7, 6, 5, and 4, AND we have an empty stack, even though R6 contains x3FFD. Why?

Because 3, 2, and 1 have been lost. That is, even though we have pushed eight values, there can be at most only five values actually available on the stack for popping. We keep track of the number of actual values on the stack in R5.

Note that R5 and R6 are known to the calling routine, so a test for underflow can be made by the calling program using R5. Furthermore, the calling program puts the value to be pushed in R0 before calling PUSH.

Your job: Complete the assembly language code shown below to implement the PUSH routine of the circular stack by filling in each of the lines: (a), (b), (c), and (d) with a missing instruction.

```
PUSH     ST R1, SAVER
         LD R1, NEGFULL
         ADD R1, R6, R1
         -------------(a)

         LD R6, BASE
SKIP     ADD R6, R6, #-1
         LD R1, MINUS5
         ADD R1, R5, R1
         BRz END
         -------------(b)

END      -------------(c)
         -------------(d)

         RET
NEGFULL  .FILL xC005      ; x-3FFB
MINUS5   .FILL xFFFB      ; #-5
BASE     .FILL x4000
SAVER    .BLKW #1
```

7.31 Memory locations x5000 to x5FFF contain 2's complement integers. What does the following program do?

```
            .ORIG x3000
            LD   R1, ARRAY
            LD   R2, LENGTH
            AND  R3, R3, #0
   AGAIN    LDR  R0, R1, #0
            AND  R0, R0, #1
            BRz  SKIP
            ADD  R3, R3, #1
   SKIP     ADD  R1, R1, #1
            ADD  R2, R2, #-1
            BRp  AGAIN
            HALT
   ARRAY    .FILL x5000
   LENGTH   .FILL x1000
            .END
```

7.32 Consider the following semi-nonsense assembly language program:

```
line 1:            .ORIG x8003
line 2:            AND R1,R1,#0
line 3:            ADD R0,R1,#5
line 4:            ST  R1,B
line 5:            LD  R1,A
line 6:            BRz SKIP
line 7:            ST  R0,B
line 8:    SKIP    TRAP x25
line 9:    A       .BLKW #7
line 10:   B       .FILL #5
line 11:   BANNER  .STRINGZ "We are done!"
line 12:   C       .FILL x0
line 13:           .END
```

A separate module will store a value in A before this program executes.

Construct the symbol table.

Show the result of assembly of lines 5 through 7 above. *Note:* the instruction at line 8 has already been assembled for you.

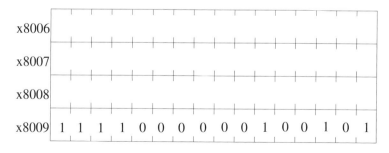

Note that two different things could cause location B to contain the value 5: the contents of line 7 or the contents of line 10. Explain the difference between line 7 causing the value 5 to be in location B and line 10 causing the value 5 to be in location B.

★**7.33** We have a program with some missing instructions, and we have a table consisting of some information and some missing information associated with five specific clock cycles of the program's execution. Your job is to complete both!

Insert the missing instructions in the program and the missing information in the table. Cycle numbering starts at 1. That is, cycle 1 is the first clock cycle of the processing of LD R0,A. Note that we have not said anything about the number of clock cycles a memory access takes. You do have enough information to figure that out for yourself. Note that we are asking for the value of the registers DURING each clock cycle.

```
        .ORIG x3000
        LD   R0, A
        LD   R1, B
        NOT  R1, R1
        ADD  R1, R1, #1
        AND  R2, R2, #0
AGAIN   -------------- (a)
        -------------- (b)
        BRnzp AGAIN
DONE    ST   R2, C
        HALT
    A   .FILL #5
    B   .FILL -------- (c)
    C   .BLKW #1
        .END
```

Cycle Number	State Number	Information					
		LD.REG: 1		DRMUX:		GateMDR:	
		LD.CC:		GateALU:		GatePC:	
16	35	LD.MDR:		MDR:		IR:	
		LD.IR:					
50		LD.REG: 1		MDR: x_4A_		DRMUX:	
		BUS: x0001				GateMDR:	
57	1	PC:		IR: x_040		GateALU:	
		BUS: x0003				GatePC:	
	23	ADDR1MUX:		ADDR2MUX:			
		LD.PC: 1		PC: x3008		PCMUX: ADDER	

What is stored in C at the end of execution for the specific operands given in memory locations A and B?

Actually, the program was written by a student, so as expected, he did not get it quite right. Almost, but not quite! Your final task on this problem is to examine the code, figure out what the student was trying to

do, and point out where he messed up and how you would fix it. It is not
necessary to write any code, just explain briefly how you would fix it.
What was the student trying to do?

How did the student mess up?

How would you fix his program?

7.34 It is often useful to find the midpoint between two values. For this
problem, assume A and B are both even numbers, and A is less than B.
For example, if A = 2 and B = 8, the midpoint is 5. The following
program finds the midpoint of two even numbers A and B by continually
incrementing the smaller number and decrementing the larger number.
You can assume that A and B have been loaded with values before this
program starts execution.
Your job: Insert the missing instructions.

```
            .ORIG  x3000
            LD     R0,A
            LD     R1,B
    X       - - - - - - - - - - - - - - - - -  (a)
            - - - - - - - - - - - - - - - - -  (b)
            ADD    R2,R2,R1
            - - - - - - - - - - - - - - - - -  (c)
            ADD    R1,R1,#-1
            - - - - - - - - - - - - - - - - -  (d)
            BRnzp  X
    DONE    ST     R1,C
            TRAP   x25
    A       .BLKW  1
    B       .BLKW  1
    C       .BLKW  1
            .END
```

★**7.35** The program stored in memory locations x3000 to x3007 loads a value
from memory location x3100, then does some processing, and then
stores a result in memory location x3101. Following is an incomplete
specification of the program. Your job: Complete the specification of the
program.

Address	Contents	Assembly code
x3000	0101 001 001 1 00000	AND R1, R1, #0
x3001	0010 000	LD R0, x3100
x3002	0000 110 000000011	BRnz x3006
x3003	0001	ADD
x3004		
x3005	0000 111	
x3006	0011 001	ST R1, x3101
x3007	1111 0000 0010 0101	HALT

To help you in this process, we have taken a snapshot of part of the
state of the machine before the first instruction executes and at several

instruction boundaries thereafter, that is, after a number of instructions executed. Part of the snapshot is shown below. Your job is to complete the snapshot. Note that the program enters the TRAP x25 service routine after executing 17 instructions. Therefore, some instructions must execute more than once.

Note that in the following table, some entries are designated xxxx. You do not have to fill in those entries. Also, you can ignore snapshots for any instructions that are not listed in the table.

Instruction #	PC	MAR	MDR	R0	R1
Initial	x3000	xxxx	xxxx	xxxx	xxxx
1	x3001	xxxx	xxxx	xxxx	
2	x3002				
3	x3003	xxxx	xxxx		
4	x3004		x1240		
5	x3005	xxxx	xxxx	x0002	
9	x3005	xxxx	xxxx	x0001	
13	x3005	xxxx	xxxx	x0000	
14	x3002	xxxx	xxxx		
15	x3006	xxxx	xxxx		
16	x3007				
17	xxxx	xxxx	xxxx		

7.36 The modulo operator (A mod B) is the remainder one gets when dividing A by B. For example, 10 mod 5 is 0, 12 mod 7 is 5.

The following program is supposed to perform A mod B, where A is in x3100 and B is in x3101. The result should be stored at location x3200. However, the programmer made a serious mistake, so the program does not work. You can assume that A and B are both positive integers.

```
        .ORIG x3000          ; Line 1
        LD R3, L2            ; 2
        LDR R0, R3, #0       ; 3
        LDR R1, R3, #1       ; 4
        NOT R2, R1           ; 5
        ADD R2, R2, #1       ; 6
L1      ADD R0, R0, R2       ; 7
        BRzp L1              ; 8
        ADD R0, R0, R1       ; 9
        ST R0, L3            ; 10
        HALT                 ; 11
L2      .FILL x3100          ; 12
L3      .FILL x3200          ; 13
        .END                 ; 14
```

After the instruction at line 6 has executed, what are the contents of R0, R1, and R2? *Note:* The correct answer in each case is one of the following: A, −A, B, −B, 0, 1, −1.

There is a bug in the program. What line is it in, and what should the correct instruction be?

★**7.37** During the processing of an LC-3 program by the data path we have been using in class, the computer stops due to a breakpoint set at x3000. The contents of certain registers and memory locations at that time are as follows:

```
R2 through R7: x0000
     M[x3000]: x1263
     M[x3003]: x0000
```

The LC-3 is restarted and executes exactly four instructions. To accomplish this, a number of clock cycles are required. In 15 of those clock cycles, the bus must be utilized. The following table lists those 15 clock cycles in sequential order, along with the values that are gated onto the LC-3 bus in each.

	BUS
1st:	x3000
2nd:	x1263
3rd:	x009A
4th:	x3001
5th:	xA000
6th:	
7th:	
8th:	
9th:	
10th:	
11th:	
12th:	
13th:	x3003
14th:	x1263
15th:	x009D

Fill in the missing entries above.

What are the four instructions that were executed?

What are the contents of R0 and R1 after the four instructions execute?

8 Data Structures

U p to now, each item of information we have processed with the computer has been a single value—either an integer, a floating point number, or an ASCII character. The real world is filled with items of information far more complex than simple, single numbers. A company's organization chart and a list of items arranged in alphabetical order are two examples. We call these complex items of information *abstract data types*, or more colloquially *data structures*. In this chapter, we will study three abstract data types: stacks, queues, and character strings. We will write programs to solve problems that require expressing information according to its structure. There are other abstract data types to be sure, but we will leave those for Chapter 15, after we have introduced you to the C programming language.

Before we get to stacks, queues, and character strings, however, we introduce a new concept that will prove very useful in manipulating data structures: *subroutines*, or what is also called *functions*.

8.1 Subroutines

It is often useful to be able to invoke a program fragment multiple times within the same program without having to specify its details in the source program each time it is needed. Also, in the real world of computer software development, it is often (usually?) the case that one software engineer writes a program that requires such fragments and another software engineer writes the fragments.

Or, one might require a fragment that has been supplied by the manufacturer or by some independent software supplier. It is almost always the case that collections of such fragments are available to user programmers to free them from having to write their own. These collections are referred to as *libraries*. An example is the Math Library, which consists of fragments that compute such functions as **square root, sine,** and **arctangent**. In fact, because the Math Library exists, user programmers can get the computer to compute those functions without even having to know how to write a program fragment to do it!

For all of these reasons, it is good to have a way to use program fragments efficiently. Such program fragments are called *subroutines,* or alternatively,
procedures, or in C terminology, *functions*.

Figure 8.1 provides a simple illustration of a part of a program—call it "piece-
of-code-A"—containing fragments that must be executed multiple times within
piece-of-code-A. Figure 8.1 will be studied in detail in Chapter 9, but for now,

```
01  START  ST    R1,SaveR1     ; Save registers needed
02         ST    R2,SaveR2     ; by this routine
03         ST    R3,SaveR3
04  ;
05         LD    R2,Newline
06  L1     LDI   R3,DSR
07         BRzp  L1            ; Loop until monitor is ready
08         STI   R2,DDR        ; Move cursor to new clean line
09  ;
0A         LEA   R1,Prompt     ; Starting address of prompt string
0B  Loop   LDR   R0,R1,#0      ; Write the input prompt
0C         BRz   Input         ; End of prompt string
0D  L2     LDI   R3,DSR
0E         BRzp  L2            ; Loop until monitor is ready
0F         STI   R0,DDR        ; Write next prompt character
10         ADD   R1,R1,#1      ; Increment prompt pointer
11         BRnzp Loop          ; Get next prompt character
12  ;
13  Input  LDI   R3,KBSR
14         BRzp  Input         ; Poll until a character is typed
15         LDI   R0,KBDR       ; Load input character into R0
16  L3     LDI   R3,DSR
17         BRzp  L3            ; Loop until monitor is ready
18         STI   R0,DDR        ; Echo input character
19  ;
1A  L4     LDI   R3,DSR
1B         BRzp  L4            ; Loop until monitor is ready
1C         STI   R2,DDR        ; Move cursor to new clean line
1D         LD    R1,SaveR1     ; Restore registers
1E         LD    R2,SaveR2     ; to original values
1F         LD    R3,SaveR3
20         JMP   R7            ; Do the program's next task
21  ;
22  SaveR1 .BLKW 1             ; Memory for registers saved
23  SaveR2 .BLKW 1
24  SaveR3 .BLKW 1
25  DSR    .FILL xFE04
26  DDR    .FILL xFE06
27  KBSR   .FILL xFE00
28  KBDR   .FILL xFE02
29  Newline .FILL x000A        ; ASCII code for newline
2A  Prompt .STRINGZ ''Input a character>''
```

Figure 8.1   Instruction sequence (Piece-of-code-A) we will study in detail in Chapter 9.

let's ignore everything about it except the three-instruction sequences starting at symbolic addresses L1, L2, L3, and L4.

Each of these four 3-instruction sequences does the following:

```
label   LDI   R3,DSR
        BRzp  label
        STI   Reg,DDR
```

Each of the four instances uses a different label (L1, L2, L3, L4), but that is not a problem since in each instance the only purpose of the label is to branch back from the BRzp instruction to the LDI instruction.

Two of the four program fragments store the contents of R0 and the other two store the contents of R2, but that is easy to take care of, as we will see. The main point is that, aside from the small nuisance of which register is being used for the source of the STI instruction, the four program fragments do exactly the same thing, and it is wasteful to require the programmer to write the code four times. The subroutine call/return mechanism enables the programmer to write the code only once.

8.1.1 The Call/Return Mechanism

The call/return mechanism allows us to execute this one three-instruction sequence multiple times by requiring us to include it as a subroutine in our program only once.

Figure 8.2 shows the instruction execution flow for a program with and without subroutines.

Note in Figure 8.2 that without subroutines, the programmer has to provide the same code A after X, after Y, and after Z. With subroutines, the programmer

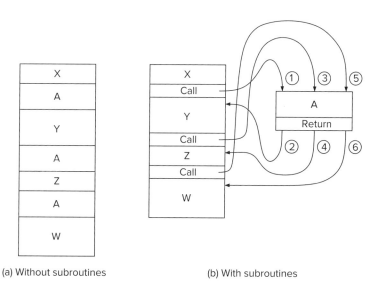

(a) Without subroutines   (b) With subroutines

Figure 8.2   Instruction execution flow with/without subroutines.

has to provide the code A only once. The programmer uses the call/return mechanism to direct the computer each time via the **call instruction** to the code A, and after the computer has executed the code A, to the **return instruction** to the proper next instruction to be executed in the program.

We refer to the program that contains the call as the *caller*, and the subroutine that contains the return as the *callee*.

The call/return mechanism consists of two instructions. The first instruction **JSR(R)** is in the caller program and does two things: It loads the PC with the starting address of the subroutine and it loads R7 with the address immediately after the address of the JSR(R) instruction. The address immediately after the address of the JSR(R) instruction is the address to come back to after executing the subroutine. We call the address we come back to the *return linkage*. The second instruction **JMP R7** is the last instruction in the subroutine (i.e., in the callee program). It loads the PC with the contents of R7, the address just after the address of the JSR instruction, completing the round trip flow of control from the caller to the callee and back.

8.1.2 JSR(R)—The Instruction That Calls the Subroutine

The LC-3 specifies one control instruction for calling subroutines; its opcode is **0100**. The instruction uses one of two addressing modes for computing the starting address of the subroutine, PC-relative addressing or Base Register addressing. The LC-3 assembly language provides two different mnemonic names for the opcode, JSR and JSRR, depending on which addressing mode is used.

The JSR(R) instruction does two things. Like all control instructions, it loads the PC, overwriting the incremented PC that was loaded during the FETCH phase of the JSR(R) instruction. In this case the starting address of the subroutine is computed and loaded into the PC. The second thing the JSR(R) instruction does is save the return address in R7. The return address is the incremented PC, which is the address of the instruction following the JSR(R) instruction in the calling program.

The JSR(R) instruction consists of three parts.

15	14	13	12	11	10	9	8	7	6	5	4	3	2	1	0
Opcode				A				Address evaluation bits							

Bits [15:12] contain the opcode, 0100. Bit [11] specifies the addressing mode, the value 1 if the addressing mode is PC-relative, and the value 0 if the addressing mode is Base Register addressing. Bits [10:0] contain information that is used to obtain the starting address of the subroutine. The only difference between JSR and JSRR is the addressing mode that is used for evaluating the starting address of the subroutine.

JSR   The JSR instruction computes the target address of the subroutine by sign-extending the 11-bit offset (bits [10:0]) of the instruction to 16 bits and adding that to the incremented PC. This addressing mode is almost identical to the addressing mode of another control instruction, the BR instruction, except eleven bits of PCoffset are used, rather than nine bits as is the case for BR.

If the following JSR instruction is stored in location x4200, its execution will cause the PC to be loaded with x3E05 (i.e., xFC04 + x4201) and R7 to be loaded with x4201.

x 4200

15	14	13	12	11	10	9	8	7	6	5	4	3	2	1	0
0	1	0	0	1	1	0	0	0	0	0	0	0	1	0	0

JSR   A   PCoffset11

JSRR   The JSRR instruction is exactly like the JSR instruction except for the addressing mode. **JSRR** obtains the starting address of the subroutine in exactly the same way the JMP instruction does; that is, bits [8:6] identify the Base Register, that contains the address to be loaded into the PC.

If the following JSRR instruction is stored in location x420A, and if R5 contains x3002, the execution of the JSRR will cause R7 to be loaded with x420B and the PC to be loaded with x3002.

Question: What important feature does the JSRR instruction provide that the JSR instruction does not provide?

x420A

15	14	13	12	11	10	9	8	7	6	5	4	3	2	1	0
0	1	0	0	0	0	0	1	0	1	0	0	0	0	0	0

JSRR   A   BaseR

R5 3002

8.1.3 Saving and Restoring Registers

We have known for a long time that every time an instruction loads a value into a register, the value that was previously in that register is lost. Thus, we need to save the value in a register

- if that value will be destroyed by some subsequent instruction, and
- if we will need it after that subsequent instruction.

This can be a problem when dealing with subroutines.

Let's examine again the piece of code in Figure 8.1. Suppose this piece of code is a subroutine called by the instruction JSR START in some caller program, which we will call CALLER.

Suppose before CALLER executes JSR START, it computes values that it loads into R1, R2, and R3. In our subroutine starting at START, the instruction on line 05 loads a value into R2, the instruction on line 06 loads a value into R3, and the instruction on line 0A loads a value into R1. What would happen if CALLER needed those values after returning from the subroutine that begins at START? Too bad! Since the subroutine destroyed the values in R1, R2, and R3 by executing the instructions in lines 05, 06, and 0A, those values are lost to CALLER when it resumes execution after the JMP R7 instruction on line 20 of the subroutine. Of course, this is unacceptable.

We prevent it from happening during the first part of our subroutine, that is, during initialization. In lines 01, 02, and 03, the contents of R1, R2, and R3 are stored in memory locations SaveR1, SaveR2, and SaveR3. Three locations in the subroutine (lines 22, 23, and 24) have been set aside for the purpose of saving those register values. And, in lines 1D, 1E, and 1F (just before the JMP R7 instruction), the values stored there are put back into R1, R2, and R3. That is, before the subroutine uses R1, R2, and R3 for its own use, the subroutine **saves** the values put there by the calling program. And, before the subroutine returns to the calling program, those values are put back (i.e., **restored**) where the calling program has a right to expect them.

We call this technique *callee save* because the subroutine (i.e., the callee) saves and restores the registers. It makes sense to have the subroutine save the registers because the subroutine knows which registers it needs to do the work of the subroutine. There really is no reason to burden the person writing the caller program to know which registers the subroutine needs.

We could of course have the caller program save all the registers before JSR START, and then the subroutine would not have to bother saving any of them. Some programs do that, and in fact, some ISAs have JSR instructions that do that as part of the execution of the JSR instruction. But if we wish to eliminate unnecessary saves and restores, we can do so in this case by having the callee save only the registers it needs.

We should also point out that since JMP START loads the return linkage in R7, whatever was in R7 is destroyed by the execution of the JMP START instruction. Therefore, if the calling program had stored a value in R7 before calling the subroutine at START, and it needed that value after returning from the subroutine, the caller program would have to save and restore R7. Why should the caller program save and restore R7? Because the caller program knows that the contents of R7 will be destroyed by execution of JMP START. We call this *caller save* because the calling program saves and restores the register value.

The message is this: If a value in a register will be needed after something else is stored in that register, we must *save* it before something else happens and *restore* it before we can subsequently use it. We save a register value by storing it in memory; we restore it by loading it back into the register.

The save/restore problem can be handled either by the calling program before the JSR occurs or by the subroutine. We will see in Section 9.3 that the same problem exists for another class of calling/called routines, those due to system calls.

In summary, we use the term *caller save* if the calling program handles the problem. We use the term *callee save* if the called program handles the problem. The appropriate one to handle the problem is the one that knows which registers will be destroyed by subsequent actions.

The callee knows which registers it needs to do the job of the called program. Therefore, before it starts, it saves those registers with a sequence of stores. After it finishes, it restores those registers with a sequence of loads. And it sets aside memory locations to save those register values.

The caller knows what damage will be done by instructions under its control. It knows that each instance of a JSR instruction will destroy what is in R7. So, before the JSR instruction is executed, R7 is saved. After the caller program resumes execution (upon completion of the subroutine), R7 is restored.

8.1.4 Library Routines

We noted early in this section that there are many uses for the call/return mechanism, among them the ability of a user program to call library subroutines that are usually delivered as part of the computer system. Libraries are provided as a convenience to the user programmer. They are legitimately advertised as *productivity enhancers* since they allow the application programmer to use them without having to know or learn much of their inner details. For example, it is often the case that a programmer knows what a square root is (we abbreviate **SQRT**), may need to use sqrt(x) for some value x, but does not have a clue as to how to write a program to perform sqrt, and probably would rather not have to learn how.

A simple example illustrates the point: We have lost our key and need to get into our apartment. We can lean a ladder up against the wall so that the ladder touches the bottom of our open window, 24 feet above the ground. There is a 10-foot flower bed on the ground along the edge of the wall, so we need to keep the base of the ladder outside the flower bed. How big a ladder do we need so that we can lean it against the wall and climb through the window? Or, stated less colorfully: If the sides of a right triangle are 24 feet and 10 feet, how big is the hypotenuse (see Figure 8.3)?

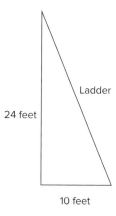

Figure 8.3 Solving for the length of the hypotenuse.

We remember from high school that Pythagoras answered that one for us:

$$c^2 = a^2 + b^2$$

Knowing a and b, we can easily solve for c by taking the square root of the sum of a^2 and b^2. Taking the sum is not hard—the LC-3 ADD instruction can do that job. The square is also not hard; we can multiply two numbers by a sequence of additions. But how does one get the square root? The structure of our solution is shown in Figure 8.4.

The subroutine SQRT has yet to be written. If it were not for the Math Library, the programmer would have to pick up a math book (or get someone to do it for him/her), check out the Newton-Raphson method, and produce the missing subroutine.

```
01                  . . .
02                  . . .
03          LD      R0,SIDE1
04          BRz     S1
05          JSR     SQUARE
06  S1      ADD     R1,R0,#0
07          LD      R0,SIDE2
08          BRz     S2
09          JSR     SQUARE
0A  S2      ADD     R0,R0,R1
0B          JSR     SQRT
0C          ST      R0,HYPOT
0D          BRnzp   NEXT_TASK
0E  SQUARE  ADD     R2,R0,#0
0F          ADD     R3,R0,#0
10  AGAIN   ADD     R2,R2,#-1
11          BRz     DONE
12          ADD     R0,R0,R3
13          BRnzp   AGAIN
14  DONE    RET
15  SQRT    . . .          ; R0 <-- SQRT(R0)
16          . . .          ;
17          . . .          ; How do we write this subroutine?
18          . . .          ;
19          . . .          ;
1A          RET
1B  SIDE1   .BLKW   1
1C  SIDE2   .BLKW   1
1D  HYPOT   .BLKW   1
1E          . . .
1F          . . .
```

Figure 8.4   A program fragment to compute the hypotenuse of a right triangle.

However, with the Math Library, the problem pretty much goes away. Since the Math Library supplies a number of subroutines (including SQRT), the user programmer can continue to be ignorant of the likes of Newton-Raphson. The user still needs to know the label of the target address of the library routine that performs the square root function, where to put the argument x, and where to expect the result SQRT(x). But these are easy conventions that can be obtained from the documentation associated with the Math Library.

If the library routine starts at address SQRT, and the argument is provided in R0 to the library routine, and the result is obtained in R0 from the library routine, Figure 8.4 reduces to Figure 8.5.

Two things are worth noting:

- *Thing 1*—The programmer no longer has to worry about how to compute the square root function. The library routine does that for us.

- *Thing 2*—The pseudo-op .EXTERNAL. We already saw in Section 7.4.2 that this pseudo-op tells the assembler that the label (SQRT), which is needed to assemble the .FILL pseudo-op in line 19, will be supplied by some other program fragment (i.e., module) and will be combined with this program

```
01                  ...
02                  ...
03                  .EXTERNAL SQRT
04                  ...
05                  ...
06                  LD      R0,SIDE1
07                  BRz     S1
08                  JSR     SQUARE
09      S1          ADD     R1,R0,#0
0A                  LD      R0,SIDE2
0B                  BRz     S2
0C                  JSR     SQUARE
0D      S2          ADD     R0,R0,R1 ; R0 contains argument x
0E                  LD      R4,BASE  ; BASE contains starting address of SQRT routine
0F                  JSRR    R4
10                  ST      R0,HYPOT
11                  BRnzp   NEXT_TASK
12      SQUARE      ADD     R2,R0,#0
13                  ADD     R3,R0,#0
14      AGAIN       ADD     R2,R2,#-1
15                  BRz     DONE
16                  ADD     R0,R0,R3
17                  BRnzp   AGAIN
18      DONE        RET
19      BASE        .FILL   SQRT
1A      SIDE1       .BLKW   1
1B      SIDE2       .BLKW   1
1C      HYPOT       .BLKW   1
1D                  ...
1E                  ...
```

Figure 8.5   The program fragment of Figure 8.4, using a library routine.

fragment (i.e., module) when the *executable image* is produced. The executable image is the binary module that actually executes. The executable image is produced at *link* time.

This notion of combining multiple modules at link time to produce an executable image is the normal case. Figure 8.6 illustrates the process. You will see concrete examples of this when we work with the programming language C in the second half of this course.

Most application software requires library routines from various libraries. It would be very inefficient for the typical programmer to produce all of them—assuming the typical programmer were able to produce such routines in the first place. We have mentioned routines from the Math Library. There are also a number of preprocessing routines for producing *pretty* graphic images. There are other routines for a number of other tasks where it would make no sense at all to have the programmer write them from scratch. It is much easier to require only (1) appropriate documentation so that the interface between the library routine and the program that calls that routine is clear, and (2) the use of the proper pseudo-ops such as .EXTERNAL in the source program. The linker can then produce an executable image at link time from the separately assembled modules.

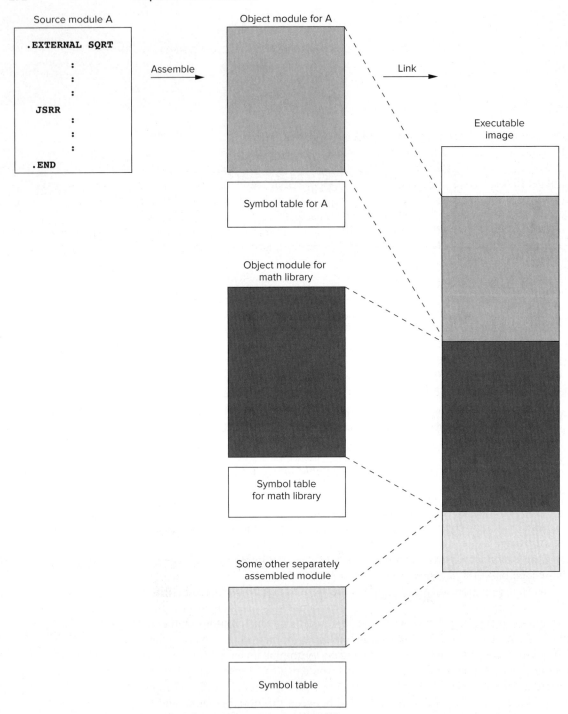

Figure 8.6   An executable image constructed from multiple files.

8.2 The Stack

Now we are ready to study some data structures. The first and most important data structure is the stack.

8.2.1 The Stack—An Abstract Data Type

Throughout your future interaction with computers (whether writing software or designing hardware), you will encounter again and again the storage mechanism known as a *stack*. Stacks can be implemented in many different ways, and we will get to that momentarily. But first, it is important to know that the concept of a stack has nothing to do with how it is implemented. The concept of a stack is the specification of how it is to be *accessed*. That is, the defining notion of a stack is that the **last** thing you stored in the stack is the **first** thing you remove from it. That is what makes a stack different from everything else in the world. Simply put: Last In, First Out, or LIFO.

In the terminology of computer programming languages, we say the stack is an example of an *abstract data type*. That is, an abstract data type is a storage mechanism that is defined by the operations performed on it and not at all by the specific manner in which it is implemented. In this section, you will see stacks implemented as sequential locations in memory.

8.2.2 Two Example Implementations

A coin holder in the armrest next to the driver of an automobile is an example of a stack. The first quarter you take to pay the highway toll is the last quarter you added to the stack of quarters. As you add quarters, you push the earlier quarters down into the coin holder.

Figure 8.7 shows the behavior of a coin holder. Initially, as shown in Figure 8.7a, the coin holder is empty. The first highway toll is 75 cents, and you give the toll collector a dollar. He gives you 25 cents change, a 1995 quarter, which you insert into the coin holder. The coin holder appears as shown in Figure 8.7b.

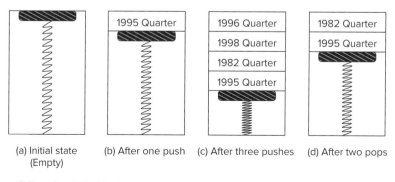

(a) Initial state (Empty)   (b) After one push   (c) After three pushes   (d) After two pops

Figure 8.7   A coin holder in an automobile armrest—example of a stack.

There are special terms for the insertion and removal of elements from a stack. We say we *push* an element onto the stack when we insert it. We say we *pop* an element from the stack when we remove it.

The second highway toll is $4.25, and you give the toll collector $5.00. She gives you 75 cents change, which you insert into the coin holder: first a 1982 quarter, then a 1998 quarter, and finally, a 1996 quarter. Now the coin holder is as shown in Figure 8.7c. The third toll is 50 cents, and you remove (pop) the top two quarters from the coin holder: the 1996 quarter first and then the 1998 quarter. The coin holder is then as shown in Figure 8.7d.

The coin holder is an example of a stack, **precisely** because it obeys the LIFO requirement. Each time you insert a quarter, you do so at the top. Each time you remove a quarter, you do so from the top. The last coin you inserted is the first coin you remove. Therefore, it is a stack.

Another implementation of a stack, sometimes referred to as a computer hardware stack, is shown in Figure 8.8. Its behavior resembles that of the coin holder we just described. It consists of some number of hardware registers, each of which can store a value. The example of Figure 8.8 contains five registers. As each value is added to the stack or removed from the stack, the values **already** on the stack **move.**

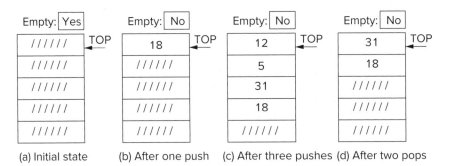

Figure 8.8   A stack, implemented in hardware—data entries move.

In Figure 8.8a, the stack is initially shown as empty. Access is always via the first element, which is labeled TOP. If the value 18 is pushed onto the stack, we have Figure 8.8b. If the three values 31, 5, and 12 are pushed (in that order), the result is as shown in Figure 8.8c. Finally, if two values are popped from the stack, we have Figure 8.8d. A distinguishing feature of the stack of Figure 8.8 is that, like the quarters in the coin holder, as each value is added or removed, **all the other values already on the stack move**.

8.2.3 Implementation in Memory

By far the most common implementation of a stack in a computer is as shown in Figure 8.9. This stack consists of a sequence of memory locations along with a mechanism, called the *stack pointer*, which keeps track of the **top** of the stack. We use R6 to contain the address of the top of the stack. That is, in the LC-3, R6 is the stack pointer.

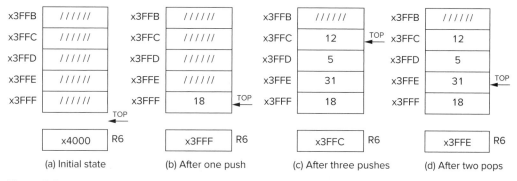

Figure 8.9 A stack, implemented in memory—data entries do not move.

In Figure 8.9, five memory locations (x3FFF to x3FFB) are provided for the stack. The actual locations comprising the stack at any single instant of time are the consecutive locations from x3FFF to the location specified in R6, that is, the top of the stack. For example, in Figure 8.9c, the stack consists of the contents of locations x3FFF, x3FFE, x3FFD, and x3FFC.

Figure 8.9a shows an initially empty stack. Since there are no values on the stack, the stack pointer contains the address x4000, the address of the memory location just after the memory locations reserved for the stack. Why this makes sense will be clear after we show the actual code for pushing values onto and popping values off of the stack. Figure 8.9b shows the stack after pushing the value 18. Note that the stack pointer contains the address x3FFF, which is the new top of the stack.

Figure 8.9c shows the stack after pushing the values 31, 5, and 12, in that order. Note that the values inserted into the stack are stored in memory locations having decreasing addresses. We say the stack *grows toward zero*. Finally, Figure 8.9d shows the stack after popping the top two elements off the stack.

Note that those two elements (the values 5 and 12) that were popped are still present in memory locations x3FFD and x3FFC. However, as we will see momentarily, those values 5 and 12 cannot be accessed from memory, as long as **every** access to memory is controlled by the stack mechanism.

Note also that, unlike the coin holder and computer hardware stack implementations discussed in the previous section, when values are pushed and popped to and from a stack implemented in sequential memory locations, the data already stored on the stack **does not physically move**.

Push We push a value onto the stack by executing the two-instruction sequence

```
PUSH            ADD   R6,R6,#-1
                STR   R0,R6,#0
```

In Figure 8.9a, R6 contains x4000, indicating that the stack is empty. To push the value 18 onto the stack, we decrement R6, the stack pointer, so the address in R6 (i.e., address x3FFF) corresponds to the location where we want to store the value we are pushing onto the stack. The actual push is done by first loading 18 into R0, and then executing STR R0,R6,#0. This stores the contents of R0 into memory location x3FFF.

That is, to push a value onto the stack, we first load that value into R0. Then we decrement R6, which contained the previous top of the stack. Then we execute STR R0,R6,#0, which stores the contents of R0 into the memory location whose address is in R6.

The three values 31, 5, and 12 are pushed onto the stack by loading each in turn into R0 and then executing the two-instruction sequence. In Figure 8.9c, R6 (the stack pointer) contains x3FFC, indicating that the top of the stack is location x3FFC and that 12 was the last value pushed.

Pop   To pop a value from the stack, the value is read and the stack pointer is incremented. The following two-instruction sequence

```
POP               LDR    R0,R6,#0
                  ADD    R6,R6,#1
```

pops the value contained in the top of the stack and loads it into R0. The stack pointer (R6) is incremented to indicate that the old value at the top of the stack has been popped and is no longer on the stack, and we have a new value at the top of the stack.

If the stack were as shown in Figure 8.9c and we executed the sequence twice, we would pop two values from the stack. In this case, we would first remove the 12, and then the 5. Assuming the purpose of popping two values is to use those two values, we would, of course, have to move the 12 from R0 to some other location before calling POP a second time.

Note that after 12 and 5 are popped, R6 contains x3FFE, indicating that 12 and 5 are no longer on the stack and that the top of the stack is 31. Figure 8.9d shows the stack after that sequence of operations.

Note that the values 12 and 5 are still stored in memory locations x3FFD and x3FFC, respectively. However, since the stack requires that we push by executing the PUSH sequence and pop by executing the POP sequence, we cannot read the values 12 and 5 if we obey the rules. The fancy name for "the rules" is the *stack protocol*.

Underflow   What happens if we now attempt to pop three values from the stack? Since only two values remain on the stack, we would have a problem. Attempting to pop items that have not been previously pushed results in an *underflow* situation. In our example, we can test for underflow by comparing the stack pointer with x4000, which would be the contents of R6 if there were nothing left on the stack to pop. If UNDERFLOW is the label of a routine that handles the underflow condition, our resulting POP sequence would be

```
POP         LD      R1,EMPTY
            ADD     R2,R6,R1        ; Compare stack
            BRz     UNDERFLOW       ; pointer with x4000.
    ;
            LDR     R0,R6,#0
            ADD     R6,R6,#1
    ;
            RET
EMPTY       .FILL   xC000           ; EMPTY <-- negative of x4000
```

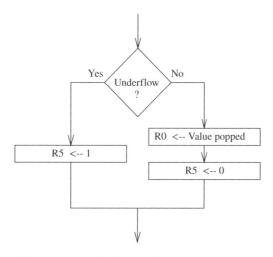

Figure 8.10   POP routine, including test for underflow.

Rather than have the POP routine immediately jump to the UNDERFLOW routine if the POP is unsuccessful, it is often useful to have the POP routine return to the calling program with the underflow information contained in a register. We will use R5 to provide success/failure information. Figure 8.10 is a flowchart showing how the POP routine could be augmented, using R5 to report this success/failure information.

Upon return from the POP routine, the calling program would examine R5 to determine whether the POP completed successfully (R5 = 0), or not (R5 = 1).

Note that since the POP routine reports success or failure in R5, whatever was stored in R5 **before** the POP routine was called is lost. Thus, it is the job of the calling program to save the contents of R5 before the JSR instruction is executed if the value stored there will be needed later. Recall from Section 8.1.3 that this is an example of a caller-save situation.

The resulting POP routine is shown in the following instruction sequence.

```
POP       AND    R5,R5,#0
          LD     R1,EMPTY
          ADD    R2,R6,R1
          BRz    Failure
          LDR    R0,R6,#0
          ADD    R6,R6,#1
          RET
Failure   ADD    R5,R5,#1
          RET
EMPTY     .FILL  xC000          ; EMPTY <-- -x4000
```

Overflow   What happens when we run out of available space and we try to push a value onto the stack? Since we cannot store values where there is no space, we have an *overflow* situation. We can test for overflow by comparing the stack pointer with (in the example of Figure 8.9) x3FFB. If they are equal, we have no place to push another value onto the stack. If OVERFLOW is the label of a routine that handles the overflow condition, our resulting PUSH sequence would be

```
PUSH        LD      R1,MAX
            ADD     R2,R6,R1
            BRz     OVERFLOW
    ;
            ADD     R6,R6,#-1
            STR     R0,R6,#0
    ;
            RET
MAX         .FILL   xC005          ; MAX <-- negative of x3FFB
```

In the same way that it is useful to have the POP routine return to the calling program with success/failure information, rather than immediately jumping to the UNDERFLOW routine, it is useful to have the PUSH routine act similarly.

We augment the PUSH routine with instructions to store 0 (success) or 1 (failure) in R5, depending on whether or not the push completed successfully. Upon return from the PUSH routine, the calling program would examine R5 to determine whether the PUSH completed successfully (R5 = 0) or not (R5 = 1).

Note again that since the PUSH routine reports success or failure in R5, we have another example of a caller-save situation. That is, since whatever was stored in R5 before the PUSH routine was called is lost, it is the job of the calling program to save the contents of R5 before the JSR instruction is executed if the value stored in R5 will be needed later.

The resulting PUSH routine is shown in the following instruction sequence.

```
PUSH        AND     R5,R5,#0
            LD      R1,MAX
            ADD     R2,R6,R1
            BRz     Failure
            ADD     R6,R6,#-1
            STR     R0,R6,#0
            RET
Failure     ADD     R5,R5,#1
    =       RET
MAX         .FILL   xC005          ; MAX <-- -x3FFB
```

8.2.4 The Complete Picture

The POP and PUSH routines allow us to use memory locations x3FFF through x3FFB as a five-entry stack. If we wish to push a value onto the stack, we simply load that value into R0 and execute JSR PUSH. To pop a value from the stack into R0, we simply execute JSR POP. If we wish to change the location or the size of the stack, we adjust BASE and MAX accordingly.

Before leaving this topic, we should be careful to clean up an important detail that we discussed in Section 8.1.3. The subroutines PUSH and POP make use of R1 and R2, and there is no reason why the calling program would know that.

Therefore, it is the job of the subroutine (callee save) to save R1 and R2 before using them, and to restore them before returning to the calling program.

The PUSH and POP routines also write to R5. But, as we have already pointed out, the calling program knows that the subroutine will report success or failure in R5, so it is the job of the calling program to save R5 before executing the JSR instruction if the value stored in R5 will be needed later. As discussed in Section 8.1.3, this is an example of caller save.

The final code for our PUSH and POP operations is shown in Figure 8.11.

```
01    ;
02    ; Subroutines for carrying out the PUSH and POP functions.  This
03    ; program works with a stack consisting of memory locations x3FFF
04    ; through x3FFB.  R6 is the stack pointer.
05    ;
06    POP           AND     R5,R5,#0        ; R5 <-- success
07                  ST      R1,Save1        ; Save registers that
08                  ST      R2,Save2        ; are needed by POP
09                  LD      R1,EMPTY        ; EMPTY contains -x4000
0B                  ADD     R2,R6,R1        ; Compare stack pointer to x4000
0C                  BRz     fail_exit       ; Branch if stack is empty
0D    ;
0E                  LDR     R0,R6,#0        ; The actual "pop"
0F                  ADD     R6,R6,#1        ; Adjust stack pointer
10                  BRnzp   success_exit
11    ;
12    PUSH          AND     R5,R5,#0
13                  ST      R1,Save1        ; Save registers that
14                  ST      R2,Save2        ; are needed by PUSH
15                  LD      R1,FULL         ; FULL contains -x3FFB
16                  ADD     R2,R6,R1        ; Compare stack pointer to x3FFB
17                  BRz     fail_exit       ; Branch if stack is full
18    ;
19                  ADD     R6,R6,#-1       ; Adjust stack pointer
1A                  STR     R0,R6,#0        ; The actual "push"
1B    success_exit  LD      R2,Save2        ; Restore original
1C                  LD      R1,Save1        ; register values
1D                  RET
1E    ;
1F    fail_exit     LD      R2,Save2        ; Restore original
20                  LD      R1,Save1        ; register values
21                  ADD     R5,R5,#1        ; R5 <-- failure
22                  RET
23    ;
24    EMPTY         .FILL   xC000           ; EMPTY contains -x4000
25    FULL          .FILL   xC005           ; FULL contains  -x3FFB
26    Save1         .FILL   x0000
27    Save2         .FILL   x0000
```

Figure 8.11　　The stack protocol.

8.3 Recursion, a Powerful Technique When Used Appropriately

Recursion is a mechanism for expressing a function *in terms of itself*. Some have referred to it as picking oneself up by one's bootstraps, since at first blush, it looks like magic—which, of course, it isn't.

When used appropriately, the expressive power of recursion is going to save us a lot of headaches. When used whimsically, recursion is going to require unnecessary activity, resulting in longer execution time and wasted energy.

The mechanism is so important that we will study it in greater detail later in the book after we have raised the level of abstraction to programming in a high-level language. However, since a critical concept needed to understand the implementation of recursion is the stack, which we have just studied, it is useful to show by means of examples just when using recursion is warranted and when using it is not a good idea.

We will examine two ill-advised uses of recursion. We will also examine a problem where using the expressive power of recursion is very helpful.

8.3.1 Bad Example Number 1: Factorial

The simplest example to illustrate recursion is the function **factorial**. The equation

$$n! = n * (n\text{-}1)!$$

says it all. We are expressing factorial in terms of factorial! How we can write a program to do this we will see momentarily.

Assume the subroutine FACT (Factorial) is supplied with a positive integer n in R0 and returns with the value n! in R0. (We will save 0! for an exercise at the end of the chapter.)

Figure 8.12 shows a pictorial view of the recursive subroutine. We represent the subroutine FACT as a hexagon, and inside the hexagon is another instance of the hexagon! We call the subroutine recursive because inside the FACT subroutine is an instruction JSR FACT.

The subroutine first tests to see if n = 1. If so, we are done, since (1)! = 1. It is important to emphasize that every recursive subroutine must have such an initial test to see if we should execute the recursive call. Without this test, the subroutine would call itself (JSR FACT) an infinite number of times! Clearly, that cannot be correct. The answer is to provide a test before the recursive JSR instruction. In the case of the subroutine FACT, if R0 is 1, we are done, since 1! = 1.

If n does not equal 1, we save the value in R1, so we can store n in R1, load R0 with n-1 and JSR FACT. When FACT returns with (n-1)! in R0, we multiply it by n (which was stored in R1), producing n!, which we load into R0, restore R1 to the value expected by the calling program, and RET.

If we assume the LC-3 has a MUL instruction, the basic structure of the FACT subroutine takes the following form:

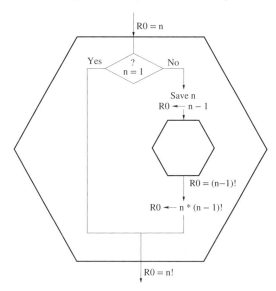

Figure 8.12 Flowchart for a recursive **FACTORIAL** subroutine.

```
FACT    ST    R1, Save1   ; Callee save R1
        ADD   R1,R0,#-1   ; Test if R0=1
        BRz   DONE        ; If R0=1, R0 also contains (1)!, so we are done
        ADD   R1,R0,#0    ; Save n in R1, to be used after we compute (n-1)!
        ADD   R0,R1, #-1  ; Set R0 to n-1, and then call FACT
B       JSR   FACT        ; On RET, R0 will contain (n-1)!
        MUL   R0,R0,R1    ; Multiply n times (n-1)!, yielding n! in R0
DONE    LD    R1, Save1   ; Callee restore R1
        RET
Save1   .BLKW 1
```

Since the LC-3 does not have a MUL instruction, this will require another subroutine call, but we are ignoring that here in order to focus on the essence of recursion.

Unfortunately, the code we have written will not work. To see why it will not work, Figure 8.13 shows the flow of instruction execution as we would like it to be. The main program calls the subroutine with a JSR instruction at address A. This causes the code labeled #1 to execute. At address B, the subroutine FACT calls itself with the instruction JSR FACT. This causes the code labeled #2 to execute, and so forth.

Note that when the main program executes the instruction JSR FACT, the return linkage A+1 is saved in R7. In the block of code labeled #1, the instruction at address B (JSR FACT) stores its return linkage B+1 in R7, destroying A+1, so there is no way to get back to the main program. Bad! In fact, very, very bad!

We can solve this problem by pushing the address A+1 onto a stack before executing JSR FACT at address B. After we subsequently return to address B+1, we can then pop the stack and load the address A+1 into R7 before we execute the instruction RET back to the main program.

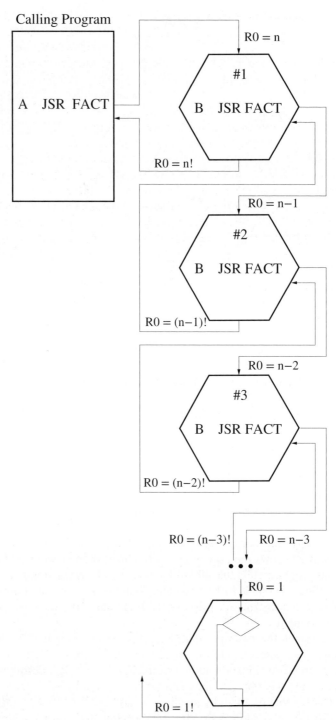

Figure 8.13   Execution flow for recursive **FACTORIAL** subroutines.

Also, note that the instruction ADD R1,R0,#0 in #1 loads the value n into R1, and in #2, the instruction ADD R1,R0,#0 loads the value n-1 into R1, thereby wiping out the value n that had been put there by the code in #1. Thus, when the instruction flow gets back to #1), where the value n is needed by the instruction MUL R0,R0,R1, it is no longer there. It was previously wiped out. Again, very, very bad!

We can solve this problem with a stack also. That is, instead of moving the value n to R1 before loading n-1 into R0, we push n onto the stack and then pop it when we need it after returning from the subroutine with (n-1)! in R0.

Finally, we note that the first instruction in our subroutine saves R1 in Save1 and the last instruction before the RET restores it to R1. We do this so that from the standpoint of the calling program, the value in R1 before the subroutine is the same as the value in R1 after the subroutine, even though the subroutine used R1 in performing its job. However, since our subroutine is recursive, when FACT is called by the JSR instruction at address B, R1 does not contain the value it had in the main program, but instead it has the value last stored in R1 by the ADD R1,R0,#0 instruction. Thus after the JSR FACT instruction is executed, the first instruction of the recursively called subroutine FACT will save that value, wiping out the value that the main program had stored in R1 when it called FACT.

We can solve this problem with a stack also. We simply replace the ST R1,Save1 with a push and LD R1,Save1 with a pop.

If we make these changes (and if the LC-3 had a MUL opcode), the recursive subroutine works as we would like it to. The resulting subroutine is shown in Figure 8.14 (with almost all instructions explained via comments):

```
FACT          ADD   R6,R6,#-1
              STR   R1,R6,#0    ; Push Caller's R1 on the stack, so we can use R1.
;
              ADD   R1,R0,#-1   ; If n=1, we are done since 1! = 1
              BRz   NO_RECURSE
;
              ADD   R6,R6,#-1
              STR   R7,R6,#0    ; Push return linkage onto stack
              ADD   R6,R6,#-1
              STR   R0,R6,#0    ; Push n on the stack
;
              ADD   R0,R0,#-1   ; Form n-1, argument of JSR
B             JSR   FACT
              LDR   R1,R6,#0    ; Pop n from the stack
              ADD   R6,R6,#1
              MUL   R0,R0,R1    ; form n*(n-1)!
;
              LDR   R7,R6,#0    ; Pop return linkage into R7
              ADD   R6,R6,#1
NO_RECURSE    LDR   R1,R6,#0    ; Pop caller's R1 back into R1
              ADD   R6,R6,#1
              RET
```

Figure 8.14   The recursive subroutine FACT.

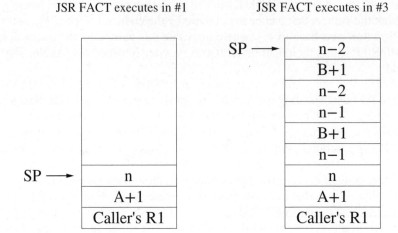

a. Contents of stack when
JSR FACT executes in #1

a. Contents of stack when
JSR FACT executes in #3

Figure 8.15   The stack during two instances of executing the FACTORIAL subroutine.

The main program calls FACT with R0 = n. The code in #1 executes, with JSR FACT being called with R0 = n-1. At this point, the stack contains the three entries pushed, as shown in Figure 8.15a. When the JSR FACT instruction in #3 executes, with R0 = n-3, the stack contains the nine entries as shown in Figure 8.15b.

The obvious question you should ask at this point is, "Why is this such a bad use of recursion, particularly when its representation n! = n * (n-1)! is so elegant?" To answer this question, we first note how many instructions are executed and how much time is wasted pushing and popping elements off the stack. AND, the second question you should ask is, "Is there a better way to compute n!?"

Consider the alternative shown in Figure 8.16:

```
FACT      ST    R1,SAVE_R1
          ADD   R1,R0,#0
          ADD   R0,R0, #-1
          BRz   DONE
AGAIN     MUL   R1,R1,R0
          ADD   R0,R0,#-1  ; R0 gets next integer for MUL
          BRnp  AGAIN
DONE      ADD   R0,R1,#0   ; Move n! to R0
          LD    R1,SAVE_R1
          RET
SAVE_R1 .BLKW 1
```

Figure 8.16   Implementing FACT iteratively (i.e., without recursion).

8.3.2 Fibonacci, an Even Worse Example

Another bad use of recursion is to evaluate the Fibonacci number FIB(n). The Fibonacci numbers are defined for all non-negative integers as follows: FIB(0)=0, FIB(1)=1, and if n > 1, FIB(n) = FIB(n-1) + FIB(n-2). The expression is beautifully elegant, but the execution time is horrendous.

Figure 8.17 shows a pictorial view of the recursive subroutine FIB. Note that the subroutine FIB is represented as a "capital F," and inside the capital F there are two more instances of the capital F.

The recursive subroutine in Figure 8.18 computes FIB(n).

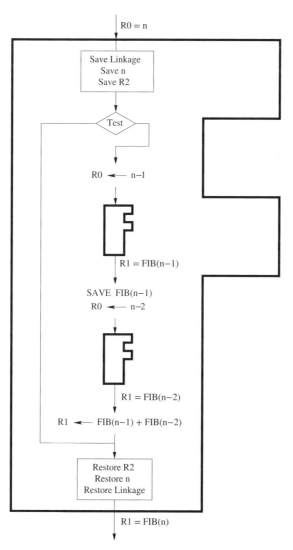

Figure 8.17   Pictorial representation of the recursive FIB subroutine.

```
;FIB subroutine
; + FIB(0) = 0
; + FIB(1) = 1
; + FIB(n) = FIB(n-1) + FIB(n-1)
;
; Input is in R0
; Return answer in R1
;
FIB     ADD R6, R6, #-1
        STR R7, R6, #0  ; Push R7, the return linkage
        ADD R6, R6, #-1
        STR R0, R6, #0  ; Push R0, the value of n
        ADD R6, R6, #-1
        STR R2, R6, #0  ; Push R2, which is needed in the subroutine

; Check for base case
        AND R2, R0, #-2
        BRnp SKIP         ; Z=0 if R0=0,1
        ADD R1, R0, #0    ; R0 is the answer
        BRnzp DONE

; Not a base case, do the recursion
SKIP    ADD R0, R0, #-1
        JSR FIB           ; R1 = FIB(n-1)
        ADD R2, R1, #0    ; Move result before calling FIB again
        ADD R0, R0, #-1
        JSR FIB           ; R1 = FIB(n-2)
        ADD R1, R2, R1    ; R1 = FIB(n-1) + FIB(n-2)

; Restore registers and return
DONE    LDR R2, R6, #0
        ADD R6, R6, #1
        LDR R0, R6, #0
        ADD R6, R6, #1
        LDR R7, R6, #0
        ADD R6, R6, #1
        RET
```

Figure 8.18   A recursive implementation of Fibonacci.

As with all recursive subroutines, we first need to test for the base cases. In this case, we AND n with xFFFE, which produces a non-zero result for all n except n = 1 and n = 0. If n = 0 or 1, we are effectively done. We move n into R1, restore R2, R0, and R7 (actually, only R2 needs to be restored), and return.

If n is not 0 or 1, we need to recursively call FIB twice, once with argument n-1 and once with argument n-2. Finally we add FIB(n-1) to FIB(n-2), put the result in R1, restore R2, R0, and R7, and return.

Note that the recursive subroutine FIB(n) calls FIB twice: once for FIB(n-1) and once for FIB(n-2). FIB(n-1) must call FIB(n-2) and FIB(n-3), and FIB(n-2) must call FIB(n-3) and FIB(n-4). That means FIB(n-2) must be evaluated twice and FIB(n-3) will have to be evaluated three times.

Question: Suppose n = 10. How many times must this recursive algorithm compute the same function FIB(5)?

Compare the recursive algorithm for Fibonacci (Figure 8.18) with a non-recursive algorithm, as shown in Figure 8.19. Much, much faster execution time!

```
FIB      ST    R1,SaveR1
         ST    R2,SaveR2
         ST    R3,SaveR3
         ST    R4,SaveR4
         ST    R5,SaveR5
;
     NOT   R0,R0
     ADD   R0,R0,#1   ; R0 contains -n
     AND   R1,R1,#0   ; Suppose n=0
     ADD   R5,R1,R0   ; R5 = 0 -n
     BRz   DONE       ; if n=0, done almost
     AND   R3,R2,#0   ; if n>0, set up R3 = FIB(0) = 0
     ADD   R1,R3,#1   ; Suppose n=1
     ADD   R5,R1,R0   ; R5 = 1-n
     BRz   DONE       ; if n=1, done almost
     ADD   R4,R1,#0   ; if n>1, set up R4 = FIB(1) = 1
;
AGAIN    ADD   R1,R1,#1   ; We begin the iteration of FIB(i)
     ADD   R2,R3,#0   : R2= FIB(i-2)
     ADD   R3,R4,#0   : R3= FIB(i-1)
     ADD   R4,R2,R3   ; R4 = FIB(i)
     ADD   R5,R1,R0   ; is R1=n ?
     BRn   AGAIN
;
     ADD   R0,R4,#0   ; if n>1, R0=FIB(n)
     BRnzp RESTORE
DONE     ADD   R0,R1,#0   ; if n=0,1, FIB(n)=n
RESTORE LD    R1,SaveR1
     LD    R2,SaveR2
     LD    R3,SaveR3
     LD    R4,SaveR4
     LD    R5,SaveR5
     RET
```

Figure 8.19   An iterative solution to Fibonacci.

8.3.3 The Maze, a Good Example

The reason for shying away from using recursion to compute factorial or Fibonacci is simply that the iterative algorithms are simple enough to understand without the horrendous execution time penalty of recursion. However, it is important to point out that there are times when the expressive beauty of recursion is useful to attack a complicated problem. Such is the case with the following problem, involving a maze: Given a maze and a starting position within the maze, write a program that determines whether or not there is a way out of the maze from your starting position.

A Maze   A maze can be any size, n by m. For example, Figure 8.20 illustrates a 6x6 maze.

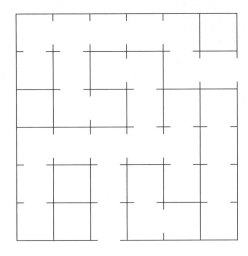

Figure 8.20   Example of a maze.

Each of the 36 cells of the maze can be characterized by whether there is a door to the north, east, south, or west, and whether there is a door from the cell to the outside world. Each cell is represented by one word of memory (Figure 8.21), as follows:

```
Bit[4]=1 if there is a door to the outside world; Bit[4]=0 if no door.
Bit[3]=1 if there is a door to the cell to the north; Bit[3]=0 if no door.
Bit[2]=1 if there is a door to the cell to the east; Bit[2]=0 if no door.
Bit[1]=1 if there is a door to the cell to the south; Bit[1]=0 if no door.
Bit[0]=1 if there is a door to the cell to the west; Bit[0]=0 if no door.
```

Figure 8.21   Specification of each cell in the maze.

The words are stored in what we call *row major* order; that is, row 1 is stored, then row 2, then row 3, etc. The complete specification of the 6 by 6 maze is shown in Figure 8.22.

```
00                    .ORIG x5000
01 MAZE               .FILL x0006
02                    .FILL x0007
03                    .FILL x0005
04                    .FILL x0005
05                    .FILL x0003
06                    .FILL x0000
07 ; second row: indices 6 to 11
08                    .FILL x0008
09                    .FILL x000A
0A                    .FILL x0004
0B                    .FILL x0003
0C                    .FILL x000C
0D                    .FILL x0015
0E ; third row: indices 12 to 17
0F                    .FILL x0000
10                    .FILL x000C
11                    .FILL x0001
12                    .FILL x000A
13                    .FILL x0002
14                    .FILL x0002
15 ; fourth row: indices 18 to 23
16                    .FILL x0006
17                    .FILL x0005
18                    .FILL x0007
19                    .FILL x000D
1A                    .FILL x000B
1B                    .FILL x000A
1C ; fifth row: indices 24 to 29
1D                    .FILL x000A
1E                    .FILL x0000
1F                    .FILL x000A
20                    .FILL x0002
21                    .FILL x0008
22                    .FILL x000A
23 ; sixth row: indices 30 to 35
24                    .FILL x0008
25                    .FILL x0000
26                    .FILL x001A
27                    .FILL x000C
28                    .FILL x0001
29                    .FILL x0008
2A                    .END
```

Figure 8.22   Specification of the maze of Figure 8.20.

A Recursive Subroutine to Exit the Maze   Our job is to develop an algorithm to determine whether we can exit a maze from a given starting position within the maze. With all the intricate paths that our attempts can take, keeping track of all that bookkeeping looks daunting. Recursion allows us to not have to keep track of the paths at all! Figure 8.23 shows a pictorial view of a recursive subroutine FIND_EXIT, an algorithm for determining whether or not we can exit the maze. Note that the subroutine FIND_EXIT is shown as an octagon, and inside the octagon there are four more instances of octagons, indicating recursive calls to FIND_EXIT. If we can exit the maze, we will return from the subroutine with R1=1; if not, we will return with R1=0.

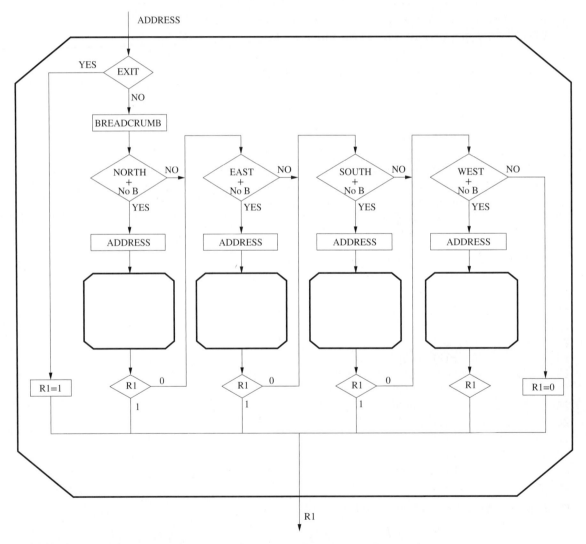

Figure 8.23   Pictorial representation of the recursive subroutine to exit the maze.

The algorithm works as follows: In each cell, we first ask if there is an exit from this cell to the outside world. If yes, we return the value 1 and return. If not, we ask whether we should try the cell to the north, the east, the south, or the west. In order to try a cell in any direction, clearly there must be a door to the cell in that direction. Furthermore, we want to be sure we do not end up in an infinite loop where for example, there are doors that allow us to go north one cell, and from there east one cell, and from there south one cell, and from there west one cell, putting us right back where we started. To prevent situations like that from happening, we put a "breadcrumb" in each cell we visit, and we only go to a cell and JSR FIND_EXIT if we have not visited that cell before.

Thus, our algorithm:

a. From our cell, we ask if we can exit. If yes, we are done. We exit with R1=1.

b. If not, we put a breadcrumb in our cell. Our breadcrumb is bit [15] of the word corresponding to our current cell. We set it to 1.

c. We ask two questions: Is there a door to the north, and have we never visited the cell to the north before? If the answer to both is yes, we set the address to the cell to the north, and JSR FIND_EXIT. We set the address to the cell to the north by simply subtracting 6 from the address of the current cell. Why 6? Because the cells are stored in row major order, and the number of columns in the maze is 6.

d. If the answer to either question is no, or if going north resulted in failure, we ask: Is there a door to the east, and have we never visited that cell before? If the answer to both is yes, we set the address to the address of the cell to the east (by adding 1 to the address) and JSR FIND_EXIT.

e. If going east does not get us out, we repeat the question for south, and if that does not work, then for west.

f. If we end up with no door to the west to a cell we have not visited, or if there is a door and we haven't visited, but it results in failure, we are done. We cannot exit the maze from our starting position. We set R1=0 and return.

Figure 8.24 shows a recursive algorithm that determines if we can exit the maze, given our starting address.

```
; Recursive subroutine that determines if there is a path from current cell
; to the outside world.
; input: R0, current cell address
; output: R1, YES (1) or NO (0)
            .ORIG x4000

01 FIND_EXIT      ; save modified registers into the stack.
02                ADD R6, R6, #-1
03                STR R2, R6, #0    ; R2 holds the cell data of the caller
04                ADD R6, R6, #-1
05                STR R3, R6, #0    ; R3 holds the cell address of the caller
06                ADD R6, R6, #-1
07                STR R7, R6, #0    ; R7 holds the PC of the caller
08
09                ; Move cell address to R3, since we need to use R0
0A                ; as the input to recursive subroutine calls.
0B                ADD R3, R0, #0
0C
0D                ; If the exit is in this cell, return YES
0E                LDR R2, R0, #0    ; R2 now holds the current cell data
0F                LD  R7, EXIT_MASK
10                AND R7, R2, R7
11                BRnp DONE_YES
12
13                ; Put breadcrumb in the current cell.
14                LD  R7, BREADCRUMB
15                ADD R2, R2, R7
16                STR R2, R0, #0
17
18                ; check the north cell for a path to exit
19 CHECK_NORTH LD  R7, NORTH_MASK
1A                AND R7, R2, R7
1B                BRz CHECK_EAST    ; If north is blocked, check east
1C                LDR R7, R3, #-6
1D                BRn CHECK_EAST    ; If a breadcrumb in the north cell, check east
1E                ADD R0, R3, #-6
1F                JSR FIND_EXIT     ; Recursively check the north cell
20                ADD R1, R1, #0
21                BRp DONE_YES      ; If a path from north cell found, return YES
22
23                ; check the north cell for a path to exit
24 CHECK_EAST  LD  R7, EAST_MASK
25                AND R7, R2, R7
26                BRz CHECK_SOUTH   ; If the way to east is blocked, check south
27                LDR R7, R3, #1
28                BRn CHECK_SOUTH   ; If a breadcrumb in the east cell, check south
29                ADD R0, R3, #1
2A                JSR FIND_EXIT     ; Recursively check the east cell
2B                ADD R1, R1, #0
2C                BRp DONE_YES      ; If a path from east cell found, return YES
2D
```

Figure 8.24   A recursive subroutine to determine if there is an exit from the maze (Fig. 8.24 continued on next page.)

```
2E                    ; check the south cell for a path to exit
2F  CHECK_SOUTH  LD   R7, SOUTH_MASK
30                AND  R7, R2, R7
31                BRz  CHECK_WEST    ; If the way to south is blocked, check west
32                LDR  R7, R3, #6
33                BRn  CHECK_WEST    ; If a breadcrumb in the south cell, check west
34                ADD  R0, R3, #6
35                JSR  FIND_EXIT     ; Recursively check the south cell
36                ADD  R1, R1, #0
37                BRp  DONE_YES      ; If a path from south cell found, return YES
38
39                    ; check the west cell for a path to exit
3A  CHECK_WEST   LD   R7, WEST_MASK
3B                AND  R7, R2, R7
3C                BRz  DONE_NO       ; If the way to west is blocked, return NO
3D                LDR  R7, R3, #-1
3E                BRn  DONE_NO       ; If a breadcrumb in the west cell, return NO
3F                ADD  R0, R3, #-1
40                JSR  FIND_EXIT     ; Recursively check the west cell
41                ADD  R1, R1, #0
42                BRp  DONE_YES      ; If a path from west cell found, return YES
43
44  DONE_NO      AND  R1, R1, #0
45                BR   RESTORE
46
47  DONE_YES     AND  R1, R1, #0
48                ADD  R1, R1, #1
49
4A  RESTORE      ADD  R0, R3, #0 ; restore R0 from R3
4B                    ; restore the rest of the modified registers from the stack.
4C                LDR  R7, R6, #0
4D                ADD  R6, R6, #1
4E                LDR  R3, R6, #0
4F                ADD  R6, R6, #1
50                LDR  R2, R6, #0
51                ADD  R6, R6, #1
52                RET
53
54  BREADCRUMB   .FILL x8000
55  EXIT_MASK    .FILL x0010
56  NORTH_MASK   .FILL x0008
57  EAST_MASK    .FILL x0004
58  SOUTH_MASK   .FILL x0002
59  WEST_MASK    .FILL x0001
5A                .END
```

Figure 8.24   A recursive subroutine to determine if there is an exit from the maze (continued Fig. 8.24 from previous page.)

8.4 The Queue

Our next data structure is the *queue*. Recall that the property that defined the concept of "stack" was LIFO, the last thing we pushed onto the stack is the first thing we pop off the stack. The defining property of the abstract data type *queue* is **FIFO**. FIFO stands for "First in First out." The data structure "queue" is like a queue in a polite supermarket, or a polite ticket counter. That is, the first person in line is the first person serviced. In the context of the data structure, this means we need to keep track of two ends of the storage structure: a FRONT pointer for servicing (i.e., removing elements from the front of the queue) and a REAR pointer for entering (i.e., inserting into the rear of the queue).

Figure 8.25 shows a block of six sequential memory locations that have been allocated for storing elements in the queue. The queue grows from x8000 to x8005. We arbitrarily assign the FRONT pointer to the location just before the first element of the queue. We assign the REAR pointer to the location containing the most recent element that was added to the queue. Let's use R3 as our FRONT pointer and R4 as our REAR pointer.

Figure 8.25a shows a queue in which five values were entered into the queue. Since FRONT = x8001, the values 45 in memory location x8000 and 17 in x8001 must have been removed, and the front element of the queue is 23, the value contained in x8002.

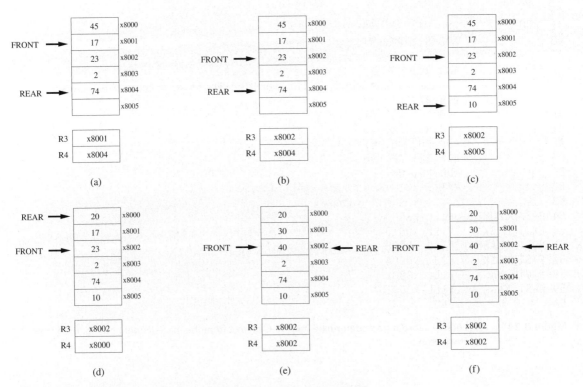

Figure 8.25   A queue allocated to memory locations x8000 to x8005.

Note that the values 45 and 17 are still contained in memory locations x8000 and x8001, even though they have been removed. Like the stack, studied already, that is the nature of load instructions. When a value is removed by means of a load instruction, what is stored in the memory location is not erased. The contents of the memory location is simply copied into the destination register. However, since FRONT contains the address x8001, there is no way to load from locations x8000 and x8001 as long as locations x8000 to x8005 behave like a queue—i.e., as long as the accesses are FIFO.

8.4.1 The Basic Operations: Remove from Front, Insert at Rear

Since FRONT points to the location just in front of the first element in the queue, we remove a value by first incrementing FRONT and then loading the value stored at that incremented address. In our example, the next value to be removed is the value 23, which is at the front of the queue, in memory location x8002. The following code *removes* 23 from the queue:

```
ADD    R3,R3,#1
LDR    R0,R3,#0
```

yielding the structure in Figure 8.25b.

Since REAR = x8004, the last value to enter the queue is 74. The values in the queue in Figure 8.25b are 2 and 74. To *insert* another element (e.g., 10) at the back of the queue, the following code is executed:

```
ADD    R4,R4,#1
STR    R0,R4,#0
```

resulting in Figure 8.25c.

8.4.2 Wrap-Around

At first blush, it looks like we cannot insert any more elements into the queue. Not so! When we remove a value from the queue, that location becomes available for storing another element. We do that by allowing the available storage locations to *wrap around*. For example, suppose we want to add 20 to the queue. Since there is nothing stored in x8000 (recall 45 had been previously removed), we can store 20 in x8000. The result is shown in Figure 8.25d.

"Wrap-around" works by having our removal and insertion algorithms test the contents of FRONT and REAR for the value x8005. If we wish to insert, and REAR contains x8005, we know we have reached the end of our available storage and we must see if x8000 is available. If we wish to remove, we must first see if FRONT contains the address x8005. If it does, the front of the queue is in x8000.

Thus, our code for remove and insert has to include a test for wrap-around. The code for remove becomes:

```
            LD    R2, LAST
            ADD   R2,R3,R2
            BRnp  SKIP_1
            LD    R3,FIRST
            BR    SKIP_2
   SKIP_1   ADD   R3,R3,#1
   SKIP_2   LDR   R0,R3,#0 ; R0 gets the front of the queue
            RET
   LAST     .FILL x7FFB  ; LAST contains the negative of 8005
   FIRST    .FILL x8000
```

The code for insert is similar. If REAR contains x8005, we need to set R4 to x8000 before we can insert an element at the rear of the queue. The code to insert is as follows:

```
            LD    R2, LAST
            ADD   R2,R4,R2
            BRnp  SKIP_1
            LD    R4,FIRST
            BR    SKIP_2
   SKIP_1   ADD   R4,R4,#1
   SKIP_2   STR   R0,R4,#0 ; R0 gets the front of the queue
            RET
   LAST     .FILL 7FFB   ; LAST contains the negative of 8005
   FIRST    .FILL x8000
```

8.4.3 How Many Elements Can We Store in a Queue?

Let's look again at Figure 8.25d. There are four values in the queue: 2, 74, 10, and 20. Suppose we insert 30 and 40 at the rear of the queue, producing Figure 8.25e. Both R3 and R4 contain the same address (x8002), and the queue is full. Now suppose we start removing elements from the front of the queue. If we remove 2, which is at the front of the queue, R3 will contain the address x8003. If we remove the remaining five elements in the queue, we will have what is shown in Figure 8.25f. Note that the FRONT and REAR pointers for e and f are identical, yet Figure 8.25e describes a full queue and Figure 8.25f describes an empty queue! Clearly that is not acceptable.

Our answer is to allow a queue to store only n-1 elements if space for n elements has been allocated. That is, if inserting an nth element into the queue would cause FRONT to equal REAR, we do not allow that insertion. We declare the queue full when there are n-1 elements in the queue.

Let's look again at the queue in Figure 8.25d. There are four elements in the queue, from front to rear: 2, 74, 10, and 20, and two empty slots, x8001 and x8002. We can insert 30 in x8001, producing Figure 8.26a. That is, 30 is the fifth element inserted in the queue. Since six words have been allocated for the queue, and we now have five elements in the queue, we declare the queue full and do not allow a sixth element to be inserted. Suppose we now start removing elements

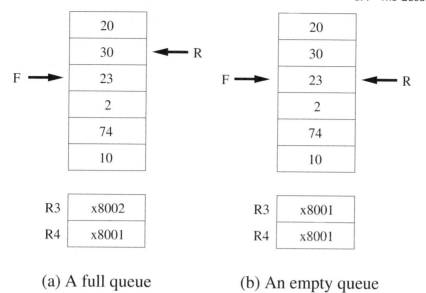

(a) A full queue   (b) An empty queue

Figure 8.26   A full queue and an empty queue.

from the queue until the queue is empty, as shown in Figure 8.26b. Now there is no ambiguity between a full and an empty queue since if the queue is empty, FRONT = REAR.

8.4.4 Tests for Underflow, Overflow

As was the case with the stack, we can only remove an element from a queue if there are elements in the queue. Likewise, we can only insert elements in the queue if it is not full. If the queue is empty and we try to remove an element, we have an *underflow* condition. If the queue is full and we try to insert an element, we have an overflow condition. In both cases, if we are using a subroutine to manage the queue, we need to report success or failure to the calling program. As with the stack, we will use R5 for this purpose.

The test for underflow is straightforward. We saw from Figure 8.26 that if FRONT = REAR, the queue is empty. Our code to test for underflow is therefore

```
            AND    R5,R5,#0   ; Initialize R5 to 0
            NOT    R2,R3
            ADD    R2,R2,#1   ; R2 contains negative of R3
            ADD    R2,R2,R4
            BRz    UNDERFLOW
            ; code to remove the front of the queue and return success.
UNDERFLOW   ADD    R5,R5,#1
            RET
```

That is, we first check to see if the queue is empty, that is, if R3 = R4. If so, we branch to UNDERFLOW, where we set R5 to failure, restore R1, and return. If not, carry out the code to remove the front of the queue.

The test for overflow is similar. To insert an element to the back of the queue, we first increment the REAR pointer. If that causes FRONT = REAR, then the queue already contains n-1 elements, which means it is full so we cannot insert any more elements. We decrement the REAR pointer, set R5 to 1, and return.

8.4.5 The Complete Story

We conclude our attention to queues with a subroutine that allows elements to be removed from the front or inserted into the rear of the queue, wraps around when one of the pointers reaches the last element, and returns with a report of success (R5 = 0) or failure (R5 = 1) depending on whether the access succeeds or the access fails due to an underflow or overflow condition.

To make this concrete, we will tie this subroutine to the queue of Figure 8.25, where we have allocated locations x8000 to x8005 for our queue, x8000 being the FIRST location and x8005 being the LAST location.

To insert, we first have to make sure the queue is not full. To do that, we increment the REAR pointer (R4) and then test REAR=FRONT. If the REAR pointer was initially x8005, we increment REAR by setting it to x8000; that is, we need to wrap around. If the queue is full, we need to set REAR back to its original value, and return, reporting failure (R5 = 1). If the queue is not full, we store the item we wish to insert (which is in R0) in REAR, and return, reporting success (R5 = 0).

To remove, we first make sure the queue is not empty by testing whether REAR=FRONT. If REAR=FRONT, the queue is empty, so we return, reporting failure. If REAR is not the same as FRONT, the queue is not empty, so we can remove the front element. To do this, we first test to see if FRONT=x8005. If it is, we set FRONT=x8000. If it isn't, we increment FRONT. In both cases, we then load the value from that memory location into R0, and return, reporting success.

Figure 8.27 shows the complete subroutine.

```
00 ;Input: R0 for item to be inserted, R3 is FRONT, R4 is REAR
01 ;Output: R0 for item to be removed
02                              ;
03 INSERT       ST    R1,SaveR1   ; Save register we need
04             AND   R5,R5,#0    ; Set R5 to success code
05                              ; Initialization complete
06             LD    R1,NEG_LAST
07             ADD   R1,R1,R4    ; R1 = REAR MINUS x8005
08             BRnp  SKIP1       ; SKIP WRAP AROUND
09             LD    R4,FIRST    ; WRAP AROUND, R4=x8000
0A             BR    SKIP2
0B SKIP1        ADD   R4,R4,#1    ; NO WRAP AROUND, R4=R4+1
0C SKIP2        NOT   R1,R4
0D             ADD   R1,R1,#1    ; R1= NEG REAR
0E             ADD   R1,R1,R3    ; R1= FRONT-REAR
0F             BRz   FULL
10             STR   R0,R4,#0    ; DO THE INSERT
11             BR    DONE
12 FULL         LD    R1,NEG_FIRST
13             ADD   R1,R1,R4    ; R1 = REAR MINUS x8000
14             BRnp  SKIP3
15             LD    R4,LAST     ; UNDO WRAP AROUND, REAR=x8005
16             BR    SKIP4
17 SKIP3        ADD   R4,R4,#-1   ; NO WRAP AROUND, R4=R4-1
18 SKIP4        ADD   R5,R5,#1    ; R5=FAILURE
19             BR    DONE
1A                              ;
1B REMOVE       ST    R1,SaveR1   ; Save register we need
1C             AND   R5,R5,#0    ; Set R5 to success code
1D                              ; Initialization complete
1E             NOT   R1,R4
1F             ADD   R1,R1,#1    ; R1= NEG REAR
20             ADD   R1,R1,R3    ; R1= FRONT-REAR
21             BRz   EMPTY
22             LD    R1, NEG_LAST
23             ADD   R1,R1,R3    ; R1= FRONT MINUS x8005
24             BRnp  SKIP5
25             LD    R3, FIRST   ; R3=x8000
26             BR    SKIP6
27 SKIP5        ADD   R3,R3,#1    ; R3=R3+1
28 SKIP6        LDR   R0,R3,#0    ; DO THE REMOVE
29             BR    DONE
2A EMPTY        ADD   R5,R5.#1    ; R5=FAILURE
2B DONE         LD    R1,SaveR1   ; Restore register
2C             RET
2D FIRST        .FILL x8000
2E NEG_FIRST   .FILL x8000
2F LAST         .FILL x8005
30 NEG_LAST    .FILL x7FFB
31 SaveR1       .BLKW 1
```

Figure 8.27   The complete queue subroutine.

8.5 Character Strings

Our final data structure: the character string!

The last data structure we will study in this chapter is the character string, where a sequence of keyboard characters (letters, digits, and other symbols) is organized as a one-dimensional array of ASCII codes, usually representing a person's name, address, or some other alphanumeric string. Figure 8.28 shows a character string representing the name of the famous late Stanford professor Bill Linvill, stored in 13 consecutive words of memory, starting at location x5000. The ASCII code for each letter of his name is stored in a separate word of memory. Since an ASCII code consists of one byte of memory, we add a leading x00 to each location. For example, x5000 contains x0042 since the ASCII code for a capital B is x42. We need 13 memory locations, one word for each of the 11 letters in his name, one word for the ASCII code x20 representing the space between his first and last names, and finally the null character x0000 to indicate that we have reached the end of the character string. Different alphanumeric strings require character strings of different lengths, but that is no problem since we allocate as many words of memory as are needed, followed by the null character x0000 to indicate the end of the character string.

x5000	x0042
	x0069
	x006C
	x006C
	x0020
	x004C
	x0069
	x006E
	x0076
	x0069
	x006C
	x006C
	x0000

Figure 8.28   Character string representing the name "Bill Linvill."

A common use of a character string is to identify a body of information associated with a particular person. Figure 8.29 shows such a body of information (often called a personnel record) associated with an employee of a company.

x4000	x6000		x6000	x004A		x4508	x004D		xCA9B	x0030		x8E25	x0045
x4001	x4508		x6001	x006F		x4509	x0061		xCA9C	x0031		x8E26	x006E
x4002	xCA9B		x6002	x006E		x450A	x0072		xCA9D	x0032		x8E27	x0067
x4003	$84,000		x6003	x0065		x450B	x0079		xCA9E	x0036		x8E28	x0069
x4004	4		x6004	x0073		x450C	x0000		xCA9F	x0035		x8E29	x006E
x4005	x8E25		x6005	x0000					xCAA0	x0034		x8E2A	x0065
									xCAA1	x0036		x8E2B	x0065
									xCAA2	x0032		x8E2C	x0072
									xCAA3	x0031		x8E2D	x0000

Figure 8.29 Mary Jones' personnel record.

Our example personnel record consists of six words of sequential memory, starting at location x4000, as follows:

1. The first word contains the starting address of a character string containing the person's last name. The pointer in location x4000 is the address x6000. The six-word character string, starting at location x6000, contains the ASCII code for "Jones," terminated with the null character.
2. The second word, at x4001, contains a pointer to the character string of the person's first name, in this case "Mary," starting at location x4508.
3. The third word, at x4002, contains a pointer (xCA9B) to her nine-digit social security number, the unique identifier for all persons working in the United States.
4. The fourth word, at x4003, contains her salary (in thousands of dollars).
5. The fifth word contains how long she has worked for the company.
6. The sixth word is a pointer (x8E25) to the character string identifying her job title, in this case "Engineer."

In summary, an employee named Mary Jones, social security number 012654621, an Engineer, has been with the company four years and earns $84,000/year salary.

One can write computer programs that examine employee records looking for various personnel information. For example, if one wanted to know an employee's salary, a program could examine employee records, looking for that employee. The program would call a subroutine that compares the character string representing an employee's social security number with the characters of the social security number of the person the subroutine is searching for. If all the characters match, the subroutine would return a success code (R5 = 0), and the program

```
STRCMP    ST      R0,SaveR0
          ST      R1,SaveR1
          ST      R2,SaveR2
          ST      R3,SaveR3
;
          AND     R5,R5,#0    ; R5 <-- Match
;
NEXTCHAR  LDR     R2,R0,#0    ; R2 contains character from 1st string
          LDR     R3,R1,#0    ; R3 contains character from 2nd string
          BRnp    COMPARE     ; String is not done, continue comparing
          ADD     R2,R2,#0
          BRz     DONE        ; If both strings done, match found
COMPARE   NOT     R2,R2
          ADD     R2,R2,#1    ; R2 contains negative of character
          ADD     R2,R2,R3    ; Compare the 2 characters
          BRnp    FAIL        ; Not equal, no match
          ADD     R0,R0,#1
          ADD     R1,R1,#1
          BRnzp   NEXTCHAR    ; Move on to next pair of characters
;
FAIL      ADD     R5,R5,#1    ; R5 <-- No match
;
DONE   LD      R0,SaveR0
          LD      R1,SaveR1
          LD      R2,SaveR2
          LD      R3,SaveR3
          RET
;
SaveR0    .BLKW   1
SaveR1    .BLKW   1
SaveR2    .BLKW   1
SaveR3    .BLKW   1
```

Figure 8.30   Subroutine to compare two character strings.

would go on to read the salary information in the fourth word of the personnel record. If all the characters do not match, the subroutine would return a failure code (R5 = 1), and the program would call the subroutine with the starting address of another employee's social security number.

Figure 8.30 is a subroutine that compares two character strings to see if they are identical.

Another Example: A Character String Representing an "Integer."   We can also represent arbitrarily long integers by means of character strings. For example, Figure 8.31 is a character string representing the integer 79,245.

Figure 8.32 is a subroutine that examines such a character string to be sure that in fact all ASCII codes represent decimal digits. If all the entries in the character string are ASCII codes of decimal digits (between x30 and x39), the subroutine returns success (R = 0). If not, the subroutine returns failure (R5 = 1).

x0037
x0039
x0032
x0034
x0035
x0000

Figure 8.31   A character string representing the integer 79,245, with one ASCII code per decimal digit.

```
; Input: R0 contains the starting address of the character string
; Output: R5=0, success; R5=1, failure.
;
TEST_INTEGER    ST    R1,SaveR1   ; Save registers needed by subroutine
                ST    R2,SaveR2
                ST    R3,SaveR3
                ST    R4,SaveR4
;
                AND   R5,R5,#0    ; Initialize success code to R5=0, success
                LD    R2,ASCII_0  ; R2=xFFD0, the negative of ASCII code x30
                LD    R3,ASCII_9  ; R3=xFFC7, the negative of ASCII code x39
;
    NEXT_CHAR   LDR   R1,R0,#0    ; Load next character
                BRz   SUCCESS
                ADD   R4,R1,R2
                BRn   BAD         ; R1 is less than x30, not a decimal digit
                ADD   R4,R1,R3
                BRp   BAD         ; R1 is greater than x39, not a decimal digit
                ADD   R0,R0,#1    ; Character good!  Prepare for next character
                BR    NEXT_CHAR
;
        BAD     ADD   R5,R5,#1    ; R5 contains failure code
    SUCCESS     LD    R4,SaveR4   ; Restore registers
                LD    R3,SaveR3
                LD    R2,SaveR2
                LD    R1,SaveR1
                RET
    ASCII_0           .FILL xFFD0
    ASCII_9           .FILL xFFC7
     SaveR1   .BLKW 1
     SaveR2   .BLKW 1
     SaveR3   .BLKW 1
     SaveR4   .BLKW 1
```

Figure 8.32   Subroutine to determine if a character string represents an integer.

Exercises

8.1   What are the defining characteristics of a stack?

8.2   What is an advantage to using the model in Figure 8.9 to implement a stack vs. the model in Figure 8.8?

8.3   The LC-3 ISA has been augmented with the following push and pop instructions. Push Rn pushes the value in Register n onto the stack. Pop Rn removes a value from the stack and loads it into Rn. The following figure shows a snapshot of the eight registers of the LC-3 BEFORE and AFTER the following six stack operations are performed. Identify (a)–(d).

	BEFORE			AFTER
R0	x0000	PUSH R4	R0	x1111
R1	x1111	PUSH (a)	R1	x1111
R2	x2222	POP (b)	R2	x3333
R3	x3333	PUSH (c)	R3	x3333
R4	x4444	POP R2	R4	x4444
R5	x5555	POP (d)	R5	x5555
R6	x6666		R6	x6666
R7	x7777		R7	x4444

8.4   Write a function that implements another stack function, peek. Peek returns the value of the first element on the stack without removing the element from the stack. Peek should also do underflow error checking. (Why is overflow error checking unnecessary?)

8.5   How would you check for underflow and overflow conditions if you implemented a stack using the model in Figure 8.8? Rewrite the PUSH and POP routines to model a stack implemented as in Figure 8.8, that is, one in which the data entries move with each operation.

8.6   Rewrite the PUSH and POP routines such that the stack on which they operate holds elements that take up two memory locations each.

8.7   Rewrite the PUSH and POP routines to handle stack elements of arbitrary sizes.

8.8   The following operations are performed on a stack:
PUSH A, PUSH B, POP, PUSH C, PUSH D, POP, PUSH E, POP, POP, PUSH F

a. What does the stack contain after the PUSH F?
b. At which point does the stack contain the most elements? Without removing the elements left on the stack from the previous operations, we perform:
PUSH G, PUSH H, PUSH I, PUSH J, POP, PUSH K, POP, POP, POP, PUSH L, POP, POP, PUSH M
c. What does the stack contain now?

8.9   The input stream of a stack is a list of all the elements we pushed onto the stack, in the order that we pushed them. The input stream from Exercise 8.8 was ABCDEFGHIJKLM

The output stream is a list of all the elements that are popped off the stack, in the order that they are popped off.

    a. What is the output stream from Exercise 8.8?
       Hint: BDE ...

    b. If the input stream is ZYXWVUTSR, create a sequence of pushes and pops such that the output stream is YXVUWZSRT.

    c. If the input stream is ZYXW, how many different output streams can be created?

★8.10 It is easier to identify borders between cities on a map if adjacent cities are colored with different colors. For example, in a map of Texas, one would not color Austin and Pflugerville with the same color, since doing so would obscure the border between the two cities.

Shown next is the recursive subroutine EXAMINE. EXAMINE examines the data structure representing a map to see if any pair of adjacent cities have the same color. Each node in the data structure contains the city's color and the addresses of the cities it borders. If no pair of adjacent cities have the same color, EXAMINE returns the value 0 in R1. If at least one pair of adjacent cities have the same color, EXAMINE returns the value 1 in R1. The main program supplies the address of a node representing one of the cities in R0 before executing JSR EXAMINE.

```
          .ORIG x4000
EXAMINE ADD R6, R6, #-1
        STR R0, R6, #0
        ADD R6, R6, #-1
        STR R2, R6, #0
        ADD R6, R6, #-1
        STR R3, R6, #0
        ADD R6, R6, #-1
        STR R7, R6, #0

        AND R1, R1, #0   ; Initialize output R1 to 0
        LDR R7, R0, #0
        BRn RESTORE      ; Skip this node if it has already been visited

        LD  R7, BREADCRUMB
        STR R7, R0, #0   ; Mark this node as visited
        LDR R2, R0, #1   ; R2 = color of current node
        ADD R3, R0, #2

AGAIN   LDR R0, R3, #0   ; R0 = neighbor node address
        BRz RESTOR
        LDR R7, R0, #1
        NOT R7, R7       ; <-- Breakpoint here
        ADD R7, R7, #1
        ADD R7, R2, R7   ; Compare current color to neighbor's color
        BRz BAD
        JSR EXAMINE      ; Recursively examine the coloring of next neighbor
        ADD R1, R1, #0
        BRp RESTORE      ; If neighbor returns R1=1, this node should return R1=1
        ADD R3, R3, #1
        BR  AGAIN        ; Try next neighbor

BAD     ADD R1, R1, #1
RESTORE LDR R7, R6, #0
        ADD R6, R6, #1
        LDR R3, R6, #0
        ADD R6, R6, #1
        LDR R2, R6, #0
        ADD R6, R6, #1
        LDR R0, R6, #0
        ADD R6, R6, #1
        RET

BREADCRUMB .FILL x8000
        .END
```

Your job is to construct the data structure representing a particular map. Before executing JSR EXAMINE, R0 is set to x6100 (the address of one of the nodes), and a breakpoint is set at x4012. The following table shows relevant information collected each time the breakpoint was encountered during the running of EXAMINE.

PC	R0	R2	R7
x4012	x6200	x0042	x0052
x4012	x6100	x0052	x0042
x4012	x6300	x0052	x0047
x4012	x6200	x0047	x0052
x4012	x6400	x0047	x0052
x4012	x6100	x0052	x0042
x4012	x6300	x0052	x0047
x4012	x6500	x0052	x0047
x4012	x6100	x0047	x0042
x4012	x6200	x0047	x0052
x4012	x6400	x0047	x0052
x4012	x6500	x0052	x0047
x4012	x6400	x0042	x0052
x4012	x6500	x0042	x0047

Construct the data structure for the particular map that corresponds to the relevant information obtained from the breakpoints. *Note:* We are asking you to construct the data structure as it exists AFTER the recursive subroutine has executed.

x6100		x6200		x6300	
x6101	x0042	x6201	x0052	x6301	
x6102	x6200	x6202		x6302	
x6103		x6203		x6303	
x6104		x6204		x6304	
x6105		x6205		x6305	
x6106		x6206		x6306	

x6400		x6500	
x6401		x6501	
x6402		x6502	
x6403		x6503	
x6404		x6504	
x6405		x6505	
x6406		x6506	

8.11 The following program needs to be assembled and stored in LC-3 memory. How many LC-3 memory locations are required to store the assembled program?

```
        .ORIG x4000
        AND   R0,R0,#0
        ADD   R1,R0,#0
        ADD   R0,R0,#4
        LD    R2,B
A       LDR   R3,R2,#0
        ADD   R1,R1,R3
        ADD   R2,R2,#1
        ADD   R0,R0,#-1
        BRnp  A
        JSR   SHIFTR
        ADD   R1,R4,#0
        JSR   SHIFTR
        ST    R4,C
        TRAP  x25
B       .BLKW 1
C       .BLKW 1
        .END
```

How many memory locations are required to store the assembled program?

What is the address of the location labeled C?

Before the program can execute, the location labeled B must be loaded by some external means. You can assume that happens before this program starts executing. You can also assume that the subroutine starting at location SHIFTR is available for this program to use. SHIFTR takes the value in R1, shifts it right one bit, and stores the result in R4.

After the program executes, what is in location C?

★**8.12** Many cities, like New York City, Stockholm, Konigsberg, etc., consist of several areas connected by bridges. The following figure shows a map of FiveParts, a city made up of five areas A, B, C, D, E, with the areas connected by nine bridges as shown.

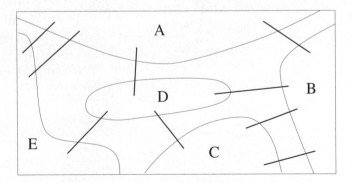

The following program prompts the user to enter two areas and then stores the number of bridges from the first area to the second in location x4500. Your job: On the next page, design the data structure for the city of FiveParts that the following program will use to count the number of bridges between two areas.

```
                .ORIG x3000
                LEA R0, FROM
                TRAP x22
                TRAP x20      ; Inputs a char without banner
                NOT R1, R0
                ADD R1, R1, #1
                LEA R0, TO
                TRAP x22
                TRAP x20
                NOT R0, R0
                ADD R0, R0, #1
                AND R5, R5, #0
                LDI R2, HEAD
SEARCH          BRz DONE
                LDR R3, R2, #0
                ADD R7, R1, R3
                BRz FOUND_FROM
                LDR R2, R2, #1
                BRnzp SEARCH
FOUND_FROM      ADD R2, R2, #2
NEXT_BRIDGE     LDR R3, R2, #0
                BRz DONE
                LDR R4, R3, #0
                ADD R7, R0, R4
                BRnp SKIP
                ADD R5, R5, #1  ; Increment Counter
SKIP            ADD R2, R2, #1
                BRnzp NEXT_BRIDGE
DONE            STI R5, ANSWER
                HALT
HEAD            .FILL x3050
ANSWER          .FILL x4500
FROM            .STRINGZ "FROM: "
TO              .STRINGZ "TO: "
                .END
```

Your job is to provide the contents of the memory locations that are needed to specify the data structure for the city of FiveParts, which is needed by the program on the previous page. We have given you the HEAD pointer for the data structure and in addition, five memory locations and the contents of those five locations. We have also supplied more than enough sequential memory locations after each of the five to enable you to finish the job. Use as many of these memory locations as you need.

8.13 Our code to compute n factorial worked for all positive integers n. As promised in the text, your assignment here: Augment the iterative solution to FACT to also work for 0!.

8.14 As you know, the LC-3 ADD instruction adds 16-bit 2's complement integers. If we wanted to add 32-bit 2's complement integers, we could do that with the program shown next. Note that the program requires calling subroutine X, which stores into R0 the carry that results from adding R1 and R2.

Fill in the missing pieces of both the program and the subroutine X, as identified by the empty boxes. Each empty box corresponds to **one** instruction or the operands of **one** instruction.

Address	Value
x4000	x0041
x4001	
x4002	
x4003	
x4004	
x4005	
x4006	

Address	Value
x3050	

Address	Value
xA243	x0042
xA244	
xA245	
xA246	
xA247	
xA248	
xA249	

Address	Value
x4100	x0043
x4101	
x4102	
x4103	
x4104	
x4105	
x4106	

Address	Value
xBBBB	x0044
xBBBC	
xBBBD	
xBBBE	
xBBBF	
xBBC0	
xBBC1	

Address	Value
x3100	x0045
x3101	
x3102	
x3103	
x3104	
x3105	
x3106	

Note that a 32-bit operand requires two 16-bit memory locations. A 32-bit operand Y has Y[15:0] stored in address A, and Y[31:16] stored in address A+1.

```
.ORIG    x3000
         LEA R3, NUM1
         LEA R4, NUM2
         LEA R5, RESULT
         LDR R1, R3, #0
         LDR   R2, R4, #0
         ADD R0, R1, R2
         STR R0, R5, #0
         --------------- (a)
         LDR ----------- (b)
         LDR ----------- (c)
         ADD R0, R1, R2
         -------------- (d)
         TRAP   x25

X        ST  R4, SAVER4
         AND   R0, R0, #0
         AND R4, R1, R2
         BRn ---------- (e)
         ADD R1, R1, #0
         BRn ---------- (f)
         ADD ---------- (g)
         BRn ADDING
         BRnzp EXIT
ADDING   ADD   R4, R1, R2
         BRn EXIT
LABEL    ADD   R0, R0, #1
EXIT     LD  R4, SAVER4
         RET

NUM1     .BLKW 2
NUM2     .BLKW 2
RESULT   .BLKW 2
SAVER4   .BLKW 1

.END
```

★**8.15**   A program encounters a breakpoint and halts. The computer operator does not change the state of the computer in any way but immediately presses the **run** button to resume execution.

The following table shows the contents of MAR and MDR for the first nine memory accesses that the LC-3 performs after resuming execution. Your job: Fill in the missing entries.

	MAR	MDR
1st:		x5020
2nd:		xF0F0
3rd:		
4th:	x2000	x020A
5th:		x040A
6th:		x61FE
7th:		
8th:		xC1C0
9th:	x4002	xF025

CHAPTER

9 I/O

U p to now we have completely ignored the details of input and output, that is, how the computer actually gets information from the keyboard (input), and how the computer actually delivers information to the monitor (output). Instead we have relied on the TRAP instruction (e.g., TRAP x23 for input and TRAP x21 for output) to accomplish these tasks. The TRAP instruction enables us to tell the operating system what we need done by means of a trap vector, and we trust the operating system to do it for us.

The more generic term for our TRAP instruction is *system call* because the TRAP instruction is calling on the operating system to do something for us while allowing us to remain completely clueless as to how it gets done. Now we are ready to examine how input and output actually work in the LC-3, what happens when the user program makes a system call by invoking the TRAP instruction, and how it all works under the control of the operating system.

We will start with the actual physical structures that are required to cause input and output to occur. But before we do that, it is useful to say a few words about the operating system and understand a few basic concepts that have not been important so far but become very important when considering what the operating system needs to do its job.

You may be familiar with Microsoft's various flavors of Windows, Apple's MacOS, and Linux. These are all examples of operating systems. They all have the same goal: to optimize the use of all the resources of the computer system while making sure that no software does harmful things to any program or data that it has no right to mess with. To better understand their job, we need to understand the notions of privilege and priority and the layout of the memory address space (i.e., the regions of memory and the purpose of each).

9.1 Privilege, Priority, and the Memory Address Space

9.1.1 Privilege and Priority

Two very different (we often say orthogonal) concepts associated with computer processing are *privilege* and *priority*.

9.1.1.1 Privilege

Privilege is all about the right to do something, such as execute a particular instruction or access a particular memory location. Not all computer programs have the right to execute all instructions. For example, if a computer system is shared among many users and the ISA contains a HALT instruction, we would not want any random program to execute that HALT instruction and stop the computer. If we did, we would have some pretty disgruntled users on our hands. Similarly, some memory locations are only available to the operating system. We would not want some random program to interfere with the data structures or code that is part of the operating system, which would in all likelihood cause the entire system to crash. In order to make sure neither of these two things happens, we designate every computer program as either privileged or unprivileged. We often say *supervisor privilege* to indicate privileged. We say a program is executing in Supervisor mode to indicate privileged, or User mode to indicate unprivileged. If a program is executing in Supervisor mode, it can execute all instructions and access all of memory. If a program is executing in User mode, it cannot. If a program executing in User mode tries to execute an instruction or access a memory location that requires being in Supervisor mode, the computer will not allow it.

9.1.1.2 Priority

Priority is all about the urgency of a program to execute. Every program is assigned a priority, specifying its urgency as compared to all other programs. This allows programs of greater urgency to interrupt programs of lesser urgency. For example, programs written by random users may be assigned a priority of 0. The keyboard may be asigned a priority of 4, and the fact that the computer is plugged into a source of energy like a wall outlet may be assigned a priority of 6. If that is the case, a random user program would be interrupted if someone sitting at a keyboard wanted to execute a program that caused data to be input into the computer. And that program would be interrupted if someone pulled the power cord out of the wall outlet, causing the computer to quickly lose its source of energy. In such an event, we would want the computer to execute some operating system program that is provided specifically to handle that situation.

9.1.1.3 Two Orthogonal Notions

We said privilege and priority are two orthogonal notions, meaning they have nothing to do with each other. We humans sometimes have a problem with that as we think of fire trucks that have the privilege of ignoring traffic lights because they must quickly reach the fire. In our daily lives, we often are given privileges because of our greater sense of urgency. Not the case with computer systems.

For example, we can have a user program that is tied to a physics experiment that needs to interrupt the computer at a specific instance of time to record information being generated by the physics experiment. If the user program does not pre-empt the program running at that instant of time, the data generated by the experiment may be lost. This is a user program, so it does not have supervisor privilege. But it does have a greater urgency, so it does have a higher priority.

Another example: The system administrator wants to execute diagnostic programs that access all memory locations and execute all instructions as part of some standard preventive maintenance. The diagnostic program needs supervisor privilege to execute all instructions and access all memory locations. But it has no sense of urgency. Whether this happens at 1 a.m. or 2 a.m. is irrelevant, compared to the urgency of other programs that need access to the computer system exactly when they need it. The diagnostic program has privilege but no priority.

Finally, an example showing that even in human activity one can have priority but not privilege. Our friend Bob works in the basement of one of those New York City skyscrapers. He is about to go to the men's room when his manager tells him to take a message immediately to the vice president on the 88th floor, and bring back a response. So Bob delays his visit to the men's room and takes the elevator to the 88th floor. The vice president keeps him waiting, causing Bob to be concerned he might have an accident. Finally, the vice president gives his response, and Bob pushes the button to summon the elevator to take him back to the basement, in pain because he needs to go to the men's room. While waiting for the elevator, another vice president appears, unlocks the executive men's room, and enters. Bob is in pain, but he cannot enter the executive men's room. Although he certainly has the priority, he does not have the privilege!

9.1.1.4 The Processor Status Register (PSR)

Each program executing on the computer has associated with it two very important registers. The Program Counter (PC) you are very familiar with. The other register, the Processor Status Register (PSR), is shown in Figure 9.1. It contains the privilege and priority assigned to that program.

Bit [15] specifies the privilege, where PSR[15]=0 means supervisor privilege, and PSR[15]=1 means unprivileged. Bits [10:8] specify the priority level (PL) of the program. The highest priority level is 7 (PL7), the lowest is PL0.

The PSR also contains the current values of the condition codes, as shown in Figure 9.1. We will see in Section 9.4 why it is important that the condition codes are included in the PSR.

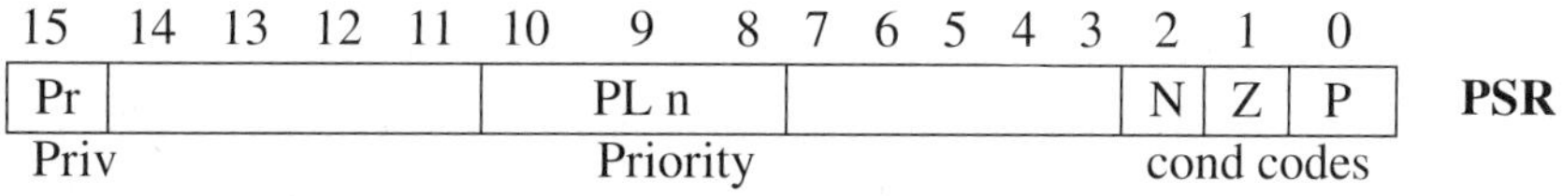

Figure 9.1   Processor status register (PSR).

9.1.2 Organization of Memory

Figure 9.2 shows the layout of the LC-3 memory.

You know that the LC-3 has a 16-bit address space; ergo, memory locations from x0000 to xFFFF. Locations x0000 to x2FFF are privileged memory locations. They contain the various data structures and code of the operating system. They require supervisor privilege to access. They are referred to as *system space*.

Locations x3000 to xFDFF are unprivileged memory locations. Supervisor privilege is not required to access these memory locations. All user programs and data use this region of memory. The region is often referred to as *user space*.

Addresses xFE00 to xFFFF do not correspond to memory locations at all. That is, the last address of a memory location is xFDFF. Addresses xFE00 to xFFFF are used to identify registers that take part in input and output functions and some special registers associated with the processor. For example, the PSR is assigned address xFFFC, and the processor's Master Control Register (MCR) is assigned address xFFFE. The benefit of assigning addresses from the memory address space will be discussed in Section 9.2.1.2. The set of addresses from xFE00 to xFFFF is usually referred to as the I/O page since most of the addresses are used for identifying registers that take part in input or output functions. Access to those registers requires supervisor privilege.

Finally, note that Figure 9.2 shows two stacks, a *supervisor stack* in system space and a *user stack* in user space. The supervisor stack is controlled by the

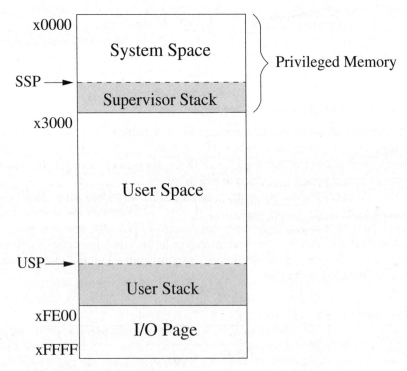

Figure 9.2   Regions of memory.

operating system and requires supervisor privilege to access. The user stack is controlled by the user program and does not require privilege to access.

Each has a stack pointer, Supervisor Stack Pointer (SSP) and User Stack Pointer (USP), to indicate the top of the stack. Since a program can only execute in Supervisor mode or User mode at any one time, only one of the two stacks is active at any one time. Register 6 is generally used as the stack pointer (SP) for the active stack. Two registers, Saved_SSP and Saved_USP, are provided to save the SP not in use. When privilege changes, for example, from Supervisor mode to User mode, the SP is stored in Saved_SSP, and the SP is loaded from Saved_USP.

9.2 Input/Output

Input and output devices (keyboards, monitors, disks, or kiosks at the shopping mall) all handle input or output data using registers that are tailored to the needs of each particular input or output device. Even the simplest I/O devices usually need at least two registers: one to hold the data being transferred between the device and the computer, and one to indicate status information about the device. An example of status information is whether the device is available or is it still busy processing the most recent I/O task.

9.2.1 Some Basic Characteristics of I/O

All I/O activity is controlled by instructions in the computer's ISA. Does the ISA need special instructions for dealing with I/O? Does the I/O device execute at the same speed as the computer, and if not, what manages the difference in speeds? Is the transfer of information between the computer and the I/O device initiated by a program executing in the computer, or is it initiated by the I/O device? Answers to these questions form some of the basic characteristics of I/O activity.

9.2.1.1 Memory-Mapped I/O vs. Special I/O Instructions

An instruction that interacts with an input or output device register must identify the particular input or output device register with which it is interacting. Two schemes have been used in the past. Some computers use special input and output instructions. Most computers prefer to use the same data movement instructions that are used to move data in and out of memory.

The very old PDP-8 (from Digital Equipment Corporation, more than 50 years ago—1965) is an example of a computer that used special input and output instructions. The 12-bit PDP-8 instruction contained a three-bit opcode. If the opcode was 110, an I/O instruction was indicated. The remaining nine bits of the PDP-8 instruction identified which I/O device register and what operation was to be performed.

Most computer designers prefer not to specify an additional set of instructions for dealing with input and output. They use the same data movement instructions that are used for loading and storing data between memory and the general purpose registers. For example, a load instruction (LD, LDI, or LDR), in which the source address is that of an input device register, is an input instruction. Similarly, a store instruction (ST, STI, or STR) in which the destination address is that of an output device register is an output instruction.

Since programmers use the same data movement instructions that are used for memory, every input device register and every output device register must be uniquely identified in the same way that memory locations are uniquely identified. Therefore, each device register is assigned an address from the memory address space of the ISA. That is, the I/O device registers are *mapped* to a set of addresses that are allocated to I/O device registers rather than to memory locations. Hence the name *memory-mapped I/O*.

The original PDP-11 ISA had a 16-bit address space. All addresses wherein bits [15:13] = 111 were allocated to I/O device registers. That is, of the 2^{16} addresses, only 57,344 corresponded to memory locations. The remaining 2^{13} were memory-mapped I/O addresses.

The LC-3 uses memory-mapped I/O. As we discussed in Section 9.1.2, addresses x0000 to xFDFF refer to actual memory locations. Addresses xFE00 to xFFFF are reserved for input/output device registers. Table A.3 lists the memory-mapped addresses of the LC-3 device registers that have been assigned so far. Future uses and future sales of LC-3 microprocessors may require the expansion of device register address assignments as new and exciting applications emerge!

9.2.1.2 Asynchronous vs. Synchronous

Most I/O is carried out at speeds very much slower than the speed of the processor. A typist, typing on a keyboard, loads an input device register with one ASCII code every time he/she types a character. A computer can read the contents of that device register every time it executes a load instruction, where the operand address is the memory-mapped address of that input device register.

Many of today's microprocessors execute instructions under the control of a clock that operates well in excess of 2 GHz. Even for a microprocessor operating at only 2 GHz, a clock cycle lasts only 0.5 nanoseconds. Suppose a processor executed one instruction at a time, and it took the processor ten clock cycles to execute the instruction that reads the input device register and stores its contents. At that rate, the processor could read the contents of the input device register once every 5 nanoseconds. Unfortunately, people do not type fast enough to keep this processor busy full-time reading characters. *Question:* How fast would a person have to type to supply input characters to the processor at the maximum rate the processor can receive them?

We could mitigate this speed disparity by designing hardware that would accept typed characters at some slower fixed rate. For example, we could design a piece of hardware that accepts one character every 200 million cycles. This would require a typing speed of 100 words/minute, assuming words on average consisted of five letters, which is certainly doable. Unfortunately, it would also require that the typist work in lockstep with the computer's clock. That is not acceptable since the typing speed (even of the same typist) varies from moment to moment.

What's the point? The point is that I/O devices usually operate at speeds very different from that of a microprocessor, and not in lockstep. We call this latter characteristic *asynchronous*. Most interaction between a processor and I/O is asynchronous. To control processing in an asynchronous world requires some protocol or *handshaking* mechanism. So it is with our keyboard and monitor. In the case of the keyboard, we will need a one-bit status register, called a *flag*, to indicate if someone has or has not typed a character. In the case of the monitor, we will need a one-bit status register to indicate whether or not the most recent character sent to the monitor has been displayed, and so the monitor can be given another character to display.

These flags are the simplest form of *synchronization*. A single flag, called the *ready bit*, is enough to synchronize the output of the typist who can type characters at the rate of 100 words/minute with the input to a processor that can accept these characters at the rate of 200 million characters/second. Each time the typist types a character, the ready bit is set to 1. Each time the computer reads a character, it clears the ready bit. By examining the ready bit before reading a character, the computer can tell whether it has already read the last character typed. If the ready bit is clear, no characters have been typed since the last time the computer read a character, and so no additional read would take place. When the computer detects that the ready bit is set, it could only have been caused by a **new** character being typed, so the computer would know to again read a character.

The single ready bit provides enough handshaking to ensure that the asynchronous transfer of information between the typist and the microprocessor can be carried out accurately.

If the typist could type at a constant speed, and we did have a piece of hardware that would accept typed characters at precise intervals (e.g., one character every 200 million cycles), then we would not need the ready bit. The computer would simply know, after 200 million cycles of doing other stuff, that the typist had typed exactly one more character, and the computer would read that character. In this hypothetical situation, the typist would be typing in lockstep with the processor, and no additional synchronization would be needed. We would say the computer and typist were operating *synchronously*. That is, the input activity was synchronous.

9.2.1.3 Interrupt-Driven vs. Polling

The processor, which is computing, and the typist, who is typing, are two separate entities. Each is doing its own thing. Still, they need to interact; that is, the data that is typed has to get into the computer. The issue of *interrupt-driven* vs. *polling* is the issue of who controls the interaction. Does the processor do its own thing until being interrupted by an announcement from the keyboard, "Hey, a key has been struck. The ASCII code is in the input device register. You need to read it." This is called *interrupt-driven I/O*, where the keyboard controls the interaction. Or, does the processor control the interaction, specifically by interrogating (usually, again and again) the ready bit until it (the processor) detects that the ready bit is set. At that point, the processor knows it is time to read the device register. This second type of interaction when the processor is in charge is called *polling*, since the ready bit is polled by the processor, asking if any key has been struck.

Section 9.2.2.2 describes how polling works. Section 9.4 explains interrupt-driven I/O.

9.2.2 Input from the Keyboard

9.2.2.1 Basic Input Registers (KBDR and KBSR)

We have already noted that in order to handle character input from the keyboard, we need two things: a data register that contains the character to be input and a synchronization mechanism to let the processor know that input has occurred. The synchronization mechanism is contained in the status register associated with the keyboard.

These two registers are called the *keyboard data register* (KBDR) and the *keyboard status register* (KBSR). They are assigned addresses from the memory address space. As shown in Table A.3, address xFE02 is assigned to the KBDR; address xFE00 is assigned to the KBSR.

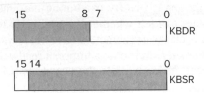

Figure 9.3   Keyboard device registers.

Even though a character needs only 8 bits and the synchronization mechanism needs only 1 bit, it is easier to assign 16 bits (like all memory addresses in the LC-3) to each. In the case of KBDR, bits [7:0] are used for the data, and bits [15:8] contain x00. In the case of KBSR, bit [15] contains the synchronization mechanism, that is, the ready bit. Figure 9.3 shows the two device registers needed by the keyboard.

9.2.2.2 The Basic Input Service Routine

KBSR[15] controls the synchronization of the slow keyboard and the fast processor. When a key on the keyboard is struck, the ASCII code for that key is loaded into KBDR[7:0], and the electronic circuits associated with the keyboard automatically set KBSR[15] to 1. When the LC-3 reads KBDR, the electronic circuits associated with the keyboard automatically clear KBSR[15], allowing another key to be struck. If KBSR[15] = 1, the ASCII code corresponding to the last key struck has not yet been read, and so the keyboard is disabled; that is, no key can be struck until the last key is read.

If input/output is controlled by the processor (i.e., via polling), then a program can repeatedly test KBSR[15] until it notes that the bit is set. At that point, the processor can load the ASCII code contained in KBDR into one of the LC-3 registers. Since the processor only loads the ASCII code if KBSR[15] is 1, there is no danger of reading a single typed character multiple times. Furthermore, since the keyboard is disabled until the previous code is read, there is no danger of the processor missing characters that were typed. In this way, KBSR[15] provides the mechanism to guarantee that each key typed will be loaded exactly once.

The following input routine loads R0 with the ASCII code that has been entered through the keyboard and then moves on to the NEXT_TASK in the program.

```
01    START   LDI     R1, A        ; Test for
02            BRzp    START        ; character input
03            LDI     R0, B
04            BRnzp   NEXT_TASK    ; Go to the next task
05    A       .FILL   xFE00        ; Address of KBSR
06    B       .FILL   xFE02        ; Address of KBDR
```

As long as KBSR[15] is 0, no key has been struck since the last time the processor read the data register. Lines 01 and 02 comprise a loop that tests bit [15] of KBSR. Note the use of the LDI instruction, which loads R1 with the contents of xFE00, the memory-mapped address of KBSR. If the ready bit, bit [15], is clear, BRzp will branch to START and another iteration of the loop. When someone strikes a key, KBDR will be loaded with the ASCII code of that key, and the ready bit of KBSR will be set. This will cause the branch to fall through, and the instruction at line 03 will be executed. Again, note the use of the LDI instruction, which this time loads R0 with the contents of xFE02, the memory-mapped address of KBDR. The input routine is now done, so the program branches unconditionally to its NEXT_TASK.

9.2.2.3 Implementation of Memory-Mapped Input

Figure 9.4 shows the additional data path required to implement memory-mapped input. You are already familiar, from Chapter 5, with the data path required to

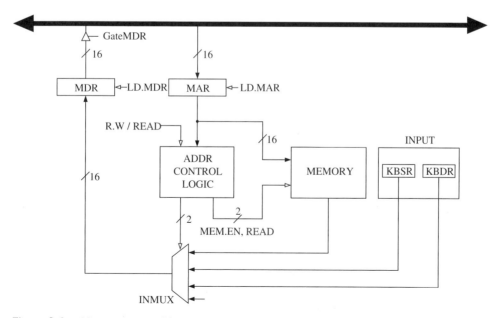

Figure 9.4   Memory-mapped input.

carry out the EXECUTE phase of the load instructions. Essentially three steps are required:

1. The MAR is loaded with the address of the memory location to be read.
2. Memory is read, resulting in MDR being loaded with the contents at the specified memory location.
3. The destination register (DR) is loaded with the contents of MDR.

In the case of memory-mapped input, the same steps are carried out, **except** instead of MAR being loaded with the address of a memory location, MAR is loaded with the address of a device register. Instead of the address control logic enabling memory to read, the address control logic selects the corresponding device register to provide input to the MDR.

9.2.3 Output to the Monitor

9.2.3.1 Basic Output Registers (DDR and DSR)

Output works in a way very similar to input, with DDR and DSR replacing the roles of KBDR and KBSR, respectively. DDR stands for Display Data Register, which drives the monitor display. DSR stands for Display Status Register. In the LC-3, DDR is assigned address xFE06. DSR is assigned address xFE04.

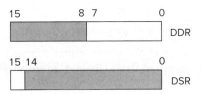

Figure 9.5   Monitor device registers.

As is the case with input, even though an output character needs only 8 bits and the synchronization mechanism needs only one bit, it is easier to assign 16 bits (like all memory addresses in the LC-3) to each output device register. In the case of DDR, bits [7:0] are used for data, and bits [15:8] contain x00. In the case of DSR, bit [15] contains the synchronization mechanism, that is, the ready bit. Figure 9.5 shows the two device registers needed by the monitor.

9.2.3.2 The Basic Output Service Routine

DSR[15] controls the synchronization of the fast processor and the slow monitor display. When the LC-3 transfers an ASCII code to DDR[7:0] for outputting, the electronics of the monitor automatically clear DSR[15] as the processing of the contents of DDR[7:0] begins. When the monitor finishes processing the character on the screen, it (the monitor) automatically sets DSR[15]. This is a signal to the processor that it (the processor) can transfer another ASCII code to DDR for outputting. As long as DSR[15] is clear, the monitor is still processing the previous character, so the monitor is disabled as far as additional output from the processor is concerned.

If input/output is controlled by the processor (i.e., via polling), a program can repeatedly test DSR[15] until it notes that the bit is set, indicating that it is OK to write a character to the screen. At that point, the processor can store the ASCII code for the character it wishes to write into DDR[7:0], setting up the transfer of that character to the monitor's display.

The following routine causes the ASCII code contained in R0 to be displayed on the monitor:

```
01      START   LDI     R1, A           ; Test to see if
02              BRzp    START           ; output register is ready
03              STI     R0, B
04              BRnzp   NEXT_TASK
05      A       .FILL   xFE04           ; Address of DSR
06      B       .FILL   xFE06           ; Address of DDR
```

Like the routine for KBDR and KBSR in Section 9.2.2.2, lines 01 and 02 repeatedly poll DSR[15] to see if the monitor electronics is finished with the last character shipped by the processor. Note the use of LDI and the indirect access to xFE04, the memory-mapped address of DSR. As long as DSR[15] is clear, the monitor electronics is still processing this character, and BRzp branches to START for another iteration of the loop. When the monitor electronics finishes with the last character shipped by the processor, it automatically sets DSR[15] to 1, which causes the branch to fall through and the instruction at line 03 to be executed. Note the use of the STI instruction, which stores R0 into xFE06, the memory-mapped address of DDR. The write to DDR also clears DSR[15], disabling for the moment DDR from further output. The monitor electronics takes over and writes the character to the screen. Since the output routine is now done, the program unconditionally branches (line 04) to its NEXT_TASK.

9.2.3.3 Implementation of Memory-Mapped Output

Figure 9.6 shows the additional data path required to implement memory-mapped output. As we discussed previously with respect to memory-mapped input, the mechanisms for handling the device registers provide very little additional complexity to what already exists for handling memory accesses.

In Chapter 5, you became familiar with the process of carrying out the EXECUTE phase of the store instructions.

1. The MAR is loaded with the address of the memory location to be written.
2. The MDR is loaded with the data to be written to memory.
3. Memory is written, resulting in the contents of MDR being stored in the specified memory location.

In the case of memory-mapped output, the same steps are carried out, **except** instead of MAR being loaded with the address of a memory location, MAR is loaded with the address of a device register. Instead of the address control logic enabling memory to write, the address control logic asserts the load enable signal of DDR.

Memory-mapped output also requires the ability to **read** output device registers. You saw in Section 9.2.3.2 that before the DDR could be loaded, the ready

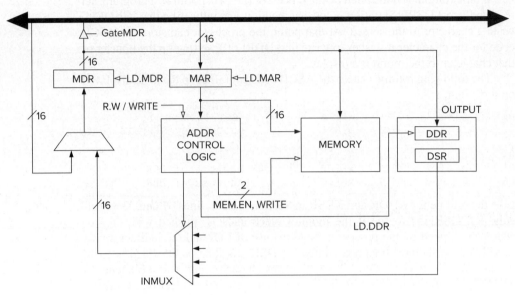

Figure 9.6   Memory-mapped output.

bit had to be in state 1, indicating that the previous character had already finished being written to the screen. The LDI and BRzp instructions on lines 01 and 02 perform that test. To do this, the LDI reads the output device register DSR, and BRzp tests bit [15]. If the MAR is loaded with xFE04 (the memory-mapped address of the DSR), the address control logic selects DSR as the input to the MDR, where it is subsequently loaded into R1, and the condition codes are set.

9.2.3.4 Example: Keyboard Echo

When we type at the keyboard, it is helpful to know exactly what characters we have typed. We can get this echo capability easily (without any sophisticated electronics) by simply combining the two routines we have discussed. The result: The key typed at the keyboard is displayed on the monitor.

```
01      START   LDI     R1, KBSR      ; Test for character input
02              BRzp    START
03              LDI     R0, KBDR
04      ECHO    LDI     R1, DSR       ; Test output register ready
05              BRzp    ECHO
06              STI     R0, DDR
07              BRnzp   NEXT_TASK
08      KBSR    .FILL   xFE00         ; Address of KBSR
09      KBDR    .FILL   xFE02         ; Address of KBDR
0A      DSR     .FILL   xFE04         ; Address of DSR
0B      DDR     .FILL   xFE06         ; Address of DDR
```

9.2.4 A More Sophisticated Input Routine

In the example of Section 9.2.2.2, the input routine would be a part of a program being executed by the computer. Presumably, the program requires character input from the keyboard. But how does the person sitting at the keyboard know when to type a character? Sitting there, the person may wonder whether or not the program is actually running, or if perhaps the computer is busy doing something else.

To let the person sitting at the keyboard know that the program is waiting for input from the keyboard, the computer typically prints a message on the monitor. Such a message is often referred to as a *prompt*. The symbols that are displayed by your operating system (e.g., % or **C:**) or by your editor (e.g., **:**) are examples of prompts.

The program fragment shown in Figure 9.7 obtains keyboard input via polling as we have shown in Section 9.2.2.2. It also includes a prompt to let the person sitting at the keyboard know when it is time to type a key. Let's examine this program fragment.

You are already familiar with lines 13 through 19 and lines 25 through 28, which correspond to the code in Section 9.2.3.4 for inputting a character via the keyboard and echoing it on the monitor.

You are also familiar with the need to save and restore registers if those registers are needed by instructions in the input routine. Lines 01 through 03 save R1, R2, and R3, lines 1D through 1F restore R1, R2, and R3, and lines 22 through 24 set aside memory locations for those register values.

This leaves lines 05 through 08, 0A through 11, 1A through 1C, 29 and 2A. These lines serve to alert the person sitting at the keyboard that it is time to type a character.

Lines 05 through 08 write the ASCII code x0A to the monitor. This is the ASCII code for a *new line*. Most ASCII codes correspond to characters that are visible on the screen. A few, like x0A, are control characters. They cause an action to occur. Specifically, the ASCII code x0A causes the cursor to move to the far left of the next line on the screen. Thus, the name *Newline*. Before attempting to write x0A, however, as is always the case, DSR[15] is tested (line 6) to see if DDR can accept a character. If DSR[15] is clear, the monitor is busy, and the loop (lines 06 and 07) is repeated. When DSR[15] is 1, the conditional branch (line 7) is not taken, and (line 8) x0A is written to DDR for outputting.

Lines 0A through 11 cause the prompt `Input a character>` to be written to the screen. The prompt is specified by the .STRINGZ pseudo-op on line 2A and is stored in 19 memory locations—18 ASCII codes, one per memory location, corresponding to the 18 characters in the prompt, and the terminating sentinel x0000.

Line 0C iteratively tests to see if the end of the string has been reached (by detecting x0000), and if not, once DDR is free, line 0F writes the next character in the input prompt into DDR. When x0000 is detected, the entire input prompt has been written to the screen, and the program branches to the code that handles the actual keyboard input (starting at line 13).

After the person at the keyboard types a character and it has been echoed (lines 13 to 19), the program writes one more new line (lines 1A through 1C) before branching to its NEXT_TASK.

```
01   START    ST      R1,SaveR1     ; Save registers needed
02            ST      R2,SaveR2     ; by this routine
03            ST      R3,SaveR3
04   ;
05            LD      R2,Newline
06   L1       LDI     R3,DSR
07            BRzp    L1            ; Loop until monitor is ready
08            STI     R2,DDR        ; Move cursor to new clean line
09   ;
0A            LEA     R1,Prompt     ; Starting address of prompt string
0B   Loop     LDR     R0,R1,#0      ; Write the input prompt
0C            BRz     Input         ; End of prompt string
0D   L2       LDI     R3,DSR
0E            BRzp    L2            ; Loop until monitor is ready
0F            STI     R0,DDR        ; Write next prompt character
10            ADD     R1,R1,#1      ; Increment prompt pointer
11            BRnzp   Loop          ; Get next prompt character
12   ;
13   Input    LDI     R3,KBSR
14            BRzp    Input         ; Poll until a character is typed
15            LDI     R0,KBDR       ; Load input character into R0
16   L3       LDI     R3,DSR
17            BRzp    L3            ; Loop until monitor is ready
18            STI     R0,DDR        ; Echo input character
19   ;
1A   L4       LDI     R3,DSR
1B            BRzp    L4            ; Loop until monitor is ready
1C            STI     R2,DDR        ; Move cursor to new clean line
1D            LD      R1,SaveR1     ; Restore registers
1E            LD      R2,SaveR2     ; to original values
1F            LD      R3,SaveR3
20            BRnzp   NEXT_TASK     ; Do the program's next task
21   ;
22   SaveR1   .BLKW   1             ; Memory for registers saved
23   SaveR2   .BLKW   1
24   SaveR3   .BLKW   1
25   DSR      .FILL   xFE04
26   DDR      .FILL   xFE06
27   KBSR     .FILL   xFE00
28   KBDR     .FILL   xFE02
29   Newline  .FILL   x000A         ; ASCII code for newline
2A   Prompt   .STRINGZ ''Input a character>''
```

Figure 9.7   The more sophisticated input routine.

9.2.5 Implementation of Memory-Mapped I/O, Revisited

We showed in Figures 9.4 and 9.6 partial implementations of the data path to handle (separately) memory-mapped input and memory-mapped output. We have also learned that in order to support interrupt-driven I/O, the two status registers must be writeable as well as readable.

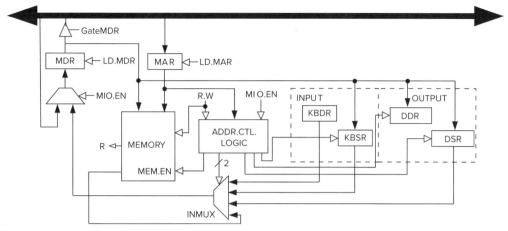

Figure 9.8   Relevant data path implementation of memory-mapped I/O.

Figure 9.8 (also shown as Figure C.3 of Appendix C) shows the data path necessary to support the full range of features we have discussed for the I/O device registers. The Address Control Logic Block controls the input or output operation. Note that there are three inputs to this block. MIO.EN indicates whether a data movement from/to memory or I/O is to take place this clock cycle. MAR contains the address of the memory location or the memory-mapped address of an I/O device register. R.W indicates whether a load or a store is to take place. Depending on the values of these three inputs, the address control logic does nothing (MIO.EN = 0), or it provides the control signals to direct the transfer of data between the MDR and the memory or between the MDR and one of the I/O registers.

If R.W indicates a load, the transfer is from memory or I/O device to the MDR. The Address Control Logic Block provides the select lines to INMUX to source the appropriate I/O device register or memory (depending on MAR) and also enables the memory if MAR contains the address of a memory location.

If R.W indicates a store, the contents of the MDR is written either to memory or to one of the device registers. The address control logic either enables a write to memory or asserts the load enable line of the device register specified by the contents of the MAR.

9.3 Operating System Service Routines (LC-3 Trap Routines)

9.3.1 Introduction

Recall Figure 9.7 of the previous section. In order for the program to successfully obtain input from the keyboard, it was necessary for the programmer to know several things:

1. The hardware data registers for both the monitor and the keyboard: the monitor so a prompt could be displayed, and the keyboard so the program would know where to get the input character.

2. The hardware status registers for both the monitor and the keyboard: the monitor so the program would know when it was OK to display the next character in the input prompt, and the keyboard so the program would know when someone had struck a key.

3. The asynchronous nature of keyboard input relative to the executing program.

This is beyond the knowledge of most application programmers. In fact, in the real world, if application programmers (or user programmers, as they are sometimes called) had to understand I/O at this level, there would be much less I/O and far fewer programmers in the business.

There is another problem with allowing user programs to perform I/O activity by directly accessing KBDR and KBSR. I/O activity involves the use of device registers that are shared by many programs. This means that if a user programmer were allowed to access the hardware registers, and he/she messed up, it could create havoc for other user programs. Thus, in general it is ill-advised to give user programmers access to these registers. That is why the addresses of hardware registers are part of the privileged memory address space and accessible only to programs that have supervisor privilege.

The simpler solution, as well as the safer solution to the problem of user programs requiring I/O, involves the TRAP instruction and the operating system, which of course has supervisor privilege.

We were first introduced to the TRAP instruction in Chapter 4 as a way to get the operating system to halt the computer. In Chapter 5 we saw that a user program could use the TRAP instruction to get the operating system to do I/O tasks for it (the user program). In fact a great benefit of the TRAP instruction, which we have already pointed out, is that it allows the user programmer to not have to know the gory details of I/O discussed earlier in this chapter. In addition, it protects user programs from the consequences of other inept user programmers.

Figure 9.9 shows a user program that, upon reaching location x4000, needs an I/O task performed. The user program uses the TRAP instruction to request the

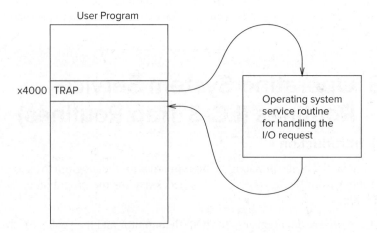

Figure 9.9   Invoking an OS service routine using the TRAP instruction.

operating system to perform the task on behalf of the user program. The operating system takes control of the computer, handles the request specified by the TRAP instruction, and then returns control back to the user program at location x4001. As we said at the start of this chapter, we usually refer to the request made by the user program as a *system call* or a *service call*.

9.3.2 The Trap Mechanism

The trap mechanism involves several elements:

1. **A set of service routines** executed on behalf of user programs by the operating system. These are part of the operating system and start at arbitrary addresses in system space. The LC-3 was designed so that up to 256 service routines can be specified. Table A.2 in Appendix A contains the LC-3's current complete list of operating system service routines.

2. **A table of the starting addresses** of these 256 service routines. This table is stored in memory locations x0000 to x00FF. The table is referred to by various names by various companies. One company calls this table the System Control Block. Another company calls it the Trap Vector Table. Figure 9.10 shows the Trap Vector Table of the LC-3, with specific starting addresses highlighted. Among the starting addresses are the one for the character output service routine (memory location x0420), which is stored in memory location x0021, the one for the keyboard input service routine (location x04A0), stored in location x0023, and the one for the machine halt service routine (location x0520), stored in location x0025.

x0000	$\vdots$
$\vdots$	
x0020	x03E0
x0021	x0420
x0022	x0460
x0023	x04A0
x0024	x04E0
x0025	x0520
$\vdots$	
x00FF	$\vdots$

Figure 9.10   The Trap Vector Table.

3. **The TRAP instruction.** When a user program wishes to have the operating system execute a specific service routine on behalf of the user program, and then return control to the user program, the user program uses the TRAP instruction (as we have been doing since Chapter 4).

4. **A linkage** back to the user program. The service routine must have a mechanism for returning control to the user program.

9.3.3 The TRAP Instruction

The TRAP instruction causes the service routine to execute by (1) changing the PC to the starting address of the relevant service routine on the basis of its trap vector, and (2) providing a way to get back to the program that executed the TRAP instruction. The "way back" is referred to as a *linkage*.

As you know, the **TRAP** instruction is made up of two parts: the TRAP opcode 1111 and the trap vector (bits [7:0]), which identifies the service routine the user program wants the operating system to execute on its behalf. Bits [11:8] must be zero.

In the following example, the trap vector is x23.

15	14	13	12	11	10	9	8	7	6	5	4	3	2	1	0
1	1	1	1	0	0	0	0	0	0	1	0	0	0	1	1

$\qquad$ TRAP $\qquad\qquad\qquad\qquad\qquad\qquad$ trap vector

The EXECUTE phase of the TRAP instruction's instruction cycle does three things:

1. The PSR and PC are both pushed onto the system stack. Since the PC was incremented during the FETCH phase of the TRAP instruction's instruction cycle, the return linkage is automatically saved in the PC. When control returns to the user program, the PC will automatically be pointing to the instruction following the TRAP instruction.
   Note that the program requesting the trap service routine can be running either in Supervisor mode or in User mode. If in User mode, R6, the stack pointer, is pointing to the user stack. Before the PSR and PC can be pushed onto the system stack, the current contents of R6 must be stored in Saved_USP, and the contents of Saved_SSP loaded into R6.

2. PSR[15] is set to 0, since the service routine is going to require supervisor privilege to execute. PSR[10:8] are left unchanged since the priority of the TRAP routine is the same as the priority of the program that requested it.

3. The 8-bit trap vector is zero-extended to 16 bits to form an address that corresponds to a location in the Trap Vector Table. For the trap vector x23, that address is x0023. Memory location x0023 contains x04A0, the starting address of the TRAP x23 service routine. The PC is loaded with x04A0, completing the instruction cycle.

Since the PC contains x04A0, processing continues at memory address x04A0.

Location x04A0 is the starting address of the operating system service routine to input a character from the keyboard. We say the trap vector "points" to the starting address of the TRAP routine. Thus, TRAP x23 causes the operating system to start executing the keyboard input service routine.

9.3.4 The RTI Instruction: To Return Control to the Calling Program

The only thing left to show is a mechanism for returning control to the calling program, once the trap service routine has finished execution.

This is accomplished by the Return from Trap or Interrupt (RTI) instruction:

15	14	13	12	11	10	9	8	7	6	5	4	3	2	1	0
1	0	0	0	0	0	0	0	0	0	0	0	0	0	0	0

RTI

The RTI instruction (opcode = **1000**, with no operands) pops the top two values on the system stack into the PC and PSR. Since the PC contains the address following the address of the TRAP instruction, control returns to the user program at the correct address.

Finally, once the PSR has been popped off the system stack, PSR[15] must be examined to see whether the processor was running in User mode or Supervisor mode when the TRAP instruction was executed. If in User mode, the stack pointers need to be adjusted to reflect that now back in User mode, the relevant stack in use is the user stack. This is done by loading the Saved_SSP with the current contents of R6, and loading R6 with the contents of Saved_USP.

9.3.5 A Summary of the Trap Service Routine Process

Figure 9.11 shows the LC-3 using the TRAP instruction and the RTI instruction to implement the example of Figure 9.9. The flow of control goes from (A) within a user program that needs a character input from the keyboard, to (B) the operating system service routine that performs that task on behalf of the user program, back to the user program (C) that presumably uses the information contained in the input character.

As we know, the computer continually executes its instruction cycle (FETCH, DECODE, etc.) on sequentially located instructions until the flow of control is changed by changing the contents of the PC during the EXECUTE phase of the current instruction. In that way, the next FETCH will be at a redirected address.

The TRAP instruction with trap vector x23 in our user program does exactly that. Execution of TRAP x23 causes the PSR and incremented PC to be pushed onto the system stack and the contents of memory location x0023 (which, in this case, contains x04A0) to be loaded into the PC. The dashed line on Figure 9.11 shows the use of the trap vector x23 to obtain the starting address of the trap service routine from the Trap Vector Table.

The next instruction cycle starts with the FETCH of the contents of x04A0, which is the first instruction of the relevant operating system service routine. The trap service routine executes to completion, ending with the RTI instruction,

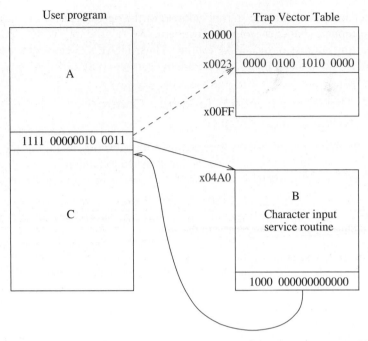

Figure 9.11　Flow of control from a user program to an OS service routine and back.

which loads the PC and PSR with the top two elements on the system stack, that is, the PSR and incremented PC that were pushed during execution of the TRAP instruction. Since the PC was incremented prior to being pushed onto the system stack, it contains the address of the instruction following the TRAP instruction in the calling program, and the user program resumes execution by fetching the instruction following the TRAP instruction.

　　The following program is provided to illustrate the use of the TRAP instruction. It can also be used to amuse the average four-year-old!

Example 9.1

Write a game program to do the following: A person is sitting at a keyboard. Each time the person types a capital letter, the program outputs the lowercase version of that letter. If the person types a 7, the program terminates.

The following LC-3 assembly language program will do the job.

```
01              .ORIG x3000
02              LD    R2,TERM  ; Load -7
03              LD    R3,ASCII ; Load ASCII difference
04      AGAIN   TRAP  x23      ; Request keyboard input
05              ADD   R1,R2,R0 ; Test for terminating
06              BRz   EXIT     ; character
07              ADD   R0,R0,R3 ; Change to lowercase
08              TRAP  x21      ; Output to the monitor
09              BRnzp AGAIN    ; ... and do it again!
0A      TERM    .FILL xFFC9    ; FFC9 is negative of ASCII 7
0B      ASCII   .FILL x0020
0C      EXIT    TRAP  x25      ; Halt
0D              .END
```

The program executes as follows: The program first loads constants xFFC9 and x0020 into R2 and R3. The constant xFFC9, which is the negative of the ASCII code for 7, is used to test the character typed at the keyboard to see if the four-year-old wants to continue playing. The constant x0020 is the zero-extended difference between the ASCII code for a capital letter and the ASCII code for that same letter's lowercase representation. For example, the ASCII code for **A** is x41; the ASCII code for **a** is x61. The ASCII codes for **Z** and **z** are x5A and x7A, respectively.

Then TRAP x23 is executed, which invokes the keyboard input service routine. When the service routine is finished, control returns to the application program (at line 05), and R0 contains the ASCII code of the character typed. The ADD and BRz instructions test for the terminating character 7. If the character typed is not a 7, the ASCII uppercase/lowercase difference (x0020) is added to the input ASCII code, storing the result in R0. Then a TRAP to the monitor output service routine is called. This causes the lowercase representation of the same letter to be displayed on the monitor. When control returns to the application program (this time at line 09), an unconditional BR to AGAIN is executed, and another request for keyboard input appears.

The correct operation of the program in this example assumes that the person sitting at the keyboard only types capital letters and the value 7. What if the person types a $? A better solution to Example 9.1 would be a program that tests the character typed to be sure it really is a capital letter from among the 26 capital letters in the alphabet or the single digit 7, and if it is not, takes corrective action.

Question: Augment this program to add the test for bad data. That is, write a program that will type the lowercase representation of any capital letter typed and will terminate if anything other than a capital letter is typed. See Exercise 9.20.

9.3.6 Trap Routines for Handling I/O

With the constructs just provided, the input routine described in Figure 9.7 can be slightly modified to be the input service routine shown in Figure 9.12. Two changes are needed: (1) We add the appropriate .ORIG and .END pseudo-ops. .ORIG specifies the starting address of the input service routine—the address found at location x0023 in the Trap Vector Table. And (2) we terminate the input service routine with the RTI instruction rather than the BR NEXT_TASK, as is done on line 20 in Figure 9.7. We use RTI because the service routine is invoked by TRAP x23. It is not part of the user program, as was the case in Figure 9.7.

The output routine of Section 9.2.3.2 can be modified in a similar way, as shown in Figure 9.13. The results are input (Figure 9.12) and output (Figure 9.13) service routines that can be invoked simply and safely by the TRAP instruction with the appropriate trap vector. In the case of input, upon completion of TRAP x23, R0 contains the ASCII code of the keyboard character typed. In the case of output, the initiating program must load R0 with the ASCII code of the character it wishes displayed on the monitor and then invoke TRAP x21.

```
01        ;  Service Routine for Keyboard Input
02        ;
03                  .ORIG    x04A0
04      START  ST     R1,SaveR1          ; Save the values in the registers
05             ST     R2,SaveR2          ; that are used so that they
06             ST     R3,SaveR3          ; can be restored before RET
07        ;
08             LD     R2,Newline
09      L1     LDI    R3,DSR             ; Check DDR --  is it free?
0A             BRzp   L1
0B             STI    R2,DDR             ; Move cursor to new clean line
0C        ;
0D             LEA    R1,Prompt          ; Prompt is starting address
0E                                       ; of prompt string
1F      Loop   LDR    R0,R1,#0           ; Get next prompt character
10             BRz    Input              ; Check for end of prompt string
11      L2     LDI    R3,DSR
12             BRzp   L2
13             STI    R0,DDR             ; Write next character of
14                                       ; prompt string
15             ADD    R1,R1,#1           ; Increment prompt pointer
16             BRnzp  Loop
17        ;
18      Input  LDI    R3,KBSR            ; Has a character been typed?
19             BRzp   Input
1A             LDI    R0,KBDR            ; Load it into R0
1B      L3     LDI    R3,DSR
1C             BRzp   L3
1D             STI    R0,DDR             ; Echo input character
1E                                       ; to the monitor
1F        ;
20      L4     LDI    R3,DSR
21             BRzp   L4
22             STI    R2,DDR             ; Move cursor to new clean line
23             LD     R1,SaveR1          ; Service routine done, restore
24             LD     R2,SaveR2          ; original values in registers.
25             LD     R3,SaveR3
26             RTI                       ; Return from Trap
27        ;
28      SaveR1 .BLKW  1
29      SaveR2 .BLKW  1
2A      SaveR3 .BLKW  1
2B      DSR    .FILL  xFE04
2C      DDR    .FILL  xFE06
2D      KBSR   .FILL  xFE00
2E      KBDR   .FILL  xFE02
2F      Newline .FILL x000A            ; ASCII code for newline
30      Prompt  .STRINGZ "Input a character>"
31              .END
```

Figure 9.12   Character input service routine.

```
01                  .ORIG    x0420       ; System call starting address
02                  ST       R1, SaveR1  ; R1 will be used to poll the DSR
03                                        ; hardware
04       ; Write the character
05       TryWrite   LDI      R1, DSR      ; Get status
06                  BRzp     TryWrite     ; Bit 15 on says display is ready
07       WriteIt    STI      R0, DDR      ; Write character
08
09       ; return from trap
0A       Return     LD       R1, SaveR1   ; Restore registers
0B                  RTI                   ; Return from trap
0C       DSR        .FILL    xFE04        ; Address of display status register
0D       DDR        .FILL    xFE06        ; Address of display data register
0E       SaveR1     .BLKW    1
0F                  .END
```

Figure 9.13   Character output service routine.

9.3.7 A Trap Routine for Halting the Computer

Recall from Section 4.5 that the RUN latch is ANDed with the crystal oscillator to produce the clock that controls the operation of the computer. We noted that if that one-bit latch was cleared, the output of the AND gate would be 0, stopping the clock.

Years ago, most ISAs had a HALT instruction for stopping the clock. Given how infrequently that instruction is executed, it seems wasteful to devote an opcode to it. In many modern computers, the RUN latch is cleared by a TRAP routine. In the LC-3, the RUN latch is bit [15] of the Master Control Register (MCR), which is memory-mapped to location xFFFE. Figure 9.14 shows the trap service routine for halting the processor, that is, for stopping the clock.

```
01                  .ORIG    x0520       ; Where this routine resides
02                  ST       R1, SaveR1  ; R1: a temp for MC register
03                  ST       R0, SaveR0  ; R0 is used as working space
04
05       ; print message that machine is halting
06
07                  LD       R0, ASCIINewLine
08                  TRAP     x21
09                  LEA      R0, Message
0A                  TRAP     x22
0B                  LD       R0, ASCIINewLine
0C                  TRAP     x21
0D       ;
0E       ; clear bit 15 at xFFFE to stop the machine
0F       ;
10                  LDI      R1, MCR      ; Load MC register into R1
11                  LD       R0, MASK     ; R0 = x7FFF
12                  AND      R0, R1, R0   ; Mask to clear the top bit
13                  STI      R0, MCR      ; Store R0 into MC register
```

Figure 9.14   HALT service routine for the LC-3 (Fig. 9.14 continued on next page.)

```
14  ;
15  ; return from HALT routine.
16  ; (how can this routine return if the machine is halted above?)
17  ;
18              LD      R1, SaveR1 ; Restore registers
19              LD      R0, SaveR0
1A              RTI
1B  ;
1C  ; Some constants
1D  ;
1E  ASCIINewLine    .FILL   x000A
1F  SaveR0          .BLKW   1
20  SaveR1          .BLKW   1
21  Message         .STRINGZ   "Halting the machine."
22  MCR             .FILL   xFFFE       ; Address of MCR
23  MASK            .FILL   x7FFF       ; Mask to clear the top bit
24                  .END
```

Figure 9.14   HALT service routine for the LC-3 (continued Fig. 9.14 from previous page.)

First (lines 02 and 03), registers R1 and R0 are saved. R1 and R0 are saved because they are needed by the service routine. Then (lines 07 through 0C), the banner *Halting the machine* is displayed on the monitor. Finally (lines 10 through 13), the RUN latch (MCR[15]) is cleared by ANDing the MCR with 0111111111111111. That is, MCR[14:0] remains unchanged, but MCR[15] is cleared. *Question*: What instruction (or trap service routine) can be used to start the clock? *Hint:* This is a trick question! :-)

9.3.8 The Trap Routine for Character Input (One Last Time)

Let's look again at the keyboard input service routine of Figure 9.12. In particular, let's look at the three-line sequence that occurs at symbolic addresses L1, L2, L3, and L4:

```
LABEL   LDI     R3,DSR
        BRzp    LABEL
        STI     Reg,DDR
```

Can the JSR/RET mechanism enable us to replace these four occurrences of the same sequence with a single subroutine? *Answer:* Yes, **almost.**

Figure 9.15, our "improved" keyboard input service routine, contains

```
JSR     WriteChar
```

at lines 04, 0A, 10, and 13, and the four-instruction subroutine

```
WriteChar   LDI     R3,DSR
            BRzp    WriteChar
            STI     R2,DDR
            RET
```

at lines 1A through 1D. Note the RET instruction (a.k.a. JMP R7) that is needed to terminate the subroutine.

```
01                      .ORIG   x04A0
02      START           JSR     SaveReg
03                      LD      R2,Newline
04                      JSR     WriteChar
05                      LEA     R1,PROMPT
06      ;
07      ;
08      Loop            LDR     R2,R1,#0     ; Get next prompt char
09                      BRz     Input
0A                      JSR     WriteChar
0B                      ADD     R1,R1,#1
0C                      BRnzp   Loop
0D      ;
0E      Input           JSR     ReadChar
0F                      ADD     R2,R0,#0     ; Move char to R2 for writing
10                      JSR     WriteChar    ; Echo to monitor
11      ;
12                      LD      R2, Newline
13                      JSR     WriteChar
14                      JSR     RestoreReg
15                      RTI                  ; RTI terminates the trap routine
16      ;
17      Newline         .FILL   x000A
18      PROMPT          .STRINGZ  "Input a character>"
19      ;
1A      WriteChar       LDI     R3,DSR
1B                      BRzp    WriteChar
1C                      STI     R2,DDR
1D                      RET                  ; JMP R7 terminates subroutine
1E      DSR             .FILL   xFE04
1F      DDR             .FILL   xFE06
20       ;
21      ReadChar        LDI     R3,KBSR
22                      BRzp    ReadChar
23                      LDI     R0,KBDR
24                      RET
25      KBSR            .FILL   xFE00
26      KBDR            .FILL   xFE02
27       ;
28       SaveReg        ST      R1,SaveR1
29                      ST      R2,SaveR2
2A                      ST      R3,SaveR3
2B                      ST      R4,SaveR4
2C                      ST      R5,SaveR5
2D                      ST      R6,SaveR6
2E                      RET
2F       ;
30       RestoreReg     LD      R1,SaveR1
31                      LD      R2,SaveR2
32                      LD      R3,SaveR3
33                      LD      R4,SaveR4
34                      LD      R5,SaveR5
35                      LD      R6,SaveR6
36                      RET
37      SaveR1          .FILL   x0000
38      SaveR2          .FILL   x0000
39      SaveR3          .FILL   x0000
3A      SaveR4          .FILL   x0000
3B      SaveR5          .FILL   x0000
3C      SaveR6          .FILL   x0000
3D                      .END
```

Figure 9.15   The LC-3 trap service routine for character input (our final answer!).

Note the hedging: *almost*. In the original sequences starting at L2 and L3, the STI instruction forwards the contents of R0 (not R2) to the DDR. We can fix that easily enough, as follows: In line 08 of Figure 9.15, we use

```
        LDR     R2,R1,#0
```

instead of

```
        LDR     R0,R1,#0
```

This causes each character in the prompt to be loaded into R2. The subroutine Writechar forwards each character from R2 to the DDR.

In line 0F of Figure 9.15, we insert the instruction

```
        ADD     R2,R0,#0
```

in order to move the keyboard input (which is in R0) into R2. The subroutine Writechar forwards it from R2 to the DDR. Note that R0 still contains the keyboard input. Furthermore, since no subsequent instruction in the service routine loads R0, R0 still contains the keyboard input after control returns to the user program.

In line 12 of Figure 9.15, we insert the instruction

```
        LD      R2,Newline
```

in order to move the "newline" character into R2. The subroutine Writechar forwards it from R2 to the DDR.

Figure 9.15 is the actual LC-3 trap service routine provided for keyboard input.

9.3.9 PUTS: Writing a Character String to the Monitor

Before we leave the example of Figure 9.15, note the code on lines 08 through 0C. This fragment of the service routine is used to write the sequence of characters *Input a character* to the monitor. A sequence of characters is often referred to as a *string of characters* or a *character string*. This fragment is also present in Figure 9.14, with the result that *Halting the machine* is written to the monitor. In fact, it is so often the case that a user program needs to write a string of characters to the monitor that this function is given its own trap service routine in the LC-3 operating system. Thus, if a user program requires a character string to be written to the monitor, it need only provide (in R0) the starting address of the character string, and then invoke TRAP x22. In LC-3 assembly language this TRAP is called *PUTS*.

PUTS (or TRAP x22) causes control to be passed to the operating system, and the trap routine shown in Figure 9.16 is executed. Note that PUTS is the code of lines 08 through 0C of Figure 9.15, with a few minor adjustments.

```
01    ; This service routine writes a NULL-terminated string to the console.
02    ; It services the PUTS service call (TRAP x22).
03    ; Inputs: R0 is a pointer to the string to print.
04    ;
05                    .ORIG   x0460
06                    ST      R0, SaveR0    ; Save registers that
07                    ST      R1, SaveR1    ; are needed by this
08                    ST      R3, SaveR3    ; trap service routine
09    ;
0A    ; Loop through each character in the array
0B    ;
0C    Loop            LDR     R1, R0, #0    ; Retrieve the character(s)
0D                    BRz     Return        ; If it is 0, done
0E    L2              LDI     R3,DSR
0F                    BRzp    L2
10                    STI     R1, DDR       ; Write the character
11                    ADD     R0, R0, #1    ; Increment pointer
12                    BRnzp   Loop          ; Do it all over again
13    ;
14    ; Return from the request for service call
15    Return          LD      R3, SaveR3
16                    LD      R1, SaveR1
17                    LD      R0, SaveR0
18                    RTI
19    ;
1A    ; Register locations
1B    DSR             .FILL   xFE04
1C    DDR             .FILL   xFE06
1D    SaveR0          .FILL   x0000
1E    SaveR1          .FILL   x0000
1F    SaveR3          .FILL   x0000
20                    .END
```

Figure 9.16   The LC-3 PUTS service routine.

9.4 Interrupts and Interrupt-Driven I/O

In Section 9.2.1.3, we noted that interaction between the processor and an I/O device can be controlled by the processor (i.e., polling) or it can be controlled by the I/O device (i.e., interrupt driven). In Sections 9.2.2, 9.2.3, and 9.2.4, we have studied several examples of polling. In each case, the processor tested the ready bit of the status register again and again, and when the ready bit was finally 1, the processor branched to the instruction that did the input or output operation.

We are now ready to study the case where the interaction is controlled by the I/O device.

9.4.1 What Is Interrupt-Driven I/O?

The essence of interrupt-driven I/O is the notion that an I/O device that may or may not have anything to do with the program that is running can (1) force the

```
                            .
                            .
                            .
          Program A is executing instruction n
          Program A is executing instruction n+1
          Program A is executing instruction n+2
     1: Interrupt signal is detected
     1: Program A is put into suspended animation
     1: PC is loaded with the starting address of Program B
     2: Program B starts satisying I/O device's needs
     2: Program B continues satisfying I/O device's needs
     2: Program B continues satisfying I/O device's needs
     2: Program B finishes satisfying I/O device's needs
     3: Program A is brought back to life

          Program A is executing instruction n+3
          Program A is executing instruction n+4
                            .
                            .
                            .
```

Figure 9.17   Instruction execution flow for interrupt-driven I/O.

running program to stop, (2) have the processor execute a program that carries out the needs of the I/O device, and then (3) have the stopped program resume execution as if nothing had happened. These three stages of the instruction execution flow are shown in Figure 9.17.

As far as Program A is concerned, the work carried out and the results computed are no different from what would have been the case if the interrupt had never happened; that is, as if the instruction execution flow had been the following:

```
                          .
                          .
                          .
        Program A is executing instruction n
        Program A is executing instruction n+1
        Program A is executing instruction n+2
        Program A is executing instruction n+3
        Program A is executing instruction n+4
                          .
                          .
                          .
```

9.4.2 Why Have Interrupt-Driven I/O?

As is undoubtedly clear, polling requires the processor to waste a lot of time spinning its wheels, re-executing again and again the LDI and BR instructions until the ready bit is set. With interrupt-driven I/O, none of that testing and branching has to go on. Interrupt-driven I/O allows the processor to spend its time doing

what is hopefully useful work, executing some other program perhaps, until it is
notified that some I/O device needs attention.

Example 9.2

Suppose we are asked to write a program that takes a sequence of 100 characters
typed on a keyboard and processes the information contained in those 100 characters.
Assume the characters are typed at the rate of 80 words/minute, which corresponds
to one character every 0.125 seconds. Assume the processing of the 100-character
sequence takes 12.49999 seconds, and that our program is to perform this process on
1000 consecutive sequences. How long will it take our program to complete the task?
(Why did we pick 12.49999? To make the numbers come out nice, of course.) :-)

We could obtain each character input by polling, as in Section 9.2.2. If we did,
we would waste a lot of time waiting for the "next" character to be typed. It would
take $100 \cdot 0.125$ or 12.5 seconds to get a 100-character sequence.

On the other hand, if we use interrupt-driven I/O, the processor does not waste
any time re-executing the LDI and BR instructions while waiting for a character to
be typed. Rather, the processor can be busy working on the previous 100-character
sequence that was typed, **except** for those very small fractions of time when it is interrupted by the I/O device to read the next character typed. Let's say that to read the next
character typed requires executing a ten-instruction program that takes on the average 0.00000001 seconds to execute each instruction. That means 0.0000001 seconds
for each character typed, or 0.00001 seconds for the entire 100-character sequence.
That is, with interrupt-driven I/O, since the processor is only needed when characters
are actually being read, the time required for each 100-character sequence is 0.00001
seconds, instead of 12.50000 seconds. The remaining 12.49999 of every 12.50000
seconds, the processor is available to do useful work. For example, it can process the
previous 100-character sequence.

The bottom line: With polling, the time to complete the entire task for each
sequence is 24.9999 seconds, 12.5 seconds to obtain the 100 characters + 12.49999
seconds to process them. With interrupt-driven I/O, the time to complete the entire
task for each sequence after the first is 12.5 seconds, 0.00001 seconds to obtain
the characters + 12.49999 seconds to process them. For 1000 sequences, that is the
difference between 7 hours and $3\frac{1}{2}$ hours.

9.4.3 Two Parts to the Process

There are two parts to interrupt-driven I/O:

1. the mechanism that enables an I/O device to interrupt the processor, and
2. the mechanism that handles the interrupt request.

9.4.4 Part I: Causing the Interrupt to Occur

Several things must be true for an I/O device to actually interrupt the program
that is running:

1. The I/O device **must want** service.
2. The device **must have the right** to request the service.
3. The device request **must be more urgent** than what the processor is
   currently doing.

If all three elements are present, the processor stops executing the program that is running and takes care of the interrupt.

9.4.4.1 The Interrupt Signal from the Device

For an I/O device to generate an interrupt request, the device must want service, and it must have the right to request that service.

The Device Must Want Service   We have discussed that already in the study of polling. It is the ready bit of the KBSR or the DSR. That is, if the I/O device is the keyboard, it wants service if someone has typed a character. If the I/O device is the monitor, it wants service (i.e., the next character to output) if the associated electronic circuits have successfully completed the display of the last character. In both cases, the I/O device wants service when the corresponding ready bit is set.

The Device Must Have the Right to Request That Service   This is the interrupt enable bit, which can be set or cleared by the processor (usually by the operating system), depending on whether or not the processor wants to give the I/O device the right to request service. In most I/O devices, this interrupt enable (IE) bit is part of the device status register. In the KBSR and DSR shown in Figure 9.18, the IE bit is bit [14]. The **interrupt request signal from the I/O device** is the logical AND of the IE bit and the ready bit, as is also shown in Figure 9.18.

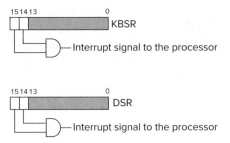

Figure 9.18   Interrupt enable bits and their use.

If the interrupt enable bit (bit [14]) is clear, it does not matter whether the ready bit is set; the I/O device will not be able to interrupt the processor because it (the I/O device) has not been given the right to interrupt the processor. In that case, the program will have to poll the I/O device to determine if it is ready.

If bit [14] is set, then interrupt-driven I/O is enabled. In that case, as soon as someone types a key (or as soon as the monitor has finished processing the last character), bit [15] is set. In this case, the device wants service, and it has been given the right to request service. The AND gate is asserted, causing an interrupt request to be generated from the I/O device.

9.4.4.2 The Urgency of the Request

The third element in the list of things that must be true for an I/O device to actually interrupt the processor is that the request must be more urgent than the program that is currently executing. Recall from Section 9.1.1.2 that each program runs at a specified level of urgency called its priority level. To interrupt the running program, the device must have a higher priority than the program that is currently running. Actually, there may be many devices that want to interrupt the processor at a specific time. To succeed, the device must have a higher priority level than all other demands for use of the processor.

Almost all computers have a set of priority levels that programs can run at. As we have already noted, the LC-3 has eight priority levels, PL0 to PL7. The higher the number, the more urgent the program. The PL of a program is usually the same as the PL (i.e., urgency) of the request to run that program. If a program is running at one PL, and a higher-level PL request wants the computer, the lower-priority program suspends processing until the higher-PL program executes and satisfies its more urgent request. For example, a computer's payroll program may run overnight, and at PL0. It has all night to finish—not terribly urgent. A program that corrects for a nuclear plant current surge may run at PL6. We are perfectly happy to let the payroll wait while the nuclear power correction keeps us from being blown to bits.

For our I/O device to successfully stop the processor and start an interrupt-driven I/O request, the priority of the request must be higher than the priority of the program it wishes to interrupt. For example, we would not normally want to allow a keyboard interrupt from a professor checking e-mail to interrupt the nuclear power correction program.

9.4.4.3 The INT Signal

To stop the processor from continuing execution of its currently running program and service an interrupt request, the INT signal must be asserted. Figure 9.19 shows what is required to assert the INT signal. Figure 9.19 shows the status registers of several devices operating at various priority levels (PL). Any device that has bits [14] and [15] both set asserts its interrupt request signal. The interrupt request signals are input to a priority encoder, a combinational logic structure that selects the highest priority request from all those asserted. If the PL of that request is higher than the PL of the currently executing program, the INT signal is asserted.

9.4.4.4 The Test for INT

Finally, the test to enable the processor to stop and handle the interrupt. Recall from Chapter 4 that the instruction cycle continually sequences through the phases of the instruction cycle (FETCH, DECODE, EVALUATE ADDRESS, FETCH OPERAND, EXECUTE, and STORE RESULT). Each instruction changes the state of the computer, and that change is completed at the end of the instruction cycle for that instruction. That is, in the last clock cycle before the computer returns to the FETCH phase for the next instruction, the computer is put in the state caused by the complete execution of the current instruction.

Interrupts can happen at any time. They are asynchronous to the synchronous finite state machine controlling the computer. For example, the interrupt signal could occur when the instruction cycle is in its FETCH OPERAND phase. If we stopped the currently executing program when the instruction cycle was in

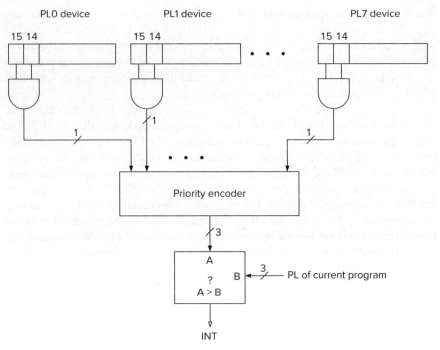

Figure 9.19   Generation of the INT signal.

its FETCH OPERAND phase, we would have to keep track of what part of the current instruction has executed and what part of the current instruction still has work to do. It makes much more sense to ignore interrupt signals except when we are at an instruction boundary; that is, the current instruction has completed, and the next instruction has not yet started. Doing that means we do not have to worry about partially executed instructions, since the state of the computer is the state created by the completion of the current instruction, period!

The additional logic to test for the interrupt signal is to augment the last state of the instruction cycle for each instruction with a test. Instead of **always** going from the last state of one instruction cycle to the first state of the FETCH phase of the next instruction, the next state depends on the INT signal. If INT is not asserted, then it is business as usual, with the control unit returning to the FETCH phase to start processing the next instruction. If INT is asserted, then the next state is the first state of Part II, handling the interrupt request.

9.4.5 Part II: Handling the Interrupt Request

Handling the interrupt request goes through three stages, as shown in Figure 9.17:

1. Initiate the interrupt (three lines numbered 1 in Figure 9.17).
2. Service the interrupt (four lines numbered 2 in Figure 9.17).
3. Return from the interrupt (one line numbered 3 in Figure 9.17).

   We will discuss each.

9.4.5.1 Initiate the Interrupt

Since the INT signal was asserted, the processor does not return to the first state of the FETCH phase of the next instruction cycle, but rather begins a sequence of actions to initiate the interrupt. The processor must do two things: (1) save the state of the interrupted program so it can pick up where it left off after the requirements of the interrupt have been completed, and (2) load the state of the higher priority interrupting program so it can start satisfying its request.

Save the State of the Interrupted Program The state of a program is a snapshot of the contents of all the program's resources. It includes the contents of the memory locations that are part of the program and the contents of all the general purpose registers. It also includes the PC and PSR.

Recall from Figure 9.1 in Section 9.1.1.4 that a program's PSR specifies the privilege level and priority level of that program. PSR[15] indicates whether the program is running in privileged (Supervisor) or unprivileged (User) mode. PSR[10:8] specifies the program's priority level (PL), from PL0 (lowest) to PL7 (highest). Also, PSR[2:0] is used to store the condition codes. PSR[2] is the N bit, PSR[1] is the Z bit, and PSR[0] is the P bit.

The first step in initiating the interrupt is to save enough of the state of the program that is running so that it can continue where it left off after the I/O device request has been satisfied. That means, in the case of the LC-3, saving the PC and the PSR. The PC must be saved since it knows which instruction should be executed next when the interrupted program resumes execution. The condition codes (the N, Z, and P flags) must be saved since they may be needed by a subsequent conditional branch instruction after the program resumes execution. The priority level of the interrupted program must be saved because it specifies the urgency of the interrupted program with respect to all other programs. When the interrupted program resumes execution, it is important to know what priority level programs can interrupt it and which ones cannot. Finally, the privilege level of the program must be saved since it specifies what processor resources the interrupted program can and cannot access.

Although many computers save the contents of the general purpose registers, we will not since we will assume that the service routine will always save the contents of any general purpose register that it needs before using it, and then restore it before returning to the interrupted program. The only state information the LC-3 saves are the PC and PSR.

The LC-3 saves this state information on the supervisor stack in the same way the PC and PSR are saved when a TRAP instruction is executed. That is, before the interrupt service routine starts, if the interrupted program is in User mode, the User Stack Pointer (USP) is stored in Saved_USP, and R6 is loaded with the Supervisor Stack Pointer (SSP) from Saved_SSP. Then the PSR and PC of the interrupted program are pushed onto the supervisor stack, where they remain unmolested while the service routine executes.

Load the State of the Interrupt Service Routine Once the state of the interrupted program has been safely saved on the supervisor stack, the second step is to load the PC and PSR of the interrupt service routine. Interrupt service routines are similar to the trap service routines we have already discussed. They are program fragments stored in system space. They service interrupt requests.

Most processors use the mechanism of *vectored interrupts*. You are familiar with this notion from your study of the trap vector contained in the TRAP instruction. In the case of interrupts, the eight-bit vector is provided by the device that is requesting the processor be interrupted. That is, the I/O device transmits to the processor an eight-bit interrupt vector along with its interrupt request signal and its priority level. The interrupt vector corresponding to the highest priority interrupt request is the one supplied to the processor. It is designated INTV.

If the interrupt is taken, the processor expands the 8-bit interrupt vector (INTV) to form a 16-bit address, which is an entry into the Interrupt Vector Table. You know that the Trap Vector Table consists of memory locations x0000 to x00FF, each containing the starting address of a trap service routine. The Interrupt Vector Table consists of memory locations x0100 to x01FF, each containing the starting address of an interrupt service routine. The processor loads the PC with the contents of the location in the Interrupt Vector Table corresponding to the address formed by expanding the interrupt vector INTV.

For example, the LC-3 keyboard could interrupt the processor every time a key is pressed by someone sitting at the keyboard. The keyboard interrupt vector would indicate the location in the interrupt vector table that contains the starting address of the keyboard interrupt service routine.

The PSR is loaded as follows: Since no instructions in the service routine have yet executed, PSR[2:0] contains no meaningful information. We arbitrarily load it initially with 010. Since the interrupt service routine runs in privileged mode, PSR[15] is set to 0. PSR[10:8] is set to the priority level associated with the interrupt request.

This completes the initiation phase, and the interrupt service routine is ready to execute.

9.4.5.2 Service the Interrupt

Since the PC contains the starting address of the interrupt service routine, the service routine will execute, and the requirements of the I/O device will be serviced.

9.4.5.3 Return from the Interrupt

The last instruction in every interrupt service routine is RTI, return from trap or interrupt. When the processor finally accesses the RTI instruction, all the requirements of the I/O device have been taken care of.

Like the return from a trap routine discussed in Section 9.3.4, execution of the **RTI** instruction (opcode = 1000) for an interrupt service routine consists simply of popping the PC and the PSR from the supervisor stack (where they have been resting peacefully) and restoring them to their rightful places in the processor. The condition codes are now restored to what they were when the program was interrupted, in case they are needed by a subsequent BR instruction in the interrupted program. PSR[15] and PSR[10:8] now reflect the privilege level and priority level of the about-to-be-resumed program. If the privilege level of the interrupted program is unprivileged, the stack pointers must be adjusted, that is, the Supervisor Stack Pointer saved, and the User Stack Pointer loaded into R6. The PC is restored to the address of the instruction that would have been executed next if the program had not been interrupted.

With all these things as they were before the interrupt occurred, the program can resume as if nothing had happened.

9.4.6 An Example

We complete the discussion of interrupt-driven I/O with an example.

Suppose program A is executing when I/O device B, having a PL higher than that of A, requests service. During the execution of the service routine for I/O device B, a still more urgent device C requests service.

Figure 9.20 shows the execution flow that must take place.

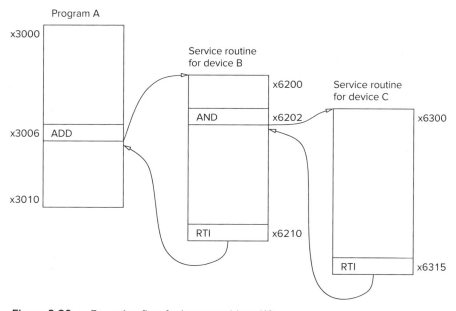

Figure 9.20   Execution flow for interrupt-driven I/O.

Program A consists of instructions in locations x3000 to x3010 and was in the middle of executing the ADD instruction at x3006 when device B sent its interrupt request signal and accompanying interrupt vector xF1, causing INT to be asserted.

Note that the interrupt service routine for device B is stored in locations x6200 to x6210; x6210 contains the RTI instruction. Note that the service routine for B was in the middle of executing the AND instruction at x6202 when device C sent its interrupt request signal and accompanying interrupt vector xF2. Since the request associated with device C is of a higher priority than that of device B, INT is again asserted.

Note that the interrupt service routine for device C is stored in locations x6300 to x6315; x6315 contains the RTI instruction.

Let us examine the order of execution by the processor. Figure 9.21 shows several snapshots of the contents of the supervisor stack and the PC during the execution of this example.

The processor executes as follows: Figure 9.21a shows the supervisor stack and the PC before program A fetches the instruction at x3006. Note that the stack pointer is shown as Saved_SSP, not R6. Since the interrupt has not yet occurred, R6 is pointing to the current contents of the user stack, which are not shown! The INT signal (caused by an interrupt from device B) is detected at the end of execution of the instruction in x3006. Since the state of program A must be

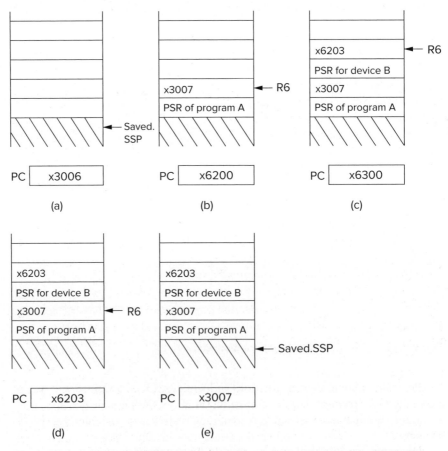

Figure 9.21   Snapshots of the contents of the supervisor stack and the PC during interrupt-driven I/O.

saved on the supervisor stack, the first step is to start using the supervisor stack. This is done by saving R6 in the Saved.UPC register and loading R6 with the contents of the Saved_SSP register. The PSR of program A, which includes the condition codes produced by the ADD instruction, is pushed on the supervisor stack. Then the address x3007, the PC for the next instruction to be executed in program A is pushed on the stack. The interrupt vector associated with device B is expanded to 16 bits x01F1, and the contents of x01F1 (x6200) is loaded into the PC. Figure 9.21b shows the stack and PC at this point.

The service routine for device B executes until a higher priority interrupt is detected at the end of execution of the instruction at x6202. The PSR of the service routine for B, which includes the condition codes produced by the AND instruction at x6202, and the address x6203 are pushed on the stack. The interrupt vector associated with device C is expanded to 16 bits (x01F2), and the contents of x01F2 (x6300) is loaded into the PC. Figure 9.21c shows the supervisor stack and PC at this point.

Assume the interrupt service routine for device C executes to completion, finishing with the RTI instruction in x6315. The supervisor stack is popped twice, restoring the PC to x6203 and the PSR of the service routine for device B, including the condition codes produced by the AND instruction in x6202. Figure 9.21d shows the stack and PC at this point.

The interrupt service routine for device B resumes execution at x6203 and runs to completion, finishing with the RTI instruction in x6210. The supervisor stack is popped twice, restoring the PC to x3007 and the PSR of program A, including the condition codes produced by the ADD instruction in x3006. Finally, since program A is in User mode, the contents of R6 is stored in Saved_SSP and R6 is loaded with the contents of Saved_USP. Figure 9.21e shows the supervisor stack and PC at this point.

Program A resumes execution with the instruction at x3007.

9.4.7 Not Just I/O Devices

We have discussed the processing of interrupts in the context of I/O devices that have higher priority than the program that is running and therefore can stop that program to enable its interrupt service routine to execute.

We must point out that not all interrupts deal with I/O devices. Any event that has a higher priority and is external to the program that is running can interrupt the computer. It does so by supplying its INT signal, its INTV vector, and its priority level. If it is the highest priority event that wishes to interrupt the computer, it does so in the same way that I/O devices do as described above.

There are many examples of such events that have nothing to do with I/O devices. For example, a *timer interrupt* interrupts the program that is running in order to note the passage of a unit of time. The *machine check* interrupt calls attention to the fact that some part of the computer system is not functioning properly. The *power failure* interrupt notifies the computer that, for example, someone has yanked the power cord out of its receptacle. Unfortunately, we will have to put off dealing with all of these until later in your coursework.

9.5 Polling Revisited, Now That We Know About Interrupts

9.5.1 The Problem

Recall our discussion of polling: We continually test the ready bit in the relevant status register, and if it is not set, we branch back to again test the ready bit. For example, suppose we are writing a character string to the monitor, and we are using polling to determine when the monitor has successfully written the current character so we can dispatch the next character. We take it for granted that the three-instruction sequence LDI (to load the ready bit of the DSR), BRzp (to test it and fall through if the device is ready), and STI (to store the next character in the DDR) acts as an atomic unit. But what if we had interrupts enabled at the same time? That is, if an interrupt occurred **within** that LDI, BRzp, STI sequence (say, just before the STI instruction), it could easily be the case that the LDI instruction indicated the DDR was ready, the BRzp instruction did not branch back, but by the time the interrupt service routine completed so the STI could write to the DDR, the DDR may no longer be ready. The computer would execute the STI, but the write would not happen.

A simple, but somewhat contrived example :-), will illustrate the problem. Suppose you are executing a "for" loop ten times, where each time the loop body prints to the monitor a particular character. Polling is used to determine that the monitor is ready before writing the next character to the DDR. Since the loop body executes ten times, this should result in the character being printed on the monitor ten times. Suppose you also have keyboard interrupts enabled, and the keyboard service routine echoes the character typed.

Suppose the loop body executes as follows: LDI loads the ready bit, BRzp falls through since the monitor is ready, and STI stores the character in DDR. In the middle of this sequence, before the STI can execute, someone types a key. The keyboard interrupt occurs, the character typed is echoed, i.e., written to the DDR, and the keyboard interrupt service routine completes.

The interrupted loop body then takes over and "knows" the monitor is ready, so it executes the STI. ... except the monitor is not ready because it has not completed the write of the keyboard service routine! The STI of the loop body writes, but since DDR is not ready, the write does not occur. The final result: Only nine characters get written, not ten.

The problem becomes more serious if the string written is in code, and the missing write prevents the code from being deciphered.

A simple way to handle this would be to disable all interrupts while polling was going on. But consider the consequences. Suppose the polling was required for a long time. If we disable interrupts while polling is going on, interrupts would be disabled for that very long time, unacceptable in an environment where one is concerned about the time between a higher priority interrupt occurring and the interrupt getting service.

9.5.2 The Solution

A better solution is shown in Figure 9.22.

The sequence we want to make noninterruptable is shown on lines 0F to 11. We accomplish this by first loading R1 with the PSR in line 09 and R2 with the PSR having interrupts disabled in line 0A. PSR[14] is the interrupt enable bit for all interrupts associated with this program. Note that PSR is memory mapped to xFFFC. We enable interrupts by storing R1 in PSR (line 0D), followed immediately by disabling interrupts by storing R2 in PSR (line 0E). With interrupts disabled, we execute the three-instruction sequence LDI, BRzp, and LDI (lines 0F, 10, and 11) if the status register indicates that the device is ready. If the device is not ready, BRzp (line 10) takes the computer back to line 0D where interrupts are again enabled.

```
01                  .ORIG x0420
02              ADD   R6,R6,#-1
03              STR   R1,R6,#0
04              ADD   R6,R6,#-1
05              STR   R2,R6,#0
06              ADD   R6,R6,#-1
07              STR   R3,R6,#0     ; Save R1,R2,R3 on the stack
08  ;
09              LDI   R1, PSR
0A              LD    R2,INTMASK
0B              AND   R2,R1,R2     ; R1=original PSR, R2=PSR with interrupts disabled
0C
0D    POLL      STI   R1,PSR    ; enable interrupts (if they were enabled to begin)
0E              STI   R2,PSR    ; disable interrupts
0F              LDI   R3,DSR
10              BRzp  POLL      ; Poll the DSR
11              STI   R0,DDR    ; Store the character into the DDR
12              STI   R1,PSR    ; Restore original PSR
13
14              LDR   R3,R6,#0
15              ADD   R6,R6,#1
16              LDR   R2,R6,#0
17              ADD   R6,R6,#1
18              LDR   R1,R6,#0
19              ADD   R6,R6,#1   ; Restore R3,R2,and R1 from the stack
1A
1B              RTI
1C
1D  INTMASK .FILL    xBFFF
1E  PSR     .FILL    xFFFC
1F  DSR     .FILL    xFE04
20  DDR     .FILL    xFE06
21
22              .END
```

Figure 9.22   Polling AND allowing interrupts.

In this way, interrupts are disabled again and again, but each time only long enough to execute the three-instruction sequence LDI, BRzp, STI (in lines 0F, 10, 0D), after which interrupts are enabled again. The result: An interrupt would have to wait for the three-instruction sequence LDI, BRzp, STI to execute, rather than for the entire polling process to complete.

Exercises

9.1   *a.* What is a device register?
     b. What is a device data register?
     c. What is a device status register?

9.2   Why is a ready bit not needed if synchronous I/O is used?

9.3   In Section 9.2.1.3, the statement is made that a typist would have trouble supplying keyboard input to a 300-MHz processor at the maximum rate (one character every 33 nanoseconds) that the processor can accept it. Assume an average word (including spaces between words) consists of six characters. How many words/minute would the typist have to type in order to exceed the processor's ability to handle the input?

9.4   Are the following interactions usually synchronous or asynchronous?

     a. Between a remote control and a television set
     b. Between the mail carrier and you, via a mailbox
     c. Between a mouse and your PC

     Under what conditions would each of them be synchronous? Under what conditions would each of them be asynchronous?

9.5   What is the purpose of bit [15] in the KBSR?

9.6   What problem could occur if a program does not check the ready bit of the KBSR before reading the KBDR?

9.7   Which of the following combinations describe the system described in Section 9.2.2.2?

     a. Memory mapped and interrupt driven
     b. Memory mapped and polling
     c. Special opcode for I/O and interrupt driven
     d. Special opcode for I/O and polling

9.8   Write a program that checks the initial value in memory location x4000 to see if it is a valid ASCII code, and if it is a valid ASCII code, prints the character. If the value in x4000 is not a valid ASCII code, the program prints nothing.

9.9   What problem is likely to occur if the keyboard hardware does not check the KBSR before writing to the KBDR?

9.10   What problem could occur if the display hardware does not check the DSR before writing to the DDR?

9.11   Which is more efficient, interrupt-driven I/O or polling? Explain.

9.12   Adam H. decided to design a variant of the LC-3 that did not need a keyboard status register. Instead, he created a readable/writable keyboard data and status register (KBDSR), which contains the same data as the KBDR. With the KBDSR, a program requiring keyboard input would wait until a nonzero value appeared in the KBDSR. The nonzero value would be the ASCII value of the last key press. Then the program would write a zero into the KBDSR, indicating that it had read the key press. Modify the basic input service of Section 8.2.2 to implement Adam's scheme.

9.13   Some computer engineering students decided to revise the LC-3 for their senior project. In designing the LC-4, they decided to conserve on device registers by combining the KBSR and the DSR into one status register: the IOSR (the input/output status register). IOSR[15] is the keyboard device ready bit and IOSR[14] is the display device ready bit. What are the implications for programs wishing to do I/O? Is this a poor design decision?

9.14   An LC-3 Load instruction specifies the address xFE02. How do we know whether to load from the KBDR or from memory location xFE02?

9.15   Name some of the advantages of doing I/O through a TRAP routine instead of writing the routine yourself each time you would like your program to perform I/O.

9.16   *a.* How many trap service routines can be implemented in the LC-3? Why?
   b. Why must a RET instruction be used to return from a TRAP routine? Why won't a BR (Unconditional Branch) instruction work instead?
   c. How many accesses to memory are made during the processing of a TRAP instruction? Assume the TRAP is already in the IR.

9.17   Refer to Figure 9.14, the HALT service routine.

   a. What starts the clock after the machine is HALTed? *Hint:* How can the HALT service routine return after bit [15] of the Master Control Register is cleared?
   b. Which instruction actually halts the machine?
   c. What is the first instruction executed when the machine is started again?
   d. Where will the RET of the HALT routine return to?

9.18 Consider the following LC-3 assembly language program:

```
        .ORIG   x3000
L1      LEA     R1, L1
        AND     R2, R2, x0
        ADD     R2, R2, x2
        LD      R3, P1
L2      LDR     R0, R1, xC
        OUT
        ADD     R3, R3, #-1
        BRz     GLUE
        ADD     R1, R1, R2
        BR      L2
GLUE    HALT
P1      .FILL   xB
        .STRINGZ "HBoeoakteSmtHaotren!s"
        .END
```

    a. After this program is assembled and loaded, what binary pattern is stored in memory location x3005?

    b. Which instruction (provide a memory address) is executed after instruction x3005 is executed?

    c. Which instruction (provide a memory address) is executed prior to instruction x3006?

    d. What is the output of this program?

9.19 The following LC-3 program is assembled and then executed. There are no assemble time or run-time errors. What is the output of this program? Assume all registers are initialized to 0 before the program executes.

```
        .ORIG   x3000
        LEA     R0, LABEL
        STR     R1, R0, #3
        TRAP    x22
        TRAP    x25
LABEL   .STRINGZ "FUNKY"
LABEL2  .STRINGZ "HELLO WORLD"
        .END
```

9.20 The correct operation of the program in Example 9.1 assumes that the person sitting at the keyboard only types capital letters and the value 7. What if the person types a $? A better program would be one that tests the character typed to be sure it really is a capital letter from among the 26 capital letters in the alphabet, and if it is not, takes corrective action. Your job: Augment the program of Example 9.1 to add a test for bad data. That is, write a program that will type the lowercase representation of any capital letter typed and will terminate if anything other than a capital letter is typed.

9.21 Assume that an integer greater than 2 and less than 32,768 is deposited in memory location A by another module before the program below is executed.

```
                    .ORIG   x3000
                    AND     R4, R4, #0
                    LD      R0, A
                    NOT     R5, R0
                    ADD     R5, R5, #2
                    ADD     R1, R4, #2
                    ;
        REMOD       JSR     MOD
                    BRz     STORE0
                    ;
                    ADD     R7, R1, R5
                    BRz     STORE1
                    ADD     R1, R1, #1
                    BR      REMOD
                    ;
        STORE1      ADD     R4, R4, #1
        STORE0      ST      R4, RESULT
                    TRAP    x25
                    ;
        MOD         ADD     R2, R0, #0
                    NOT     R3, R1
                    ADD     R3, R3, #1
        DEC         ADD     R2, R2, R3
                    BRp     DEC
                    RET
                    ;
        A           .BLKW  1
        RESULT      .BLKW  1
                    .END
```

In 20 words or fewer, what does the above program do?

9.22 Recall the machine busy example. Suppose the bit pattern indicating which machines are busy and which are free is stored in memory location x4001. Write subroutines that do the following:

  a. Check if no machines are busy, and return 1 if none are busy.
  b. Check if all machines are busy, and return 1 if all are busy.
  c. Check how many machines are busy, and return the number of busy machines.
  d. Check how many machines are free, and return the number of free machines.
  e. Check if a certain machine number, passed as an argument in R5, is busy, and return 1 if that machine is busy.
  f. Return the number of a machine that is not busy.

9.23 The starting address of the trap routine is stored at the address specified in the TRAP instruction. Why isn't the first instruction of the trap routine stored at that address instead? Assume each trap service routine requires at most 16 instructions. Modify the semantics of the LC-3 TRAP instruction so that the trap vector provides the starting address of the service routine.

9.24 Following is part of a program that was fed to the LC-3 assembler. The program is supposed to read a series of input lines from the console into a buffer, search for a particular character, and output the number of times that character occurs in the text. The input text is terminated by an EOT and is guaranteed to be no more than 1000 characters in length. After the text has been input, the program reads the character to count.

The subroutine labeled COUNT that actually does the counting was written by another person and is located at address x3500. When called, the subroutine expects the address of the buffer to be in R5 and the address of the character to count to be in R6. The buffer should have a NULL to mark the end of the text. It returns the count in R6.

The OUTPUT subroutine that converts the binary count to ASCII digits and displays them was also written by another person and is at address x3600. It expects the number to print to be in R6.

Here is the code that reads the input and calls COUNT:

```
        .ORIG   x3000
        LEA     R1, BUFFER
G_TEXT  TRAP    x20                 ; Get input text
        ADD     R2, R0, x-4
        BRz     G_CHAR
        STR     R0, R1, #0
        ADD     R1, R1, #1
        BRnzp   G_TEXT
G_CHAR  STR     R2, R1, #0          ; x0000 terminates buffer
        TRAP    x20                 ; Get character to count
        ST      R0, S_CHAR
        LEA     R5, BUFFER
        LEA     R6, S_CHAR
        LD      R4, CADDR
        JSRR    R4                  ; Count character
        LD      R4, OADDR
        JSRR    R4                  ; Convert R6 and display
        TRAP    x25
CADDR   .FILL   x3500               ; Address of COUNT
OADDR   .FILL   x3600               ; Address of OUTPUT
BUFFER  .BLKW   1001
S_CHAR  .FILL   x0000
        .END
```

There is a problem with this code. What is it, and how might it be fixed? (The problem is *not* that the code for COUNT and OUTPUT is missing.)

9.25 Consider the following LC-3 assembly language program:

```
            .ORIG   x3000
            LEA     R0,DATA
            AND     R1,R1,#0
            ADD     R1,R1,#9
LOOP1       ADD     R2,R0,#0
            ADD     R3,R1,#0
LOOP2       JSR     SUB1
            ADD     R4,R4,#0
            BRzp    LABEL
            JSR     SUB2
LABEL       ADD     R2,R2,#1
            ADD     R3,R3,#-1
            BRP     LOOP2
            ADD     R1,R1,#-1
            BRp     LOOP1
            HALT
DATA        .BLKW   10 x0000
SUB1        LDR     R5,R2,#0
            NOT     R5,R5
            ADD     R5,R5,#1
            LDR     R6,R2,#1
            ADD     R4,R5,R6
            RET
SUB2        LDR     R4,R2,#0
            LDR     R5,R2,#1
            STR     R4,R2,#1
            STR     R5,R2,#0
            RET
            .END
```

Assuming that the memory locations at DATA get filled in before the program executes, what is the relationship between the final values at DATA and the initial values at DATA?

9.26 The following program is supposed to print the number 5 on the screen. It does not work. Why? Answer in no more than ten words, please.

```
            .ORIG   x3000
            JSR     A
            OUT
            BRnzp   DONE
A           AND     R0,R0,#0
            ADD     R0,R0,#5
            JSR     B
            RET
DONE        HALT
ASCII       .FILL   x0030
B           LD      R1,ASCII
            ADD     R0,R0,R1
            RET
            .END
```

9.27   Figure 9.14 shows a service routine to stop the computer by clearing the RUN latch, bit [15] of the Master Control Register. The latch is cleared by the instruction in line 14, and the computer stops. What purpose is served by the instructions on lines 19 through 1C?

9.28   Suppose we define a new service routine starting at memory location x4000. This routine reads in a character and echoes it to the screen. Suppose memory location x0072 contains the value x4000. The service routine is shown below.

```
              .ORIG x4000
              ST R7, SaveR7
              GETC
              OUT
              LD R7, SaveR7
              RET
      SaveR7  .FILL x0000
```

   a. Identify the instruction that will invoke this routine.
   b. Will this service routine work? Explain.

9.29   The two code sequences *a* and *b* are assembled separately. There are two errors that will be caught at assemble time or at link time. Identify the bugs, and describe why the bug will cause an error, and whether it will be detected at assemble time or link time.

   a.
```
                    .ORIG x3500
          SQRT      ADD    R0, R0, #0
                    ; code to perform square
                    ; root function and
                    ; return the result in R0
                    RET
                    .END
```
   b.
```
                    .EXTERNAL SQRT
                    .ORIG    x3000
                    LD       R0,VALUE
                    JSR      SQRT
                    ST       R0,DEST
                    HALT
          VALUE     .FILL    x30000
          DEST      .FILL    x0025
                    .END
```

9.30 Shown below is a partially constructed program. The program asks the user his/her name and stores the sentence "Hello, name" as a string starting from the memory location indicated by the symbol HELLO. The program then outputs that sentence to the screen. The program assumes that the user has finished entering his/her name when he/she presses the Enter key, whose ASCII code is x0A. The name is restricted to be not more than 25 characters.

Assuming that the user enters Onur followed by a carriage return when prompted to enter his/her name, the output of the program looks exactly like:

```
Please enter your name: Onur
Hello, Onur
```

Insert instructions at (a)–(d) that will complete the program.

```
                .ORIG  x3000
                LEA    R1,HELLO
        AGAIN   LDR    R2,R1,#0
                BRz    NEXT
                ADD    R1,R1,#1
                BR     AGAIN
        NEXT    LEA    R0,PROMPT
                TRAP   x22          ; PUTS
                ----------- (a)
        AGAIN2  TRAP   x20          ; GETC
                TRAP   x21          ; OUT
                ADD    R2,R0,R3
                BRz    CONT
                ----------- (b)
                ----------- (c)
                BR     AGAIN2
        CONT    AND    R2,R2,#0
                ----------- (d)
                LEA    R0, HELLO
                TRAP   x22          ; PUTS
                TRAP   x25          ; HALT
        NEGENTER .FILL xFFF6        ; -x0A
        PROMPT  .STRINGZ "Please enter your name: "
        HELLO   .STRINGZ "Hello, "
                .BLKW  #25
                .END
```

9.31 The program below, when complete, should print the following to the monitor:

ABCFGH

Insert instructions at (a)–(d) that will complete the program.

```
                .ORIG x3000
                LEA   R1, TESTOUT
BACK_1          LDR   R0, R1, #0
                BRz   NEXT_1
                TRAP  x21
                ------------ (a)
                BRnzp BACK_1
                ;
NEXT_1          LEA   R1, TESTOUT
BACK_2          LDR   R0, R1, #0
                BRz   NEXT_2
                JSR   SUB_1
                ADD   R1, R1, #1
                BRnzp BACK_2
                ;
NEXT_2          ------------ (b)
                ;
SUB_1           ------------ (c)

K               LDI   R2, DSR
                ------------ (d)

                STI   R0, DDR
                RET
DSR             .FILL xFE04
DDR             .FILL xFE06
TESTOUT         .STRINGZ "ABC"
                .END
```

9.32 A local company has decided to build a real LC-3 computer. In order to make the computer work in a network, four interrupt-driven I/O devices are connected. To request service, a device asserts its interrupt request signal (IRQ). This causes a bit to get set in a special LC-3 memory-mapped interrupt control register called INTCTL, which is mapped to address xFF00. The INTCTL register is shown below. When a device requests service, the INT signal in the LC-3 data path is asserted. The LC-3 interrupt service routine determines which device has requested service and calls the appropriate subroutine for that device. If more than one device asserts its IRQ signal at the same time, only the subroutine for the highest priority device is executed. During execution of the subroutine, the corresponding bit in INTCTL is cleared.

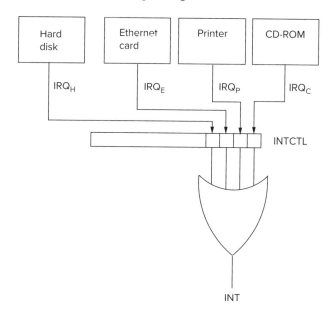

The following labels are used to identify the first instruction of each device subroutine:

HARDDISK ETHERNET PRINTER CDROM

For example, if the highest priority device requesting service is the printer, the interrupt service routine will call the printer subroutine with the following instruction:

JSR PRINTER

Finish the code in the LC-3 interrupt service routine for the following priority scheme by filling in the spaces labeled (a)–(k). The lower the number, the higher the priority of the device.

1. Hard disk
2. Ethernet card
3. Printer
4. CD-ROM

```
              LDI    R1, INTCTL
      DEV0    LD     R2, ------ (a)
              AND    R2, R2, R1
              BRnz   DEV1
              JSR    ---------- (b)
              --------------- (c)
       ;
      DEV1    LD     R2, ------ (d)
              AND    R2, R2,  R1
              BRnz   DEV2
              JSR    ---------- (e)
              --------------- (f)
       ;
      DEV2    LD     R2, ------ (g)
              AND    R2, R2, R1
              BRnz   DEV3
              JSR    ---------- (h)
              --------------- (i)
       ;
      DEV3    JSR    ---------- (j)
       ;
      END     --------------- (k)

      INTCTL  .FILL  xFF00
      MASK8   .FILL  x0008
      MASK4   .FILL  x0004
      MASK2   .FILL  x0002
      MASK1   .FILL  x0001
```

9.33 Interrupt-driven I/O:

   a. What does the following LC-3 program do?

```
              .ORIG   x3000
              LD      R3, A
              STI     R3, KBSR
      AGAIN   LD      R0, B
              TRAP    x21
              BRnzp   AGAIN
      A       .FILL   x4000
      B       .FILL   x0032
      KBSR    .FILL   xFE00
              .END
```

b. If someone strikes a key, the program will be interrupted and the keyboard interrupt service routine will be executed as shown below. What does the keyboard interrupt service routine do?

```
          .ORIG     x1000
          LDI       R0, KBDR
          TRAP      x21
          TRAP      x21
          RTI
KBDR      .FILL     xFE02
          .END
```

Note: RTI is an instruction that enables the computer to return to executing the program that was interrupted. It will be studied in Chapter 10. The only thing you need to know about it now is that it loads the PC with the address of the instruction that was about to be fetched when the interrupt occurred.

c. Finally, suppose the program of part *a* started executing, and someone sitting at the keyboard struck a key. What would you see on the screen?

d. In part c, how many times is the digit typed shown on the screen? Why is the correct answer: "I cannot say for sure."

9.34 What does the following LC-3 program do?

```
          .ORIG     x3000
          LD        R0,ASCII
          LD        R1,NEG
AGAIN     LDI       R2,DSR
          BRzp      AGAIN
          STI       R0,DDR
          ADD       R0,R0,#1
          ADD       R2,R0,R1
          BRnp      AGAIN
          HALT
ASCII     .FILL     x0041
NEG       .FILL     xFFB6     ; -x004A
DSR       .FILL     xFE04
DDR       .FILL     xFE06
          .END
```

9.35 During the initiation of the interrupt service routine, the N, Z, and P condition codes are saved on the stack. Show by means of a simple example how incorrect results would be generated if the condition codes were not saved.

9.36 In the example of Section 9.4.6, what are the contents of locations x01F1 and x01F2? They are part of a larger structure. Provide a name for that structure. (*Hint:* See Table A.3.)

9.37 Expand the example of Section 9.4.6 to include an interrupt by a still more urgent device D while the service routine of device C is executing the instruction at x6310. Assume device D's interrupt vector is xF3. Assume the interrupt service routine is stored in locations x6400 to x6412. Show the contents of the stack and PC at each relevant point in the execution flow.

9.38   Suppose device D in Exercise 9.37 has a lower priority than device C but a higher priority than device B. Rework Exercise 9.37 with this new wrinkle.

9.39   Write an interrupt handler to accept keyboard input as follows: A buffer is allocated to memory locations x4000 through x40FE. The interrupt handler must accept the next character typed and store it in the next "empty" location in the buffer. Memory location x40FF is used as a pointer to the next available empty buffer location. If the buffer is full (i.e., if a character has been stored in location x40FE), the interrupt handler must display on the screen: "Character cannot be accepted; input buffer full."

9.40   Consider the interrupt handler of Exercise 9.39. The buffer is modified as follows: The buffer is allocated to memory locations x4000 through x40FC. Location x40FF contains, as before, the address of the next available empty location in the buffer. Location x40FE contains the address of the oldest character in the buffer. Location x40FD contains the number of characters in the buffer. Other programs can remove characters from the buffer. Modify the interrupt handler so that, after x40FC is filled, the next location filled is x4000, assuming the character in x4000 has been previously removed. As before, if the buffer is full, the interrupt handler must display on the screen: "Character cannot be accepted; input buffer full."

9.41   Consider the modified interrupt handler of Exercise 9.40, used in conjunction with a program that removes characters from the buffer. Can you think of any problem that might prevent the interrupt handler that is adding characters to the buffer and the program that is removing characters from the buffer from working correctly together?

9.42   Suppose the keyboard interrupt vector is x34 and the keyboard interrupt service routine starts at location x1000. What can you infer about the contents of any memory location from the above statement?

9.43   Two students wrote interrupt service routines for an assignment. Both service routines did exactly the same work, but the first student accidentally used RET at the end of his routine, while the second student correctly used RTI. There are three errors that arose in the first student's program due to his mistake. Describe any two of them.

★9.44   Since ASCII codes consist of eight bits each, we can store two ASCII codes in one word of LC-3 memory. If a user types $2n$ characters on the keyboard, followed by the Enter key, the subroutine PACK on the next page will store the corresponding ASCII codes into n sequential memory locations, two per memory location, starting at location A.
You may assume that a user never enters an odd number of characters.
Your job: Fill in the blanks in the program.

If a user types the string **Please help!** followed by the Enter key, what does the program do?

```
             .ORIG x7020
PACK    ST R7, SAVER7
        ST R6, SAVER6
        ST R4, SAVER4
        ST R3, SAVER3
        LEA R6, A        ; R6 is the pointer
        AND R4, R4, #0
        ADD R4, R4, #8 ; R4 is our counter
        AND R3, R3, #0
        LEA R0, PROMPT
        TRAP x22
POLL    --------------- (a)
        BRzp POLL
        -------------- (b)
        LD R0, NEG_LF
        ADD R0, R7, R0
        --------------- (c)
        ADD R4, R4, #0
        BRz NOSHIFT
SHIFT   ADD R7, R7, R7
        ADD R4, R4, #-1
        BRp SHIFT
        ADD R3, R7, #0
        BRnzp POLL
NOSHIFT ADD R3, R3, R7
        -------------- (d)
        ADD R6, R6, #1
        ADD R4, R4, #8
        BRnzp POLL
DONE    LD R7, SAVER7
        LD R6, SAVER6
        LD R4, SAVER4
        LD R3, SAVER3
        LEA R0, A        ; Returns a pointer to the characters
        RET
KBSR    .FILL xFE00
KBDR    .FILL xFE02
NEG_LF  .FILL xFFF6
PROMPT  .STINGZ "Please enter a string: "
A       .BLKW #5
SAVER7  .BLKW #1
SAVER6  .BLKW #1
SAVER4  .BLKW #1
SAVER3  .BLKW #1
        .END
```

★9.45   We want to support eight input keyboards instead of one. To do this, we
         need eight ready bits in KBSR, and eight separate KBDRs. We will use
         the eight odd-numbered bits in the KBSR as ready bits for the eight
         keyboards, as shown below. We will set the other eight bits in the KBSR
         to 0.

The eight memory-mapped keyboard data registers and their
corresponding ready bits are as follows:

FE04:	KBSR	
FE06:	KBDR1,	Ready bit is KBSR[1]
FE08:	KBDR2,	Ready bit is KBSR[3]
FE0A:	KBDR3,	Ready bit is KBSR[5]
FE0C:	KBDR4,	Ready bit is KBSR[7]
FE0E:	KBDR5,	Ready bit is KBSR[9]
FE10:	KBDR6,	Ready bit is KBSR[11]
FE12:	KBDR7,	Ready bit is KBSR[13]
FE14:	KBDR8,	Ready bit is KBSR[15]

We wish to write a program that polls the keyboards and loads the ASCII
code typed by the highest priority keyboard into R0. That is, if someone
had previously typed a key on keyboard 1, we want to load the ASCII
code in KBDR1 into R0. If no key was typed on keyboard 1, but a key
had been typed on keyboard 2, we want to load the ASCII code in
KBDR2 into R0. ... and so on. That is, KB1 has higher priority than
KB2, which has higher priority than KB3, which has higher priority than
KB4, etc. KB8 has the lowest priority.
The following program will do the job AFTER you fill in the missing
instructions. Your job: Fill in the missing instructions.

```
        .ORIG X3000
        LD    R0, KBDR1
POLL    LDI   R1, KBSR
        BRz   POLL
        AND   R2, R2, #0
        ADD   R2, R2, #2
AGAIN   ---------------- (a)
        BRnp    FOUND
        ADD     R0, R0, #2
        ---------------- (b)
        ---------------- (c)
        BRnp    AGAIN
        HALT
FOUND   ---------------- (d)
        HALT
KBSR    .FILL   xFE04
KBDR1   .FILL   xFE06
        .END
```

★**9.46** The following program pushes elements onto a stack with JSR PUSH
      and pops elements off the stack with JSR POP.

```
                .ORIG X3000
                LEA   R6, STACK\_BASE

X               TRAP  x20           ;GETC
                TRAP  x21           ;OUT
                ADD   R1, R0, x-0A  ;x0A is ASCII code for line feed,
                                    ;x-0A is the negative of x0A
                BRz   Y
                JSR   PUSH
                BRnzp  X

Y               LEA   R2, STACK\_BASE
                NOT   R2, R2
                ADD   R2, R2, #1
                ADD   R3, R2, R6
                BRz   DONE
                JSR   POP
                TRAP  x21           ;OUT
                BRnzp  Y

DONE            TRAP  x25           ;HALT
STACK           .BLKW  5
STACK\_BASE .FILL  xOFFF

PUSH            ADD   R6, R6, #-1
                STR   R0, R6, #0
                RET

POP             LDR   R0, R6, #0
                ADD   R6, R6, #1
                RET

                .END
```

What will appear on the screen if a user, sitting at a keyboard, typed the
three keys a, b, c, followed by the Enter key?

What will happen if a user, sitting at a keyboard, typed the eight keys
a, b, c, d, e, f, g, h, followed by the Enter key?

9.47 We wish to add a new TRAP service routine, which will be called by the instruction TRAP x9A. The new trap routine will wait for someone to type a lowercase letter, then echo on the screen the corresponding capital letter. Assume the user will not type anything except a lowercase letter. The assembly language code for this trap service routine is shown below:

```
        .ORIG       x2055
        ---------------- (a)
        ST R1, SaveR1
        ST R0, SaveR0
        TRAP x20
        LD R1, A
        ---------------- (b)
        TRAP x21
        ---------------- (c)
        LD R1, SaveR1
        LD R0, SaveR0
        JMP R7
SaveR1  .BLKW 1
SaveR0  .BLKW 1
A       .FILL ----------- (d)
_____   .BLKW           ; (e) a missing label

        .END
```

In order for TRAP x9A to call this service routine, what must be contained in the memory location having what address?
Fill in the missing information in the assembly language program, that is, the three missing instructions, the one missing label, and the operand of the .FILL pseudo-op.

9.48 A programmer wrote the following program that was assembled and executed. Execution started with PC at x3000.

```
        .ORIG x3000

        LEA R0, Message
        TRAP x01
        TRAP x22   ; What is the output here?
        TRAP x25

Message .STRINGZ "Cat in the hat."

        .END
```

Assume that the Trap Vector Table includes the following entries in addition to the ones we have previously used:

Memory Address	Memory Contents
x0000	x0100
x0001	x0102
x0002	x0107
x0003	x010A

Assume further that additional trap service routines have been loaded previously in memory as specified below:

```
        .ORIG x0100

        LD R7, SaveR7
        RET
        ST R7, SaveR7
        TRAP x02
        AND R1, R1, #0
        STR R1, R0, #3
        RET
        AND R1, R1, #0
        STR R1, R0, #5
        TRAP x00
        RET
SaveR7  .BLKW #1

        .END
```

What is the result of execution of this program?

★9.49 The state machine shown below will produce an output sequence if it receives an input sequence. The initial state is S0.

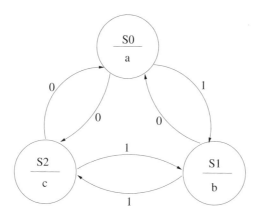

For example, the input sequence 100 produces the output sequence bac. We have written a program that simulates this state machine. Inputs are requested from the keyboard, and the corresponding outputs are shown on the screen. For example, for the input sequence shown above, the monitor would display

```
INPUT (either 0 or 1): 1
OUTPUT: b
INPUT (either 0 or 1): 0
OUTPUT: a
INPUT (either 0 or 1): 0
OUTPUT: c
```

Complete the program that simulates the state machine by filling in each blank with **one** missing line of LC-3 assembly language code. You can assume the person at the keyboard can type a 1 or a 0 without error (i.e., you do not have to test for wrong input).

```
           .ORIG        x3000
           LEA          R6, S0
Loop       ----------------- (a)
           TRAP         x22
           TRAP         x20              ; inputs a character
           TRAP         x21

           LD           R1, NEGASCII
           ADD          R0, R0, R1
           ----------------- (b)
           LDR          R6, R6,#0
           LD           R0, NEWLINE
           TRAP         x21
           LEA          R0, OUTPUT
           TRAP         x22
           ----------------- (c)
           TRAP         x21
           LD           R0, NEWLINE
           TRAP         x21
           BRnzp        LOOP

S0         .FILL        S2
           .FILL        S1
           .FILL        x0061

S1         .FILL        S0
           .FILL        S2
           .FILL        x0062
S2         .FILL        _____ (d)
           .FILL        _____ (e)
           .FILL        _____ (f)

NEGASCII .FILL          xFFD0                    ; the value -48
OUTPUT   .STRINGZ        "OUTPUT:"
INPUT    .STRINGZ        "INPUT (either 0 or 1):"
NEWLINE  .FILL          x000A

         .END
```

★9.50 Up to now, we have only had one output device, the monitor, with xFE04
and xFE06 used to address its two device registers. We now introduce a
second output device, a light that requires a single device register, to
which we assign the address xFE08. Storing a 1 in xFE08 turns the light
on, storing a 0 in xFE08 turns the light off.

An Aggie decided to write a program that would control this light by a
keyboard interrupt as follows: Pressing the key 0 would turn the light off.
Pressing the key 1 would cause the light to flash on and off repeatedly.
Shown below is the Aggie's code and his keyboard interrupt service
routine.

```
The User Program:
                .ORIG x3000
0               LEA  R7, LOOP
1       LOOP    LDI  R0, ENABLE
2               LD   R1, NEG_OFF
3               ADD  R0, R0, R1   ; check if switch is on
4               BRnp BLINK
        ;
5               AND  R0, R0, #0
6               STI  R0, LIGHT       ; turn light off
7               RET
        ;
8       BLINK   ST   R7, SAVE_R7    ; save linkage
9               LDI  R0, LIGHT
A               ADD  R0, R0, #1
B               AND  R0, R0, #1     ; toggle LIGHT between 0 and 1
C               STI  R0, LIGHT
D               JSR  DELAY          ; 1 second delay
E               LD   R7, SAVE_R7
F               RET                 ; <-- Breakpoint here
        ;
        LIGHT    .FILL xFE08
        ENABLE   .FILL x4000
        NEG_OFF  .FILL x-30
        SAVE_R7  .BLKW #1
                 .END

The Keyboard Interrupt Routine:
                .ORIG   x1500
0               ADD R6, R6, #-1     ; <-- Breakpoint here
1               STR R0, R6, #0      ; save R0 on stack
2               ADD R6, R6, #-1
3               STR R7, R6, #0      ; save R7 on stack
        ;
4               TRAP x20
5               STI  R0, ENABLE2
        ;
6               RTI                 ; <-- Breakpoint here
7       ENABLE2 .FILL x4000
                .END
```

The DELAY subroutine was inserted in his program in order to separate
the turning on and off of the light by one second in order to make the

on-off behavior visible to the naked eye. The DELAY subroutine does not modify any registers.

Unfortunately, per usual, the Aggie made a mistake in his program, and things do not work as he intended. So he decided to debug his program (see the next page).

He set three breakpoints, at x1500, at x1506, and at x300F. He initialized the PC to x3000, the keyboard IE bit to 1, and memory location x0180 to x1500.

Then he hit the Run button, which stopped executing when the PC reached x1500. He hit the Run button three more times, each time the computer stopping when the PC reached a breakpoint. While the program was running, he pressed a key on the keyboard EXACTLY ONCE.

The table below shows the data in various registers and memory locations each time a breakpoint was encountered. *Note:* Assume, when an interrupt is initiated, the PSR is pushed onto the system stack before the PC.

Complete the table.

	Initial	Breakpoint 1	Breakpoint 2	Breakpoint 3	Breakpoint 4
PC	x3000	x1500	x1506	x1506	x300F
R0	x1234		x0030		
R6	x3000				
R7	x1234				
M[x2FFC]	x0000				
M[x2FFD]	x0000				
M[x2FFE]	x0000	x300D			
M[x2FFF]	x0000	x8001			
M[x4000]	x0031				
M[xFE00]	x4000				

★9.51   The following user program (priority 0) is assembled and loaded into memory.

```
        .ORIG x8000
        LD R0, Z
AGAIN   ADD R0, R0, #-1
        BRnp AGAIN
        LD R0, W
        BRp L1
        LD R0, X
        TRAP x21
        BRnzp DONE
L1      LEA R0, Y
        TRAP x22
DONE    HALT

X       .FILL x34
Y       .STRINGZ "OOOOPS!"
Z       .FILL x100
W       .BLKW #1
        .END
```

Before this code executes, two things happen: (a) another program loads a value into W, and (b) a breakpoint is set at the address DONE. Then the run switch is hit and the program starts executing. Before the computer stops due to the breakpoint, several interrupts occur and their corresponding service routines are executed. Finally, the LC-3 stops due to the breakpoint. We examine the memory shown, and R6, the Supervisor Stack Pointer.

	Memory
x2FF8	x0601
x2FF9	x0601
x2FFA	x0500
x2FFB	x0504
x2FFC	x0204
x2FFD	x0201
x2FFE	x8004
x2FFF	x8002
x3000	x8010
x3001	x8012

R6 | x3000 |

What does the user program write to the monitor? How do you know that?

★9.52 Your job in this problem will be to add the missing instructions to a program that detects palindromes. Recall that a palindrome is a string of characters that are identical when read from left to right or from right to left—for example, racecar and 112282211. In this program, we will have no spaces and no capital letters in our input string—just a string of lowercase letters.

The program will make use of both a stack and a queue. The subroutines for accessing the stack and queue are shown below. Recall that elements are PUSHed (added) and POPped (removed) from the stack. Elements are ENQUEUEd (added) to the back of a queue and DEQUEUEd (removed) from the front of the queue.

```
        .ORIG x3050                      .ORIG x3080
PUSH    ADD R6, R6, #-1     ENQUEUE ADD R5, R5, #1
        STR R0, R6, #0              STR R0, R5, #0
        RET                        RET
POP     LDR R0, R6, #0      DEQUEUE LDR R0, R4, #0
        ADD R6, R6, #1             ADD R4, R4, #1
        RET                        RET
STACK   .BLKW #20           QUEUE   .BLKW #20
        .END                       .END
```

The program is carried out in two phases. Phase 1 enables a user to input a character string one keyboard character at a time. The character string is terminated when the user types the Enter key (line feed). In Phase 1, the ASCII code of each character input is pushed onto a stack, and its negative value is inserted at the back of a queue. Inserting an element at the back of a queue we call enqueuing.

In Phase 2, the characters on the stack and in the queue are examined by removing them one by one from their respective data structures (i.e., stack and queue). If the string is a palindrome, the program stores a 1 in memory location RESULT. If not, the program stores a 0 in memory location RESULT. The PUSH and POP routines for the stack as well as the ENQUEUE and DEQUEUE routines for the queue are shown below. You may assume the user never inputs more than 20 characters.

```
            .ORIG  X3000
            LEA    R4, QUEUE
            LEA    R5, QUEUE
            ADD    R5, R5, #-1
            LEA    R6, ENQUEUE            ; Initialize SP
            LD     R1, ENTER
            AND    R3, R3, #0
            ----------------- (a)
            TRAP   x22
PHASE1      TRAP   x20
            ----------------- (b)
            BRz PHASE2
            JSR PUSH
            ----------------- (c)
            ----------------- (d)
            JSR ENQUEUE
            ADD R3, R3, #1
            BRnzp PHASE1
    ;
PHASE2      JSR POP
            ----------------- (e)
            JSR DEQUEUE
            ADD R1, R0, R1
            BRnp FALSE
            ----------------- (f)
            ----------------- (g)
            BRnzp PHASE2
    ;
TRUE        AND R0, R0, #0
            ADD R0, R0, #1
            ST R0, RESULT
            HALT
FALSE       AND R0, R0, #0
            ST R0, RESULT
            HALT
RESULT      .BLKW #1
ENTER       .FILL x-0A
PROMPT      .STRINGZ "Enter an input string: "
            .END
```

★9.53 Now that the keyboard interrupt is old stuff for you, it is time to introduce two interrupts for the LC-3: INTA and INTB. The necessary hardware has been added to allow them to happen. INTA has priority 2

and an interrupt vector of x50. INTB has priority 4 and an interrupt
vector of x60.

Recall that the priority is specified in bits [10:8] of the PSR. In fact, the
full PSR specification is:

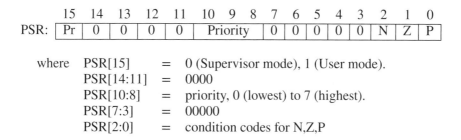

	15	14	13	12	11	10 9 8	7	6	5	4	3	2	1	0
PSR:	Pr	0	0	0	0	Priority	0	0	0	0	0	N	Z	P

where PSR[15]   = 0 (Supervisor mode), 1 (User mode).
       PSR[14:11] = 0000
       PSR[10:8]   = priority, 0 (lowest) to 7 (highest).
       PSR[7:3]   = 00000
       PSR[2:0]   = condition codes for N,Z,P

In this problem, you are given the user program and the two interrupt
service routines. The user program starts executing at cycle 1 and runs at
priority 0.

User program:

```
        .ORIG x3000
        AND R0,R0,#0
        ADD R0,R0,#5
        LD R1,COUNT
        NOT R0,R0
        ADD R0,R0,#1
AGAIN   ADD R2,R0,R1
        BRz DONE
        ADD R1,R1,#-1
        BRnzp AGAIN
DONE    TRAP x25
COUNT   .FILL x000F
        .END
```

INTA service routine:

```
        .ORIG x1000
        AND R5,R4,#0
        ADD R5,R5,#-1
        LD R3,VAL
        ADD R3,R3,R5
        ST R3,VAL
        RTI
VAL     .BLKW 1
        .END
```

INTB service routine:

```
        .ORIG x2000
        LDI R4,VAL2
        NOT R4,R4
        ADD R4,R4,#1
        STI R4,VAL2
        RTI
VAL2    .FILL xFE08
        .END
```

Assume both interrupts are enabled. Assume 22 cycles are needed to
initiate an interrupt when you are in User mode, that is, from the time the
test is taken until the interrupt service routine starts executing. Assume it
takes 21 cycles if you are in privileged (Supervisor) mode. You already
know from problem 1 the number of cycles individual instructions take.
In order to support INTA and INTB, the interrupt vector table must have
entries. Show the addresses of these entries and the contents of those
memory locations.

Memory address	Content

Suppose INTA requests service at cycle 30 and INTB requests service at cycle 68. In which cycle does each **service routine** start executing? The following table shows the contents of a section of memory (locations x2FFA to x3002) before the user program starts executing. Show the contents of these locations and the contents of the stack pointer in cycle 100.

	Initial	At the end of cycle 100
x2FFA	x0001	
x2FFB	x0010	
x2FFC	x0100	
x2FFD	x1000	
x2FFE	x1100	
x2FFF	x1110	
x3000	x5020	
x3001	x1025	
x3002	x2207	
Stack Pointer	x3000	

★9.54 Consider a two-player game where the players must think quickly each time it is their turn to make a move. Each player has a total allotted amount of time to make all his/her moves. Two clocks display the remaining time for each player. While a player is thinking of his/her move, his clock counts down. If time runs out, the other player wins. As soon as a player makes his/her move, he hits a button, which serves to stop counting down his clock and start counting down the other player's clock.

The program on the next page implements this mechanism. The main program keeps track of the time remaining for each player by decrementing the proper counter once per second while the player is thinking. When a player's counter reaches zero, a message is printed on the screen declaring the winner. When a player hits the button, an interrupt is taken. The interrupt service routine takes such action as to enable the main program (after returning from the interrupt) to start decrementing the other counter.

The interrupt vector for the button is x35. The priority level of the button is #2. Assume that the operating system has set the interrupt enable bit of the button to enable it to interrupt. Assume the main program runs at priority #1 and executes in User mode.

In order for the interrupt service routine to be executed when the button is pushed, what memory location must contain what value?

Assume a player hits the button while the instruction at line 16 is being executed. What two values (in hex) will be pushed onto the stack?

Fill in the missing instructions in the user program.

This program has a bug that will only occur if an interrupt is taken at an inappropriate time. Write down the line number of an instruction such that if the button is pressed while that instruction is executing, unintended behavior will result.

How could we fix this bug?

```
; Interrupt Service Routine
        .ORIG x1550
        NOT    R0, R0
        RTI
        .END

; User Program
        .ORIG x3000
        AND    R0, R0, #0      ; Line 1
        LD     R1, TIME        ; Line 2
        LD     R2, TIME        ; Line 3

NEXT    ------------------- (a)
        ------------------- (b)
        BRn    P2_DEC          ; Line 6
        ADD    R1, R1, #-1     ; Line 7
        ------------------- (c)
        LEA    R0, P2WINS      ; Line 9
        BRnzp  END             ; Line 10
P2_DEC  ADD    R2, R2, #-1     ; Line 11
        ------------------- (d)
        LEA    R0, P1WINS      ; Line 13
END     PUTS                   ; Line 14
        HALT                   ; Line 15
COUNT   LD     R3, SECOND      ; Line 16
LOOP    ADD    R3, R3, #-1     ; Line 17
        BRp    LOOP            ; Line 18
        ------------------- (e)
TIME    .FILL   #300
SECOND  .FILL   #25000         ; 1 second
P1WINS  .STRINGZ "Player 1 Wins."
P2WINS  .STRINGZ "Player 2 Wins."
        .END
```

★9.55 A program is running in privilege mode (PSR[15] = 0). We set a breakpoint at location x2000. The operator immediately pushes the run button. What are the subsequent MAR/MDR values?

MAR	MDR
	x8000
	x1050
	x0004
	xBCAE
x2800	x2C04
x1052	x3C4D
	x2C0A

CHAPTER

10   A Calculator

Before we leave LC-3 assembly language and raise the level of abstraction to the C programming language, it is useful to step back and pull together much of what we have learned with a comprehensive example. The intent is to demonstrate the use of many of the concepts discussed thus far, as well as to show an example of well-documented, clearly written code, where the example is much more complicated than what can fit on one or two pages.

Our example is a program that simulates the actions of a calculator that a person can use to add, subtract, and multiply 2's complement integers. The person will enter numbers into the calculator-simulator by typing keys on the keyboard. Results of a computation will be displayed on the monitor. The calculator simulation consists of a main program and eleven separate subroutines. You are encouraged to study this example before moving on to Chapter 11 and high-level language programming.

Two topics we have not discussed thus far are needed to understand the workings of the calculator simulation: (1) the conversion of integers between ASCII strings and 2's complement, and (2) arithmetic using a stack, the method most calculators use.

The reason for two data types and conversion between them: We need one data type for input/output and another for doing arithmetic. Numbers entered via the keyboard and displayed on the monitor use ASCII codes to represent the numbers. Arithmetic uses 2's complement integers.

We will need to convert the number the person types from ASCII codes to a 2's complement integer, and we will need to convert the result of the computation from a 2's complement integer to ASCII codes in order to display it on the monitor. Section 10.1 deals with data type conversion.

With respect to the way calculators perform arithmetic, the mechanism used by most calculators is very different from the way most desktop and laptop computers perform arithmetic. The ISAs of most desktops and laptops are like the LC-3, where arithmetic instructions get their source operands from general purpose registers and store the results of the arithmetic operations in general purpose registers. Our simulation of a calculator, like most calculators, does not use general purpose registers. Instead it uses a stack. Source operands are popped from the stack, and the result of the operation is pushed back onto the stack. Section 10.2 deals with arithmetic using a stack instead of general purpose registers.

Finally, Section 10.3 contains a full discussion of the calculator-simulator, along with all the subroutines that are needed to make it work.

10.1 Data Type Conversion

It has been a long time since we talked about data types. We have already been exposed to several data types: unsigned integers for address arithmetic, 2's complement integers for integer arithmetic, 16-bit binary strings for logical operations, floating point numbers for scientific computation, and ASCII codes for interaction with input and output devices.

It is important that every instruction be provided with source operands of the data type that the instruction requires. For example, an ALU requires operands that are 2's complement integers to perform an **ADD**. If the ALU were supplied with floating point operands, the ALU would produce garbage results.

It is not uncommon in high-level language programs to find an instruction of the form $A = R + I$ where R (floating point) and I (2's complement integer) are represented in different data types.

If the operation is to be performed by a floating point adder, then we have a problem with I. To handle the problem, one must first convert the value I from its original data type (2's complement integer) to the data type required by the functional unit performing the operation (floating point). For those programming in some high-level language, the compiler generally produces the code to do that conversion so the programmer does not even have to think about it.

Even in our "character count problem" way back in Chapter 5, we had to deal with data type conversion. Our program entered a character from the keyboard, scanned a file counting the number of occurrences of that character, and then displayed the count on the monitor. Recall that before we could display our final count on the monitor, we had to convert our 2's complement integer to an ASCII code. Why? Because when we were counting, we were performing arithmetic on 2's complement integers. But when we were displaying, we needed to represent our count as an ASCII code. You remember we restricted our program to work only on files where the total count was not greater than 9, so our conversion from a 2's complement integer to an ASCII code could be obtained by simply adding x30 to the 2's complement integer to get the ASCII code. For example, the 2's complement representation for 6 (in one byte) is 00000110, or x06. The ASCII code for 6, on the other hand, is 00110110, or x36.

That was a severe limitation to put on our count, restricting it to a single decimal digit. But that was Chapter 5, and now we are in Chapter 10! If our number is represented by more than one decimal digit, simply adding x30 does not work. For example, consider the two decimal digit number 25. If we enter 25 via the keyboard, we input the ASCII code x32, followed by the ASCII code x35. The bit stream is 0011001000110101. To perform arithmetic on this integer, we must first convert it to 0000000000011001, the 2's complement integer representation of 25. Displaying the result of some arithmetic computation on the monitor causes a similar problem. To do that, we must first convert the result of the arithmetic (a 2's complement integer) to an ASCII string.

In this section, we develop routines to convert integers consisting of more than one decimal digit from a string of ASCII codes to 2's complement, and from 2's complement to a string of ASCII codes.

10.1.1 Example: A Bogus Program: 2 + 3 = e

Before we get into the actual conversion routines, it is worth looking at a simple, concrete example that illustrates their importance. Figure 10.1 shows how we can get into trouble if we do not pay attention to the data types that we are working with.

Suppose we want to enter two single-digit integers from the keyboard, add them, and display the result on the monitor. At first blush, we write the simple program of Figure 10.1. What happens?

```
01    TRAP   x23          ; Input from the keyboard.
02    ADD    R1,R0,#0      ; Make room for another input.
03    TRAP   x23          ; Input another character.
04    ADD    R0,R1,R0      ; Add the two inputs.
05    TRAP   x21          ; Display result on the monitor.
06    TRAP   x25          ; Halt.
```

Figure 10.1   ADDITION without paying attention to data types.

Suppose the first digit entered via the keyboard is a 2 and the second digit entered via the keyboard is a 3. What will be displayed on the monitor before the program terminates? The value loaded into R0 as a result of entering a 2 is the ASCII code for 2, which is x0032. When the 3 is entered, the ASCII code for 3, which is x0033, is loaded into R0 (after the ASCII code for 2 is moved to R1, of course). Thus, the ADD instruction adds the two binary strings x0032 and x0033, producing x0065. When that value is displayed on the monitor, it is treated as an ASCII code. Since x0065 is the ASCII code for a lowercase *e*, a lowercase e is displayed on the monitor.

The reason we did not get 5 (which, at last calculation, is the correct result when adding 2 + 3) is that (a) we didn't convert the two input characters from ASCII to 2's complement integers before performing the addition and (b) we didn't convert the result back to ASCII before displaying it on the monitor.

Exercise: Correct Figure 10.1 so that it will add two single-digit positive integers and produce the correct single-digit positive sum. Assume that the two digits being added do in fact produce a single-digit sum.

10.1.2 Input Data (ASCII to Binary)

Figure 10.2 shows the ASCII representation of the three-decimal-digit integer 295, stored as an ASCII string in three consecutive LC-3 memory locations, starting at ASCIIBUFF. R1 contains the number of decimal digits in the positive integer. Our ASCII to binary subroutine restricts integers to the range 0 to 999.

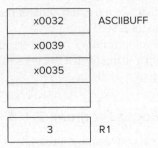

Figure 10.2   The ASCII representation of 295 stored in consecutive memory
                locations.

ASCIIBUFF is the address of the first memory location of a sequence of four memory locations that we have allocated (a) to store the ASCII codes of decimal digits entered from the keyboard, and (b) to store the ASCII codes corresponding to the result of arithmetic operations in preparation for writing it (the result) to the monitor.

You might ask why, in Figure 10.2, we used a whole 16-bit word to store the ASCII code of each decimal digit when a byte would have been enough. In fact, typically, one does store each ASCII code in a single byte of memory. In this example, we decided to give each ASCII character its own word of memory in order to simplify the algorithm.

Since we are restricting input to positive integers consisting of at most three decimal digits, you might also ask why we are allocating four words of memory to ASCIIBUFF. Wouldn't three words be enough? For input yes, but you will see in Section 10.1.3 that in preparation for output, we will need one more word for the sign (positive or negative) of the result, since the result of the arithmetic could be negative.

Figure 10.3 shows the flowchart for a subroutine that converts the ASCII representation of an integer, stored in Figure 10.2, into a binary integer.

The subroutine systematically takes each digit, converts it from its ASCII code to its binary code by stripping away all but the last four bits, and then uses those four bits to index into a table of ten binary values. Since we are restricting conversion to integers consisting of at most three decimal digits, only two tables are needed, one for the tens digit and one for the hundreds digit. Each entry in each table corresponds to the value of one of the ten digits. For example, the entry for index 6 in the hundreds table is the value #600, which is in binary 0000001001011000. That value is then added to R0. R0 is used to accumulate the contributions of all the digits. The result is returned in R0.

Question: If we wanted to be able to convert four decimal-digit integers, would we need a table of *thousands digits*? Or, is there a way to convert larger numbers represented as larger decimal strings into their binary form without requiring a table of *thousands* digits, *ten-thousands* digits, etc.?

Exercise: [Challenging] Suppose the decimal number is arbitrarily long. Rather than store a table of 10 values for the thousands-place digit, another table for the 10 ten-thousands-place digit, and so on, design an algorithm to do the conversion without requiring any tables at all. See Exercise 10.4.

Figure 10.4 shows the LC-3 code that implements this subroutine.

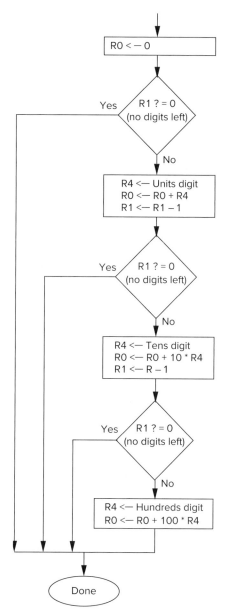

Figure 10.3 Flowchart, subroutine for ASCII-to-binary conversion.

There are two points that we need to make about the subroutines in Chapter 10, which are all part of our calculator simulation, described fully in Section 10.3. First, they cannot be assembled individually, and second (because of that) we need to be sure that no label is used more than once.

Why cannot the subroutine of Figure 10.4 be assembled by itself? Answer: Line 36 specifies a .FILL having the value ASCIIBUFF, but there is no location

```
01    ;
02    ;   This subroutine takes an ASCII string of up to three decimal digits and
03    ;   converts it into a binary number.  R0 is used to collect the result.
04    ;   R1 keeps track of how many digits are left to process.  ASCIIBUFF
05    ;   contains the most significant digit in the ASCII string.
06    ;
07    ASCIItoBinary  ST     R1,AtoB_Save1
08                   ST     R2,AtoB_Save2
09                   ST     R3,AtoB_Save3
0A                   ST     R4,AtoB_Save4
0B                   AND    R0,R0,#0        ; R0 will be used for our result.
0C                   ADD    R1,R1,#0        ; Test number of digits.
0D                   BRz    AtoB_Done       ; There are no digits, result is 0.
0E    ;
0F                   LD     R2,AtoB_ASCIIBUFF ; R2 points to ASCIIBUFF
10                   ADD    R2,R2,R1
11                   ADD    R2,R2,#-1       ; R2 now points to "ones" digit.
12    ;
13                   LDR    R4,R2,#0        ; R4 <-- "ones" digit
14                   AND    R4,R4,x000F     ; Strip off the ASCII template.
15                   ADD    R0,R0,R4        ; Add ones contribution.
16    ;
17                   ADD    R1,R1,#-1
18                   BRz    AtoB_Done       ; The original number had one digit.
19                   ADD    R2,R2,#-1       ; R2  now points to "tens" digit.
1A    ;
1B                   LDR    R4,R2,#0        ; R4 <-- "tens" digit
1C                   AND    R4,R4,x000F     ; Strip off ASCII template.
1D                   LEA    R3,LookUp10     ; LookUp10 is BASE of tens values.
1E                   ADD    R3,R3,R4        ; R3 points to the right tens value.
1F                   LDR    R4,R3,#0
20                   ADD    R0,R0,R4        ; Add tens contribution to total.
21    ;
22                   ADD    R1,R1,#-1
23                   BRz    AtoB_Done       ; The original number had two digits.
24                   ADD    R2,R2,#-1       ; R2 now points to "hundreds" digit.
25    ;
26                   LDR    R4,R2,#0        ; R4 <-- "hundreds" digit
27                   AND    R4,R4,x000F     ; Strip off ASCII template.
28                   LEA    R3,LookUp100    ; LookUp100 is hundreds BASE.
29                   ADD    R3,R3,R4        ; R3 points to hundreds value.
2A                   LDR    R4,R3,#0
2B                   ADD    R0,R0,R4        ; Add hundreds contribution to total.
2C    ;
2D    AtoB_Done      LD     R1,AtoB_Save1
2E                   LD     R2,AtoB_Save2
2F                   LD     R3,AtoB_Save3
```

Figure 10.4   ASCII-to-binary conversion subroutine (Fig. 10.4 continued on next page.)

```
30                      LD      R4,AtoB_Save4
31                      RET
32      ;
33      AtoB_ASCIIBUFF  .FILL   ASCIIBUFF
34      AtoB_Save1      .BLKW   #1
35      AtoB_Save2      .BLKW   #1
36      AtoB_Save3      .BLKW   #1
37      AtoB_Save4      .BLKW   #1
38      LookUp10        .FILL   #0
39                      .FILL   #10
3A                      .FILL   #20
3B                      .FILL   #30
3C                      .FILL   #40
3D                      .FILL   #50
3E                      .FILL   #60
3F                      .FILL   #70
40                      .FILL   #80
41                      .FILL   #90
42      ;
43      LookUp100       .FILL   #0
44                      .FILL   #100
45                      .FILL   #200
46                      .FILL   #300
47                      .FILL   #400
48                      .FILL   #500
49                      .FILL   #600
4A                      .FILL   #700
4B                      .FILL   #800
4C                      .FILL   #900
```

Figure 10.4   ASCII-to-binary conversion subroutine (continued Fig. 10.4 from previous page.)

in the subroutine labeled ASCIIBUFF. Therefore, trying to assemble the subroutine by itself will fail. We could have used .EXTERNAL, discussed briefly in Chapter 7, to enable the subroutines to be assembled individually, but we chose to not do that, preferring to assemble the entire calculator-simulator program including its eleven subroutines as a single entity. As you would expect, line 43 in the code of Figure 10.15 contains the label ASCIIBUFF.

Second, if we are to assemble the main program and all the subroutines as a single unit, we need to be sure to not use the same label in more than one subroutine. Note that in Figure 10.4, most labels start with "AtoB_." As expected, the same pattern of labeling is used in the rest of the subroutines.

10.1.3 Display Result (Binary to ASCII)

To display the result of a computation on the monitor, we must first convert the 2's complement integer result into an ASCII string. Figure 10.5 shows the subroutine

```
01    ; This subroutine converts a 2's complement integer within the range
02    ; -999 to +999 (located in R0) into an ASCII character string consisting
03    ; of a sign digit, followed by three decimal digits, and stores the
04    ; character string into the four memory locations starting at ASCIIBUFF
05    ; (see Figure 10.4).
06    ;
07    BinarytoASCII   ST    R0,BtoA_Save0
08                    ST    R1,BtoA_Save1
09                    ST    R2,BtoA_Save2
0A                    ST    R3,BtoA_Save3
0B                    LD    R1,BtoA_ASCIIBUFF   ; R1 keeps track of output string.
0C                    ADD   R0,R0,#0            ; R0 contains the binary value.
0D                    BRn   NegSign             ;
0E                    LD    R2,ASCIIplus        ; First store the ASCII plus sign.
0F                    STR   R2,R1,#0
10                    BRnzp Begin100
11    NegSign         LD    R2,ASCIIminus       ; First store ASCII minus sign.
12                    STR   R2,R1,#0
13                    NOT   R0,R0               ; Convert the number to absolute
14                    ADD   R0,R0,#1            ; value; it is easier to work with.
15    ;
16    Begin100        LD    R2,ASCIIoffset      ; Prepare for "hundreds" digit.
17    ;
18                    LD    R3,Neg100           ; Determine the hundreds digit.
19    Loop100         ADD   R0,R0,R3
1A                    BRn   End100
1B                    ADD   R2,R2,#1
1C                    BRnzp Loop100
1D    ;
1E    End100          STR   R2,R1,#1   ; Store ASCII code for hundreds digit.
1F                    LD    R3,Pos100
20                    ADD   R0,R0,R3    ; Correct R0 for one-too-many subtracts.
21    ;
22                    LD    R2,ASCIIoffset ; Prepare for "tens" digit.
23    ;
24    Loop10          ADD   R0,R0,#-10     ; Determine the tens digit.
25                    BRn   End10
26                    ADD   R2,R2,#1
27                    BRnzp Loop10
28    ;
29    End10           STR   R2,R1,#2    ; Store ASCII code for tens digit.
2A                    ADD   R0,R0,#10   ; Correct R0 for one-too-many subtracts.
2B    Begin1          LD    R2,ASCIIoffset ; Prepare for "ones" digit.
2C                    ADD   R2,R2,R0
2D                    STR   R2,R1,#3
2E                    LD    R0,BtoA_Save0
2F                    LD    R1,BtoA_Save1
30                    LD    R2,BtoA_Save2
31                    LD    R3,BtoA_Save3
32                    RET
33    ;
34    ASCIIplus       .FILL   x002B
35    ASCIIminus      .FILL   x002D
36    ASCIIoffset     .FILL   x0030
37    Neg100          .FILL   #-100
38    Pos100          .FILL   #100
39    BtoA_Save0      .BLKW   #1
3A    BtoA_Save1      .BLKW   #1
3B    BtoA_Save2      .BLKW   #1
3C    BtoA_Save3      .BLKW   #1
3D    BtoA_ASCIIBUFF  .FILL   ASCIIBUFF
```

Figure 10.5   Binary-to-ASCII conversion subroutine.

for converting a 2's complement integer stored in R0 into an ASCII string stored in the four consecutive memory locations starting at ASCIIBUFF. The value initially in R0 is restricted to the range −999 to +999. After the subroutine completes execution, ASCIIBUFF contains the sign (+ or −) of the value initially stored in R0, followed by three locations that contain the ASCII codes corresponding to the decimal digits representing its magnitude.

The subroutine works as follows: First, the sign of the result to be displayed is determined, and the ASCII code for + or − is stored in ASCIIBUFF. The result (in R0) is replaced by its absolute value. The algorithm determines the hundreds-place digit by repeatedly subtracting #100 from R0 until the result goes negative. This is next repeated for the tens-place digit. The value left is the ones digit.

Exercise: This subroutine always produces a string of four characters independent of the sign and magnitude of the integer being converted. Devise an algorithm that eliminates unnecessary characters; that is, eliminate leading zeros and eliminate a leading + sign. See Exercise 10.6.

10.2 Arithmetic Using a Stack

10.2.1 The Stack as Temporary Storage

You know that the LC-3 ADD instruction takes two source operands that are stored in registers, performs an addition, and stores the result into one of the LC-3's eight general purpose registers. We call the register where the result is stored the *destination register*. The eight general purpose registers R0 to R7 comprise the temporary storage that allows operate instructions like ADD to access both source registers and the destination register much more quickly than if the computer had to access memory for the operands. Because the three locations are specified explicitly,

```
ADD   R0,R1,R2
```

we call the LC-3 a three-address machine. Most desktop and laptop computers are either *three-address machines* like the LC-3 or *two-address machines* like the x86 ISA that is implemented in many of your laptop and desktop computers. In a two-address machine, two locations are specified explicitly. An example of an x86 ADD instruction is

```
ADD   EAX,EBX
```

where EAX and EBX are two of the eight general purpose registers in the x86 ISA. In this case, EAX serves as both the location of one of the source operands and the location of the destination operand. With a two-address machine, one of the source registers is overwritten with the result of the operation.

There are also ISAs that do not use general purpose registers at all to store either source operands or the results of operate instructions. The most common of these are called *stack machines* because a stack is used for temporary storage. Most calculators, including the one we will simulate in Section 10.3, use a stack for temporary storage rather than a set of general purpose registers.

Source operands are obtained by popping the top two elements from the stack. The result (i.e., the destination operand) is subsequently pushed onto the stack. Since the computer always pops and pushes operands from the stack, no addresses need to be specified explicitly. Therefore, stack machines are sometimes referred to as zero-address machines. The instruction would simply be

ADD

and the computer would know where to find the operands. For a calculator, that is convenient because a person can cause an ADD to be performed by simply pressing the + button on the calculator. Note that the pop, push, and add are not part of the ISA of the computer, and therefore they are available to the programmer. They are control signals that the hardware uses to make the actual pop, push, and add occur. The control signals are part of the microarchitecture, similar to the load enable signals and mux select signals we discussed in Chapters 4 and 5. As is the case with LC-3 instructions LD and ST, and control signals PCMUX and LD.MDR, the programmer simply instructs the computer to ADD, and the microarchitecture does the rest.

10.2.2 An Example

Suppose we want to evaluate $(A + B) \cdot (C + D)$, where A contains 25, B contains 17, C contains 3, and D contains 2, and store the result in E. If the LC-3 had a multiply instruction (we would probably call it MUL), we could use the following program:

```
LD     R0,A
LD     R1,B
ADD    R0,R0,R1
LD     R2,C
LD     R3,D
ADD    R2,R2,R3
MUL    R0,R0,R2
ST     R0,E
```

With a calculator, we would execute the following eight operations:

```
(1)    push      25
(2)    push      17
(3)    add
(4)    push      3
(5)    push      2
(6)    add
(7)    multiply
(8)    pop       E
```

with the final result popped (i.e., 210) being the result of the computation. Figure 10.6 shows a snapshot of the stack after each of the eight operations. Note that in this example we have allocated memory locations x3FFB to x3FFF for our stack, and the stack pointer is initially at x4000, indicating that there is nothing initially on the stack.

In Section 10.3, we write a program that causes the LC-3 (with keyboard and monitor) to act like such a calculator. We say the LC-3 *simulates* the calculator

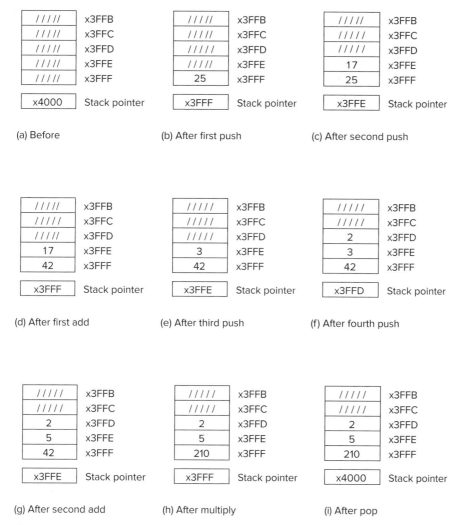

Figure 10.6   Stack usage during the computation of $(25 + 17) \cdot (3 + 2)$.

when it executes that program. To do this, our program will need subroutines to perform the various arithmetic operations.

10.2.3 OpAdd, OpMult, and OpNeg

The program we write in Section 10.3 to simulate a calculator will need three subroutines to be able to perform addition, subtraction, and multiplication. They are:

1. OpAdd, which will pop two values from the stack, add them, and push the result onto the stack.

2. OpMult, which will pop two values from the stack, multiply them, and push the result onto the stack.

3. OpNeg, which will pop the top value, form its 2's complement negative value, and push the result onto the stack. This will allow us to subtract two numbers A minus B by first forming −B and then adding the result to A.

The OpAdd Subroutine   Figure 10.7 shows the flowchart of the OpAdd subroutine. Basically, it attempts to pop two values off the stack and, if successful, add them. If the result is within the range of acceptable values (i.e., an integer between −999 and +999), then the result is pushed onto the stack.

There are two things that could prevent OpAdd from completing successfully: Fewer than two values are available on the stack for source operands, or

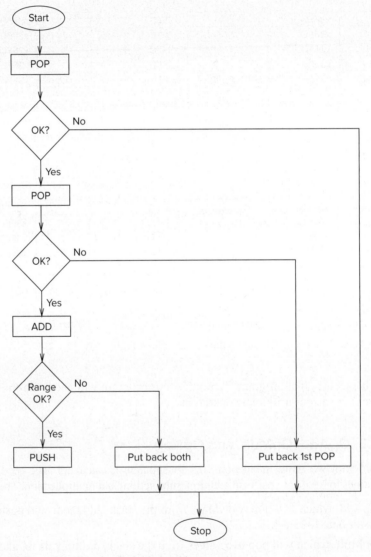

Figure 10.7   Flowchart for OpAdd algorithm.

the result is out of range. In both cases, the stack is put back to the way it was at the start of the OpAdd subroutine. If the first pop is unsuccessful, the stack is not changed since the POP routine leaves the stack as it was. If the second of the two pops reports back unsuccessfully, the stack pointer is decremented, which effectively returns the first value popped to the top of the stack. If the result is outside the range of acceptable values, then the stack pointer is decremented twice, returning both values to the top of the stack.

The OpAdd subroutine is shown in Figure 10.8.

Note that the OpAdd subroutine calls the RangeCheck subroutine. This is a simple test to be sure the result of the computation is within what can successfully be stored in a single stack location. For our purposes, we restrict values to integers in the range −999 to +999. This will come in handy in Section 10.3 when we design our home-brew calculator. The flowchart for the RangeCheck subroutine is shown in Figure 10.9. The LC-3 program that implements this subroutine is shown in Figure 10.10.

```
01    ;
02    ;         Subroutine to pop the top two elements from the stack,
03    ;         add them, and push the sum onto the stack.  R6 is
04    ;         the stack pointer.
05    ;
06    OpAdd           ST    R0,OpAdd_Save0
07                    ST    R1,OpAdd_Save1
08                    ST    R5,OpAdd_Save5
09                    ST    R7,OpAdd_Save7
0A                    JSR   POP              ; Get first source operand.
0B                    ADD   R5,R5,#0         ; Test if POP was successful.
0C                    BRp   OpAdd_Exit       ; Branch if not successful.
0D                    ADD   R1,R0,#0         ; Make room for second operand.
0E                    JSR   POP              ; Get second source operand.
0F                    ADD   R5,R5,#0         ; Test if POP was successful.
10                    BRp   OpAdd_Restore1   ; Not successful, put back first.
11                    ADD   R0,R0,R1         ; THE Add.
12                    JSR   RangeCheck       ; Check size of result.
13                    ADD   R5,R5,#0         ; Check R5 for success/failure.
14                    BRp   OpAdd_Restore2   ; Out of range, restore both.
15                    JSR   PUSH             ; Push sum on the stack.
16                    BRnzp OpAdd_Exit       ; On to the next task...
17    OpAdd_Restore2  ADD   R6,R6,#-1        ; Decrement stack pointer.
18    OpAdd_Restore1  ADD   R6,R6,#-1        ; Decrement stack pointer.
19    OpAdd_Exit      LD    R0,OpAdd_Save0
1A                    LD    R1,OpAdd_Save1
1B                    LD    R5,OpAdd_Save5
1C                    LD    R7,OpAdd_Save7
1D                    RET
1E    OpAdd_Save0     .BLKW #1
1F    OpAdd_Save1     .BLKW #1
20    OpAdd_Save5     .BLKW #1
21    OpAdd_Save7     .BLKW #1
```

Figure 10.8   The OpAdd Subroutine.

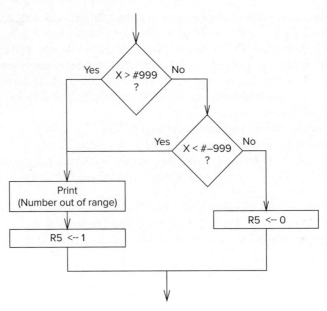

Figure 10.9   The RangeCheck algorithm flowchart.

```
01    ;
02    ;       Subroutine to check that a value is
03    ;       between -999 and +999.
04    ;
05    RangeCheck        LD        R5,Neg999
06                      ADD       R5,R0,R5        ; Recall that R0 contains the
07                      BRp       BadRange        ; result being checked.
08                      LD        R5,Pos999
09                      ADD       R5,R0,R5
0A                      BRn       BadRange
0B                      AND       R5,R5,#0        ; R5 <-- success
0C                      RET
0D    BadRange          ST        R0,RangeCheck_Save0
0E                      LEA       R0,RangeErrorMsg
0F                      TRAP      x22             ; Output character string
10                      AND       R5,R5,#0        ;
11                      ADD       R5,R5,#1        ; R5 <-- failure
12                      LD        R0,RangeCheck_Save0
13                      RET
14    Neg999            .FILL     #-999
15    Pos999            .FILL     #999
16    RangeErrorMsg     .FILL     x000A
17                      .STRINGZ  "Error: Number is out of range."
18    RangeCheck_Save0 .BLKW      #1
```

Figure 10.10   The RangeCheck Subroutine.

The OpMult Subroutine Figure 10.11 shows the flowchart of the OpMult subroutine, and Figure 10.12 shows the LC-3 program that implements it. Similar to the OpAdd subroutine, the OpMult subroutine attempts to pop two values off the stack and, if successful, multiplies them. Since the LC-3 does not have a multiply

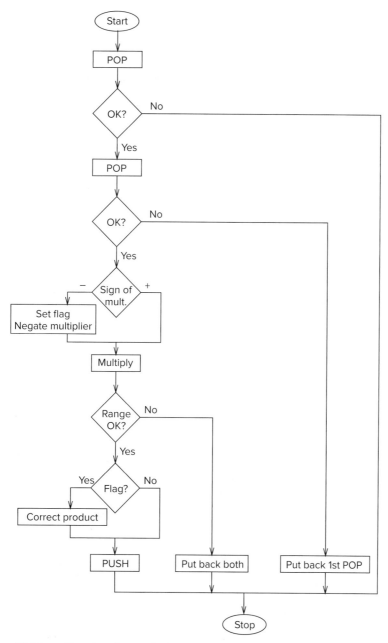

Figure 10.11 Flowchart for the OpMult subroutine.

```
01    ;
02    ;       Two values are popped from the stack, multiplied, and if
03    ;       their product is within the acceptable range, the result
04    ;       is pushed onto the stack.  R6 is the stack pointer.
05    ;
06    OpMult          ST      R0,OpMult_Save0
07                    ST      R1,OpMult_Save1
08                    ST      R2,OpMult_Save2
09                    ST      R3,OpMult_Save3
0A                    ST      R5,OpMult_Save5
0B                    ST      R7,OpMult_Save7
0C                    AND     R3,R3,#0        ; R3 holds sign of multiplier.
0D                    JSR     POP             ; Get first source from stack.
0E                    ADD     R5,R5,#0        ; Test for successful POP.
0F                    BRp     OpMult_Exit     ; Failure
10                    ADD     R1,R0,#0        ; Make room for next POP.
11                    JSR     POP             ; Get second source operand.
12                    ADD     R5,R5,#0        ; Test for successful POP.
13                    BRp     OpMult_Restore1 ; Failure; restore first POP.
14                    ADD     R2,R0,#0        ; Moves multiplier, tests sign.
15                    BRzp    PosMultiplier
16                    ADD     R3,R3,#1        ; Sets FLAG: Multiplier is neg.
17                    NOT     R2,R2
18                    ADD     R2,R2,#1        ; R2 contains -(multiplier).
19    PosMultiplier   AND     R0,R0,#0        ; Clear product register.
1A                    ADD     R2,R2,#0
1B                    BRz     PushMult        ; Multiplier = 0, Done.
1C    ;
1D    MultLoop        ADD     R0,R0,R1        ; THE actual "multiply"
1E                    ADD     R2,R2,#-1       ; Iteration Control
1F                    BRp     MultLoop
20    ;
21                    JSR     RangeCheck
22                    ADD     R5,R5,#0        ; R5 contains success/failure.
23                    BRp     OpMult_Restore2
24    ;
25                    ADD     R3,R3,#0        ; Test for negative multiplier.
26                    BRz     PushMult
27                    NOT     R0,R0           ; Adjust for
28                    ADD     R0,R0,#1        ; sign of result.
29    PushMult        JSR     PUSH            ; Push product on the stack.
2A                    BRnzp   OpMult_Exit
2B    OpMult_Restore2 ADD     R6,R6,#-1       ; Adjust stack pointer.
2C    OpMult_Restore1 ADD     R6,R6,#-1       ; Adjust stack pointer.
2D    OpMult_Exit     LD      R0,OpMult_Save0
2E                    LD      R1,OpMult_Save1
2F                    LD      R2,OpMult_Save2
30                    LD      R3,OpMult_Save3
31                    LD      R5,OpMult_Save5
32                    LD      R7,OpMult_Save7
33                    RET
34    OpMult_Save0    .BLKW   #1
35    OpMult_Save1    .BLKW   #1
36    OpMult_Save2    .BLKW   #1
37    OpMult_Save3    .BLKW   #1
38    OpMult_Save5    .BLKW   #1
39    OpMult_Save7    .BLKW   #1
```

Figure 10.12   The OpMult subroutine.

instruction, multiplication is performed as we have done in the past as a sequence of adds. Lines 17 to 19 of Figure 10.12 contain the crux of the actual multiply. If the result is within the range of acceptable values, then the result is pushed onto the stack.

If the second of the two pops reports back unsuccessfully, the stack pointer is decremented, which effectively returns the first value popped to the top of the stack. If the result is outside the range of acceptable values, which as before will be indicated by a 1 in R5, then the stack pointer is decremented twice, returning both values to the top of the stack.

The OpNeg Subroutine To perform subtraction with the top two elements on the stack, we first replace the top element on the stack with its negative and then use OpADD. That is, if the top of the stack contains A, and the second element on the stack contains B, we can push B−A on the stack by first negating the top of the stack and then performing OpAdd. The subroutine OpNeg for computing the negative of the element on the top of the stack is shown in Figure 10.13.

```
01    ; Subroutine to pop the top of the stack, form its negative,
02    ; and push the result onto the stack.
03    ;
04    OpNeg          ST      R0,OpNeg_Save0
05                   ST      R5,OpNeg_Save5
06                   ST      R7,OpNeg_Save7
07                   JSR     POP         ; Get the source operand.
08                   ADD     R5,R5,#0    ; Test for successful pop
09                   BRp     OpNeg_Exit  ; Branch if failure.
0A                   NOT     R0,R0
0B                   ADD     R0,R0,#1    ; Form the negative of source.
0C                   JSR     PUSH        ; Push result onto the stack.
0D    OpNeg_Exit     LD      R0,OpNeg_Save0
0E                   LD      R5,OpNeg_Save5
0F                   LD      R7,OpNeg_Save7
10                   RET
11    OpNeg_Save0    .BLKW   #1
12    OpNeg_Save5    .BLKW   #1
13    OpNeg_Save7    .BLKW   #1
```

Figure 10.13 The OpNeg subroutine.

10.3 The Calculator

10.3.1 Functionality

We are now ready to specify all the code for our calculator. As we already said, our calculator is not very sophisticated by today's standards. It will allow a user to enter positive integers consisting of not more than three decimal digits, perform basic arithmetic (addition, subtraction, and multiplication) on these integers, and display the decimal result (which will also be limited to at most three decimal digits).

We will use the keyboard to tell the calculator what to do. We can enter positive integers having up to three decimal digits, the arithmetic operators + (for ADD), * (for MUL), and − (for negative), and three additional commands D (to display the result of the calculation on the monitor), C (to erase all values entered), and X (to turn off the calculator).

The calculator algorithm works as follows: We use the keyboard to input commands and decimal values. We use the monitor to display results. We use a stack to hold source operands for performing arithmetic operations and the results of those arithmetic operations, as described in Section 10.2. Values entered and displayed are restricted to three decimal digits, that is, only values between −999 and +999, inclusive.

Figure 10.14 is a flowchart that provides an overview of our algorithm that simulates a calculator. Simulation of the calculator starts with initialization, which includes setting R6, the stack pointer, to an empty stack. Then the user sitting at the keyboard is prompted with: "Enter a Command."

The following commands are available to the user.

X Exit the simulation.

D Display the value at the top of the stack.

C Clear all values from the stack.

+ Pop the top two elements A,B off the stack and push A+B.

* Pop the top two elements A,B off the stack and push A*B.

− Pop the top element A off the stack and push "minus" A.

Enter or **LF** Push the value typed on the keyboard onto the top of the stack.

If the user wants to enter a number, he/she types the number (up to three decimal digits) followed by <Enter> or <Line Feed (LF)>.

Input is echoed, and the calculator simulation systematically tests the character to identify the user's command. Depending on the user's command, the calculator calls the appropriate subroutine to carry out the work specified. After the work is carried out, the subroutine returns, followed by a prompt for another command. The calculator simulation continues in this way until the user presses X, signaling that the user is finished with the calculator.

For example, to calculate

```
(51 - 49) * (172 + 205) - (17 * 2)
```

and display the result 720 on the monitor, one types the following sequence of keys on the keyboard:
5,1,LF,4,9,LF,−,+,1,7,2,LF,2,0,5,LF,+,*,1,7,LF,2,LF,*,−,+,D.

10.3.2 Code

Twelve routines comprise the calculator simulation. Figure 10.15 is the main algorithm, supported by eleven subroutines. Note the three global labels, Stack-Max, StackBase, and ASCIIBUFF, are all part of the main algorithm, shown in Figure 10.15. They provide the symbol table entries needed by the subroutines that reference those locations. Note also that the stack has been allocated ten

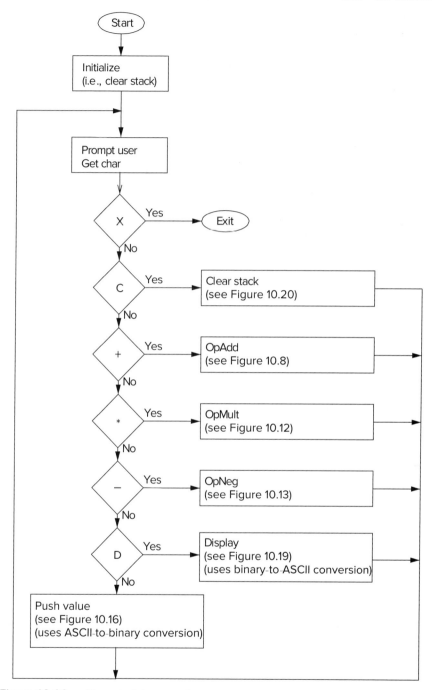

Figure 10.14   The calculator, overview.

```
01      ;
02      ;   The Calculator, Main Algorithm
03      ;
04                      LEA         R6,StackBase    ; Initialize the Stack Pointer.
05                      ADD         R6,R6,#1        ; R6 = StackBase + 1 --> empty stack
06
07      NewCommand      LEA         R0,PromptMsg
08                      PUTS
09                      GETC
0A                      OUT
0B      ;
0C      ; Check the command
0D      ;
0E      TestX           LD          R1,NegX         ; Check for X.
0F                      ADD         R1,R1,R0
10                      BRnp        TestC
11                      HALT
12      ;
13      TestC           LD          R1,NegC         ; Check for C.
14                      ADD         R1,R1,R0
15                      BRnp        TestAdd
16                      JSR         OpClear         ; See Figure 10.20
17                      BRnzp       NewCommand
18      ;
19      TestAdd         LD          R1,NegPlus      ; Check for +
1A                      ADD         R1,R1,R0
1B                      BRnp        TestMult
1C                      JSR         OpAdd           ; See Figure 10.8
1D                      BRnzp       NewCommand
1E      ;
1F      TestMult        LD          R1,NegMult      ; Check for *
20                      ADD         R1,R1,R0
21                      BRnp        TestMinus
22                      JSR         OpMult          ; See Figure 10.12
23                      BRnzp       NewCommand
24      ;
25      TestMinus       LD          R1,NegMinus     ; Check for -
26                      ADD         R1,R1,R0
27                      BRnp        TestD
28                      JSR         OpNeg           ; See Figure 10.13
29                      BRnzp       NewCommand
2A      ;
2B      TestD           LD          R1,NegD         ; Check for D
2C                      ADD         R1,R1,R0
2D                      BRnp        EnterNumber
2E                      JSR         OpDisplay       ; See Figure 10.19
2F                      BRnzp       NewCommand
30      ;
31      ; Then we must be entering an integer
32      ;
33      EnterNumber JSR             PushValue       ; See Figure 10.16
34                      BRnzp       NewCommand
35      ;
36      PromptMsg       .FILL       x000A
37                      .STRINGZ "Enter a command:"
38      NegX            .FILL       xFFA8
39      NegC            .FILL       xFFBD
3A      NegPlus         .FILL       xFFD5
3B      NegMinus        .FILL       xFFD3
3C      NegMult         .FILL       xFFD6
3D      NegD            .FILL       xFFBC
3E
3F      ; Globals
40      StackMax        .BLKW       #9
41      StackBase       .BLKW       #1
42      ASCIIBUFF       .BLKW       #4
43                      .FILL       x0000 ; ASCIIBUFF sentinel
```

Figure 10.15   The calculator's main algorithm.

entries in the main algorithm, and R6, the stack pointer, is initialized to an empty stack in line 05.

Figure 10.16 takes an ASCII string of characters terminating by a LF, checks to be sure it corresponds to a string of not more than three decimal digits, and if so, converts it to a binary number, then pushes the binary number onto the top of the stack. Figure 10.4 provides the ASCII-to-binary conversion routine. Figure 10.19 pops the entry on the top of the stack, converts it to an ASCII character string, and displays the ASCII string on the monitor. Figure 10.5 provides the binary-to-ASCII conversion routine. Figures 10.8 (OpAdd), 10.12 (OpMult), and 10.13 (OpNeg) supply the basic arithmetic algorithms using a stack. Figures 10.17 and 10.18 contain the basic POP and PUSH routines Finally, Figure 10.20 clears the stack.

```
01      ; This subroutine takes a sequence of not more than three decimal digits
02      ; typed by the user, converts its ASCII string to a binary value using the
03      ; ASCIItoBinary subroutine, and pushes the binary value onto the stack.
04      ; Anything else typed results in an error message.
05      ;
06      PushValue       ST      R0,PushValue_Save0
07                      ST      R1,PushValue_Save1
08                      ST      R2,PushValue_Save2
09                      ST      R7,PushValue_Save7
0A                      LD      R1,PushValue_ASCIIBUFF  ; R1 points to string being
0B                      LD      R2,MaxDigits            ; generated.
0C      ;
0D      ValueLoop       ADD     R3,R0,x-0A      ; Test for line feed, x0A
0E                      BRz     GoodInput
0F                      ADD     R2,R2,#0
10                      BRz     TooLargeInput
11                      LD      R3,NEGASCII0
12                      ADD     R3,R0,R3
13                      BRn     NotInteger
14                      LD      R3,NEGASCII9
15                      ADD     R3,R0,R3
16                      BRp     NotInteger
17                      ADD     R2,R2,#-1       ; Still room for more digits.
18                      STR     R0,R1,#0        ; Store last character read.
19                      ADD     R1,R1,#1
1A                      GETC
1B                      OUT                     ; Echo it.
1C                      BRnzp   ValueLoop
1D      ;
1E      GoodInput       LD      R2,PushValue_ASCIIBUFF
1F                      NOT     R2,R2
20                      ADD     R2,R2,#1
21                      ADD     R1,R1,R2        ; R1 now contains no. of char.
22                      BRz     NoDigit
23                      JSR     ASCIItoBinary
24                      JSR     PUSH
25                      BRnzp   PushValue_Done
```

Figure 10.16   The calculator's PushValue routine (Fig. 10.16 continued on next page.)

```
26    NoDigit            LEA        R0,NoDigitMsg
27                       PUTS
28                       BRnzp      PushValue_Done
29    NotInteger         GETC                        ; Spin until carriage return.
2A                       OUT
2B                       ADD        R3,R0,x-0A     ; Test for line feed, x0A
2C                       BRnp       NotInteger
2D                       LEA        R0,NotIntegerMsg
2E                       PUTS
2F                       BRnzp      PushValue_Done
30    TooLargeInput      GETC                        ; Spin until carriage return.
31                       OUT
32                       ADD        R3,R0,x-0A     ; Test for line feed, x0A
33                       BRnp       TooLargeInput
34                       LEA        R0,TooManyDigits
35                       PUTS
36    PushValue_Done     LD         R0,PushValue_Save0
37                       LD         R1,PushValue_Save1
38                       LD         R2,PushValue_Save2
39                       LD         R7,PushValue_Save7
3A                       RET
3B    TooManyDigits      .FILL      x000A
3C                       .STRINGZ   "Too many digits"
3D    NoDigitMsg         .FILL      x000A
3E                       .STRINGZ   "No number entered"
3F    NotIntegerMsg      .FILL      x000A
40                       .STRINGZ   "Not an integer"
41    MaxDigits          .FILL      x0003
42    NegASCII0          .FILL      x-30
43    NegASCII9          .FILL      x-39
44    PushValue_ASCIIBUFF .FILL     ASCIIBUFF
45    PushValue_Save0    .BLKW      #1
46    PushValue_Save1    .BLKW      #1
47    PushValue_Save2    .BLKW      #1
48    PushValue_Save7    .BLKW      #1
```

Figure 10.16   The calculator's PushValue routine (continued Fig. 10.16 from previous page.)

```
01      ;  This subroutine POPs a value from the stack and puts it in
02      ;  R0 before returning to the calling program.  R5 is used to
03      ;  report success (R5 = 0) or failure (R5 = 1) of the POP operation.
04      POP             LD      R0,POP_StackBase
05                      NOT     R0,R0               ; R0 = -(addr. of StackBase + 1)
06                      ADD     R0,R0,R6            ; R6 = StackPointer
07                      BRz     Underflow
08                      LDR     R0,R6,#0            ; The actual POP
09                      ADD     R6,R6,#1            ; Adjust StackPointer
0A                      AND     R5,R5,#0            ; R5 <-- success
0B                      RET
0C      Underflow       LEA     R0,UnderflowMsg
0D                      PUTS                        ; Print error message.
0E                      AND     R5,R5,#0
0F                      ADD     R5,R5,#1            ; R5 <-- failure
10                      RET
11      UnderflowMsg    .FILL   x000A
12                      .STRINGZ "Error: Too Few Values on the Stack."
13      POP_StackBase   .FILL   StackBase
```

Figure 10.17   The calculator's POP routine.

```
01      ;  This subroutine PUSHes on the stack the value stored in R0.
02      ;  R5 is used to report success (R5 = 0) or failure (R5 = 1) of
03      ;  the PUSH operation.
04      PUSH            ST      R1,PUSH_Save1 ; R1 is needed by this routine.
05                      LD      R1,PUSH_StackMax
06                      NOT     R1,R1
07                      ADD     R1,R1,#1            ; R1 = - addr. of StackMax
08                      ADD     R1,R1,R6            ; R6 = StackPointer
09                      BRz     Overflow
0A                      ADD     R6,R6,#-1           ; Adjust StackPointer for PUSH.
0B                      STR     R0,R6,#0            ; The actual PUSH
0C                      LD      R1,PUSH_Save1 ; Restore R1.
0D                      AND     R5,R5,#0            ; R5 <-- success
0E                      RET
0F      Overflow        LEA     R0,OverflowMsg
10                      PUTS
11                      LD      R1,PUSH_Save1 ; Restore R1.
12                      AND     R5,R5,#0
13                      ADD     R5,R5,#1            ; R5 <-- failure
14                      RET
15      PUSH_Save1      .BLKW   #1
16      OverflowMsg     .FILL   x000A
17                      .STRINGZ "Error: Stack is Full."
18      PUSH_StackMax   .FILL   StackMax
```

Figure 10.18   The calculator's PUSH routine.

```
01    ; This subroutine calls BinarytoASCII to convert the 2's complement
02    ; number on the top of the stack into an ASCII character string, and
03    ; then calls PUTS to display that number on the screen.
04    OpDisplay          ST      R0,OpDisplay_Save0
05                       ST      R5,OpDisplay_Save5
06                       ST      R7,OpDisplay_Save7
07                       JSR     POP             ; R0 gets the value to be displayed.
08                       ADD     R5,R5,#0
09                       BRp     OpDisplay_DONE  ; POP failed, nothing on the stack.
0A                       JSR     BinarytoASCII
0B                       LD      R0,NewlineChar
0C                       OUT
0D                       LD      R0,OpDisplay_ASCIIBUFF
0E                       PUTS
0F                       ADD     R6,R6,#-1       ; Push displayed number back on stack.
10    OpDisplay_DONE     LD      R0,OpDisplay_Save0
11                       LD      R5,OpDisplay_Save5
12                       LD      R7,OpDisplay_Save7
13                       RET
14    NewlineChar            .FILL    x000A
15    OpDisplay_ASCIIBUFF .FILL    ASCIIBUFF
16    OpDisplay_Save0        .BLKW    #1
17    OpDisplay_Save5        .BLKW    #1
18    OpDisplay_Save7        .BLKW    #1
```

Figure 10.19   The calculator's display routine.

```
01 ;
02 ; This routine clears the stack by resetting the stack pointer (R6).
03 ;
04 OpClear             LD    R6,OpClear_StackBase  ; Initialize the Stack Pointer.
05                     ADD   R6,R6,#1              ; R6 = StackBase + 1 --> empty stack
06                     RET
07 OpClear_StackBase .FILL StackBase
```

Figure 10.20   The OpClear routine.

Exercises

10.1 Describe, in your own words, how the Multiply step of the OpMult algorithm in Figure 10.14 works. How many instructions are executed to perform the Multiply step? Express your answer in terms of n, the value of the multiplier. (*Note:* If an instruction executes five times, it contributes five to the total count.) Write a program fragment that performs the Multiply step in fewer instructions if the value of the multiplier is less than 25. How many?

10.2 Correct Figure 10.1 so that it will add two single-digit positive integers and produce a single-digit positive sum. Assume that the two digits being added do in fact produce a single-digit sum.

10.3 Modify Figure 10.1, assuming that the input numbers are one-digit positive hex numbers. Assume that the two hex digits being added together do in fact produce a single hex-digit sum.

10.4   Figure 10.4 provides an algorithm for converting ASCII strings to binary values. Suppose the decimal number is arbitrarily long. Rather than store a table of 10 values for the thousands-place digit, another table for the 10 ten-thousands-place digit, and so on, design an algorithm to do the conversion without resorting to any tables whatsoever.

10.5   The code in Figure 10.4 converts a decimal number represented as ASCII digits into binary. Extend this code to also convert a hexadecimal number represented in ASCII into binary. If the number is preceded by an x, then the subsequent ASCII digits (three at most) represent a hex number; otherwise, it is decimal.

10.6   The algorithm of Figure 10.5 always produces a string of four characters independent of the sign and magnitude of the integer being converted. Devise an algorithm that eliminates unnecessary characters in common representations, that is, an algorithm that does not store leading 0s nor a leading + sign.

10.7   What does the following LC-3 program do?

```
            .ORIG     x3000
            LEA       R6, STACKBASE
            LEA       R0, PROMPT
            TRAP      x22            ; PUTS
            AND       R1, R1, #0
LOOP        TRAP      x20            ; IN
            TRAP      x21
            ADD       R3, R0, #-10   ; Check for newline
            BRz       INPUTDONE
            JSR       PUSH
            ADD       R1, R1, #1
            BRnzp     LOOP
INPUTDONE   ADD       R1, R1, #0
            BRz       DONE
LOOP2       JSR       POP
            TRAP      x21
            ADD       R1, R1, #-1
            BRp       LOOP2
DONE        TRAP      x25            ; HALT

PUSH        ADD       R6, R6, #-2
            STR       R0, R6, #0
            RET

POP         LDR       R0, R6, #0
            ADD       R6, R6, #2
            RET
PROMPT      .STRINGZ  ''Please enter a sentence: ''
STACKSPAC   .BLKW #50
STACKBASE   .FILL #0
            .END
```

★**10.8** The calculator program assumes that if the user did not type one of the characters X,C,+,−,*,D, then it must be pushing a value and so executes BRnzp PushValue. Modify the program so it is more robust; that is, if the user typed something other than a digit, the main program would load R0 with the ASCII code for X, and branch to Test. If the user typed a digit, the main program would branch to PushValue.

★**10.9** For the calculator program in Exercise 10.8, improve the robustness by modifying PushValue to make sure all the characters typed are digits.

11 Introduction to C/C++ Programming

11.1 Our Objective

Congratulations, and welcome to the second half of the book! We've just completed an introduction to the basic underlying structure of modern computing devices. Be it on a smartphone or in a smart car, the underlying mechanisms for processing digital data are very much the same. With these foundational concepts solidly in place, we are now well prepared to explore programming in a high-level programming language.

In the second half of this book, we will discuss high-level programming concepts in the context of the C and C++ programming languages. At every step, with every new high-level concept, we will be able to make a connection to the lower levels of the digital system. Our perspective is that nothing should be left abstract or mysterious. If we can deconstruct new concepts into operations carried out by the underlying layers, we become more proficient developers and engineers who are better at building new hardware and software systems.

Let's begin with a quick overview of the first half. In the first ten chapters, we described the LC-3, a simple computing architecture that has all the important characteristics of a more complex, real system. A basic idea behind the LC-3 (and indeed, behind all modern digital systems) is that simple elements are systematically interconnected to form elements with more complex capabilities. MOS transistors are connected to build logic gates. Logic gates are used to build memory and data path elements. Memory and data path elements are interconnected to build the LC-3. This systematic connection of simple elements to create something more sophisticated is an important concept that is pervasive throughout computing, not only in hardware design but also in software design. It is this construction principle that enables us to build digital computing systems that are, as a whole, mind-bogglingly complex.

After describing the hardware of the LC-3, we programmed it in the 1s and 0s of its native machine language. Having gotten a taste of the error-prone and unnatural process of programming in machine language, we quickly moved to the more user-friendly LC-3 assembly language. We described how to decompose a programming problem systematically into pieces that could be easily coded on the LC-3. We examined how low-level TRAP subroutines perform commonly needed tasks, such as input and output, on behalf of the programmer. Systematic decomposition and subroutines are prevalent design paradigms for software. We will continue to see examples of these concepts before we are through.

In this half of the book, our primary objectives are to introduce fundamental high-level programming constructs—variables, control structures, functions, arrays, pointers, recursion, simple data structures—and to teach a good problem-solving methodology for attacking programming problems. Our primary vehicles for doing so are the C and C++ programming languages.

It is not our objective to provide complete coverage of C or C++. Both C and C++ are vast programming languages (particularly C++) that have evolved over decades to support the building of large-scale software. Billions of lines of code have been written in these languages. Some of the most widely used apps, cloud services, and devices are built using C or C++. These languages contain many features that enable stable, maintainable, scalable software development by teams of developers, but it is not necessary to cover many of these features for a first exposure to these languages.

Our objective will be to explore the **core** elements of C initially, and later C++. These core elements are the entry points of these languages, and they will enable us to write interesting and challenging programs consisting of 100 or so lines of code contained in a single file.

We must start somewhere. So in this chapter, we make the transition from programming in low-level assembly language to high-level language programming in C. The C and C++ programming languages have a fascinating history. We'll explore how and why these languages came about and why they are so widely popular even nearly 50 years after their introduction. We'll dive headfirst into C by examining a simple example program. Let us begin!

11.2 Bridging the Gap

It is almost always the software that enables a digital system to do its thing. The hardware provides the general fabric, and the software provides the specific capabilities. In devices we might not consider to be software-driven, such as a smart speaker or Bluetooth headphones, there is a large body of software embedded in the device to implement its features. It's the software that animates the device.

Enabling these sophisticated capabilities requires larger and more complex bodies of software. A typical smartphone app might consist of hundreds of thousands of lines of code, a web browser several million, and the code to power a modern automobile (nonautonomous) might range in the hundreds of millions of lines. Over time, from generation to generation, the software needed to power these devices has grown in complexity. As the underlying hardware becomes faster and our demand for additional capabilities grows, we expect the amount of software needed to continue to grow as well. Examine Figure 11.1. It provides a graphical view of the sizes of software systems for various applications.

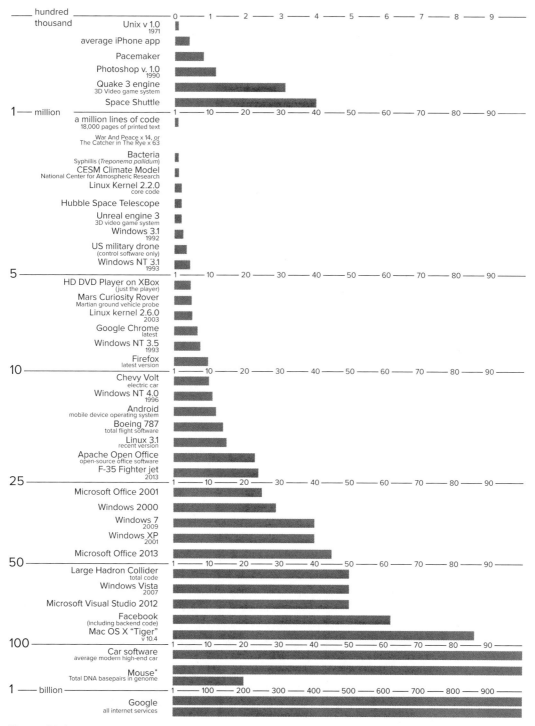

Figure 11.1   The size in estimated lines of code of various computing applications. Certain applications require large bodies of code. And, looking at specific items, such as the Windows operating system, we can see that their complexity grows with each new version. Codebases: Millions of Line of Code, concept and design by David McCandless, research by Pearl Doughty-White and Miriam Quick. Informationisbeautiful.net, September 24, 2015. David McCandless@informationisbeautiful.net. Used with permission.

Programming languages such as C and C++ were created for one primary purpose: to increase programmer productivity. The most commonly used languages enable teams of programmers to more rapidly and maintainably develop correctly working code. Without effective programming languages and corresponding development environments, our ability to create these incredible devices would be severely diminished. Just as building a 100-story skyscraper or a Boeing 787 aircraft is an engineering feat requiring their own sets of technologies and tools, so are developing and maintaining a web service requiring ten million lines of code.

Clearly, LC-3 assembly language isn't going to be the language of choice for developing most real-world software (nor are the assembly languages for x86 or ARM, which are the two most widespread instruction set architectures today, powering nearly all of our PCs, servers, and mobile devices). But it is the case that whatever the development language, C or C++ or Java or Python, the code is ultimately, and automatically, translated into the instruction set of the underlying hardware (be it ARM or x86 or LC-3). So the conceptual process here is that the programming language enables us humans to express code in a much more human-friendly way and in a manner that can be automatically, and unambiguously, translated into a machine-executable form. Ideally we might wish to express things in a human language, but we know how ambiguous and error-prone that would be. So we choose more precise, machine-oriented languages like C and C++.

As we made the transition from LC-3 machine language in Chapters 5 and 6 to LC-3 assembly language in Chapter 7, you no doubt noticed and appreciated how assembly language simplified programming the LC-3. The 1s and 0s became mnemonics, and memory addresses became symbolic labels. Both instructions and memory addresses took on a form more comfortable for the human than for the machinery. The assembler filled some of the *gap* between the algorithm level and the ISA level in the levels of transformation (see Figure 1.6). We would like the language level to fill more of that gap. High-level languages do just that. They help make the job of programming easier. Let's look at some ways in which they help.

• **High-level languages help manage the values upon which we are computing.** When programming in machine language, if we want to keep track of the iteration count of a loop, we need to set aside a memory location or a register in which to store the counter value. To update the counter, we need to remember the spot where we last stored it, load it, operate, and store it back in that location. The process is easier in assembly language because we can assign a meaningful label to the counter's memory location. In a higher-level language such as C, the programmer simply gives the value a meaningful symbolic name and the programming language takes care of allocating storage for it and performing the appropriate data movement operations whenever we refer to it in our code. Since most programs contain lots of values, having such a convenient way to handle these values is critical to enhancing programmer productivity.

• **High-level languages provide a human-friendly way to express computation.** Most humans are more comfortable describing the interaction of objects in the real world than describing the interaction of objects such as integers, characters, and floating point numbers in the digital world. Because of their human-friendly orientation, high-level languages enable the programmer to be more expressive. In a high-level language, the programmer can express complex tasks with a smaller amount of code, with the code itself looking more like a human language. For example, if we wanted to calculate the area of a triangle in C, we would write:

```
area = 0.5 * base * height;
```

Here's another example: We often write code to test a condition and do something if the condition is true or do something else if the condition is false. In high-level languages, such common tasks can be simply stated in an English-like form. For example, if we want to get(Umbrella) if the condition isItCloudy is true, otherwise get(Sunglasses) if it is false, then in C we would use the following *control structure*:

```
if (isItCloudy)
   get(Umbrella);
else
   get(Sunglasses);
```

This expressiveness enables us to achieve more with fewer lines than with assembly code. And this dramatically enhances our productivity as programmers.

• **High-level languages provide an abstraction of the underlying hardware.** High-level languages provide a uniform programmer interface independent of underlying hardware. And this provides two distinct advantages. First, our code becomes *portable*. C or C++ or Java code can be easily and efficiently targeted for a variety of different devices, independent of their hardware. Code written directly in assembly language takes advantage of the specifics of a particular hardware system and isn't as easy to run on different hardware. It's easy to understand why portability is important: An app developer who has written an app for Android will want to quickly port the app to iOS to take advantage of the large base of Apple devices.

The second advantage is that we use operations that aren't natively supported by the hardware. For example, in the LC-3, there is no single instruction that performs an integer multiplication. Instead, an LC-3 assembly language programmer must write a small piece of code to perform multiplication. The set of operations supported by a high-level language is usually larger than the set supported by the ISA. The language will generate the necessary code to carry out the operation whenever the programmer uses it. The programmer can concentrate on the actual programming task knowing that these high-level operations will be performed correctly and without having to deal with the low-level implementation.

• **High-level languages enhance maintainability.** Since common control structures are expressed using simple, English-like statements, the program itself becomes easier to read and therefore easier for others to modify and fix. One can look at a program in a high-level language, notice loops and decision constructs, and understand the code with less effort than with a program written in assembly language. No doubt you've had to get reacquainted with your own LC-3 assembly code after spending even a couple of hours away from it. It's no fun! Often as programmers, we are given the task of debugging or building upon someone else's code. If the organization of the language is human-friendly to begin with, then understanding code in that language is a much simpler task.

- **Many high-level languages provide safeguards against bugs.** By making the programmer adhere to a stricter set of rules, the language can make checks as the program is translated or as it is executed. If certain rules or conditions are violated, an error message will direct the programmer to the spot in the code where the bug is likely to exist. In this manner, the language helps programmers to get their programs working more quickly.

11.3 Translating High-Level Language Programs

Just as LC-3 assembly language programs need to be translated (or more specifically, assembled) into machine language, so must all programs written in high-level languages. After all, the underlying hardware can only execute machine code. How this translation is done depends on the design of the particular high-level language. One translation technique is called *interpretation*. With interpretation, a translation program called an *interpreter* reads in the high-level language program and performs the operations indicated by the programmer. The high-level language program does not directly execute but rather is executed by the interpreter program. The other technique is called *compilation*, and the translator is a *compiler*. The compilation process completely translates the high-level language program into machine language, or a form very close to machine language. An executable image is an output of the compilation process. It can directly execute on the hardware. Keep in mind that both interpreters and compilers are themselves pieces of software running on some device.

11.3.1 Interpretation

If you've ever run Python code, you've run an interpreter. With interpretation, a high-level language program is a set of "commands" for the interpreter program. The interpreter reads in the commands and carries them out as defined by the language. The high-level language program is not directly executed by the hardware but is in fact just input data for the interpreter. The interpreter is a *virtual machine* that executes the program in an isolated sandbox.

Many interpreters translate the high-level language program section by section, one line, command, or subroutine at a time. For example, the interpreter might read a single line of the high-level language program and directly carry out the effects of that line on the underlying hardware. If the line said, "Take the square root of B and store it into C," the interpreter will carry out the square root by issuing the correct stream of instructions in the ISA of the computer to perform square root. Once the current line is processed, the interpreter moves on to the next line and executes it. This process continues until the entire high-level language program is done.

11.3.2 Compilation

With compilation, on the other hand, a high-level language program is translated into machine code that can be directly executed on the hardware. To do this effectively, the compiler must analyze the source program as a larger unit (usually, the entire source file) before producing the translated version. A program need only be compiled once, and it can be executed many times. Many programming languages, including C, C++, and their variants are typically compiled. A compiler *processes* the file (or files) containing the high-level language program and produces an executable image. The compiler does not execute the program (although some sophisticated compilers do execute the program in order to better optimize its performance), but instead only transforms it from the high-level language into the computer's native machine language.

11.3.3 Pros and Cons

There are advantages and disadvantages with either translation technique. With interpretation, developing and debugging a program are usually easier. Interpreters often permit the execution of a program one section (a single line, for example) at a time. This allows the programmer to examine intermediate results and make code modifications on the fly. Often the debugging is easier with interpretation. Interpreted code is more easily portable across different computing systems. However, with interpretation, programs take longer to execute because there is an intermediary, the interpreter, which is actually doing the work. With compilation, the programmer can produce code that executes more quickly and uses memory more efficiently. Since compilation produces more efficient code, most production software tends to be programmed in compiled languages.

11.4 The C/C++ Programming Languages

11.4.1 The Origins of C and C++

Let's cover a bit of history. The C programming language was developed in the early 1970s by Dennis Ritchie at Bell Laboratories. Ritchie was part of a group at Bell Labs developing the Unix operating system. C was created to meet the need for a programming language that was powerful, yet compact enough for a simple compiler to generate efficient code. The computer systems being used by Ritchie and his team had very little memory, so the code generated by the compiler had to be small, and all with a compiler that was small, too! It was this pragmatic bent that gave rise to the popularity of C and propelled it to become one of the most popular production programming languages of its time.

It's remarkable that anything in the computing industry can still be useful 50 years after its introduction. (The authors of this textbook are an exception to this, of course.) The C programming language is going strong, and it is still among the top languages for software development.

In 1979, shortly after C was introduced, a computer scientist named Bjarne Stroustrup, also at Bell Labs, working alongside Ritchie and his colleagues, introduced a set of improvements to the C language that helped programmers to better organize their C code, particularly for large and complex programs. Stroustrup introduced the notion of *classes* to C, and he thereby created the C++ programming language. C++ uses the basic types, syntax, and constructs of C, so it is as efficient as C, but it also has additional features, such as classes and templates, that are essential for creating the building blocks for large-scale coding projects. C has enabled us to create computing applications consisting of hundreds of thousands of lines of code, and C++ has enabled us to create applications with hundreds of millions of lines.

11.4.2 How We Will Approach C and C++

Because of their popularity and close-to-the-metal, low-level approach, C and C++ are the ideal languages for our bottom-up exploration. We'll spend the bulk of our time with the C language in Chapters 11 through 19, and we will introduce some core C++ concepts in Chapter 20. Because C++ is based on C, the C-specific material we cover will help in our understanding of C++.

Both C and C++ are highly developed, heavily evolved languages that support large-scale programming. We will not be covering all aspects of C or C++ in this textbook; instead, we will cover the common core subset that will enable you to write code on the order of hundreds of lines by yourself in a single source code file. Our objective is to give you a grounding in digital systems, hardware, and software. This grounding will be useful in your subsequent courses in data structures and software engineering for more complex software projects.

All of the examples and specific details of C presented in this text are based on a standard version of C called ANSI C, or C18. As with many programming languages, several variants of C have been introduced throughout the years. The American National Standards Institute (ANSI) approves "an unambiguous and machine-independent definition of the language C" in order to standardize the language, promoting portability of C code across different systems and compilers. The most recently adopted version of ANSI C is from 2018 and is thus referred to as C18. Likewise, we'll use ISO C++, often called Standard C++, in our examples involving C++ code.

Many of the new C and C++ concepts we present will be coupled with LC-3 code generated by a hypothetical LC-3 C compiler. In some cases, we will describe what actually happens when this code is executed. Keep in mind that you are not likely to be using an LC-3–based computer but rather one based on a real ISA such as the x86 or ARM. For example, if you are using a Windows-based PC, then it is likely that your compiler will generate x86 code, not LC-3 code. Many of the examples we provide are complete programs that you can compile and execute. For the sake of clearer illustration, some of the examples we provide are not quite complete programs and need to be completed before they can be compiled. In order to keep things straight, we'll refer to these partial code examples as *code segments*.

11.4.3 The Compilation Process

Both C and C++ are compiled languages. The C or C++ compiler follows the typical mode of translation from a source program to an *executable image*. An executable image (refer to Section 7.4.1 for a refresher on this concept) is a machine language representation of a program that is ready to be loaded into memory and executed. The compilation mechanism involves several distinct components, notably the preprocessor, the compiler itself, and the linker. Figure 11.2 shows the overall compilation process for C. Let's briefly take a look at each of the major components.

11.4.3.1 The Preprocessor

As its name implies, the preprocessor "preprocesses" the source program before handing it off to the compiler. The preprocessor scans through the source files (the source files contain the actual C program) looking for and acting upon preprocessor directives. These directives are similar to pseudo-ops in LC-3 assembly language. They instruct the preprocessor to transform the source file in some controlled manner. For example, we can direct the preprocessor to substitute the character string DAYS_THIS_MONTH with the string 30 or direct it to insert the contents of file stdio.h into the source file at the current line. We'll discuss why both of these actions are useful in later chapters. All preprocessor directives begin with a pound sign, #, as the first character. All useful C and C++ programs rely on the preprocessor in some way.

11.4.3.2 The Compiler

After the preprocessor transforms the input source file, the program is ready to be handed over to the compiler. The compiler transforms the preprocessed program into an *object module*. Recall from Section 7.4.2 that an object module is the machine code for one section of the entire program. There are two major phases of compilation: analysis, in which the source program is broken down or *parsed* into its constituent parts, and synthesis, in which a machine code version of the program is generated. It is the job of the analysis phase to read in, parse, and build an internal representation of the original program. The synthesis phase generates machine code and, if directed, tries to optimize this code to execute more quickly and efficiently on the computer on which it will be run. Each of these two phases is typically divided into subphases where specific tasks, such as parsing, register allocation, or instruction scheduling, are accomplished. Some compilers generate assembly code and use an assembler to complete the translation to machine code.

One of the most important internal bookkeeping mechanisms the compiler uses in translating a program is the *symbol table*. A symbol table is the compiler's internal bookkeeping method for keeping track of all the symbolic names the

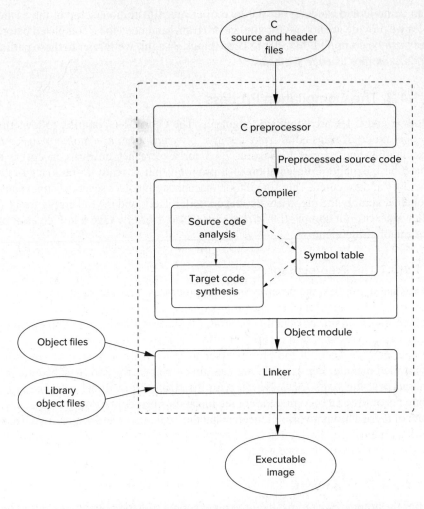

Figure 11.2   The dotted box indicates the overall compilation process—the preprocessor, the compiler, and the linker. The entire process is called compilation even though the compiler is only one part of it. The inputs are C source and header files and various object files. The output is an executable image.

programmer has used in the program. The compiler's symbol table is very similar to the symbol table maintained by the LC-3 assembler (see Section 7.3.3). We'll examine the compiler's symbol table in more detail in Chapter 8.

11.4.3.3 The Linker

The linker takes over after the compiler has translated the source file into object code. It is the linker's job to link together all object modules to form an executable image of the program. The executable image is a version of the program that can be loaded into memory and executed by the underlying hardware. When you click

In this example, the first grouping of statements (lines 24–26) displays a message and prompts the user to input an integer number. Once the user enters a number, the program enters the last statement, which is a `for` loop (a type of iteration construct that we will discuss in Chapter 13). The loop counts downward from the number typed by the user to 0. For example, if the user entered the number 5, the program's output would look as follows:

```
===== Countdown Program =====
Enter a positive integer: 5
5
4
3
2
1
0
```

Notice in this example that many lines of the source code are terminated by semicolons, ;. In C, semicolons are used to terminate declarations and statements; they are necessary for the compiler to parse the program down unambiguously into its constituents.

11.5.2 Formatting, Comments, and Style

C is a free-format language. That is, white space (spaces and tabs and line breaks) between words and between lines within a program does not change the meaning of the program. The programmer is free to structure the program in whatever manner he or she sees fit while obeying the syntactic rules of C. Programmers use this freedom to format the code in a manner that makes it easier to read. In the example program (Figure 11.3), notice that the `for` loop is indented in such a manner that the statement being iterated is easier to identify. Also in the example, notice the use of blank lines to separate different regions of code in the function `main`. These blank lines are not necessary but are used to provide visual separation of the code. Often, statements that together accomplish a larger task are grouped together into a visually identifiable unit.

The C code examples throughout this book use a conventional indentation style typical for C. Styles vary. Programmers sometimes use style as a means of expression. Feel free to define your own style, keeping in mind that the objective is to help convey the meaning of the program through its formatting.

Comments in C are different than in LC-3 assembly language. Comments in C begin with // and proceed through the end of the line. Notice that this example program contains several lines of comments and also source lines with comments at the end of them. Comments in C++ can also begin with the sequence // and extend to the end of the line, and this is one of the many ways in which the two languages are similar.

Every programming language provides a way for the programmer to express comments. These comments enable programmers to describe in human terms what their code does. Proper commenting of code is an important part of the software development process. Good comments enhance code readability, allowing someone not familiar with the code to understand it more quickly. Since programming tasks often involve working in teams, code very often gets shared or borrowed between programmers. In order to work effectively on a programming team, or to write code that is worth sharing, you must adopt a good commenting style early on.

One aspect of good commenting style is to provide information at the beginning of each source file that describes the code contained within it, the date it was last modified, and by whom. Furthermore, each function (see function `main` in the example) should have a brief description of what the function accomplishes, along with a description of its inputs and outputs. Also, comments are usually interspersed within the code to explain the intent of the various sections of the code. But over-commenting can be detrimental because it can clutter up your code, making it harder to read. In particular, watch out for comments that provide no additional information beyond what is obvious from the code.

11.5.3 The C Preprocessor

We briefly mentioned the preprocessor in Section 11.4.3. Recall that it transforms the original source program before it is handed off to the compiler. Our simple example contains two commonly used preprocessor directives: #define and #include. The C and C++ examples in this book rely only on these two directives. The #define directive is a simple yet powerful directive that instructs the preprocessor to replace occurrences of any text that matches X with text Y. That is, the X gets *substituted* with Y. In the example, the #define causes the text STOP to be substituted with the text 0. So the following source line

```
for (counter = startPoint; counter >= STOP; counter--)
```

is transformed (internally, only between the preprocessor and compiler) into

```
for (counter = startPoint; counter >= 0; counter--)
```

Why is this helpful? Often, the #define directive is used to create fixed values within a program. Following are several examples.

```
#define NUMBER_OF_STUDENTS   25
#define MAX_LENGTH           80
#define LENGTH_OF_GAME       300
#define PRICE_OF_FUEL        1.49
#define COLOR_OF_EYES        brown
```

So for example, we can symbolically refer to the price of fuel as PRICE_OF_FUEL. If the price of fuel were to change, we would simply modify the definition of PRICE_OF_FUEL and the preprocessor would handle the actual substitution throughout the code for us. This can be very convenient—if the cost of fuel was used heavily within a program, we would only need to modify one line in the source code to change the price throughout the code. Notice that the last example is slightly different from the others. In this example, one string of characters COLOR_OF_EYES is being substituted for another, brown. The common C and C++ programming style is to use uppercase for the name being substituted.

The other directive we'll encounter is the #include directive. It instructs the preprocessor literally to insert another source file into the code at the point where the #include appears. Essentially, the #include directive itself is replaced by the contents of another file. At this point, the usefulness of this command may not be completely apparent to you, but as we progress deeper into the C and C++ languages, you will understand how *header files* can be used to hold #defines and declarations that are useful among multiple source files.

We'll often encounter the following example: #include <stdio.h> in our C programs. All C programs that perform typical input and output must include C's input/output library's header file stdio.h. This file defines some relevant information about the I/O functions in the library. The preprocessor directive #include <stdio.h> is used to insert the header file before compilation begins.

There are two variations of the #include directive:

```
#include <stdio.h>
#include "program.h"
```

The first variation uses angle brackets (< >) around the filename. This tells the preprocessor that the header file can be found in a predefined system directory. This is usually determined by the configuration of the system, and it contains many common system-related header files, such as stdio.h. Often we want to include header files we have created ourselves for the particular program we are writing. The second variation, using double quotes (" ") around the filename, tells the preprocessor that the header file can be found in the same directory as the C source file or in some other directory known to the compiler.

Notice that none of the preprocessor macros end with a semicolon. Since #define and #include are preprocessor directives and not C statements, they are not required to be terminated by semicolons.

11.5.4 Input and Output

We close this chapter by describing how to perform input and output from within a C program. In C, I/O is accomplished through a set of I/O functions. We describe these functions at a high level now and save the details for Chapter 18, when we have introduced enough background material to understand C I/O down to a low level. Since all useful programs perform some form of I/O, getting familiar with the I/O capabilities of C is an important first step.

The C I/O functions are similar to the IN and OUT trap routines provided by the LC-3 system software. Three lines of the example program in Figure 11.3 perform output using the C library function printf or *print formatted* (refer to lines 24, 25, and 30). The function printf performs output to the standard output device, which is typically the display device. It requires a *format string* in which we provide two things: (1) text to print out and (2) some specifications on how to print out program values within that text. For example, the statement

```
printf("43 is a prime number.");
```

prints out the following text to the output device:

```
43 is a prime number.
```

In addition to text, it is often useful to print out values generated within the code. Specifications within the format string indicate how we want these values to be printed out. Let's examine a few examples.

```
printf("%d is a prime number.", 43);
```

This first example contains the format specification %d in its format string. It causes the value listed after the format string to be embedded in the output as a decimal number in place of the %d. The resulting output would be

```
43 is a prime number.
```

The following examples show other variants of the same printf.

```
printf("43 plus 59 in decimal is %d.", 43 + 59);
printf("43 plus 59 in hexadecimal is %x.", 43 + 59);
printf("43 plus 59 as a character is %c.", 43 + 59);
```

In the first example above, the format specification causes the value 102 to be embedded in the text because the result of "43 + 59" is printed as a decimal number. In the next example, the format specification %x causes 66 (because 102 equals x66) to be embedded in the text. Similarly, in the third example, the format specification of %c displays the value interpreted as an ASCII character that, in this case, would be lowercase f. The output of this statement would be

```
43 plus 59 as a character is f.
```

What is important is that the binary pattern being supplied to printf after the format string is the same for all three statements. Here, printf interprets the binary pattern 0110 0110 (decimal 102) as a decimal number in the first example, as a hexadecimal number in the second example, and as an ASCII character in the third. The C output function printf converts the bit pattern into the proper sequence of ASCII characters based on the format specifications we provide it. All format specifications begin with the percent sign, %.

The final example demonstrates a very common and powerful use of printf.

```
printf("The wind speed is %d km/hr.", windSpeed);
```

Here, a value generated during the execution of the program, in this case the variable windSpeed, is output as a decimal number. The value displayed depends on the value of windSpeed when this line of code is executed. So if windSpeed were to equal 2 when the statement containing printf is executed, the following output would result:

```
The wind speed is 2 km/hr.
```

If we want line breaks to appear, we must put them explicitly within the format string in the places we want them to occur. New lines, tabs, and other special characters require the use of a special backslash (\) sequence. For example, to print a new line character (and thus cause a line break), we use the special sequence \n. Consider the following statements:

```
printf("%d is a prime number.\n", 43);
printf("43 plus 59 in decimal is %d.\n", 43 + 59);
printf("The wind speed is %d km/hr.\n", windSpeed);
```

Notice that each format string ends by printing the new line character \n, so each subsequent printf will begin on a new line. The output generated by these five statements would look as follows:

```
43 is a prime number.
43 plus 59 in decimal is 102.
The wind speed is 2 km/hr.
```

In our sample program in Figure 11.3, printf appears three times in the source. The first two versions display only text and no values (thus, they have no format specifications). The third version prints out the value of variable counter. Generally speaking, we can display as many values as we like within a single printf. The number of format specifications (e.g., %d) must equal the number of values that follow the format string.

Question: What happens if we replace the third printf in the example program with the following? The expression "startPoint - counter" calculates the value of startPoint minus the value of counter.

```
printf("%d %d\n", counter, startPoint - counter);
```

Let's turn our attention to the input function scanf. The function scanf performs input from the standard input device, which is typically the keyboard. It requires a format string (similar to the one required by printf) and a list of variables into which the values input from the keyboard should be stored. The function scanf reads input from the keyboard and, according to the conversion characters in the format string, converts the input and assigns the converted values to the variables listed.

In the example program in Figure 11.3, we use scanf to read in a single decimal number using the format specification %d. Recall from our discussion on LC-3 keyboard input that the value received via the keyboard is in ASCII. The format specification %d informs scanf to expect a sequence of *numeric* ASCII keystrokes (i.e., the digits 0 to 9). This sequence is interpreted as a decimal number and converted into an integer. The resulting binary pattern will be stored in the variable called startPoint. The function scanf automatically performs type conversions (in this case, from ASCII to integer) for us! The format specification %d is one of several that can be used with scanf. There are specifications to read in a single character, a floating point value, an integer expressed as a hexadecimal value, and so forth.

One important point to note about scanf : Variables that are being modified by the scanf function (e.g., startPoint) must be preceded by the & (ampersand) character. We will discuss why this is required when we discuss pointers in Chapter 16.

Following are several more examples of scanf.

```
// Reads in a character and stores it in nextChar
scanf("%c", &nextChar);

// Reads in a floating point number into radius
scanf("%f", &radius);

// Reads two decimal numbers into length and width
scanf("%d %d", &length, &width);
```

11.6 Summary

In this chapter, we have introduced some key characteristics of high-level programming languages, C and C++ in particular, and provided an initial exposure to the C programming language. We covered the following major topics:

• **High-Level Programming Languages.** High-level languages aim to make the programming process easier by providing human-friendly abstractions for the bits and memory that a digital system natively operates upon. Because computers can only execute machine code, programs in high-level languages must be translated using the process of compilation or interpretation into a form native to the hardware.

• **The C and C++ Programming Languages.** C and C++ are ideal languages for a bottom-up exposure to computing because of their low-level, close-to-the-metal nature. They are also two of the most popular programming languages in use today. The C/C++ compilation process involves a preprocessor, a compiler, and a linker.

• **Our First C Program.** We provided a very simple program to illustrate several basic features of C programs. Comments, indentation, and style can help convey the meaning of a program to someone trying to understand the code. Many C programs use the preprocessor macros #define and #include. The execution of a C program begins at the function main, which itself consists of variable declarations and statements. Finally, I/O in C can be accomplished using the library functions printf and scanf.

Exercises

11.1 Describe some problems or inconveniences you encountered when programming in lower-level languages.

11.2 How do higher-level languages help reduce the tedium of programming in lower-level languages?

11.3 What are some disadvantages to programming in a higher-level language?

11.4 Compare and contrast the execution process of an interpreter with the execution process of a compiled binary. What effect does interpretation have on performance?

11.5 A language is portable if its source code can run on different computing systems, say with different ISAs. What makes interpreted languages more portable than compiled languages?

11.6 A command line interface is an interpreter. Why can't it be a compiler?

11.7 Is the LC-3 simulator a compiler or an interpreter?

11.8 Another advantage of compilation over interpretation is that a compiler can optimize code more thoroughly. Since a compiler can examine the entire program when generating machine code, it can reduce the amount of computation by analyzing what the program is trying to do.

The following algorithm performs some very straightforward arithmetic based on values typed at the keyboard. It outputs a single result.

1. Get W from the keyboard
2. X·W + W
3. Y·X + X
4. Z·Y + Y
5. Print Z to the screen

   a. An interpreter would execute the program statement by statement. In total, five statements would execute. If the underlying ISA were capable of all arithmetic operations (i.e., addition, subtraction, multiplication, division), at least how many operations would be needed to carry out this program? State what the operations would be.

   b. A compiler would analyze the entire program before generating machine code, and it would possibly optimize the code. If the underlying ISA were capable of all arithmetic operations (i.e., addition, subtraction, multiplication, division), at least how many operations would be needed to carry out this program? State what the operations would be.

11.9 For this exercise, refer to Figure 11.2.

   a. Describe the input to the C preprocessor.
   b. Describe the input to the C compiler.
   c. Describe the input to the linker.

11.10 What happens if we change the second-to-last line of the program in Figure 11.3 from `printf("%d\n", counter);` to:

   a. `printf("%c\n", counter + 'A');`
   b. `printf("%d\n%d\n", counter, startPoint + counter);`
   c. `printf("%x\n", counter);`

11.11   The function scanf reads in a character from the keyboard, and the function printf prints it out. What do the following two statements accomplish?

```
scanf("%c", &nextChar);
printf("%d\n", nextChar);
```

11.12   The following lines of C code appear in a program. What will be the output of each printf statement?

```
#define LETTER '1'
#define ZERO 0
#define NUMBER 123
printf("%c", 'a');
printf("x%x", 12288);
printf("$%d.%c%d n", NUMBER, LETTER, ZERO);
```

11.13   Describe a program (at this point, we do not expect you to be able to write working C code) that reads a decimal number from the keyboard and prints out its hexadecimal equivalent.

CHAPTER

12 Variables and Operators

12.1 Introduction

In this chapter, we cover two basic concepts of high-level language programming, variables and operators. *Variables* hold the values upon which a program acts, and *operators* are the language constructs for manipulating these values. Variables and operators together allow the programmer to more easily express the work that a program is to carry out.

The following line of C code is a statement that involves both variables and operators. In this statement, the addition operator + is used to add 3 to the original value of the variable score. This new value is then assigned using the assignment operator = back to score. If score was equal to 7 before this statement was executed, it would equal 10 afterwards.

```
score = score + 3;
```

In the first part of this chapter, we'll take a closer look at variables in the C programming language. Variables in C are straightforward: The four most basic flavors are integers, characters, floating point numbers, and boolean values (i.e., variables that take on the value 0 or 1). After variables, we'll cover C's rich set of operators, providing plenty of code examples to illustrate their operations. One unique feature of our approach is that we can connect these high-level concepts back to the lower levels. In the third part of the chapter, we'll examine the compiler translations of C code with variables and operators. We close this chapter by writing some simple C code involving variables and operators.

12.2 Variables

A value is any data item upon which a program performs an operation. Examples of values include the iteration counter for a loop, an input value entered by a user, or the partial sum of a series of numbers that are being added together.

Because keeping track of them requires considerable programmer effort, high-level languages make the process of managing them easier on the programmer. High-level languages enable the programmer to refer to values *symbolically*, by a name rather than the storage location where the value resides. To operate on the value, referring to the symbolic name suffices, and the actual storage location is abstracted away. The compiler generates the full set of data movement operations to access the value from wherever it resides in memory. The programmer can focus on writing the logic of the program without concern about where values are currently stored. In high-level languages, these symbolically named values are called *variables*.

Variables are the most basic type of *memory object*. We'll elaborate on that concept as we progress though the C and C++ programming languages. For now, an object is a named unit of data stored in memory with certain characteristics and behaviors. The evolution of C into C++ and to languages such as Java and C# extends our ability to create and manage more general forms of objects in our code. But for now, let's focus on the simplest form of memory objects: variables.

In order to properly track the variables in a program, the C or C++ compiler needs to know several characteristics about each variable, which are ultimately provided by the programmer. The compiler needs to know the symbolic name of the variable. It needs to know what type of information the variable will contain. It needs to know where in the code the variable will be accessible. In C and C++, this information is provided by the variable's *declaration*.

Let's look at an example. The following declares a variable called echo that will contain an integer value.

```
int echo;
```

Based on this declaration, the compiler reserves enough memory for echo to hold an integer. Whenever echo is referred to in the subsequent C code, the compiler generates the appropriate machine code to access it. (In some cases, the compiler can optimize the program such that echo is stored in a register and therefore does not require a memory location, but that is a subject for later.)

12.2.1 Four Basic Data Types

Here's a concept that we've seen repeatedly, in various forms: The meaning of a particular bit pattern depends on the data type imposed on the pattern. For example, the binary pattern 0110 0110 might represent the lowercase f or it might represent the decimal number 102, depending on whether we treat the pattern as an ASCII data type or as a 2's complement integer data type. A variable's declaration informs the compiler about the variable's type. The compiler uses a variable's type information to allocate a proper amount of storage for the variable. Also, type indicates how operations on the variable are to be performed at the machine level. For instance, performing an addition on two integer variables can be done on the LC-3 with one ADD instruction. If the two variables are of floating point type, the LC-3 compiler would generate a sequence of instructions to perform the addition because no single LC-3 instruction performs a floating point addition.

C supports four basic data types: integers, characters, floating point numbers, and boolean values. Variables of these types can be created with the type specifiers `int`, `char`, `float` (or `double`), and `_Bool` (or `bool`).

int

The following line of code declares an integer variable called `numberOfSeconds`. This declaration causes the compiler to allocate storage for one integer's worth of data (in the case of the LC-3, one memory location).

```
int numberOfSeconds;
```

It should be no surprise that variables of integer type are often used in programs. They conveniently represent the discrete real-world data we want our programs to process. If we wanted to represent time in seconds, for example, an integer variable might be appropriate. In an application that tracks whale migration, an integer might be useful to represent the sizes of pods of gray whales seen off the California coast. Integers are also useful for program control. An integer can be useful as the iteration counter for a counter-controlled loop.

The internal representation and range of values of an `int` depend on the ISA of the underlying hardware. In the LC-3, for example, an `int` is a 16-bit 2's complement integer that can represent values between −32,768 and +32,767. On an x86-based system, an `int` is likely to be a 32-bit 2's complement number that can represent values between −2,147,483,648 and +2,147,483,647. In most cases, an `int` is a 2's complement integer in the word length of the underlying ISA.

char

The `char` type specifier declares a variable whose data value represents a character. In the following example, the first declaration creates a variable named `lock`. The second one declares `key`. The second declaration is slightly different; it also contains an *initializer*. In C, any variable can be set to an initial value directly in its declaration. In this example, the variable `key` will have the initial value of the ASCII code for uppercase *Q*. Also notice that the uppercase *Q* is surrounded by single quotes, `' '`. In C, characters that are to be interpreted as ASCII *literals* are surrounded by single quotes. What about `lock`? What initial value will it have? We'll examine this question in depth later in this chapter.

```
char lock;
char key = 'Q';
```

Although eight bits are sufficient to hold an ASCII character, for purposes of simplifying the examples in this textbook, all `char` variables will occupy 16 bits on the LC-3. That is, `chars`, like `ints`, will each occupy one LC-3 memory location.

float / double

The type specifier `float` declares a single-precision floating point number, and the type specifier `double` declares a double-precision floating point number. The representation of these numbers is similar to what we examined in Section 2.7.1.

Floating point numbers allow us to conveniently deal with numbers that have fractional components or numbers that are very large or very small. Recall from our discussion in Section 2.7.1 that at the lowest level, a floating point number is a bit pattern where one of the bits represents the sign of the number, several other bits represent the mantissa, and the remaining bits represent the exponent. Here are three examples of variables of type `double`:

```
double costPerLiter;
double electronsPerSecond;
double averageTemp;
```

As with `int`s and `char`s, we can also optionally initialize a floating point variable within its declaration. Floating point values are a little more complicated than integers and characters, though. Floating point *literals* are represented containing either a decimal point or an exponent, or both, as demonstrated in the example code that follows. The exponent is signified by the character *e* or *E* and can be positive or negative. It represents the power of ten by which the fractional part (the part that precedes the *e* or *E*) is multiplied. Note that the exponent must be an integer value.

```
double twoPointOne = 2.1;          // This is 2.1
double twoHundredTen = 2.1E2;      // This is 210.0
double twoHundred = 2E2;           // This is 200.0
double twoTenths = 2E-1;           // This is 0.2
double minusTwoTenths = -2E-1;     // This is -0.2
double extTemp = -0.2;             // This is -0.2
```

The precision of a floating point number depends on the number of bits of the representation allocated to the fraction. In C, depending on the compiler and the ISA, a `double` may have more bits allocated for the fraction than a `float`, but never fewer. The size of the `double` is dependent upon the ISA and the compiler. Usually, a `double` is 64 bits long and a `float` is 32 bits in compliance with the IEEE 754 floating point standard.

_Bool / bool

The `_Bool` type is a more recent addition to the C language and is now part of the ANSI standard. A variable of the `_Bool` type takes on the values 0 or 1, representing a value that can be false or true. This type was supported natively by C++, and later supported by C, and it provides a representation for a commonly occurring value in our code.

The C type specifier for a boolean type is `_Bool`. A more convenient way to accomplish the same is to use the use the `bool` specifier. To do so, we need to include the `stdbool.h` header file. This header file also defines true to symbolically map to 1, and false to map to 0.

```
_Bool flag = 1;       // Initialized to 1 or true
bool test = false;    // Initialized to false, which is symbolically
                      // defined to 0.  Requires stdbool.h
```

12.2.2 Choosing Identifiers

Most high-level languages have flexible rules for the variable names, or more generally, *identifiers*, that can be chosen by the programmer. C allows you to create identifiers composed of letters of the alphabet, digits, and the underscore character, _. Only letters and the underscore character, however, can be used to begin an identifier. Uppercase is distinct from lowercase, so Capital is different from capital. As for length, ANSI C places no limit on the length of an identifier. Also, identifiers cannot be *keywords*—words that already have reserved meaning within the language (words like int, for example).

Here are several tips on standard C naming conventions: Variables beginning with an underscore (e.g., _index_) conventionally are used only in special library code. Variables are almost never declared in all uppercase letters. The convention of all uppercase is used solely for symbolic values created using the preprocessor directive #define. Programmers like to visually partition variables that consist of multiple words. In this book, we use uppercase (e.g., wordsPerSecond). Other programmers prefer underscores (e.g., words_per_second).

Giving variables meaningful names is important for writing good code. Variable names should be chosen to reflect a characteristic of the value they represent, allowing the programmer to more easily recall what the value is used for. For example, a value representing the speed of an object could be named metersPerSecond rather than x.

12.2.3 Scope: Local vs. Global

As we mentioned, a variable's declaration assists the compiler in managing the storage of that variable. In C, a variable's declaration conveys three pieces of information to the compiler: the variable's *identifier*, its *type*, and its *scope*. The first two of these, identifier and type, the C compiler gets explicitly from the variable's declaration. The third piece, scope, the compiler infers from the position of the declaration within the code.

The scope of a variable is the region of the program in which the variable is "alive" and accessible. The good news is that in C, there are only two basic types of scope for a variable. Either the variable is *global* to the entire program, or it is *local*, or private, to a particular block of code.

12.2.3.1 Local Variables

In C, all variables must be declared before they can be used. If a variable is declared within a block, it is visible up through the end of the block. In C, a *block* is any subsection of a program beginning with the open brace character, {, and ending with the closing brace character, }. These variables are *local* to the block in which they are declared.

The following code is a simple C program that gets a number from the keyboard and redisplays it on the screen. The integer variable echo is declared within the block that contains the code for function main. It is only visible to the function main. If the program contained any other functions besides main, the variable would not be accessible from those other functions. ANSI C allows local variables to be declared basically anywhere within the block in which they are in scope, prior to their use. For the examples in this textbook, we will follow a simple, more structured style where variables are declared at the beginning of the block in which they are used.

```c
#include <stdio.h>

int main(void)
{
    int echo;

    scanf("%d", &echo);
    printf("%d\n", echo);
}
```

It is sometimes useful to declare two different variables with the same name within different blocks of the same function. For instance, it might be convenient to use the name count for the counter variable for several different loops within the same program. C allows this, as long as the different variables sharing the same name are declared in separate blocks. Figure 12.1, which we discuss in the next section, provides an example of this.

12.2.3.2 Global Variables

In contrast to local variables, which can only be accessed within the block in which they are declared, global variables can be accessed throughout the

```c
 1 #include <stdio.h>
 2
 3 int globalVar = 2;        // This variable is a global variable
 4
 5 int main(void)
 6 {
 7     int localVar = 3;     // This variable is local to main
 8
 9     printf("globalVar = %d, localVar = %d\n", globalVar, localVar);
10
11     // Creating a new sub-block within main
12     {
13         int localVar = 4; // This local to the sub-block within main
14
15         printf("globalVar = %d, localVar = %d\n", globalVar, localVar);
16     }
17
18     printf("globalVar = %d, localVar = %d\n", globalVar, localVar);
19 }
```

Figure 12.1   A C program that demonstrates nested scope.

program.[1] They retain their storage and values throughout the duration of the program.

Global variables can be tempting to use! They are often an easy solution to various conundrums we encounter when writing code. But even the modest use of globals can introduce problems for large-scale coding projects. Because global variables can be modified from anywhere within the code, they open the door for bugs. They create challenges for code maintenance. They make the code more difficult to extend and modify. For these reasons, production coding rules often restrict the use of global variables. We'll shy away from the use of globals in this textbook.

Let's look at a comprehensive example involving globals and locals. The C program in Figure 12.1 contains a global variable globalVar that can be accessed directly from anywhere in our code. We also have two flavors of local variable, both with the same name: The first localVar declared at line 7 is local to the function main. The second localVar declared at line 13 is local to the sub-block starting at the curly brace at line 12 and extending to line 16. If we compile and execute this code, the output generated looks as follows:

```
globalVar = 2, localVar = 3
globalVar = 2, localVar = 4
globalVar = 2, localVar = 3
```

12.2.3.3 Initialization of Variables

What initial value will a variable have if it has no initializer? In C, by default, local variables start with an undefined value. That is, local variables have garbage values in them, unless we explicitly initialize them in our code. Global variables, in contrast, are initialized to 0. It is standard coding practice to explicitly initialize local variables within their declarations.

12.2.4 More Examples

The following code provides examples of the four basic types discussed in this chapter. Some declarations have no initializers; some do. Notice how floating point and character literals are expressed in C.

```
double width;
double pType = 9.44;
double mass = 6.34E2;
double verySmallAmount = 9.1094E-31;
double veryLargeAmount = 7.334553E102;
int average = 12;
int windChillIndex = -21;
int unknownValue;
int mysteryAmount;
bool flag = false;
char car = 'A';        // single quotes specify a single ASCII character
char number = '4';     // single quotes specify a single ASCII character
```

---

[1]This is a slight simplification. C also allows globals to be global to a particular source file and not the entire program, but this detail is not relevant for our discussion here.

12.3 Operators

C, like many other high-level languages, supports a rich set of operators that allow the programmer to manipulate variables. Some operators perform arithmetic operations, some perform logic functions, and others perform comparisons between values. These operators allow the programmer to express a computation in a more natural, convenient, and compact manner using symbols that we are already accustomed to using. This is much more user-friendly than expressing an operation as a sequence of assembly language instructions!

Given some C code, the compiler's job is to convert it into machine code that the underlying hardware can execute. Our hypothetical LC-3 C compiler must translate whatever operations the program might contain into the LC-3 instruction set—clearly not an easy task given that the LC-3 supports very few native operations (AND, ADD, NOT). To help illustrate this point, we examine the code generated by a simple C statement in which two integers are multiplied together. In the following code segment, x, y, and z are integer variables where x and y are multiplied and the result *assigned* to z.

```
z = x * y;
```

Since there is no single LC-3 instruction to multiply two values, our LC-3 compiler must generate a sequence of code that accomplishes the multiplication of two (possibly negative) integers. One possible manner in which this can be accomplished is by repeatedly adding the value of x to itself a total of y times, as accomplished in the calculator example in Chapter 10.

Figure 12.2 provides the resulting LC-3 code generated by the LC-3 compiler. Assume that R5 contains the memory address where variable x is allocated. Immediately prior to that location is where variable y is allocated (i.e., R5-1), and immediately prior to that is where variable z resides. This allocation is very deliberate and follows a system we will describe later in Section 12.5.2.

```
        AND R0, R0, #0    ; R0 <= 0
        LDR R1, R5, #0    ; load value of x
        LDR R2, R5, #-1   ; load value of y
        BRz DONE          ; if y is zero, we're done
        BRp LOOP          ; if y is positive, start mult

                          ; y is negative
        NOT R1, R1
        ADD R1, R1, #1    ; R1 <= -x

        NOT R2, R2
        ADD R2, R2, #1    ; R2 <= -y (-y is positive)

LOOP    ADD R0, R0, R1    ; Multiply loop
        ADD R2, R2, #-1   ; The result is in R2
        BRp LOOP

DONE    STR R0, R5, #-2   ; z = x * y;
```

Figure 12.2   The LC-3 code for C multiplication.

12.3.1 Expressions and Statements

Before we proceed, let's cover some C syntax. We can combine variables and literal values with operators, such as the multiply operator from the previous example, to form a C *expression*. In the previous example, x * y is an expression. Expressions can be grouped together to form a *statement*. For example, z = x * y; is a statement. Statements in C are like complete sentences in English. Just as a sentence captures a complete thought or action, a C statement expresses a complete unit of work to be carried out by the digital hardware. All single statements in C end with a semicolon character ;. The semicolon terminates the end of a statement in much the same way a punctuation mark terminates a sentence in English. During program execution, statements are executed in order from first to last, starting with the first statement in main.

One or more simple statements plus declarations can be grouped together to form a compound statement, or *block*, by enclosing the declarations and statements within curly braces,{ }. Syntactically, compound statements are equivalent to simple statements.

The following code provides some illustrations.

```
z = x * y;        // This statement accomplishes some work

{                 // This is a compound statement
    a = b + c;
    i = p * r * t;
}

k = k + 1;        // This is another simple statement
```

12.3.2 The Assignment Operator

We've already seen examples of C's assignment operator. Its symbol is the equal sign, =. The operator works by first evaluating the right-hand side of the assignment, and then assigning the value to the *object* (such as a variable) specified on the left-hand side. For example, in the C statement

```
a = b + c;
```

the value of variable a will be set equal to the value of the expression b + c. Notice that even though the arithmetic symbol for equality is the same as the C symbol for assignment, they have different meanings. In mathematics, by using the equal sign, =, one is making the assertion that the right-hand and left-hand expressions are equivalent. In C, using the = operator causes the compiler to generate code that will make the left-hand side change its value to equal the value of the right-hand side. In other words, the left-hand side is *assigned* the value of the right-hand side.

Let's examine what happens when the LC-3 C compiler generates code for a statement containing the assignment operator. The following C statement represents incrementing by 4 the integer variable x.

```
x = x + 4;
```

The LC-3 code for this statement is straightforward. Here, assume R5 contains the address of variable x.

```
LDR R0, R5, #0 ; Get the value of x
ADD R0, R0, #4 ; calculate x + 4
STR R0, R5, #0 ; x = x + 4;
```

In C, all expressions evaluate to a value of a particular type. From the previous example, the expression x + 4 evaluates to an integral value because we are adding an integer 4 to another integer (the variable x). This integer result is then assigned to an integer variable. What would happen if we constructed an expression of mixed type, for example x + 4.3? The general rule in C is that the mixed expressions like this one will be *converted* from integer to floating point. If an expression contains both integer and character types, it will be promoted to integer type. In general, in C shorter types are converted to longer types.

What if we tried to assign an expression of one type to a variable of another, for example x = x + 4.3? In C, the type of a variable remains immutable (meaning it cannot be changed), so the expression is converted to the type of the variable. In this case, the floating point expression x + 4.3 is converted to integer. In C, floating point values are rounded into integers by dropping the fractional part. For example, 4.3 will be rounded to 4 when converting from a floating point into an integer; 5.9 will be rounded to 5.

12.3.3 Arithmetic Operators

The arithmetic operators are easy to understand. Many of the operations and corresponding symbols are ones to which we are accustomed, having used them since learning arithmetic in grade school. For instance, + performs addition, - performs subtraction, * performs multiplication (which is different from the symbol we are accustomed to for multiplication in order to avoid ambiguity with the letter x), and / performs division. Just as when doing arithmetic by hand, there is an order in which expressions are evaluated. Multiplication and division are evaluated first, followed by addition and subtraction. The order in which operators are evaluated is called *precedence*, and we discuss it in more detail in Section 12.3.4. Following are several C statements formed using the arithmetic operators and the assignment operator:

```
distance = rate * time;
netIncome = income - taxesPaid;
fuelEconomy = milesTraveled / fuelConsumed;
area = 3.14159 * radius * radius;
y = a*x*x + b*x + c;
```

C has another arithmetic operator that might not be as familiar to you as +, -, *, and /. It is the integer remainder operator, %. To illustrate its operation, consider what happens when we divide two integer values. When performing an integer divide in C, the fractional part is dropped and the integral part is the result.

The expression `11 / 4` evaluates to 2. The modulus operator % can be used to calculate the integer remainder. For example, `11 % 4` evaluates to 3. Said another way, `(11 / 4) * 4 + (11 % 4)` is equal to 11. In the following example, all variables are integers.

```
quotient = x / y;   // if x = 7 and y = 2, quotient = 3
remainder = x % y;  // if x = 7 and y = 2, remainder = 1
```

Table 12.1 lists all the arithmetic operations and their symbols. Multiplication, division, and modulus have higher precedence than addition and subtraction.

Table 12.1	Arithmetic Operators in C	
Operator symbol	Operation	Example usage
*	multiplication	x * y
/	division	x / y
%	integer remainder	x % y
+	addition	x + y
-	subtraction	x - y

12.3.4 Order of Evaluation

What value is stored in x as a result of the following statement? Unless we create some rules around the order of evaluation, the result would be ambiguous.

```
x = 2 + 3 * 4;
```

12.3.4.1 Precedence

Just as when doing arithmetic by hand, there is an order to which expressions are evaluated. And this order is called operator *precedence*. For instance, when doing arithmetic, multiplication and division have higher precedence than addition and subtraction. For the arithmetic operators, the C precedence rules are the same as we were taught in grade-school arithmetic. In the preceding statement, x is assigned the value 14 because the multiplication operator has higher precedence than addition. That is, the expression evaluates as if it were 2 + (3 * 4).

12.3.4.2 Associativity

But what about operators of equal precedence? What does the following statement evaluate to?

```
x = 2 + 3 - 4 + 5;
```

Depending on which operator we evaluate first, the value of the expression `2 + 3 - 4 + 5` could equal 6 or it could equal −4. Since the precedence of both operators is the same (i.e., addition has the same precedence as subtraction in C), we clearly need a rule on how such expressions should be evaluated in C. For operations of equal precedence, their *associativity* determines the order in which they are evaluated. In the case of addition and subtraction, both associate from left to right. Therefore `2 + 3 - 4 + 5` evaluates as if it were `((2 + 3) - 4) + 5`.

The complete set of precedence and associativity rules for all operators in C is provided in Table 12.5 at the end of this chapter. We suggest that you do not try to memorize this table (unless you enjoy reciting C trivia to your friends). Instead, it is important to realize that the precedence rules exist and to roughly comprehend the logic behind them. You can always refer to the table whenever you need to know the relationship between particular operators. There is a safeguard, however: parentheses.

12.3.4.3 Parentheses

Parentheses override the evaluation rules by specifying explicitly which operations are to be performed ahead of others. As in arithmetic, evaluation always begins at the innermost set of parentheses. We can surround a subexpression with parentheses if we want that subexpression to be evaluated first. So in the following example, say the variables a, b, c, and d are all equal to 4. The statement

```
x = a * b + c * d / 2;
```

could be written equivalently as

```
x = (a * b) + ((c * d) / 4);
```

For both statements, x is set to the value of 20. Here the program will always evaluate the innermost subexpression first and move outward before falling back on the precedence rules. What value would the following expression evaluate to if a, b, c, and d equal 4?

```
x = a * (b + c) * d / 4;
```

Parentheses can help make code more readable, too. Most people reading your code are unlikely to have memorized C's precedence rules. For this reason, for long or complex expressions, it is often stylistically preferable to use parentheses, even if the code works fine without them.

12.3.5 Bitwise Operators

We now return to our discussion of C operators. C has a set of operators called *bitwise* operators that manipulate bits of a value. That is, they perform a logical operation such as AND, OR, NOT, XOR across the individual bits of a value. For example, the C bitwise operator & performs an operation similar to the LC-3 AND instruction. That is, the & operator performs an AND operation bit by bit across the two input operands. The C operator | performs a bitwise OR. The operator ˜ performs a bitwise NOT and takes only one operand (i.e., it is a unary operator). The operator | performs a bitwise XOR. Examples of expressions using these operators on 16-bit values follow. In C, the prefix "0x" designates a hexadecimal value.

```
0x1234 | 0x5678    // equals 0x567C
0x1234 & 0x5678    // equals 0x1230
0x1234 ^ 0x5678    // equals 0x444C
˜0x1234            // equals 0xEDCB
1234 & 5678        // equals 1026
```

C's set of bitwise operators includes two shift operators: <<, which performs a left shift, and >>, which performs a right shift. Both are binary operators, meaning they require two operands. The first operand is the value to be shifted and the second operand indicates the number of bit positions to shift by. On a left shift, the vacated bit positions of the value are filled with zeros; on a right shift, the value is sign-extended. The result is the value of the expression; neither of the two original operand values is modified. The following expressions provide examples of these two operators operating on 16-bit integers.

```
0x1234 << 3    // equals 0x91A0
0x1234 >> 2    // equals 0x048D
1234 << 3      // equals 9872
1234 >> 2      // equals 308
0x1234 << 5    // equals 0x4680 (result is 16 bits)
0xFEDC >> 3    // equals 0xFFDB (from sign-extension)
```

Here we show several C statements formed using the bitwise operators. For all of C's bitwise operators, both operands must be integral values; neither can be a floating point value. For these statements, f, g, and h are integers.

```
h = f & g;      // if f = 7, g = 8, h will equal 0
h = f | g;      // if f = 7, g = 8, h will equal 15
h = f << 1;     // if f = 7, g = 8, h will equal 14
h = g << f;     // if f = 7, g = 8, h will equal 1024
h = ~f | ~g;    // if f = 7, g = 8, h will equal -1
                // because h is a signed integer
```

Table 12.2 lists all the bitwise operations and their symbols. The operators are listed in order of precedence, the NOT operator having highest precedence, and the left and right shift operators having equal precedence, followed by AND, then XOR, then OR. They all associate from left to right. See Table 12.5 for a complete listing of operator precedence.

Table 12.2	Bitwise Operators in C	
Operator symbol	Operation	Example usage
~	bitwise NOT	~x
&	bitwise AND	x & y
|	bitwise OR	x | y
^	bitwise XOR	x ^y
<<	left shift	x << y
>>	right shift	x >> y

12.3.6 Relational Operators

C has several operators to test the relationship between two values. As we will see in Chapter 13, these operators are useful for creating conditional constructs, which change the flow of statement execution. The equality operator, ==, is an example of C's relational operators. This operator tests if two values are equal. If they are equal, the expression evaluates to a 1, and if they are not, the expression evaluates to 0.

The following shows two examples:

```
q = (312 = = 83); // q will equal 0
z = (x = = y);    // z will equal 1 if x equals y
```

In the second example, the right-hand side of the assignment operator = is the expression x == y, which evaluates to a 1 or a 0, depending on whether x and y are equal.

Opposite of the equality operator, the inequality operator, !=, evaluates to a 1 if the operands are not equal. Other relational operators test for greater than, less than, and so on, as described in the following examples. For these examples, the variables f, g, and h are integers. The variable f has the value 7, and g is 8.

```
h = f = = g;   // Equal To operator.    h will equal 0
h = f > g;     // Greater Than operator. h will equal 0
h = f != g;    // Not Equal To operator. h will equal 1
h = f <= g;    // Less Than Or Equal To. h will equal 1
```

The next example is a preview of coming attractions. The C relational operators are particularly useful for performing tests on variables in order to change the flow of the program. In the following code, a message is printed only if the variable tankLevel is equal to zero. The example uses the C if statement, which we'll cover extensively in Chapter 13. The concept of an if construct is quite familiar to us, having seen the notion during programming of the LC-3.

```
if (tankLevel == 0)
    printf("Warning: Tank Empty!!\n");
```

Table 12.3 lists all the relational operators and provides a simple example of each. The first four operators have higher precedence than the last two. Both sets associate from left to right.

Table 12.3	Relational Operators in C	
Operator symbol	Operation	Example usage
>	greater than	x > y
>=	greater than or equal	x >= y
<	less than	x < y
<=	less than or equal	x <= y
==	equal	x == y
!=	not equal	x != y

12.3.7 Logical Operators

C's logical operators appear at first glance to be exactly like some of the bitwise operators, and many intro programmers sometimes confuse the two. Unlike the bitwise operators, the logical operators only generate the integer values 1 or 0, depending on whether the test is true or false. This is consistent with the bool datatype, where 1 is true and 0 false.

C supports three logical operators: &&, | |, and !. The && operator performs a logical AND of its two operands; it evaluates to an integer value if both of its operands are nonzero. It evaluates to 0 otherwise. For example, 3 && 4 evaluates to a 1, whereas 3 && 0 evaluates to 0.

The || operator is C's logical OR operator. The expression x || y evaluates to a 1 if either x OR y is nonzero. For example, 3 || 4 evaluates to a 1. Also, 3 || 0 evaluates to 1.

The negation operator ! evaluates to the other logical state of its operand. So !x is 1 only if x equals 0. It is 0 otherwise. These logical operators are useful for constructing logical conditions within a program. For example, we can determine if a variable is within a particular range of values using a combination of relational and logical operators. To check if x is between 10 and 20, inclusive, we can use the following expression:

```
(10 <= x) && (x <= 20)
```

Or to test if a character c is a letter of the alphabet:

```
(('a' <= c) && (c <= 'z')) || (('A' <= c) && (c <= 'Z'))
```

Here are some examples of the logical operators, with several previous examples of bitwise operators included to highlight the difference. As in the previous examples, the variables f, g, and h are integers. The variable f has the value 7, and g is 8.

```
h = f & g;      // bitwise operator: h will equal 0
h = f && g;     // logical operator: h will equal 1
h = f | g;      // bitwise operator: h will equal 15
h = f || g;     // logical operator: h will equal 1
h = ~f | ~g;    // bitwise operator: h will equal -1
h = !f && !g;   // logical operator: h will equal 0
h = 29 || -52;  // logical operator: h will equal 1
```

Table 12.4 lists logical operators in C and their symbols. The logical NOT operator has the highest precedence, then logical AND, then logical OR. See Table 12.5 for a complete listing of operator precedence.

Table 12.4	Logical Operators in C	
Operator symbol	Operation	Example usage
!	logical NOT	!x
&&	logical AND	x && y
||	logical OR	x || y

12.3.8 Increment /Decrement Operators

Because incrementing and decrementing variables is such a commonly performed operation, the designers of the C programming language decided to include special operators to perform them. The ++ operator *increments* a variable to the next

Table 12.5	Operator Precedence and Associativity in C	

Precedence Group	Associativity	Operators
1 (highest)	left-to-right	`()` (function call) `[ ]` (array index) `.` (structure member) `->` (structure pointer dereference)
2	right-to-left	`++` `--` (postfix versions)
3	right-to-left	`++` `--` (prefix versions)
4	right-to-left	`*` (indirection) `&` (address of) `+` (unary) `-` (unary) `~` (bitwise NOT) `!` (logical NOT) `sizeof`
5	right-to-left	`(type)` (type cast)
6	left-to-right	`*` (multiplication) `/` (division) `%` (integer division)
7	left-to-right	`+` (addition) `-` (subtraction)
8	left-to-right	`«` (left shift) `»` (right shift)
9	left-to-right	`<` (less than) `>` (greater than) `<=` (less than or equal) `>=` (greater than or equal)
10	left-to-right	`==` (equals) `!=` (not equals)
11	left-to-right	`&` (bitwise AND)
12	left-to-right	`^` (bitwise XOR)
13	left-to-right	`|` (bitwise OR)
14	left-to-right	`&&` (logical AND)
15	left-to-right	`||` (logical OR)
16	left-to-right	`& :` (conditional expression)
17 (lowest)	right-to-left	`= += -= *= etc..` (assignment operators)

higher value. The `--` operator *decrements* it. For example, the expression $x++$ increments the value of integer variable x by 1. The expression $x--$ decrements the value of x by 1. Keep in mind that these operators modify the value of the variable itself. That is, $x++$ is similar to the operation $x = x + 1$. These operators became such a distinctive feature of the C language that the improved version of C was named C++ as a play on that language feature.

The ++ and `--` operators can be used on either side of a variable, either before the variable as a pre-increment (or pre-decrement), or after as a post-increment (or post-decrement). The expression $++x$ operates in a subtly different fashion than $x++$. We can illustrate the difference by examining the sequence of statements:

```
x = 4;
y = x++;
```

After this code executes, the variable x will be 5, and y will be 4. That is, the increment happens *after* the value of the subexpression $x++$ is determined. The subexpression $x++$ evaluates to 4, which is subsequently assigned to y. Then, the variable x is incremented.

The following code segment illustrates pre-increment, to contrast.

```
x = 4;
y = ++x;
```

The expression $++x$ is evaluated after the variable x is incremented. In this case, the value of both y and x will be 5.

That said, a standard coding style in C and C++ is to avoid writing code where the difference between the post- and pre- matters. It is difficult for someone reading and building upon your code to grasp the difference in usage, so you should avoid it. Most coders tend to consistently use one form throughout their code.

12.3.9 Expressions with Multiple Operators

Thus far we've only seen examples of expressions with one or two operators. Real and useful expressions sometimes have more. We can combine various operators and operands to form complex expressions. The following example demonstrates a peculiar blend of operators forming a complex expression.

```
y = x & z + 3 || 9 - w % 6;
```

In order to figure out what this statement evaluates to, we need to examine the order of evaluation of operators. Table 12.5 lists all the C operators (including some that we have not yet covered but will cover later in this textbook) and their order of evaluation. According to precedence rules, this statement is equivalent to the following:

```
y = (x & (z + 3)) || (9 - (w % 6));
```

Another more useful expression that consists of multiple operators is given in the example that follows. In this example, if the value of the variable `age` is between 18 and 25, the expression evaluates to 1. Otherwise it is 0. Notice that even though the parentheses are not required to make the expression evaluate as we described, they do help make the code easier to read.

```
(18 <= age) && (age <= 25)
```

12.4 Problem Solving Using Operators

Let's apply what we have covered to this point to solve a coding problem. For this problem, we are to create a program that performs a simple network calculation: It calculates the amount of time required to transfer some number of bytes across a network with a particular transfer rate (provided in bytes per second). The twist to this problem is that transfer time is to be displayed in hours, minutes, and seconds.

We approach this problem by applying the decomposition techniques described in Chapter 6. That is, we will start with a top-level description of our approach and continually refine it using the sequential, decision, and iteration constructs (see Chapter 6 if you need a refresher) until we arrive at something from which we can easily write C code. This technique is called *top-down decomposition* because we start with a high-level description of the algorithm and refine it by breaking larger steps into smaller ones, eventually arriving at a form that is easy to render into C code.

Before we start the decomposition process, let's think about how we will represent the data items that the program will need to manipulate. At this point, we get to select from the four basic C types: integer, character, floating point, and boolean. Since it's an arithmetic calculation we are performing, the most natural types for us to consider are either floating point values or integers. The problem is ultimately about calculating number of hours, minutes, and seconds, so any fractional components of time are unnecessary. Displaying the total transfer time as 10.1 hours, 12.7 minutes, 9.3 seconds does not make sense, and 10 hours, 18 minutes, 51 seconds is the preferred output. The better choice of data type for the time calculation is integer (yes, there are rounding issues, but say we can ignore them for this calculation).

With our choice of data representation completed, we can apply stepwise refinement to decompose the problem into C code. Figure 12.3 shows the decomposition of this programming problem. Step 1 in the figure shows the initial formulation of the problem. It involves three phases: get input, calculate results, output results. In the first phase, we will query the user about the amount of data

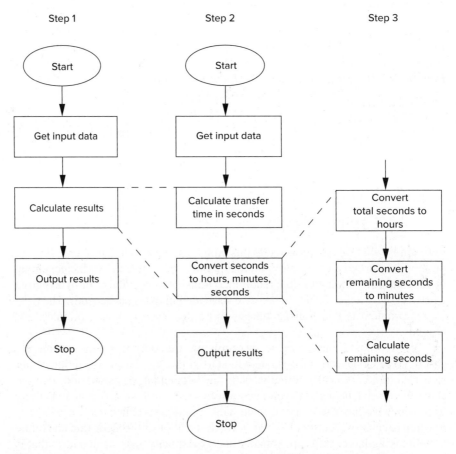

Figure 12.3   **Stepwise refinement of a simple network transfer time calculation.**

to be transferred (in bytes) and the transfer rate of the network (in bytes per second). In the second phase, we will perform all necessary calculations, which we will then output in the third phase.

Step 1 is not detailed enough to translate directly into C code, and therefore we perform another refinement of it in Step 2. Here we realize that the calculation phase can be further refined into a subphase that first calculates total time in seconds—which is an easy calculation given the input data—and a subphase to convert total time in seconds into hours, minutes, and seconds. Step 2 is still not complete enough for mapping into C, so we perform another refinement of it in Step 3. Most phases of Step 2 are simple enough to convert into C, except for the conversion of seconds into hours, minutes, and seconds. In Step 3, we refine this phase into three subphases. First, we will calculate total hours based on the total number of seconds. Second, we will use the remaining seconds to calculate minutes. Finally, we determine the remaining number of seconds after the minutes have been calculated. Going from Step 3 into C code is a straightforward translation.

The complete C program for this problem is presented in Figure 12.4.

```
1  #include <stdio.h>
2  int main(void)
3  {
4      int amount;       // The number of bytes to be transferred
5      int rate;         // The average network transfer rate
6      int time;         // The time, in seconds, for the transfer
7      int hours;        // The number of hours for the transfer
8      int minutes;      // The number of mins for the transfer
9      int seconds;      // The number of secs for the transfer
10
11     // Get input: number of bytes and network transfer rate
12     printf("How many bytes of data to be transferred? ");
13     scanf("%d", &amount);
14     printf("What is the transfer rate (in bytes/sec)? ");
15     scanf("%d", &rate);
16
17     // Calculate total time in seconds
18     time = amount / rate;
19
20     // Convert time into hours, minutes, seconds
21     hours = time / 3600;            // 3600 seconds in an hour
22     minutes = (time % 3600) / 60;   // 60 seconds in a minute
23     seconds = ((time % 3600) % 60); // remainder is seconds
24
25     // Output results
26     printf("Time : %dh %dm %ds\n", hours, minutes, seconds);
27 }
```

Figure 12.4   A C program that performs a simple network rate calculation.

12.5 Tying It All Together

We've now covered all the basic C types and most of the operators that we plan to use throughout this textbook. Variables are memory objects that require storage in memory. Operators express the computation that is to be performed on those memory objects. Our C compiler's task will be to properly allocate memory for those objects (specifically in our case, variables) and to generate the proper sequence of LC-3 code corresponding to the C statements. Performing the translation from C to LC-3 correctly in all cases will require the compiler to be systematic about these objects and where they are allocated. The compiler will use a *symbol table* to keep track of objects that are declared in our code. The compiler also uses a *memory map* to systematically allocate these objects in memory. Let's take a closer look.

12.5.1 Symbol Table

In Chapter 7, we examined how the assembler systematically keeps track of labels within an assembly program by using a symbol table. Like the LC-3 assembler, our C compiler keeps track of variables in a program with a symbol table. Whenever the compiler reads a variable declaration, it creates a new entry in its symbol table corresponding to the variable being declared. The entry contains enough information for the compiler to manage the storage allocation for the variable and generation of the proper sequence of machine code whenever the variable is used in the program. For now, we'll consider that each symbol table entry for a variable contains (1) its identifier, (2) its type, (3) the place in memory the variable has been allocated storage, and (4) the scope of the variable, which for our purposes will be the line numbers in the code corresponding to where the variable is in scope.

Figure 12.5 shows the symbol table entries corresponding to the variables declared in the network rate calculation program in Figure 12.4. Since this program contains six variable declarations, the compiler ends up with six entries in its symbol table, one for each. Notice that the compiler records a variable's location in memory as an offset, with most offsets being negative. This offset indicates

Identifier	Type	Location (as an offset)	Scope	Other info...
amount	int	0	main	...
hours	int	−3	main	...
minutes	int	−4	main	...
rate	int	−1	main	...
seconds	int	−5	main	...
time	int	−2	main	...

Figure 12.5   The compiler's symbol table when it compiles the code in Figure 12.4.

the relative position of the variable within the region of memory in which it is allocated. Important concept. Let us elaborate.

12.5.2 Allocating Space for Variables

There are two regions of memory in which declared variables in C are allocated storage: the *global data section* and the *run-time stack*.[2] Variables that are global are allocated storage in the global data section. Local variables are allocated storage on the run-time stack. The offset field in the symbol table enables the compiler to precisely locate those variables in either of those two regions. The offset field indicates how many locations from the *base* of the section a variable is allocated storage. For instance, if a global variable earth has an offset of 4 and the global data section starts at memory location 0x5000, then earth is stored in location 0x5004. If R4 contained the address of the beginning of the global data section, then loading the variable earth into R3 can be accomplished with the following LC-3 instruction:

```
LDR R3, R4, #4
```

If earth is instead a local variable, say for example in the function main, the variable is on the run-time stack, in units of allocation called *activation records* or *stack frames*. Whenever a function starts to execute, its stack frame is added to the run-time stack in a process we will describe in Chapter 14. A stack frame is a region of contiguous memory locations that contains all the local variables for a given function.

Whenever a particular function is executing, the highest numbered memory address of its stack frame will be stored in R5—which is called the *frame pointer*. For example, the stack frame for the function main from the code in Figure 12.4 is shown in Figure 12.6. The variables are allocated in the record in the reverse of the order in which they are declared. Since the variable amount is declared first, it appears closest to the frame pointer R5.

If we make a reference to a particular local variable, the compiler will use the variable's symbol table entry to generate the proper code to access it. The offset in the variable's symbol table entry indicates where in the stack the variable has been allocated storage. To access the variable seconds, the compiler would generate the instruction

```
LDR R0, R5, #-5
```

A preview of things to come: Whenever we call a function in C (functions are C's notion of subroutines), the stack frame for the function is pushed onto the run-time stack. That is, the function's stack frame is allocated on top of the stack. R5 is appropriately adjusted to point to the base of the record—therefore, any code within the function that accesses local variables will now work correctly using the offsets as recorded in the symbol table. Whenever the function completes and

---

[2]For examples in this textbook, all variables will be assigned a memory location. However, real compilers perform code optimizations that attempt to allocate variables in registers. Since registers take less time to access than memory, the program will run faster if frequently accessed values are put into registers.

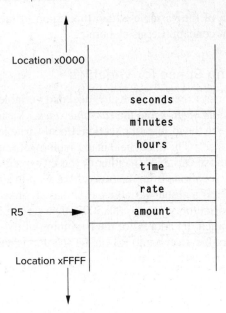

Location x0000

| seconds |
| minutes |
| hours |
| time |
| rate |
R5 ———→ | amount |

Location xFFFF

Figure 12.6   An example of the stack frame from function main of the code in
Figure 12.4. This function has five local variables. R5 is the frame
pointer and points to the first local variable.

control is about to return to the caller, the activation record is popped off the stack.
R5 is adjusted to point to the caller's activation record. Throughout all of this, R6
always contains the address of the top of the run-time stack—it is called the *stack
pointer*. We will go through this process in more detail in Chapter 14.

Figure 12.7 shows the organization of the LC-3's memory when a program is
running. The program itself occupies a region of memory (labeled Program text
in the diagram); so does the run-time stack and the global data section. There
is another region reserved for dynamically allocated data called the *heap* (we
will discuss this region in Chapter 19). Both the run-time stack and the heap can
change size as the program executes. For example, whenever one function calls
another, the run-time stack grows because we push another activation record onto
the stack—in fact, it grows toward memory address x0000. In contrast, the heap
grows toward 0xFFFF. Since the stack grows toward x0000, the organization of
an activation record appears to be "upside-down"; that is, the first local variable
appears at the memory location pointed to by R5, the next one at R5 - 1, the
subsequent one at R5 - 2, and so forth (as opposed to R5, R5 + 1, R5 + 2, etc.).

During execution, the PC points to a location in the program text, R4 points
to the beginning of the global data section, R5 points within the run-time stack,
and R6 points to the very top of the run-time stack. There are certain regions of
memory, marked System space in Figure 12.7, that are reserved for the operating
system, for things such as TRAP routines, vector tables, I/O registers, and boot
code.

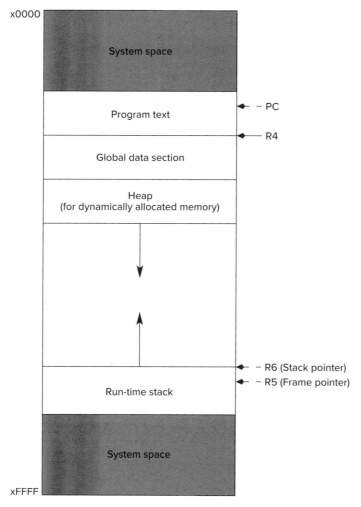

Figure 12.7   The LC-3 memory map showing various sections active during program execution.

12.5.3 A Comprehensive Example

In this section, we will take a comprehensive look at some C code and its LC-3 translation to illustrate how everything we've discussed in this chapter ties together. Figure 12.8 is the source code for a complete C program that performs some simple operations on integer variables and then outputs the results of these operations. The program contains one global variable, inGlobal, and three local variables, inLocal, outLocalA, and outLocalB, which are local to the function main. The program starts off by assigning initial values to inLocal (which is initialized in the declaration) and inGlobal. After the initialization step, the variables outLocalA and outLocalB are updated based on two calculations performed using inLocal and inGlobal. After the calculation step, the values of outLocalA and outLocalB are output using the printf library function. Notice

```
1  #include <stdio.h>
2
3  int inGlobal;    // inGlobal is a global variable.
4                   // It is declared outside of all blocks
5
6  int main(void)
7  {
8      int inLocal = 5;   // inLocal, outLocalA, outLocalB are all
9      int outLocalA;     // local to main
10     int outLocalB;
11
12     // Initialize
13     inGlobal = 3;
14
15     // Perform calculations
16     outLocalA = inLocal & ~inGlobal;
17     outLocalB = (inLocal + inGlobal) - (inLocal - inGlobal);
18
19     // Print results
20     printf("outLocalA = %d, outLocalB = %d\n", outLocalA, outLocalB);
21 }
```

Figure 12.8   A C program that performs simple operations. The output of this code is "outLocalA = 4, outLocalB = 6".

that because we are using `printf`, we must include the standard I/O library header file, `stdio.h`.

When analyzing this code, the LC-3 C compiler will assign the global variable `inGlobal` the first available spot in the global data section, which is at offset 0. When analyzing the function `main`, it will assign `inLocalA` to offset 0, `outLocalA` to offset −1, and `outLocalB` to offset −2 within `main`'s stack frame. A snapshot of the compiler's symbol table corresponding to this program along with the activation record of `main` is shown in Figure 12.9. The resulting assembly

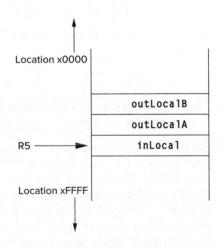

Identifier	Type	Location (as an offset)	Scope	Other info...
inGlobal	int	0	global	...
inLocal	int	0	main	...
outLocalA	int	−1	main	...
outLocalB	int	−2	main	...

(a) Symbol table   (b) Activation record for main

Figure 12.9   The LC-3 C compiler's symbol table when compiling the program in Figure 12.8 and the stack frame format for its function `main`.

```
 1 main:
 2 :
 3 :
 4 <startup code>
 5 :
 6 :
 7 AND R0, R0, #0
 8 ADD R0, R0, #5      ; inLocal is at offset 0
 9 STR R0, R5, #0      ; inLocal = 5;
10
11 AND R0, R0, #0
12 ADD R0, R0, #3      ; inGlobal is at offset 0, in globals
13 STR R0, R4, #0      ; inGlobal = 3;
14
15 LDR R0, R5, #0      ; get value of inLocal
16 LDR R1, R4, #0      ; get value of inGlobal
17 NOT R1, R1          ; ~inGlobal
18 AND R2, R0, R1      ; calculate inLocal & ~inGlobal
19 STR R2, R5, #-1     ; outLocalA = inLocal & ~inGlobal;
20                     ; outLocalA is at offset -1
21
22 LDR R0, R5, #0      ; get value of inLocal
23 LDR R1, R4, #0      ; get value of inGlobal
24 ADD R0, R0, R1      ; calculate inLocal + inGlobal
25
26 LDR R2, R5, #0      ; get value of inLocal
27 LDR R3, R4, #0      ; get value of inGlobal
28 NOT R3
29 ADD R3, R3, #1      ; calculate -inGlobal
30
31 ADD R2, R2, R3      ; calculate inLocal - inGlobal
32 NOT R2
33 ADD R2, R2, #1      ; calculate -(inLocal - inGlobal)
34
35 ADD R0, R0, R2      ; (inLocal + inGlobal) - (inLocal - inGlobal)
36 STR R0, R5, #-2     ; outLocalB = ...
37                     ; outLocalB is at offset -2
38 :
39 :
40 <code for calling the function printf>
41 :
42 :
```

Figure 12.10   The LC-3 code for the C program in Figure 12.8.

code generated by the LC-3 C compiler is listed in Figure 12.10. Execution starts
at the instruction labeled main.

12.6 Additional Topics

The last major section of this chapter involves a set of additional topics involving variables and operators. Some of the topics are advanced issues involving
concepts we covered earlier in the chapter; some of the topics are miscellaneous
features of C. We provide this section in order to provide a fuller coverage of

commonly used features of C. This material is not essential to your understanding of the material in later chapters. For those of you interested in a more complete coverage of variables and operators in C, read on!

12.6.1 Variations of the Basic Types

C gives the programmer the ability to specify larger or smaller versions of the basic types int, char, float, and double. The modifiers long and short can be attached to int with the intent of extending or shortening the default size. For example, a long int can declare an integer that has twice the number of bits of a regular int, thereby allowing us to represent a larger range of integers in a C program. Similarly, the specifier long can be attached to the double type to create a larger floating point type (if supported by the particular system) with greater range and precision.

The modifier short can be used to create variables that are smaller than the default size, which can be useful when trying to conserve on memory space when handling data that does not require the full range of the default data type. The following example illustrates how the variations are declared:

```
long double particlesInUniverse;
long int worldPopulation;
short int ageOfStudent;
```

Because the size of the three basic C types is closely tied to the types supported by the underlying ISA, many compilers only support these modifiers long and short if the device's ISA supports these size variations. Even though a variable can be declared as a long int, it may be equivalent to a regular int if the underlying ISA has no support for longer versions of the integer data type.

Another useful variation of the basic int data type is the unsigned integer. We can declare an unsigned integer using the unsigned type modifier. With unsigned integers, all bits are used to represent nonnegative integers (i.e., positive numbers and zero). In the LC-3, for instance, which has 16-bit data types, an unsigned integer has a value between 0 and 65,535. When dealing with real-world objects that by nature do not take on negative values, unsigned integers might be the data type of choice. The following are examples of unsigned integers:

```
unsigned int numberOfDays;
unsigned int populationSize;
```

Following are some sample variations of the three arithmetic basic types:

```
long int ounces;
short int gallons;
long double veryVeryLargeNumber = 4.12936E361;
unsigned int sizeOfClass = 900;
float tonsOfGrain = 2.998E8;
```

```
 1  #include <stdio.h>
 2
 3  #define RADIUS 15.0                    // This value is in centimeters
 4
 5  int main(void)
 6  {
 7      const double pi = 3.14159;
 8      double area;
 9      double circumference;
10
11      // Calculations
12      area = pi * RADIUS * RADIUS;       // area = pi*r^2
13
14      circumference = 2 * pi * RADIUS;   // circumference = 2*pi*r
15
16      printf("Area of circle with radius %f cm is %f cm^2\n", RADIUS, area);
17      printf("Circumference of the circle is %f cm\n", circumference);
18  }
```

Figure 12.11   A C program that computes the area and circumference of a circle with a radius of 15 cm.

12.6.2 Literals, Constants, and Symbolic Values

In C, variables can also be declared as *constants* by adding the `const` qualifier before the type specifier. These constants are types whose values cannot be modified during the execution of a program; they are read-only. For example, in writing a program that calculates the area and circumference of a circle of a given radius, it might be useful to create a floating point constant called `pi` initialized to the value 3.14159. Figure 12.11 contains an example of such a program. This example is useful for making a distinction between three types of constant values that often appear in C code. *Literal* constants are unnamed values that appear *literally* in the source code. In the circle example, the values 2 and 3.14159 are examples of *literal* constants. In C, we can represent literal constants in hexadecimal by prepending a `0x` in front of them, for example `0x1DB`. ASCII literals require single quotes around them, as for example `'R'`, which is the ASCII value of the character R. Floating point literals can be the exponential notation described in Section 12.2.1. An example of the second type of constant value is `pi`, which is declared as a constant value using a variable declaration with the `const` qualifier. The third type of constant value is created using the preprocessor directive `#define`, an example of which is the symbolic value `RADIUS`. All three types create values that do not change during the execution of a program.

The distinction between constants declared using `const` and symbolic values defined using `#define` might seem a little subtle to you. Using one vs. another is really a matter of programming style rather than function. Declared constants are used for things we traditionally think of as constant values, which are values that never change. The constant `pi` is an example. Physical constants such as the speed of light, or the number of days in a week, are conventionally represented by declared constants.

Values that stay constant during a single execution of the program but which might be different from user to user, or possibly from invocation to invocation, are represented by symbolic values using #define. Such values can be thought of as parameters for the program. For example, RADIUS in Figure 12.11 can be changed and the program recompiled, then re-executed. In general, naming a constant using const or #define is preferred over leaving the constant as a literal in your code. Names convey more meaning about your code than unnamed literal values.

12.6.3 Additional C Operators

The C programming language has a collection of unusual operators, some of which have become woven into common C programming style. They occur often in existing C and C++ code, and there they are worth our notice. Most of these operators are combinations of operators we have already seen. The combinations simplify the expression of commonly used computations.

12.6.3.1 Assignment Operators

C allows for arithmetic and bitwise operators to be combined with the assignment operator, creating an "update and assign" operation. For instance, if we wanted to add 29 to variable x, we could use the shorthand operator += as follows:

```
x += 29;
```

This code is equivalent to

```
x = x + 29;
```

More examples are as follows:

```
h += g;  // Equivalent to h = h + g;
h %= f;  // Equivalent to h = h % f;
h <<= 3; // Equivalent to h = h << 3;
```

Table 12.6 lists some of the special operators provided by C

Table 12.6	Special Operators in C	
Operator Symbol	**Operation**	**Example Usage**
+=	add and assign	x += y
-=	subtract and assign	x -= y
*=	multiply and assign	x *= y
/=	divide and assign	x /= y
%=, &=, |=, ^=, etc	other operate and assign	x &= y

12.6.3.2 Conditional Expressions

Conditional expressions are a unique feature of C that allow for simple decisions to be made with a simple expression. The symbols for the conditional expression are the question mark and colon, ? and :. The following is an example:

```
x = a ? b : c;
```

Here variable x will get either the value of b **or** the value of c based on the logical value of a. If a is nonzero, x will get the value of b. Otherwise, it will get the value of c.

So if we wanted to have the variable maxValue be assigned the maximum of two values, valueA and valueB, we could write:

```
maxValue = (valuaA > valueB) ? valueA : valueB;
```

12.7 Summary

We conclude this chapter by summarizing the three key concepts we covered.

• **Variables in C.** The C programming language supports variables of four basic types: integers (int), characters (char), floating point numbers (float and double), and booleans (_Bool or bool). C, like all other high-level languages, enables the programmer to give symbolic names to these variables. Variables in C can be locally declared within a block of code (such as a function) or globally visible by all blocks.

• **Operators in C.** C's operators can be categorized by the function they perform: assignment, arithmetic, bitwise manipulations, logical and relational tests. We can form expressions using variables and operators such that the expressions are evaluated according to precedence and associativity rules. Expressions are grouped into statements, which express the work the program is to perform.

• **Translating C Variables and Operators into LC-3 Code.** Using a symbol table to keep track of variable declarations, a compiler will allocate local variables for a function within a stack frame for the function. The stack frame, or activation record, for the function is pushed onto the run-time stack whenever the function is executed. Global variables in a program are allocated in the global data section.

Exercises

12.1 Generate the compiler's symbol table for the following code. Assume all variables occupy one location in memory.

```
{
        double ff;
        char cc;
        int ii;
        char dd;
        bool zz;
}
```

12.2 The following variable declaration appears in a program:

```
int r;
```

a. If r is a local variable, to what value will it be initialized?
b. If r is a global variable, to what value will it be initialized?

12.3　What are the value ranges for the following two variables if they are stored as 32-bit quantities?

```
int plusOrMinus;
unsigned int positive;
```

12.4　Evaluate the following floating point literals. Write their values in standard decimal notation.

　a.　111 E −11
　b.　−0.00021 E 4
　c.　101.101 E 0

12.5　Write the LC-3 code that would result if the following local variable declarations were compiled using the LC-3 C compiler:

```
char c = 'a';
int x = 3;
int y;
int z = 10;
```

12.6　For the following code, state the values that are printed out by each `printf` statement. The statements are executed in the order A, B, C, D.

```
int t; // This variable is global
{
    int t = 2;
    printf("%d\n", t);    // A
    {
    printf("%d\n", t);    // B
    t = 3;
    }
    printf("%d\n", t);    // C
}
{
    printf("%d\n", t);    // D
}
```

12.7　Given that a and b are both integers equal to the values 6 and 9, respectively, what is the value of each of the following expressions? Also, if the value of a or b changes, provide their new value.

　a.　a | b
　b.　a || b
　c.　a & b
　d.　a && b
　e.　!(a + b)
　f.　a % b
　g.　b / a
　h.　a = b
　i.　a = b = 5
　j.　++a + b--
　k.　a = (++b < 3) ? a : b
　l.　a <<= b

12.8   For the following questions, write a C expression to perform the following relational test on the character variable `letter`.

   a. Test if `letter` is any alphabetic character or a number.
   b. Test if `letter` is any character except an alphabetic character or a number.

12.9   *a.* What does the following statement accomplish? The variable `letter` is a character variable.

```
letter = ((letter >= 'a' && letter <= 'z') ? '!' : letter);
```

   b. Modify the statement in part *a* so that it converts lowercase to uppercase.

12.10   Write a program that reads an integer from the keyboard and displays a 1 if it is divisible by 3 or a 0 otherwise.

12.11   Explain the differences between the following C statements:

   a. `j = i++;`
   b. `j = ++i;`
   c. `j = i + 1;`
   d. `i += 1;`
   e. `j = i += 1;`
   f. Which statements modify the value of `i`? Which ones modify the value of `j`? If `i = 1` and `j = 0` initially, what will the values of `i` and `j` be after each statement is run separately?

12.12   Say variables `a` and `b` are both declared locally as `long int`.

   a. Translate the expression `a + b` into LC-3 code, assuming an `int` occupies two bytes. Assume `a` is allocated at offset 0 and `b` is at offset -1 in the activation record for their function.
   b. Translate the same expression, assuming an `int` occupies four bytes, `a` is allocated at offset 0, and `b` is at offset −2.

12.13   If initially, `a = 1, b = 1, c = 3`, and `result = 999`, what are the values of the variables after the following C statement is executed?

```
result = b + 1 | c + a;
```

12.14   Recall the machine busy example from Chapter 2. Say the integer variable `machineBusy` tracks the busyness of all 16 machines. Recall that a 0 in a particular bit position indicates the machine is busy and a 1 in that position indicates the machine is idle.

   a. Write a C statement to make machine 5 busy.
   b. Write a C statement to make machine 10 idle.
   c. Write a C statement to make machine n busy. That is, the machine that has become busy is an integer variable `n`.
   d. Write a C expression to check if machine 3 is idle. If it is idle, the expression returns a 1. If it is busy, the expression returns a 0.

> *e.* Write a C expression that evaluates to the number of idle machines. For example, if the binary pattern in `machineBusy` were 1011 0010 1110 1001, then the expression would evaluate to 9.

12.15 What purpose does the semicolon serve in C?

12.16 Say we are designing a new computer programming language that includes the operators @, #, $ and U. How would the expression w @ x # y $ z U a get evaluated under the following constraints?

> *a.* The precedence of @ is higher than # is higher than $ is higher than U. Use parentheses to indicate the order.
> *b.* The precedence of # is higher than U is higher than @ is higher than $.
> *c.* Their precedence is all the same, but they associate left to right.
> *d.* Their precedence is all the same, but they associate right to left.

12.17 Notice that the C assignment operators have the lowest precedence. Say we have developed a new programming language called *Q* that works exactly like C, except that the assignment operator has the highest precedence.

> *a.* What is the result of the following Q statement? In other words, what would the value of x be after it is executed?
>
> ```
> x = x + 1;
> ```
>
> *b.* How would we change this Q statement so that it works the same way as it would in C?

12.18 Modify the example program in Chapter 11 (Figure 11.3) so that it prompts the user to type a character and then prints every character from that character down to the character ! in the order in which they appear in the ASCII table.

12.19 Write a C program to calculate the sales tax on a purchase transaction. Prompt the user to enter the amount of the purchase and the tax rate. Output the amount of sales tax and the total amount (including tax) on the whole purchase.

12.20 Suppose a program contains the two integer variables x and y, which have values 3 and 4, respectively. Write C statements that will exchange the values in x and y so that after the statements are executed, x is equal to 4 and y is equal to 3.

> *a.* First, write this routine using a temporary variable for storage.
> *b.* Now rewrite this routine without using a temporary variable.

CHAPTER

13 Control Structures

13.1 Introduction

In Chapter 6, we introduced our top-down problem-solving methodology where a problem is systematically refined into smaller, more detailed subtasks using three programming constructs: the sequential construct, the conditional construct, and the iteration construct.

We applied this methodology in Chapter 12 to derive a simple C program that calculates network transfer time. The problem's refinement into a program only required the use of the sequential construct. For transforming more complex problems into C code, we will need a way to create the conditional and iteration constructs. In this chapter, we cover C's versions of these two constructs.

We begin this chapter by describing C's conditional constructs. The `if` and `if-else` statements allow us to conditionally execute a statement. After conditional constructs, we move on to C's iteration constructs: the `for`, the `while`, and the `do-while` statements, all of which allow us to express loops. With many of these constructs, we will present the corresponding LC-3 code generated by our hypothetical LC-3 C compiler to better illustrate how these constructs behave at the lower levels. C also provides additional control constructs, such as the `switch`, `break`, and `continue` statements, all of which provide a convenient way to represent some particular control tasks. We discuss these in Section 13.5. In the final part of the chapter, we'll use the top-down problem-solving methodology to solve some complex coding problems that require the use of control structures.

13.2 Conditional Constructs

Conditional constructs allow a programmer to select an action based on some condition. This is a very common programming idiom, and every useful programming language provides a convenient way of expressing it. C provides two types of basic conditional constructs: `if` and `if-else`.

13.2.1 The `if` Statement

The `if` statement is quite simple. It performs an action if a condition is true. The action is a C statement, and it is executed only if the condition, which is a C expression, evaluates to a non-zero (logically true) value. Let's take a look at an example.

```
if (x <= 10)
    y = x * x + 5;
```

The statement y = x . * x + 5; is only executed if the expression x <= 10 is non-zero, or logically true. Recall from our discussion of the <= operator (the less than or equal to operator) that it evaluates to 1 if the relationship is true, 0 otherwise. The statement following the condition can also be a *compound statement*, or *block*, which is a sequence of statements beginning with an open brace and ending with a closing brace. Compound statements are used to group one or more simple statements into a single entity. This entity is itself equivalent to a simple statement. Using compound statements with an `if` statement, we can conditionally execute several statements on a single condition. For example, in the following code, both y and z will be modified if x is less than or equal to 10.

```
if (x <= 10) {
    y = x * x + 5;
    z = (2 * y) / 3;
}
```

As with all statements in C, the format of the `if` statement is flexible. The line breaks and indentation used in the preceding example are a common style for an `if` statement. This style allows someone reading the code to quickly identify the portion that executes if the condition is true. Keep in mind that the use of indentation does not affect the behavior of the program, even though we might want it to. The following code is indented like the previous code, but it behaves differently. The second statement, z = (2 * y) / 3; is not associated with the `if` and will execute regardless of the condition.

```
if (x <= 10)
    y = x * x + 5;
    z = (2 * y) / 3;
```

Figure 13.1 shows the control flow of an `if` statement. The diagram corresponds to the following code:

```
if (condition)
    action;
```

Syntactically, the condition is surrounded by parentheses so that the compiler can unambiguously separate the condition from the rest of the `if` statement. The action must be a simple or compound statement.

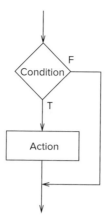

Figure 13.1   The C if statement, pictorially represented.

Here are more examples of if statements. They demonstrate programming situations where this decision construct might be useful.

```
if (temperature <= 0)
   printf("At or below freezing point.\n");

if ('a' <= key && key <= 'z')
   numLowerCase++;

if (current > currentLimit)
   blownFuse = 1;

if (loadMAR & clock)
   registerMAR = bus;

if (month==4 || month==6 || month==9 || month==11)
   printf("The month has 30 days\n");

if (x = 2)    // This condition is always true. Why?
   y = 5;     // The variable y will always be 5
```

The last example in the preceding code illustrates a common mistake made when programming in C. The condition uses the assignment operator = rather than the equality operator ==, which causes the value of x to change to 2. This condition is always true: expressions containing the assignment operator evaluate to the value being assigned (in this case, 2). Since the condition is always non-zero, y will always get assigned the value 5 and x will always be assigned 2.

Even though they look similar at first glance, the following code is a "repaired" version of the previous code.

```
if (x == 2)
   y = 5;
```

Let's look at the LC-3 code that is generated for this code, assuming that x and y are integers that are locally declared. This means that R5 will point to the variable x and R5 - 1 will point to y.

```
        LDR R0, R5, #0    ; load x into R0
        ADD R0, R0, #-2   ; subtract 2 from x
        BRnp NOT_TRUE     ; If condition is not true,
                          ; then skip the assignment

        AND R0, R0, #0    ; R0 <- 0
        ADD R0, R0, #5    ; R0 <- 5
        STR R0, R5, #-1   ; y = 5;
NOT_TRUE                  ; the rest of the program
        :
        :
```

Notice that it is most straightforward for the LC-3 C compiler to generate code that tests for the opposite of the original condition (x not equal to 2) and to branch based on its outcome.

The if statement is itself a statement. Therefore, it is legal to *nest* an if statement within another if statement, as demonstrated in the following C code. Since the statement following the first if is a simple statement (i.e., composed of only one statement), no braces are required on the outer if.

```
if (x == 3)
    if (y != 6) {
        z = z + 1;
        w = w + 2;
    }
```

The inner if statement only executes if x is equal to 3. There is an easier way to express this code. The following code does it with a single if.

```
if ((x == 3) && (y != 6)) {
    z = z + 1;
    w = w + 2;
}
```

13.2.2 The if-else Statement

If we wanted to perform one set of actions if a condition were true and another set if the same condition were false, we could use the following sequence of if statements:

```
if (temperature <= 0)
    printf("At or below freezing point.\n");
if (temperature > 0)
    printf("Above freezing.\n");
```

Here, a single message is printed depending on whether the variable temperature is less than or equal to zero or if it is greater than zero. It turns out that this type of conditional execution is a very useful construct in programming that is natively supported in C via the `if-else` statement. The following code is equivalent to the previous code segment. Here, the statement appearing immediately after the `else` keyword executes only if the condition is false.

```
if (temperature <= 0)
    printf("At or below freezing point.\n");
else
    printf("Above freezing.\n");
```

The flow diagram for the `if-else` is shown in Figure 13.2. The figure corresponds to the following code:

```
if (condition)
    action_if;
else
    action_else;
```

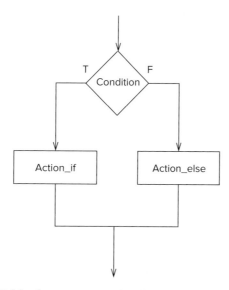

Figure 13.2   The C `if-else` statement, pictorially represented.

The lines `action_if` and `action_else` can correspond to compound statements and thus consist of multiple statements, as in the following example.

```
if (x) {
    y++;
    z--;
}
else {
    y--;
    z++;
}
```

If the variable x is non-zero, the `if`'s condition is true, y is incremented, and z is decremented. Otherwise, y is decremented and z incremented. The LC-3 code

```
1        LDR R0, R5, #0      ; load the value of x
2        BRz ELSE            ; if x equals 0, perform else part
3
4        LDR R0, R5, #-1     ; load y into R0
5        ADD R0, R0, #1
6        STR R0, R5, #-1     ; y++;
7
8        LDR R0, R5, #-2     ; load z into R0
9        ADD R0, R0, #-1
10       STR R0, R5, #-2     ; z--;
11       BR DONE
12
13  ELSE: LDR R0, R5, #-1    ; load y into R0
14       ADD R0, R0, #-1
15       STR R0, R5, #-1     ; y--;
16
17       LDR R0, R5, #-2     ; load z into R0
18       ADD R0, R0, #1
19       STR R0, R5, #-2     ; z++;
20  DONE:
21       :
```

Figure 13.3   The LC-3 code generated for an if-else statement.

generated by our LC-3 C compiler is listed in Figure 13.3. The three variables x, y, and z are locally declared integers.

We can connect conditional constructs together to form a longer sequence of conditional tests. The example in Figure 13.4 shows a complex decision structure

```
1   #include <stdio.h>
2
3   int main(void)
4   {
5       int month;
6
7       printf("Enter the number of the month: ");
8       scanf("%d", &month);
9
10      if (month==4 || month==6 || month==9 || month==11)
11          printf("The month has 30 days\n");
12      else if (month==1 || month==3 || month==5 ||
13              month==7 || month==8 || month==10 || month==12)
14              printf("The month has 31 days\n");
15      else if (month==2)
16          printf("The month has either 28 days or 29 days\n");
17      else
18          printf("Don't know that month\n");
19  }
```

Figure 13.4   A program that determines the number of days in a given month.

created using only the if and if-else statements. No other control structures are used. This program requests a number of a month from the user and outputs the number of days in that month.

At this point, we should clarify how elses are associated with ifs in the C / C++ programming languages: An else is associated with the closest unassociated if. The following example points out why this is important.

```
if (x != 10)
    if (y > 3)
        z = z / 2;
    else
        z = z * 2;
```

Without this rule, it would be ambiguous whether the else should be paired with the *outer* if or the *inner* if. For this situation, the rule states that the else is coupled with the inner if because it is closer than the outer if and the inner if statement has not already been coupled to another else (i.e., it is unassociated). The code is equivalent to the following:

```
if (x != 10) {
    if (y > 3)
        z = z / 2;
    else
        z = z * 2;
}
```

Just as parentheses can be used to modify the order of evaluation of expressions, curly braces can be used to associate statements. If we wanted to associate the else with the outer if, we could write the code as

```
if (x != 10) {
    if (y > 3)
        z = z / 2;
}
else
    z = z * 2;
```

We finish our discussion on if and if-else constructs with a simple example, provided in Figure 13.5. This example illustrates a common use for conditional constructs. In the code, we perform a simple division based on two numbers read as input from the keyboard. Because division by 0 is undefined, if the user enters a 0 divisor, a message is displayed indicating the result cannot be generated. The if-else statement serves nicely for the purpose of checking for the error case. Notice that the non-error case appears first and the error case second. Although we could have coded this either way, having the common, non-error case first provides a visual cue to someone reading the code that the error case is the uncommon one.

```
1    #include <stdio.h>
2
3    int main(void)
4    {
5        int dividend;
6        int divisor;
7        int result;
8
9        printf("Enter the dividend: ");
10       scanf("%d", &dividend);
11
12       printf("Enter the divisor: ");
13       scanf("%d", &divisor);
14
15       if (divisor != 0) {
16           result = dividend / divisor;
17           printf("The result of the division is %d\n", result);
18       }
19       else
20           printf("A divisor of zero is not allowed\n");
21   }
```

Figure 13.5   A program that has error-checking code.

13.3 Iteration Constructs

The power of computing comes in no small part from the ability to compute via iteration. All useful programs perform some form of iteration. C and C++, as with all programming languages, provide native constructs for expressing iterative computation. In C/C++, there are three iteration constructs, each a slight variant of the others: the `while` statement, the `for` statement, and the `do-while` statement. Let's examine each.

13.3.1 The `while` Statement

We begin by describing C's simplest iteration statement. A `while` loop executes a statement repeatedly *while* a condition is true. Before each iteration of the statement, the condition is checked. If the condition evaluates to a logical true (non-zero) value, the statement is executed again. In the following example program, the loop keeps iterating while the value of variable x is less than 10. It produces the following output:

```
0 1 2 3 4 5 6 7 8 9
```

```
#include <stdio.h>

int main(void)
{
    int x = 0;

    while (x < 10) {
        printf("%d ", x);
        x = x + 1;
    }
}
```

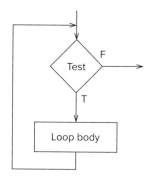

Figure 13.6 The C while statement, pictorially represented.

The while statement consists of two components. The test condition is an expression used to determine whether or not to continue executing the loop. It is tested *before* each execution of the loop_body. The loop_body is a statement that expresses the work to be done within the loop. Like all statements, it can be a compound statement.

```
while (test)
    loop_body;
```

Figure 13.6 shows the control flow using the notation of systematic decomposition. Two branches are required: one conditional branch to exit the loop after test and one unconditional branch after loop_body back to test to determine whether or not to execute another iteration. The LC-3 code generated by our compiler for the previous while example that counts from 0 to 9 is listed in Figure 13.7.

```
1                AND R0, R0, #0    ;   clear out R0
2                STR R0, R5, #0    ;   x = 0;
3
4                ; while (x < 10)
5     LOOP       LDR R0, R5, #0    ;   perform the test
6                ADD R0, R0, #-10
7                BRpz DONE         ;   x is not less than 10
8
9                ; loop body
10               :
11               <code for calling the function printf>
12               :
13               LDR R0, R5, #0    ;   R0 <- x
14               ADD R0, R0, #1    ;   x + 1
15               STR R0, R5, #0    ;   x = x + 1;
16               BR LOOP           ;   end of iteration
17    DONE
18               :
```

Figure 13.7 The LC-3 code generated for a while loop that counts to 9.

The `while` statement is useful for coding loops where the iteration process involves testing for a *sentinel* condition. That is, we don't know the number of iterations beforehand, but we wish to keep looping until some event (i.e., the sentinel) occurs. For example, when we wrote the character counting program in Chapters 5 and 7, we created a loop that terminated when the sentinel EOT character (a character with ASCII code 4) was detected. If we were coding that program in C rather than LC-3 assembly language, we would use a `while` loop. The program in Figure 13.8 uses the `while` statement to test for a sentinel condition.[1]

```
 1  #include <stdio.h>
 2
 3  int main(void)
 4  {
 5      char echo = 'A'; // Initialize char variable echo
 6
 7      while (echo != '\n') {
 8          scanf("%c", &echo);
 9          printf("%c", echo);
10      }
11  }
```

Figure 13.8   Another program with a simple `while` loop.

We end our discussion of the `while` statement by pointing out a common programming bug involving `while` loops. The following program will never terminate because the loop body does not change the looping condition. In this case, the condition always remains true, and the loop never terminates. Such loops are called *infinite loops*, and they are usually (but not always) unintentional, created due to programmer error.

```
#include <stdio.h>
int main()
{
    int x = 0;
    while (x < 10)
        printf("%d ", x);
}
```

13.3.2 The `for` Statement

Just as the `while` loop is a perfect match for a sentinel-controlled loop, the C `for` loop is a perfect match for a counter-controlled loop. In fact, the `for` loop is a special case of the `while` loop that happens to work well when the number of iterations is known ahead of time.

---

[1] This program behaves a bit differently than you might expect. You might expect it to print out each input character as the user types it in, just as the LC-3 version did. Because of the way C deals with keyboard I/O, the program does not get any input until the user hits the Enter key. We explain why this is so when dealing with the low-level issues surrounding I/O in Chapter 18.

In its most straightforward form, the `for` statement allows us to repeat a statement a specified number of times. For example,

```c
#include <stdio.h>
int main(void)
{
    int x;
    for (x = 0; x < 10; x++)
        printf("%d ", x);
}
```

will produce the following output. It loops exactly ten times.

```
0 1 2 3 4 5 6 7 8 9
```

The syntax for the C `for` statement may look a little perplexing at first. It is composed of four components, as follows:

```c
for (init; test; update)
    loop_body;
```

The three components within the parentheses, `init`, `test`, and `update`, control the behavior of the loop and must be separated by semicolons. The final component, `loop_body`, specifies the actual computation to be executed in each iteration.

Let's take a look at each component of the `for` loop in detail. The `init` component is an expression (and optionally also a declaration) that is evaluated before the *first* iteration. It is typically used to declare and initialize variables in preparation for executing the loop. The `test` is an expression that gets evaluated before *every* iteration to determine if another iteration should be executed. If the `test` expression evaluates to zero, the `for` terminates, and the control flow passes to the statement immediately following the `for`. If the expression is non-zero, another iteration of the `loop_body` is performed. Therefore, in the previous code example, the test expression `x < 10` causes the loop to keep repeating as long as `x` is less than 10. The `update` component is an expression that is evaluated at the end of *every* iteration. It is used to update things in preparation for the next iteration. In the previous code example, the variable `x` is incremented by 1 in the `update` step. The `loop_body` is a statement that defines the work to be performed in each iteration, and it works much the same way as the loop body in a `while` statement. It can be a compound statement.

We mention that that `init` can optionally be a declaration. If it is a declaration, the declared variable's scope is the `for` statement itself. This makes it very convenient to create loops where the iteration variable is self-contained within the loop itself. The following example is a common usage for a `for` statement, where the iteration variable is declared in the loop. There are some strong benefits to doing this—for one thing, stray iteration variables don't end up cluttering our code. They are declared and used within the few lines of the loop itself. There is a difference between the previous version of this code and this one. What is it? *Hint:* It isn't a difference in output.

```
#include <stdio.h>
int main(void)
{
    for (int x = 0; x < 10; x++)
        printf("%d ", x);
}
```

Figure 13.9 shows the flow diagram of the for statement. There are four blocks, one for each of the four components of the for statement. There is a conditional branch that determines whether to exit the loop based on the outcome of the test expression or to proceed with another iteration. An unconditional branch loops back to the test at the end of each iteration, after the update expression is evaluated.

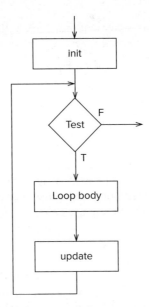

Figure 13.9   The C for statement, pictorially represented.

Even though the syntax of a for statement allows it to be very flexible, most of the for loops you will encounter (or will write) will be of the counter-controlled variety, that is, loops that iterate for a certain number of iterations. Following are some commonly encountered examples of for loops, including counter-controlled loops and loops with locally declared variables.

```
// --- What does the loop output? ---
for (int x = 0; x <= 10; x++)
    printf("%d ", x);

// --- What does this one output? ---
char letter = 'a';
for (char c = 0; c < 26; c++)
    printf("%c ", letter + c);
```

```
// --- What does this loop do? ---
int numberOfOnes = 0;
for (int bitNum = 0; bitNum < 16; bitNum++) {
   if (inputValue & (1 << bitNum))
      numberOfOnes++;
}
```

Let's take a look at the LC-3 translation of a simple for loop. The program is a simple one: It calculates the sum of all integers between 0 and 9.

```
#include <stdio.h>
int main(void)
{
    int x;
    int sum = 0;
    for (x - 0; x < 10; x++)
       sum = sum + x;
}
```

The LC-3 code generated by the compiler is shown in Figure 13.10. The following code contains an easy-to-make mistake involving for loops.

```
1               AND R0, R0, #0    ;   clear out R0
2               STR R0, R5, #-1   ;   sum = 0;
3
4               ; init
5               AND R0, R0, #0    ;   clear out R0
6               STR R0, R5, #0    ;   init (x = 0)
7
8               ; test
9     LOOP      LDR R0, R5, #0    ;   perform the test
10              ADD R0, R0, #-10
11              BRpz DONE         ;   x is not less than 10
12
13              ; loop body
14              LDR R0, R5, #0    ;   get x
15              LDR R1, R5, #-1   ;   get sum
16              ADD R1, R1, R0    ;   sum + x
17              STR R0, R5, #-1   ;   sum = sum + x;
18
19              ; reinit
20              LDR R0, R5, #0    ;   get x
21              ADD R0, R0, #1
22              STR R0, R5, #0    ;   x++
23              BR LOOP
24
25    DONE
26              :
```

Figure 13.10   The LC-3 code generated for a for statement.

```
sum = 0;
for (x = 0; x < 10; x++);
    sum = sum + x;
printf("sum = %d\n", sum);
printf("x = %d\n", x);
```

What is output by the first `printf`? The answer is `sum` = 10. Why? The second `printf` outputs `x` = 10. Why? If you look carefully, you might be able to notice a misplaced semicolon.

A `for` loop can be constructed using a `while` loop (actually, vice versa as well). When programming, they can be used interchangeably, to a degree. Which construct to use in which situation may seem puzzling at first, but keep in mind the general rule that `while` is best suited for loops that involve sentinel conditions, whereas `for` fits situations where the number of iterations is known beforehand.

13.3.2.1 Nested Loops

Figure 13.11 contains an example of a `for` where the loop body is composed of another `for` loop. This construct is referred to as a *nested loop* because the inner loop is nested within the outer. In this example, the program prints out a multiplication table for the numbers 0 through 9. Each iteration of the inner loop prints out a single product in the table. That is, the inner loop iterates ten times for each iteration of the outer loop. An entire row is printed for each iteration of the outer loop. Notice that the `printf` at line 9 contains a special character sequence in its format string. The `\t` sequence causes a tab character to be printed out. The tab helps align the columns of the multiplication table so the output looks neater.

```
1    #include <stdio.h>
2
3    int main(void)
4    {
5        // Outer Loop
6        for (int multiplicand = 0; multiplicand < 10; multiplicand++) {
7            // Inner Loop
8            for (int multiplier = 0; multiplier < 10; multiplier++)
9                printf("%d\t", multiplier * multiplicand);
10           printf("\n");
11       }
12   }
```

Figure 13.11   **A program that prints out a multiplication table.**

Figure 13.12 contains a slightly more complex example. The number of iterations of the inner loop depends on the value of `outer` as determined by the outer loop. The inner loop will first execute zero time, then one time, then two times, etc. There is a wide range of interesting algorithms that we'll encounter in this book that have similar iteration structures.

```
1    #include <stdio.h>
2
3    int main(void)
4    {
5        int sum = 0;     // Initial the result variable
6        int input;       // Holds user input
7
8        // Get input
9        printf("Input an integer: ");
10       scanf("%d", &input);
11
12       // Perform calculation
13       for (int outer = 1; outer <= input; outer++) {
14           for (int inner = 0; inner < outer; inner++) {
15               sum += inner;
16           }
17       }
18
19       // Output result
20       printf("The result is %d\n", sum);
21   }
```

Figure 13.12   A program with a nested for **loop.**

13.3.3 The do-while Statement

With a while loop, the condition is always checked *before* an iteration is performed. Therefore, it is possible for the while loop to execute zero iterations (i.e., when the condition is false from the start). There is a slight variant of the while statement in C called do-while, which always performs at least one iteration. In a do-while loop, the condition is evaluated *after* the first iteration is performed. The operation of the do-while is demonstrated in the following example:

```
x = 0;
do {
    printf("%d \n", x);
    x = x + 1;
} while (x < 10);
```

Here, the conditional test, x < 10, is evaluated at the end of each iteration. Thus, the loop body will execute at least once. The next iteration is performed only if the test evaluates to a non-zero value. This code produces the following output:

```
0 1 2 3 4 5 6 7 8 9
```

Syntactically, a do-while is composed of two components, exactly like the while.

```
do
    loop_body;
while (test);
```

The loop_body component is a statement (simple or compound) that describes the computation to be performed by the loop. The test is an expression

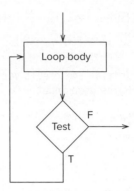

Figure 13.13   The C `do-while` statement, pictorially represented.

that determines whether another iteration is to be performed. Figure 13.13 shows the control flow of the `do-while` loop. Notice the slight change from the flow of a `while` loop. The loop body and the test are interchanged. A conditional branch loops back to the top of the loop body, initiating another iteration.

At this point, the differences between the three types of C iteration constructs may seem very subtle, but once you become comfortable with them and build up experience using these constructs, you will more easily be able to pick the right construct to fit the situation. To a large degree, these constructs can be used interchangeably. Stylistically, there are times when one construct makes more sense to use than another—often the type of loop you choose will convey information about the intent of the loop to someone reading your code.

13.4 Problem Solving Using Control Structures

Armed with a new arsenal of control structures, we can now try to solve complex programming problems. In this section, we will apply our top-down problem-solving methodology to four problems requiring the use of C control structures.

Being effective at solving programming problems requires that you understand the basic primitives of the system on which you are programming. The art of programming is often creative uses of those basic primitives in clever ways. At this point, our set of C primitives includes variables of the three basic types, operators, two decision structures, and three control structures. It's a pretty powerful set with which we can achieve a lot.

13.4.1 Problem 1: Approximating the Value of π

For our first programming problem, we will calculate the value of π using the following series expansion:

$$\pi = 4 - \frac{4}{3} + \frac{4}{5} - \frac{4}{7} + \cdots + (-1)^{n-1} \frac{4}{2n+1}$$

We'll write C code to evaluate this series for the number of terms indicated by the user. If the user enters 3, the program will evaluate $4 - \frac{4}{3} + \frac{4}{5}$. The series is an infinite series, and the more terms we evaluate, the more accurate our approximation of π. This is not a very rapidly converging series, so we'll need to evaluate a lot of terms to generate a good approximation.

As we did for the problem-solving example in Chapter 12, we first invoke step 0: We select a representation for the data involved in the computation. Since the series deals with fractional numbers, we use the `double` floating point type for any variables directly involved in the series calculation.

Now we invoke stepwise refinement to decompose a roughly stated algorithm into a C program. Roughly, we want the program to first initialize everything, then prompt the user to input the number of terms of the series to evaluate, then evaluate the series for the given number of terms, and finally print out the result. We have defined the problem as a set of sequential constructs. Figure 13.14 shows this initial decomposition. Most of the sequential constructs in Figure 13.14 are very straightforward, and converting them into C code is quite simple.

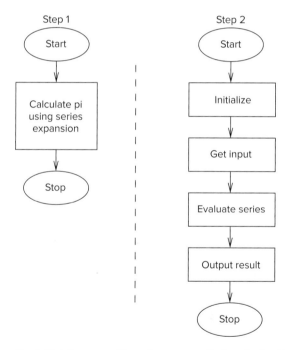

Figure 13.14 The initial decomposition of a program that evaluates the series expansion for π for a given number of terms.

One of the elements in the figure, however, requires some additional refinement. We need to put a little thought into the subtask labeled *Evaluate series*. For this subtask, we essentially want to *iterate* through the series, term by term, until we evaluate exactly the number of terms indicated by the user. We want

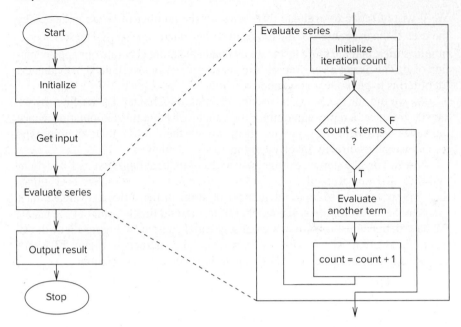

Figure 13.15 The refinement of the subtask Evaluate series into an iteration construct that iterates a given number of times. Within this loop, we evaluate terms for a series expansion for π.

to use a counter-controlled iteration construct since we know exactly the number of iterations to execute. Figure 13.15 shows the refined decomposition. We maintain a counter for the current loop iteration. If the counter is less than the limit indicated by the user, then we evaluate another term. Notice that the refined version of the subtask looks like the flow diagram for a `for` loop. The only non-trivial subtask remaining is *Evaluate another term*. Notice that all even terms in the series are subtracted, and all odd terms are added. Within this subtask, we need to determine if the particular term being evaluated is odd or even and then factor it into the current value of the approximation. This involves using a decision construct as shown in Figure 13.16. The complete code resulting from this stepwise refinement is shown in Figure 13.17.

13.4.2 Problem 2: Finding Prime Numbers Less Than 100

Our next problem-solving example involves finding all the prime numbers that are less than 100. A number is prime only if the numbers that evenly divide it are 1 and itself.

Step 0, as with our previous examples, is to select an appropriate data representation for the various variables associated with the problem. Since primality only applies to integers, using the integer data type for the main computation seems the best choice. Next, we approach this problem by first stating it as a single

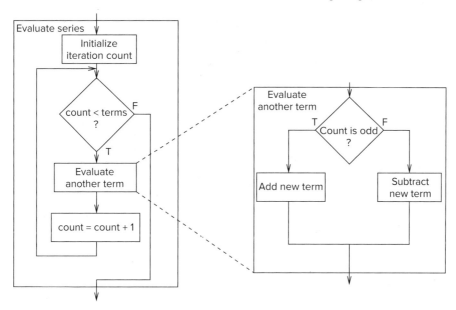

Figure 13.16   Incorporate the current term based on whether it is odd or even.

```
1    #include <stdio.h>
2
3    int main(void)
4    {
5        int numOfTerms;    // Number of terms to evaluate
6        double pi = 0;     // approximation of pi
7
8        printf("Number of terms (must be 1 or larger) : ");
9        scanf("%d", &numOfTerms);
10
11       for (int count = 1; count <= numOfTerms; count++) {
12           if (count % 2)
13               pi = pi + (4.0 / (2.0 * count - 1)); // Odd term
14           else
15               pi = pi - (4.0 / (2.0 * count - 1)); // Even term
16       }
17
18       printf("The approximate value of pi is %f\n", pi);
19   }
```

Figure 13.17   A program to calculate π.

task (step 1). We then refine this single task into two separate sequential subtasks: Initialize and then perform the calculation (step 2). Performing the *Calculation* subtask is the bulk of the coding effort. Essentially, the *Calculation* subtask can be stated as follows: We will iterate through every integer between 2 and 100

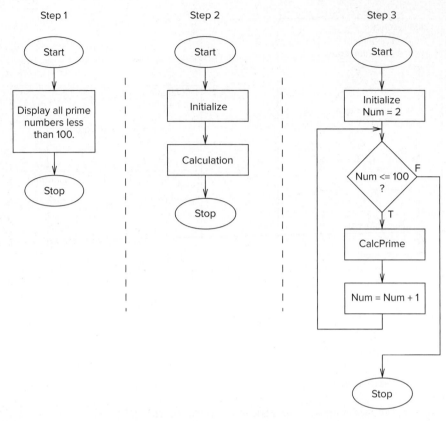

Figure 13.18   Decomposing a problem to compute prime numbers less than 100. The first three steps involve creating a loop that iterates between the 2 and 100.

to determine if it is prime, printing out only those that are. A counter-controlled loop should work just fine for this purpose because we know the iteration space precisely. We can further refine the *Calculation* subtask into smaller subtasks, as shown in Figure 13.18. Notice that the flow diagram has the shape of a for loop. Already, the problem is starting to resolve into C code. We still need to refine the *CalcPrime* subtask but determine if the current number is prime or not. Here, we rely on the fact that any number between 2 and 100 that is *not* prime will have at least one divisor between 2 and 10 that is not itself.

We can refine this subtask as shown in Figure 13.19. Basically, we will determine if each number is divisible by an integer between 2 and 10 (being careful to exclude the number itself). If it has no divisors between 2 and 10, except perhaps itself, then the number is prime.

Finally, we need to refine the *Divide number by integers 2 through 10* subtask. It involves dividing the current number by all integers between 2 and 10 and determining if any of them evenly divide it. A simple way to do this is to use

Step 3

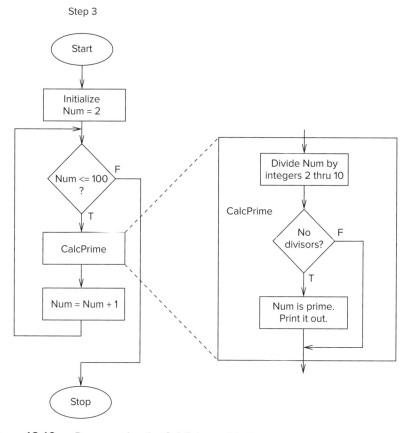

Figure 13.19   Decomposing the CalcPrime subtask.

another counter-controlled loop to cycle through all the integers between 2 and 10. Figure 13.20 shows the decomposition using an iteration construct.

Now, we have a representation of the program that can easily be reduced to C code. The program is listed in Figure 13.21. There are two `for` loops within the program, one of which is nested within the other. The outer loop sequences through all the integers between 2 and 100; it corresponds to the loop created when we decomposed the *Calculation* subtask. An inner loop determines if the number generated by the outer loop has any divisors; it corresponds to the loop created when we decomposed the *Divide number by integers 2 through 10* subtask.

13.4.3 Problem 3: Analyzing an E-mail Address

Our final problem in this section involves analyzing an e-mail address typed in at the keyboard to determine if it is of valid format. For this problem, we'll use a simple definition of validity: An e-mail address is a sequence of characters that must contain an at sign, "@", and a period, ".", with the @ symbol preceding the period.

As before, we start by choosing an appropriate data representation for the underlying data of the problem. Here, we are processing text data entered by

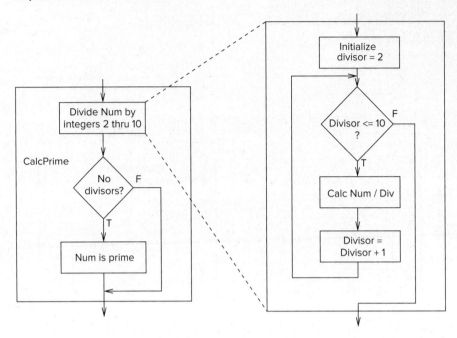

Figure 13.20   Decomposing the Divide numbers by integers 2 through 10 subtask.

```
 1  #include <stdio.h>
 2  #include <stdbool.h>
 3
 4  int main(void)
 5  {
 6      bool prime = true;
 7
 8      // Start at 2 and go until 0
 9      for (int num = 2; num <= 100; num++) {
10          prime = true;     // Assume the number is prime
11
12          // Test if the candidate number is a prime
13          for (int divisor = 2; divisor <= 10; divisor++)
14              if (((num % divisor)==0) && num != divisor)
15                  prime = false;
16
17          if (prime)
18              printf("The number %d is prime\n", num);
19      }
20  }
```

Figure 13.21   A program that finds all prime numbers between 2 and 100.

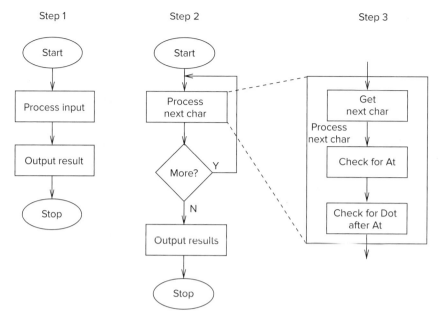

Figure 13.22   A stepwise refinement of the analyze e-mail address program.

the user. The type best suited for text is the ASCII character type, `char`. Actually, the best representation for input text is an array of characters, or *character string*, but because we have not yet introduced arrays into our lexicon of primitive elements (and we will in Chapter 16), we instead target our solution to use a single variable of the `char` type.

Next, we apply the stepwise refinement process. The entire process is diagrammed in Figure 13.22. We start with a rough flow of the program where we have two tasks (step 1): *Process input* and *Output results*. Here, the *Output results* task is straightforward. We output the validity of the input sequence of characters.

The *Process input* task requires more refinement, however. In decomposing the *Process input* task (step 2), we need to keep in mind that our choice of data representation (variable of the char type) implies that we will need to read and process the user's input one character at a time. We will keep processing, character by character, until we have reached the end of the e-mail address, implying that we'll need a sentinel-controlled loop. Step 2 of the decomposition divides the *Process input* task into a sentinel-controlled iteration construct that terminates when the end of an e-mail address is encountered, which we'll say is either a space or a newline character, `\n`.

The next step (step 3) of the decomposition involves detailing what processing occurs within the loop. Here, we need to check each character within the e-mail address and record if we have seen the @ symbol and a period in the proper order. To do this, we will use two variables to record each symbol's occurrence. When the loop terminates and we are ready to display the result, we can examine these variables to display the appropriate output message.

```
1    #include <stdio.h>
2    #include <stdbool.h>
3
4    int main(void)
5    {
6        char nextChar;        // Next character in e-mail address
7        bool gotAt = false;   // Indicates if At @ was found
8        bool gotDot = false;  // Indicates if Dot . was found
9
10       printf("Enter your e-mail address: ");
11
12       do {
13          scanf("%c", &nextChar);
14
15          if (nextChar=='@')
16             gotAt = true;
17
18          if (nextChar=='.' && gotAt)
19             gotDot = true;
20       }
21       while (nextChar != ' ' && nextChar != '\n');
22
23       if (gotAt && gotDot)
24          printf("Your e-mail address appears to be valid.\n");
25       else
26          printf("Your e-mail address is not valid!\n");
27   }
```

Figure 13.23   A C program to perform a simple test for validity of e-mail addresses.

At this point, we are not far from C code. Notice that the loop structure is very similar to the flow diagram of the `do-while` statement, and therefore we choose to use it as the iteration construct. The C code for this problem is provided in Figure 13.23.

13.5 Additional C Control Structures

We complete our coverage of the C control structures by examining the `switch`, `break`, and `continue` statements. These three statements provide specialized program control that programmers occasionally find useful for very particular programming situations. We provide them here primarily for completeness; none of the examples in the remainder of the textbook use any of these three constructs.

13.5.1 The `switch` Statement

Occasionally, we run into programming situations where we want to do one of *n* different things based on the value of a particular variable. For example, in the following code, we test the character variable `keypress` to see which of several possible character values it equals and do one outcome based on its value.

```
// keypress is a char variable

if (keyPress == 'a')
   // Do statement A
else if (keyPress == 'b')
   // Do statement B
else if (keyPress == 'x')
   // Do statement C
else if (keyPress == 'y')
   // Do statement D
```

In this code, one (or none) of the statements labeled A, B, C, or D will execute, depending on the value of the variable `keyPress`. If `keyPress` is equal to the character a, then statement A is executed, if it is equal to the character b, then statement B is executed, and so forth. If `keyPress` does not equal a or b or x or y, then none of the statements are executed. If there are many of these conditions to check, then many tests will be required in order to find the "matching" one. To simplify this particular programming idiom, C provides the `switch` statement. The following code segment behaves the same as the code in the previous example. It uses a `switch` statement instead of cascaded `if-else` statements.

```
switch (keyPress) {
case 'a':
   // Do statement A
   break;

case 'b':
   // Do statement B
   break;

case 'x':
   // Do statement C
   break;

case 'y':
   // Do statement D
   break;
}
```

Notice that the `switch` statement contains several lines beginning with the keyword `case`, followed by a label and colon `:`. If the value of any of the following case labels matches the value of `keypress`, then associated statements are executed.

Let's go through the `switch` construct step by step. The `switch` keyword precedes the expression on which to base the decision. This expression must be of integral type (e.g., an `int` or a `char`). If one of the `case` labels matches the value of the expression, then program control passes to the statement or block immediately following that `case` label. Each `case` consists of a sequence of zero or more statements similar to a compound statement, but no delimiting braces are required. The place within this compound statement to start executing is determined by which `case` matches the value of the `switch` expression. Each `case` label within a `switch` statement must be unique, and identical labels are not allowed. Furthermore, each `case` label must be a constant expression. It cannot be based on a value that changes as the program is executing.

In the preceding `switch` example, each `case` ends with a `break` statement. The `break` exits the `switch` construct by jumping the flow of control to the closing brace of the `switch`, essentially exiting the `switch`. The `break` statements are optional. If they are not used (which is rarely the case), then control will go from the current `case` to the next. We can optionally also include a `default` case. This case is selected if the `switch` expression matches none of the `case` constants. If no `default` case is given, and the expression matches none of the constants, none of the `cases` are executed.

A stylistic note: The last `case` of a `switch` does not need to end with a `break` since execution of the `switch` ends there, anyway. However, including a `break` for the final `case` is good programming practice. If another `case` is ever added to the end of the `switch`, then you will not have to remember to add the `break` to the previous `case`.

13.5.2 The `break` and `continue` Statements

In Section 13.5.1, we saw an example of how the C `break` statement is used with `switch`. The `break` statement and also the `continue` statement are occasionally used with iteration constructs. The `break` statement causes the compiler to generate code that will immediately exit a loop or a `switch` statement. When used within a loop body, `break` causes the loop to terminate by jumping out to the end of the loop statement. No more iterations are executed. The `continue` statement, on the other hand, causes the current iteration to end. The next iteration might then execute, depending on the looping conditions. Both of these statements can occur within a loop body and apply to the iteration construct immediately enclosing them. Essentially, the break and continue statements cause the compiler to generate an unconditional branch instruction that leaves the loop or loop iteration from somewhere in the loop body. Following are two example C code segments that use `break` and `continue`.

```
// This code segment produces the output: 0 1 2 3 4
for (i = 0; i < 10; i++) {
    if (i==5)
        break;
    printf("%d ", i);
}

// This code produces the output: 0 1 2 3 4 6 7 8 9
for (i = 0; i < 10; i++) {
    if (i==5)
        continue;
    printf("%d ", i);
}
```

13.5.3 An Example: Simple Calculator

The program in Figure 13.24 performs a function similar to the calculator example from Chapter 10. The user is prompted for three items: an integer operand,

```
1    #include <stdio.h>
2
3    int main(void)
4    {
5        int operand1, operand2;  // Input values
6        int result = 0;          // Result of the operation
7        char operation;          // operation to perform
8
9        // Get the input values
10       printf("Enter first operand: ");
11       scanf("%d", &operand1);
12       printf("Enter operation to perform (+, -, *, /): ");
13       scanf("\n%c", &operation);
14       printf("Enter second operand: ");
15       scanf("%d", &operand2);
16
17       // Perform the calculation
18       switch(operation) {
19       case '+':
20          result = operand1 + operand2;
21          break;
22
23       case '-':
24          result = operand1 - operand2;
25          break;
26
27       case '*':
28          result = operand1 * operand2;
29          break;
30
31       case '/':
32          if (operand2 != 0)   // Error-checking code.
33             result = operand1 / operand2;
34          else
35             printf("Divide by 0 error!\n");
36          break;
37
38       default:
39          printf("Invalid operation!\n");
40          break;
41    }
42
43    printf("The answer is %d\n", result);
44 }
```

Figure 13.24   Calculator program in C.

an operation to perform, and another integer operand. The program performs the operation on the two input values and displays the result. The program makes use of a switch to base its computation on the operator the user has selected.

13.6 Summary

We conclude this chapter by summarizing the key concepts we've covered. The basic objective of this chapter was to enlarge our set of problem-solving primitives by exploring the various control structures supported by the C programming language.

- **Decision Constructs in C.** We covered two basic C decision statements: `if` and `if-else`. Both of these statements *conditionally* execute a statement, depending on whether a specified expression is true or false.

- **Iteration Constructs in C.** C provides three iteration statements: `while`, `for`, and `do-while`. All of these statements execute a statement multiple times based on some iteration criteria or condition. The `while` and `do-while` statements are particularly well-suited for expressing sentinel-controlled loops. The `for` statement works well for expressing counter-controlled loops.

- **Problem Solving Using Control Structures.** To our arsenal of primitives for problem solving (which already includes the three basic C types, variables, operators, and I/O using `printf` and `scanf`), we added control constructs. We practiced some problem-solving examples that required application of these control constructs.

Exercises

13.1 Re-create the LC-3 compiler's symbol table when it compiles the calculator program listed in Figure 13.24.

13.2 *a.* What does the following code look like after it is processed by the preprocessor?

```
#define VERO -2

if (VERO)
    printf("True!");
else
    printf("False!");
```

   b. What is the output produced when this code is run?
   c. If we modified the code to the following, does the code behave differently? If so, how?

```
#define VERO -2

if (VERO)
    printf("True!");
else if (!VERO)
    printf("False!");
```

13.3 An if-else statement can be used in place of the C conditional operator (see Section 12.6.3). Rewrite the following statement using an if-else rather than the conditional operator.

```
x = a ? b : c;
```

13.4 Describe the behavior of the following statements for the case when x equals 0 and when x equals 1. Assume all variables are integer types.

a.
```
if (x = 0)
    printf("x equals 0\n");
else
    printf("x does not equal 0\n");
```

b.
```
if (x == 0)
    printf("x equals 0\n");
else
    printf("x does not equal 0\n");
```

c.
```
if (x == 0)
    printf("A\n");
else if (x != 1)
    printf("B\n");
else if (x < 1)
    printf("C\n");
else if (x)
    printf("D\n");
```

d.
```
switch (x) {
case 0:
    y = 3;
case 1:
    y = 4;
    break;
default:
    y = 5;
    break;
}
```

e. What happens if x is not equal to 0 or 1 for part *d*?

13.5 Provide the LC-3 code generated by our LC-3 C compiler when it compiles the switch statement in part *d* of Exercise 13.4.

13.6 Figure 13.12 contains a C program with a nested for loop.

a. Mathematically state the series that this program calculates.
b. Write a program to calculate the following function:

$$f(n) = f(n-1) + f(n-2)$$

with the following initial conditions,

$$f(0) = 1, f(1) = 1$$

13.7   Can the following if-else statement be converted into a `switch`? If yes, convert it. If no, why not?

```
if (x == 0)
    y = 3;
else if (x == 1)
    y = 4;
else if (x == 2)
    y = 5;
else if (x == y)
    y = 6;
else
    y = 7;
```

13.8   At least how many times will the statement called `loopBody` execute the following constructs?

a. `while (condition)`
          `loopBody;`

b. `do`
          `loopBody;`
    `while (condition);`

c. `for (init; condition; update)`
          `loopBody;`

d. `while (condition1)`
          `for (init; condition2; reinit)`
              `loopBody;`

e. `do`
        `do`
            `loopBody;`
        `while (condition1);`
    `while (condition2);`

13.9   What is the output of each of the following code segments?

a. `a = 2;`
    `while (a > 0)`
        `a--;`
    `printf("%d", a);`

b. `a = 2;`
    `do {`
        `a--;`
    `} while (a > 0)`
    `printf("%d", a);`

c. `b = 0;`
    `for (a = 3; a < 10; a += 2)`
        `b = b + 1;`
    `printf("%d %d", a, b);`

13.10 Convert the program in Figure 13.4 into one that uses a `switch` statement instead of `if-else`.

13.11 Modify the e-mail address validation program in Figure 13.23 to check that a valid e-mail address has at least one alphabetic character preceding the @ (at sign), at least one between the @ and the period, and at least one after the period.

13.12 For the following questions, x is an integer with the value 4.

a. What output is generated by the following code segment?

```
if (7 > x > 2)
    printf("True.");
else
    printf("False.");
```

b. Why doesn't the following code cause an infinite loop?

```
while (x > 0)
    x++;
```

c. What is the value of x after the following code has executed?

```
for (x = 4; x < 4; x--) {
    if (x < 2)
        break;
    else if (x == 2)
        continue;
    x = -1;
}
```

13.13 Change this program so that it uses a do-while loop instead of a for loop.

```
int main(void)
{
    int sum;

    for (int i = 0; i <= 100; i++) {
        if (i % 4 == 0)
            sum = sum + 2;
        else if (i % 4 == 1)
            sum = sum - 6;
        else if (i % 4 == 2)
            sum = sum * 3;
        else if (i % 4 == 3)
            sum = sum / 2;
    }
    printf("%d\n", sum);
}
```

13.14 Write a C program that accepts as input a single integer k, then writes a pattern consisting of a single 1 on the first line, two 2s on the second line, three 3s on the third line, and so forth, until it writes k occurrences of k on the last line.

For example, if the input is 5, the output should be the following:

```
1
2 2
3 3 3
4 4 4 4
5 5 5 5 5
```

13.15   *a.*   Convert the following `while` loop into a `for` loop.

```
while (condition)
    loopBody;
```

       b.   Convert the following `for` loop into a `while` loop.

```
for (init; condition; update)
    loopBody;
```

13.16   What is the output of the following code?

```
int w = 12;
int sum = 0;

for (int r = 1; r <= w; r++)
    for (int s = r; s <= w; s++)
        sum = sum + s;
printf("sum =%d\n", sum);
```

13.17   The following code performs something quite specific. Describe its output.

```
int i;
scanf("%d", &i);

for (int j = 0; j < 16; j++) {
    if (i & (1 << j))
        count++;
}
printf("%d\n", count);
```

13.18   Provide the output of each of the following code segments.

       a.
```
int x = 20;
int y = 10;

while ((x > 10) && (y & 15)) {
    y = y + 1;
    x = x - 1;
    printf("*");
}
```

       b.
```
for (int x = 10; x ; x = x - 1)
    printf("*");
```

c.
```
for (int x = 0; x < 10; x = x + 1)
    if (x % 2)
        printf("*");
```

d.
```
int x = 0;

while (x < 10) {
    for (int i = 0; i < x; i = x + 1)
        printf("*");
    x = x + 1;
}
```

13.19 Why does C not permit declaration of variables in `while` loops similar to `for` loops?

```
while (int x < 10) {
    // Loop body
    x = x + 1;
}
```

CHAPTER

14 Functions

14.1 Introduction

Functions are the basic building blocks for large-scale code development today. They enable the software developer to extend the set of constructs natively supported by the language to include new primitives. Functions are such a necessary and important concept that we build support for them directly in the hardware at the instruction set architecture level.

Why are they so important? Functions (or procedures, or subroutines, or methods—all of which are variations of the same theme) enable *abstraction*. That is, they increase our ability to separate the operation performed by a component from the details of how it performs that operation. Once the component is created and we understand its construction, we can use the component as a building block without giving much thought to its detailed implementation. Without abstraction, our ability to create complex, sophisticated digital systems would be seriously impaired.

Functions are not new to us. We have been using variants of functions ever since we programmed subroutines in LC-3 assembly language. While there are syntactic differences between subroutines in LC-3 assembly and functions in C, the concepts behind them are largely the same. The C programming language is heavily oriented around functions. A C program is essentially a collection of functions. Every statement belongs to one (and only one) function. All C programs start and finish execution in the function `main`. The function `main` might call other functions along the way, and they might, in turn, call more functions. Control eventually returns to the function `main`, and when `main` ends, the program ends. And the C++ language takes the idea of functions even further by enabling the programmer to associate functions with specific types to build objects. But that is a subject for Chapter 20.

In this chapter, we examine C functions in detail. We begin by creating several short programs in order to get a sense of the C syntax around functions. From there we move on to how functions are implemented, examining the low-level operations necessary for functions to work. In the last part of the chapter, we apply our problem-solving methodology to some programming problems that benefit from the use of functions.

14.2 Functions in C

Let's start off with a simple example of a C program involving functions. Figure 14.1 is a program that prints a message using a function named PrintBanner. This program begins execution at the function main, which then calls the function PrintBanner. This function prints a line of text consisting of the = character to the output device. PrintBanner is the simplest form of a function: It requires no input from its caller to do its job, and it provides its caller with no output data (not counting the banner printed to the screen). In other words, no arguments are passed from main to PrintBanner and no value is returned from PrintBanner to main. More formally, we refer to the function main as the *caller* and to PrintBanner as the *callee*.

```
1    #include <stdio.h>
2
3    void PrintBanner();     // Function declaration
4
5    int main(void)
6    {
7        PrintBanner();        // Function call
8        printf("A simple C program.\n");
9        PrintBanner();
10   }
11
12   void PrintBanner()     // Function definition
13   {
14       printf("=============================\n");
15   }
```

Figure 14.1   A C program that uses a function to print a banner message.

14.2.1 A Function with a Parameter

The fact that PrintBanner and main require no exchange of information simplifies their interface. In general, however, we'd like to be able to pass information between the caller and the callee. The next example demonstrates how this is accomplished in C. The code in Figure 14.2 contains a function Factorial that performs an operation based on an input argument.

Factorial performs a multiplication of all integers between 1 and n, where n is the value provided by the caller function (in this case main). The calculation performed by this function can be algebraically stated as:

$$\text{factorial}(n) = n! = 1 \times 2 \times 3 \times \ldots \times n$$

```
1   #include <stdio.h>
2
3   int Factorial(int n);          // Function Declaration
4
5   int main(void)                 // Definition for main
6   {
7       int number;                // Number from user
8       int answer;                // Answer of factorial
9
10      printf("Input a number: ");  // Call to printf
11
12      scanf("%d", &number);        // Call to scanf
13
14      answer = Factorial(number);  // Call to factorial
15
16      printf("The factorial of %d is %d\n", number, answer);
17  }
18
19  int Factorial(int n)           // Function Definition
20  {
21      int result = 1;            // Initialized result
22
23      for (int i = 1; i <= n; i++)  // Calculate factorial
24          result = result * i;
25
26      return result;             // Return to caller
27  }
```

Figure 14.2   A C program to calculate factorial.

The value calculated by this function is named `result` in the C code in Figure 14.2. Its value is returned (using the `return` statement) to the caller. We say that the function `Factorial` requires a single integer *argument* from its caller, and it *returns* an integer value back to its caller. In this particular example, the variable `answer` in the caller is assigned the return value from `Factorial` (line 14).

Let's take a closer look at the syntax. In the code in Figure 14.2, there are four lines that are of particular interest to us. The *declaration* for `Factorial` is at line 3. Its *definition* starts at line 19. The call to `Factorial` is at line 14; this statement invokes the function. The return from `Factorial` back to its caller is at line 26.

14.2.1.1 The Declaration

The function declaration for `Factorial` appears at line 3, looking kind of lonely. What is the purpose of a this line? It informs the compiler about some relevant properties of the function in the same way a variable's declaration informs the compiler about a variable. Sometimes called a *function prototype*, a function declaration contains the name of the function, the type of value it returns, and a list of input arguments it expects along with their associated types. The function declaration ends with a semicolon.

The first item appearing in a function's declaration is the type of the value the function returns. The type can be any C data type (e.g., `int`, `char`, `double`). This type describes the type of the single output value that the function produces. Not all functions return values. For example, the function `PrintBanner` from the previous example did not return a value. If a function does not return a value, then its return type should be declared as `void`, indicating to the compiler that the function returns nothing.

The next item in the declaration is the function's name. A function's name can be any legal C identifier. Often, programmers choose function names rather carefully to reflect the actions performed by the function. `Factorial`, for example, is a good choice for the function in our example because the mathematical term for the operation it performs is *factorial*. Also, it is good style to use a naming convention where the names of functions and the names of variables are easily distinguishable. In the examples in this book, we do this by capitalizing the first character of all function names, such as `Factorial`.

A function's declaration also describes the type and order of the input *arguments* required by the function. These are the types of values that the function expects to receive from its callers and the order in which it expects to receive them. We can optionally specify (and often do) the name of each parameter in the declaration. For example, the function `Factorial` takes one integer value as an input argument, and it refers to this value internally as `n`. Some functions may not require any input. The function `PrintBanner` requires no input arguments; therefore, its argument list is empty.

14.2.1.2 The Call

Line 14 in our example is the function call that invokes `Factorial`. In this statement, the function `main` calls `Factorial`. Before `Factorial` can start, however, `main` must transmit a single integer value to `Factorial`. Such values within the caller that are transmitted to the callee are called *arguments*. Arguments can be any legal expression, but they should match the type expected by the callee. These arguments are enclosed in parentheses immediately after the callee's name. In this example, the function `main` passes the value of the variable `number` as the argument. The value returned by `Factorial` is then assigned to the integer variable `answer`.

14.2.1.3 The Definition

The code beginning at line 19 is the function definition for `Factorial`. Notice that the first line of the definition matches the function declaration (minus the semicolon). Within the parentheses after the name of the function is the function's *formal parameter list*. The formal parameter list is a list of variable declarations, where each variable will be initialized with the corresponding argument provided by the caller. In this example, when `Factorial` is called on line 14, the parameter `n` will be initialized to the value of `number` from `main`. From every place in the program where a function is called, the actual arguments appearing in each call should match the type and ordering of the formal parameter list. The function's body appears in the braces following the parameter list. A function's body consists of declarations and statements that define the computation the function performs. Any variable declared within these braces is local to the function, visible and modifiable only within the function itself. In C, the arguments of the caller are *passed as values* to the callee. What this means is that Factorial cannot modify the variable number because only the value of number is passed to Factorial.

14.2.1.4 The Return Value

Control passes back from Factorial to the caller main on line 26. Since Factorial is returning a value, an expression must follow the return keyword, and the type of this expression should match the return type declared for the function. In the case of Factorial, the statement return result; transmits the calculated value stored in result back to the caller. In general, functions that return a value must include at least one return statement in their body. Functions that do not return a value—functions declared as type void—do not need a return statement; the return is optional. For these functions, control passes back to the caller after the last statement has executed.

What about the function main? Its return type is int (as required by the ANSI standard), yet it does not contain a return. Strictly speaking, we should include a return 0 at the end of main in the examples we've seen thus far. In C, if a non-void function does not explicitly return a value, the value of the last statement is returned to the caller. For the simple code that we describe in this textbook, the return value from main is unnecessary, so we've omitted an explicit return in the text to make our examples more compact. Also, the formal parameter list for main in this example is void. It turns out we can pass main arguments, and oftentimes it's useful to do so. For most examples in this textbook, main will not use those arguments; we designate main's parameter list as void.

Let's summarize these various syntactic components: A function declaration informs the compiler about the function, indicating its name, the number and types of parameters the function expects from a caller, and the type of value the function returns. A function definition is the actual source code for the function. The definition includes a formal parameter list, which indicates the names of the function's parameters and the order in which they will be expected from the caller. A function is invoked via a function call. Input values, or arguments, for the function are listed within the parentheses of the function call. Literally, the value of each argument listed in the function call is assigned to the corresponding parameter in the parameter list, the first argument assigned to the first parameter, the second argument to the second parameter, and so forth. The return value is the output of the function, and it is passed back to the caller function.

14.2.2 Example: Area of a Ring

We further demonstrate C function syntax with a short example in Figure 14.3. This C program calculates the area of a circle that has a smaller circle removed from it. In other words, it calculates the area of a ring with a specified outer and

```
1    #include <stdio.h>
2
3    // Function declarations
4    double AreaOfCircle(double radius);
5
6    int main(void)
7    {
8        double outer;        // Inner radius
9        double inner;        // Outer radius
10       double areaOfRing;   // Area of ring
11
12       printf("Enter inner radius: ");
13       scanf("%lf", &inner);
14
15       printf("Enter outer radius: ");
16       scanf("%lf", &outer);
17
18       areaOfRing = AreaOfCircle(outer) - AreaOfCircle(inner);
19       printf("The area of the ring is %f\n", areaOfRing);
20   }
21
22   // Calculate area of circle given a radius
23   double AreaOfCircle(double radius)
24   {
25       double pi = 3.14159265; // This can be optionally declared as a const
26
27       return pi * radius * radius;
28   }
```

Figure 14.3   A C program that calculates the area of a ring.

inner radius. In this program, a function is used to calculate the area of a circle with a given radius. The function AreaOfCircle takes a single argument of type double and returns a double value back to the caller. The following point is important for us to reiterate: when function AreaOfCircle is active, it can "see" and modify its local variable pi and its parameter radius. It cannot, however, directly modify any of the variables within the function main. The function AreaOfCircle in this example has a slightly different usage than the functions that we've seen in the previous examples in this chapter. Notice that there are multiple calls to AreaOfCircle from the function main. In this case, AreaOfCircle performs a useful, primitive computation such that encapsulating it into a function is beneficial.

On a larger scale, real programs will include functions that are called from hundreds or thousands of different places. By forming AreaOfCircle and similar primitive operations into functions, we potentially save on the amount of source code in the program, which is beneficial for code maintenance. The program also takes on a better structure. With AreaOfCircle, the intent of the code is more visibly apparent than if the formula were directly embedded in-line.

14.3 Implementing Functions in C

Every C feature we've encountered (and will encounter in the future) must be translated into machine-executable form in order for it to be of consequence. Functions in C are the high-level equivalent of subroutines at the LC-3 machine level. Functions in C are implemented using a similar set of mechanisms as assembly level subroutines. In this section, we'll explore the full process in detail.

There are four basic phases in the execution of a function call: (1) Argument values from the caller are passed to the callee, (2) control is transferred to the callee, (3) the callee executes its task, and (4) control is passed back to the caller, along with a return value. In C, each function is required to be *caller-independent*. That is, a function should be callable from any function. With this requirement, functions become composable building blocks that we can use from anywhere in our code. In this section, we will examine how all of this is accomplished on the LC-3.

14.3.1 Run-Time Stack

At the assembly level, a function is just a sequence of instructions that is called using a JSR instruction. The RET instruction returns control back to the caller. That is the simple part. We need to address some of the stickier issues, too, in order to complete the translation framework. These sticky issues include how arguments are passed, how the return value is returned, and the allocation of local variables. The solution to these issues involves something that has become the cornerstone of digital systems architecture: the run-time stack.

We need a way to "activate" a function when it is called. That is, when a function starts executing, its local variables must be allocated somewhere in memory. There are many possible solutions, and here we'll explore two options.

Option 1: The compiler could systematically assign places in memory for each function to place its local variables. Function A might be assigned the memory chunk starting at X for its local values, function B might be assigned the memory chunk starting at location Y, and so forth, provided, of course, that these memory chunks do not overlap. While this seems like the most straightforward way to manage the allocation, it has some limitations. What happens if function A calls itself? We call this *recursion*, which we saw initially in Section 8.3. We'll dedicate all of Chapter 17 to the idea of recursion in C. If function A calls itself, then the callee version of function A will overwrite the local values of the caller version of function A, and the program will not behave as we expect it to. For the C programming language, which allows recursive functions, option 1 will not work. Also it's a wasteful allocation of memory because a function will require storage (potentially a lot of storage) even if it isn't executing.

Option 2: What if instead of allocating the space for local variables statically (i.e., in a fixed place in memory), the space is allocated once the function starts executing? And when the function returns to the caller, its space is reclaimed to be assigned later to another function. And if the function is called from itself, the new invocation of the function will get its own space that is distinct from its other currently active invocations. This solves the issues raised with Option 1.

How should this allocation be done? We can utilize the idea that the calling pattern of functions can easily be tracked with a stack data structure. Each function has a memory template where it stores its local variables, some bookkeeping information, and its parameter variables (we'll mention more about the parameters and bookkeeping information later in this chapter). This template is called its stack frame or activation record. Whenever a function is called, its stack frame will be allocated somewhere in memory. And because the calling pattern of functions naturally follows a stack-like pattern, this allocation and deallocation will follow the pushes and pops of a stack.

Let us demonstrate with an example. The code in Figure 14.4 contains three functions, main, Watt, and Volt. What each function does is not important for this example, so we've omitted some of their details but provided enough so that the calling pattern between them is apparent. The function main calls Watt, and Watt calls Volt. Eventually, control returns to main, which then calls Volt.

```
1   int main(void)
2   {
3       int a;
4       int b;
5
6       :
7       b = Watt(a);        // main calls Watt first
8       b = Volt(a, b);     // then calls Volt
9   }
10
11  int Watt(int a)
12  {
13      int w;
14
15      :
16      w = Volt(w, 10);    // Watt calls Volt
17
18      return w;
19  }
20
21  int Volt(int q; int r)
22  {
23      int k;
24      int m;
25
26      :
27      return k;
28  }
```

Figure 14.4   Code example that demonstrates the stack-like nature of function calls.

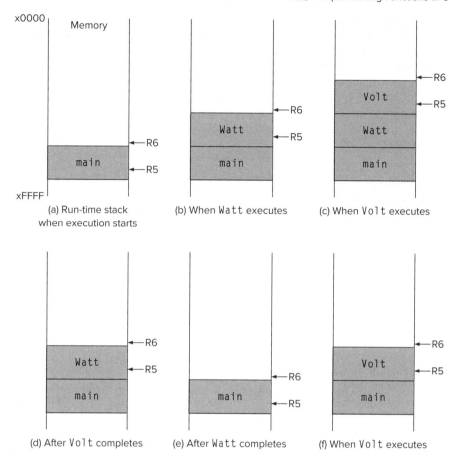

Figure 14.5 Several snapshots of the run-time stack while the program outlined in Figure 14.4 executes.

This is illustrated in the diagrams of Figure 14.5. Each of the shaded regions represents the activation record or stack frame of a particular function call. The sequence of figures shows how the run-time stack grows and shrinks as the various functions are called and return to their caller. Keep in mind that, as we push items onto the stack, the top of the stack moves, or "grows," toward lower-numbered memory locations.

Figure 14.5a is a picture of the run-time stack when the program starts execution. Since the execution of a C program starts in main, the stack frame for main is the first to be allocated on the stack. Figure 14.5b shows the run-time stack immediately after Watt is called by main. Notice that the stack frames are allocated in a stack-like fashion. That is, whenever a function is called, its stack frame is *pushed* onto the stack. Whenever the function returns, its frame is *popped* off the stack. Figure 14.5 parts (c) through (f) show the state of the run-time stack at various points during the execution of this code.

We ultimately want to map this process into LC-3 assembly code, so we'll need some easy way to access the data in each function's stack frame and also to manage the pushing and popping of stack frames. For this, we will use R5 and R6. Notice that R5 points to some internal location within the stack frame at the top of the stack—it points to the base of the local variables for the currently executing function. We call it the *frame pointer*. Also notice how R6 always points to the very top of the stack. We call it the *stack pointer*. Both of these registers have a key role to play in the implementation of the run-time stack and of functions in C in general.

14.3.2 Getting It All to Work

It is clear that there is a lot of work going on at the machine level when a function is called. Arguments must be passed, stack frames pushed and popped, control moved from one function to another. As involved as it may seem, the implementation of this is rather straightforward, and we will spend the remainder of this section going through the details of the C run-time stack protocol on the LC-3.

We'll partition this protocol into four steps. Step 1: The caller function copies arguments for the callee onto the run-time stack and passes control to the callee. Step 2: The callee function pushes space for local variables and other information onto the run-time stack, essentially creating its stack frame on top of the stack. Step 3: The callee executes. Step 4: Once it is ready to return, the callee removes, or pops, its stack frame off the run-time stack and returns the return value and control to the caller.

We'll examine the LC-3 implementation of each of these steps in detail by looking at the code generated to accomplish the following line of code:

```
w = Volt(w, 10);
```

which is line 16 from the code in Figure 14.4.

14.3.2.1 The Call

In the statement w = Volt(w, 10);, the function Volt is called with two arguments. The value returned by Volt is then assigned to the local integer variable w. In translating this function call, the compiler generates LC-3 code that does the following:

1. Transmits the value of the two arguments to the function Volt by pushing them directly onto the top of the run-time stack. Recall that R6 points to the top of the run-time stack. It is the stack pointer. That is, it contains the address of the memory location that is actively holding the topmost data item on the stack. To push an item onto the stack, we first decrement R6 and then store the data value using R6 as a base address. In our stack protocol, the arguments of a C function call are pushed onto the stack from

right to left in the order in which they appear in the function call. In the case of Watt, we will first push the value 10 (rightmost argument) and then the value of w.

2. Transfers control to Volt via the JSR instruction.

The following LC-3 code performs the call to Volt from Watt. Instructions 1 through 4 perform the push of the argument 10, and instructions 6 through 8 push the argument w. Notice that w itself is a local variable in Watt and must be loaded from Watt's stack frame. More on this soon.

```
1   AND R0, R0, #0   ; R0 <- 0
2   ADD R0, R0, #10  ; R0 <- 10
3   ADD R6, R6, #-1  ;
4   STR R0, R6, #0   ; Push 10 onto stack
5
6   LDR R0, R5, #0   ; Load w
7   ADD R6, R6, #-1  ;
8   STR R0, R6, #0   ; Push w
9   JSR Volt
```

Figure 14.6 illustrates the modifications made to the run-time stack by these instructions. Notice that the argument values are pushed immediately on top of the stack frame of the caller (Watt). The stack frame for the callee (Volt) will be constructed on the stack directly on top of the stack frame of the caller.

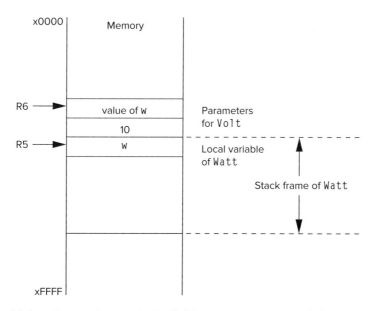

Figure 14.6   The run-time stack after Watt pushes arguments to Volt.

14.3.2.2 Starting the Callee Function

The instruction executed immediately after the JSR in the function Watt is the first instruction in the callee function Volt. Before we begin to execute the actual work in Volt described by the C code, we need to set the stage for Volt to execute. We need to properly allocate the stack frame for Volt and properly set the stack pointer R6 and the frame pointer R5 so that the code of Volt can execute correctly.

At this point, the stack contains the two arguments for Volt at the top. The purpose of the preamble code of Volt is to prepare the stack such that it also contains a spot for the return value of Volt, the return address of Watt, Watt's frame pointer, and all of the local variables of Volt. This will be accomplished in four steps, which we describe next, each as a single action:

1. Save space on the stack for callee's return value. The return value is located immediately on top of the parameters for the callee. Later, when the callee is ready to pass control back to the caller, the return value is written into this location.

2. Push a copy of the return address in R7 onto the stack. Recall that R7 will hold the return address whenever a JSR is used to initiate a subroutine call. This will ensure that we can return to the caller even if the callee calls another function.

3. Push a copy of the caller's frame pointer in R5 onto the stack. By saving a copy of R5, we will be able to restore the stack frame of the caller in such a way that the caller can easily resume execution after the function call is complete. If either the caller's return address or the frame pointer is destroyed, then we will have trouble restarting the caller correctly when the callee finishes. Therefore, it is important that we make copies of both in memory.

4. Allocate space on the stack for the callee's local variables, and adjust R5 to point to the base of the local variables and R6 to point to the top of the stack.

The preamble code to accomplish this for Volt is provided below. This code appears first before any of the code for statements in Volt.

```
 1  Volt: ADD R6, R6, #-1    ; Allocate spot for the return value
 2
 3        ADD R6, R6, #-1    ;
 4        STR R7, R6, #0     ; Push R7 (Return address)
 5
 6        ADD R6, R6, #-1    ;
 7        STR R5, R6, #0     ; Push R5 (Caller's frame pointer)
 8
 9        ADD R5, R6, #-1    ; Set frame pointer for Volt
10        ADD R6, R6, #-2    ; Allocate memory for Volt's local variables
```

Figure 14.7 summarizes the changes to memory accomplished by the function call code we have encountered so far. The layout in memory of these stack frames—one for Watt and one for Volt—is apparent. Notice that some entries of the stack frame of Volt are written by Watt. In particular, the parameter fields of Volt's stack frame are initialized using the argument values from Watt. Watt writes the value of its local variable w as the first argument and the value 10 for the second argument. Keep in mind that these values are pushed from right to left

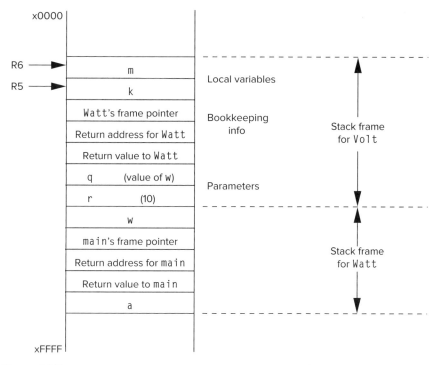

Figure 14.7   The run-time stack after the stack frame for Volt is pushed onto the stack.

according to their position in the function call. Therefore, the value of w appears on top of the value 10. Once invoked, Volt will refer to these values as the parameters q and r. Question: What are the initial values of Volt's local variable? Recall from Chapter 11 that local variables such as these are uninitialized.

Notice that each stack frame on the stack has the same structure. Each contains locations for the function's local variables, for the bookkeeping information (consisting of the caller's return address and caller's frame pointer), the return value, and the function's parameters.

14.3.2.3 Ending the Callee Function

Once the callee function has completed its work, we prepare to return to the caller. This essentially involves tearing down the stack frame and restoring the run-time stack to the state it was in when the caller initiated its function call. To accomplish this, we use the following four actions:

1. If there is a return value, it is written into the return value entry of the active stack frame.
2. The local variables for the callee are popped off the stack. This can be accomplished by individually popping them, or simply by setting the stack pointer R6 to the location immediately after the frame pointer R5.

3. The caller frame pointer and return address are restored.

4. Control to the caller function via the RET instruction.

The LC-3 instructions corresponding to this for Volt are as follows. Keep in mind that even though the stack frame for Volt is popped off the stack, its values remain in memory until they are explicitly overwritten.

```
1    LDR R0, R5, #0    ; Load local variable k
2    STR R0, R5, #3    ; Write it in return value slot, which will always
3                      ; be at location R5 + 3
4
5    ADD R6, R5, #1    ; Pop local variables
6
7    LDR R5, R6, #0    ; Pop the frame pointer
8    ADD R6, R6, #1    ;
9
10   LDR R7, R6, #0    ; Pop the return address
11   ADD R6, R6, #1    ;
12   RET
```

14.3.2.4 Returning to the Caller Function

After the callee function executes the RET instruction, control is passed back to the caller function. In some cases, there is no return value (if the callee is declared of type void) and, in some cases, the caller function ignores the return value. Again, from our previous example, the return value is assigned to the variable w in Watt. In particular, there are two actions to be performed:

1. The return value (if there is one) is popped off the stack.

2. The arguments are popped off the stack.

The code after the JSR looks like the following. Once this code starts executing, R6 points to the top of the stack, which is the return value, and R5 is again the frame pointer of Watt.

```
1    JSR Volt
2    LDR R0, R6, #0    ; Load the return value
3    STR R0, R5, #0    ; w = Volt(w, 10);
4    ADD R6, R6, #1    ; Pop return value
5
6    ADD R6, R6, #2    ; Pop arguments
```

Once this code is done, the call is now complete, and the caller function can resume its normal operation. Notice that prior to the return, the callee restores the environment of the caller. From the caller's perspective, it appears as if nothing has changed except that a new value (the return value) has been pushed onto the stack.

14.3.2.5 Caller Save/Callee Save

Before we complete our discussion of the implementation of functions, we need to cover a topic that we've so far swept under the rug. During the execution of a function, R0 through R3 can contain temporary values that are part of an ongoing computation. Registers R4 through R7 are reserved for other purposes: R4 is the pointer to the global data section, R5 is the frame pointer, R6 is the stack pointer, and R7 is used to hold return addresses. If we make a function call, based on the calling convention we've described, R4 through R7 do not change, or they change in a predetermined fashion. But what happens to registers R0, R1, R2, and R3? To address this, digital systems typically adopt one of two strategies: (1) The caller will save these registers by pushing them onto its stack frame. This is the *caller-save* convention. (We also discussed this in Section 8.1.1.) When control is returned to the caller, the caller will restore these registers by popping them off the stack. (2) Alternatively, the callee can save these registers by adding four fields in the bookkeeping area of its record. This is called the *callee-save* convention. When the callee is initiated, it will save R0 through R3 and R5 and R7 into the bookkeeping region and restore these registers before returning to the caller.

14.3.3 Tying It All Together

The code for the function call in Watt and the beginning and end of Volt is listed in Figure 14.8. The LC-3 code segments presented in the previous sections are all combined, showing the overall structure of the code. This code is more optimized than the previous individual code segments. We've combined the manipulation of the stack pointer R6 associated with pushing and popping the return value into single instructions.

Let's summarize our LC-3 C function call protocol. The caller function pushes the value of each argument onto the stack and performs a Jump To Subroutine (JSR) to the callee. The callee allocates a space for the return value, saves the caller's frame pointer and return address, and then allocates space on the stack for its local variables. The callee then proceeds to carry out its task. When the task is complete, the callee writes the return value into the space reserved for it, pops and restores frame pointer and return value for the caller, and returns to the caller. The caller then pops the return value and arguments from the stack and resumes its execution.

You might be wondering why we would go through all these steps just to make a function call. That is, is all this code really required, and couldn't the calling convention be made simpler? One of the characteristics of real calling conventions is that in the general case, any function should be able to call any other function. To enable this, the calling convention should be organized so that a caller does not need to know anything about a callee except its interface (i.e., the type of value the callee returns and the types of values it expects as arguments). Likewise, a callee is written to be independent of the functions that call it. Because of this generality, the functional calling protocol needs these steps. It is all part of the overhead required to make functions an essential building block for large-scale software.

```
 1 Watt:
 2        ...
 3        AND R0, R0, #0   ; R0 <- 0
 4        ADD R0, R0, #10  ; R0 <- 10
 5        ADD R6, R6, #-1  ;
 6        STR R0, R6, #0   ; Push 10 onto stack
 7
 8        LDR R0, R5, #0   ; Load w
 9        ADD R6, R6, #-1  ;
10        STR R0, R6, #0   ; Push w
11        JSR Volt
12
13        LDR R0, R6, #0   ; Load the return value
14        STR R0, R5, #0   ; w = Volt(w, 10);
15        ADD R6, R6, #3   ; Pop return value and arguments
16        ...
17
18 Volt: ADD R6, R6, #-1  ; Allocate spot for the return value
19
20        ADD R6, R6, #-1  ;
21        STR R7, R6, #0   ; Push R7 (Return address)
22
23        ADD R6, R6, #-1  ;
24        STR R5, R6, #0   ; Push R5 (Caller's frame pointer)
25
26        ADD R5, R6, #-1  ; Set frame pointer for Volt
27        ADD R6, R6, #-2  ; Allocate memory for Volt's local variables
28
29        ...              ; Volt performs its work
30
31        LDR R0, R5, #0   ; Load local variable k
32        STR R0, R5, #3   ; Write it in return value slot, which will always
33                         ; be at location R5 + 3
34
35        ADD R6, R5, #1   ; Pop local variables
36
37        LDR R5, R6, #0   ; Pop the frame pointer
38        ADD R6, R6, #1   ;
39
40        LDR R7, R6, #0   ; Pop the return address
41        ADD R6, R6, #1   ;
42        RET
```

Figure 14.8   The LC-3 code corresponding to a C function call and return.

14.4 Problem Solving Using Functions

For functions to be useful to us, we must somehow integrate them into our programming problem-solving methodology. In this section, we will demonstrate the use of functions through two example problems, with each example demonstrating a slightly different manner in which functions are applied.

Conceptually, functions are a good point of division during the top-down design of an algorithm from a problem. As we decompose a problem, natural "components" will appear in the tasks that are to be performed by the algorithm. These components are natural candidates for functions. Our first example involves converting text from lowercase into uppercase, and it presents an example of a component function that is naturally apparent during the top-down design process.

Functions are also useful for encapsulating primitive operations that the program requires at various spots in the code. By creating such functions, we are in a sense extending the set of operations of the programming language, tailoring them to the specific problem at hand. In the case of the second problem, which determines Pythagorean Triples, we will develop a primitive function to calculate x^2 to assist with the calculation.

14.4.1 Problem 1: Case Conversion

In this section, we go through the development of a program that reads input from the keyboard and echoes it back to the screen, similar to the program in Figure 13.8. We throw in a slight twist in this version: We want the program to convert lowercase characters into uppercase before echoing them onto the screen.

Our approach to solving this problem is to use the echo program from Figure 13.8 as a starting point. The previous code used a `while` loop to read an input character from the keyboard and then print it to the output device. To this basic structure, we want to add a component that checks if a character is lowercase and converts it to uppercase if it is. We could add code to perform this directly into the while loop, but given the self-contained nature of this component, we will create a function to do this job.

The conversion function is called after each character is scanned from the keyboard and before it is displayed to the screen. The function requires a single character as an argument and either returns the same character (if the character is already uppercase or is not a character of the alphabet) or returns an uppercase version of the character. Figure 14.9 shows the flow of this program. The flowchart of the original echo program is shaded. To this original flowchart, we are adding a component function to perform the conversion.

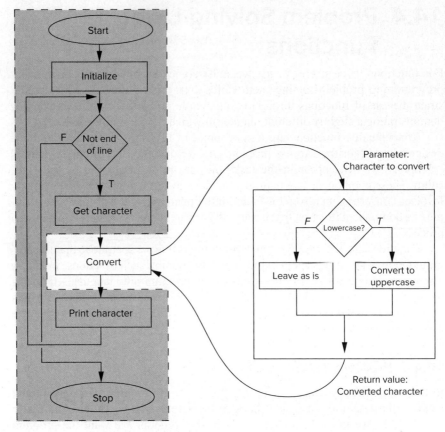

Figure 14.9   The decomposition into smaller subtasks of a program that converts input characters into uppercase.

Figure 14.10 shows the complete C code. It takes input from the keyboard, converts each input character into uppercase, and prints out the result. When the input character is the new line character, the program terminates. The conversion process from lowercase to uppercase is done by the function ToUpper. Notice the use of ASCII literals in the function body to perform the actual conversion. Keep in mind that a character in single quotes (e.g., 'A') is evaluated as the ASCII value of that character. The expression 'a' - 'A' is therefore the ASCII value of the character a minus the ASCII of A.

14.4.2 Problem 2: Pythagorean Triples

Now we'll attempt a programming problem involving calculating all Pythagorean Triples less than a particular input value. A Pythagorean Triple is a set of three **integer** values a, b, and c that satisfy the property $c^2 = a^2 + b^2$. In other words, a and b are the lengths of the sides of a right triangle where c is the hypotenuse. For example, 3, 4, and 5 is a Pythagorean Triple. The problem here is to calculate

```
 1  #include <stdio.h>
 2
 3  char ToUpper(char inchar);  // Function Declaration
 4
 5  // Prompt for a line of text, Read one character,
 6  // convert to uppercase, print it out, then get another
 7  int main(void)
 8  {
 9     char echo = 'A';    // Initialize input character
10     char upcase;        // Converted character
11
12     printf("Type input: ");
13     while (echo != '\n') {
14        scanf("%c", &echo);
15        upcase = ToUpper(echo);
16        printf("%c", upcase);
17     }
18  }
19
20  // If the parameter is lowercase, return
21  // its uppercase ASCII value
22  char ToUpper(char inchar)
23  {
24     char outchar;
25
26     if ('a' <= inchar && inchar <= 'z')
27        outchar = inchar - ('a' - 'A');
28     else
29        outchar = inchar;
30
31     return outchar;
32  }
```

Figure 14.10   **A program with a function to convert lowercase letters to uppercase.**

all Triples *a*, *b*, and *c* where all are less than a certain number provided by the user.

For this problem, we will try to find all Triples by brute force. That is, if the limit indicated by the user is max, we will check all combinations of three integers less than max to see if they satisfy the Triple property. In order to check all combinations, we will want to vary each sideA, sideB, and sideC from 1 to max. This implies the use of counter-controlled loops. More exactly, we will want to use a for loop to vary sideC, another to vary sideB, and another to vary sideA, each *nested* within the other. At the core of these loops, we will check to see if the property holds for the three values, and if so, we'll print them out.

Now, in performing the Triple check, we will need to evaluate the following expression:

```
(sideC * sideC == (sideA * sideA + sideB * sideB))
```

```
1  #include <stdio.h>
2
3  int Squared(int x);
4
5  int main(void)
6  {
7      int maxC;
8
9      printf("Enter the maximum length of hypotenuse: ");
10     scanf("%d", &maxC);
11
12     for (int sideC = 1; sideC <= maxC; sideC++) {
13        for (int sideB = 1; sideB <= maxC; sideB++) {
14           for (int sideA = 1; sideA <= maxC; sideA++) {
15              if (Squared(sideC) == Squared(sideA) + Squared(sideB))
16                 printf("%d %d %d\n", sideA, sideB, sideC);
17           }
18        }
19     }
20  }
21
22  // Calculate the square of a number
23  int Squared(int x)
24  {
25     return x * x;
26  }
```

Figure 14.11   A C program that calculates Pythagorean Triples.

Because the square operation is a primitive operation for this problem—meaning it is required in several spots—we will encapsulate it into a function `Squared` that returns the square of its integer parameter. The preceding expression will be rewritten as follows. Notice that this code gives a clearer indication of what is being calculated.

```
(Squared(sideC) == Squared(sideA) + Squared(sideB))
```

The C program for this is provided in Figure 14.11. There are better ways to calculate Triples than with a brute-force technique of checking all combinations (Can you modify the code to run more efficiently?); the brute-force technique suits our purposes of demonstrating the use of functions.

14.5 Summary

In this chapter, we introduced the concept of functions in C. The general notion of subprograms such as functions has been part of programming languages since the earliest days of programming. Functions are useful because they allow us to create new primitive building blocks that might be useful for a particular programming task (or for a variety of tasks). In a sense, they allow us to extend the native operations and constructs supported by the language with additional primitive functions. The key notions that you should take away from this chapter are:

- **Syntax of functions in C.** To use a function in C, we must declare the function using a function declaration (which we typically do at the beginning of our code) that indicates the function's name, the type of value the function returns, and the types and order of values the function expects as inputs. A function's definition contains the actual code for the function. A function is invoked when a call to it is executed. A function call contains arguments—values that are to be passed to the function.

- **Implementation of C functions at the lower level.** Part of the complexity associated with implementing functions is that in C, a function can be called from any other function in the source file (and even from functions in other object files). To assist in dealing with this, we adopt a general calling convention for calling one function from another. To assist with the fact that some functions might even call themselves, we base this calling convention on the run-time stack. The calling convention involves the caller passing the value of its arguments by pushing them onto the stack, then calling the callee. The arguments written by the caller become the parameters of the callee's stack frame. The callee does its task and then pops its stack frame off the stack, leaving behind its return value for the caller.

- **Using functions when programming.** It is possible to write all your programs without ever using functions. The result would be that your code would be hard to read, maintain, and extend, and it would probably be buggier than it would if your code used functions. Functions enable abstraction: We can write a function to perform a particular task, debug it, test it, and then use it within the program wherever it is needed.

Exercises

14.1   What is the significance of the function `main`? Why must all programs contain this function?

14.2   Refer to the structure of a stack frame to answer these questions.

    a. What is the purpose of the frame pointer?
    b. What is the purpose of the return address?
    c. What is the purpose of the return value?

14.3   Refer to the C syntax of functions to answer these questions.

    a. What is a function declaration? What is its purpose?
    b. What is a function prototype?
    c. What is a function definition?
    d. What are arguments?
    e. What are parameters?

14.4   For each of the following items, identify whether the caller function or the callee function performs the action.

    a. Writing the arguments into the stack frame.
    b. Writing the return value.
    c. Writing the frame pointer.
    d. Modifying the value in R5 to point within the callee function's stack frame.

14.5   What is the output of the following program? Explain.

```c
void MyFunc(int z);

int main(void)
{
    int z = 2;
    MyFunc(z);
    MyFunc(z);
}

void MyFunc(int z)
{
    printf("%d ", z);
    z++;
}
```

14.6   What is the output of the following program?

```c
#include <stdio.h>
int Multiply(int d, int b);

int d = 3;
int main()
{
    int a = 1, b = 2, c;
    int e = 4;

    c = Multiply(a, b);
    printf("%d %d %d %d %d\n", a, b, c, d, e);
}

int Multiply(int d, int b)
{
    int a = 2;
    b = 3;
    return (a * b);
}
```

14.7   Following is the code for a C function named Bump.

```c
int Bump(int x)
{
    int a;
    a = x + 1;
    return a;
}
```

      a. Draw the stack frame for `Bump`.

      b. Write one of the following in each entry of the stack frame to indicate what is stored there.

         (1) Local variable

         (2) Argument

         (3) Address of an instruction

         (4) Address of data

         (5) Other

      c. Some of the entries in the stack frame for `Bump` are written by the function that calls `Bump`; some are written by `Bump` itself. Identify the entries written by `Bump`.

14.8 What is the output of the following code? Explain why the function `Swap` behaves the way it does.

```
void Swap(int x, int y);

int main(void)
{
    int x = 1;
    int y = 2;

    Swap(x, y);
    printf("x = %d  y = %d\n", x, y);
}

void Swap(int y, int x)
{
    int temp

    temp = x;
    x = y;
    y = temp;
}
```

14.9 Are the arguments to a function placed on the stack before or after the JSR to that function? Why?

14.10 A C program containing the function `food` has been compiled into LC-3 assembly language. The partial translation of the function into LC-3 is:

```
food:
    ADD  R6, R6, #-2  ;
    STR  R7, R6, #0   ;
    ADD  R6, R6, #-1  ;
    STR  R5, R6, #0   ;
    ADD  R5, R6, #-1  ;
    ADD  R6, R6, #-4  ;
    ...
```

      a. How many local variables does this function have?

      b. Say this function has two integer parameters x and y. Generate the code to evaluate the expression x + y.

14.11 Following is the code for a C function named `Unit`.

```c
int Init(int x);
int Unit(int x);
int main()
{
    int a = 1;
    int b = 2;

    a = Init(a);
    b = Unit(b);
    printf("a = %d b = %d\n", a, b);
}

int Init(int x)
{
    int y = 2;
    return y + x;
}

int Unit(int x)
{
    int z;
    return z + x;
}
```

     a. What is the output of this program?

     b. What determines the value of local variable `z` when function `Unit` starts execution?

14.12 Modify the example in Figure 14.10 to also convert each character to lowercase. The new program should print out both the lower- and uppercase versions of each input character.

14.13 Write a function to print out an integer value in base 4 (using only the digits 0, 1, 2, 3). Use this function to write a program that reads two integers from the keyboard and displays both numbers and their sum in base 4 on the screen.

14.14 Write a function that returns a 1 if the first integer input parameter is evenly divisible by the second. Using this function, write a program to find the smallest number that is evenly divisible by all integers less than 10.

14.15 The following C program is compiled into LC-3 machine language and loaded into address x3000 before execution. Not counting the JSRs to library routines for I/O, the object code contains three JSRs (one to function `f`, one to `g`, and one to `h`). Suppose the addresses of the three JSR instructions are x3102, x3301, and x3304. Also suppose the user provides 4 5 6 as input values. Draw a picture of the run-time stack, providing the contents of locations, if possible, when the program is about to return from function `f`. Assume the base of the run-time stack is location xEFFF.

```c
#include <stdio.h>
int f(int x, int y, int z);
int g(int arg);
int h(int arg1, int arg2);

int main(void)
{
    int a, b, c;

    printf("Type three numbers: ");
    scanf("%d %d %d", &a, &b, &c);
    printf("%d", f(a, b, c));
}

int f(int x, int y, int z)
{
    int x1;

    x1 = g(x);
    return h(y, z) * x1;
}

int g(int arg)
{
    return arg * arg;
}

int h(int arg1, int arg2)
{
    return arg1 / arg2;
}
```

14.16 Referring once again to the machine-busy example from previous chapters, remember that we represent the busyness of a set of 16 machines with a bit pattern. Recall that a 0 in a particular bit position indicates the corresponding machine is busy and a 1 in that position indicates that machine is idle.

  a. Write a function to count the number of busy machines for a given busyness pattern. The input to this function will be a bit pattern (which can be represented by an integer variable), and the output will be an integer corresponding to the number of busy machines.

  b. Write a function to take two busyness patterns and determine which machines have changed state, that is, gone from busy to idle, or idle to busy. The output of this function is simply another bit pattern with a 1 in each position corresponding to a machine that has changed its state.

  c. Write a program that reads a sequence of ten busyness patterns from the keyboard and determines the average number of busy machines and the average number of machines that change state from one pattern to the next. The user signals the end of busyness patterns by entering a pattern of all 1s (all machines idle). Use the functions you developed for parts 1 and 2 to write your program.

14.17 *a.* Write a C function that mimics the behavior of a 4-to-1 multiplexer. See Figure 3.13 for a description of a 4-to-1 mux.

       b. Write a C function that mimics the behavior of the LC-3 ALU.

14.18 Notice that on a numeric keypad for your phone, the keys labeled 2, 3, 4, . . . , 9 also have letters associated with them. For example, the key labeled 2 corresponds to the letters *A*, *B*, and *C*. Write a program that will map a seven-digit telephone number into all possible character sequences that the phone number can represent. For this program, use a function that performs the mapping between digits and characters. The digits 1 and 0 map to nothing.

14.19 The following C program uses a combination of global variables and local variables with different scope. What is the output?

```c
#include <stdio.h>

int t = 1; // Global variable

int sub1(int fluff);

int main (void)
{
    int t = 2;
    int z;
    z = t;
    z = z + 1;
    printf("A: The variable z equals %d\n", z);
    {
        z = t;
        t = 3;
        {
            int t = 4;
            z = t;
            z = z + 1;
            printf("B: The variable z equals %d\n", z);
        }
        z = sub1(z);
        z = z + 1;
        printf("C: The variable z equals %d\n", z);
    }
    z = t;
    z = z + 1;
    printf("D: The variable z equals %d\n", z);
}

int sub1(int fluff)
{
    int i;
    i = t;
    return (fluff + i);
}
```

CHAPTER

15

Testing and Debugging

15.1 Introduction

December 1999, NASA mission controllers lost contact with the *Mars Polar Lander* as it approached the Martian surface. The *Mars Polar Lander* was on a mission to study the southern polar region of the Red Planet. Contact was never reestablished, and NASA subsequently announced that the spacecraft most probably crashed onto the planet's surface during the landing process. After evaluating the situation, investigators concluded that the likely cause was faulty control software that prematurely caused the onboard engines to shut down when the probe was 40 meters above the surface rather than when the probe had actually landed. It is suspected that a software error incorrectly identified vibrations from deployment of the landing gear as touchdown on the surface, triggering thruster shutdown.

Just a few months earlier, another NASA mission to Mars, the *Mars Climate Orbiter*, was lost during orbital insertion due to a different software bug. A ground-based software subsystem that controlled the *Orbiter*'s thrusters was calculating measurements in imperial units instead of metric units, as required by the other systems on the spacecraft, sending the *Orbiter* on a catastrophic trajectory. The end result of this infamous bug was the loss of a $655 million space probe.

The physical complexities of sending probes into space are astounding, and the software systems that control these spacecraft are no less complex. Software is just as integral to a system as any mechanical or electrical subsystem, and all the more difficult to make correct because it is "invisible." It cannot be visually observed or quantitatively measured as easily as, say, a propulsion system or landing system. It's an obvious fact that software plays a vital and critical part in our digital world. Even something as nondigital as turning on the water faucet requires the processing of hundreds of thousands of lines of code to track the delivery and flow of water into your water glass.

With software playing such a vital role, it is important that this software behave correctly according to specifications. Designing working code is not automatic. Programs are not correct by construction, particularly code written in C or C++. We must actively test and debug software as an integral part of the development process.

Anecdotally, experienced coders spend more than half of their time debugging code as opposed to writing code. The best programmers are those who have mastered debugging. Concepts in testing and debugging code are as important to understand as basic ideas in coding. In this chapter, we introduce basic notions of testing and debugging to help give you essential skills in being an effective programmer.

Testing is the process of exposing bugs, and debugging is the process of fixing them. Testing a piece of code involves subjecting it to as many input conditions as possible, in order to stress the software into revealing its bugs. For example, in testing the function `ToUpper` from Chapter 14 (this function returns the uppercase version of an alphabetic character passed as the argument), we might want to pass every possible ASCII value as an input argument and observe the function's output in order to determine if the function behaves according to specifications. If the function produces incorrect output for a particular input, then we've discovered a bug. It is better to find the bug while the code is still in development than to have an unsuspecting user stumble on the bug inadvertently. It would have been better for the NASA software engineers to find the bug in the *Mars Polar Lander* on the surface of the Earth rather than encounter it 40 meters above the surface of Mars.

Using information about a program and its execution, a programmer can apply common sense to deduce where things are going awry. Just as a crime detective cracks a case by examining evidence, a programmer must examine the available clues in order to track down the source of the bug. Debugging code is much easier if you know how to gather information about it—such as the value of key variables during the execution of the program—in a systematic way.

In this chapter, we describe several techniques you can use to find and fix bugs in a program. We first describe some broad categories of errors that can creep into programs. We then describe testing methods for quickly finding these errors. We finally describe some debugging techniques for isolating and repairing these errors, and we provide some defensive programming techniques to minimize bugs in the code you write.

15.2 Types of Errors

To better understand how to find and fix errors in our code, or to avoid errors in the first place, it's helpful to build a taxonomy of types of errors. There are four broad categories of errors that programmers introduce into code. *Syntactic errors* are the easiest to deal with because they are caught by the compiler. The compiler notifies us of such errors when it tries to translate the source code into machine code, often pointing out exactly in which line the error occurred. *Semantic errors*, on the other hand, are problems that can often be very difficult to repair. They occur when the program is syntactically correct but does not behave exactly as we intended. Both syntactic and semantic errors are generally typographic in nature—they occur when we write something we did not mean to write. *Algorithmic errors*, on the other hand, are less casual mistakes. They are errors in which our approach to solving a problem is wrong. They are costly to the overall software development process because they are hard to detect and often hard to fix. *Specification errors* are due to poorly defined program requirements, or misinterpretations of those requirements by the person or team implementing them.

As far as overall digital systems go, bugs can be anywhere, and they aren't limited to the software side of the house. The hardware can have bugs, sensors can be flaky, and physical systems can fail, which can manifest in the device not working properly. And any of these systems can fail transiently due to an adverse operating situation—the device can fail for just a brief moment and then resume correct operation. It's important that the overall system be robust and bug-free, and as system designers we want a good methodology for testing and debugging. For now we will focus on software testing and debugging. You'll find that many of the ideas we'll develop here will translate into testing and debugging hardware, too.

Another aspect that we will not explore in this chapter is the idea of security bugs. Many digital devices hold and process personal and private information, and they have design requirements to keep this information secure, particularly from malicious attackers. To meet these requirements, hardware and software systems are carefully designed and tested to provide a basic layer of security against clever attackers. Nonetheless, security holes exist and have been exploited. Some of these exploits have become famous (Heartbleed, Meltdown, Spectre, and many others) and have had costly consequences. In this chapter, we'll keep our attention on general software bugs, focusing on the fundamentals of testing and debugging. System security is a major topic worthy of subsequent study.

15.2.1 Syntactic Errors

In C and C++ and all programming languages, syntactic errors (or *syntax errors* or *parse errors*) are always caught by the compiler or other translator. These types of errors occur when we ask the compiler to translate code that does not conform to the C/C++ specification. For instance, the code listed in Figure 15.1 contains a syntax error, which the compiler will flag when the code is compiled. The declaration for the variable j is missing a semicolon. For anyone learning a new programming language, incorrect syntax accounts for a good number of errors. The good news is that these types of errors are easy to find because the compiler detects them, and they are rather simple to fix. In compiling the code in Figure 15.1, the compiler will inform us of the syntax error (sometimes cryptically, because it gets confused and is unable to pinpoint the root cause) and will indicate the spot in the code where things went awry.

15.2.2 Semantic Errors

Semantic errors are similar to syntactic errors. They occur for the same reason: Our minds and our fingers are not completely coordinated when writing code.

```
1    #include <stdio.h>
2
3    int main(void)
4    {
5        int i
6        int j;
7
8        for (i = 0; i <= 10; i++) {
9            j = i * 7;
10           printf("%d x 7 = %d\n", i, j);
11       }
12   }
```

Figure 15.1   This program contains a syntax error.

Semantic errors do not involve incorrect syntax; therefore, the program gets translated and we can execute it. It is not until we analyze the output that we discover that the program is not performing as expected. Figure 15.2 lists an example of the same program as Figure 15.1 with a simple semantic error (the syntax error is fixed). The program should print out a multiplication table for the number 7. Here, a single execution of the program reveals the problem. Only one entry of the multiplication table is printed.

```
1    #include <stdio.h>
2
3    int main(void)
4    {
5        int i;
6        int j;
7
8        for (i = 0; i <= 10; i++)
9            j = i * 7;
10           printf("%d x 7 = %d\n", i, j);
11   }
```

Figure 15.2   A program with a semantic error.

You should be able to deduce, given your knowledge of C, why this program behaves incorrectly. Why is the following line the only output?

```
11 x 7 = 70
```

This code demonstrates something called a *control flow* error. Here, the program's control flow, or the order in which statements are executed, is different than we intended.

The code listed in Figure 15.3 also contains a semantic error. It is intended to calculate the sum of all integers less than or equal to the number input from the keyboard (i.e., it calculates $1 + 2 + 3 + \ldots + n$). It contains a common but tricky semantic error. Try executing this program and you will notice that the output is not what you might expect. This code has an uninitialized variable, or *initialization error*, in variable result in AllSum.

```
 1  #include <stdio.h>
 2
 3  int AllSum(int n);
 4
 5  int main(void)
 6  {
 7      int in;                 // Input value
 8      int sum;                // Value of 1+2+3+..+ n
 9
10      printf("Input a number: ");
11      scanf("%d", &in);
12
13      sum = AllSum(in);
14      printf("The AllSum of %d is %d\n", in, sum);
15  }
16
17
18  int AllSum(int n)
19  {
20      int result;             // Result to be returned
21      int i;                  // Iteration count
22
23      for (i = 1; i <= n; i++) // This calculates sum
24          result = result + i;
25
26      return result;          // Return to caller
27  }
```

Figure 15.3   A program with a bug involving local variables.

Some errors are caught during execution because an illegal action is performed by the program. All digital systems have certain protected regions of memory. These regions require the appropriate privilege level for access, and they can't be accessed by all code. For example, system memory can only be accessed by code with system-level privilege. In this way, we can protect the system from application code with bugs or from potentially malicious code that is accessing memory that it shouldn't. When such an illegal action is performed by a program, the operating system terminates its execution. We can easily create such code. Modify the scanf statement from the AllSum example to the following:

```
scanf("%d", in);
```

The ampersand character, &, as we shall see in Chapter 16, is a special operator in the C language. Omitting it here causes a run-time error because the program has tried to modify a memory location it lacks the privilege to access. We will look at this example and the reasons for the error in more detail in later chapters.

15.2.3 Algorithmic Errors

Algorithmic errors are the result of an incorrectly designed piece of code. That is, the program itself behaves exactly as we designed, but the design itself was flawed. These types of errors can be hidden; they may not appear until many trials of the program have been run. Even when they are detected and isolated, they can be very hard to repair. The good news is that these types of errors can often be reduced and even eliminated by proper planning during the design phase, before any code is written.

The space of algorithmic errors is broad. They can range from simple, isolated errors to complex ones involving large portions of functionality. We'll start by examining a simple, somewhat common algorithmic error made by novice and experienced programmers alike. We call it an *off-by-one error* because something in our code is off by one (or by a similar, small amount). This something can be the number of iterations of a loop, the amount of storage for a data object, or another such value. In the code in Figure 15.4, the number of iterations to perform is off by one. Instead of performing ten iterations, if we input 10, it will perform only nine. Clearly, this bug is easy to fix. As coders we are naturally apt to miscalculate the ending conditions of loops, or the sizes of objects in memory, or other similar calculations in our program logic. And often, these miscalculations are off by one (or a small number).

```
1   #include <stdio.h>
2
3   int main(void)
4   {
5       int iterations;        // Input value
6
7       printf("How many iterations? ");
8       scanf("%d", &iterations);
9
10      for (int i = 1; i < iterations; i++)
11          printf("Executing iteration %d\n" , i);
12  }
```

Figure 15.4   A program with an off-by-one error.

Another, deeper example of an algorithmic flaw, this time involving program logic, is provided in Figure 15.5. This code takes as input the number of a calendar year and determines if that year is a leap year or not. At first glance, this code appears to be correct. Leap years do occur every four years. However, they are skipped at the turn of every century, **except** every fourth century (i.e., the year 2000 was a leap year, but 2100, 2200, and 2300 will not be). The code works for almost all years, except those falling into these exceptional cases. We categorize this as an algorithmic error.

15.2.4 Specification Errors

Perhaps the most infamous software bug of all was the Year 2000 computer bug, or Y2K bug. Many early computer systems had small memories, and this required programmers to economize on the size of data items they stored in memory. When storing dates, many early software systems only stored enough bits to represent the last two digits of the year; for example, in storing the year 1975, only 75

```
1    #include <stdio.h>
2
3    int main(void)
4    {
5        int year;
6
7        printf("Input a year (i.e., 1942): ");
8        scanf("%d", &year);
9
10       if ((year % 4) == 0)
11           printf("This year is a leap year\n");
12       else
13           printf("This year is not a leap year\n");
14   }
```

Figure 15.5   This program to determine leap years has an algorithmic bug.

was stored, with the century being implicitly the 1900s. With this shortcut, the year 2000 became indistinguishable from the year 1900 (or 1800 or 2100, for that matter). This presented a worldwide challenge as we anticipated the current year transitioning into the 2000s after December 31, 1999. Plenty of software written originally on memory-constrained systems was still functional, and this software needed fixing in order to properly roll over with the century changeover. As a consequence, a lot of money and effort were invested in tracking down Y2K-related bugs before January 1, 2000, rolled around.

We call this type of bug a specification bug. The software worked as specified, but the specification itself was flawed. The software architects of the day decided that it was OK to encode only the last two digits of a year because they didn't expect the software would still be operational at the end of 1999.

Specification errors can arise from poor specifications that don't properly anticipate the operating requirements for the software, and the Y2K bug is an example of this. Specification errors can also arise from poor communication of those specifications. Often, we write down the working requirements in specification documents, and if those documents are poorly or incorrectly written, software errors can arise. Even with a well-conceived and well-written set of requirements, specification errors can arise due to poor interpretation on the part of the coding team. Specifications are a human-oriented concept, and they are susceptible to human errors throughout the process.

15.3 Testing

There is an adage among seasoned programmers that any line of code that is untested is probably buggy. Good testing techniques are crucial to writing good software. What is testing? With testing, we basically put the software through "synthetic trails." We apply synthetic inputs, observe how the software behaves, and try to discover bugs before the software is released into the wild. Real-world software might undergo millions of trials before it is released.

In an ideal world, we could test a program by examining its operation under every possible input condition. For most programs, testing for every input combination is impossible. For example, if we wanted to test a program that finds prime numbers between integers A and B, where A and B are 32-bit input values, there would be $(2^{32})^2$ possible input combinations. If we could run one million trials in one second, it would take half a million years to completely test the program. Clearly, testing each input combination is not an option.

Which input combinations do we test with? We could randomly pick inputs in hopes that some of those random patterns will expose the program's bugs. And such a strategy is good, but it is often not enough to provide high degrees of assurance that the code meets specifications. The modern software development process views testing more systematically. In particular, black-box testing is used to check if the code meets its specifications, and white-box testing targets various facets of the program's implementation in order to provide some assurance that many lines (if not every line) of code are tested.

15.3.1 Black-Box Testing

With black-box testing, we examine if the program meets its input and output specifications, disregarding the internals of the program. We treat the software being tested as a black box where the internals are not visible to us. That is, with black-box testing, we are concerned with what the program does and not how it does it. For example, a black-box test of the program AllSum in Figure 15.3 might involve running the program, typing an input number, and comparing the resulting output to what you calculated by hand. If the two do not match, then either the program contains a bug or your arithmetic skills are shoddy. We might continue attempting trials until we are reasonably confident that the program is functional.

For testing larger programs, the testing process is *automated* in order to run more tests per unit time. That is, we automatically run the original program, provide some random inputs, check that the output meets specifications, and repeat. With such a process, we can clearly run many more trials than we could if a person performed each trial.

To automate the black-box test process, we need a way to automatically verify whether the program output meets specifications given a particular testing input. Oftentimes, we'll need to develop a checker program that can perform a computation similar to the program being tested but developed independently. Because such a program is developed independently, it is less likely to have the same bug in the same place, and the two programs can jointly serve to detect bugs. Black-box testers who write checker programs are often not permitted to see the code within the black box they are testing so that we get a truly independent version of the checker.

15.3.2 White-Box Testing

For larger software systems, black-box testing is supplemented with additional techniques to raise the effectiveness of the testing process. With black-box testing, it is not possible to know which lines of code have been tested and which have not, and therefore, according to the adage, all are presumed to be buggy.

Software developers supplement black-box testing with white-box tests. White-box tests isolate various internal components of the software and test whether the components conform to their intended design. That is, we test knowing how the software is constructed. For example, knowing that the code consists of several different functions and testing each function in isolation (perhaps as a black box) is a white-box process. We can apply the same type of testing to loops and other subconstructs within a function.

How might a white-box test be constructed? For many types of white-box tests, we modify the code itself. For example, in order to see whether a function is working correctly, we might add extra code to call the function a few extra times with different inputs and check whether its outputs match the expected results. We might add extra `printf` statements to the code with which we can observe values of internal variables to see if things are working as expected. Once the code is complete and ready for release, these `printf` statements can be disabled, or not selected for compilation, or removed outright.

Another common white-box strategy is the use of error-detecting code strategically placed within an application. This code might check for conditions that indicate that the application is not working correctly. When an incorrect situation is detected, the code takes some corrective actions, such as shutting down some portion of the app, or terminating or restarting the application. Since this error-detecting code *asserts* that certain conditions hold during program execution, we generally call these checks *assertions*. For example, assertions can be used to check whether a function returns a value within an expected range. If the return value is out of range, then some action is triggered.

In the following example, we check whether the function `CalculateArea` generates a value that is a reasonable value. In this case, the function takes as input some geometric object represented by two height values and two width values. Not knowing anything else about the function, we can include a check that assures that the value generated by `CalculateArea` is never negative, which it shouldn't be unless something has gone awry.

```
area = CaculateArea(height1, heigth2, width1, width2);
if (area < 0)
    printf("Error in function CalculateArea!\n");
```

Most practical testing methodologies enforce the use of both black-box and white-box testing together. White-box tests alone do not cover the complete functionality of the software—even if all white-box tests pass and we individually cover each line of code, there might be a portion of the operating specifications that is left uncovered. Similarly, black-box tests alone do not guarantee that every line of code is tested. The two together provide a powerful mechanism for testing through the vast operating space of real-world software systems.

15.4 Debugging

Once bug is detected, it must be isolated, fixed, and the fix verified. This is what we refer to as debugging our code. Debugging an error requires the use of our reasoning skills, often intense use. We observe a symptom of the error, such as incorrect output, and perhaps even a set of input that triggers the error. We might even have a general idea of where in the code the bug is located, but often not. From this limited information, we apply our powers of deduction to isolate the exact location of the bug in order to address it.

The key to effective debugging is being able to quickly gather information that will lead to identification and resolution of the bug, similar to the way a detective might gather evidence at a crime scene or the way a skilled physician might perform a series of tests in order to diagnose a patient's illness. There are a number of methodologies programmers use to gather information for debugging purposes. These range from quick and dirty ad hoc techniques to those that are more systematic, involving the use of software debugging tools.

15.4.1 Ad Hoc Techniques

The easiest and most natural technique for debugging is visual inspection of the source code. Sometimes the nature of the failure tips us off to the region of the code where the bug is likely to exist. Looking through the code in that region and checking for simple mistakes, such as initialization errors and off-by-one errors and other semantic errors, is an effective first measure for debugging our code. This technique is fine if the region of source code is small and you are very familiar with the code.

We can complement this technique with another ad hoc technique of inserting statements within the code to print out additional information during execution. Printing out values of key variables can provide quick insights into what is going wrong in the program logic. Adding `printf` statements to track control flow can tell us which statements are executing and in which order. For example, if you wanted to quickly determine if a counter-controlled loop is iterating for the correct number of iterations, you could place a `printf` statement within the loop body. For simple programs, such ad hoc techniques are easy and reasonable to use. Large or more complex programs, which can have intricate bugs, require the use of more heavy-duty techniques.

15.4.2 Source-Level Debuggers

Ad hoc techniques require additional work, code, and compilations to gather debugging information, and they are time-intensive on the part of the programmer. Simplifying the debugging process would go a long way toward improving programmer productivity. Source-level debuggers do just that by making the ad hoc techniques easier on the programmer. Source-level debuggers are software development tools that enable us to examine variables, memory objects, registers, and memory at any point during the execution of our code.

A source-level debugger can allow us to execute our code one C statement at a time and examine the values of any program state (variables, registers, memory, run-time stack, etc.) along the way. Source-level debuggers are similar to the LC-3 debugger that we used previously, except that a source-level debugger operates in relation to high-level source code rather than LC-3 assembly code.

For a source-level debugger to be used on a program, the program must be compiled such that the compiler augments the executable image with enough additional information for the debugger to do its job. Among other things, the debugger will need information from the compilation process in order to map every machine language instruction to its corresponding statement in the high-level source code. The debugger also needs information about variable names and their locations in memory (i.e., the symbol table). This is required so that a programmer can examine the value of any variable within the program using its name in the source code.

Most programmers today use an integrated development environment (IDE) for developing their code. These environments integrate the common tools needed to develop code, such as code repository, editor, and compilation system, into a single user interface. Examples of IDEs include Windows Visual Studio, Xcode for Apple devices, Android Studio for Android devices, and Eclipse for cross-platform development. All of these IDEs provide access to a source-level debugger. While the specifics of the debugger depend on the IDE itself, there is a core set of operations that nearly every IDE's debugger will support. In this section, we will step through this core set. The core debugger commands fall into two categories: those that let you control the execution of the program and those that let you examine the value of variables and memory during the execution.

15.4.2.1 Breakpoints

Breakpoints allow us to specify points during the execution of a program when the program should be temporarily stopped so that we can examine or modify the state of the program. This is useful because it helps us examine the program's execution in the region of the code where the bug occurs. For example, we can add a breakpoint at a particular line in the source code or at a particular function. When execution reaches that line, program execution is frozen in time, and we can examine everything about that program at that particular instance. How a breakpoint is added is specific to the user interface of the IDE, usually by clicking on the line of code where we want the breakpoint to be inserted. Sometimes it is useful to stop at a line only if a certain condition is true. Such conditional breakpoints are useful for isolating specific situations in which we suspect buggy behavior. For example, if we suspect that the function PerformCalculation works incorrectly when its input argument is 16, then we might want to add a breakpoint that stops execution only when x is equal to 16 in the following code:

```
for (x = 0; x < 100; x++)
   PerformCalculation(x);
```

Alternatively, we can set a *watchpoint* to stop the program at any point where a particular condition is true. For example, we can use a watchpoint to stop execution whenever the variable LastItem is equal to 4. This will cause the debugger to stop execution at any statement that causes LastItem to equal 4. Unlike breakpoints, watchpoints are not associated with any single line of the code but apply to every line.

15.4.2.2 Single-Stepping

Once the debugger reaches a breakpoint (or watchpoint), it temporarily suspends program execution and awaits our next command. At this point we can examine program state, such as values of variables, or we can continue with execution. It is often useful to proceed from a breakpoint one statement at time, a process referred to as *single-stepping*. The LC-3 debugger has a command that executes a single LC-3 instruction and similarly a C source-level debugger that allows execution to proceed one C statement at a time. The single-step command executes the current source line and then suspends the program again. Single-stepping through a program is very useful, particularly when isolating a bug down to a single source code line. We can set a breakpoint near the suspected region and then check the values of variables as we single-step through the code. A common use of single-stepping is to verify that the control flow of the program does what we expect. We can single-step through a loop to verify that it performs the correct number of iterations, or we can single-step through an `if-else` to verify that we have programmed the condition correctly.

Variations of single-stepping exist that allow us to skip over functions or to skip to the last iteration of a loop. These variations are useful for skipping over code that we do not suspect to contain errors but that is in the execution path between a breakpoint and the error itself.

15.4.2.3 Examining Values

The art of debugging is about gathering the information required to logically deduce the source of the error. A source-level debugger is the tool of choice for gathering information when debugging large programs. While execution is suspended at a breakpoint, we can gather information about the bug by examining the values of variables related to the suspected bug. Generally speaking, we can examine all execution states of the program at the breakpoint. We can examine the values of variables, memory, the stack, and even the registers. The specifics on how these things can be examined depend on the user interface of the particular IDE being used. Some IDEs allow you to mouse over a variable in the source code window, causing a pop-up window to display the variable's current value. We encourage you to familiarize yourself with the source-level debugger in your IDE. At the end of this chapter, we provide several problems that you can use to gain some experience with this useful debugging tool.

15.5 Programming for Correctness

Knowing how to test and debug your code is a prerequisite for being a good programmer. Great programmers know how to avoid many error-causing situations in the first place. Poor programming methodologies give rise to buggy code, particularly on projects developed by teams of coders. Being aware of some defensive programming techniques can help reduce the amount of time required to get a piece of code up and running. The battle against bugs starts before any line of code is written. Here, we provide three general methods for catching errors even before they become errors.

15.5.1 Nailing Down the Specifications

Many bugs arise from poor or incomplete program specifications. Specifications sometimes do not cover all possible operating scenarios, and thus they leave some conditions open for interpretation by the programmer. For example, recall the factorial example from Chapter 14. Figure 14.2 is a program that calculates the factorial of a number typed at the keyboard. The specification for this program might have simply been, "Write a program to take an integer value from the keyboard and calculate its factorial." As such, the specification is incomplete. What if the user enters a negative number? Or zero? What if the user enters a number that is too large and results in an overflow? In these cases, the code as written will not perform correctly, and it is therefore buggy. To fix this, we need to modify the specifications of the program to allow the program to indicate an error if the input is less than or equal to zero, or if the input is such that $n! > 2^{31}$, implying that n must be less than or equal to 31. In the code in Figure 15.6, we have added an input range check to the Factorial function. Now the function returns a -1 if its input parameter is out of the correct operating range.

```
1   int Factorial(int n)      // Function Definition
2   {
3       int result = 1;        // Initialized result
4
5       if ((n < 1) || (n > 31))   // Bad parameter
6           return -1;
7
8       for (int i = 1; i <= n; i++) // Calculate factorial
9           result = result * i;
10
11      return result;         // Return to caller
12  }
```

Figure 15.6   Factorial function with a check for valid input parameter range.

15.5.2 Modular Design

Functions are useful for extending the functionality of the programming language. With functions we can add new operations and constructs that are helpful for a particular programming task. In this manner, functions enable us to write programs in a modular fashion.

   Once a function is complete, we can test it independently in isolation (i.e., as a white-box test) and determine that it is working as we expect. Since a typical function performs a smaller task than the complete program, it is easier to test than the entire program. Once we have tested and debugged each function in isolation, we will have an easier chance getting the program to work when everything is integrated.

This modular design concept of building a program out of simple, pretested, working components is a fundamental concept in systems design. In subsequent chapters, we will introduce the concept of a *library*. A library is a collection of pretested components that all programmers can use in writing their code. Modern programming practices are heavily oriented around the use of libraries because of the benefits inherent to modular design. We not only design software, but circuits, hardware, and various other layers of the computing system using a similar modular design philosophy.

15.5.3 Defensive Programming

All seasoned programmers have techniques to prevent bugs from creeping into their code. They construct their code in a such a way that those errors that they suspect might affect the program are eliminated by design. That is, they program *defensively*. We provide a short list of general defensive programming techniques that you should adopt to avoid problems with the programs you write.

- Comment your code. Writing comments makes you think about the code you've written. Code documentation is not only a way to inform others about how your code works but also a process that makes you reflect on and reconsider your code. During this process, you might discover that you forgot a special case or operating condition that will ultimately break your code.

- Adopt a consistent coding style. For instance, aligning opening and closing braces will let you identify simple semantic errors associated with missing braces. Along these lines, also be consistent in variable naming. The name of a variable should convey some meaningful information about the value the variable contains.

- Avoid assumptions. It is tempting to make simple, innocent assumptions when writing code, but these can ultimately lead to broken code. For example, in writing a function, we might assume that the input parameter will always be within a certain range. If this assumption is not grounded in the program's specifications, then the possibility for an error has been introduced. Write code that is free of such assumptions—or at least use assertions and spot checks to indicate when the assumptions do not hold.

- Avoid global variables. While some experienced programmers rely heavily on global variables, many software engineers advocate avoiding them whenever possible. Global variables can make some programming tasks easier. However, they often make code more difficult to understand and extend, and when a bug is detected, harder to analyze.

- Rely on the compiler. Most good compilers have an option to carefully check your program for suspicious code (e.g., an uninitialized variable) or commonly misapplied code constructs (e.g., using the assignment operator = instead of the equality operator ==). While these checks are not thorough, they do help identify some commonly made programming mistakes. The defensive techniques mentioned here are particular to the programming concepts we've already discussed. In subsequent chapters, after we introduce new programming concepts, we also discuss how to use defensive techniques when writing programs that use them.

15.6 Summary

In this chapter, we presented methodologies for finding and fixing bugs within your code. Digital systems are increasingly reliant on software, and modern software is often very complex. In order to prevent software bugs from often rendering our personal devices unusable or from occasionally causing space probes to crash, it is important that software tightly conform to its specifications. The key concepts that we covered in this chapter are:

- **Testing.** Finding bugs in code is not easy, particularly when the program is large. Software engineers use systematic testing to find errors in software. Black-box testing is done to validate that the behavior of a program conforms to specifications. White-box testing targets the structure of a program and provides some assurance that every line of code has undergone some level of testing.

- **Debugging.** Debugging an error requires the ability to take the available information and deduce the source of the error. While ad hoc techniques can provide us with a little additional information about the bug, the source-level debugger is the software engineering tool of choice for most debugging tasks. Source-level debuggers allow a programmer to execute a program in a controlled environment and examine various values and states within the program during execution.

- **Programming for correctness.** Experienced programmers try to avoid bugs even before the first line of code is written. Often, the specification of the program is the source of bugs, and nailing down loose ends will help eliminate bugs after the code has been written. Modular design involves writing a larger program out of simple pretested functions and helps reduce the difficulty in testing a large program. Following a defensive programming style helps reduce situations that lead to buggy code.

Exercises

15.1   The following programs each have a single error that prevents them from operating as specified. With as few changes as possible, correct the programs. They all should output a single number: the sum of the integers from 1 to 10, inclusive.

a.
```c
#include <stdio.h>
int main(void)
{
    int i = 1;
    int sum = 0;

    while (i < 11) {
        sum = sum + i;
        ++i;
        printf("%d\n", sum);
    }
}
```

b.
```c
#include <stdio.h>
int main(void)
{
    int sum = 0;

    for (int i = 0; i >= 10; ++i)
        sum = sum + i;
    printf("%d\n", sum);
}
```

c.
```c
#include <stdio.h>
int main(void)
{
    int i = 0;
    int sum = 0;

    while (i <= 11)
        sum = sum + i++;
    printf("%d\n", sum);
}
```

d.
```c
#include <stdio.h>
int main(void)
{
    int sum = 0;
    for (int i = 0; i <= 10;)
        sum = sum + ++i;
    printf("%d\n", sum);
}
```

15.2   The following program fragments have syntax errors and therefore will not compile. Assume that all variables have been properly declared. Fix the errors so that the fragments will not cause compiler errors.

a.
```
i = 0;
j = 0;
while (i < 5)
{
    j = j + 1;
    i = j >> 1
}
```

b.
```
if (cont == 0)
    a = 2;
    b = 3;
else
    a = -2;
    b = -3;
```

c.
```
#define LIMIT 5;
if (LIMIT)
    printf("True");
else
    printf("False");
```

15.3   The following C code was written to find the minimum of a set of positive integers that a user enters from the keyboard. The user signifies the end of the set by entering the value -1. Once all the numbers have been entered and processed, the program outputs the minimum. However, the code contains an error. Identify and suggest ways to fix the error. Use a source-level debugger, if needed, to find it.

```
#include <stdio.h>
int main(void)
{
    int smallestNumber = 0;
    int nextInput;
    // Get the first input number
    scanf("%d", &nextInput);

    // Keep reading inputs until user enters -1
    while (nextInput != -1) {
        if (nextInput < smallestNumber)
            smallestNumber = nextInput;
        scanf("%d", &nextInput);
    }
    printf("The smallest number is %d\n", smallestNumber);
}
```

15.4   The following program reads in a line of characters from the keyboard and echoes only the alphabetic characters within the line. For example, if the input were "`Let's meet at 6:00pm.`", then the output should be "`Letsmeetatpm`" However, the program has a bug. Can you identify and fix the bug?

```
#include <stdio.h>
int main(void)
{
    char echo = '0';

    while (echo != '\n') {
        scanf("%c", &echo);
        if ((echo > 'a' || echo < 'z') &&
            (echo > 'A' || echo < 'Z'))
            printf("%c", echo);
    }
}
```

15.5   Use a source-level debugger to monitor the execution of the following code:

```
#include <stdio.h>
int IsDivisibleBy(int dividend, int divisor);

int main(void)
{
    int f; // The number of integer factors of a number
    for (int i = 2; i < 1000; i++) {
        f = 0;
        for (int j = 2; j < i; j++) {
            if (IsDivisibleBy(i, j))
                f++;
        }
        printf("The number %d has %d factors\n", i, f);
    }
}

int IsDivisibleBy(int dividend, int divisor)
{
    if (dividend % divisor == 0)
        return 1;
    else
        return 0;
}
```

a. Set a breakpoint at the beginning of function `IsDivisibleBy` and examine the parameter values for the first ten calls. What are they?

b. What is the value of `f` after the inner `for` loop ends and the value of `i` equals 660?

c. Can this program be written more efficiently? *Hint:* Monitor the value of the arguments when the return value of `IsDivisibleBy` is 1.

15.6 Using a source-level debugger, determine for what values of arguments the function `Mystery` returns a zero.

```
#include <stdio.h>
int Mystery(int a, int b, int c);

int main(void)
{
    int sum = 0; // running sum of Mystery
    for (int i = 100; i > 0; i--) {
        for (int j = 1; j < i; j++) {
            for (int k = j; k < 100; k++)
                sum = sum + Mystery(i, j, k);
        }
    }
}

int Mystery(int a, int b, int c)
{
    int out;

    out = 3*a*a + 7*a - 5*b*b + 4*b + 5*c ;
    return out;
}
```

15.7   The following program manages flight reservations for a small airline that has only one plane. This plane has SEATS number of seats for passengers. This program processes ticket reservation requests from the airline's website. The command *R* requests a reservation. If there is a seat available, the reservation is approved. If there are no seats, the reservation is denied. Subsequently, a passenger with a reservation can purchase a ticket using the *P* command. This means that for every *P* command, there must be a preceding *R* command; however, not every *R* will materialize into a purchased ticket. The program ends when the *X* command is entered. Following is the program, but it contains serious design errors. Identify the errors. Propose and implement a correct solution.

```c
#include <stdio.h>
#define SEATS 10

int main(void)
{
    int seatsAvailable = SEATS;
    char request = 'O';
    while (request != 'X') {
        scanf("%c", &request);
        if (request == 'R') {
            if (seatsAvailable)
                printf("Reservation Approved!\n");
            else
                printf("Sorry, flight fully booked.\n");
        }
        if (request == 'P') {
            seatsAvailable--;
            printf("Ticket purchased!\n");
        }
    }
    printf("Done! %d seats not sold\n", seatsAvailable);
}
```

CHAPTER

16 Pointers and Arrays

16.1 Introduction

In this chapter, we introduce (actually, reintroduce) two simple but powerful types of data objects: pointers and arrays. We first encountered the idea of pointers and arrays when writing LC-3 code. Now we formalize them in the context of high-level programming languages. A pointer is simply the address of a memory object, such as a variable. With pointers, we can *indirectly* access these objects, which provides for some very useful capabilities. For example, with pointers, we can create functions that modify the arguments passed by the caller. With pointers, we can create sophisticated data organizations that grow and shrink (like the run-time stack) during a program's execution.

An array is a list of data objects of the same type arranged sequentially in memory. For example, in a few of the LC-3 examples from the first half of the book, we represented a file of characters as a sequence of characters arranged sequentially in memory. This sequential arrangement of characters is more formally known as an *array*. To access a particular item in an array, we specify which element we want to access by providing its index. So, an expression like a[4] will access the fifth element in the array named a—it is the fifth element because we start numbering the array at element 0. Arrays are useful because they allow us to conveniently process groups of data such as vectors, matrices, lists, and character strings, which are naturally representative of certain objects in the real world.

16.2 Pointers

We begin our discussion of pointers with a classic example of their utility. In the C program in Figure 16.1, the function Swap is designed to switch the value of its two arguments. The function Swap is called from main with the arguments valueA, which in this case equals 3, and valueB, which equals 4. Once Swap returns control to main, we expect valueA and valueB to have their values

```
1    #include <stdio.h>
2
3    // Swap has no return value thus is declared as void
4    void Swap(int firstVal, int secondVal);
5
6    int main(void)
7    {
8        int valueA = 3;
9        int valueB = 4;
10
11       printf("Before Swap ");
12       printf("valueA = %d and valueB = %d\n", valueA, valueB);
13
14       Swap(valueA, valueB);
15
16       printf("After Swap  ");
17       printf("valueA = %d and valueB = %d\n", valueA, valueB);
18   }
19
20   void Swap(int firstVal, int secondVal)
21   {
22       int tempVal;      // Holds firstVal when swapping
23
24       tempVal = firstVal;
25       firstVal = secondVal;
26       secondVal = tempVal;
27   }
```

Figure 16.1   The function `Swap` attempts to swap the values of its two parameters.

swapped. However, compile and execute the code and you will notice that those variables in `Swap` remain unchanged. To analyze why, let's examine the run-time stack during the execution of `Swap`. Figure 16.2 shows the state of the run-time stack just prior to the completion of the function, just after the statement on line 25 has executed but before control returns to function `main`. Notice that the function `Swap` has modified the values of its parameters `firstVal` and `secondVal` within its own stack frame. When `Swap` finishes and control returns to `main`, these modified values are lost when the stack frame for `Swap` is popped off the stack. The values from `main`'s perspective have not been swapped. And we are left with a buggy program.

In C, arguments are always passed from the caller function to the callee *by value*. C evaluates each argument that appears in a function call as an expression and pushes the value of the expression onto the run-time stack in order to pass them to the function being called. In the callee, the argument values then become values for the function's parameter variables. For `Swap` to modify the arguments that the caller passes to it, it must have access to the caller function's stack frame—it must access the locations at which the arguments are stored in order to modify their values. The function `Swap` needs the *addresses* of `valueA` and `valueB` in `main` in order to change their values. As we shall see

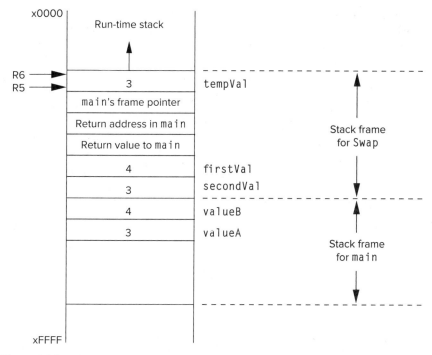

Figure 16.2   A snapshot of the run-time stack when the function Swap is about to return control to main.

in the next few sections, pointers and their associated operators enable this to happen.

16.2.1 Declaring Pointer Variables

Just as an integer variable contains a bit pattern that is treated and interpreted as an integer value, a pointer variable contains a bit pattern that is treated as an address of a memory object, such as a variable. A pointer is said to *point* to the variable whose address it contains. Associated with a pointer variable is the *type* of object to which it points. So, for instance, an integer pointer points to an integer variable. To declare a pointer variable in C, we use the following syntax:

```
int *ptr;
```

Here we have declared a variable named ptr that points to an integer. The asterisk (*) indicates that the identifier that follows is a pointer variable. C programmers will often say that ptr is of type int *star*. Similarly, we can declare

```
char *cp;
double *dp;
```

The variable cp points to a character and dp points to a double-precision float-ing point number. Pointer variables are initialized in a manner similar to all other variables. If a pointer variable is declared as a local variable, it will not be initialized automatically. The syntax of declaring a pointer variable using * may seem a bit odd at first, but once we have gone through the pointer operators, the rationale behind the syntax will become more clear.

16.2.2 Pointer Operators

C has two operators for pointer-related manipulations, the address operator & and the indirection operator *.

16.2.2.1 The Address Operator &

The address operator, whose symbol is an ampersand, &, generates the memory address of its operand, which must be a memory object such as a variable. In the following code sequence, the pointer variable ptr will point to the integer variable object. The expression on the right-hand side of the second assignment statement generates the memory address of object.

```
int object;
int *ptr;

object = 4;
ptr = &object;
```

Let's examine the LC-3 code for this sequence. Both declared variables are local variables allocated on the run-time stack. Recall that R5, the base pointer, points to the first declared local variable, or object in this case.

```
AND R0, R0, #0  ; Clear R0
ADD R0, R0, #4  ; R0 = 4
STR R0, R5, #0  ; object = 4;
ADD R0, R5, #0  ; Generate memory address of object
STR R0, R5, #-1 ; Ptr = &object;
```

Figure 16.3 shows the stack frame of the function containing this code immediately after the statement ptr = &object; has executed. In order to make things more concrete, each memory location is labeled with an address, which we've arbitrarily selected to be in the xEFF0 range. The base pointer R5 currently points to xEFF2. Notice that object contains the integer value 4 and ptr contains the memory address of object.

16.2.2.2 The Indirection Operator *

The second pointer operator is called the *indirection*, or *dereference*, operator, and its symbol is the asterisk, * (pronounced *star* in this context). This operator allows us to indirectly manipulate the value of a memory object. From our previous

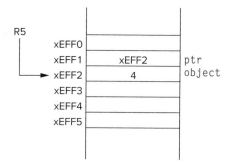

Figure 16.3 The run-time stack frame containing `object` and `ptr` after the statement `ptr = &object` has executed.

example: `*ptr` refers to the value stored in variable `object`. The expression `*ptr` refers to the value pointed to by the pointer variable `ptr`. Here, `*ptr` and `object` can be used interchangeably. Adding to the previous C code example,

```
int object;
int *ptr;

object = 4;
ptr = &object;
*ptr = *ptr + 1;
```

The statement `*ptr = *ptr + 1;` accomplishes the same thing as `object = object + 1;`. The expression `*ptr` means different things depending on which side of the assignment operator it appears on. On the right-hand side of the assignment operator, it refers to the value that appears at that location (in this case the value 4). On the left-hand side, it specifies the location that gets modified (in this case, the address of `object`). Let's examine the LC-3 code for the last statement in the preceding code.

```
LDR R0, R5, #-1 ; R0 contains the value of ptr
LDR R1, R0, #0  ; R1 <- *ptr
ADD R1, R1, #1  ; *ptr + 1
STR R1, R0, #0  ; *ptr = *ptr + 1;
```

Notice that this code is different from what would be generated if the final C statement had been `object = object + 1;`. With the pointer dereference, the compiler generates two `LDR` instructions for the indirection operator on the right-hand side, one to load the value of `ptr`, which is a memory address, and another to get the value stored at that address. With the dereference on the left-hand side, the compiler generates a `STR R1, R0, #0`. Had the statement been `object = *ptr + 1;`, the compiler would have generated `STR R1, R5, #0`.

16.2.3 Passing a Reference Using Pointers

Using the address and indirection operator, we can repair the `Swap` function from Figure 16.1, which did not quite accomplish the swap of its two input arguments. Figure 16.4 lists the same program with a revised version of `Swap` called `NewSwap`.

```
1    #include <stdio.h>
2
3    void NewSwap(int *firstVal, int *secondVal);
4
5    int main(void)
6    {
7      int valueA = 3;
8      int valueB = 4;
9
10     printf("Before Swap ");
11     printf("valueA = %d and valueB = %d\n", valueA, valueB);
12
13     NewSwap(&valueA, &valueB);
14
15     printf("After Swap ");
16     printf("valueA = %d and valueB = %d\n", valueA, valueB);
17   }
18
19   void NewSwap(int *firstVal, int *secondVal)
20   {
21     int tempVal;    // Holds firstVal when swapping */
22
23     tempVal = *firstVal;
24     *firstVal = *secondVal;
25     *secondVal = tempVal;
26   }
```

Figure 16.4   The function `NewSwap` swaps the values of its two arguments.

The first modification we've made is that the parameters of `NewSwap` are no longer integers but are now pointers to integers (`int *`). These two parameters are the memory addresses of the two variables that are to be swapped. Within the function body of `NewSwap`, we use the indirection operator `*` to obtain the values that these pointers point to.

Now when we call `NewSwap` from `main`, we need to supply the *addresses* for the two variables we want swapped, rather than the *values* of the variables as we did in the previous version of the code. For this, the `&` operator does the trick. Figure 16.5 shows the run-time stack when various statements of the function `NewSwap` are executed. The three subfigures (A–C) correspond to the run-time stack after lines 23, 24, and 25 execute. By design, C passes information from the caller function to the callee by value; that is, each argument expression in the call statement is evaluated, and the resulting value is passed to the callee via the run-time stack. However, in `NewSwap` we created a *call by reference* for the two arguments by using the address operator `&`. When an argument is passed as a reference, its **address** is passed to the callee function—for this to be valid, the argument must be a variable or other memory object (i.e., it must have an address). The callee function then can use the indirection operator `*` to access (and modify) the original value of the object.

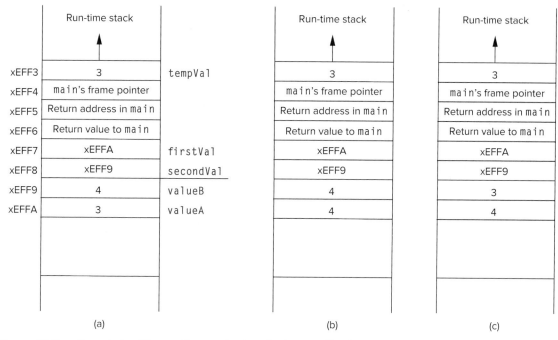

Figure 16.5 Snapshots of the run-time stack when the function NewSwap executes the statements in (a) line 23, (b) line 24, (c) line 25.

16.2.4 Null Pointers

Sometimes it is convenient for us to have a pointer point to nothing so that we can differentiate it from an actual pointer value. A pointer that points to nothing is a *null* pointer. In C, we make this designation with the following assignment:

```
int *ptr;
ptr = NULL;
```

Here, we are assigning the value of NULL to the pointer variable ptr. In C, NULL is a specially defined preprocessor macro that contains a value 0. So by convention, we consider a pointer that points to memory address 0 to be a special case pointer that points to nothing. Having such a pointer will be quite useful for dynamic data structures, which we will discuss in Chapter 19.

16.2.5 Demystifying the Syntax

Let's revisit some notation that we introduced in Chapter 11. Considering our discussion of pass-by-reference in C, let's re-examine the I/O library function scanf. In following example,

```
scanf("%d", &input);
```

the function scanf needs to update the variable input with the decimal value read from the keyboard. Therefore, scanf needs the address of input and not its value. To accomplish this, the address operator & is required. If we omit the address operator, the program terminates with an error. Can you come up with a plausible reason why this happens? Why is it not possible for scanf to work correctly without the use of a reference?

Before we complete our introduction to pointers, let's try to make sense of the pointer declaration syntax. To declare a pointer variable, we use a declaration of the following form:

```
type *ptr;
```

where type can be any of the predefined (or programmer-defined) types such as int, char, float, double, and so forth. The name ptr is simply any legal variable identifier. With this declaration, we are declaring a variable that, when the dereference (*) operator is applied to it, generates a value of type type. That is, *ptr is of type type.

As with all other operators, the address and indirection operators are evaluated according to the C precedence and associativity rules. The precedence and associativity of these and all other operators are listed in Table 12.5. Notice that both of the pointer operators have very high precedence.

16.2.6 An Example Problem Involving Pointers

Say we want to develop a C program that calculates the quotient and remainder given an integer dividend and integer divisor. That is, our code will calculate *dividend / divisor* and *dividend % divisor* . The structure of this program is very simple and requires only the sequential construct—no iteration required. The twist, however, is that we want the calculation of quotient and remainder to be performed by a single C function.

We can easily construct a function to generate a single output value (say, quotient) that we can pass back to the caller using the return value mechanism. A function that calculates only the quotient, for example, could consist of the single statement return dividend / divisor;. To provide the caller with multiple values, however, we will make use of the call by reference mechanism using pointer variables.

The code in Figure 16.6 contains a function that does just that. The function IntDivide has four parameters, two of which are integers and two of which are pointers to integers. The function divides the first parameter x by the second parameter y. The integer portion of the result is assigned to the memory location pointed to by quoPtr, and the integer remainder is assigned to the memory location pointed to by remPtr. Using call-by-reference with pointers, we can create a function that "returns" multiple output values back to its caller.

Notice that the function IntDivide also returns a value to indicate its status: It returns a −1 if the divisor is zero, indicating to the caller that an error has occurred. It returns a zero otherwise, indicating to the caller that the computation proceeded successfully. The function main, upon return, checks the return value to determine if the values in quotient and remainder are correct. Using the return value to signal error conditions during a function call is a common programming convention, particularly for complex functions.

```
1    include <stdio.h>
2
3    int IntDivide(int x, int y, int *quoPtr, int *remPtr);
4
5    int main(void)
6    {
7        int dividend;    // The number to be divided
8        int divisor;     // The number to divide by
9        int quotient;    // Integer result of division
10       int remainder;   // Integer remainder of division
11       int error;       // Did something go wrong?
12
13       printf("Input dividend: ");
14       scanf("%d", &dividend);
15       printf("Input divisor: ");
16       scanf("%d", &divisor);
17
18       error = IntDivide(dividend,divisor,&quotient,&remainder);
19
20       if (!error)      // !error indicates no error
21           printf("Answer: %d remainder %d\n", quotient, remainder);
22       else
23           printf("IntDivide failed.\n");
24   }
25
26   int IntDivide(int x, int y, int *quoPtr, int *remPtr)
27   {
28       if (y != 0) {
29           *quoPtr = x / y;   // Modify *quoPtr
30           *remPtr = x % y;   // Modify *remPtr
31           return 0;
32       }
33       else
34           return -1;
35   }
```

Figure 16.6   The function `IntDivide` calculates the integer portion and remainder of an integer divide; it returns a −1 if the divisor is zero.

16.3 Arrays

Consider a program that keeps track of the final exam scores for each of the 50 students in a computer engineering course. The most convenient way to store data in this code would be to declare a single memory object, say the variable `examScore`, in which we can store 50 different integer values. We can access a particular exam score within this variable using an offset from the beginning of the object. For example, `examScore[32]` provides the exam score for the 33rd student, and `examScore[19]` would be the exam score for the 20th student (the very first student's score stored in `examScore[0]`). The object `examScore` in this example is an *array* of integers. An array is a collection of similar data items that are stored sequentially in memory and accessible through a single name or identifier. Specifically, all the elements in the array are of the same type (e.g., int, char, etc.) and accessible through the name of the array.

Arrays are most useful when the data upon which the program operates is naturally expressed as a contiguous sequence of values. Because real-world data falls into this category (such as exam scores for students in a course), arrays are incredibly useful data structures. Also, from a computational perspective, being able to access the individual array elements using indices that can potentially themselves be computed creates a powerful capability for complex computational patterns. For instance, if we wanted to write a program to take a sequence of 100 numbers entered from the keyboard and *sort* them into ascending order, then an array would be the natural choice for storing these numbers in memory. The program would be almost impossible to write using the simple (non-array) variables. And the indices for the array elements can be computed using iteration constructs, making the sorting code much more compact and expressive.

16.3.1 Declaring and Using Arrays

First, let's examine how to declare an array in C. As with all other declarations, arrays must have a type associated with them. The type indicates the properties of the values stored in the array. The following declaration creates an array of ten integers:

```
int grid[10];
```

The keyword int indicates that we are declaring something of integer type named grid. The brackets indicate we are declaring an array, and the 10 indicates that the array is to contain ten integers, all of which will be consecutively located in memory. Figure 16.7 shows a pictorial representation of how grid is allocated. The first element, grid[0], is allocated in the lowest memory address and the last

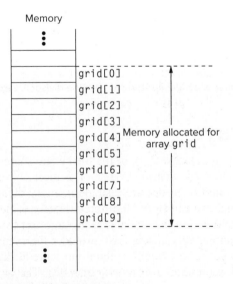

Figure 16.7   The array grid allocated in memory.

element, grid[9], in the highest address. If the array grid were a local variable, then its memory space would be allocated on the run-time stack. To access a particular element, we provide an *index* within brackets. For example,

```
grid[6] = grid[3] + 1;
```

The statement reads the value stored in the fourth element of grid (remember, we start numbering with 0), adds 1 to it, and stores the result into the seventh element of grid. Let's look at the LC-3 code for this example. Let's say that grid is the only local variable allocated on the run-time stack. By our run-time stack convention, this means that the frame pointer R5 will point to grid[9], or the last element in the array.

```
ADD R0, R5, #-9    ; Put the base address of grid into R0
LDR R1, R0, #3     ; R1 <-- grid[3]
ADD R1, R1, #1     ; R1 <-- grid[3] + 1
STR R1, R0, #6     ; grid[6] = grid[3] + 1;
```

Notice that the first instruction calculates the base address of the array, which is the address of grid[0], and puts it into R0. The base address of an array in general is the address of the first element of the array. We can access any element in the array by adding the index of the desired element to the base address.

The power of arrays comes from being able to compute an array index using a C integral expression. The following example demonstrates this. Here we are accessing the array grid using another variable x.

```
grid[x+1] = grid[x] + 2;
```

Let's look at the LC-3 code for this statement. Assume x is allocated on the run-time stack directly on top of the array grid.

```
LDR R0, R5, #-10   ; Load the value of x
ADD R1, R5, #-9    ; Put the base address of grid into R1
ADD R1, R0, R1     ; Calculate address of grid[x]
LDR R2, R1, #0     ; R2 <-- grid[x]
ADD R2, R2, #2     ; R2 <-- grid[x] + 2
LDR R0, R5, #-10   ; Load the value of x
ADD R0, R0, #1     ; R0 <-- x + 1
ADD R1, R5, #-9    ; Put the base address of grid into R1
ADD R1, R0, R1     ; Calculate address of grid[x+1]
STR R2, R1, #0     ; grid[x+1] = grid[x] + 2;
```

16.3.2 Examples Using Arrays

We start off with a simple C program that adds two arrays together by adding the corresponding elements from each array to form the sum. Each array represents a list of exam scores for students in a course. Each array contains an element for each student's score. To generate the cumulative points for each student, we effectively want to perform Total[i] = Exam1[i] + Exam2[i]. Figure 16.8 contains the C code to read in two ten-element integer arrays, add them together into another ten-element array, and print out the sum.

```
1    #include <stdio.h>
2    #define NUM_STUDENTS 10
3
4    int main(void)
5    {
6        int Exam1[NUM_STUDENTS];
7        int Exam2[NUM_STUDENTS];
8        int Total[NUM_STUDENTS];
9
10       // Input Exam 1 scores
11       for (int i = 0; i < NUM_STUDENTS; i++) {
12           printf("Input Exam 1 score for student %d : ", i);
13           scanf("%d", &Exam1[i]);
14       }
15       printf("\n");
16
17       // Input Exam 2 scores
18       for (int i = 0; i < NUM_STUDENTS; i++) {
19           printf("Input Exam 2 score for student %d : ", i);
20           scanf("%d", &Exam2[i]);
21       }
22       printf("\n");
23
24       // Calculate Total Points
25       for (int i = 0; i < NUM_STUDENTS; i++) {
26           Total[i] = Exam1[i] + Exam2[i];
27       }
28
29       // Output the Total Points
30       for (int i = 0; i < NUM_STUDENTS; i++) {
31           printf("Total for Student %d = %d\n", i, Total[i]);
32       }
33   }
```

Figure 16.8   A C program that calculates the sum of two ten-element arrays.

Notice the use of the preprocessor macro NUM_STUDENTS to represent a constant value of the size of the input set. This is a common use for preprocessor macros, which are usually found at the beginning of the source file (or within C header files). Now, if we want to increase the size of the array, for example if the student enrollment changes, we simply change the definition of the macro (one change) and recompile the program. If we did not use the macro, changing the array size would require changes to the code in multiple places. The changes could be potentially difficult to track down, and forgetting to do one would likely result in a program that did not work correctly.

Now onto a slightly more complex array example. Figure 16.9 lists a C program that reads in a sequence of decimal numbers (in total MAX_NUMS of them) from the keyboard and determines the number of times each input number is repeated within the sequence. The program then prints out each number, along with the number of times it repeats.

```
1    #include <stdio.h>
2    #define MAX_NUMS 10
3
4    int main(void)
5    {
6
7        int repIndex;          // Loop variable for rep loop
8        int numbers[MAX_NUMS]; // Original input numbers
9        int repeats[MAX_NUMS]; // Number of repeats
10
11       // Get input
12       printf("Enter %d numbers.\n", MAX_NUMS);
13       for (int index = 0; index < MAX_NUMS; index++) {
14           printf("Input number %d : ", index);
15           scanf("%d", &numbers[index]);
16       }
17
18       // Scan through entire array, counting number of
19       // repeats per element within the original array
20       for (int index = 0; index < MAX_NUMS; index++) {
21           repeats[index] = 0;
22           for (repIndex = 0; repIndex < MAX_NUMS; repIndex++) {
23               if (numbers[repIndex] == numbers[index])
24                   repeats[index]++;
25           }
26       }
27
28       // Print the results
29       for (int index = 0; index < MAX_NUMS; index++)
30           printf("Original number %d. Number of repeats %d\n",
31                   numbers[index], repeats[index]);
32   }
```

Figure 16.9   A C program that determines the number of repeated values in an array.

In this program, we use two arrays, numbers and repeats. Both are declared to contain MAX_NUMS integer values. The array numbers stores the input sequence. The array repeats is calculated by the program to contain the number of times the corresponding element in numbers is repeated in the input sequence. For example, if numbers[3] equals 115, and there are a total of four 115s in the input sequence, then repeats[3] will equal 4.

This program consists of three loops, one at line 13, one at line 20, and one at 29. The first and last for loops are simple loops that get keyboard input (line 13) and print out the results (line 29). The middle for loop (line 20) contains a nested loop—a loop within a loop. This nested loop computes the number of repeats of each element of the number array. The outer loop iterates the variable index from 0 through MAX_NUMS. We use index to scan through the array from the first element numbers[0] through the last element numbers[MAX_NUMS]. That is, the outer loop iterates through each element of number. The inner loop also iterates from 0 through MAX_NUMS; we use this loop to scan through the number array again, this time determining how many of the elements equal the element selected by the outer loop (i.e., `numbers[index]`). Each time a copy is detected through the expression

```
(numbers[repIndex] == numbers[index]),
```

the corresponding element in the `repeats` array is incremented (line 24).

16.3.3 Arrays as Parameters

Passing arrays between functions is a useful thing because it allows us to create functions that operate on arrays. Say we want to create a set of functions that calculates the mean and median on an array of integers. We would need either (1) to pass the entire array of values from one function to another or (2) to pass a reference to the array. If the array contains a large number of elements, copying each element from one stack frame onto another could be very costly in execution time. Fortunately, C naturally passes arrays by reference. Figure 16.10 is a C program

```
 1   #include <stdio.h>
 2   #define MAX_NUMS 10
 3
 4   int Average(int input_values[]);
 5
 6   int main(void)
 7   {
 8       int mean;                  // Average of numbers
 9       int numbers[MAX_NUMS]; // Original input numbers
10
11
12       // Get input
13       printf("Enter %d numbers.\n", MAX_NUMS);
14       for (int index = 0; index < MAX_NUMS; index++) {
15           printf("Input number %d : ", index);
16           scanf("%d", &numbers[index]);
17       }
18
19       mean = Average(numbers);
20
21       printf("The average of these numbers is %d\n", mean);
22   }
23
24   int Average(int inputValues[])
25   {
26       int sum = 0;
27
28       for (int index = 0; index < MAX_NUMS; index++) {
29           sum = sum + inputValues[index];
30       }
31
32       return (sum / MAX_NUMS);
33   }
```

Figure 16.10   An example of an array as a parameter to a function.

that contains a function Average whose single parameter is an array of integers. When calling the function Average from main, we use as the argument the name of the array numbers. Here, we are not using the standard notation involving brackets [ ] that we normally use for arrays. In C, an array's name refers to the address of the base element of the array. The name numbers is equivalent to &numbers[0]. The type of numbers is similar to int *, because numbers is a pointer to something of integer type. In using numbers as the argument to the function Average, we are causing the address of the array numbers to be pushed onto the stack and passed to the function Average. Within the function Average, the parameter inputValues is assigned the address of the array. Within Average we can access the elements of the original array using standard array notation. Figure 16.11 shows the run-time stack just prior to the execution of the return from Average (line 34 of the program).

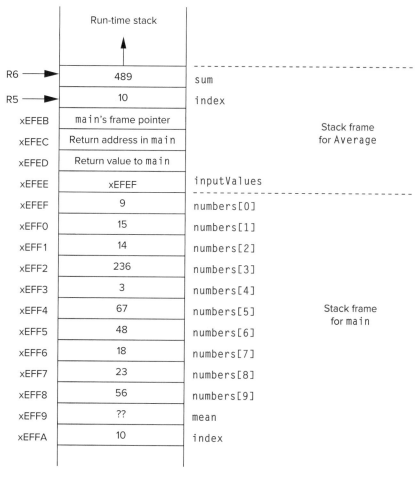

Figure 16.11   The run-time stack prior to the execution of the return from Average.

Notice how the input parameter inputValues is specified in the declaration of the function Average. The brackets [ ] indicate to the compiler that the corresponding parameter will be the base address to an array of the specified type, in this case an array of integers. Since arrays are passed by reference in C, any modifications to the array values made by the called function will be visible to the caller once control returns to it. How would we go about passing only a single element of an array by value? How about by reference?

16.3.4 Strings in C

Strings are sequences of characters that represent text. Strings in C are simply arrays of character type, with each subsequent element containing the next character of the string. For example,

```
char word[10];
```

declares an array that can contain a string of up to ten characters. Longer strings require larger arrays. In our example, the array word can contain the strings "elephant" or "giraffe", but not the entirety of "hippopotamus".

The word "giraffe" requires seven actual characters to be stored in the array, with the remaining three character slots in **word** unused. If we don't treat those three unused elements in a special manner, then we may end up not knowing where "giraffe" ends. To avoid any ambiguity, we adopt a special protocol for strings in C where the end of a string is denoted by the null character whose ASCII value is 0. This character serves as a sentinel that identifies the end of the string. Such strings are also called *null-terminated strings*. '\0' is the special character sequence that we can use in our C code to designate the null character. Continuing with our previous declaration,

```
char word[10];

word[0] = 'g';
word[1] = 'i';
word[2] = 'r';
word[3] = 'a';
word[4] = 'f';
word[5] = 'f';
word[6] = 'e';
word[7] = '\0';
printf("%s", word);
```

Here, we are assigning each element of the array individually such that the string will contain "giraffe". Notice that the end-of-string character itself is a character that occupies an element of the array. Even though the array is declared for ten elements, we must reserve one element for the null character, and therefore strings that are longer than nine characters cannot be stored in this array. The word "rhinoceros" could not be stored in word because there would be no room available for storing the null character designating the end of the string.

We also used a new printf format specification %s in this example. This specification prints out a string of characters, starting with the character pointed to by the corresponding parameter and ending at the end-of-string character '\0'. C also allows strings to be initialized within their declarations.

For instance, the preceding example can be rewritten to the following:

```
char word[10] = "Hello";
printf("%s", word);
```

Make note of two things here: First, character strings are distinguished from single characters with double quotes," ". Single quotes are used for single characters, such as 'A'. Second, the null character is automatically added to the end of the string.

16.3.4.1 Examples of Strings

Figure 16.12 contains C code that performs a common, useful primitive operation on strings: It calculates the length of a string. Since the size of the array that contains the string does not indicate the actual length of the string (it does, however, tell us the maximum length of the string), we need to examine the string itself to calculate its length. The algorithm for determining string length is easy. Starting with the first element, we count the number of characters before the null character. The function StringLength in Figure 16.12 performs this calculation. Notice

```
1    #include <stdio.h>
2    #define MAX_STRING 20
3
4    int StringLength(char string[]);
5
6    int main(void)
7    {
8        char input[MAX_STRING];   // Input string
9        int length = 0;
10
11       printf("Input a word (less than 20 characters): ");
12       scanf("%s", input);
13
14       length = StringLength(input);
15       printf("The word contains %d characters\n", length);
16   }
17
18   int StringLength(char string[])
19   {
20       int index = 0;
21
22       while (string[index] != '\0')
23           index = index + 1;
24
25       return index;
26   }
```

Figure 16.12   A program that calculates the length of a string.

that we are using the format specification %s in the scanf statement. This specification causes scanf to read in a string of characters from the keyboard until the
first *white space* character. In C, any space, tab, new line, carriage return, vertical
tab, or form-feed character is considered white space. So if the user types (from
The New Colossus, by Emma Lazarus)

```
Not like the brazen giant of Greek fame,
With conquering limbs astride from land to land;
```

only the word *Not* is stored in the array input. The remainder of the text
line is reserved for subsequent scanf calls to read. So if we perform another
scanf("%s", input), the word *like* will be stored in the array input. Notice
that the white space is automatically discarded by this %s specification. We examine this I/O behavior more closely in Chapter 18 when we take a deeper look into
I/O in C. Notice that the maximum word size is 20 characters. What happens if
the first word is longer? The scanf function has no information on the size of the
array input and will keep storing characters to the array address it was provided
until white space is encountered.

So what then happens if the first word is longer than 20 characters? Any
local variables that are allocated after the array input in the function main will
be overwritten. Draw out the stack frame before and after the call to scanf to see
why. In the exercises at the end of this chapter, we provide a problem where you
need to modify this program in order to catch the scenario where the user enters
a word longer than what fits into the input array.

Let's examine a slightly more complex example that uses functions we
developed in previous code examples in this chapter. In the code example in
Figure 16.13, we read an input string from the keyboard using scanf, then call a
function to reverse the string. The reversed string is then printed out. The function Reverse first determines the length of the string using the StringLength
function from the previous example. Then it performs the reversal by swapping
the first character with the last, the second character with the second to last, the
third character with the third to last, and so on. To perform the swap, it uses the
NewSwap function from Figure 16.4 modified to operate on characters. The reversal loop calls the function CharSwap on pairs of characters within the string. First,
CharSwap is called on the first and last character, then on the second and second to
last character, and so forth. The C standard library provides many prewritten functions for strings. For example, functions to copy strings, merge strings together,
compare them, or calculate their length can be found in the C standard library, and
the declarations for these functions can be included via the <string.h> header
file.

16.3.5 The Relationship Between Arrays and Pointers in C

You might have noticed that there is a similarity between an array's name and a
pointer variable to an element of the same type as the array. For instance,

```
char word[10];
char *cptr;
cptr = word;
```

```
1    #include <stdio.h>
2    #define MAX_STRING 20
3
4    int StringLength(char string[]);
5    void CharSwap(char *firstVal, char *secondVal);
6    void Reverse(char string[]);
7
8    int main(void)
9    {
10       char input[MAX_STRING];    // Input string
11
12       printf("Input a word (less than 20 characters): ");
13       scanf("%s", input);
14
15       Reverse(input);
16       printf("The word reversed is %s.\n", input);
17   }
18
19   int StringLength(char string[])
20   {
21       int index = 0;
22
23       while (string[index] != '\0')
24           index = index + 1;
25
26       return index;
27   }
28
29   void CharSwap(char *firstVal, char *secondVal)
30   {
31       char tempVal;              // Temporary location for swapping
32
33       tempVal = *firstVal;
34       *firstVal = *secondVal;
35       *secondVal = tempVal;
36   }
37
38   void Reverse(char string[])
39   {
40       int length;
41
42       length = StringLength(string);
43
44       for (int index = 0; index < (length / 2); index++)
45           CharSwap(&string[index], &string[length - (index + 1)]);
46   }
```

Figure 16.13   A program that reverses a string.

is a legal, and sometimes useful, sequence of code. Here we have assigned the pointer variable `cptr` to point to the base address of the array `word`. Because they are both pointers to characters, `cptr` and `word` can be used interchangeably. For example, we can access the fourth character within the string by using either `word[3]` or `*(cptr + 3)`.

One difference between the two, though, is that `cptr` is a variable and can be reassigned (i.e., it can appear on the left-hand side of an assignment operator). The array identifier `word`, on the other hand, cannot be reassigned. For example, the following statement is illegal: `word = newArray`. It generates a compiler error. The identifier always points to a fixed spot in memory where the compiler has placed the array. Once it has been allocated, it cannot be moved.

Table 16.1 shows the equivalence of several expressions involving pointer and array notation. Rows in the table are expressions with similar meanings.

Table 16.1	Expressions with Similar Meanings		
	Using a Pointer	**Using Name of Array**	**Using Array Notation**
Address of array	`cptr`	`word`	`&word[0]`
0th element	`*cptr`	`*word`	`word[0]`
Address of element n	`(cptr + n)`	`(word + n)`	`&word[n]`
Element n	`*(cptr + n)`	`*(word + n)`	`word[n]`

Here we assume `cptr` is a `char *` and `word` is a `char` array and `cptr = &word[0];`

16.3.6 Problem Solving: Insertion Sort

With this initial exposure to arrays under our belt, we can now attempt an interesting and sizeable (and useful!) problem: We will write C code to *sort* an array of integers into ascending order. That is, the code should arrange the data in array `a[]` such that `a[0]` $\leq$ `a[1]` $\leq$ `a[2]` . . . .

To accomplish this, we will use an algorithm for sorting called Insertion Sort. Sorting is an important primitive operation in computing, and considerable energy has been devoted over the years to understanding, analyzing, and refining the sorting process. There are many algorithms for sorting, and you will encounter various techniques in later computing courses. We use insertion sort here because it parallels how we might sort items in the physical world, with real objects. And it is quite straightforward enough for us to develop C code for it.

Insertion sort is best described by an example. Say we want to sort the books on a bookshelf into alphabetical order by author. Conceptually, we divide the books on the shelf into two groups, those that are already sorted and those that are not. Initially, the sorted group would be empty because all the books would be unsorted. The sorting process proceeds by taking a book from the unsorted group and *inserting* it into the proper position among the sorted books. For example, if the sorted group contained three books, one by Faulkner, one by Fitzgerald, and one by Steinbeck, then sorting the book by Hemingway would mean inserting it between Fitzgerald and Steinbeck. We keep sorting one book at a time until all books in the unsorted group have been inserted. This is insertion sort.

How would we go about applying this technique to sort an array of integers? Applying systematic decomposition to the preceding algorithm, we see that the core of the program involves iterating through the elements of the array, inserting each element into the proper spot in a new array where all items are in ascending order. This process continues until all elements of the original array have been inserted into the new array. Once this is done, the new array will contain the same elements as the first array, except in sorted order.

For this technique we need to represent two groups of items, the original unsorted elements and the sorted elements. For this we could use two separate arrays. It turns out, however, that we can represent both groups of elements within the original array. Doing so results in code that requires less memory and is more compact, though slightly more complex. The initial part of the array contains the sorted elements and the remainder of the array contains the unsorted elements. We pick the next unsorted item and insert it into the sorted part at the correct point. We keep doing this until we have gone through the entire array.

The actual `InsertionSort` routine (shown in Figure 16.14) contains a nested loop. The outer loop scans through all the unsorted items (analogous to going through the unsorted books, one by one). The inner loop scans through the already sorted items, scanning for the place at which to insert the new item. Once we detect an already sorted element that is larger than the one we are inserting, we insert the new element between the larger and the one before it.

Let's take a closer look by examining what happens during an iteration of the actual sorting code at lines 33–43. The outer loop at line 33 iterates the variable `unsorted` through the sequence 1, 2, 3, 4,..., 9. During the fourth iteration, at line 34, the variable `unsorted` is 4, and say the array `list` contains the following ten elements, and therefore `unsortedItem = 15`:

```
list = [2 16 68 69 15 9 10 7 82 19]
unsorted = 4
unsortedItem = 15
```

During this iteration, the code inserts the value of `list[4]`, which is 15, into the sorted portion of the array, which at this point is the elements `list[0]` through `list[3]`. The inner loop at lines 38–41 iterates the variable `sorted` through the list of already sorted elements. It does this from the highest numbered element down to 0, in this case starting at 3 down to 0. Notice that the condition on the `for` loop terminates the loop once a list item *less* than the current item, 15, is found.

In each iteration of this inner loop (lines 38–41), an element in the sorted group is copied to the subsequent position in the array (line 41) in order to make space for the new element to be inserted. In the first iteration, `list[3]` is copied to `list[4]`. Upon the completion of line 43, the variables values are:

```
list = [2 16 68 69 69 9 10 7 82 19]
unsorted = 4
unsortedItem = 15
sorted = 3
```

Notice that we have overwritten `list[4]` and lost the value 15 that was stored there. This is OK because we have a copy of its value in the variable

```c
1   #include <stdio.h>
2   #define MAX_NUMS 10
3
4   void InsertionSort(int list[]);
5
6   int main(void)
7   {
8
9       int numbers[MAX_NUMS]; // List of numbers to be sorted
10
11      // Get input
12      printf("Enter %d numbers.\n", MAX_NUMS);
13      for (int index = 0; index < MAX_NUMS; index++) {
14          printf("Input number %d : ", index);
15          scanf("%d", &numbers[index]);
16      }
17
18      InsertionSort(numbers); // Call sorting routine
19
20      // Print sorted list
21      printf("\nThe input set, in ascending order:\n");
22      for (int index = 0; index < MAX_NUMS; index++)
23          printf("%d\n", numbers[index]);
24  }
25
26  void InsertionSort(int list[])
27  {
28      int unsorted;      // Index for unsorted list items
29      int sorted;        // Index for sorted items
30      int unsortedItem;  // Current item to be sorted
31
32      // This loop iterates from 1 thru MAX_NUMS
33      for (unsorted = 1; unsorted < MAX_NUMS; unsorted++) {
34          unsortedItem = list[unsorted];
35
36          // This loop iterates from unsorted thru 0, unless
37          // we hit an element smaller than current item
38          for (sorted = unsorted - 1;
39              (sorted >= 0) && (list[sorted] > unsortedItem);
40              sorted--)
41              list[sorted + 1] = list[sorted];
42
43          list[sorted + 1] = unsortedItem; // Insert item
44      }
45  }
```

Figure 16.14   Insertion sort in C.

unsortedItem (from line 34). After the second iteration, and the completion of line 43, the variables contain:

```
list = [2 16 68 68 69 9 10 7 82 19]
unsorted = 4
unsortedItem = 15
sorted = 2
```

After the third iteration, after the completion of line 43, the variables contain:

```
list = [2 16 16 68 69 9 10 7 82 19]
unsorted = 4
unsortedItem = 15
sorted = 1
```

For the fourth iteration, sorted is set to 0. The inner for loop at line 38 terminates because the evaluation condition is no longer true. More specifically, list[sorted] > unsortedItem is not true. The current sorted list item list[0], which is 2, is not larger than the current unsorted item unsortedItem, which is 15. Now the inner loop terminates, and the statement at line 43, list[sorted + 1] = unsortedItem; executes. Now list contains, and the sorted part of the array contains, one more element.

```
list = [2 15 16 68 69 9 10 7 82 19]
```

This process continues until all items have been sorted, meaning the outer loop has iterated through all elements of the array list.

16.3.7 Common Pitfalls with Arrays in C

Unlike some other modern programming languages, C does not provide protection against exceeding the size (or bounds) of an array. Recall that C originated during an era when memory and computer processing power were precious resources, and programmers had to be very economical in the operations their code performed. In the spirit of minimizing overhead, C performs no size enforcement on arrays. This enables programs written in C to be fast and efficient, but at the cost of potential bugs. Programmer beware!

In the valid C expression a[i], the index i can access a memory location beyond the end of the array. The code in Figure 16.15 illustrates a situation where exceeding the size of an array can generate puzzling, erroneous results. Run this code and enter a number larger than the array size. Analyze this program by drawing out the run-time stack, and you will see more clearly why this bug causes the behavior it does. Writing beyond the end of the array causes some unexpected behavior in this code.

16.3.8 Variable-Length Arrays

In all of our discussion of arrays up until this point, we've worked under the assumption that an array in C is of fixed size. That is, the size of the array is fixed and is known when the code is compiled. In order to allocate an array on the run-time stack, the compiler needs to know the exact size. If the exact size is not

```
1   #include <stdio.h>
2   #define MAX_SIZE 10
3
4   int main(void)
5   {
6       int index;
7       int array[MAX_SIZE];
8       int limit;
9
10      printf("Enter limit (integer): ");
11      scanf("%d", &limit);
12
13      for(index = 0; index < limit; index++) {
14          array[index] = 0;
15          printf("array[%d] is set to 0\n", index);
16      }
17  }
```

Figure 16.15   This C program has peculiar behavior if the user enters a number that
is too large.

known, then the offsets from the frame pointer (R5) for the array and other variables in the stack frame cannot be properly determined, and everything falls apart.

But this particular restriction proves to be quite limiting. Often we want to size our arrays based on the particular situation we've encountered during execution. For example, referring back to our InsertionSort example in Figure 16.14, we may want our algorithm to be flexible enough to handle as much data as we want to throw at it. The example is hard-coded to work only on ten data items.

Starting in 1999, the ANSI C standard adopted support for variable-length arrays. Variable-length arrays are arrays whose sizes are variable integer expressions, rather than constants. The following code fragment

```
int Calculate(int len)
{
    int data[len];
```

illustrates the declaration of a variable-length array. The size of the array data can only be determined during execution of the code, and it is not known at compile time. The array data is still allocated on the run-time stack in this case but using a different type of allocation scheme than with standard, statically sized arrays. This protocol requires additional instructions during allocation and access, which adds performance overheard. Variable-length arrays are a nice programming convenience at the expense of additional performance.

Variable-length arrays work nicely for many of the examples in this textbook because the examples tend to be simple. We'll use them occasionally throughout the remaining chapters. While variable-length arrays address a limitation of statically sized arrays, they themselves are limited in that once they are declared, we can't modify their size. For this, dynamically sized arrays in C and vectors in C++ are the more general, thus more commonly used, solution. We'll discuss both in the final few chapters of this textbook.

16.3.9 Multidimensional Arrays in C

Nearly everyone alive today has taken or will take a picture with a smartphone. It's an activity that's simple enough for a person to accomplish, but it triggers an incredible amount of activity within a smartphone. Some of this activity involves physics and optics, as light from the scene being captured enters the lens of the phone to form an image on a device called a CMOS image sensor (think of it as the digital retina of the phone's camera). Much of this activity is digital; the image sensor and a slew of associated software on the phone convert the signals captured by the sensor into a high-quality picture. What exactly is this picture? Each element of the picture, or image, is called a *pixel*, and it represents the intensity of green, blue, and red at a particular point in the image. The image itself is a collection of these pixels (short for picture elements), arranged in a two-dimensional grid, with each pixel belonging to a particular row and column within the image. For example, an image might have 1080 rows and 1920 columns of pixels and would contain about two million pixels altogether. For the sake of this example, let's say we can represent each pixel with an integer value in C. How would we represent the overall image in C?

We can easily extend our idea of arrays to incorporate multidimensional concepts like images. In C, the syntax for doing so is simple:

```
int image[1080][1920];
```

This declaration creates an array called `image` that is organized as a two-dimensional array. The first dimension is of size 1080, or the number of rows of pixels, and the second dimension is of size 1920, and it represents the number of columns of pixels. Instead of providing a single index value to access elements of a single dimensional array, we now need to provide two, one for the row and one for the column. So, the expression:

```
image[38][283]
```

accesses the pixel in the 284th column of the 39th row of the image. Remember, numbering of arrays in C always starts with 0.

This 2D array will need to be mapped into memory somehow, just as we did with a simple 1D array. In the 1D case, the mapping is easy because the arrangement in memory corresponds to increasing indices of the array. In the 2D case, we have two options. Either we can map consecutive elements of each column into consecutive memory locations, or we can map consecutive elements of each row into consecutive memory locations. With C and C++, consecutive elements of **each column are in adjacent memory locations**, which is an ordering often called *row-major order*. Figure 16.16 provides a diagram of how this ordering applies to the array `image`. The image is so large that it won't fit into the LC-3's 16-bit address space. The LC-3 only has 2^{16} or 65,536 locations, and this image requires 2,073,600. We need a larger address space! So for this figure, we extended the address space to be 32 bits to make the example work.

Let's take a look at a simple image processing function that operates on images represented as 2D arrays. Using our example of an image, let's say that each element of the image array is an integer, and this integer represents the intensity of light at that position in the image. The higher the value, the brighter that

x0001 EA00	image[0][0]
x0001 EA01	image[0][1]
x0001 EA02	image[0][2]
x0001 EA03	image[0][3]
⋮	⋮
x0001 F17E	image[0][1918]
x0001 F17F	image[0][1919]
x0001 F180	image[1][0]
x0001 F181	image[1][1]
⋮	⋮
x0001 F8FE	image[1][1918]
x0001 F8FF	image[1][1919]
x0001 F900	image[2][0]
x0001 F901	image[2][1]
⋮	⋮

Figure 16.16   How a two-dimensional array is mapped into memory in C.

particular pixel. As such, the value represents the "white value" of the pixel. More generally, we'd incorporate color into the representation, but for now we'll keep it simple. The function Adjust in Figure 16.17 divides each pixel value by 2. When viewed visually, what would you expect in the resulting image?

```
1    #define ROWS 1080
2    #define COLS 1920
3
4    int Adjust(int image[ROWS][COLS])
5    {
6       for (int row = 0; row < ROWS; row++) {
7          for (int col = 0; col < COLS; col++) {
8             image[row][col] = image[row][col] / 2;
9          }
10      }
11   }
```

Figure 16.17   A simple image processing function based on 2D arrays in C.

The idea of multidimensional arrays in C extends beyond 2D arrays, too. We can declare a 3D array by attaching another set of brackets to the declaration, thus adding a dimension.

```
int dataVolume[40][50][60];  // This declares 120,000 elements
```

The layout in memory of a 3D array in C follows the same pattern as a 2D array: Consecutive elements of the rightmost index are allocated sequentially in memory. And we move through the indices right to left. So immediately in memory after `dataVolume[0][0][59]` will be `dataVolume[0][1][0]`.

16.4 Summary

In this chapter we covered two important high-level programming constructs: pointers and arrays. Both constructs enable us to access memory *indirectly*. The key notions we covered in this chapter are:

- **Pointers.** Pointers are variables that contain addresses of other memory objects (such as other variables). With pointers we can indirectly access and manipulate these other objects. A very simple application of pointers is to use them to pass parameters by reference. Pointers have more substantial applications, and we will see them in subsequent chapters.

- **Arrays.** An array is a collection of elements of the same type arranged sequentially in memory. We can access a particular element within an array by providing an index to the element that is its offset from the beginning of the array. Many real-world objects are best represented within a computer program as an array of items, thus making the array a significant structure for organizing data. With arrays, we can represent character strings that hold text data, for example. We examined several important array operations, including the sorting operation via insertion sort. C also supports variable-length arrays. With a variable-length array, we can declare an array whose size is determined during program execution. We also examined multidimensional arrays in C.

Exercises

16.1 Write a C function that takes as a parameter a character string of unknown length, containing a single word. Your function should translate this string from English into Pig Latin. This translation is performed by removing the first letter of the string, appending it onto the end, and concatenating the letters *ay*. You can assume that the array contains enough space for you to add the extra characters. For example, if your function is passed the string "Hello," after your function returns, the string should have the value "elloHay." The first character of the string should be "e."

16.2 Write a C program that accepts a list of numbers from the user until a number is repeated (i.e., is the same as the number preceding it). The program then prints out the number of numbers entered (excluding the last) and their sum. When the program is run, the prompts and responses will look like the following:

```
Number: 5
Number: -6
Number: 0
Number: 45
Number: 45
4 numbers were entered and their sum is 44
```

16.3   What is the output when the following code is compiled and run?

```
int x;
int main(void)
{
    int *px = &x;
    int x = 7;

    *px = 4;
    printf("x = %d\n", x);
}
```

16.4   Create a string function that takes two input strings, stringA and stringB, and returns a 0 if both strings are the same, a 1 if stringA appears before stringB in the sorted order of a dictionary, or a 2 if stringB appears before stringA.

16.5   Using the function developed for Exercise 16.4, modify the Insertion Sort program so that it operates upon strings instead of integers.

16.6   Translate the following C function into LC-3 assembly language.

```
int main(void)
{
    int a[5], i;
    i = 4;
    while (i >= 0) {
        a[i] = i;
        i--;
    }
}
```

16.7   For this question, examine the following program. Notice that the variable ind is a pointer variable that points to another pointer variable. Such a construction is legal in C.

```
#include <stdio.h>
int main(void)
{
    int apple;
    int *ptr;
    int **ind;
    ind = &ptr;

    *ind = &apple;
    **ind = 123;
    ind++;
    *ptr++;
    apple++;
    printf("%x %x %d\n", ind, ptr, apple);
}
```

Analyze what this program performs by drawing out the run-time stack at the point just after the statement apple++; executes.

16.8 The following code contains a call to the function `triple`. What is the minimum size of the stack frame of `triple`?

```
int main(void)
{
    int array[3];

    array[0] = 1;
    array[1] = 2;
    array[2] = 3;
    triple(array);
}
```

16.9 Write a program to remove any duplicates from a sequence of numbers. For example, if the list consisted of the numbers 5, 4, 5, 5, and 3, the program would output 5, 4, 3.

16.10 Write a program to find the median of a set of numbers. Recall that the median is a number within the set in which half the numbers are larger and half are smaller. *Hint:* To perform this, you may need to sort the list first.

16.11 For this question, refer to the following C program:

```
int FindLen(char *);
int main(void)
{
    char str[10];

    printf("Enter a string : ");
    scanf("%s", str);
    printf("%s has %d characters\n", str, FindLen(str));
}

int FindLen(char * s)
{
    int len=0;
    while (*s != '\0') {
        len++;
        s++;
    }
    return len;
}
```

a. What is the size of the stack frame for the functions `main` and `FindLen`?

b. Show the contents of the stack just before `FindLen` returns if the input string is `apple`.

c. What would the stack frame look like if the program were run and the user typed a string of length greater than ten characters? What would happen to the program?

16.12 The following code reads a string from the keyboard and prints out a version with any uppercase characters converted to lowercase. However, it has a flaw. Identify it.

```c
#include <stdio.h>
#define MAX_LEN 10

char *LowerCase(char *s);
int main(void)
{
    char str[MAX_LEN];
    printf("Enter a string : ");
    scanf("%s", str);
    printf("Lowercase: %s \n", LowerCase(str));
}

char *LowerCase(char *s)
{
    char newStr[MAX_LEN];
    for (int index = 0; index < MAX_LEN; index++) {
        if ('A' <= s[index] && s[index] <= 'Z')
            newStr[index] = s[index] + ('a' - 'A');
        else
            newStr[index] = s[index];
    }
    return newStr;
}
```

16.13 Consider the following declarations.

```c
#define STACK_SIZE 100
int stack[STACK_SIZE];
int topOfStack;
int Push(int item);
```

a. Write a funtion `Push` (the declaration is provided) that will push the value of `item` onto the top of the stack. If the stack is full and the item cannot be added, the function should return a 1. If the item is successfully pushed, the function should return a 0.

b. Write a function `Pop` that will pop an item from the top of the stack. Like `Push`, this function will return a 1 if the operation is unsuccessful. That is, a `Pop` was attempted on an empty stack. It should return a 0 if successful. Consider carefully how the popped value can be returned to the caller.

16.14 Write a function that takes an image represented as 2-dimensional array of integers, where each integer represents the intensity of the corresponding pixel and creates a histogram of that counts the frequency of intensity values. For simplicity assume that the intensity values are only between 0 and 15, and only 16 bins need to be created in the histogram.

    a. Write the function assuming that the image dimensions are fixed and can be hard-coded.

    b. Write the function assuming that the image dimensions are provided as parameters to the function.

CHAPTER

17 Recursion

17.1 Introduction

Suppose we want to find a particular student's exam in a stack of exams that are already sorted into alphabetical order. Our procedure for doing so could be as follows: Pick a random point in the stack, and check for a match. If we find a match, great! We are done. If we don't find the exam (which is the more likely case, initially), we now know the exam we're looking for is either in the upper stack or in the lower stack based on whether the name occurs alphabetically before or after the name at the random point. Here's the key: We can now repeat the same procedure on a stack of exams (lower or upper) that is necessarily smaller than our original stack. For example, say we are looking for Mira's exam. We find at our selected random point Salina's exam. We clearly didn't find Mira's exam, but we know that it must in the portion of the stack that precedes Salina's exam. We repeat our search on that smaller substack. Fairly quickly, we will locate Mira's exam, if it exists in the set.

The technique we've described is *recursive*. We are solving the problem (finding an exam in a stack of exams) by stating that we'll solve it on successively smaller versions of the problem (find the exam on this smaller stack). We examined recursion first in Chapter 8, in the context of subroutines in LC-3 assembly language. Now that we've raised the level of programming abstraction, it's worthwhile for us to revisit recursion in the context of the C programming language.

Recursion is similar to iteration in that both describe a repeating flow of computation. The power of recursion lies in its ability to elegantly express the computation flow for certain programming tasks. There are some programming problems for which the recursive solution is far simpler than the corresponding iterative solution. Nearly always, recursion comes at the cost of additional execution overhead compared to iteration. So recursion must be applied carefully with a thorough understanding of the underlying costs.

In this chapter, we introduce the concept of recursion via several different examples. As we did in Chapter 8, we'll examine how recursive functions are implemented on the LC-3, this time with the run-time stack facilitating the recursion. The elegance of the run-time stack mechanism is that recursive functions require no special handling—they execute in the same manner as any other function. The main purpose of this chapter is to provide an initial but deep exposure to recursion so that you can start implementing recursive algorithms in your code.

17.2 What Is Recursion?

Let's revisit the basic idea of recursion through a simple toy example. A function that calls itself is a recursive function. The function RunningSum in Figure 17.1 is an example. This function calculates the sum of all the integers between the input parameter n and 1, inclusive. For example, RunningSum(4) calculates 4+3+2+1. However, it does the calculation recursively. Notice that the running sum of 4 is really 4 plus the running sum of 3. Likewise, the running sum of 3 is 3 plus the running sum of 2. This *recursive* definition is the basis for a recursive algorithm. In other words,

$$\text{RunningSum}(n) = n + \text{RunningSum}(n-1)$$

In mathematics, we use *recurrence equations* to express such functions. The preceding equation is a recurrence equation for RunningSum. In order to complete the evaluation of this equation, we must also supply an initial case. So in addition to the preceding formula, we need to state

$$\text{RunningSum}(1) = 1$$

before we can completely evaluate the recurrence. Now we can fully evaluate RunningSum(4):

$$\text{RunningSum}(4) = 4 + \text{RunningSum}(3)$$
$$= 4 + 3 + \text{RunningSum}(2)$$
$$= 4 + 3 + 2 + \text{RunningSum}(1)$$
$$= 4 + 3 + 2 + 1$$

The C version of RunningSum works in the same manner as the recurrence equation. During execution of the function call RunningSum(4), RunningSum makes a function call to itself, with an argument of 3 (i.e., RunningSum(3)). However, before RunningSum(3) ends, it makes a call to RunningSum(2). And before

```
1   int RunningSum(int n)
2   {
3       if (n == 1)
4           return 1;
5       else
6           return (n + RunningSum(n-1));
7   }
```

Figure 17.1   An example of a simple recursive function.

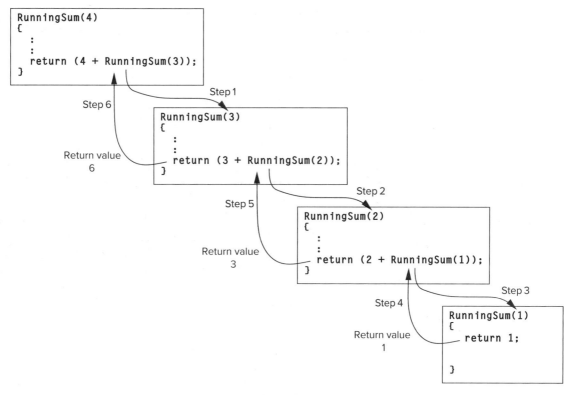

Figure 17.2 The flow of control when `RunningSum(4)` is executed.

`RunningSum(2)` ends, it makes a call to `RunningSum(1)`. `RunningSum(1)`, however, makes no additional recursive calls and returns the value 1 to `RunningSum(2)`, which enables `RunningSum(2)` to end and return the value 2 + 1 back to `RunningSum(3)`. This enables `RunningSum(3)` to end and pass a value of 3 + 2 + 1 to `RunningSum(4)`. Figure 17.2 pictorially shows how the execution of `RunningSum(4)` proceeds.

17.3 Recursion vs. Iteration

Clearly, we could have (and should have) written `RunningSum` using a `for` loop, and the code would have been more straightforward than its recursive counterpart. We provided a recursive version here in order to demonstrate a recursive call in the context of an easy-to-understand example.

There is a parallel between using recursion and using conventional iteration (such as `for` and `while` loops) in programming. All recursive functions can be written using iteration. For certain programming problems, however, the recursive version is simpler and more elegant than the iterative version. Solutions to certain problems are naturally expressed in a recursive manner, such as problems that are expressed with recurrence equations. It is because of such problems that recursion is an indispensable programming technique. Knowing which problems require recursion and which are better solved with iteration is part of the art of computer programming, and it is a skill one develops through coding experience.

Recursion, as useful as it is, comes at a cost. As an experiment, write an iterative version of `RunningSum` and compare the running time for large n with the recursive version. To do this you can use library functions to get the time of day (e.g., `gettimeofday`) before the function starts and when it ends. Plot the running time for a variety of values of n and you will notice that the recursive version is relatively slower (provided the compiler did not optimize away the recursion, which it can do through a simple transformation that converts certain types of recursive code to iterative code when the recursion is the last operation in the function, i.e., it occurs at the tail of the function). Recursive functions incur function call overhead that iterative solutions do not. Understanding the underlying overheads of recursion is something we cleanly explore with our bottom-up approach, and it will assist you in knowing when, and when not, to apply recursion for a particular programming task.

17.4 Towers of Hanoi

One problem for which the recursive solution is simpler than iteration is the classic puzzle Towers of Hanoi. The puzzle involves a platform with three posts. On one of the posts sit a number of wooden disks, each smaller than the one below it. The objective is to move all the disks from their current post to one of the other posts. However, there are two rules for moving disks: Only one disk can be moved at a time, and a larger disk can never be placed on top of a smaller disk. For example, Figure 17.3 shows a puzzle where five disks are on post 1. To solve this puzzle, these five disks must be moved to one of the other posts obeying the two rules. As the legend associated with the puzzle goes, when the world was created, the priests at the Temple of Brahma were given the task of moving 64 disks from one post to another. When they completed their task, the world would end.

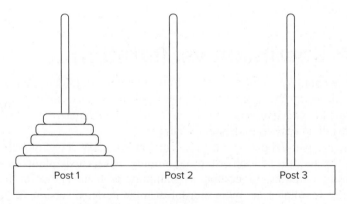

Figure 17.3 The Towers of Hanoi puzzle with five disks.

Now how would we go about writing C code to solve this puzzle? If we view the problem from the end first, we can make the following observation: The final sequence of moves **must** involve moving the largest disk from post 1 to the target post, say post 3, and then moving all of the other disks back on top of it. Conceptually, we need to move all $n - 1$ disks off the largest disk and onto the intermediate post, then move the largest disk onto the target post. Finally, we move all $n - 1$ disks from the intermediate post onto the target post. Moving $n - 1$ disks in one move is not a singular, legal move. However, we have stated the problem in such a manner that we can solve by solving two smaller subproblems. We now have a recursive definition of the problem: In order to move n disks to the target post, which we symbolically represent as `Move(n, target)`, we first move $n - 1$ disks to the intermediate post, `Move(n-1, intermediate)`, then move the nth disk to the target, which is a singular move, and finally move $n - 1$ disks from the intermediate to the target, `Move(n-1, target)`. So in order to `Move(n, target)`, two recursive calls are made to solve two smaller subproblems involving $n - 1$ disks.

As with recurrence equations in mathematics, all recursive definitions require a *base case*, which ends the recursion. In the way we have formulated the problem, the base case involves moving the smallest disk (disk 1). Moving disk 1 requires no other disks to be moved since it is always on top and can be moved directly from one post to any another without moving any other disks. Without a base case, a recursive function would never end, similar to an infinite loop in conventional iteration. Taking our recursive definition to C code is fairly straightforward. Figure 17.4 is a recursive C function of this algorithm.

```
1    // diskNumber is the disk to be moved (disk1 is smallest)
2    // startPost is the post the disk is currently on
3    // endPost is the post we want the disk to end on
4    // midPost is the intermediate post
5    void MoveDisk(int diskNumber, int startPost, int endPost, int midPost)
6    {
7        if (diskNumber > 1) {
8            // Move n-1 disks off the current disk on
9            // startPost and put them on the midPost
10           MoveDisk(diskNumber-1, startPost, midPost, endPost);
11
12           printf("Move disk %d from post %d to post %d.\n",
13                   diskNumber, startPost, endPost);
14
15           // Move all n-1 disks from midPost onto endPost
16           MoveDisk(diskNumber-1, midPost, endPost, startPost);
17       }
18       else
19           printf("Move disk 1 from post %d to post %d.\n",
20                   startPost, endPost);
21   }
```

Figure 17.4   A recursive function to solve the Towers of Hanoi puzzle.

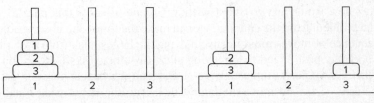

Figure 17.5   The Towers of Hanoi puzzle, initial configuration.

Figure 17.6   The Towers of Hanoi puzzle, after first move.

Let's see what happens when we solve the puzzle with three disks. Following is the initial function call to MoveDisk. We start off by saying that we want to move disk 3 (the largest disk) from post 1 to post 3, using post 2 as the intermediate storage post. That is, we want to solve a three-disk Towers of Hanoi puzzle. See Figure 17.5.

```
// diskNumber 3; startPost 1; endPost 3; midPost 2
MoveDisk(3, 1, 3, 2)
```

This call invokes another call to MoveDisk to move disks 1 and 2 off disk 3 and onto post 2 using post 3 as intermediate storage. The call is performed at line 10 in the source code.

```
// diskNumber 2; startPost 1; endPost 2; midPost 3
MoveDisk(2, 1, 2, 3)
```

To move disk 2 from post 1 to post 2, we first move disk 1 off disk 2 and onto post 3 (the intermediate post). This triggers another call to MoveDisk again from the call on line 10.

```
// diskNumber 1; startPost 1; endPost 3; midPost 2
MoveDisk(1, 1, 3, 2)
```

For this call, the condition of the if statement on line 7 will not be true, and disk 1 can be moved directly to the target post. The printf statement on lines 19–20 is executed. See Figure 17.6.

```
Move disk 1 from post 1 to post 3.
```

This invocation of MoveDisk returns to its caller, which was the call MoveDisk(2, 1, 2, 3). Recall that we were waiting for all disks on top of disk 2 to be moved to post 3. Since that is now complete, we can move disk 2 from post 1 to post 2. The printf on lines 19–20 is the next statement to execute, signaling another disk to be moved. See Figure 17.7.

```
Move disk 2 from post 1 to post 2.
```

Next, a call is made to move all disks that were on disk 2 back onto disk 2. This happens at the call on line 16 of the source code for MoveDisk.

```
// diskNumber 1; startPost 2; endPost 3; midPost 1
MoveDisk(1, 2, 3, 1)
```

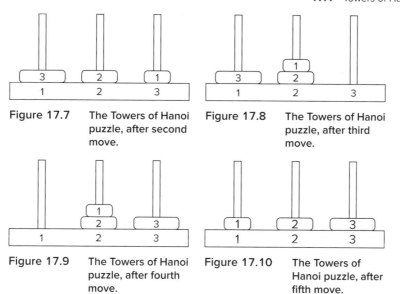

| Figure 17.7 | The Towers of Hanoi puzzle, after second move. | Figure 17.8 | The Towers of Hanoi puzzle, after third move. |

| Figure 17.9 | The Towers of Hanoi puzzle, after fourth move. | Figure 17.10 | The Towers of Hanoi puzzle, after fifth move. |

Again, since disk 1 has no disks on top of it, we see the move printed. See Figure 17.8.

```
Move disk number 1 from post 3 to post 2.
```

Control passes back to the call `MoveDisk(2, 1, 2, 3)` which, having completed its task of moving disk 2 (and all disks on top of it) from post 1 to post 2, returns to its caller. Its caller is `MoveDisk(3, 1, 3, 2)`. All disks have been moved off disk 3 and onto post 2. Disk 3 can be moved from post 1 onto post 3. The `printf` is the next statement executed. See Figure 17.9.

```
Move disk 3 from post 1 to post 3.
```

The next subtask remaining is to move disk 2 (and all disks on top of it) from post 2 onto post 3. We can use post 1 for intermediate storage. The following call occurs on line 16 of the source code.

```
// diskNumber 2; startPost 2; endPost 3; midPost 1
MoveDisk(2, 2, 3, 1)
```

In order to do so, we must first move disk 1 from post 2 onto post 1, via the call on line 16.

```
// diskNumber 1; startPost 2; endPost 1; midPost 3
MoveDisk(1, 2, 1, 3)
```

The move requires no submoves. See Figure 17.10.

```
Move disk 1 from post 2 to post 1.
```

Return passes back to the caller `MoveDisk(2, 2, 3, 1)`, and disk 2 is moved onto post 3. See Figure 17.11.

```
Move disk 2 from post 2 to post 3.
```

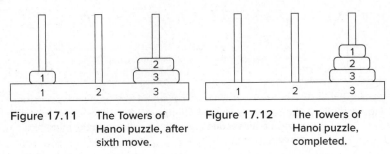

Figure 17.11   The Towers of
                 Hanoi puzzle, after
                 sixth move.

Figure 17.12   The Towers of
                 Hanoi puzzle,
                 completed.

The only thing remaining is to move all disks that were on disk 2 back on
top.

```
// diskNumber 1; startPost 1; endPost 3; midPost 2
MoveDisk(1, 1, 3, 2)
```

The move is done immediately. See Figure 17.12.

```
Move disk 1 from post 1 to post 3.
```

and the puzzle is completed!

Let's summarize the action of the recursion by examining the sequence of
function calls that were made in solving the three-disk puzzle:

```
MoveDisk(3, 1, 3, 2)    // Initial Call
MoveDisk(2, 1, 2, 3)
MoveDisk(1, 1, 3, 2)
MoveDisk(1, 2, 3, 1)
MoveDisk(2, 2, 3, 1)
MoveDisk(1, 2, 1, 3)
MoveDisk(1, 1, 3, 2)
```

Consider how you would write an iterative version of a solver for this puzzle. You'll no doubt quickly appreciate the simplicity of the recursive version.
Returning to the legend of the Towers of Hanoi: The world will end when the
monks finish solving a 64-disk version of the puzzle. For a three-disk puzzle, the
solution required seven moves. If each move takes one second, how long will it
take the monks to solve the 64-disk puzzle? Would the number of moves for an
iterative version be any different?

17.5 Fibonacci Numbers

Let's revisit an example from Section 8.3.2. We considered this a bad application
of recursion when we introduced it for the LC-3, and it still is in C! But this example is worth reexamining. It's simple enough to express with a short C function,
yet complex enough to have interesting stack behavior during execution. Also,
we can view a complete translation to LC-3 assembly and take note of how the
recursion is handled by the run-time stack.

The following recurrence equations generate a well-known sequence of numbers called the *Fibonacci numbers*, which has some interesting mathematical,
geometrical, and natural properties.

$$f(n) = f(n-1) + f(n-2)$$
$$f(1) = 1$$
$$f(0) = 1$$

The nth Fibonacci number is the sum of the previous two. The series is 1, 1, 2, 3, 5, 8, 13, ... This series was popularized by the Italian mathematician Leonardo of Pisa around the year 1200 (it is thought to have first been described by Indian mathematicians around 200 BC). His father's name was Bonacci, and thus he often called himself Fibonacci as a shortening of *filius Bonacci*, or son of Bonacci. Fibonacci formulated this series as a way of estimating breeding rabbit populations. We have since discovered some fascinating ways in which the series models some other natural phenomena such as the structure of a spiral shell or the pattern of petals on a flower. The ratios of successive numbers in the sequence approximate the Golden Ratio.

We can formulate a recursive function to calculate the nth Fibonacci number directly from the recurrence equations. Fibonacci(n) is recursively calculated by Fibonacci(n-1) + Fibonacci(n-2). The base case of the recursion is simply the fact that Fibonacci(1) and Fibonacci(0) both equal 1. Figure 17.13 lists the recursive code to calculate the nth Fibonacci number.

```
1   #include <stdio.h>
2
3   int Fibonacci(int n);
4
5   int main(void)
6   {
7       int in;
8       int number;
9
10      printf("Which Fibonacci number? ");
11      scanf("%d", &in);
12
13      number = Fibonacci(in);
14      printf("That Fibonacci number is %d\n", number);
15  }
16
17  int Fibonacci(int n)
18  {
19      int sum;
20
21      if (n == 0 || n == 1)
22          return 1;
23      else {
24          sum = (Fibonacci(n-1) + Fibonacci(n-2));
25          return sum;
26  }
```

Figure 17.13   A recursive C function to calculate the nth Fibonacci number.

This example is simple enough for us to take a deeper look into how recursion actually is implemented at the lower levels. In particular, we will examine the run-time stack mechanism and see how it naturally handles recursive calls. Whenever a function is called, whether from itself or another function, a new copy of its stack frame is pushed onto the run-time stack. That is, each invocation of the function gets a new, private copy of parameters and local variables. And once each invocation completes, this private copy must be deallocated. The run-time stack enables this in a natural fashion. If the variables of a recursive function were statically allocated in memory, each recursive call to Fibonacci would overwrite the values of the previous call.

Let's take a look at the run-time stack when we call the function Fibonacci with the parameter 3, Fibonacci(3). We start off with the stack frame for Fibonacci(3) on top of the run-time stack. Figure 17.14 shows the progression of the stack as the original function call is evaluated. The function call Fibonacci(3) will first calculate Fibonacci(3-1) as the expression Fibonacci(n-1) + Fibonacci(n-2) is evaluated left to right. Therefore, a call is first made to Fibonacci(2), and a stack frame for Fibonacci(2) is pushed onto the run-time stack (see Figure 17.14, step 2). For Fibonacci(2), the parameter n equals 2 and does not meet the terminal condition; therefore, a call is made to Fibonacci(1) (see Figure 17.14, step 3). This call is made in the course of evaluating Fibonacci(2-1) + Fibonacci(2-2). The call Fibonacci(1) results in no more recursive calls because the parameter n meets the terminal condition. The value 1 is returned to Fibonacci(2), which now can complete the evaluation of Fibonacci(1) + Fibonacci(0) by calling Fibonacci(0) (see Figure 17.14, step 4). The call Fibonacci(0) immediately returns a 1. Now, the call Fibonacci(2) can complete and return its subcalculation (its result is 2) to its caller, Fibonacci(3). Having completed the left-hand component of the expression Fibonacci(2) + Fibonacci(1), Fibonacci(3) calls Fibonacci(1) (see Figure 17.14, step 5), which immediately returns the value 1. Now Fibonacci(3) is done—its result is 3 (Figure 17.14, step 6). We could state the recursion of Fibonacci(3) algebraically, as follows:

```
Fibonacci(3) = Fibonacci(2) + Fibonacci(1)
             = (Fibonacci(1) + Fibonacci(0)) + Fibonacci(1)
             = 1 + 1 + 1 = 3
```

The sequence of function calls made during the evaluation of Fibonacci(3) is as follows:

```
Fibonacci(3)
Fibonacci(2)
Fibonacci(1)
Fibonacci(0)
Fibonacci(1)
```

Walk through the execution of Fibonacci(4) and you will notice that the sequence of calls made by Fibonacci(3) is a subset of the calls made by Fibonacci(4). No surprise, since Fibonacci(4) = Fibonacci(3) + Fibonacci(2). Likewise, the sequence of calls made by Fibonacci(4) is a subset of the calls made by Fibonacci(5). There is an exercise at the end of this

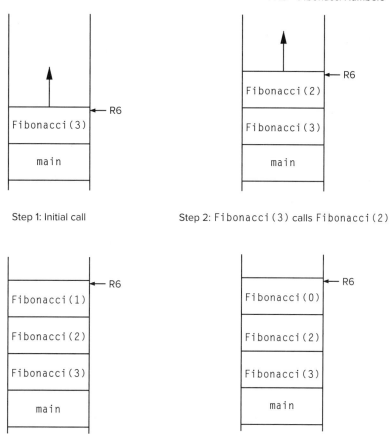

Step 1: Initial call

Step 2: Fibonacci(3) calls Fibonacci(2)

Step 3: Fibonacci(2) calls Fibonacci(1)

Step 4: Fibonacci(2) calls Fibonacci(0)

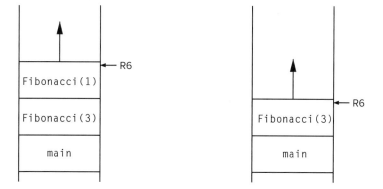

Step 5: Fibonacci(3) calls Fibonacci(1)

Step 6: Back to the starting point

Figure 17.14 **Snapshots of the run-time stack for the function call** Fibonacci(3).

chapter involving calculating the number of function calls made during the evaluation of Fibonacci(n). As we did in Section 8.3.2, it's worthwhile to compare the running time of the recursive version of Fibonnaci in C to an iterative version. The simple recursive version, while it falls directly out of the recurrence equations and is easy to code, is far more costly than its iterative counterpart. It is more expensive not only because of the function call overhead, but also because the recursive solution has a significant number of repeated calculations that the iterative version does not.

Figure 17.15 lists the LC-3 C compiler generated for this Fibonacci program. Notice that no special treatment was required to handle the program's recursive nature. Because of the run-time stack mechanism for activating functions, a recursive function gets treated like every other function. If you examine this code closely, you will notice that the compiler generated a temporary variable in order to translate line 24 of Fibonacci properly. Most compilers will generate such temporaries when compiling complex expressions and will allocate storage in the stack frame on top of programmer-declared local variables.

```
1  Fibonacci:
2      ADD R6, R6, #-2    ; push return value/address
3      STR R7, R6, #0     ; store return address
4      ADD R6, R6, #-1    ; push caller's frame pointer
5      STR R5, R6, #0     ;
6      ADD R5, R6, #-1    ; set new frame pointer
7      ADD R6, R6, #-2    ; allocate space for locals and temps
8
9      LDR R0, R5, #4     ; load the parameter n
10     BRZ FIB_BASE       ; check for n == 0
11     ADD R0, R0, #-1    ;
12     BRZ FIB_BASE       ; n==1
13
14     LDR R0, R5, #4     ; load the parameter n
15     ADD R0, R0, #-1    ; calculate n-1
16     ADD R6, R6, #-1    ; push n-1
17     STR R0, R6, #0     ;
18     JSR Fibonacci      ; call to Fibonacci(n-1)
19
20     LDR R0, R6, #0     ; read the return value at top of stack
21     ADD R6, R6, #-1    ; pop return value
22     STR R0, R5, #-1    ; store it into temporary value
23     LDR R0, R5, #4     ; load the parameter n
24     ADD R0, R0, #-2    ; calculate n-2
25     ADD R6, R6, #-1    ; push n-2
26     STR R0, R6, #0     ;
27     JSR Fibonacci      ; call to Fibonacci(n-2)
28
```

Figure 17.15   Fibonacci in LC-3 assembly code (Fig. 17.15 continued on next page.)

```
29        LDR R0, R6, #0     ; read the return value at top of stack
30        ADD R6, R6, #-1    ; pop return value
31        LDR R1, R5, #-1    ; read temporary value: Fibonacci(n-1)
32        ADD R0, R0, R1     ; Fibonacci(n-1) + Fibonacci(n-2)
33        BR FIB_END         ; branch to end of code
34
35 FIB_BASE:
36        AND R0, R0, #0     ; clear R0
37        ADD R0, R0, #1     ; R0 = 1
38
39 FIB_END:
40        STR R0, R5, #3     ; write the return value
41        ADD R6, R5, #1     ; pop local variables
42        LDR R5, R6, #0     ; restore caller's frame pointer
43        ADD R6, R6, #1     ;
44        LDR R7, R6, #0     ; pop return address
45        ADD R6, R6, #1     ;
46        RET
```

Figure 17.15   `Fibonacci` **in LC-3 assembly code (continued Fig. 17.15 from previous page.)**

17.6 Binary Search

We started this chapter by describing a recursive technique for finding a particular exam in a set of exams that are in alphabetical order. The technique is called *binary search*, and it is a rapid way of finding a particular element within a list of elements in sorted order. At this point, given our understanding of recursion and of arrays, we can code a recursive function in C to perform binary search.

Say we want to find a particular integer value in an array of integers that is in ascending order. The function should return the index of the integer, or a -1 if the integer does not exist. To accomplish this, we will use the binary search technique as follows: Given an array and an integer to search for, we will examine the midpoint of the array and determine if the integer is (1) equal to the value at the midpoint, (2) less than the value at the midpoint, or (3) greater than the value at the midpoint. If it is equal, we are done. If it is less than, we perform the search again, but this time only on the first half of the array. If it is greater than, we perform the search only on the second half of the array. Notice that we can express cases (2) and (3) using recursive calls.

What happens if the value we are searching for does not exist within the array? Given this recursive technique of performing searches on smaller and smaller subarrays of the original array, we eventually perform a search on an array that has no elements (e.g., of size 0) if the item we are searching for does not exist. If we encounter this situation, we will return a -1. This will be a base case in the recursion.

Figure 17.16 contains the recursive implementation of the binary search algorithm in C. Notice that in order to determine the size of the array at each step, we pass the starting and ending points of the subarray along with each call to `BinarySearch`. Each call refines the variables `start` and `end` to search smaller

```
1    // This function returns the position of 'item' if it exists
2    // between list[start] and list[end], or -1 if it does not.
3    int BinarySearch(int item, int list[], int start, int end)
4    {
5        int middle = (end + start) / 2;
6
7        // Did we not find what we are looking for?
8        if (end < start)
9            return -1;
10
11        // Did we find the item?
12        else if (list[middle] == item)
13            return middle;
14
15        // Should we search the first half of the array?
16        else if (item < list[middle])
17            return BinarySearch(item, list, start, middle - 1);
18
19        // Or should we search the second half of the array?
20        else
21            return BinarySearch(item, list, middle + 1, end);
22    }
```

Figure 17.16   A recursive C function to perform binary search.

and smaller subarrays of the original array list. The variable start contains the array index of the first data item, and the variable end contains the index of the last data item.

Figure 17.17 provides an illustration of this code during execution. The array list contains eleven elements as shown. The initial call to BinarySearch passes the value we are searching for (item) and the array to be searched. (Recall from Chapter 16 that this is the address of the very first element, or base address, of the array.) Along with the array, we provide the *extent* of the array. That is, we provide the starting and ending points of the portion of the array to be searched. In every subsequent recursive call to BinarySearch, this extent is made smaller, eventually reaching a point where the subset of the array we are searching has either only one element or no elements at all. These two situations are the base cases of the recursion.

A more straightforward search technique would be to sequentially search through the array. That is, we could examine list[0], then list[1], then list[2], etc., and eventually either find the item or determine that it does not exist. Binary search, however, will require fewer comparisons and can potentially execute faster if the array is large enough. In subsequent computing courses, you will analyze binary search and determine that its running time is proportional to $\log_2 n$, where n is the size of the array. Sequential search, on the other hand, is proportional to n. For sufficiently large values of n, $\log_2 n$ is much smaller than n. For example, if $n = 1,000,000$, then $\log_2 n$ is 19.93. Note that we aren't saying that recursive binary search is more efficient than iterative binary search, because it

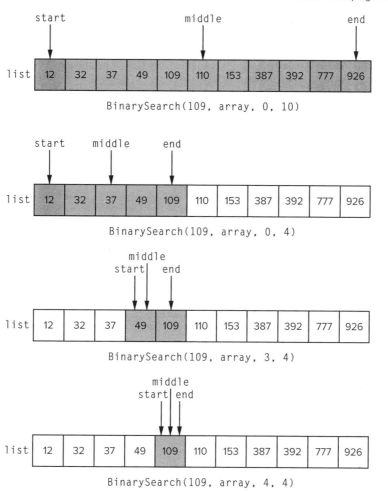

Figure 17.17   `BinarySearch` **performed on an array of eleven elements. We are searching for the element 109.**

isn't (due to function call overhead). But we are saying that binary search (iterative or recursive) is more efficient than sequential search, and significantly so.

17.7 Escaping a Maze

Recursion is commonly applied in solving games and puzzles. Recursion allows for a systematic search through all possibilities, making it useful for solving problems where it is feasible to examine every possible solution in search of the right one. Solving a Soduku puzzle, or finding a path through a maze, for example, are problems that are amenable to recursive search.

We wrote a simple maze solver in Chapter 8 in LC-3 assembly, and we'll revisit the problem again in the context of C. There are many ways we can approach a maze solver, but the recursive approach is perhaps the simplest. Let's start by considering how to represent a maze in C. As we did in Chapter 8, we'll use a two-dimensional array, with each element in the array representing whether the maze position is blocked (because it contains a wall), is open, or contains an exit. The maze will be a character array, where each element of the array contains the character *X* for a blocked space, a space ' ' character for an open space, and the character *E* for an exit. Our maze solver will take this 2D array as input, along with coordinates of the initial starting point, and will search through the maze to find a path to the exit, if it exists. Figure 17.18 shows an example of a simple 4 × 4 maze represented in our 2D array format. In this example, maze[3][0] = 'E' designates the exit, and maze[0][2] = 'X' is an example of a space that is blocked. If we set the initial position to maze[1][2], then there exists a path to the exit.

	X	X	
X			X
		X	
E	X		

Figure 17.18   An example of how to represent a maze with a two-dimensional character array.

Now the question is, how might a maze solver compute the path to the exit? We can use the following idea: From the starting point, if a path to the exit exists, it must go through the space either directly to the left, directly to the right, directly up, or directly down from the initial point. So we set the new position to one of those spaces and recursively solve the maze from there. That is, from the new point, if a solution exists, it must go through space to the left, to the right, directly up, or directly down from the new point.

Eventually, we'll hit a blocked space *X* or the exit *E*. And these designate base cases for the recursion. We'll also need to mark spaces that we've already visited with a *V*. This will enable us to skip over spaces that we've already evaluated, and it will prevent us from going in circles (literally!). This will also be a base case.

Figure 17.19 provides the C code implementation of the ExitMaze function. It takes as its parameters a maze represented as a 2D character array of dimensions MAZE_HEIGHT by MAZE_WIDTH, and two integers that represent the current position as *x* and *y* indices in the maze array. The initial portion of the function checks to see if we've hit any of our terminal conditions: Either xpos or ypos is out of the maze, or the current position is the exit or corresponds to a space in the maze that has already been visited or is blocked. If not, we mark the current position as visited and recursively check the neighboring positions.

This algorithm performs something called a *depth-first search* through all the possible paths through the maze. We can represent the recursive calls as a graph, where each node in the graph corresponds to an invocation of the function ExitMaze. In the general case, each invocation of ExitMaze can make up to four

```
1    #define MAZE_HEIGHT 4
2    #define MAZE_WIDTH 4
3
4    int ExitMaze(char maze[MAZE_HEIGHT][MAZE_WIDTH], int xpos, int ypos)
5    {
6        if (xpos < 0 || xpos >= MAZE_HEIGHT || ypos < 0 || ypos >= MAZE_WIDTH)
7            return 0;
8
9        if (maze[xpos][ypos] == 'E')  // Found the Exit!
10           return 1;
11
12       if (maze[xpos][ypos] != ' ')  // Space is not empty (possibly X or V)
13           return 0;
14
15       maze[xpos][ypos]='V';          // Mark this space as visited
16
17       // Go Down
18       if (ExitMaze(maze, xpos + 1, ypos)) {
19           maze[xpos][ypos]='P';
20           return 1;
21       }
22
23       // Go Right
24       if (ExitMaze(maze, xpos, ypos + 1)) {
25           maze[xpos][ypos]='P';
26           return 1;
27       }
28
29       // Go Up
30       if (ExitMaze(maze, xpos - 1, ypos)) {
31           maze[xpos][ypos]='P';
32           return 1;
33       }
34
35       // Go Left
36       if (ExitMaze(maze, xpos, ypos - 1)) {
37           maze[xpos][ypos]='P';
38           return 1;
39       }
40
41       // No path to Exit
42       return 0;
43   }
```

Figure 17.19   A recursive C function to find an escape path in a maze.

recursive calls (one call for each direction). So each node can end up creating up to four new invocations of ExitMaze. Figure 17.20 provides a graphical depiction of ExitMaze in action. The initial call shows the initial maze configuration, along with the starting point (maze[1][2]). That initial call generates four new calls,

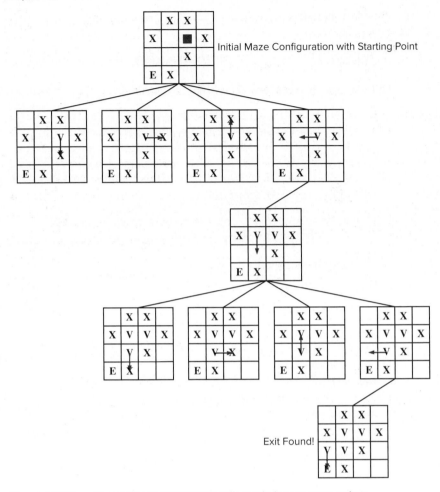

Figure 17.20   The total set of recursive calls made by our maze solver.

each evaluated one after the other. The first call (move down) returns immediately, as does the next call (move right), as does the third call (move up). The fourth call (move left) is a move into an open space, and thus it causes new calls to be generated.

17.8 Summary

We initially examined recursion in the context of LC-3 assembly language in Chapter 8. In this chapter, we examine it again in the context of C. With recursion, it is important for us to develop an understanding of the types of problems that are amenable to a recursive solution and also to understand the overheads involved with recursion.

We can solve a problem recursively by using a function that calls itself on smaller subproblems. With recursion, we state the function, say $f(n)$, in terms of the same function on smaller values of n, say for example, $f(n-1)$. The Fibonacci series, for example, is recursively stated as

$$\text{Fibonacci}(n) = \text{Fibonacci}(n-1) + \text{Fibonacci}(n-2);$$

For the recursion to eventually terminate, recursive calls require a base case. Recursion is a powerful programming tool that, when applied to the right problem, can make the task of programming considerably easier. For example, the Towers of Hanoi puzzle can be solved in a simple manner with recursion. It is much harder to formulate using iteration. In future courses, you will examine ways of organizing data involving pointers (e.g., trees and graphs) where the simplest techniques to manipulate the data structure involve recursive functions. At the lower levels, recursive functions are handled in exactly the same manner as any other function call. The run-time stack mechanism enables this by systematically allocating a stack frame for each function invocation, providing storage for each invocation such that it doesn't interfere with storage for any other invocation.

Exercises

17.1 For these questions, refer to the examples that appear in the chapter.

    a. How many calls to `RunningSum` are made for the call `RunningSum(10)`?

    b. How about for the call `RunningSum(n)`? Give your answer in terms of n.

    c. How many calls to `MoveDisk` are made in the Towers of Hanoi problem if the initial call is `MoveDisk(4, 1, 3, 2)`? This call plays out a four-disk game.

    d. How many calls are made for an n-disk game?

    e. How many calls to `Fibonacci` (see Figure 17.13) are made for the initial call `Fibonacci(10)`?

    f. How many calls are required for the nth Fibonacci number?

    g Is a square with a 'P' ever encountered at line 12 of the `ExitMaze` code?

17.2 Is the return address for a recursive function always the same at each function call? Why or why not?

17.3 What is the maximum number of recursive calls made to solve a maze using `ExitMaze`?

17.4   What does the following function produce for `count(20)`?

```
int count(int arg)
{
    if (arg < 1)
        return 0;
    else if (arg % 2)
        return(1 + count(arg - 2));
    else
        return(1 + count(arg - 1));
}
```

17.5   Consider the following C program, and the run-time stack in Figure 17.21:

```
#include <stdio.h>
int Power(int a, int b);
int main(void)
{
    int x, y, z;

    printf("Input two numbers: ");
    scanf("%d %d", &x, &y);
    if ((x > 0) && (y > 0))
        z = Power(x,y);
    else
        z = 0;
    printf("The result is %d.\n", z);
}

int Power(int a, int b)
{
    if (a < b)
        return 0;
    else
        return 1 + Power(a/b, b);
}
```

a. State the complete output if the input is
   (1) 4 9
   (2) 27 5
   (3) −1 3
b. What does the function `Power` compute?
c. Figure 17.21 is a snapshot of the stack after a call to the function `Power`. Two stack frames are shown, with some of the entries filled in. Assume the snapshot was taken just before execution of one of the `return` statements in `Power`. What are the values in the entries marked with a question mark? If an entry contains an address, use an arrow to indicate the location the address refers to.

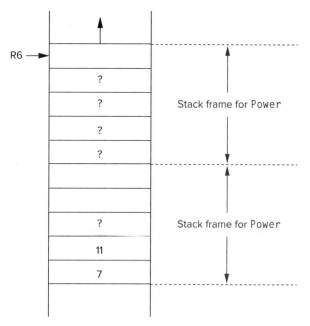

Figure 17.21   **Run-time stack after the function** Power **is called.**

17.6   Consider the following C function:

```
int Sigma( int k )
{
    int l;
    l = k - 1;
    if (k==0)
        return 0;
    else
        return (k + Sigma(l));
}
```

     a. Convert the recursive function into a nonrecursive function. Assume
       Sigma() will always be called with a nonnegative argument.

     b. Exactly 1 KB of contiguous memory is available for the run-time
       stack, and addresses and integers are 16 bits wide. How many
       recursive function calls can be made before the program runs out
       of stack space? Assume no storage is needed for temporary values.

17.7   The following C program is compiled and executed on the LC-3. When the program is executed, the run-time stack starts at memory location xFEFF and grows toward xC000 (the stack can occupy up to 16 KB of memory).

```
int SevenUp(int x)
{
    if (x == 1)
        return 7;
    else
        return (7 + sevenUp(x - 1));
}

int main(void)
{
    int a;

    printf("Input a number \n");
    scanf("%d", &a);
    a = SevenUp(a);
    printf("%d is 7 times the number\n", a);
}
```

      a. What is the largest input value for which this program will run correctly? Explain your answer.

      b. If the run-time stack can occupy only 4 KB of memory, what is the largest input value for which this program will run correctly?

17.8   Write an iterative version of a function to find the *n*th Fibonacci number. Plot the running time of this iterative version to the running time of the recursive version on a variety of values for *n*. Why is the recursive version significantly slower?

17.9   The binary search routine shown in Figure 17.16 searches through an array that is in ascending order. Rewrite the code so that it works for arrays in descending order.

17.10   Following is a very famous algorithm whose recursive version is significantly easier to express than the iterative one. It was originally proposed by the Greek mathematician Euclid! For the following subproblems, provide the final value returned by the function.

```
int ea(int x, int y)
{
    if (y == 0)
        return x;
    else
        return ea(y, x % y);
}
```

      a. ea(12, 15)
      b. ea(6, 10)
      c. ea(110, 24)

    d. What does this function calculate? Consider how you might construct an iterative version to calculate the same thing.

17.11 Write a program without recursive functions equivalent to the following C program:

```
int main(void)
{
    printf("%d", M());
}

void M()
{
    int num, x;
    printf("Type a number: ");
    scanf("%d", &num);
    if (num <= 0)
        return 0;
    else {
        x = M();
        if (num > x)
            return num;
        else
            return x;
    }
}
```

17.12 Consider the following recursive function:

```
int func (int arg)
{
    if (arg % 2 != 0)
        return func(arg - 1);
    if (arg <= 0)
        return 1;
    return func(arg/2) + 1;
}
```

    a. Is there a value of `arg` that causes an infinite recursion? If so, what is it?

    b. Suppose that the function `func` is part of a program whose `main` function is as follows. How many function calls are made to `func` when the program is executed?

```
int main(void)
{
    printf("The value is %d\n", func(10));
}
```

    c. What value is output by the program?

17.13 A magic square is an $n \times n$ grid where each cell contains one of the integers between 1 and n^2. Each cell contains a different integer, and the sum of the cells in a column, in a row, and on each diagonal is equal. Given a partial solution to a magic square (provided as a 2D integer array), find a complete solution if it exists. Use a recursive technique to build a solver.

17.14 What is the output of the following C program?

```
#include <stdio.h>
void Magic(int in);
int Even(int n);

int main(void)
{
    Magic(10);
}

void Magic(int in)
{
    if (in == 0)
        return;
    if (Even(in))
        printf("%i\n", in);
    Magic(in - 1);
    if (!Even(in))
        printf("%i\n", in);
    return;
}

int Even(int n)
{
    if (n % 2) return 1 else 0;
}
```

CHAPTER

18 I/O in C

18.1 Introduction

Whether it be to the screen, to a file, or to another computer across a network, all useful programs perform output of some sort or another. Most programs also require some form of input. As is the case with many other modern programming languages, input and output are not directly supported by C. Instead input/output (I/O) is handled by a set of standard library functions that extend the base language. The behavior of these standard library functions is precisely defined by the ANSI C standard.

In this chapter, we will discuss several functions in the C standard library that support simple I/O. The functions `putchar` and `printf` write to the output device, and `getchar` and `scanf` read from the input device. The more general functions `fprintf` and `fscanf` perform file I/O, such as to a file on disk. We have used `printf` and `scanf` extensively throughout the second half of this book. In this chapter, we examine the details of how these functions work. Along the way, we will introduce the notion of variable argument lists and demonstrate how parameter-passing on the LC-3 run-time stack handles function calls with a variable number of arguments.

18.2 The C Standard Library

The C standard library is a major extension of the C programming language. It provides support for input/ouput, character string manipulations, mathematical functions, file access functions, and various system utilities that are not specifically required for a single program but are generally useful in many programs. The standard library is intended to be a repository of useful, primitive functions that serve as *components* for building complex software. This component-based library approach is a characteristic of many contemporary programming languages such as C++, Java, and Python, which also have similar standard libraries of primitive functions, types, and other facilities.

We provide a short description of some useful C library functions in Appendix D.9. The library's functions are typically developed by the designers of the underlying device and system—the Android smartphone, for example—and are optimized for the system on which they are developed.

To use a function defined within the C standard library, we must include the appropriate header file (.h file). The functions within the standard library are grouped according to their functionality. Each of these groups has a header file associated with it. For example, mathematical functions such as `sin` and `tan` use the common header file `math.h`. The standard I/O functions use the header file `stdio.h`. These header files contain, among other things, function declarations for the I/O functions and preprocessor macros relating to I/O. A library header file does *not* contain the source code for library functions.

If the header files do not contain source code, how does the machine code for, say, `printf` get added to our applications? Each library function called within a program is linked in when the executable image is formed. The object files containing the library functions are stored somewhere on the system and are accessed by the linker, which links together the various function binaries into a single executable program. We refer to this as static linking.

Libraries can be linked *dynamically* into the application. With certain types of libraries (dynamically linked libraries, or DLLs), the machine code for a library isn't directly integrated into the executable image but is "linked" on demand, while the program executes. This has a number of advantages over a statically linked library. It reduces the size of the executable, it enables multiple programs to link the same code, thereby reducing memory requirements, and it allows the library to be upgraded independently from the application.

18.3 I/O, One Character at a Time

We'll start by examining two of the simplest I/O functions provided by the C library. The functions `getchar` and `putchar` perform input and output on a single character at a time. Input is read in as ASCII and output is written out as ASCII, in a manner similar to the `IN` and `OUT` TRAP routines of the LC-3.

18.3.1 I/O Streams

Conceptually, all character-based input and output is performed in *streams*. The sequence of ASCII characters typed by the user at the keyboard is an example of an input stream. As each character is typed, it is added to the end of the stream. Whenever a program reads keyboard input, it reads from the beginning of the stream. The sequence of ASCII characters printed by a program, similarly, is added to the end of the output stream. In other words, this stream abstraction allows us to further decouple the producer from the consumer, which is helpful because the two are usually operating at different rates (see Chapter 8). For example, if a program wants to perform some output, it adds characters to the end of the output stream without being required to wait for the output device to finish displaying the previous character. Many other popular languages, such as C++, provide a similar stream-based abstraction for I/O.

In C, the standard input stream is referred to as `stdin` and is mapped to the keyboard by default. The standard output stream is referred to as `stdout` and is mapped by default to the display. The functions `getchar` and `putchar` operate on these two streams.

18.3.2 `putchar`

The function `putchar` is the high-level language equivalent of the LC-3 `OUT` TRAP routine. The function `putchar` displays on the `stdout` output stream the ASCII value of the parameter passed to it. It performs no type conversions—the value passed to it is assumed to be ASCII and is added directly to the output stream. All the calls to `putchar` in the following code segment cause the same character (lowercase h) to be displayed. A `putchar` function call is treated like any other function call, except here the function resides within the standard library. The function declaration for `putchar` appears in the `stdio.h` header file. Its code will be linked into the executable during the compiler's link phase.

```
char c = 'h';
:
putchar(c);
putchar('h');
putchar(104);
```

18.3.3 `getchar`

The function `getchar` is the high-level language equivalent of the LC-3 `IN` TRAP function. It returns the ASCII value of the next input character appearing in the `stdin` input stream. By default, the `stdin` input stream is simply the stream of characters typed at the keyboard. In the following code segment, `getchar` returns the ASCII value of the next character typed at the keyboard. This return value is assigned to the variable `c`.

```
char c;

c = getchar();
```

18.3.4 Buffered I/O

Run the C code in Figure 18.1 and you will notice something peculiar. The program prompts the user for the first input character and waits for that input to be typed in. Type in a single character (say *z*, for example) and nothing happens. The second prompt does not appear, as if the call to `getchar` has missed the keystroke. In fact, the program seems to make no progress at all until the Enter/Return key is pressed. Such behavior seems unexpected considering that `getchar` is specified to read only a single character from the keyboard input stream. This unexpected behavior is due to *buffering* of the keyboard input stream. On most devices, I/O

```
1    #include <stdio.h>
2
3    int main(void)
4    {
5        char inChar1;
6        char inChar2;
7
8        printf("Input character 1:\n");
9        inChar1 = getchar();
10
11       printf("Input character 2:\n");
12       inChar2 = getchar();
13
14       printf("Character 1 is %c\n", inChar1);
15       printf("Character 2 is %c\n", inChar2);
16   }
```

Figure 18.1   An example of buffered input.

streams are buffered. Every key typed on the keyboard is captured by the lower levels of the system software and kept in a *buffer*, which is a small array or queue (see Section 8.4), until it is released into the stream. In the case of the input stream, the buffer is released when the user presses Enter. The Enter key itself appears as a newline character in the input stream. So in the example in Figure 18.1, if the user types the character *A* and presses Enter, the variable inChar1 will equal the ASCII value of *A* (which is 65) and the variable inChar2 will equal the ASCII value of newline (which is 10). There is a good reason for buffering, particularly for keyboard input: Pressing the Enter key allows the user to *confirm* the input. Say you mistyped some input and wanted to correct it before the program detects it. You can edit what you type using the Backspace and Delete keys, and then confirm your input by pressing Enter.

The output stream is similarly buffered. Observe by running the program in Figure 18.2. This program uses a new library function called sleep that suspends the execution of the program for approximately the number of seconds provided as the integer argument, which in this case is 5. This library function requires that

```
1    #include <stdio.h>
2    #include <unistd.h>
3
4    int main()
5    {
6        putchar('a');
7
8        sleep(5);
9
10       putchar('b');
11       putchar('\n');
12   }
```

Figure 18.2   An example of buffered output.

we include the `unistd.h` header file. Run this code and you will notice that the output of the character a does not happen quite as you might expect. Instead of appearing prior to the five-second delay, the character a appears *afterwards*, only after the newline character releases the output buffer to the output stream. We say that the `putchar('\n')` causes output to be *flushed*. Add a `putchar('\n')` statement immediately after line 6 and the program will behave differently.

Despite the slightly complex behavior of buffered I/O streams, the underlying mechanism used to make this happen is the device's native I/O functionality, which in the case of the LC-3 is the `IN` and `OUT` TRAP routines described in Chapter 8. The buffering of streams is accomplished by the interrupt service routines that handle the arrival of input data, or the OUT service routine.

18.4 Formatted I/O

The functions `putchar` and `getchar` suffice for simple I/O tasks but are cumbersome for performing non-ASCII I/O. The functions `printf` and `scanf` perform more sophisticated *formatted* I/O, and they are designed to more conveniently handle I/O of integer and floating point values.

18.4.1 `printf`

The function `printf` writes formatted text to the output stream. Using `printf`, we can print out ASCII text embedded with values generated by the running program. The `printf` function takes care of all of the type conversions necessary for this to occur. For example, the following code prints out the value of integer variable x. In doing so, the `printf` must convert the integer value of x into a sequence of ASCII characters that can be embedded in the output stream.

```
int x;

printf("The value is %d\n", x);
```

Generally speaking, `printf` writes its first parameter to the output stream. The first parameter is the *format string*. It is a character string (i.e., of type `char *`) containing text to be displayed on the output device. Embedded within the format string are zero or more *conversion specifications*.

The conversion specifications indicate how to print out any of the parameters that follow the format string in the function call. Conversion specifications all begin with a % character. As their name implies, they indicate how the values of the parameters that follow the format string should be treated when converted to ASCII. In many of the examples we have encountered so far, integers have been printed out as decimal numbers using the `%d` specification. We could also use the `%x` specification to print integers as hexadecimal numbers, or `%b` to print them as binary numbers (represented as ASCII text, of course). Other conversions include `%c`, which causes a value to be interpreted as straight ASCII, and `%s`, which is used for strings and causes characters stored consecutively in memory to be output (for this the corresponding parameter is expected to be of type `char*`).

The specification %f interprets the corresponding parameter as a floating point number and displays it in a floating point format. What if we wanted to print out the % character itself? We use the sequence %%. See Appendix D for a full listing of conversion specifiers.

As mentioned in Chapter 11, when we first encountered C I/O functions, special characters such as newline can also be embedded in the format string. The \n prints a new line, and a \t character prints a tab; both are examples of these special characters. All special characters begin with a \ and they can appear anywhere within a format string. To print out a backslash character, we use a \\. See Table D.1 in Appendix D for a list of special characters.

Here are some examples of various format specifications:

```
int  a = 102;
int  b = 65;
char c = 'z';
char banner[10] = "Hola!";
double pi = 3.14159;

printf("The variable 'a' decimal : %d\n", a);
printf("The variable 'a' hex : %x\n", a);
printf("The variable 'a' binary : %b\n", a);
printf("'a' plus 'b' as character : %c\n", a + b);
printf("Char %c.\t String %s\n Float %f\n", c, banner, pi);
```

The function printf begins by examining the format string a single character at a time. If the current character is not a % or \, then the character is directly written to the output stream. (Recall that the output stream is buffered, so the output might not appear on the display until a new line is written.) If the character is a \, then the next character indicates the particular special character to print out. For instance, the escape sequence \n indicates a newline character. If the current character is a %, indicating a conversion specification, then the next character indicates how the next pending parameter should be interpreted. For instance, if the conversion specification is a %d and the next pending parameter has a value that corresponds to the bit pattern 0000000001101000, then the number 104 is written to the output stream. If the conversion character is a %c, then the character h is written. A different value is printed if %f is the conversion specification. The conversion specifier indicates to printf how the next parameter should be interpreted. It is important to realize that, within the printf routine, there is no relationship between a conversion specification and the type of a parameter. The programmer is free to choose how things are to be interpreted as they are displayed to the screen. *Question:* What happens with the following function call?

```
printf("The value of nothing is %d\n");
```

There is no argument corresponding to the %d specification. When the printf routine is called, it assumes the correct number of values was written onto the stack, so it blindly reads a value off the stack for the %d spec, assuming it was intentionally placed there by the caller. Here, a garbage value is displayed to the screen, in decimal.

18.4.2 `scanf`

The function `scanf` is used to read formatted ASCII data from the input stream. A call to `scanf` is similar to a call to `printf`. Both calls require a format string as the first argument followed by a variable number of other arguments. Both functions are controlled by characters within the format string. The function `scanf` differs in that all arguments following the format string *must* be pointers. As we discussed in Chapter 16, `scanf` must be able to access the original locations of the objects in memory in order to assign new values to them.

The format string for `scanf` contains ASCII text and conversion specifications, just like the format string for `printf`. The conversion characters are similar to those used for `printf`. A table of these specifications can be found in Appendix D. Essentially, the format string represents the format of the input stream. For example, the format string `"%d"` indicates to `scanf` that the next sequence of non–white space characters (white space is defined as spaces, tabs, new lines, carriage returns, vertical tabs, and form feeds) is a sequence of digits in ASCII representing an integer in decimal notation. After this decimal number is read from the input stream, it is converted into an integer and stored in the corresponding argument. Since `scanf` modifies the values of the variables passed to it, arguments are passed *by reference* using the & operator. In addition to conversion specifications, the format string also can contain plain text, which `scanf` tries to match with the input stream. We use the following code to demonstrate.

```
char name[100];
int month, day, year;
double gpa;

printf("Enter : lastname birthdate grade_point_average\n");
scanf("%s %d/%d/%d %lf", name, &month, &day, &year, &gpa);

printf("\n");
printf("Name : %s\n", name);
printf("Birthday : %d/%d/%d\n", month, day, year);
printf("GPA : %f\n", gpa);
```

In this `scanf` statement, the first specification is a `%s` that scans a string of characters from the input stream. In this context, all characters starting from the first non–white space character and ending with the next white space character (conceptually, the next *word* in the input stream) are stored in memory starting at the address of `name`. An `\0` character is automatically added to signify the end of the string. Since the argument `name` is an array, it is automatically passed by reference; that is, the address of the first element of the array is passed to `scanf`.

The next specification is for a decimal number, `%d`. Now `scanf` expects to find a sequence of digits (at least one digit) as the next set of non–white space characters in the standard input stream. Characters from standard input are analyzed, white space characters are discarded, and the decimal number (i.e., a sequence of digits terminated by a nondigit) is read in. The number is converted from a sequence of ASCII characters into a binary integer and stored in the memory location indicated by the argument `&month`.

The next input field is the ASCII character /. Now, scanf expects to find this character, possibly surrounded by white space, in the input stream. Since this input field is not a conversion specification, it is not assigned to any variable. Once it is read in from the input stream, it is discarded, and scanf moves onto the next field of the format string. Similarly, the next three input fields %d/%d read in two decimal numbers separated by a /. These values are converted into integers and are assigned to the locations indicated by the pointers appearing as the next two arguments (which correspond to the addresses of the variables day and year).

The last field in the format string specifies that the input stream contains a *long* floating point number, which is the specification used to read in a value of type double. For this specifier, scanf expects to see a sequence of decimal numbers, and possibly a decimal point, possibly an E or e signifying exponential notation, in the input stream (see Appendix D.2.4). This field is terminated once a nondigit (excluding the first E, or the decimal point or a plus or minus sign for the fraction or exponent) or white space is detected. The scanf routine takes this sequence of ASCII characters and converts them into a properly expressed, double-precision floating point number and stores it into gpa.

Once it is done processing the format string, scanf returns to the caller. It also returns an integer value. The number of format specifications that were successfully scanned in the input stream is passed back to the caller. In this case, if everything went correctly, scanf would return the value 5. In the preceding code example, we chose to ignore the return value.

So, for example, the following line of input yields the following output:

```
Enter : lastname birthdate grade_point_average
Mudd 02/16/69 3.02

Name : Mudd
Birthday : 2/16/69
GPA : 3.02
```

Since scanf ignores white space for this format string, the following input stream yields the same results. Remember, newline characters are considered white space.

```
Enter : lastname birthdate grade_point_average
Mudd 02
/
16 / 69 3.02

Name : Mudd
Birthday : 2/16/69
GPA : 3.02
```

What if the format of the input stream does not match the format string? For instance, what happens with the following stream?

```
Enter : lastname birthdate grade_point_average
Mudd 02 16 69 3.02
```

Here, the input stream does not contain the / characters encoded in the format string. In this case, `scanf` returns the value 2, since the variables `name` and `month` are correctly assigned before the mismatch between the format string and the input stream is detected. The remaining variables go unmodified. Since the input stream is buffered, unused input is not discarded, and subsequent reads of the input stream begin where the last call left off.

If the next two reads of the input stream are

```
a = getchar();
b = getchar();
```

what do `a` and `b` contain? The answer ' ' (the space character) and 1 should be no surprise.

18.4.3 Variable Argument Lists

Do you notice something different about the functions `printf` and `scanf` from all other functions we have described thus far? These two functions have a *variable* number of arguments passed to them. The number of arguments passed to `printf` and `scanf` depends on the number of items being printed or scanned. We say such functions have *variable argument lists*. In the case of `printf` and `scanf`, there is a one-to-one correspondence between each conversion specification in the format string and each argument that appears after the format string in such function calls. The following `printf` statement is from one of our previous examples:

```
printf("Char %c.\t String %s\n Float %f\n", c, banner, pi);
```

The format string contains three format specifications; therefore, three arguments should follow it in the function call. The `%c` spec in the string is associated with the first argument that follows (the variable c). The `%s` is associated with `banner`, and `%f` with `pi`. There are three values to be printed; therefore, this call contains four arguments altogether. If we want to print five values, the `printf` call should contain six arguments.

Recall from Chapter 14 that our LC-3 calling convention pushed items onto the run-time stack from *right to left* of the order in which they appear on the function call. This places the pointer to the format string immediately at the top of the stack when `printf` or `scanf` takes over. Since it is the leftmost argument, it will always be the last item pushed onto the stack before the function call (JSR instruction) occurs. Once `printf` or `scanf` takes over, it can access the first parameter directly off the top of the stack. Once this parameter (which is the format string) is analyzed, the functions can determine the other parameters on the stack. If the arguments on a function call were pushed from left to right, it would be much more difficult for `printf` and `scanf` to discern the location of the format string parameter.

Figure 18.3 shows two diagrams of the run-time stack. In diagram (a), the arguments to the call for `printf` are passed from right to left, and in (b) they are passed from left to right. Consider for which case the resulting LC-3 code for `printf` will be simpler. In version (a), the offset of the format string from the

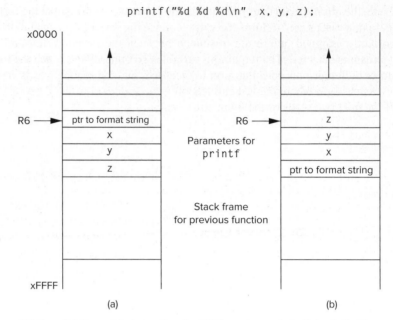

Figure 18.3   Subfigure (a) shows the stack if the arguments to the printf call are pushed from right to left. Subfigure (b) shows the stack if the arguments are pushed left to right.

stack pointer will always be zero, regardless of the number of other parameters on the stack. In version (b), the offset of the format string from the stack pointer depends on the number of parameters on the stack. The format string, like all other strings embedded within a program's source code, is stored in a special region of memory reserved for constants, or *literal values*.

18.5 I/O from Files

Say we wanted to process a large set of data, such as the daily closing price of Apple stock for the last 20 years. To ask the user to type this in on a keyboard would render it very "user-unfriendly." Instead, we would want the program to read the data from a file and possibly write its output to another file. I/O in C is based on streams, as we described earlier, and these streams are conceptually all bound to files.

The functions printf and scanf are in fact special cases of more general-purpose C I/O functions. These two functions operate specifically on two special files called stdin and stdout. In C, stdin and stdout are mapped by default to the keyboard and the display.

The general-purpose version of printf is called fprintf, and the general-purpose version of scanf is called fscanf. The functions fprintf and fscanf work like their counterparts, with the main difference being that they allow us to specify the stream on which they act. For example, we can tell `fprintf` to write its output to a specific file with a particular name at a precise location on the device. Let's examine how this is done.

The first step in performing file I/O is to declare a *file pointer* for each file we want to manipulate. Typically, files are stored on the file system of the device, which provides protected and secure access to all the documents, images, executables, videos, text files, and other data stored on the devices. In C, we can declare a file pointer called `infile` as follows:

```
FILE *infile;
```

Here we are declaring a pointer to something of type `FILE`. The type `FILE` is defined within the header file `stdio.h`. Its details are not important for current purposes. Once the file pointer is declared, we need to map it to a file on the device's file system. The C library call `fopen` performs this mapping. Each `fopen` call requires two arguments: the name of the file to open and the description of what type of operation we want to perform on the file. An example follows.

```
FILE *infile;

infile = fopen("aapl_stock_prices", "r");
```

The first argument to `fopen` is the string `aapl_stock_prices`, which is the name of the file to open. The second argument is the operation we want to perform on this file. Several useful *modes* are `"r"` for reading, `"w"` for writing (a file opened with this mode will lose its previous contents), `"a"` for appending (here, previous contents is not lost; new data is added to the end of the file), and `"r+"` for reading and writing. Note that both arguments must be character strings; therefore, they are surrounded by double quotes in this example. In this case, we are opening the file called `"aapl_stock_prices"` for reading.

If the `fopen` call is successful, the function returns a file pointer to the physical file. If the open for some reason fails (as in a case when the file cannot be found), then the function returns a null pointer. Recall that a null pointer is an invalid pointer that has the value `NULL`. It is *always* good practice to check to determine if the `fopen` call was successful.

```
FILE *infile;

infile = fopen("ibm_stock_prices", "r");

if (infile == NULL)
   printf("fopen unsuccessful!\n");
```

Now with the file pointer properly mapped to a physical file, we can use `fscanf` and `fprintf` to read and write it just as we used `printf` and `scanf` to read the standard devices. The functions `fscanf` and `fprintf` both require a file pointer as their first argument to indicate on which stream the operations are to be performed. The example in Figure 18.4 demonstrates this.

Here, we are reading from an ASCII text file called `aapl_stock_prices` and writing to a file called `buy_hold_or_sell`. The input file contains the stock

```
1    #include <stdio.h>
2    #define LIMIT 10000
3
4    int main()
5    {
6
7        FILE *infile;
8        FILE *outfile;
9        double prices[LIMIT];
10       char answer[10];
11       int i = 0;
12
13       infile = fopen("aapl_stock_prices", "r");
14       outfile = fopen("buy_hold_or_sell", "w");
15
16       if (infile != NULL && outfile != NULL) {
17           // Read the input data
18           while ((fscanf(infile, "%lf", &prices[i]) != EOF) && i < LIMIT)
19               i++;
20
21           printf("%d prices read from the data file", i);
22
23           // Process the data...
24           :
25           :
26           answer = ...
27
28           // Write the output
29           fprintf(outfile, "%s", answer);
30       }
31       else
32           printf("fopen unsuccessful!\n");
33   }
```

Figure 18.4   An example of a program that performs file I/O.

prices represented as floating point data, each separated by white space. Even though the file can contain more, our program will process at most 10,000 items. The fscanf function returns a special value when no more data can be read from the input file, indicating the end of file has been reached. We can check the return value of fscanf against this special character, which is defined to the preprocessor macro EOF. The while loop terminates once we encounter the EOF character, or if we reach the data limit of 10,000 items. After reading the input file, the program processes the input data and generates the string answer, which is then written to the output file. The function printf is equivalent to calling fprintf using stdout as the file pointer. Likewise, scanf is equivalent to calling fscanf using stdin.

18.6 Summary

In this chapter, we examined the C facilities for performing input and output. Like many other current programming languages, C provides no direct support for input and output. Rather, standard library functions are provided for I/O. At their core, these functions perform I/O one character at a time using the IN and OUT routines supported by the underlying machine. The key concepts that you should take away from this chapter are:

* **Input and output in streams.** Modern programming languages create a useful abstraction for thinking about I/O. Input and output occur in streams. The producer adds data to the stream, and the consumer reads data from the stream. With this relationship, both can operate at their own rate without waiting for the other to be ready to conduct the I/O. For example, a program generating output for the display writes data into the output stream without necessarily waiting for the display to keep pace.

* **The four basic I/O functions.** We discuss the operation, at a fairly detailed level, of four basic I/O functions: putchar, getchar, printf, and scanf. The latter two functions require the use of variable argument lists, which our LC-3 calling convention can easily handle because of the order in which we push arguments onto the run-time stack.

* **File I/O.** The standard C I/O functions treat all I/O streams as file I/O. Functions like printf and scanf are special cases where the I/O files are the standard output and input devices. The more general functions fprintf and fscanf enable us to specify a file pointer to which the corresponding operations are to be performed. We can bind a file pointer to a physical file on the file system using fopen.

Exercises

18.1 Write an I/O function call to handle the following tasks. All can be handled by a single call.

  a. Print out an integer followed by a string followed by a floating point number.

  b. Print out a phone number in (XXX)-XXX-XXXX format. Internally, the phone number is stored as three integers.

  c. Print out a student ID number in XXX-XX-XXXX format. Internally, the ID number is stored as three character strings.

  d. Read a student ID number in XXX-XX-XXXX format. The number is to be stored internally as three integers.

  e. Read in a line of input containing Last name, First name, Middle initial age sex. The name fields are separated by commas. The middle initial and sex should be stored as characters. Age is an integer.

18.2   What does the value returned by `scanf` represent?

18.3   Why is buffering of the keyboard input stream useful?

18.4   What must happen when a program tries to read from the input stream but the stream is empty?

18.5   Why does the following code print out a strange value (such as 1073741824)?

```
float x = 192.27163;
printf("The value of x is %d\n", x);
```

18.6   What is the value of `input` for the following function call:

```
scanf("%d", &input);
```

if the input stream contains

```
This is not the input you are looking for.
```

18.7   Consider the following program:

```
#include <stdio.h>

int main(void)
{
    int x = 0;
    int y = 0;
    char label[10];

    scanf("%d %d", &x, &y);
    scanf("%s", label);

    printf("%d %d %s\n", x, y, label);
}
```

a. What gets printed out if the input stream is 46 29 BlueMoon?
b. What gets printed out if the input stream is 46 BlueMoon?
c. What gets printed out if the input stream is 111 999 888?

18.8   Write a program to read in a C source file and write it back to a file called "condensed_program" with all *white space* removed.

18.9   Write a program to read in a text file and provide a count of

a. The number of strings in the file, where a string begins with a non–white space character and ends with a white space character.
b. The number of words in the file, where a word begins with an alphabetic character (e.g., a–z or A–Z) and ends with a nonalphabetic character.
c. The number of unique words in the file. Words are as defined in part *b*. The set of unique words has no duplicates.
d. The frequency of words in order of most frequent to least frequent. In other words, analyze the text file, count the number of times each word occurs, and display these counts from most frequent word to least frequent.

19 Dynamic Data Structures in C

19.1 Introduction

C at its core provides support for just a few fundamental types of data. That is, C natively supports the allocation of variables of integers, floating point values, characters, and booleans. C also supports operators that manipulate these types, such as + for addition and * for multiplication. With C, we can quite easily declare variables of these native types, and we can also create arrays of them and pointers to them.

Ultimately, though, when we write code, we often deal with things that cannot be easily described by an integer, or floating point value, or character, or boolean, or even by arrays of them. If we are, for example, modeling an aircraft wing or developing the path planner for an autonomous vehicle, we need more sophisticated types in order to map the real world (or virtual world) into the digital world of the computing device.

The next two chapters deal primarily with the framework that C and C++ provide for creating and organizing more complex data types. We'll discover that the fundamental data types, as limited as they are, form the building blocks with which we can build nearly any general, complex type we might need. Creating these types, organizing them, connecting them together, and defining operations to manipulate them are a large part of the coding process.

In this chapter, we first explore the C framework for building more complex data types. In C, we can create a new type that is a collection of basic types by using a *structure*. Structures provide us with a convenient way of representing objects that are best represented by combinations of the basic types. For example, an employee might be represented as a structure containing a name (character string), job title (character string), department (perhaps integer), and employee ID (integer) within a corporate database. With this structure, we can declare a single memory object representing an employee just as simply as we can declare an integer variable.

In addition to structures, we'll explore dynamic memory allocation in C, which is a framework for allocating memory objects that are more persistent than those allocated on the run-time stack. With the pairing of structures and dynamic memory allocation, we can create dynamic data structures that can grow and shrink and persist in memory across different function calls. This capability is so incredibly useful that it forms the basis of most software development.

19.2 Structures

Let's leap straight into an example. Let's say we wanted to track airborne aircraft around a particular geographic point, say the city of Urbana, Illinois. There are several characteristic features that we would want to associate with each aircraft. The aircraft's registration number, which is useful for identification, can be represented by a character string. The altitude, longitude, latitude, and heading of the flight are also useful, and these could each be represented as an integer value. Airspeed could be represented by a floating point value (say a `double`, for example). Depending on the specifics of the tracker application, there could also be other items worth associating with each aircraft.

For our application, associated with each aircraft, we'd want the following values:

```
char ID[7];              // Max 6 characters
int altitude;            // in meters
int longitude;           // in tenths of degrees
int latitude;            // in tenths of degrees
int heading;             // in tenths of degrees
double airSpeed;         // in kilometers/hour
```

If we wanted to track multiple aircraft around Urbana, what sort of data structure would we use? Our natural choice might be to use a collection of arrays, one for each value. If we were to go with this approach, it's not difficult to imagine how cumbersome it would be to juggle this in our code.

To assist in the creation and management of such types that are collections of basic types, C provides "structures." Structures allow the programmer to define a new type that consists of a combination of other, simpler types such as `int`, `char`, and `double`, as well as pointers to them and arrays of them. Structure variables are declared in the same way variables of fundamental data types are declared. Before any structure variables are declared, however, the structure itself needs to be defined.

For our aircraft tracking app, we could create a structure definition as such:

```
struct flightType {
    char ID[7];          // Max 6 characters
    int altitude;        // in meters
    int longitude;       // in tenths of degrees
    int latitude;        // in tenths of degrees
    int heading;         // in tenths of degrees
    double airSpeed;     // in kilometers/hour
};
```

With this structure definition, we create a new type consisting of six values, or *members*. If we were to declare something of this new type, it would be allocated in contiguous storage, with enough space for all its members. To declare a variable of this new type, we do the following:

```
struct flightType plane;
```

This declares a variable called `plane` that consists of the six members defined in the structure definition.

We can access the individual members of this structure variable using the following syntax:

```
struct flightType plane;

plane.airSpeed = 800.00;
plane.altitude = 10000;
```

Each member can be accessed using the variable's name as the base name followed by a dot "." followed by the member name.

The variable `plane` gcts allocated onto the stack just like any other local variable, and it occupies a contiguous region of memory large enough to hold all member elements. In this case, if each of the basic types occupied one LC-3 memory location, the variable `plane` would occupy 12 locations (7 for the character string, 5 for the integers, and 1 for the double). Figure 19.1 shows a portion of the run-time stack when a function that contains the following declarations is invoked.

```
int x;
struct flightType plane;
int y;
```

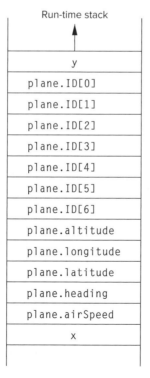

Run-time stack

y
plane.ID[0]
plane.ID[1]
plane.ID[2]
plane.ID[3]
plane.ID[4]
plane.ID[5]
plane.ID[6]
plane.altitude
plane.longitude
plane.latitude
plane.heading
plane.airSpeed
x

Figure 19.1 The run-time stack showing an allocation of a variable of structure type.

More generally, the syntax for a structure declaration is as follows:

```
struct tag {
    type1 member1;
    type2 member2;
    ...
    typeN memberN
} identifiers;
```

The `tag` field provides a handle for referring to the structure later in the code, as in the case of declaring variables of the structure's format. The list of members defines the organization of a structure and is syntactically a list of declarations in types that have been previously defined. A member can be of any type, including another structure type. We can optionally include identifiers in a structure's declaration to actually declare variables of that structure's type. These appear after the closing brace of the structure declaration, prior to the semicolon.

19.2.1 `typedef`

C structures enable programmers to define their own aggregate types. C `typedef` enables programmers to name their own types. It has the general form

```
typedef type name;
```

It's not so much a type *definition*, as its name implies, as it is a type *synonym*. This statement causes the identifier `name` to be synonymous with the type `type`, which can be any basic type or aggregate type (e.g., a structure). For instance,

```
typedef int Color;
```

allows us to define variables of type `Color`, which will now be synonymous with integer. Using this definition, we can declare:

```
Color pixels[200][100];
```

which could be used to represent an image, for example, of size 200×100 pixels.

The `typedef` facility is particularly useful when dealing with structures. For example, we can create a simpler, more meaningful name for our airborne aircraft structure.

```
struct flightType {
    char ID[7];          // Max 6 characters
    int altitude;        // in meters
    int longitude;       // in tenths of degrees
    int latitude;        // in tenths of degrees
    int heading;         // in tenths of degrees
    double airSpeed;     // in kilometers/hour
};
typedef struct flightType Flight;
```

Now we can declare structure variables using the type name `Flight`. For example,

```
Flight plane;
```

is now equivalent to the declaration used previously:

```
struct flightType plane;
```

The `typedef` declaration provides no additional functionality. However, its purpose is to provide additional clarity to our code, particularly code that is heavy with programmer-defined types. Well-chosen type names connote properties of the variables they declare even beyond what can be expressed by the names of the variables themselves.

19.2.2 Implementing Structures in C

As useful as structures are, they are a fairly simple concept built atop the basic framework provided by C. A structure variable is a regular variable like an `int`, `char`, or `float`, but with more moving parts. Each of these parts is necessarily a simpler type that can be directly manipulated using existing operators. For example, in the following code, the member `altitude` of the structure variable of type `Flight` is accessed.

```
int x;
Flight plane;
int y;

plane.altitude = 0;
```

Here, the variable `plane` is of type `Flight`, meaning it contains the six member fields we defined previously. The member field labeled `altitude` is accessed using the variable's name followed by a period, followed by the member field label. The compiler, knowing the layout of the structure, generates code that accesses the structure's member field using the appropriate offset. Figure 19.1 shows the layout of the portion of the stack frame for this function. The compiler keeps track, in its symbol table, of the position of each variable in relation to the base pointer R5, and if the variable is an aggregate data type, it also tracks the position of each field within the variable. Notice that for the particular reference `plane.altitude = 0;`, the compiler must generate code to access the second variable on the stack and the second member element of that variable. Following is the code generated by the LC-3 C compiler for the assignment statement `plane.altitude = 0;`.

```
AND R1, R1, #0    ; zero out R1
ADD R0, R5, #-12  ; R0 contains base address of plane
STR R1, R0, #7    ; plane.altitude = 0;
```

19.3 Arrays of Structures

Let's continue to build on this example by considering how we might build an application to track all the airborne aircraft over a particular location, such as Urbana, Illinois. The core data structure for our tool would be some sort of collection of memory objects (i.e., variables) of the `flightType` structure. This data structure should give us easy access to all aircraft in flight over Urbana at any point in time and should support the addition and removal of aircraft as they take off and land, or as they otherwise enter and exit the airspace.

An easy, straightforward way to represent the set of airborne aircraft would be to use an array. We are already familiar with arrays for building contiguous collections of simple variables, and here we'll apply the same concept to objects of `flightType`. We quickly run into a design issue in that we need to pick a size for the array, either statically or using a variable-sized array (see Section 16.3.8). For the sake of example, let's make the determination that no more than 100 aircraft will exist in this airspace (but what if we are wrong?). For this the following declaration suffices:

```
Flight aircraft[100];
```

This declaration is like a declaration of a regular array, except instead of declaring 100 integer values, we have declared a contiguous region of memory containing 100 structures, each of which is composed of the six members indicated in the declaration `struct flightType`. The reference `aircraft[12]`, for example, would refer to the 13th object in the region of 100 such objects in memory.

Each object contains enough storage for its six constituent member elements. Each object in this array is of type `Flight` (which is a synonym of `struct flightType`) and can be accessed using standard array notation. For example, accessing the flight characteristics of the first aircraft can be done using the identifier `aircraft[0]`. Accessing a member field is done by accessing an element of the array and then specifying a field:

```
aircraft[0].heading
```

The following code segment provides an example. It finds the average airspeed of all 100 aircraft in the airspace.

```
double sum = 0;
double averageAirSpeed;

for (int i = 0; i < 100; i++)
    sum = sum + plane[i].airSpeed;

averageAirSpeed = sum / 100;
```

What if there are fewer than 100 aircraft? We'd need some convenient way of tracking the actual number of airborne aircraft in our array. More on this later.

We can also create pointers to structures. The following declaration creates a pointer variable that contains the address of a variable of type `Flight`.

```
Flight *aircraftPtr;
```

We can assign this variable as we would any pointer variable.

```
aircraftPtr = &aircraft[34];
```

If we want to access any of the member fields pointed to by this pointer variable, we could use an expression such as the following:

```
(*aircraftPtr).longitude
```

Let's decode this expression. We are dereferencing the variable `aircraftPtr`. It points to something of type `Flight`, which is a structure. We can access one of the member elements of this structure by using the dot operator (`.`). Pointers to structures are an incredibly powerful and therefore commonly used concept, so the creators of the C programming language provided for a simple, intuitive syntax for this type of dereferencing. The previous expression is equivalent to:

```
aircraftPtr->longitude
```

That is, the expression -> is like the dereference operator *, except it is used for directly dereferencing a member element of a structure type. The symbol -> visually evokes that something is being pointed at.

Let's develop our running example a little further. Say we want to add some functionality that determines, for each aircraft, which of the other aircraft is closest in physical distance. To accomplish this, we need to examine the position and altitude of each aircraft and determine the one that is closest to the reference aircraft. In Figure 19.2, the function NearestNeighbor calls the function AirDistance on pairs of aircraft to determine distance and finds the minimum of

```
1    #include <stdio.h>
2    #define TOTAL_FLIGHTS 100
3
4    // Structure definition
5    struct flightType {
6        char ID[7];          // Max 6 characters
7        int altitude;        // in meters
8        int longitude;       // in tenths of degrees
9        int latitude;        // in tenths of degrees
10       int heading;         // in tenths of degrees
11       double airSpeed;     // in kilometers/hour
12   };
13   typedef struct flightType Flight;
14
15   double AirDistance(Flight *aircraftA, Flight *aircraftB)
16   {
17       // This function calculates Euclidean distance
18       // in meters in 3-space of two aircraft given
19       // their altitude, longitude and latitude.
20       return distance;
21   }
22
23   void NearestNeighbor(Flight aircraft[TOTAL_AIRCRAFT])
24   {
25       double minD;
26       Flight *closest;
27
28       for (int i = 0; i < TOTAL_AIRCRAFT; i++) {
29           closestAircraft = NULL;   // Initialize
30           minD = MAX_DISTANCE;      // Initialize
31           for (int j = 0; j < TOTAL_AIRCRAFT; j++) {
32               if (i != j) {
33                   if (AirDistance(&aircraft[i], &aircraft[j]) < minD)
34                       closest = &aircraft[j];
35               }
36           }
37           printf("The closest aircraft to %s is %s.\n",
38                   aircraft[i].flightNum, closest->flightNum);
39       }
40   }
```

Figure 19.2   Tracking airborne aircraft using an array based on the type Flight.

all pairs. The function `AirDistance` isn't completely coded. It uses the position and altitude of each of its two arguments to determine their distance apart.

Notice that `NearestNeighbor` passes `AirDistance` two pointers rather than the structures themselves. While it is possible to pass structures, passing pointers is more efficient because it involves less pushing of data onto the run-time stack; that is, in this case two pointers are pushed rather than 24 locations' worth of data for two objects of type `Flight`.

19.4 Dynamic Memory Allocation

The choice of array of `Flight` types for our core data structure is quite problematic for several reasons. We needed to choose a size for this array and hard-code that size into our code. If the number of aircraft is fewer than that size, then we are okay, except that we have more space allocated than we actually need. Yes, we also need a means for identifying which array elements contain real aircraft and which are unused. But if we had more than that number of aircraft in the sky, then our code would not function correctly. Such rigid assumptions make our code brittle. When the assumptions don't hold, our code is likely to fail. It would be better if we could make our sizing choice flexible to accommodate however many aircraft are in the air.

Another reason that the array of `Flight` types is a poor choice of core structure arises from the dynamic nature of airborne aircraft. They tend to land, take off, exit the airspace, or enter it with relatively high frequency. Our core data structure will need to add and remove aircraft as they enter and exit the airspace. Adding or removing a data item from the middle of an array is easy enough to code, but it requires moving all the items that follow in the array over one spot, which amounts to a lot of data movement over time, which could slow down our app or put a higher load on our device's battery.

The solution to these issues (the fixed data structure size and the inefficient delete of objects) is to use a dynamic data structure. In the next section, we will introduce the idea of a linked data structure that addresses both of these issues head on. But before we get there, we need to discuss the idea of dynamic memory allocation.

Memory objects (e.g., variables) in C programs are allocated to one of three spots in memory: the run-time stack, the global data section, or the *heap*. Variables declared local to functions are allocated during execution onto the run-time stack by default. Global variables are allocated to the global data section and are accessible from all parts of a program. Dynamically allocated data objects are allocated onto the heap, and their allocation and deallocation are determined completely by the logic of our code.

At a high level, dynamic memory allocation works as follows: A memory allocator (which is a C system library function named `malloc`) manages an area of memory called the heap. During execution, a program can make a request to the memory allocator for blocks of memory of a particular size in bytes. The memory allocator locates a contiguous block of this size, reserves this block by marking it as allocated, and returns a pointer to this block. For example, if we wanted to store 1000 aircraft's worth of data in our aircraft tracker code, we could request the allocator for this space in bytes. If enough space exists in the heap, the allocator will return a pointer to it. We'll work through a detailed example momentarily.

A block of memory that is allocated on the heap stays allocated until we decide to explicitly deallocate it by calling the memory deallocator (it works in concert with the allocator and is also a C system library function. It's named `free`). The deallocator adds the block back onto the heap for subsequent reallocation.

Figure 19.3 is a copy of Figure 12.7; it shows the relationship of the various regions of memory, including the heap. Notice that as blocks are allocated and deallocated, the heap grows and shrinks. The heap and the stack both grow toward each other. The size of the stack is based on the depth of the current function call, whereas the size of the heap is based on how much memory the memory allocator has reserved for the requests it has received.

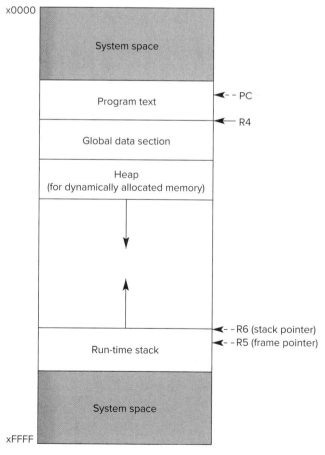

Figure 19.3   The LC-3 memory map showing the heap region of memory.

Objects that are allocated in the heap stay "alive" until we, the programmer, explicitly deallocate them. This is unlike the stack, where objects are deallocated once the code blocks (e.g., functions) in which they are declared have exited. This additional programmer control is invaluable. It will enable us to create data structures that are persistent across multiple functions and across large spans of program execution.

19.4.1 Dynamically Sized Arrays

Dynamic allocation and deallocation are handled by the C standard library functions `malloc` and `free`. They both have simple interfaces—they each take one argument (their internals are quite complex, but that is a topic for a subsequent course). We'll see how they are used via a simple example involving dynamically sized arrays.

```
int numAircraft;
Flight *planes;

printf("Total number of aircraft?");
scanf("%d", &numAircraft);
planes = malloc(24 * numAircraft);
```

The function `malloc` allocates a contiguous region of memory on the heap of the size in bytes indicated by the single parameter. If the heap has enough unclaimed memory and the call is successful, `malloc` returns a pointer to the allocated region. Here we allocate a chunk of memory consisting of `24 * numAircraft` bytes, where `numAircraft` is the number of aircraft in the air.

What about the 24? Recall that the type `Flight` is composed of six members—an array of seven characters, four integers, and a double, each occupying a single two-byte location on the LC-3. Each structure requires 24 bytes of memory on the LC-3. But this same structure on a Windows PC might require 31 bytes, due to the different sizes of integers, characters, and double types. As a necessary convenience for programmers, the C language supports a compile-time operator called `sizeof`. This operator returns the size, in bytes, of the memory object or type on the particular system being compiled for. For example, `sizeof(Flight)` will return the number of bytes occupied by an object of type `Flight` on the particular device the code is being compiled for. In this way, we can create more portable code that works on different systems without having to modify it.

If all the memory on the heap has been allocated and the current allocation cannot be accomplished, `malloc` returns the value `NULL`. Recall that the symbol `NULL` is a preprocessor macro symbol that represents a null pointer. It is good programming practice to check that the return value from `malloc` indicates that the memory allocation was successful.

The function `malloc` returns a pointer, but of what type? In the preceding example, we are treating the pointer that is returned by `malloc` as a pointer to some variable of type `Flight`. In other places, we might want `malloc` to allocate an array of integers, characters, or of some other type. In other words, `malloc` needs to return a *generic pointer* of type `void *`. This generic pointer needs to be *type cast* to the appropriate type during assignment. That is, whenever we call the memory allocator, we need to convert the `void *` pointer from `malloc` to the type of the pointer variable we are assigning it to. In the preceding example, we assigned the pointer to `planes`, which is of type `Flight *`; we therefore should cast the pointer to type `Flight *`. To do otherwise makes the code less portable, and most compilers generate a warning message because we are assigning a pointer value of one type to a pointer variable of another.

To type cast a value from one type to a `newType`, we use the following syntax. The variable `var` should be of `newType`.

```
var = (newType) expression;
```

Now that we've discussed type casting, the `sizeof` operation, and error checking of the return value from `malloc`, the correct way to write the code from the previous example is:

```
int numAircraft;
Flight *planes;

printf("Total number of aircraft?");
scanf("%d", &numAircraft);
planes = (Flight *) malloc(sizeof(Flight) * numAircraft);
if (planes == NULL) {
   printf("Error in malloc...\n");
   :
   :
```

Since the region that is allocated by `malloc` is contiguous in memory, we can switch between pointer notation and array notation. Now we can use the expression `planes[29]` to access the characteristics of the 30th aircraft (provided that `numAircraft` was larger than 30, of course). Notice that we smoothly switched from pointer notation to array notation; this is an example of the equivalence between array and pointer notation that we discussed in Section 16.3.5.

What about deallocation? To deallocate memory and return it to the heap, we can use the function `free`. It takes as an argument a pointer to a block that was previously allocated by `malloc` and deallocates it. After a region has been `free`'d, it is once again eligible for allocation. We'll see some examples that use `free` in the next section.

The function `malloc` is only one of several memory allocation functions in the standard library. The function `calloc` allocates memory and initializes it to the value 0. The function `realloc` attempts to grow or shrink previously allocated regions of memory. To use the memory allocation functions of the C standard library, we need to include the `stdlib.h` header file.

We can use `realloc` to create an array that adapts to the data size. For example, the function `AddMoreAircraft()` could double the size of our core aircraft array if the current size of the `planes` were too small. Likewise, we could use `ReduceAircraft()` when the size of the array is larger than what is required. Both of these functions would call `realloc` to adjust the array's size.

Notice that with this dynamic allocation functionality, we've created something similar, but not exactly the same as the variable-length arrays natively supported in C (recall from Section 16.3.8). Dynamically sized arrays (or dynamic arrays) are allocated on the heap, which means that we can access them throughout our code and not just within a single function, which is the case with stack-allocated variable-sized arrays. Dynamic arrays can also grow and shrink, whereas variable-length arrays are of fixed size throughout program execution. Even if we chose to use variable-length arrays for our aircraft tracker code, if the number of aircraft in our airspace surged, our code might not have enough space to track all aircraft.

Now let's take a step back. We started Section 19.4 by pointing out that our choice of data structure was rather poor because it required that we chose a fixed size for the array, and also because it wasn't efficient at deleting aircraft after they left our airspace or them adding once they entered. We addressed the dynamic sizing requirement by sketching a solution using dynamic memory allocation and dynamically sized arrays. But the issue of deleting and adding aircraft persists. One approach to resolving this is to use a linked data structure, which we are now fully prepared to explore in the next section!

19.5 Linked Lists

A *linked list* is a data structure that is similar to an array in that both can be used for data that is a sequential list of elements. In an array, each element (except the last) has a next element that follows it consecutively in memory. Likewise in a linked list, each element has a next element (except the last), but the elements need not be adjacent in memory. Rather, each element in a linked list contains a pointer to the next element, which enables the next element to be placed anywhere in relation. The pointer is used to reconstruct the sequential order.

A linked list is a collection of elements, or *nodes*, where each node is one "unit" of data, such as the Flight structure for tracking airborne aircraft, plus a pointer to the next node. Given a starting node, we can traverse the list from one node to another by following the pointers. The following code shows how this is accomplished in C. Here we have added a single new member element to the structure, the pointer Flight * next. As a side note, we rearranged this code slightly from the example in Figure 19.2 by moving the typedef to precede the structure definition. Why? This enables us to use the more convenient Flight * rather than struct flightType * as the type for next.

```
1    // Structure definition
2    typedef struct flightType Flight;
3    struct flightType {
4        char ID[7];         // Max 6 characters
5        int altitude;       // in meters
6        int longitude;      // in tenths of degrees
7        int latitude;       // in tenths of degrees
8        int heading;        // in tenths of degrees
9        double airSpeed;    // in kilometers/hour
10       Flight *next;       // Pointer to next element
11   };
```

Like an array, a linked list has a beginning and an end. Its beginning, or *head*, is accessed using a pointer called the *head pointer*. The final node in the list, or

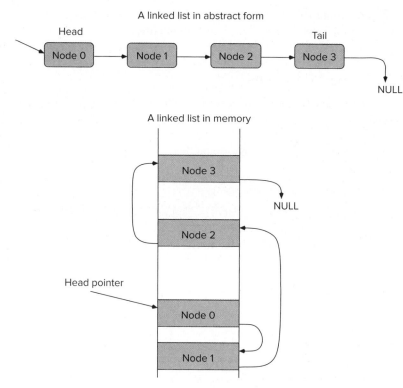

Figure 19.4   Two representations for a linked list.

tail, points to the NULL value, which signifies that no additional elements follow, similar to the way the NULL character indicates the end of a string. Figure 19.4 shows two representations of a linked list data structure: an abstract depiction where nodes are represented as blocks and pointers are represented by arrows, and a more physical representation that shows what the data structure might look like in memory. Nodes can appear anywhere, and it is the pointers that help recreate the linear order. Given a head pointer, we can access all elements in the list by traversing from one node to the next via the next pointer.

Despite their similarities, arrays and linked lists have fundamental differences. An array can be accessed in random order. We can access element number 4, followed by element 911, followed by 45, for example, by providing the index of the element we wish to access. A simple linked list must be traversed sequentially starting at its head; if we wanted to access node 29, then we would have to start at node 0 (the head node) and then go to node 1, then to node 2, and so forth. This sequential access may seem like a disadvantage, and it is! But there is a strong benefit to linked lists, which we discuss next.

Linked lists are dynamic in nature; additional nodes can be added or deleted without movement of the other nodes. Existing nodes stay in place, with the new node added, or old node deleted, by rearranging the node-to-node links. Both add and delete are accomplished by rearranging pointers, and they don't require copying or moving data. While it is straightforward to dynamically size an array (see Section 19.4.1 on using `malloc`), it is more costly to add or remove a single element in an array.

19.5.1 Support Functions

Let's redevelop the core data structure for our flight tracker app, this time using a linked list instead of an array as we did in Figure 19.2. There are two basic functions we'll develop in this example, `AddFlight`, which will add an aircraft to the linked list as it enters our airspace, and `DeleteFlight` to remove an aircraft. Our starting point will be the variable

```
Flight *airspace = NULL;
```

and it will replace the array we used in Figure 19.2. It is initially empty, as signified by its initialization to `NULL`.

Before we dive into the linked list itself, let's build up the code surrounding the `AddFlight` and `DeleteFlight` functions. Figure 19.5 lists the C source code

```
1    #include <stdio.h>
2    #include <stdlib.h>
3    #include <string.h>
4
5    // Structure definition
6    typedef struct flightType Flight;
7    struct flightType {
8        char ID[7];          // Max 6 characters
9        int altitude;        // in meters
10       int longitude;       // in tenths of degrees
11       int latitude;        // in tenths of degrees
12       int heading;         // in tenths of degrees
13       double airSpeed;     // in kilometers/hour
14       Flight *next;        // Pointer to next element
15   };
16
17   Flight *CreateFlight(char *ID, int altitude, int longitude,
18                        int latitude, int heading, double airspeed)
19   {
20       Flight *newFlight;
21
22       newFlight = (Flight *)malloc(sizeof(Flight));
23       strcpy(newFlight->ID, ID);
24       newFlight->altitude = altitude;
25       newFlight->longitude = longitude;
26       newFlight->latitude = latitude;
27       newFlight->heading = heading;
28       newFlight->airSpeed = airspeed;
29   }
30
31   void PrintAirspace(Flight *list)
```

Figure 19.5   The support functions for our airspace tracker (Fig. 19.5 continued on next page.)

```
32  {
33      int count = 1;
34
35      printf("Aircraft in Airspace -------------------------\n");
36      while (list != NULL) {
37          printf("Aircraft : %d\n", count);
38          printf("ID       : %s\n", list->ID);
39          printf("Altitude : %d\n", list->altitude);
40          printf("Longitude: %d\n", list->longitude);
41          printf("Heading  : %d\n", list->heading);
42          printf("Airspeed : %f\n", list->airSpeed);
43          printf("---------------------------\n");
44          count = count + 1;
45          list = list->next;
46      }
47      printf("\n\n");
48  }
49
50  int main(void)
51  {
52      Flight *airspace = NULL;
53      Flight *newPlane = NULL;
54
55      newPlane = CreateFlight("ZA123", 1000, 3233,
56                              2516, 392, 3493.20);
57      if (AddFlight(newPlane, &airspace) == 0)
58          printf("Successful add of flight %s\n",newPlane->ID);
59      .
60      .
61      .
62      if (DeleteFlight("ZA123", &airspace) == 0)
63          printf("Successful removal of flight %s\n", "ZZ");
64      .
65      .
66      .
67  }
```

Figure 19.5   The support functions for our airspace tracker (continued Fig. 19.5 from previous page.)

for the support functions for our linked list–based flight tracker. The structure definition is just as we developed previously, with the addition of the Flight *next pointer to enable us to link nodes together.

The function CreateFlight takes as arguments the various properties of an aircraft to create a new node via malloc. The function then returns a pointer to this new node.

The function PrintAirspace prints all the aircraft in the airspace by traversing the linked list, which is provided as an input parameter. Notice that the while loop is the analog of the for loop we would typically use for traversing a fixed-size array. Since we don't know the number of nodes in the list, we use a while loop to keep traversing from node to node until we reach the NULL pointer. And instead of the i++ which is typical of a for loop, the iteration is accomplished by list = list ->next;.

The function main orchestrates everything, and it contains example calls to the functions AddFlight and DeleteFlight.

One note about the code in Figure 19.5 is that we needed to include two additional header files from the C standard library. The header file stdlib.h contains the definitions for the memory allocation functions that we'll use, e.g., malloc and free. The header file string.h contains various string functions, including strcmp, which we'll use in the functions to add and delete aircraft to and from our linked list.

19.5.2 Adding a Node to a Linked List

Since the linked list of aircraft will be maintained in sorted order by aircraft ID, there is a precise spot within the list where each new aircraft should be added. For example, if our list contains two aircraft, one with ID A, followed by one with ID C, then the new aircraft B will be inserted in between those two aircraft. The new list will be A, B, C.

The basic insertion algorithm is simple: the next pointer of A, which currently points to C, should be changed to point to the new aircraft B, and the next pointer of B should be changed to point to C. Only two values are modified in order to add the new node. Compare this to what is required to add a node to a sorted array!

Let's start off with some code to represent this particular situation. Keep in mind that this code is not complete, as we'll elaborate later, but it does provide the basic structure of the algorithm, and it is important for us to understand before we develop the full code.

We want to traverse the list, searching for the spot in the list at which to insert B. We'll use a while loop, as we did for the PrintAirspace support function, to traverse the list. We're searching for a node with an ID that is greater than B because that indicates we've found the spot at which to insert B. In this case, A is not greater than B, so we keep iterating. C is greater than B, and therefore we insert B just before C.

Note that because ID is represented as a character string, we'll use the C standard string function strcmp, which compares two strings, stringX and stringY:

```
comp = strcmp(stringX, stringY);
```

It returns a 0 if both are equal, or a value <0 if stringX appears before stringY in alphabetical order, according to ASCII, or a value >0 if stringX appears after stringY.

To insert B prior to node C, we need to modify the next pointer of A, which is prior to node C. To accomplish this, we need to retain a "previous" pointer that points to the node prior to node C. In other words, the current pointer serves as our index through the linked list, and the previous pointer lags it by one node. The current pointer helps us locate the point of insertion, and the previous pointer

```
1    int AddFlight(Flight *newPlane, Flight *list)
2    {
3        Flight *previous = NULL;
4        Flight *current = list;
5        int IDcompare;
6
7        while (current != NULL) {
8            IDcompare = strcmp(newPlane->ID, current->ID);
9            // returns 0 if equal
10           // < 0 if newPlane->ID is less than current->ID
11           // > 0 if newPlane->ID is greater than current->ID
12
13           if (IDcompare < 0) {
14               // Add newPlane in between previous and current nodes
15               newPlane->next = current;
16               previous->next = newPlane;
17               return 0;
18           }
19           // Continue traversing thru the list
20           previous = current;
21           current = current->next;
22       }
23   }
```

Figure 19.6   Our first version of AddFlight. It handles the simple case of adding a node to the middle of the list.

assists in the insertion by providing a way to access the node whose next pointer needs to be modified.

The code provided in Figure 19.6 provides the basic structure, albeit incomplete, of our code. Notice that the while loop iterates through the nodes in the linked list using the pointer variable current. The pointer variable previous lags current by one node.

This code is incomplete. It doesn't take into account some of the different cases we will encounter during use. How does the preceding situation change if C doesn't exist, or if A doesn't exist, or if neither exists? Let's walk through the permutations of A and C (and B) existing in the list prior to the insertion of B.

We've already covered the situation where both A and C are in the list in the code in Figure 19.6. Here B is inserted in between two existing nodes. We'll call this the "**Add to Middle**" case. Let's consider the other cases.

Empty List: What if neither A nor C exists prior to the insertion of B? Here we are adding B to an empty list. We want to change the value of the head pointer of the list (allAircraft in the function main), which currently points to NULL, to point instead to B. The next pointer of B will point to NULL. The list now contains a single aircraft, B.

Add at Tail: What if A exists, but C does not? In this case, we will be adding B to the end, or tail, of the list. The next pointer of A will be modified to point to B instead of NULL. B's next pointer will be set to NULL.

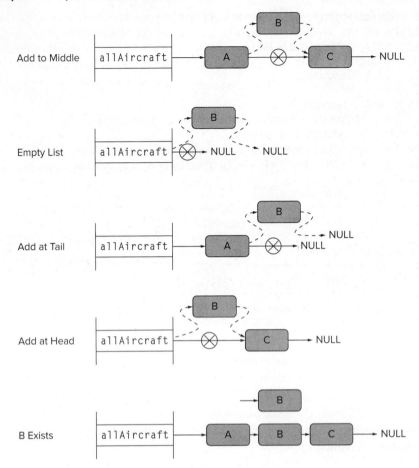

Figure 19.7   Inserting a node into a linked list. The dashed lines indicate newly formed links.

Add at Head: What if C exists, but A does not? In this case, B will be inserted prior to C. This requires modifying the head pointer of the list (`allAircraft` in the function `main`), which currently points to C, to point to B instead. B's next pointer will be set to point to C.

B Exists: What if A and C exist, but so does B? In this case, we will not insert a duplicate of B; instead we will signal that a special condition has occurred.

Figure 19.7 provides another view of each of these five cases. We'll have to ensure that our `AddFlight` code from Figure 19.6 handles all five of these situations. Some of these cases are rather easy to address, such as "**B Exists**". "**Add at Tail**" is also rather simple. Here we exit the `while` loop without having added B. At this point, we know that B will be added to the tail, which requires modifying the `previous` node to point to B and having B point to `NULL`.

The other two cases, **Add at Head** and **Empty List**, are more problematic. They both require modifying the parameter `list` to point to a new node.

To address this issue, we'll need to pass `list` by reference to `AddFlight` (see Section 16.2.3). That is, we'll need to pass a *pointer* to it, instead of the value itself. We've seen how to do this for typical variables, but it gets a little confusing when dealing with pointer variables. In C, this parameter would be expressed as a pointer to a variable of type `Flight *`, or as expressed as code:

```
Flight **list;
```

It's often distractingly difficult to clearly think about what this actually means. The double asterisks can require some mental processing for most programmers to decode. It is helpful to keep in mind that the concept is just the same as if we were passing an integer variable by reference:

```
int *x;
```

And in order to modify the variable `x`, say by incrementing it, we can use the following notation:

```
*x = *x + 1;
```

Likewise, to modify a pointer variable passed by reference, we can use the following notation:

```
*list = *list->next;
```

We've provided the complete version of `AddFlight` in Figure 19.8. The places in the code where we handle each of the five different cases are identified in the comments.

19.5.3 Deleting Node from a Linked List

Our function to delete a node from the list follows the template set `AddFlight` quite closely. The delete function requires an ID of the aircraft to be deleted. The corresponding node can exist somewhere within the list, at the head of the list, at the tail of the list, or it might not exist at all. As with our code to add an element to the list, our delete code needs to handle each of these cases.

We traverse the list looking for the node to delete. If found, the node previous to it is modified to point to the node following it. The node to delete is then deallocated using the `free` function. As with the add function, `DeleteFlight` returns a 0 if the delete proceeded successfully or a −1 if it didn't.

When deleting a node from a linked list, we can encounter situations analogous to those we encountered when adding a node: **Delete from Middle**, **Empty List**, **Delete from Tail**, **Delete from Head**, and **Doesn't Exist**.

Each of these situations is simple to code on top of the basic `while` loop structure. Some of these cases are similar to each other: **Empty List** and **Doesn't Exist** are in effect the same. Neither actually performs a delete, and each returns a −1 to signal an error. Also, **Delete from Middle** and **Delete from Tail** are the same due to the type similarity between a NULL pointer and a pointer to a real node. The **Delete from Head** case requires that we modify the parameter `list` in

```
1   int AddFlight(Flight *newPlane, Flight **list)
2   {
3      Flight *previous = NULL;
4      Flight *current = *list;
5      int IDcompare;
6
7      while (current != NULL) {
8         IDcompare = strcmp(newPlane->ID, current->ID);
9         // returns 0 if equal
10        // < 0 if newPlane->ID is less than current->ID
11        // > 0 if newPlane->ID is greater than current->ID
12
13        if (IDcompare == 0)
14           return -1;                        // Exists!
15        }
16        else if (IDcompare < 0) {
17           // Add newPlane in between previous and current nodes
18           newPlane->next = current;
19           if (previous == NULL)
20              *list = newPlane;              // Add At Head
21           else
22              previous->next = newPlane;     // Add to Middle
23           return 0;
24        }
25        else {
26           // Continue traversing thru the list
27           previous = current;
28           current = current->next;
29        }
30     }
31     newPlane->next = NULL;
32     if (previous == NULL)
33        *list = newPlane;                    // Empty List
34     else
35        previous->next = newPlane;           // Add At Tail
36     return 0;
37  }
```

Figure 19.8   Source code for complete AddFlight **function.**

order to assign a new head node after the delete operation. Figure 19.9 provides the complete source code for DeleteFlight.

19.5.4 Arrays vs. Linked Lists

We can now replace our core array data structure in our flight tracker app with the more dynamic linked list. Throughout this chapter, we've discussed some of the advantages in doing so. But as with many things in computing, there are tradeoffs involved: linked lists provide some advantages over arrays, but they also have some disadvantages. Wisely choosing which method of data organization to

```
1   int DeleteFlight(char *planeID, Flight **list)
2   {
3       Flight *previous = NULL;
4       Flight *current = *list;
5       int IDcompare;
6
7       while (current != NULL) {
8           IDcompare = strcmp(planeID, current->ID);
9           // returns 0 if equal
10          // < 0 if Plane->ID is less than current->ID
11          // > 0 if Plane->ID is greater than current->ID
12          if (IDcompare == 0) {
13              // Found node to remove!
14              if (previous == NULL)
15                  *list = current->next;          // Del At Head
16              else
17                  previous->next = current->next; // Del from Mid/Tail
18              free(current);
19              return 0;
20          }
21          else if (IDcompare < 0)
22              return -1;                          // Doesn't Exist
23          else {
24              // Continue traversing thru the list
25              previous = current;
26              current = current->next;
27          }
28      }
29      // Traversed the whole list. Doesn't Exist
30      return -1;
31  }
```

Figure 19.9   Source code for complete DeleteFlight function.

use in a particular situation requires consideration of these tradeoffs (and also a deeper sense of how these structures are implemented at the lower level).

Let's first examine the impact to memory space. Arrays are quite memory efficient. If we create an array of 1000 integers, we will be allocated 1000 integers' worth of memory space. Additional storage is not required. If the array is dynamically allocated on the heap, there is likely some additional overhead to keep track of the block of memory, but that is small in relation to the actual array. Linked lists, in contrast, require a pointer per node to link to the next node. Also, since the nodes are individually allocated on the heap, each node will incur additional dynamic allocation overhead. If the node size is small, then this overhead can be a significant fraction of overall data structure size. While arrays are efficient in terms of allocation, they suffer in our inability to precisely size them to our needs. We often need to declare strings that are long enough to hold the longest string we expect to encounter, which is larger than necessary for the typical case.

Now, what if we wanted to add an element, or delete an element, or search the structure for a particular element? These are primitive operations that we may want to perform on any list of data. For adding and deleting elements, which we've examined when developing our flight tracker app, a linked list offers the ability to dynamically add and remove nodes by rearranging links. And because the data structure need not be contiguous in memory, we can dynamically allocate nodes to fit the actual run-time needs of the application. With arrays, adding an element requires that enough space exists for it in the array; if there is enough space, existing elements must then be moved around to create a spot for the new data. Likewise, when deleting an element from an array, we need to fill the vacated spot by moving data elements in order to keep data contiguous. As for searching, linked lists require sequential traversal, whereas with an array, we can use binary search (see Section 17.6), which is a highly efficient algorithm for searching a sorted list.

These differences arise because we've improved the add and delete operations at the expense of random access. Array elements can be randomly accessed, whereas nodes in a linked list require sequential traversal. This in turn affects our ability to do efficient search.

Arrays and linked lists form the opposite ends of a spectrum of data structure choices. There is a near continuum of variations created by inventive programmers and computer scientists to fit particular situations, each of which provides some advantages of one end of the spectrum without the disadvantages of the other. A subsequent course in data structures and algorithmic analysis will provide deeper exposure to the data structure zoo.

19.6 Summary

We conclude this chapter by a summarizing the three key concepts we covered.

- **Structures in C.** The primary objective of this chapter was to introduce the concept of user-defined aggregate types in C, or structures. C structures allow us to create new data types by grouping together data of more primitive types. C structures take us a big step toward the idea of objects in C++, which we'll discuss in Chapter 20.

- **Dynamic memory allocation.** The concept of dynamic memory allocation is an important prerequisite for advanced programming concepts. In particular, dynamic data structures that grow and shrink during program execution require some form of memory allocation. C provides some standard memory allocation functions such as `malloc` and `free`.

- **Linked lists.** We combine the concepts of structures and dynamic memory allocation to introduce a fundamental new data structure called a linked list. It is similar to an array in that it contains data that is best organized in a list fashion. Why is the linked list such an important data structure? For one thing, it is a dynamic structure that can be expanded or shrunk during execution. This dynamic quality makes it appealing to use in certain situations where the static nature of arrays would be wasteful. The concept of connecting data elements together using pointers is fundamental, and you will encounter it often when dealing with advanced structures such as hash tables, trees, and graphs.

19.1   Is there a bug in the following program? Explain.

```
struct node {
    int count;
    struct node *next;
};

int main(void)
{
    int data = 0;
    struct node *getdata;
    getdata->count = data + 1;
    printf("%d", getdata->count);
}
```

19.2   The following are a few lines of a C program:

```
struct node {
    int count;
    struct node *next;
};

int main(void)
{
    int data = 0;
    struct node *getdata;
    :
    :
    getdata = getdata->next;
    :
    :
}
```

Write, in LC-3 assembly language, the instructions that are generated by the compiler for the line getdata = getdata->next;.

19.3   The code for NearestNeighbor in Figure 19.2 performs a pairwise check of all aircraft currently in the airspace. If there are *n* aircraft in the airspace, how many checks are performed?

19.4 The following program is compiled on a computing device in which
each basic data type (pointer, character, integer, floating point) occupies
one location of memory.

```c
typedef element_t Element;
struct element_t {
    char name[25];
    int atomic_number;
    float atomic_mass;
};

int NobleElement(Element *t)
{
    if ((t->atomic_number==2) ||
        (t->atomic_number==10) ||
        (t->atomic_number==18) ||
        (t->atomic_number==36) ||
        (t->atomic_number==54) ||
        (t->atomic_number==86))
        return 1;
    else
        return 0;
}

int main(void)
{
    int x, y;
    Element periodic_table[110];
    :
    :
    // Determine if the yth element is noble
    x = NobleElement(_____);
    :
    :
}
```

  a. How many locations will the stack frame of the function
      `NobleElement` contain?
  b. Assuming that `periodic_table`, x, and y are the only local
      variables, how many locations in the stack frame for `main` will be
      devoted to local variables?
  c. Fill in the missing blank in the function call to `NobleElement` in
      `main`.

19.5   The following C program is compiled into the LC-3 machine language and executed. The run-time stack begins at xEFFF. The user types the input `abac` followed by a return.

```c
#include <stdio.h>
#define MAX 4

typedef Rec
struct rec_t {
    char ch;
    struct Rec *back;
};

int main(void)
{
    struct Rec *ptr, pat[MAX+2];
    int i = 1, j = 1;
    printf("Pattern: ");
    pat[1].back = pat;
    ptr = pat;
    while ((pat[i].ch = getchar()) != '\n') {
        ptr[++i].back = ++ptr;
        if (i > MAX) break;
    }
    while (j <= i)
        printf("%d ", pat[j++].back - pat);
        // Note the pointer arithmetic here: subtraction
        // of pointers to structures gives the number of
        // structure elements, not the number
        // of memory locations
}
```

   a. Show the contents of the stack frame for `main` when the program terminates.

   b. What is the output of this program for the input `abac`?

19.6   Write a basic version of `malloc` and `free`. Assume that `malloc` is initialized whenever a program is started and points to an empty (unallocated) heap. Initially, don't be concerned about efficiency or reallocating blocks of memory after they've been freed. Develop something that is functional, and then improve it from there.

20 Introduction to C++

20.1 Essential C++

We can think of programming languages as the scaffolding with which the digital world is constructed. Building more sophisticated apps and services that are safe, secure, and reliable requires that our programming systems—languages and tools—are oriented toward programmer productivity. If coding in a particular language is tedious, overly complicated, error prone, or hard to extend, then the applications that can be created will be limited, and the language will be unlikely to be widely used. Many languages have come and gone, and very few have endured as long as C and C++. Both are very effective languages for large-scale software development for performance-hungry, core system code.

C++ was born out of a desire to help C programmers to create more sophisticated programs. C programs at scale tend to become large, messy collections of types, structures, and functions. The C language itself doesn't provide support for systematic organization of these code entities. As coding projects become large, involving teams of people, this lack of programming organization can render the code hard to extend and maintain, creating lots of headaches for software engineering management.

C++ addresses some core limitations of large programs that have lots of defined types, structures, and functions created by multiple programmers. C++ creator Bjarne Stroustrup had the foresight in the late 1970s to address these limitations by creating an extension of C that provided a formalized way of organizing types, structures, and functions into *classes*. Classes are the logical evolution of the C structure we introduced in Chapter 19. With classes, code tends to be much more extendable and reusable. Large C++ projects today can reach tens of millions of lines or more, and C++ is as widely used as any other language out there, particularly for applications that require high performance or a high degree of optimization.

C++ is a vast language that evolved over the years from C with classes (in fact, the original name for it was C with Classes!) to include a variety of advanced language features that would require another 1,000 pages to treat thoroughly. But don't fret—we'll cover what we consider the essential C++ in this single chapter. It will be enough to provide you with a very strong start on writing fairly complex C++ code. Consider this chapter to be a C++ starting point from which you can explore further in subsequent courses.

The good news is that nearly everything we've described in the previous chapters on C translates directly into C++. C++ was originally built on top of C. Basic types, variables, code constructs, and functions are largely the same or similar to what we've discussed with C. We could go back and change all mentions of C with C++ and Chapters 11 through 19 would largely remain correct.

It will help to keep one simple concept in mind: C++ code compiles down to the same execution model as C. C's model is a collection of functions, starting with `main`, that execute sequentially based on the call structure of the code, with the run-time stack used for passing arguments and for local variable (or object) allocation, the heap providing for dynamic allocation, and the global section providing for global allocation. The same framework will apply to our compiled C++ code. The same binary representations, basic types, constructs, and execution model applies. It will be helpful to keep this in mind as we discuss the various features of C++. Much of the magic of C++ is handled at the compilation layer. The C++ compiler is doing more work on our behalf to generate the executable code, enabling the level of software abstraction to be raised and thereby making the task of programming more convenient for us.

20.2 Going from C to C++

C++ gained rapid popularity shortly after its introduction, partly on the idea that it was a better version of C, which was the most popular programming language of the time. C++ kept the structural concepts of C while addressing some major shortcomings from a software engineering perspective. It was based on the idea that a program should be organized around the objects it will operate on through a notion called *classes*. We'll talk about classes shortly.

In its revision of C, the C++ language also addressed other shortcomings of C, which were not as significant a change as adding classes, but helped with the overall ease of programming. In this section, we'll start off by introducing some of these smaller but commonly used changes from C that are provided by the C++ language. Throughout the book, it has been our style to introduce big new concepts with simple code examples. So we'll dive directly into C++ with an example in Figure 20.1. Let's go through some of the changes from C in this code.

20.2.1 Compiling C++ Code

The code in Figure 20.1 looks very similar in syntax and structure to a program in C. Again, C++ is based on C, so most of what we've learned about C can be applied to C++. In fact, because we are familiar with C, we can guess with reasonable accuracy what this program does by reading the C++ code. It's quite similar to the code we saw in Figure 16.4 when we discussed pointers in C for

```
 1  #include <iostream>
 2
 3  void swap(int &x, int &y)
 4  {
 5      int temp = x;
 6      x = y;
 7      y = temp;
 8  }
 9
10  void swap(char &x, char &y)
11  {
12      char temp = x;
13      x = y;
14      y = temp;
15  }
16
17  void swap(double &x, double &y)
18  {
19      double temp = x;
20      x = y;
21      y = temp;
22  }
23
24  int main (void)
25  {
26      // Variable declarations
27      int a = 4, b =5;
28      char c = 'c', d = 'd';
29      double x = 3.14, y = 1.41;
30
31      // Before the swaps
32      std::cout << "a = " << a << "   b = " << b << std::endl;
33      std::cout << "c = " << c << "   d = " << d << std::endl;
34      std::cout << "x = " << x << "   y = " << y << std::endl;
35
36      swap(a, b);
37      swap(c, d);
38      swap(x, y);
29
40      // After the swaps
41      std::cout << "a = " << a << "   b = " << b << std::endl;
42      std::cout << "c = " << c << "   d = " << d << std::endl;
43      std::cout << "x = " << x << "   y = " << y << std::endl;
44  }
```

Figure 20.1   A simple C++ code example.

the first time. You might be perplexed by the three variants of the function swap that appear in the code. More on that later.

Because the two languages are similar, most Integrated Development Environments, or IDEs, that provide a C development environment will also compile C++ code (they are really C++ environments that also support C code development). For the few C++ examples we provide in this text, we've adhered to standard coding conventions using ISO, or Standard C++. Now would be an appropriate moment to experiment with compiling some simple C++ code, such as the code from Figure 20.1, in your favorite IDE.

20.2.2 Namespaces

The concept of a namespace doesn't quite have a C counterpart. A namespace is an advanced C++ concept that applies to software projects that consist of many lines of code in multiple files developed by many people.

With larger programs written by teams of programmers, it is common to run into naming conflicts. Functions, global variables, and structure types will inevitably be named the same thing at some point. To resolve these naming collisions, new names must be selected somewhere by someone. It can be an awkward, painful process. To solve this systematically in C requires adopting an onerous naming convention.

Namespaces provide a better path. In C++, we can create a namespace where all identifiers are distinct from those in all other namespaces. This lets us create names and make them unique to a particular region of code, very similar to scope (see Section 12.2.3). This is essential for large code bodies.

For those who are just starting with C++, often the default global namespace suffices. It's what we are accustomed to as C programmers. For most intro programs we write, everything we create will be added to the global namespace. For example, the function swap in Figure 20.1 will be part of the global namespace.

We can use named entities (types, functions, global values) from other namespaces, such as the std namespace for the C++ Standard Library (more on this later). To do this, we use the std:: extension on the identifier in question. This appears in several spots in the code in Figure 20.1. This indicates that these identifiers were defined within a different namespace and used in the current one. The :: is called the scope operator in C++, and it lets us explicitly choose which namespace a particular identifier originates. We'll see it again when we discuss classes.

20.2.3 Input and Output

Keeping our attention on the lines that contain the std:: operator, each of these lines performs output in C++. C++ significantly simplifies formatted input and output compared to C by providing an easy mechanism for doing typical formatted I/O operations. C++ defines two streams: cin, which is similar to stdin in C, and cout, which is similar to stdout. These streams are defined within the iostream header file, which is included on line 1.

Instead of using printf and scanf to perform basic formatted I/O, C++ uses a set of operators to remove items from the cin input stream and to add items to the cout data stream. The operator >> is used to extract from an input stream, and the operator << is used to insert into the output stream. For example, on lines 32 to 34 and 41 to 43, we use the << operator to insert various strings and variables into the standard output stream cout. We can also add a new line character via the endl constant. Each of the items is displayed on the standard output device, character by character, in the order in which they are added to the output stream. Since each of these is defined within the std namespace in the C++ Standard Library, we need to precede each with the std:: namespace tag. Whenever a variable is inserted into the output stream, it is converted into ASCII based on its original type (integers are converted into decimal characters, etc.).

Input happens in a similar fashion using the standard input stream std::cin and the extraction operator >>. For example, the following lines of code assign a value from cin to the variable input.

```
int input;

std::cout << "Provide an integer value: ";
std::cin >> input;
```

While the I/O functionality of C++ looks drastically different than C, the underlying functionality is similar. Instead of using printf and scanf, we are using the << and >> operators in conjunction with cout and cin. The preceding code is translated into an appropriate function call with a set of arguments similar to those in C. In other words, much of this functionality is provided for the syntactic convenience of the programmer. Ultimately, I/O functions need to be called, and a system call (e.g., TRAP) to perform the physical I/O needs to be performed.

20.2.4 Pass by Reference

Passing by reference in C can be a challenging proposition. Consider for example our linked list code from Chapter 19. For the AddFlight function, we needed to pass in the address of the head pointer, instead of the head pointer itself, to handle the case when the list was empty or a new aircraft was being added to the front of the list. This required using a pointer to a pointer (Flight **list) and careful use of the dereference operator within the AddFlight function to modify the correct memory location. Also, we must modify both the function and all the call sites to designate a parameter as a reference in C.

C++ provides direct syntax to designate a parameter as reference within a function's definition. Notice line 3 in the code in Figure 20.1. The two parameters to swap are both prefixed with an ampersand &, indicating that they are references to integer variables, instead of the integer values themselves. Now within the code of swap (lines 5 and 7) we treat those values syntactically as if we have access to the original variable (i.e., in the stack frame for main), instead of as dereferenced pointers as we did with C. The C++ compiler generates the appropriate code, based on whether the identifiers are references or values.

For example, the LC-3 translation for the following line of code (line 6):

```
x = y; // Equivalent to *x = *y in C
```

is

```
LDR R0, R5, 4    ; Load x, which is a reference
LDR R1, R5, 5    ; Load y, which is a reference
LDR R2, R1, 0    ; Load *y
STR R2, R0, 0    ; Perform *x = *y
```

This is another case where the cumbersome and challenging-to-read syntax of C is replaced by something simpler and more straightforward in C++. With the C++ approach, if a parameter needs to be a reference, we only need to change the function itself and not the places it is called. During compilation, each argument at each call site can be selected to be passed as a value or as a reference without requiring explicit coding from the programmer. The compiler picks the appropriate thing to pass based on the function's declaration.

20.2.5 Function Overloading

We deferred our discussion on why there are three versions of the same function swap in the code in Figure 20.1. You may have noticed that the code for each is mostly the same except for the types of the input parameters and the internal temporary variable. They all perform the same set of internal operations.

C++ lets us create functions with the same name (three versions of swap) provided they have a different parameter list, in terms of sequence of types. The three versions of swap are each different in that one takes two integers by reference, another takes two characters, and the third requires two doubles. At each call site for swap, the types of the argument are used by the compiler to select which one to actually call. That is, the argument list is matched with the parameter list.

This facility is called function *overloading*. Any function can have multiple versions, with different sets of parameters. You can think about this as a naming trick performed by the compilation system where each function's name is appended with the types of the parameters in the order they appear. So swap_int_int is different than swap_char_char. And this happens transparently, under the hood, as the code is compiled.

Why is function overloading a useful thing? Consider the swap function. It's useful to be able to provide general swap capabilities, regardless of type. We'd like to be able to swap two integer values, two character values, or two doubles. With overloading we can keep the simple, intuitive name swap and create variants that handle each basic type, as we did in Figure 20.1.

Let's go one step further. The three versions of swap are very similar, with each performing the same underlying operations on different types. In the spirit of reusing code, and reducing source code footprint, another approach would be to make this code independent of type by using a *template*. We'll discuss templates later in Section 20.4.

20.2.6 Dynamic Allocation

In C, we used `malloc` to dynamically allocate a block of memory on the heap. Once we are done with that block, we use `free` to return that block to the heap for subsequent reallocation. Both `malloc` and `free` are library functions, provided by the C Standard Library.

In C++, dynamic allocation is accomplished by the `new` and `delete` operators. Here's how they work:

```
1   int *p;
2
3   p = new int;
4   :
5   :
6   delete p;
```

On line 3, we are allocating an integer's worth of space using the `new` operator. And on line 6, we are deallocating p using `free`. In C++, both `new` and `delete` are operators rather than functions as `malloc` and `free` are in C, and they also call the constructor or destructor of the type they create. More on that in Section 20.3.2.

20.2.7 Compilation to Machine Version

We've touched on a small but essential set of changes from C in this section. There are more concepts we certainly could have discussed, but our intention is not to provide complete exposure, just enough to jump-start the development of small but powerful C++ coding projects. When combined with what we've discussed with C, which is a subset, this is a fairly substantial set of C++.

C++ uses the same run-time model as C. Like a C program, a C++ program compiles down to a section of functions. The code in Figure 20.1 compiles down into four functions plus library functions. The function `main` calls the equivalent of `printf` for each of the formatted output statements involving `std::cout`, then calls the version of `swap` for integer parameters (`swap_int_int`), then swap for characters (`swap_char_char`), then `swap` for doubles (`swap_double_double`), and so forth.

20.3 Classes

One of the original innovations of C++ over C was the introduction of classes. Classes are a refinement on the idea of a structure as a programmer-defined type. C++ extends the idea of C structures by adding functions as member elements, incorporating hierarchy, and supporting well-defined interfaces. The memory items that are declared using classes are no longer simple *variables*, they are *objects* that have a richer set of operations associated with them. These ideas were borrowed from other languages that predate C++, but they were embedded within C, which was very popular at the time.

```
// C++ code                        // C code
class Triangle {                   struct Triangle {
    double sideA;                      double sideA;
    double sideB;                      double sideB;
    double sideC;                      double sideC;
};                                 };

Triangle t1;                       struct Triangle t2;
```

Figure 20.2   Comparing Triangles in C++ and C.

There is a very clear and pragmatic benefit of classes. C programs are a flat collection of types, values, and functions. As programs grow in complexity, this flat collection becomes a soupy mess that inhibits forward progress from a development perspective. Classes are primarily an organizational construct that enable us to associate similar functionality together. They provide a strong software engineering benefit. It is no surprise that many of the successful languages that followed, such as Java, also provide support for classes.

We'll start off with an example of a simple class called `Triangle` in Figure 20.2. As we did with structures in Chapter 19, we can define our own type with classes. The type `Triangle` will contain several member elements to describe a particular triangle, specifically the lengths of each of its three sides. This is quite similar to what we would have done in C using structures. Both versions of the code in Figure 20.2 create new types. The C++ class `Triangle` enables us to declare the object `t1`. In C, the structure Triangle enables us to declare the memory item `t2`. In C++, objects are the memory items that are defined by classes.

20.3.1 Methods

Let's take one step deeper into the realm of objects. We can associate specific functions with objects that are of `Triangle` class. These functions can only be called when operating on objects of that class. They have no meaning otherwise. Such functions are called *methods*. In our `Triangle` example, we might want to calculate the area and the perimeter of a triangle.

Specifically, we'll add two functions to the class structure (in the next section, we'll add another), one to calculate the perimeter and one to calculate the area of a given triangle. These are methods within the class `Triangle`. Figure 20.3 contains an expanded definition of the class. We've added lines 5, 6, and 7. We'll discuss line 5 shortly, in the next section. Lines 6 and 7 within the class definition declare two methods to be part of the class. Both return double values, and both have empty parameter lists.

Lines 10 through 13 define the method `perimeter`, and lines 15 through 21 define the method `area`. These are function definitions as we saw in C, with an essential restriction: these methods can only be called in reference to a specific object of `Triangle` type. We'll elaborate on this shortly. For now, both are methods similar to the functions we created in C.

The name of each method is preceded in the definition by `Triangle::`, which signifies to the C++ compiler that they belong to the class `Triangle` (i.e., their

```
1  class Triangle {
2     double sideA;
3     double sideB;
4     double sideC;
5   public:
6     double area();
7     double perimeter();
8  };
9
10 double Triangle::perimeter()
11 {
12     return sideA + sideB + sideC;
13 }
14
15 double Triangle::area()
16 {
17     double s = perimeter() / 2;
18
19     // Heron's Formula
20     return sqrt(s*(s - sideA)*(s - sideB)*(s - sideC));
21 }
```

Figure 20.3 The class `Triangle` with two methods.

scope is `Triangle`). The method `perimeter` performs a simple calculation of adding the lengths of the three sides. But the three sides of what? The method `area` actually calls `perimeter` (on what?) and uses the semi-perimeter in conjunction with the three sides (again, of what) to calculate the total area using Heron's Formula.

The code in Figure 20.3 is only the class definition. We aren't creating any objects with this code. Let's create a `Triangle` object and use it! The code in Figure 20.4 is a portion of a `main` function, where an object of `Triangle` type, `t1`, is declared. This object is allocated in the stack frame for `main`, with enough storage for the data members of `Triangle`, in this case the three doubles for the lengths of the three sides. Notice that what gets allocated in memory for the C++ class version of `Triangle` is exactly the same as what would get allocated for the C structure from Figure 20.2. From this perspective, nothing has changed.

```
1  int main(void)
2  {
3     Triangle t1;
4     double p1;
5     :
6     :
7     p1 = t1.perimeter();
8     :
9  }
```

Figure 20.4 A method call in C++.

Line 7 has a call to the method `perimeter` on the object `Triangle t1`. This C++ code is translated into lower-level assembly code that looks like a typical function call in C. Parameters are pushed, stack frames are built, `JSR` is used to transfer control, `RET` is used to return back, etc.

Unlike a typical C function, though, `perimeter` can only be called in relation to a `Triangle` object, as is the case in line 7. Calling `perimeter` or `area` directly will result in a compilation error. The idea is that a method is a special kind of function that is directly tied to a particular class type.

The method `perimeter` requires a reference to a `Triangle` object in order to calculate its result. If the method `perimeter` is just a regular subroutine at the assembly level, and it takes no parameters, how will it know which `Triangle` to operate on? For instance, how will the triangle t1 be operated upon when `area` is called on line 7? To make this happen, on a C++ method call, a reference to the particular object in question is passed implicitly to the method as an extra parameter. In C++, this implicit reference is called the `this` pointer, and we can use it within any method.

So the method call is translated like a standard function call in C, with the exception that we'll push the `this` pointer first onto the stack frame, as an implicit argument to the method. This happens for any and all method calls in C++. Figure 20.5 provides the LC-3 code that corresponds to line 7 above and also a portion of the method `perimeter`. In the method `perimeter`, all expressions that access member elements of the `Triangle` class are actually based on the `this` pointer.

20.3.2 Access Specifiers

One of the benefits of classes in C++ is that they encourage the use of abstraction in the software development process. Abstraction has been a major theme throughout this textbook because it is foundational to the architecture of digital systems. Abstraction enables us to hide the complexity at one level behind a well-defined interface in order to create building blocks for the next level. For example, interconnected MOS transistors form a NOT gate, which is a more composable abstraction for building an adder. In C, this abstraction primarily happens around the use of functions: a function provides some complex functionality, but it is accessed by a simple interface (parameters, etc.). The details of the function can be hidden once the functionality is understood.

C++ extends and formalizes this idea through the use of classes. Classes have well-defined interfaces, and those interfaces are specified by *access specifiers* in the class definition. We can declare member elements to be accessible from the outside (i.e., on the interface) or as purely internal (i.e., part of the implementation). We can hide the internals and focus on the interface if we want to use a particular class in our code.

There are a variety of access specifiers in C++. Of these, we'll focus on two: public and private. Private members can only be accessed within the class, and public members can be accessed from within and also from the outside.

Notice in the class definition for `Triangle` in Figure 20.3, on line 5, we use the `public` specifier. The following two member elements `area` and `perimeter`

```
 1  perimeter
 2          ADD R6, R6, #-1  ; Allocate spot for the return value
 3
 4          ADD R6, R6, #-1  ;
 5          STR R7, R6, #0   ; Push R7 (Return address)
 6
 7          ADD R6, R6, #-1  ;
 8          STR R5, R6, #0   ; Push R5 (Caller's frame pointer)
 9
10          ADD R5, R6, #-1  ; Set frame pointer for perimeter
11
12          LDR R0, R5, #-4  ; Load this pointer
13          AND R1, R1, #0   ; Zero out R1
14          LDR R2, R0, #0   ; Load this->sideA
15          ADD R1, R1, R2   ; Add to perimeter
16          LDR R2, R0, #1   ; Load this->sideB
17          ADD R1, R1, R2   ; Add to perimeter
18          LDR R2, R0, #2   ; Load this->sideC
19          ADD R1, R1, R2   ; Add to perimeter
20
21          STR R1, R5, #3   ; Write it in return value slot
22          ADD R6, R5, #1   ; Pop local variables
23
24          LDR R5, R6, #0   ; Pop the frame pointer
25          ADD R6, R6, #1   ;
26
27          LDR R7, R6, #0   ; Pop the return address
28          ADD R6, R6, #1   ;
29          RET
30          ...
31  main
32          ...
33          ADD R0, R5, #0   ; Load address of t1 into R0
34          ADD R6, R6, #-1  ;
35          STR R0, R6, #0   ; Push &t1
36          JSR perimeter
37
38          LDR R0, R6, #0   ; Load the return value from perimeter
39          STR R0, R5, #1   ; p1 = t1.perimeter();
40          ADD R6, R6, #2   ; Pop return value and argument
41          ...
```

Figure 20.5   The LC-3 code corresponding to the method call in Figure 20.4.

are both public, and they can be accessed from anywhere in our code that the Triangle class is visible. These two members happen to be methods, but we could have chosen any member element to be public. In contrast, because we didn't provide a specifier for sideA, sideB, sideC, the default is that they are private. These three member elements can only be accessed by methods within the Triangle class definition. In other words, they are hidden. With this, we can create an object of `Triangle` type, and the only access we get is via the `area` and `perimeter` methods. They are on the interface. Everything else is an implementation detail and is abstracted away.

It's important to note that the public and private designations are only compile-time constructs and are very similar in concept to scope. They do not affect the behavior of the code during run time. If we access a private member from a non-class method (i.e., outside of the `Triangle::` naming scope), the compiler will generate an error, as is the case with line 7 in the following example. In line 7, we are accessing `sideA`, which is a `private` member.

```
1   int main(void)
2   {
3      Triangle t1;
4      double a1;
5      :
6      :
7      t1.sideA = 10;    // This will generate an error
8      a1 = t1.area();
9      :
10  }
```

20.3.3 Constructors

If the code in the preceding example doesn't work, then how do we initialize a `Triangle` object? By defining a *constructor* method. A constructor is a special method within a class that is called *implicitly* whenever an object of that class is created. For example, if we declare an object as local within a function, an instance of that object is allocated on the stack whenever the function is called, and also a constructor method for that class is called.

We can define a constructor using the following syntax, shown as an extension to the class `Triangle`. A method with the same name as the class name is considered the class constructor, and by definition it never returns anything. On line 6, we declare the method `Triangle`, and on line 11, we define it. This method takes three `double` values and initializes the three sides of a newly allocated `Triangle`.

```
1   class Triangle {
2      double sideA;
3      double sideB;
4      double sideC;
5   public:
6      Triangle(double a, double b, double c);
7      double area();
8      double perimeter();
9   };
10
11  Triangle::Triangle(double a, double b, double c)
12  {
13     sideA = a;
14     sideB = b;
15     sideC = c;
16  }
```

A class's constructor is called whenever an object is allocated on the run-time stack, or on the heap via dynamic allocation. In the following code, we create two objects. The first `t1` is declared as a local variable and allocated on the run-time stack. As part of the allocation of this object, the constructor `Triangle::Triangle` is called implicitly.

On line 2, we declare a pointer variable `t2` to a `Triangle`, which initially has no real storage that it is pointing to. On line 4, we allocate storage to it using `new` (see Section 20.2.6). Once the memory is allocated by `new`, the constructor for the class for `Triangle` is called, which then initializes the values of the internal members based on the supplied arguments.

```
1   Triangle t1(2.0, 2.0, 3.0);
2   Triangle *t2;
3
4   t2 = new Triangle(4.2, 7.8, 10.2);
```

The idea of a constructor, which is an implicitly invoked function, is a departure from how things work in C. C's philosophy is to give a large degree of control to the programmer, keeping the source code relatively close to the hardware. C++ relaxes that language philosophy slightly, with the goal of creating a more extensible structure to our code.

There is enough flexibility in C++ to put whatever code we like into a class's constructor method. In practice, constructors are used to initialize the internal logic/data of a class. C++ also provides support for a corresponding method for when an object is destroyed (when it is deallocated via `delete`, or when the block in which it was declared exits) called a destructor, but that is a topic for later.

The complete code of our running example is provided in Figure 20.6.

20.3.4 Advanced Topics

We are just scratching the surface on classes in C++. What we have covered thus far in this chapter are the core class concepts that are used most frequently in C++. Before we end this topic, let's touch upon the next realm: inheritance.

Programmer-defined types tend to multiply as a coding project matures and grows. New classes get added that are similar to but slightly different from existing ones, the net result of which is replicated code in the form of similar class definitions, methods, and functions. To address this tendency toward code bloating, the C++ class system provides the notion of inheritance, where classes can be derived from other classes.

Let's consider our `Triangle` example. As we extend our code, we may discover that we'd like to handle quadrilaterals and pentagons, too, and form data structures that contain a mixture of polygons. It's easy to imagine how these classes could contain a lot of common code, with differences in how specific methods are implemented. Each would have different `area` and `perimeter` methods, for example.

For this particular situation, we could create a base class for a `Polygon`, from which `Triangle`, `Quadrilateral`, and `Pentagon` are derived. Common functionality and data members could be placed in the `Polygon` class. The `Triangle`,

```
1  #include <iostream>
2  #include <math.h>
3
4  class Triangle {
5      double sideA;
6      double sideB;
7      double sideC;
8    public:
9      Triangle(double a, double b, double c);
10     double area();
11     double perimeter();
12 };
13
14 Triangle::Triangle(double a, double b, double c)
15 {
16     sideA = a;
17     sideB = b;
18     sideC = c;
19 }
20
21 double Triangle::perimeter()
22 {
23     return sideA + sideB + sideC;
24 }
25
26 double Triangle::area()
27 {
28     double s = perimeter() / 2;
29
30     // Heron's Formula
31     return sqrt(s*(s - sideA)*(s - sideB)*(s - sideC));
32 }
33
34 int main (void)
35 {
36     Triangle t1(2.0, 2.0, 3.0);
37     Triangle *t2;
38
39     t2 = new Triangle(4.2, 7.8, 10.2);
40
41
42     std::cout << "Tri 1 Area " << t1.area() << std::endl;
43     std::cout << "Tri 1 Perim " << t1.perimeter() << std::endl;
44
45     std::cout << "Tri 2 Area " << t2->area() << std::endl;
46     std::cout << "Tri 2 Perim " << t2->perimeter() << std::endl;
47 }
```

Figure 20.6   A complete example involving the Triangle class in C++.

Quadrilateral, and Pentagon class would inherit these common portions, requiring only the portions that are unique to be provided as additional code.

This type of hierarchy enables programmers to develop a rich set of class structures where code from one can be leveraged to create another similar but distinct derived class. This concept in general is called inheritance. This avoids the soupy, redundant mess in C where each structure requires its own definition and support functions no matter how similar it might be to another existing structure.

As with other parts of the class system within C++, inheritance is a compile-time construct. The programmer can build sophisticated classes that are derived from other classes. The compiler weaves them together as a combination of data elements and methods. At the end of the day, it's all a memory layout for the data elements and a JSR to the appropriate method whenever an invocation is made.

20.4 Containers and Templates

When creating a new type (struct in C or class in C++), we are quickly tempted to take into account the data structure that we want to store that type. Consider for instance our Triangle type from the previous section. If we want to store objects of this type as a linked data structure of triangles, we need to include additional data members in the class definition to store the links. If we later decide to change to a different structure, then the class or structure itself must be reworked. If both data structures are required in different places in the code, then we're faced with the prospect of replicating our type definition, creating redundant code.

The idea of containers enables us to separate the data type from the data structure. We can define the type independently from the structure containing that type. Because the two have different design constraints, enabling the programmer to think about them separately is a big benefit to programming productivity. In general, the idea of a flexible data structure code that can hold an object of any type is a *container*.

C++ provides containers via the C++ Standard Template Library, or STL. Of all the features of C++, many experienced programmers consider the STL one of the most useful. The STL provides a set of prebuilt container classes that enable programmers to quickly build data structures such as dynamic, resizable arrays, linked lists, stacks, queues, and maps without having to write much code.

20.4.1 Vectors

We will focus our attention on one particular STL container: the vector. Its utility will be readily apparent to us having dealt with the limitations of arrays in C. The vector container enables us to create arrays that can be easily resized—that is, dynamic arrays. We've explored this concept previously (Section 19.4.1), and we know that C's support for dynamic arrays is fairly minimal. Fully implementing a dynamic array in C requires additional code for each new type of dynamic array we create, which increases the burden on the programmer.

```
1   int main (void)
2   {
3       std::vector<Triangle> triVector(10);   // Vector of 10 tris
4       std::vector<int> intVector(20);        // Vector of 20 ints
5
6       for (int i = 1; i < intVector.size(); i++)
7           intVector[i] = intVector[i - 1] + i;
8
9       // Print out vector
10      std::cout << "intVector[" << intVector.size() << "] = ";
11          for (int i = 1; i < intVector.size(); i++)
12              std::cout << intVector[i] << " ";
13      std::cout << std::endl;
14
15      // Let's resize!
16      intVector.resize(50);
17
18      // Print out vector
19      std::cout << "intVector[" << intVector.size() << "] = ";
20      for (int i = 1; i < intVector.size(); i++)
21          std::cout << intVector[i] << " ";
22      std::cout << std::endl;
23  }
```

Figure 20.7   An example using the C++ vector container from the C++ Standard Template Library.

The C++ vector container provides a rich set of array functionality, and it can be used with any type we create in our code. Figure 20.7 contains a simple piece of code that declares two vectors, one of `Triangle` type, and one of `int` type. Notice the new syntax for declaration on lines 3 and 4. The `std::` prefix indicates that we are using the namespace of the Standard Library, and the `vector` indicates the container class we are using.

There are a number of prebuilt methods provided by the STL `vector` container class. Table 20.1 provides a brief description of some of them. So with very little code, we can create a data structure with a fairly sophisticated set of prebuilt functionality. All we do is provide the type!

Table 20.1	Some Useful Methods of the C++ STL Vector Class	
	Description	Example
size()	Return size of vector	intVector.size();
resize()	Change size of vector	intVector.resize(newSize);
insert()	Add elements to vector	intVector.insert(where, value);
erase()	Remove elements from vector	intVector.erase(where);
push_back()	Add new element at end of vector	intVector.push_back(value);
front()	Access first element	y = intVector.front() - 1;
back()	Access last element	intVector.back() = 3;

20.4.2 Templates

The container classes in C++ are built using templates. A template is a programming language feature that enables us to write code that is type independent. For example, we can rewrite the code for swap from our initial C++ code in Figure 20.1 using templates and create only a single version of swap, thereby reducing code replication. The template version causes the compiler to stamp out multiple versions, differing based on the template's parameters. Creating templates is an advanced C++ concept that is done rather infrequently in day-to-day programming. On the other hand, using containers from the Standard Template Library is quite common.

Given our bottom-up perspective, it's worth noting again that templates, containers, and the STL are all compiler-oriented features. The C++ source code is enabling the compiler to combine and mix-and-match things to ultimately generate the same type of assembly code that we generated with C. In other words, many of these features can be directly translated from C++ code to equivalent C code.

20.5 Summary

We conclude this chapter by summarizing some of the key C++ concepts we covered.

- **C to C++.** C++ was originally created to enable C programmers to be more productive. The underlying execution framework of C++ is the same as C. Ultimately C++ code, like C code, is translated to machine code that is an assemblage of functions that are called starting with main, with a run-time stack for passing arguments and return values, allocation of local values, and a heap for dynamic allocation. C++ provides some syntactic updates to C, with simpler formatted I/O, function overloading, and pass by reference.

- **Classes.** The natural evolution of structures in C are classes in C++. Classes extend the idea of structures to include member elements that are functions (methods) with strict interfaces and with inheritance. Also, classes have some implicit behavior, such as invocation of a class's constructor method whenever an object of that class is allocated.

- **Containers.** Separating data type from data structure is a powerful concept. Containers in C++ enable us to accomplish this, and the C++ Standard Library (STL) provides a number of useful data structures that can "contain" the classes we build in our code. We explored the vector container class, which can be used to implement arrays. Vectors are richer than standard C arrays with their prebuilt functionality for resizing, inserting elements, removing elements, and so on. Container classes in C are built using C++ templates.

Exercises

20.1   Modify the code in Figure 20.1 to include a swap function for boolean types.

20.2   Modify the code in Figure 20.1 to include a swap function for swapping two pointers to integers (`int *`).

20.3   In the following code, which version of `funcA` will get called?

```
int funcA(int a);                    // Version A
int funcA(int a, int b);             // Version B
int funcA(int a, int b, int c);      // Version C

// Which funcA will get called here?
x = funcA(x, y, 2);
```

20.4   Draw the memory layout of the objects/variables allocated on lines 3 and 4 of Figure 20.4.

20.5   Add a method to the Triangle class to calculate the height of the `Triangle`, given that `sideC` is the base.

20.6   What is the net result if we remove line 8 from the code in Figure 20.6?

20.7   Convert the aircraft tracking code from Chapter 19, Figures 19.5, 19.8, and 19.9 to the equivalent version in C++ using classes instead of structures.

20.8   Write C++ code that contains a quadrilateral class similar to the `Triangle` class of Figure 20.6 with methods for area and perimeter.

20.9   Extend your code from Exercise 20.8 to include pentagons.

20.10   Write the LC-3 code that accomplishes the local object allocation on line 36 in Figure 20.6

20.11   Consider the following code:

```
int main (void)
{
    std::vector<int> intVector(0);        // Vector of 0 ints

    intVector.pushback(1);
    intVector.pushback(2);
    intVector.pushback(3);
}
```

     a. Draw the memory layout of `intVector` when the code is finished.
     b. Where in memory is `intVector` allocated?

20.12   Write a C++ program that uses vectors to read in a character string from the keyboard and print it out in reverse.

20.13 Write a C++ program using vectors that reads in a line of text from the keyboard and removes all the redundant words from it. For example, if the input line is:

This line of this line text text contains no copied copied no words.

Then the output would be:

This line of text contains no copied words.

APPENDIX

The LC-3 ISA

A.1 Overview

The instruction set architecture (ISA) of the LC-3 is defined as follows:

Memory address space 16 bits, corresponding to 2^{16} locations, each
containing one word (16 bits). Addresses are numbered from 0 (i.e., x0000)
to 65,535 (i.e., xFFFF). Addresses are used to identify memory locations
and memory-mapped I/O device registers. Certain regions of memory are
reserved for special uses, as described in Figure A.1.
Locations x0000 to x2FFF comprise privileged memory and are only
accessible if the process is executing in Supervisor mode (PSR[15]=0).
Locations x3000 to xFDFF comprise memory available to User mode and

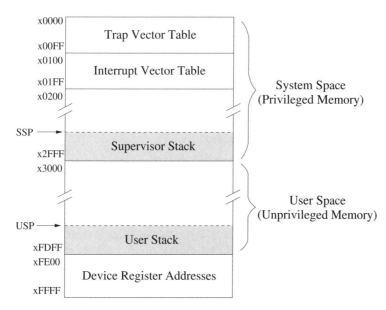

Figure A.1   Memory map of the LC-3

Table A.1   Device Register Assignments

Address	I/O Register Name	I/O Register Function
xFE00	Keyboard status register (KBSR)	The ready bit (bit [15]) indicates if the keyboard has received a new character.
xFE02	Keyboard data register (KBDR)	Bits [7:0] contain the last character typed on the keyboard.
xFE04	Display status register (DSR)	The ready bit (bit [15]) indicates if the display device is ready to receive another character to print on the screen.
xFE06	Display data register (DDR)	A character written in bits [7:0] will be displayed on the screen.
xFFFC	Processor Status Register (PSR)	Contains privilege mode, priority level and condition codes of the currently executing process.
xFFFE	Machine control register (MCR)	Bit [15] is the clock enable bit. When cleared, instruction processing stops.

data. Addresses xFE00 to xFFFF specify input and output device registers and special internal processor registers that are also only accessible if the process is executing in Supervisor mode (PSR[15]=0). For purposes of controlling access to these device registers, their addresses are also considered part of privileged memory.

Memory-mapped I/O Input and output are handled by load/store (LD/ST, LDI/STI, LDR/STR) instructions using memory addresses from xFE00 to xFFFF to designate each device register. Table A.1 lists the input and output device registers and internal processor registers that have been specified for the LC-3 thus far, along with their corresponding assigned addresses from the memory address space.

Bit numbering Bits of all quantities are numbered, from right to left, starting with bit 0. The leftmost bit of the contents of a memory location is bit 15.

Instructions Instructions are 16 bits wide. Bits [15:12] specify the opcode (operation to be performed); bits [11:0] provide further information that is needed to execute the instruction. The specific operation of each LC-3 instruction is described in Section A.2.

Illegal opcode exception Bits [15:12] = 1101 has not been specified. If an instruction contains 1101 in bits [15:12], an illegal opcode exception occurs. Section A.3 explains what happens.

Program counter A 16-bit register containing the address of the next instruction to be processed.

General purpose registers Eight 16-bit registers, numbered from 000 to 111 (R0 to R7).

Condition codes Three 1-bit registers: N (negative), Z (zero), and P (positive). Load instructions (LD, LDI, and LDR) and operate instructions (ADD, AND, and NOT) each load a result into one of the eight general purpose registers. The condition codes are set, based on whether that result, taken as a 16-bit 2's complement integer, is negative ($N = 1; Z, P = 0$), zero ($Z = 1; N, P = 0$), or positive ($P = 1; N, Z = 0$). All other LC-3 instructions leave the condition codes unchanged.

Interrupt processing I/O devices have the capability of interrupting the processor. Section A.3 describes the mechanism.

Priority level The LC-3 supports eight levels of priority. Priority level 7 (PL7) is the highest, PL0 is the lowest. The priority level of the currently executing process is specified in bits PSR[10:8].

Processor status register (PSR) A 16-bit register, containing status information about the currently executing process. Seven bits of the PSR have been defined thus far. PSR[15] specifies the privilege mode of the executing process. PSR[10:8] specifies the priority level of the currently executing process. PSR[2:0] contains the condition codes. PSR[2] is N, PSR[1] is Z, and PSR[0] is P.

Supervisor mode The LC-3 specifies two modes of operation, Supervisor mode (privileged) and User mode (unprivileged). Interrupt service routines and trap service routines (i.e., system calls) execute in Supervisor mode. The privilege mode is specified by PSR[15]. PSR[15]=0 indicates Supervisor mode; PSR[15]=1 indicates User mode.

Privilege mode exception The RTI instruction executes in Supervisor mode. If the processor attempts to execute the RTI instruction while in User mode, a privilege mode exception occurs. Section A.3 explains what happens.

Access Control Violation (ACV) exception An ACV exception occurs if a process attempts to access a location in privileged memory (either a location in system space or a device register having an address from xFE00 to xFFFF) while operating in User mode. Section A.3 explains what happens.

Supervisor stack A region of memory in system space accessible via the Supervisor Stack Pointer (SSP). When PSR[15]=0, the stack pointer (R6) is SSP. When the processor is operating in User mode (PSR[15]=1), the SSP is stored in Saved_SSP.

User stack A region of memory in user space accessible via the User Stack Pointer (USP). When PSR[15]=1, the stack pointer (R6) is USP. When the processor is operating in Supervisor mode (PSR[15]=0), the USP is stored in Saved_USP.

A.2 The Instruction Set

The LC-3 supports a rich, but lean, instruction set. Each 16-bit instruction consists of an opcode (bits[15:12]) plus 12 additional bits to specify the other information that is needed to carry out that instruction. Figure A.2 summarizes the 15 different opcodes in the LC-3 and the specification of the remaining bits of each instruction. The 16th four-bit opcode is not specified but is reserved for future use.

In the following pages, the instructions will be described in greater detail. Table A.2 is provided to help you to understand those descriptions. For each instruction, we show the assembly language representation, the format of the 16-bit instruction, the operation of the instruction, an English-language description of its operation, and one or more examples of the instruction. Where relevant, additional notes about the instruction are also provided.

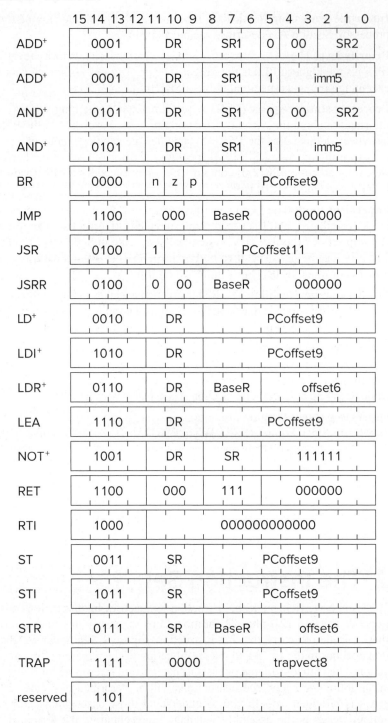

Figure A.2   Format of the entire LC-3 instruction set. *Note:* + indicates instructions that modify condition codes

Table A.2	Notational Conventions

Notation	Meaning
xNumber	The number in hexadecimal notation. Example: xF2A1
#Number	The number in decimal notation. Example #793
bNumber	The number in binary. Example b10011
A[l:r]	The field delimited by bit [l] on the left and bit [r] on the right, of the datum A. For example, if PC contains 0011001100111111, then PC[15:9] is 0011001. PC[2:2] is 1. If l and r are the same bit number, we generally write PC[2].
BaseR	Base Register; one of R0..R7, specified by bits [8:6] of the instruction, used in conjunction with a six-bit offset to compute Base+offset addresses (LDR and STR), or alone to identify the target address of a control instruction (JMP and JSRR).
DR	Destination Register; one of R0..R7, which specifies the register a result should be written to.
imm5	A five-bit immediate value (bits [4:0] of an instruction), when used as a literal (immediate) value. Taken as a five-bit, 2's complement integer, it is sign-extended to 16 bits before it is used. Range: −16..15.
INTV	An eight-bit value, supplied along with an interrupting event; used to determine the starting address of an interrupt service routine. The eight bits form an offset from the starting address of the interrupt vector table. The corresponding location in the interrupt vector table contains the starting address of the corresponding interrupt service routine. Range 0..255.
LABEL	An assembly language construct that identifies a location symbolically (i.e., by means of a name, rather than its 16-bit address).
mem[address]	Denotes the contents of memory at the given address.
offset6	A six-bit signed 2's complement integer (bits [5:0] of an instruction), used with the Base+offset addressing mode. Bits [5:0] are sign-extended to 16 bits and then added to the Base Register to form an address. Range: −32..31.
PC	Program Counter; 16-bit register that contains the memory address of the next instruction to be fetched. For example, if the instruction at address A is not a control instruction, during its execution, the PC contains the address A + 1, indicating that the next instruction to be executed is contained in memory location A + 1.
PCoffset9	A nine-bit signed 2's complement integer (bits [8:0] of an instruction), used with the PC+offset addressing mode. Bits [8:0] are sign-extended to 16 bits and then added to the incremented PC to form an address. Range −256..255.
PCoffset11	An eleven-bit signed 2's complement integer (bits [10:0] of an instruction), used with the JSR opcode to compute the target address of a subroutine call. Bits [10:0] are sign-extended to 16 bits and then added to the incremented PC to form the target address. Range −1024..1023.
PSR	Processor Status Register. A 16-bit register that contains status information of the process that is executing. Seven bits of the PSR have been specified. PSR[15] = privilege mode. PSR[10:8] = Priority Level. PSR[2:0] contains the condition codes. PSR[2] = N, PSR[1] = Z, PSR[0] = P.
Saved_SSP	Saved Supervisor Stack Pointer. The processor is executing in either Supervisor mode or User mode. If in User mode, R6, the stack pointer, is the User Stack Pointer (USP). The Supervisor Stack Pointer (SSP) is stored in Saved_SSP. When the privilege mode changes from User mode to Supervisor mode, Saved_USP is loaded with R6 and R6 is loaded with Saved_SSP.
Saved_USP	Saved User Stack Pointer. The User Stack Pointer is stored in Saved_USP when the processor is executing in Supervisor mode. See Saved_SSP.
setcc()	Indicates that condition codes N, Z, and P are set based on the value of the result written to DR.
SEXT(A)	Sign-extend A. The most significant bit of A is replicated as many times as necessary to extend A to 16 bits. For example, if A = 110000, then SEXT(A) = 1111 1111 1111 0000.
SP	The current stack pointer. R6 is the current stack pointer. There are two stacks, one for each privilege mode. SP is SSP if PSR[15] = 0; SP is USP if PSR[15] = 1.
SR, SR1, SR2	Source register; one of R0..R7 that specifies the register from which a source operand is obtained.
SSP	The Supervisor Stack Pointer.
trapvect8	An eight-bit value (bits [7:0] of an instruction), used with the TRAP opcode to determine the starting address of a trap service routine. Bits [7:0] are taken as an unsigned integer and zero-extended to 16 bits. This is the address of the memory location containing the starting address of the corresponding service routine. Range 0..255.
USP	The User Stack Pointer.
ZEXT(A)	Zero-extend A. Zeros are appended to the leftmost bit of A to extend it to 16 bits. For example, if A = 110000, then ZEXT(A) = 0000 0000 0011 0000.

ADD   Addition

Assembler Formats

    ADD   DR, SR1, SR2
    ADD   DR, SR1, imm5

Encodings

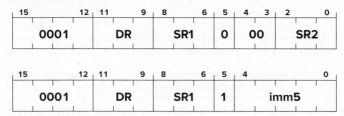

Operation

```
if (bit[5] == 0)
     DR = SR1 + SR2;
else
     DR = SR1 + SEXT(imm5);
setcc();
```

Description

If bit [5] is 0, the second source operand is obtained from SR2. If bit [5] is 1, the second source operand is obtained by sign-extending the imm5 field to 16 bits. In both cases, the second source operand is added to the contents of SR1 and the result stored in DR. The condition codes are set, based on whether the result is negative, zero, or positive.

Examples

    ADD   R2, R3, R4   ; R2 ← R3 + R4
    ADD   R2, R3, #7   ; R2 ← R3 + 7

AND   Bit-wise Logical AND

Assembler Formats

```
AND   DR, SR1, SR2
AND   DR, SR1, imm5
```

Encodings

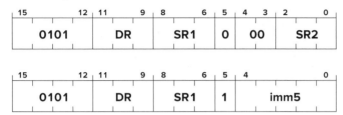

Operation

```
if (bit[5] == 0)
     DR=SR1 AND SR2;
else
     DR=SR1 AND SEXT(imm5);
setcc();
```

Description

If bit [5] is 0, the second source operand is obtained from SR2. If bit [5] is 1, the second source operand is obtained by sign-extending the imm5 field to 16 bits. In either case, the second source operand and the contents of SR1 are bit-wise ANDed and the result stored in DR. The condition codes are set, based on whether the binary value produced, taken as a 2's complement integer, is negative, zero, or positive.

Examples

```
AND   R2, R3, R4     ;R2 ← R3 AND R4
AND   R2, R3, #7     ;R2 ← R3 AND 7
```

BR

Conditional Branch

Assembler Formats

BRn	LABEL	BRzp	LABEL
BRz	LABEL	BRnp	LABEL
BRp	LABEL	BRnz	LABEL
BR[†]	LABEL	BRnzp	LABEL

Encoding

15 12	11	10	9	8 0
0000	n	z	p	PCoffset9

Operation

```
if ((n AND N) OR (z AND Z) OR (p AND P))
   PC = PC‡ + SEXT(PCoffset9);
```

Description

The condition codes specified by bits [11:9] are tested. If bit [11] is 1, N is tested; if bit [11] is 0, N is not tested. If bit [10] is 1, Z is tested, etc. If any of the condition codes tested is 1, the program branches to the memory location specified by adding the sign-extended PCoffset9 field to the incremented PC.

Examples

BRzp	LOOP	; Branch to LOOP if the last result was zero or positive.
BR[†]	NEXT	; Unconditionally branch to NEXT.

[†]The assembly language opcode BR is interpreted the same as BRnzp; that is, always branch to the target address.

[‡]This is the incremented PC.

JMP

RET

Jump

Return from Subroutine

Assembler Formats

    JMP   BaseR
    RET

Encoding

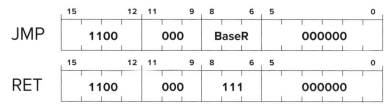

Operation

```
PC = BaseR;
```

Description

The program unconditionally jumps to the location specified by the contents of the base register. Bits [8:6] identify the base register.

Examples

    JMP   R2   ; PC ← R2
    RET   ; PC ← R7

Note

The RET instruction is a special case of the JMP instruction, normally used in the return from a subroutine. The PC is loaded with the contents of R7, which contains the linkage back to the instruction following the subroutine call instruction.

JSR
JSRR

Jump to Subroutine

Assembler Formats

    JSR   LABEL
    JSRR   BaseR

Encoding

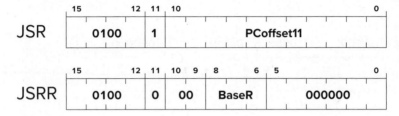

Operation

```
TEMP = PC;†
if (bit[11] == 0)
    PC = BaseR;
else
    PC = PC† + SEXT(PCoffset11);
R7 = TEMP;
```

Description

First, the incremented PC is saved in a temporary location. Then the PC is loaded with the address of the first instruction of the subroutine, which will cause an unconditional jump to that address after the current instruction completes execution. The address of the subroutine is obtained from the base register (if bit [11] is 0), or the address is computed by sign-extending bits [10:0] and adding this value to the incremented PC (if bit [11] is 1). Finally, R7 is loaded with the value stored in the temporary location. This is the linkage back to the calling routine.

Examples

    JSR   QUEUE ; Put the address of the instruction following JSR into R7;
                  ; Jump to QUEUE.
    JSRR R3   ; Put the address of the instruction following JSRR into R7;
                  ; Jump to the address contained in R3.

---

†This is the incremented PC.

LD

Load

Assembler Format

LD   DR, LABEL

Encoding

15 12	11 9	8 0
0010	DR	PCoffset9

Operation

```
if (computed address is in privileged memory AND PSR[15] == 1)
   Initiate ACV exception;
else
   DR = mem[PC† + SEXT(PCoffset9)];
   setcc();
```

Description

An address is computed by sign-extending bits [8:0] to 16 bits and adding this value to the incremented PC. If the address is to privileged memory and PSR[15]=1, initiate ACV exception. If not, the contents of memory at this address is loaded into DR. The condition codes are set, based on whether the value loaded is negative, zero, or positive.

Example

LD   R4, VALUE   ; R4 ← mem[VALUE]

---

†This is the incremented PC.

LDI

Load Indirect

Assembler Format

    LDI DR, LABEL

Encoding

15 12	11 9	8 0
1010	DR	PCoffset9

Operation

```
if (either computed address is in privileged memory AND PSR[15] == 1)
    Initiate ACV exception;
else
    DR = mem[mem[PC† + SEXT(PCoffset9)]];
    setcc();
```

Description

An address is computed by sign-extending bits [8:0] to 16 bits and adding this value to the incremented PC. What is stored in memory at this address is the address of the data to be loaded into DR. If either address is to privileged memory and PSR[15]=1, initiate ACV exception. If not, the data is loaded and the condition codes are set, based on whether the value loaded is negative, zero, or positive.

Example

    LDI R4, ONEMORE   ; R4 ← mem[mem[ONEMORE]]

---

†This is the incremented PC.

LDR

Load Base+offset

Assembler Format

LDR   DR, BaseR, offset6

Encoding

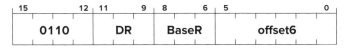

15 12	11 9	8 6	5 0
0110	DR	BaseR	offset6

Operation

```
If (computed address is in privileged memory AND PSR[15] == 1)
   Initiate ACV exception;
else
   DR = mem[BaseR + SEXT(offset6)];
   setcc();
```

Description

An address is computed by sign-extending bits [5:0] to 16 bits and adding this value to the contents of the register specified by bits [8:6]. If the computed address is to privileged memory and PSR[15]=1, initiate ACV exception. If not, the contents of memory at this address is loaded into DR. The condition codes are set, based on whether the value loaded is negative, zero, or positive.

Example

LDR   R4, R2, #−5   ; R4 ← mem[R2 − 5]

LEA   Load Effective Address

Assembler Format

    LEA   DR, LABEL

Encoding

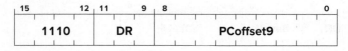

Operation

DR = PC† + SEXT(PCoffset9);

Description

An address is computed by sign-extending bits [8:0] to 16 bits and adding this value to the incremented PC. This address is loaded into DR.‡

Example

    LEA   R4, TARGET   ; R4 ← address of TARGET.

---

†This is the incremented PC.

‡The LEA instruction computes an address but does NOT read memory. Instead, the address itself is loaded into DR.

NOT

Bit-Wise Complement

Assembler Format

    NOT   DR, SR

Encoding

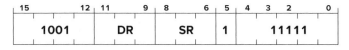

15 12	11 9	8 6	5	4 3 2 0
1001	DR	SR	1	11111

Operation

```
DR = NOT(SR);
setcc();
```

Description

The bit-wise complement of the contents of SR is stored in DR. The condition codes are set, based on whether the binary value produced, taken as a 2's complement integer, is negative, zero, or positive.

Example

    NOT   R4, R2   ; R4 ← NOT(R2)

RET   Return from Subroutine

Assembler Format

RET[†]

Encoding

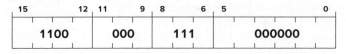

Operation

PC = R7;

Description

The PC is loaded with the value in R7. Its normal use is to cause a return from a previous JSR(R) instruction.

Example

RET   ; PC ← R7

[†]The RET instruction is a specific encoding of the JMP instruction. See also JMP.

RTI

Return from Trap or Interrupt

Assembler Format

    RTI

Encoding

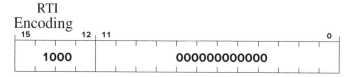

15 12	11 0
1000	**000000000000**

Operation

```
if (PSR[15] == 1)
    Initiate a privilege mode exception;
else
    PC=mem[R6]; R6 is the SSP, PC is restored
    R6=R6+1;
    TEMP=mem[R6];
    R6=R6+1; system stack completes POP before saved PSR is restored
    PSR=TEMP; PSR is restored
    if (PSR[15] == 1)
        Saved_SSP=R6 and R6=Saved_USP;
```

Description

If the processor is running in User mode, a privilege mode exception occurs. If in Supervisor mode, the top two elements on the system stack are popped and loaded into PC, PSR. After PSR is restored, if the processor is running in User mode, the SSP is saved in Saved_SSP, and R6 is loaded with Saved_USP.

Example

    RTI   ; PC, PSR ← top two values popped off stack.

Note

RTI is the last instruction in both interrupt and trap service routines and returns control to the program that was running. In both cases, the relevant service routine is initiated by first pushing the PSR and PC of the program that is running onto the system stack. Then the starting address of the appropriate service routine is loaded into the PC, and the service routine executes with supervisor privilege. The last instruction in the service routine is RTI, which returns control to the interrupted program by popping two values off the supervisor stack to restore the PC and PSR. In the case of an interrupt, the PC is restored to the address of the instruction that was about to be processed when the interrupt was initiated. In the case of an exception, the PC is restored to either the address of the instruction that caused the exception or the address of the following instruction, depending on whether the instruction that caused the exception is to be re-executed. In the case of a TRAP service routine, the PC is restored to the instruction following the TRAP instruction in the calling routine. In the case of an interrupt or TRAP, the PSR is restored to the value it had when the interrupt was initiated. In the case of an exception, the PSR is restored to the value it had when the exception occurred or to some modified value, depending on the exception. See also Section A.3.

ST

Store

Assembler Format

    ST   SR, LABEL

Encoding

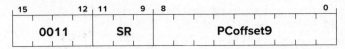

Operation

```
if (computed address is in privileged memory AND PSR[15] == 1)
   Initiate ACV exception;
else
   mem[PC† + SEXT(PCoffset9)] = SR;
```

Description

If the computed address is to privileged memory and PSR[15]=1, initiate ACV exception. If not, the contents of the register specified by SR is stored in the memory location whose address is computed by sign-extending bits [8:0] to 16 bits and adding this value to the incremented PC.

Example

    ST   R4, HERE   ; mem[HERE] ← R4

---

†This is the incremented PC.

STI   Store Indirect

Assembler Format

STI   SR, LABEL

Encoding

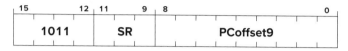

Operation

```
if (either computed address is in privileged memory AND PSR[15] == 1)
    Initiate ACV exception;
else
    mem[mem[PC† + SEXT(PCoffset9)]] = SR;
```

Description

If either computed address is to privileged memory and PSR[15]=1, initiate ACV exception. If not, the contents of the register specified by SR is stored in the memory location whose address is obtained as follows: Bits [8:0] are sign-extended to 16 bits and added to the incremented PC. What is in memory at this address is the address of the location to which the data in SR is stored.

Example

STI   R4, NOT_HERE   ; mem[mem[NOT_HERE]] ← R4

---

†This is the incremented PC.

STR

Store Base+offset

Assembler Format

STR   SR, BaseR, offset6

Encoding

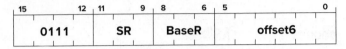

15	12	11	9	8	6	5	0
0111		SR		BaseR		offset6	

Operation

```
if (computed address is in privileged memory AND PSR[15] == 1)
    Initiate ACV exception;
else
    mem[BaseR + SEXT(offset6)] = SR;
```

Description

If the computed address is to privileged memory and PSR[15]=1, initiate ACV exception. If not, the contents of the register specified by SR is stored in the memory location whose address is computed by sign-extending bits [5:0] to 16 bits and adding this value to the contents of the register specified by bits [8:6].

Example

STR   R4, R2, #5   ; mem[R2+5] ← R4

TRAP System Call

Assembler Format

> TRAP   trapvector8

Encoding

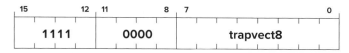

Operation

```
TEMP=PSR;
if (PSR[15] == 1)
    Saved_USP=R6 and R6=Saved_SSP;
    PSR[15]=0;
Push TEMP,PC† on the system stack
PC=mem[ZEXT(trapvect8)];
```

Description

If the the program is executing in User mode, the User Stack Pointer must be saved and the System Stack Pointer loaded. Then the PSR and PC are pushed on the system stack. (This enables a return to the instruction physically following the TRAP instruction in the original program after the last instruction in the service routine (RTI) has completed execution.) Then the PC is loaded with the starting address of the system call specified by trapvector8. The starting address is contained in the memory location whose address is obtained by zero-extending trapvector8 to 16 bits.

Example

> TRAP   x23   ; Directs the operating system to execute the **IN** system call.
>   ; The starting address of this system call is contained in
>   ; memory location x0023.

Note:

Memory locations x0000 through x00FF, 256 in all, are available to contain starting addresses for system calls specified by their corresponding trap vectors. This region of memory is called the Trap Vector Table. Table A.3 describes the functions performed by the service routines corresponding to trap vectors x20 to x25.

---

†This is the incremented PC.

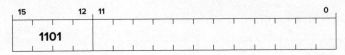

Assembler Format

Encoding

15	12	11												0
1101														

Operation

Initiate an illegal opcode exception.

Description

If an illegal opcode is encountered, an illegal opcode exception occurs.

Note:

The opcode 1101 has been reserved for future use. It is currently not defined. If the instruction currently executing has bits [15:12] = 1101, an illegal opcode exception occurs. Section A.3 describes what happens.

Table A.3	Trap Service Routines	
Trap Vector	**Assembler Name**	**Description**
x20	GETC	Read a single character from the keyboard. The character is not echoed onto the console. Its ASCII code is copied into R0. The high eight bits of R0 are cleared.
x21	OUT	Write a character in R0[7:0] to the console display.
x22	PUTS	Write a string of ASCII characters to the console display. The characters are contained in consecutive memory locations, one character per memory location, starting with the address specified in R0. Writing terminates with the occurrence of x0000 in a memory location.
x23	IN	Print a prompt on the screen and read a single character from the keyboard. The character is echoed onto the console monitor, and its ASCII code is copied into R0. The high eight bits of R0 are cleared.
x24	PUTSP	Write a string of ASCII characters to the console. The characters are contained in consecutive memory locations, two characters per memory location, starting with the address specified in R0. The ASCII code contained in bits [7:0] of a memory location is written to the console first. Then the ASCII code contained in bits [15:8] of that memory location is written to the console. (A character string consisting of an odd number of characters to be written will have x00 in bits [15:8] of the memory location containing the last character to be written.) Writing terminates with the occurrence of x0000 in a memory location.
x25	HALT	Halt execution and print a message on the console.

A.3 Interrupt and Exception Processing

As has been discussed in detail in Chapter 9, events external to the program that is running can interrupt the processor. A common example of an external event is interrupt-driven I/O. It is also the case that the processor can be interrupted by exceptional events that occur while the program is running that are caused by the program itself. An example of such an "internal" event is the presence of an unused opcode in the computer program that is running.

Associated with each event that can interrupt the processor is an eight-bit vector that provides an entry point into a 256-entry *interrupt vector table*. The starting address of the interrupt vector table is x0100. That is, the interrupt vector table occupies memory locations x0100 to x01FF. Each entry in the interrupt vector table contains the starting address of the service routine that handles the needs of the corresponding event. These service routines execute in Supervisor mode.

Half (128) of these entries, locations x0100 to x017F, provide the starting addresses of routines that service events caused by the running program itself. These routines are called *exception service routines* because they handle exceptional events, that is, events that prevent the program from executing normally. The other half of the entries, locations x0180 to x01FF, provide the starting addresses of routines that service events that are external to the program that is running, such as requests from I/O devices. These routines are called *interrupt service routines*.

A.3.1 Interrupts

At this time, an LC-3 computer system provides only one I/O device that can interrupt the processor. That device is the keyboard. It interrupts at priority level PL4 and supplies the interrupt vector x80.

An I/O device can interrupt the processor if it wants service, if its interrupt enable (IE) bit is set, and if the priority of its request is greater than the priority of any other event that wants to interrupt and greater than the priority of the program that is running.

Assume a program is running at a priority level less than 4, and someone strikes a key on the keyboard. If the IE bit of the KBSR is 1, the currently executing program is interrupted at the end of the current instruction cycle. The interrupt service routine is **initiated** as follows:

1. The PSR of the interrupted process is saved in TEMP.
2. The processor sets the privilege mode to Supervisor mode (PSR[15]=0).
3. The processor sets the priority level to PL4, the priority level of the interrupting device (PSR[10:8]=100).
4. If the interrupted process is in User mode, R6 is saved in Saved_USP and R6 is loaded with the Supervisor Stack Pointer (SSP).
5. TEMP and the PC of the interrupted process are pushed onto the supervisor stack.
6. The keyboard supplies its eight-bit interrupt vector, in this case x80.
7. The processor expands that vector to x0180, the corresponding 16-bit address in the interrupt vector table.
8. The PC is loaded with the contents of memory location x0180, the address of the first instruction in the keyboard interrupt service routine.

The processor then begins execution of the interrupt service routine.

The last instruction executed in an interrupt service routine is RTI. The top two elements of the supervisor stack are popped and loaded into the PC and PSR registers. R6 is loaded with the appropriate stack pointer, depending on the new value of PSR[15]. Processing then continues where the interrupted program left off.

A.3.2 Exceptions

At this time, the LC-3 ISA specifies three exception conditions: privilege mode violation, illegal opcode, and access control violation (ACV). The privilege mode violation occurs if the processor attempts to execute the RTI instruction while running in User mode. The illegal opcode exception occurs if the processor attempts to execute an instruction having the unused opcode (bits [15:12] = 1101). The ACV exception occurs if the processor attempts to access privileged memory (i.e., a memory location in system space or a device register having an address from xFE00 to xFFFF while running in User mode).

Exceptions are handled as soon as they are detected. They are *initiated* very much like interrupts are initiated, that is:

1. The PSR of the process causing the exception is saved in TEMP.

2. The processor sets the privilege mode to Supervisor mode (PSR[15]=0).

3. If the process causing the exception is in User mode, R6 is saved in Saved_USP and R6 is loaded with the SSP.

4. TEMP and the PC of the process causing the exception are pushed onto the supervisor stack.

5. The exception supplies its eight-bit vector. In the case of the privilege mode violation, that vector is x00. In the case of the illegal opcode, that vector is x01. In the case of the ACV exception, that vector is x02.

6. The processor expands that vector to x0100, x0101, or x0102, the corresponding 16-bit address in the interrupt vector table.

7. The PC is loaded with the contents of memory location x0100, x0101, or x0102, the address of the first instruction in the corresponding exception service routine.

The processor then begins execution of the exception service routine.

The details of the exception service routine depend on the exception and the way in which the operating system wishes to handle that exception.

In many cases, the exception service routine can correct any problem caused by the exceptional event and then continue processing the original program. In those cases, the last instruction in the exception service routine is RTI, which pops the top two elements from the supervisor stack and loads them into the PC and PSR registers. The program then resumes execution with the problem corrected.

In some cases, the cause of the exceptional event is sufficiently catastrophic that the exception service routine removes the program from further processing.

Another difference between the handling of interrupts and the handling of exceptions is the priority level of the processor during the execution of the service routine. In the case of exceptions, we normally do not change the priority level when we service the exception. The priority level of a program is the urgency with which it needs to be executed. In the case of the exceptions specified by the LC-3 ISA, the urgency of a program is not changed by the fact that a privilege mode violation occurred or there was an illegal opcode in the program or the program attempted to access privileged memory while it was in User mode.

B

From LC-3 to x86

As you know, the ISA of the LC-3 explicitly specifies the interface between what the LC-3 machine language programmer or LC-3 compilers produce and what a microarchitecture of the LC-3 can accept and process. Among those things specified are the address space and addressability of memory, the number and size of the registers, the format of the instructions, the opcodes, the data types that are the encodings used to represent information, and the addressing modes that are available for determining the location of an operand.

The ISA of the microprocessor in your PC also specifies an interface between the compilers and the microarchitecture. However, in the case of the PC, the ISA is not the LC-3. Rather it is the x86. Intel introduced the first member of this ISA in 1979. It was called the 8086, and the "normal" size of the addresses and data elements it processed was 16 bits, the same size as the LC-3. Today, the typical size of addresses and data is 64 bits. With special vector extensions, instructions can operate on vectors that can be of size 128, 256, and 512 bits. Because there are a lot of old programs and data expressed in 32 bits, the x86 is able to process instructions in what we call 64-bit mode or 32-bit mode. That is, in 32-bit mode, the x86 restricts itself to a 32-bit address space and 32-bit elements.

From the 8086 to the present time, Intel has continued implementations of the x86 ISA, among them the 386 (in 1985), 486 (in 1989), Pentium (in 1992), Pentium Pro (in 1995), Pentium II (in 1997), Pentium IV (in 2001), "1st Generation Core i7-9xx Series," codename Nehalem (in 2008), "4th Generation Core i7-4xxx Series," codename Haswell (in 2013), and "8th Generation Core i7-8086K," codename: Coffee Lake (in 2018).

The ISA of the x86 is much more complicated than that of the LC-3. There are more opcodes, more data types, more addressing modes, a more complicated memory structure, and a more complicated encoding of instructions into 0s and 1s. However, fundamentally, they have the same basic ingredients.

You have spent a good deal of time understanding computing within the context of the LC-3. Some may feel that it would be good to learn about a *real* ISA. One way to do that would be to have some company such as Intel mass-produce LC-3 microprocessors, some other company like Dell put them in their PCs, and a third company such as Microsoft compile Windows NT into the ISA of the LC-3. An easier way to introduce you to a *real* ISA is by way of this appendix.

We present here elements of the x86, a very complicated ISA. We do so in spite of its complexity because it is one of the most pervasive of all ISAs available in the marketplace.

We make no attempt to provide a complete specification of the x86 ISA. That would require a whole book by itself, and to appreciate it, a deeper understanding of operating systems, compilers, and computer systems than we think is reasonable at this point in your education. If one wants a complete treatment, we recommend the *Intel Architecture Software Developer's Manual*. In this appendix, we restrict ourselves to some of the characteristics that are relevant to application programs. Our intent is to give you a sense of the richness of the x86 ISA. We introduce these characteristics within the context of the LC-3 ISA, which at this point you are very familiar with.

B.1 LC-3 Features and Corresponding x86 Features

B.1.1 Instruction Set

An instruction set is made up of instructions, each of which has an opcode and zero or more operands. The number of operands depends on how many are needed by the corresponding opcode. Each operand is a data element and is encoded according to its data type. The location of an operand is determined by evaluating its addressing mode.

The LC-3 instruction set contains one data type, 15 opcodes, and three addressing modes: PC-relative (LD, ST), indirect (LDI, STI), and register-plus-offset (LDR, STR). The x86 instruction set has more than a dozen data types, more than a thousand opcodes, and more than two dozen addressing modes (depending on how you count).

B.1.1.1 Data Types

Recall that a data type is a representation of information such that the ISA provides opcodes that operate on information that is encoded in that representation.

The LC-3 supports only one data type, 16-bit 2's-complement integers. This is not enough for efficient processing in the real world. Scientific applications need numbers that are represented by the floating point data type. Multimedia applications require information that is represented by a different data type. Commercial applications written years ago, but still active today, require an additional data type, referred to as *packed decimal*. Some applications require a greater range of values and a greater precision of each value than other applications.

As a result of all these requirements, the x86 is designed with instructions that operate on (for example) 8-bit integers, 16-bit integers, and 32-bit integers, 32-bit and 64-bit floating point numbers, 64-bit, 128-bit, 256-bit, and 512-bit multimedia values. Figure B.1 shows some of the data types present in the x86 ISA.

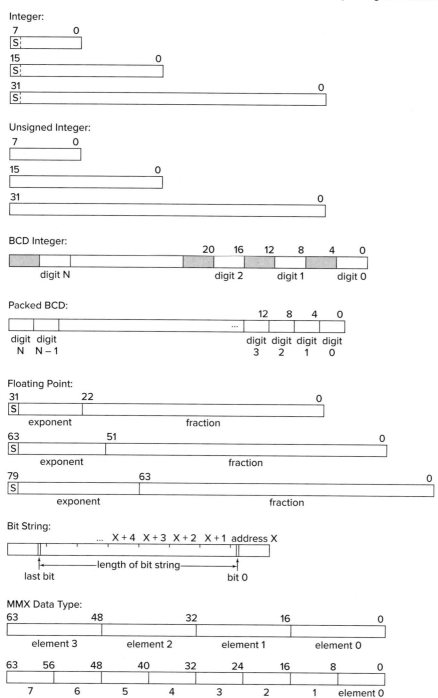

Figure B.1 A sample of x86 data types.

B.1.1.2 Opcodes

The LC-3 comprises 15 opcodes; the x86 instruction set comprises more than a thousand. Recall that the three basic instruction types are operates, data movement, and control. Operates process information, data movement opcodes move information from one place to another (including input and output), and control opcodes change the flow of the instruction stream.

In addition, we should add a fourth category to handle functions that must be performed in the real world because a user program runs in the context of an operating system that is controlling a computer system, rather than in isolation. These instructions deal with computer security, system management, hardware performance monitoring, and various other issues that are beyond what the typical application program pays attention to. We will ignore those instructions in this appendix, but please realize that they do exist, and you will see them as your studies progress. Here we will concentrate on the three basic instruction types: operates, data movement, and control.

Operates   The LC-3 has three operate instructions: ADD, AND, and NOT. The ADD opcode is the only LC-3 opcode that performs arithmetic. If one wants to subtract, one obtains the negative of an operand and then adds. If one wants to multiply, one can write a program with a loop to ADD a number some specified number of times. However, this is too time-consuming for a real microprocessor. So the x86 has separate SUB and MUL, as well as DIV, INC (increment), DEC (decrement), and ADC (add with carry), to name a few.

A useful feature of an ISA is to extend the size of the integers on which it can operate. To do this, one writes a program to operate on such *long* integers. The ADC opcode, which adds two operands plus the carry from the previous add, is a very useful opcode for extending the size of integers.

In addition, the x86 has, for each data type, its own set of opcodes to operate on that data type. For example, multimedia instructions (collectively called the MMX instructions) often require *saturating arithmetic*, which is very different from the arithmetic we are used to. PADDS is an opcode that adds two operands with saturating arithmetic.

Saturating arithmetic can be explained as follows: Suppose we represent the degree of grayness of an element in a figure with a digit from 0 to 9, where 0 is white and 9 is black. Suppose we want to add some darkness to an existing value of grayness of that figure. An element could start out with a grayness value of 7, and we might wish to add a 5 worth of darkness to it. In normal arithmetic, $7 + 5$ is 2 (with a carry), which is lighter than either 7 or 5. Something is wrong! With saturating arithmetic, when we reach 9, we stay there—we do not generate a carry. So, for example, $7 + 5 = 9$ and $9 + n = 9$. Saturating arithmetic is a different kind of arithmetic, and the x86 has opcodes (MMX instructions) that perform this type of arithmetic.

Scientific applications require opcodes that operate on values represented in the floating point data type. FADD, FMUL, FSIN, FSQRT are examples of floating point opcodes in the x86 ISA.

The AND and NOT opcodes are the only LC-3 opcodes that perform logical functions. One can construct any logical expression using these two opcodes.

Table B.1	Operate Instructions, x86 ISA
Instruction	**Explanation**
ADC x, y	x, y, and the carry retained from the last relevant operation (in CF) are added and the result stored in x.
MUL x	The value in EAX is multiplied by x, and the result is stored in the 64-bit register formed by EDX, EAX.
SAR x	x is right shifted (arithmetic shift) n bits, and the result is stored in x. The value of n can be 1, an immediate operand, or the count in the CL register.
XOR x, y	A bit-wise exclusive-OR is performed on x, y and the result is stored in x.
DAA	After adding two packed decimal numbers, AL contains two BCD values, which may be incorrect due to propagation of the carry bit after 15, rather than after 9. DAA corrects the two BCD digits in AL.
FSIN	The top of the stack (call it x) is popped. The sin(x) is computed and pushed onto the stack.
FADD	The top two elements on the stack are popped, added, and their result pushed onto the stack.
PANDN x, y	A bit-wise AND-NOT operation is performed on MMX values x, y, and the result is stored in x.
PADDS x, y	Saturating addition is performed on packed MMX values x, y, and the result is stored in x.

However, as is the case with arithmetic, this also is too time-consuming. The x86 has in addition separate OR, XOR, AND-NOT, and separate logical operators for different data types.

Furthermore, the x86 has a number of other operate instructions that set and clear registers, convert a value from one data type to another, shift or rotate the bits of a data element, and so on. Table B.1 lists some of the operate opcodes in the x86 instruction set.

Data Movement The LC-3 has six data movement opcodes: LD, LDI, ST, STI, LDR, and STR. They all copy information between memory (and memory-mapped device registers) and the eight general purpose registers, R0 to R7.

Although the x86 does not have LDI or STI opcodes, it does have the other four, and in addition to these, many other data movement opcodes. XCHG can swap the contents of two locations. PUSHA pushes all eight general purpose registers onto the stack. IN and OUT move data between input and output ports and the processor. CMOVcc copies a value from one location to another only if a previously computed condition is true. Table B.2 lists some of the data movement opcodes in the x86 instruction set.

Control The LC-3 has five control opcodes: BR, JSR/JSRR, JMP, RTI, and TRAP. x86 has all these and more. Table B.3 lists some of the control opcodes in the x86 instruction set.

B.1.1.3 Two Address vs. Three Address

The LC-3 is a three-address ISA. This description reflects the number of operands explicitly specified by the ADD instruction. An add operation requires two source operands (the numbers to be added) and one destination operand to store

Table B.2	Data Movement Instructions, x86 ISA
Instruction	**Explanation**
MOV x, y	The value stored in y is copied into x.
XCHG x, y	The values stored in x and y are swapped.
PUSHA	All the registers are pushed onto the top of the stack.
PUSH	Push a register onto the top of the stack.
POP	Pop a register from the top of the stack.
MOVS	The element in the DS segment pointed to by ESI is copied into the location in the ES segment pointed to by EDI. After the copy has been performed, ESI and EDI are both incremented.
REP MOVS	Perform the MOVS. Then decrement ECX. Repeat this instruction until ECX = 0. (This allows a string to be copied in a single instruction, after initializing ECX.)
LODS	The element in the DS segment pointed to by ESI is loaded into EAX, and ESI is incremented or decremented, according to the value of the DF flag.
INS	Data from the I/O port specified by the DX register is loaded into the EAX register (or AX or AL, if the size of the data is 16 bits or 8 bits, respectively).
CMOVZ x, y	If ZF = 1, the value stored in y is copied into x. If ZF = 0, the instruction acts like a no-op.
LEA x, y	The address y is stored in x. This is very much like the LC-3 instruction of the same name.

Table B.3	Control Instructions, x86 ISA
Instruction	**Explanation**
Jcond x	Branch based on the condition specified by cond. If cond is true, the IP is loaded with x.
JMP x	IP is loaded with the address x. This is very much like the LC-3 instruction of the same name.
CALL x	The IP is pushed onto the stack, and a new IP is loaded with x.
RET	The stack is popped, and the value popped is loaded into IP.
LOOP x	ECX is decremented. If ECX is not 0 and ZF = 1, the IP is loaded with x.
INT n	The value n is an index into a table of descriptors that specify operating system service routines. The end result of this instruction is that IP is loaded with the starting result of the corresponding service routine. This is very much like the TRAP instruction in the LC-3.

the result. In the LC-3, all three must be specified explicitly, hence the name three-address ISA.

Even if the same location is to be used both for one of the sources and for the destination, the three addresses are all specified. For example, the LC-3

```
ADD R1,R1,R2
```

identifies R1 as both a source and the destination.

The x86 is mostly (except for special instructions defined as SSE or AVX instructions) a two-address ISA. Since the add operation needs three operands, the location of one of the sources must also be used to store the result. For example, the corresponding 16-bit ADD instruction in the x86 ISA would be

```
ADD AX,BX
```

where AX and BX are names of two of the x86's eight 16-bit general purpose registers. AX and BX are the sources, and AX is the destination.

Since the result of the operate is stored in the location that originally contained one of the sources, that source operand is no longer available after that instruction is executed. If that source operand is needed later, it must be saved before the operate instruction is executed.

B.1.1.4 Memory Operands

A major difference between the LC-3 instruction set and the x86 instruction set is the restriction on where operate instructions can get their operands. An LC-3 operate instruction must obtain its source operands from registers and write the result to a destination register. An x86 instruction, on the other hand, can obtain one of its sources from memory and/or write its result to memory. In other words, the x86 can read a value from memory, operate on that value, and store the result in memory all in a single instruction. The LC-3 cannot.

The LC-3 program requires a separate load instruction to read the value from memory before operating on it, and a separate store instruction to write the result in memory after the operate instruction. An ISA, like the LC-3, that has this restriction is called a *load-store* ISA. The x86 is not a load-store ISA.

B.1.2 Memory

The LC-3 memory consists of 2^{16} locations, each containing 16 bits of information. We say the LC-3 has a 16-bit address space, since one can uniquely address its 2^{16} locations with 16 bits of address. We say the LC-3 has an addressability of 16 bits, since each memory location contains 16 bits of information.

The x86 memory has a 64-bit address space and an addressability of eight bits. Since one byte contains eight bits, we say the x86 memory is byte addressable. Since each location contains only eight bits, four contiguous locations in memory are needed to store a 32-bit data element, say locations X, X+1, X+2, and X+3. We designate X as the address of the 32-bit data element. In actuality, X only contains bits [7:0], X+1 contains bits [15:8], X+2 contains bits [23:16], and X+3 contains bits [31:24] of the 32-bit value.

One can determine an LC-3 memory location by simply obtaining its address from the instruction, using one of the three addressing modes available in the instruction set. An x86 instruction has available to it more than two dozen addressing modes that it can use to specify the memory address of an operand. We examine the addressing modes of an x86 instruction in Section B.2.

In addition to the larger number of addressing modes, the x86 contains a mechanism called *segmentation* that provides a measure of protection against unwanted accesses to particular memory addresses. The address produced by an instruction's addressing mode, rather than being an address in its own right, is used as an address within a segment of memory. Access to that memory location must take into account the segment register that controls access to that segment. The details of how the protection mechanism works will have to wait for later in your studies.

However, Figure B.2 does show how an address is calculated for the register+offset addressing mode, both for the LC-3 and for the x86, with

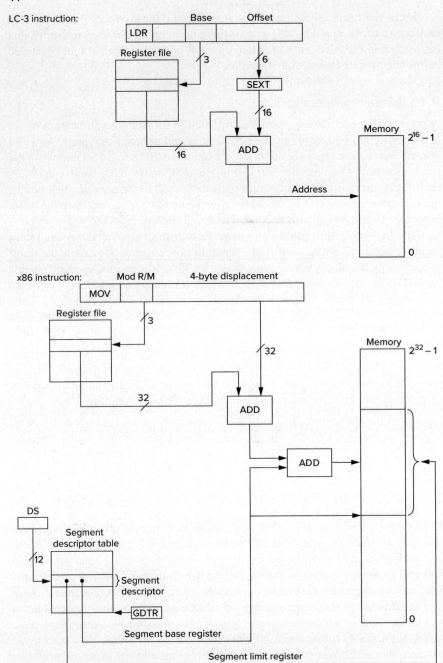

Figure B.2   **Register+offset addressing mode in LC-3 and x86 ISAs.**

segmentation. In both cases, the opcode is to move data from memory to a general purpose register. The LC-3 uses the LDR instruction. The x86 uses the MOV instruction. In the case of the x86, the address calculated is in the DS segment, which is accessed via the DS register. That access is done through a 16-bit *selector*, which indexes into a segment descriptor table, yielding the *segment descriptor* for that segment. The segment descriptor contains a *segment base register*, a *segment limit register*, and protection information. The memory address obtained from the addressing mode of the instruction is added to the segment base register to provide the actual memory address, as shown in Figure B.2.

B.1.3 Internal State

The internal state of the LC-3 consists of eight 16-bit general purpose registers, R0 to R7, a 16-bit PC, and a 16-bit PSR that specifies the privilege mode, priority, and three 1-bit condition codes (N, Z, and P). The user-visible internal state of the x86 consists of 64-bit application-visible registers, a 64-bit Instruction pointer (RIP), a 64-bit RFLAGS register, and the 16-bit segment registers.

B.1.3.1 Application-Visible Registers

Figure B.3 shows some of the application-visible registers in the x86 ISA.

In 64-bit mode, the x86 has 16 general purpose registers: RAX, RBX, RCX, RDX, RSP, RBP, RCI, RDI, and R8 through R15. Each register contains 64 bits reflecting the normal size of operands. In 32-bit mode, there are eight general purpose registers: EAX, EBX, ECX, EDX, ESP, EBP, ECI, and EDI, which use bits [31:0] of the corresponding 64-bit registers. Also, since some x86 opcodes process 16-bit and 8-bit operands, x86 also specifies 16-bit registers AX, BX, ...DI by using bits [15:0] of the 64-bit registers, and 8 bit registers AL, BL, CL, and DL using bits [7:0] and AH, BH, CH, and DH, using bits [15:8] of the corresponding 64-bit registers. The x86 also provides 128-bit, 256-bit, and 512-bit SIMD registers for operands needed by SSE and AVX operations. They are, respectively, XMM0 to XMM31 for 128 bits, YMM0 to YMM31 for 256 bits, and ZMM0 to ZMM31 for 512 bits.

B.1.3.2 System Registers

The LC-3 has two system-level registers—the PC and the PSR. The user-visible x86 has these and more. Figure B.4 shows some of the user-visible system registers in the x86 ISA.

Instruction Pointer (RIP) The x86 has the equivalent of the LC-3's 16-bit program counter. The x86 calls it an *instruction pointer* (RIP). Since the address space of the x86 is 64 bits, the RIP is a 64-bit register. In 32-bit mode, since the address space is only 32 bits, the instruction pointer (EIP) uses bits [31:0] of the RIP.

RFLAGS Register Corresponding to the LC-3's N, Z, and P condition codes, the x86 has a one-bit SF (sign flag) register and a one-bit ZF (zero flag) register.

General Purpose Registers

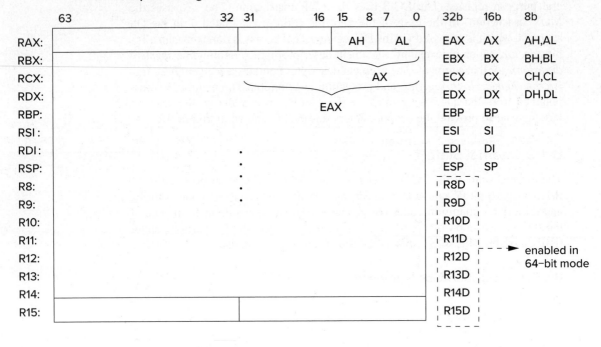

SIMD Registers

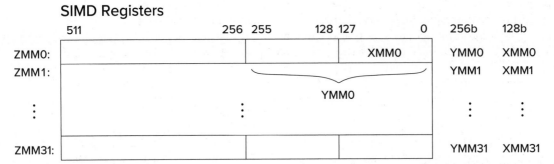

Figure B.3   Some x86 application-visible registers.

SF and ZF provide exactly the same functions as the N and Z condition codes of the LC-3. The x86 does not have the equivalent of the LC-3's P condition code. In fact, the P condition code is redundant since, if one knows the values of N and Z, one knows the value of P. We included it in the LC-3 ISA anyway, for the convenience of assembly language programmers and compiler writers.

The x86 collects other one-bit values in addition to N and Z. These one-bit values (which Intel calls *flags*, rather than condition codes) are contained in a 64-bit register called RFLAGS. Several of these flags are discussed in the following paragraphs.

Instruction Pointer

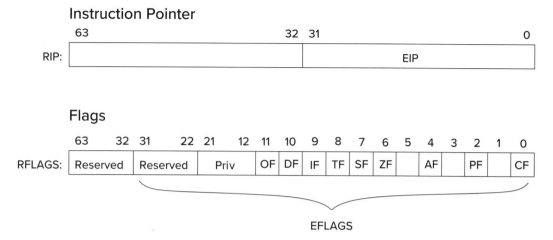

Flags

	63	32	31	22	21	12	11	10	9	8	7	6	5	4	3	2	1	0
RFLAGS:	Reserved		Reserved		Priv		OF	DF	IF	TF	SF	ZF		AF		PF		CF

EFLAGS

Segment Registers (Selectors)

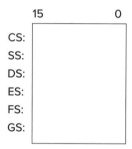

Figure B.4   x86 system registers.

The CF flag stores the *carry* produced by the last relevant operation that generated a carry. As we said earlier, together with the ADC instruction, CF facilitates the generation of procedures, which allows the software to deal with larger integers than the ISA supports.

The OF flag stores an *overflow* condition if the last relevant operate generated a value too large to store in the available number of bits. Recall the discussion of overflow in Section 2.5.3.

The DF flag indicates the *direction* in which string operations are to process strings. If DF = 0, the string is processed from the high-address byte down (i.e., the pointer keeping track of the element in the string to be processed next is decremented). If DF = 1, the string is processed from the low-address byte up (i.e., the string pointer is incremented).

Two flags not usually considered as part of the application state are the IF (*interrupt*) flag and the TF (*trap*) flag. Both correspond to functions with which you are familiar.

IF is very similar to the IE (interrupt enable) bit in the KBSR and DSR, discussed in Section 9.4.4.1. If IF = 1, the processor can recognize external interrupts (like keyboard input, for example). If IF = 0, these external interrupts have no effect on the process that is executing. We say the interrupts are *disabled*.

TF is very similar to *single-step mode* in the LC-3 simulator, only in this case it is part of the ISA. If TF = 1, the processor halts after every instruction so the state of the system can be examined. If TF = 0, the processor ignores the trap and processes the next instruction.

Segment Registers   When operating in its preferred operating mode (called *protected mode*), the address calculated by the instruction is really an offset from the starting address of a segment, which is specified by some *segment base register*. These segment base registers are part of their corresponding *data segment descriptors*, which are contained in the *segment descriptor table*. At each instant of time, six of these segments are active. They are called, respectively, the *code segment* (CS), *stack segment* (SS), and four data segments (DS, ES, FS, and GS). The six active segments are accessed via their corresponding segment registers shown in Figure B.4, which contain pointers to their respective segment descriptors.

B.2 The Format and Specification of x86 Instructions

The LC-3 instruction is a 16-bit instruction. Bits [15:12] always contain the opcode; the remaining 12 bits of each instruction are used to support the needs of that opcode.

The length of an x86 instruction is not fixed. It consists of from 1 to 16 bytes, depending on the needs of that instruction. A lot of information can be packed into one x86 instruction. Figure B.5 shows the format of an x86 instruction.

The two key parts of an x86 instruction are the opcode and, where necessary, the ModR/M byte. The opcode specifies the operation the instruction is to perform. The ModR/M byte specifies how to obtain the operands it needs. The ModR/M byte specifies one of several addressing modes, some of which require

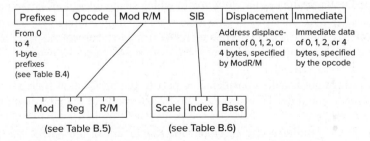

Figure B.5   Format of the x86 instruction.

the use of registers, a one-, two-, or four-byte displacement, and additional register information contained in an optional SIB byte.

Some opcodes specify an immediate operand and also specify the number of bytes of the instruction that is used to store that immediate information. The immediate value (when one is specified) is the last element of the instruction.

Finally, instructions assume certain default information with respect to the semantics of an instruction, such as address size, operand size, segment to be used, and so forth. The instruction can change this default information by means of one or more prefixes, which are located at the beginning of the instruction.

Each part of an x86 instruction is discussed in more detail in Sections B.2.1 through B.2.6.

B.2.1 Prefix

Prefixes provide additional information that is used to process the instruction. There are four classes of prefix information, and each instruction can have from zero to four prefixes, depending on its needs. Fundamentally, a prefix overrides the usual interpretation of the instruction.

The four classes of prefixes are lock and repeat, segment override, operand override, and address override. Table B.4 describes the four types of prefixes.

B.2.2 Opcode

The opcode byte (or bytes—some opcodes are represented by two bytes) specifies a large amount of information about the needs of that instruction. The

Table B.4	Prefixes, x86 ISA
Repeat/Lock	
xF0 (LOCK)	This prefix guarantees that the instruction will have exclusive use of all shared memory until the instruction completes execution.
xF2, xF3 (REP/REPE/REPNE)	This prefix allows the instruction (a string instruction) to be repeated some specified number of times. The iteration count is specified by ECX. The instruction is also terminated on the occurrence of a specified value of ZF.
Segment override	
x2E(CS), x36(SS), x3E(DS), x26(ES), x64(FS), x65(GS)	This prefix causes the memory access to use the specified segment, instead of the default segment expected for that instruction.
Operand size override	
x66	This prefix changes the size of data expected for this instruction. That is, instructions expecting 32-bit data elements use 16-bit data elements. And instructions expecting 16-bit data elements use 32-bit data elements.
Address size override	
x67	This prefix changes the size of operand addresses expected for this instruction. That is, instructions expecting a 32-bit address use 16-bit addresses. And instructions expecting 16-bit addresses use 32-bit addresses.

opcode byte (or bytes) specifies, among other things, the operation to be performed, whether the operands are to be obtained from memory or from registers, the size of the operands, whether or not one of the source operands is an immediate value in the instruction, and if so, the size of that immediate operand.

Some opcodes are formed by combining the opcode byte with bits [5:3] of the ModR/M byte, if those bits are not needed to provide addressing mode information. The ModR/M byte is described in Section B.2.3.

B.2.3 ModR/M Byte

The ModR/M byte, shown in Figure B.5, provides addressing mode information for two operands, when necessary, or for one operand, if that is all that is needed. If two operands are needed, one may be in memory, the other in a register, or both may be in registers. If one operand is needed, it can be either in a register or in memory. The ModR/M byte supports all cases.

The ModR/M byte is essentially partitioned into two parts. The first part consists of bits [7:6] and bits [2:0]. The second part consists of bits [5:3].

If bits [7:6] = 00, 01, or 10, the first part specifies the addressing mode of a memory operand, and the combined five bits ([7:6],[2:0]) identify which addressing mode. If bits [7:6] = 11, there is no memory operand, and bits [2:0] specify a register operand.

Bits [5:3] specify the register number of the other operand, if the opcode requires two operands. If the opcode only requires one operand, bits [5:3] are available as a subopcode to differentiate among eight opcodes that have the same opcode byte, as described in Section B.2.2.

Table B.5 lists some of the interpretations of the ModR/M byte.

Table B.5			ModR/M Byte, Examples		
Mod	Reg	R/M	Eff. Addr.	Reg	Explanation
00	011	000	[EAX]	EBX	EAX contains the address of the memory operand. EBX contains the register operand.
01	010	000	disp8[EAX]	EDX	Memory operand's address is obtained by adding the displacement byte of the instruction to the contents of EAX. EDX contains the register operand.
10	000	100	disp32[-][-]	EAX	Memory operand's address is obtained by adding the four-byte (32 bits) displacement of the instruction to an address that will need an SIB byte to compute. (See Section B.2.4 for the discussion of the SIB byte.) EAX contains the register operand.
11	001	110	ESI	ECX	If the opcode requires two operands, both are in registers (ESI and ECX). If the opcode requires one operand, it is in ESI. In that case, 001 (bits [5:3]) are part of the opcode.

Table B.6			SIB Byte, Examples	
Scale	Index	Base	Computation	Explanation
00	011	000	EBX+EAX	The contents of EBX is added to the contents of EAX. The result is added to whatever is specified by the ModR/M byte.
01	000	001	2 · EAX + ECX	The contents of EAX is multiplied by 2, and the result is added to the contents of ECX. This is then added to whatever is specified by the ModR/M byte.
01	100	001	ECX	The contents of ECX is added to whatever is specified by the ModR/M byte.
10	110	010	4 · ESI + EDX	The contents of ESI is multiplied by 4, and the result is added to the contents of EDX. This is then added to whatever is specified by the ModR/M byte.

B.2.4 SIB Byte

If the opcode specifies that an operand is to be obtained from memory, the ModR/M byte specifies the addressing mode, that is, the information that is needed to calculate the address of that operand. Some addressing modes require more information than can be specified by the ModR/M byte alone. Those operand specifiers (see the third entry in Table B.5) specify the inclusion of an SIB byte in the instruction. The SIB byte (for scaled-index-base), shown in Figure B.5, provides scaling information and identifies which register is to be used as an index register and/or which register is to be used as a base register. Taken together, the SIB byte computes scale · index + base, where base and/or index can be zero, and scale can be 1. Table B.6 lists some of the interpretations of the SIB byte.

B.2.5 Displacement

If the ModR/M byte specifies that the address calculation requires a displacement, the displacement (one, two, or four bytes) is contained in the instruction. The opcode and/or ModR/M byte specifies the size of the displacement.

Figure B.6 shows the addressing mode calculation for the source operand if the instruction is as shown. The prefix x26 overrides the segment register and specifies using the ES segment. The ModR/M and SIB bytes specify that a four-byte displacement is to be added to the base register ECX + the index register EBX after its contents is multiplied by 4.

B.2.6 Immediate

Recall that the LC-3 allowed small immediate values to be present in the instruction, by setting inst[5:5] to 1. The x86 also permits immediate values in the instruction. As stated previously, if the opcode specifies that a source operand is an immediate value in the instruction, it also specifies the number of bytes of the instruction used to represent the operand. That is, an immediate can be

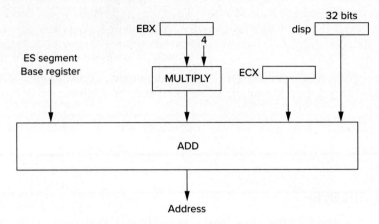

Prefix	Opcode	ModR/M	SIB	Displacement
00100110	00000011	10000100	10011001	32 bits
ES	ADD	disp32 [][]	EBX * 4 + ECX	
override	r32, m32	EAX		

Figure B.6   Addressing mode calculation for Base+ScaledIndes+disp32.

represented in the instruction with one, two, or four bytes. Since the opcode also specifies the size of the operand, immediate values that can be stored in fewer bytes than the operand size are first sign-extended to their full size before being operated on. Figure B.7 shows the use of the immediate operand with the ADD instruction. The example is ADD EAX, $5. We are very familiar with the corresponding LC-3 instruction: ADD R0,R0,#5.

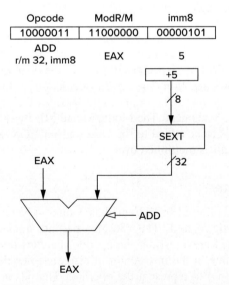

Opcode	ModR/M	imm8
10000011	11000000	00000101
ADD	EAX	5
r/m 32, imm8		

Figure B.7   Example x86 instruction in 32-bit mode: ADD EAX, $5.

B.3 An Example

We conclude this appendix with an example. The problem is one we have dealt with extensively in Chapter 14. Given an input character string consisting of text, numbers, and punctuation, write a C program to convert all the lowercase letters to uppercase. Figure B.8 shows a C program that solves this problem. Figure B.9 shows the annotated LC-3 assembly language code that a C compiler would generate. Figure B.10 shows the corresponding annotated x86 assembly language code, assuming we are operating the x86 in 32-bit mode. For readability, we show assembly language representations of the LC-3 and x86 programs rather than the machine code.

```c
#include <stdio.h>

void UpcaseString(char inputString[]);

int main (void)
{
    char string[8];

    scanf("%s", string);
    UpcaseString(string);
}

void UpcaseString(char inputString[])
{
  int i = 0;

  while(inputString[i]) {
    if (('a' <= inputString[i]) && (inputString[i] <= 'z'))
      inputString[i] = inputString[i] - ('a' - 'A');
    i++;
  }
}
```

Figure B.8   C source code for the upper-/lowercase program.

```
; uppercase:  converts lower- to uppercase
                .ORIG   x3000
                LEA     R6, STACK
MAIN            ADD     R1, R6, #3
READCHAR        IN                          ; read in input string: scanf
                OUT
                STR     R0, R1, #0
                ADD     R1, R1, #1
                ADD     R2, R0, x-A
                BRnp    READCHAR
                ADD     R1, R1, #-1
                STR     R2, R1, #0          ; put in NULL char to mark the "end"
                ADD     R1, R6, #3          ; get the starting address of the string
                STR     R1, R6, #14         ; pass the parameter
                STR     R6, R6, #13
                ADD     R6, R6, #11
                JSR     UPPERCASE
                HALT
UPPERCASE       STR     R7, R6, #1
                AND     R1, R1, #0
                STR     R1, R6, #4
                LDR     R2, R6, #3
CONVERT         ADD     R3, R1, R2          ; add index to starting addr of string
                LDR     R4, R3, #0
                BRz     DONE                ; Done if NULL char reached
                LD      R5, a
                ADD     R5, R5, R4          ; 'a' <= input string
                BRn     NEXT
                LD      R5, z
                ADD     R5, R4, R5          ; input string <= 'z'
                BRp     NEXT
                LD      R5, asubA           ; convert to uppercase
                ADD     R4, R4, R5
                STR     R4, R3, #0
NEXT            ADD     R1, R1, #1          ; increment the array index, i
                STR     R1, R6, #4
                BRnzp   CONVERT
DONE            LDR     R7, R6, #1
                LDR     R6, R6, #2
                RET
a               .FILL   #-97
z               .FILL   #-122
asubA           .FILL   #-32
STACK           .BLKW   100
                .END
```

Figure B.9   LC-3 assembly language code for the upper-/lowercase program.

```
        .386P
        .model FLAT

_DATA   SEGMENT                 ; The NULL-terminated scanf format
$SG397  DB      '%s', 00H       ; string is stored in global data space.
_DATA   ENDS


_TEXT   SEGMENT

_string$ = -8                   ; Location of "string" in local stack
_main   PROC NEAR
        sub     esp, 8          ; Allocate stack space to store "string"
        lea     eax, DWORD PTR _string$[esp+8]
        push    eax             ; Push arguments to scanf
        push    OFFSET FLAT:$SG397
        call    _scanf

        lea     ecx, DWORD PTR _string$[esp+16]
        push    ecx             ; Push argument to UpcaseString
        call    _UpcaseString

        add     esp, 20         ; Release local stack space
        ret     0
_main   ENDP

_inputString$ = 8              ; "inputString" location in local stack
_UpcaseString PROC NEAR
        mov     ecx, DWORD PTR _inputString$[esp-4]
        cmp     BYTE PTR [ecx], 0
        je      SHORT $L404      ; If inputString[0]=0, skip the loop
$L403:  mov     al, BYTE PTR [ecx]  ; Load inputString[i] into AL
        cmp     al, 97           ; 97 == 'a'
        jl      SHORT $L405
        cmp     al, 122          ; 122 == 'z'
        jg      SHORT $L405
        sub     al, 32           ; 32 == 'a' - 'A'
        mov     BYTE PTR [ecx], al
$L405:  inc     ecx              ; i++ %$
        mov     al, BYTE PTR [ecx]
        test    al, al
        jne     SHORT $L403      ; Loop if inputString[i] != 0
$L404:  ret     0
_UpcaseString ENDP
_TEXT   ENDS
END
```

Figure B.10   x86 assembly language code for the upper-/lowercase program.

The Microarchitecture of the LC-3

We have seen in Chapters 4 and 5 the several stages of the instruction cycle that must occur in order for the computer to process each instruction. If a microarchitecture is to implement an ISA, it must be able to carry out this instruction cycle for every instruction in the ISA. This appendix illustrates one example of a microarchitecture that can do that for the LC-3 ISA. Many of the details of the microarchitecture and the reasons for each design decision are well beyond the scope of an introductory course. However, for those who want to understand **how** a microarchitecture can carry out the requirements of each instruction of the LC-3 ISA, this appendix is provided.

C.1 Overview

Figure C.1 shows the two main components of a microarchitecture: the *data path*, which contains all the components that actually process the instructions, and the *control*, which contains all the components that generate the set of control signals that are needed to control the processing at each instant of time.

We say, "at each instant of time," but we really mean **during each clock cycle**. That is, time is divided into *clock cycles*. The cycle time of a microprocessor is the duration of a clock cycle. A common cycle time for a microprocessor today is 0.33 nanoseconds, which corresponds to 3 billion clock cycles each second. We say that such a microprocessor is operating at a frequency of 3 gigahertz, or 3 GHz.

At each instant of time—or, rather, during each clock cycle—the 52 control signals (as shown in Figure C.1) control both the processing in the data path and the generation of the control signals for the next clock cycle. Processing in the data path is controlled by 42 bits, and the generation of the control signals for the next clock cycle is controlled by 10 bits.

Note that the hardware that determines which control signals are needed each clock cycle does not operate in a vacuum. On the contrary, the control signals needed in the "next" clock cycle depend on the following:

1. The control signals that are present during the current clock cycle.
2. The LC-3 instruction that is being executed.

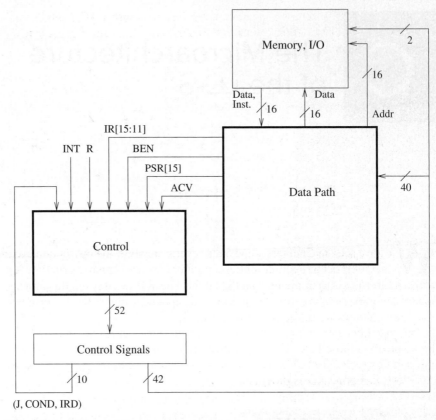

Figure C.1   Microarchitecture of the LC-3, major components.

3. The privilege mode of the program that is executing, and whether the processor has the right to access a particular memory location.

4. If that LC-3 instruction is a BR, whether the conditions for the branch have been met (i.e., the state of the relevant condition codes).

5. Whether or not an external device is requesting that the processor be interrupted.

6. If a memory operation is in progress, whether it is completing during this cycle.

Figure C.1 identifies the specific information in our implementation of the LC-3 that corresponds to these six items. They are, respectively:

1. J[5:0], COND[2:0], and IRD—ten bits of control signals provided by the current clock cycle.

2. inst[15:12], which identifies the opcode, and inst[11:11], which differentiates JSR from JSRR (i.e., the addressing mode for the target of the subroutine call).

3. PSR[15], bit [15] of the Processor Status Register, which indicates whether the current program is executing with supervisor or user privileges, and ACV, a signal that informs the processor that a process operating in User

mode is trying to access a location in privileged memory. ACV stands for Access Control Violation. When asserted, it denies the process access to the privileged memory location.

4. BEN to indicate whether or not a BR should be taken.

5. INT to indicate that some external device of higher priority than the executing process requests service.

6. R to indicate the end of a memory operation.

C.2 The State Machine

The behavior of the LC-3 microarchitecture during a given clock cycle is completely determined by the 52 control signals, combined with ten bits of additional information (inst[15:11], PSR[15], ACV, BEN, INT, and R), as shown in Figure C.1. We have said that during each clock cycle, 42 of these control signals determine the processing of information in the data path and the other ten control signals combine with the ten bits of additional information to determine which set of control signals will be required in the next clock cycle.

We say that these 52 control signals specify the *state* of the control structure of the LC-3 microarchitecture. We can completely describe the behavior of the LC-3 microarchitecture by means of a directed graph that consists of nodes (one corresponding to each state) and arcs (showing the flow from each state to the one[s] it goes to next). We call such a graph a *state machine*.

Figure C.2, combined with Figure C.7, is the state machine for our implementation of the LC-3. The state machine describes what happens during each clock cycle in which the computer is running. Each state is active for exactly one clock cycle before control passes to the next state. The state machine shows the step-by-step (clock cycle–by–clock cycle) process that each instruction goes through from the start of its FETCH phase to the end of its instruction cycle, as described in Section 4.3.2. Each node in the state machine corresponds to the activity that the processor carries out during a single clock cycle. The actual processing that is performed in the data path is contained inside the node. The step-by-step flow is conveyed by the arcs that take the processor from one state to the next.

Let's start our study of Figure C.2 by examining the FETCH phase of the instruction cycle. As you know, every instruction goes through the same FETCH phase in its instruction cycle. Recall from Chapter 4 that the FETCH phase starts with a memory access to read the instruction at the address specified by the PC. Note that in the state numbered 18, the MAR is loaded with the address contained in PC, and the PC is incremented in preparation for the FETCH of the next LC-3 instruction after the current instruction finishes its instruction cycle. If the content of MAR specifies privileged memory, and PSR[15] = 1, indicating User mode, the access of the instruction will not be allowed. That would be an access control violation, so ACV is set. Finally, if there is no interrupt request present (INT = 0), the flow passes to the state numbered 33. We will describe in Section C.7 the flow of control if INT = 1, that is, if an external device is requesting an interrupt.

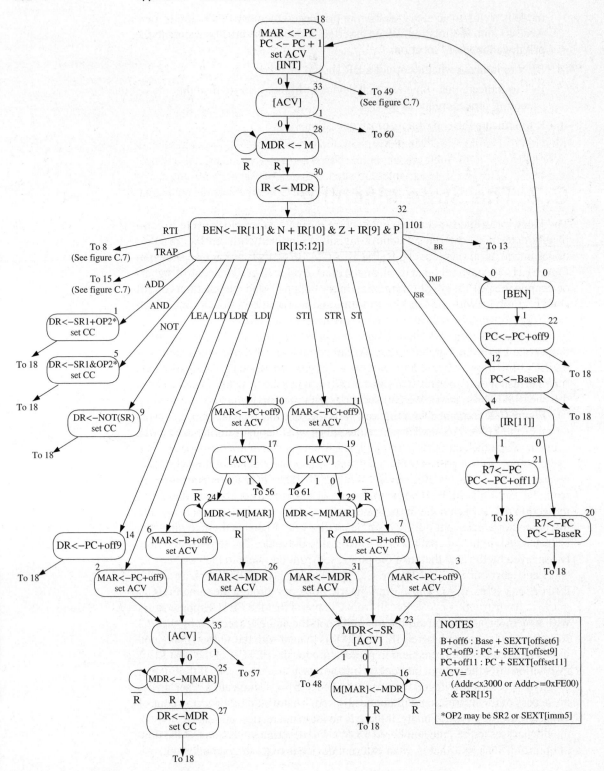

Figure C.2 A state machine for the LC-3.

Before we get into what happens during the clock cycle when the processor is in the state numbered 33, we should explain the numbering system—that is, why are states numbered 18 and 33. Recall, from our discussion of finite state machines in Chapter 3, that each state must be uniquely specified and that this unique specification is accomplished by means of state variables. Our state machine that implements the LC-3 ISA requires 59 distinct states to implement the entire behavior of the LC-3. Figure C.2 shows 31 of them plus pointers to seven others (states 8, 13, 15, 48, 49, 57, and 60). Figure C.7 shows the other 28 states (including the seven that are pointed to in Figure C.2). We will visit all of them as we go through this appendix. Since k logical variables can uniquely identify 2^k items, six state variables are needed to uniquely specify 59 states. The number next to each node in Figure C.2 and Figure C.7 is the decimal equivalent of the values (0 or 1) of the six state variables for the corresponding state. Thus, for example, the state numbered 18 has state variable values 010010.

Now, back to what happens after the clock cycle in which the activity of state 18 has finished. As we said, if no external device is requesting an interrupt, the flow passes to state 33 (i.e., 100001). From state 33, control passes to state 60 if the processor is trying to access privileged memory while in User mode, or to state 28, if the memory access is allowed, that is, if there is no ACV violation. We will discuss what happens if there is an ACV violation in Section C.7.

In state 28, since the MAR contains the address of the instruction to be processed, this instruction is read from memory and loaded into the MDR. Since this memory access can take multiple cycles, this state continues to execute until a ready signal from the memory (R) is asserted, indicating that the memory access has completed. Thus, the MDR contains the valid contents of the memory location specified by MAR. The state machine then moves on to state 30, where the instruction is loaded into the instruction register (IR), completing the fetch phase of the instruction cycle.

The state machine then moves to state 32, where DECODE takes place. Note that there are 13 arcs emanating from state 32, each one corresponding to bits [15:12] of the LC-3 instruction. These are the opcode bits that direct the state machine to one of 16 paths to carry out the instruction cycle of the particular instruction that has just been fetched. Note that the arc from the last state of each instruction cycle (i.e., the state that completes the processing of that LC-3 instruction) takes us to state 18 (to begin the instruction cycle of the next LC-3 instruction).

C.3 The Data Path

The data path consists of all components that actually process the information during each clock cycle—the functional units that operate on the information, the registers that store information at the end of one cycle so it will be available for further use in subsequent cycles, and the buses and wires that carry information from one point to another in the data path. Figure C.3, an expanded version of what you have already encountered in Figure 5.18, illustrates the data path of our microarchitecture of the LC-3.

Note the control signals that are associated with each component in the data path. For example, ALUK, consisting of two control signals, is associated with

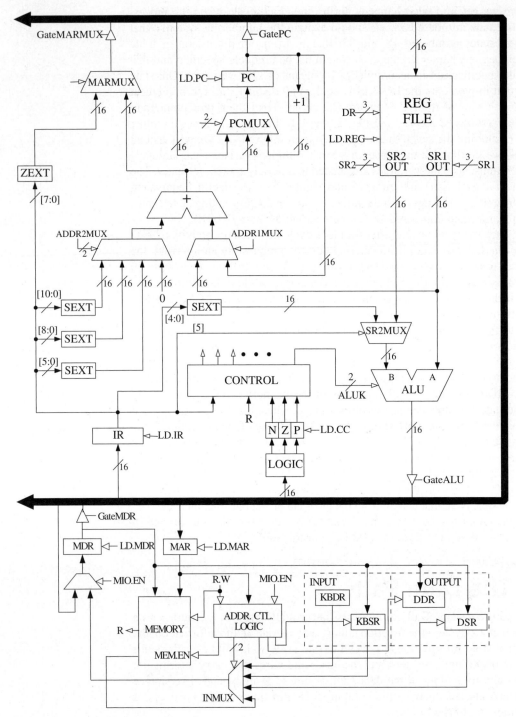

Figure C.3   The LC-3 data path.

Table C.1	Data Path Control Signals
Signal Name	**Signal Values**

LD.MAR/1:	NO, LOAD	
LD.MDR/1:	NO, LOAD	
LD.IR/1:	NO, LOAD	
LD.BEN/1:	NO, LOAD	
LD.REG/1:	NO, LOAD	
LD.CC/1:	NO, LOAD	
LD.PC/1:	NO, LOAD	
LD.Priv/1:	NO, LOAD	
LD.Priority/1:	NO, LOAD	
LD.SavedSSP/1:	NO, LOAD	
LD.SavedUSP/1:	NO, LOAD	
LD.ACV/1:	NO, LOAD	
LD.Vector/1:	NO, LOAD	
GatePC/1:	NO, YES	
GateMDR/1:	NO, YES	
GateALU/1:	NO, YES	
GateMARMUX/1:	NO, YES	
GateVector/1:	NO, YES	
GatePC-1/1:	NO, YES	
GatePSR/1:	NO, YES	
GateSP/1:	NO, YES	
PCMUX/2:	PC+1	;select pc+1
	BUS	;select value from bus
	ADDER	;select output of address adder
DRMUX/2:	11.9	;destination IR[11:9]
	R7	;destination R7
	SP	;destination R6
SR1MUX/2:	11.9	;source IR[11:9]
	8.6	;source IR[8:6]
	SP	;source R6
ADDR1MUX/1:	PC, BaseR	
ADDR2MUX/2:	ZERO	;select the value zero
	offset6	;select SEXT[IR[5:0]]
	PCoffset9	;select SEXT[IR[8:0]]
	PCoffset11	;select SEXT[IR[10:0]]
SPMUX/2:	SP+1	;select stack pointer+1
	SP−1	;select stack pointer−1
	Saved SSP	;select saved Supervisor Stack Pointer
	Saved USP	;select saved User Stack Pointer
MARMUX/1:	7.0	;select ZEXT[IR[7:0]]
	ADDER	;select output of address adder
TableMUX/1:	x00, x01	
VectorMUX/2:	INTV	
	Priv.exception	
	Opc.exception	
	ACV.exception	
PSRMUX/1:	individual settings, BUS	
ALUK/2:	ADD, AND, NOT, PASSA	
MIO.EN/1:	NO, YES	
R.W/1:	RD, WR	
Set.Priv/1:	0	;Supervisor mode
	1	;User mode

the ALU. These control signals determine how that component (the ALU) will be used each cycle. Table C.1 lists the set of 42 control signals that control the elements of the data path and the set of values that each control signal can have. (Actually, for readability, we provide a symbolic name for each value, rather than the binary value.) For example, since ALUK consists of two bits, it can have one of four values. Which value it has during any particular clock cycle depends on whether the ALU is required to ADD, AND, NOT, or simply pass one of its inputs to the output during that clock cycle. PCMUX also consists of two control signals and specifies which input to the MUX is required during a given clock cycle. LD.PC is a single-bit control signal and is a 0 (NO) or a 1 (YES), depending on whether or not the PC is to be loaded during the given clock cycle.

During each clock cycle, corresponding to the "current state" in the state machine, the 42 bits of control direct the processing of all components in the data path that are required during that clock cycle. As we have said, the processing that takes place in the data path during that clock cycle is specified inside the node representing the state.

C.4 The Control Structure

The control structure of a microarchitecture is specified by its state machine. As described earlier, the state machine (Figure C.2 and Figure C.7) determines which control signals are needed each clock cycle to process information in the data path and which control signals are needed each clock cycle to direct the flow of control from the currently active state to its successor state.

Figure C.4 shows a block diagram of the control structure of our implementation of the LC-3. Many implementations are possible, and the design considerations that must be studied to determine which of many possible implementations should be used is the subject of a full course in computer architecture.

We have chosen here a straightforward microprogrammed implementation. Each state of the control structure requires 42 bits to control the processing in the data path and 10 bits to help determine which state comes next. These 52 bits are collectively known as a *microinstruction*. Each microinstruction (i.e., each state of the state machine) is stored in one 52-bit location of a special memory called the control store. There are 59 distinct states. Since each state corresponds to one microinstruction in the control store, the control store for our microprogrammed implementation requires six bits to specify the address of each microinstruction. Those six bits correspond to the state number associated with each state in the state machine. For example, the microinstruction associated with state 18 is the set of 52 control signals stored in address 18 of the control store.

Table C.2 lists the function of the ten bits of control information that help determine which state comes next. Figure C.5 shows the logic of the microsequencer. The purpose of the microsequencer is to determine the address in the control store that corresponds to the next state, that is, the location where the 52 bits of control information for the next state are stored.

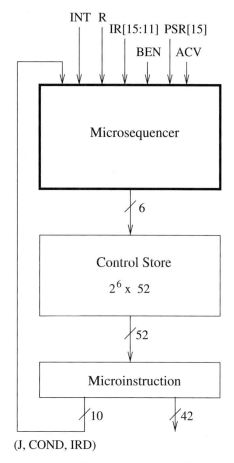

Figure C.4 The control structure of a microprogrammed implementation, overall block diagram.

Table C.2	Microsequencer Control Signals	
Signal Name	**Signal Values**	
J/6:		
COND/3:	COND0	;Unconditional
	COND1	;Memory Ready
	COND2	;Branch
	COND3	;Addressing Mode
	COND4	;Privilege Mode
	COND5	;Interrupt test
	COND6	;ACV Test
IRD/1:	NO, YES	

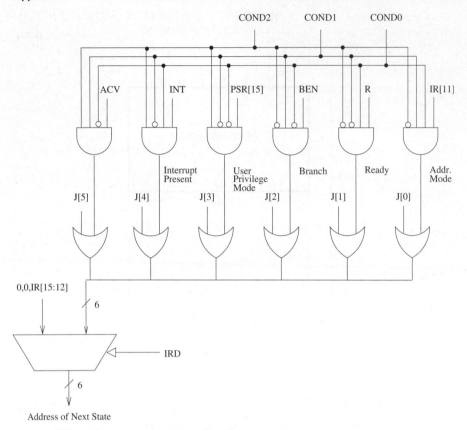

Figure C.5   The microsequencer of the LC-3.

As we said, state 32 of the state machine (Figure C.2) performs the DECODE phase of the instruction cycle. It has 16 "next" states, depending on the LC-3 instruction being executed during the current instruction cycle. If the IRD control signal in the microinstruction corresponding to state 32 is 1, the output MUX of the microsequencer (Figure C.5) will take its source from the six bits formed by 00 concatenated with the four opcode bits IR[15:12]. Since IR[15:12] specifies the opcode of the current LC-3 instruction being processed, the next address of the control store will be one of 16 addresses, corresponding to the 15 opcodes plus the one unused opcode, IR[15:12] = 1101. That is, each of the 16 next states after state 32 is the first state to be carried out after the instruction has been decoded in state 32. For example, if the instruction being processed is ADD, the address of the next state is state 1, whose microinstruction is stored at location 000001. Recall that IR[15:12] for ADD is 0001.

If, somehow, the instruction inadvertently contained IR[15:12] = 1101, the unused opcode, the microarchitecture would execute a sequence of microinstructions, starting at state 13. These microinstructions would respond to the fact that an instruction with an illegal opcode had been fetched. Section C.7.3 describes what happens in that case.

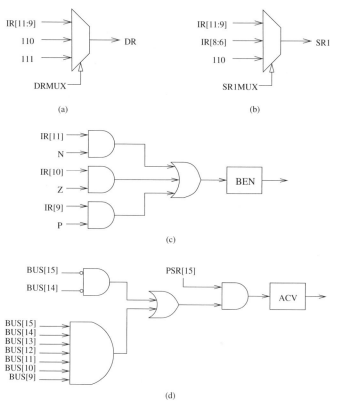

Figure C.6   Additional logic required to provide control signals.

Several signals necessary to control the data path and the microsequencer are not among those listed in Tables C.1 and C.2. They are DR, SR1, BEN, INT, ACV, and R. Figure C.6 shows the additional logic needed to generate DR, SR1, BEN, and ACV.

The INT signal is supplied by some event external to the normal instruction processing, indicating that normal instruction processing should be interrupted and this external event dealt with. The interrupt mechanism was described in Chapter 9. The corresponding flow of control within the microarchitecture is described in Section C.7.

The remaining signal, R, is a signal generated by the memory in order to allow the LC-3 to operate correctly with a memory that takes multiple clock cycles to read or store a value.

Suppose it takes memory five cycles to read a value. That is, once MAR contains the address to be read and the microinstruction asserts READ, it will take five cycles before the contents of the specified location in memory is available to be loaded into MDR. (Note that the microinstruction asserts READ by means of two control signals: MIO.EN/YES and R.W/RD; see Figure C.3.)

Recall our discussion in Section C.2 of the function of state 28, which accesses an instruction from memory during the FETCH phase of each instruction cycle. If the memory takes five cycles to read a value, for the LC-3 to operate correctly, state 28 must execute five times before moving on to state 30. That is, until MDR contains valid data from the memory location specified by the contents of MAR, we want state 28 to continue to re-execute. After five clock cycles, the memory has completed the "read," resulting in valid data in MDR, so the processor can move on to state 30. What if the microarchitecture did not wait for the memory to complete the read operation before moving on to state 30? Since the contents of MDR would still be garbage, the microarchitecture would put garbage into the IR in state 30.

The ready signal (R) enables the memory read to execute correctly. Since the memory knows it needs five clock cycles to complete the read, it asserts a ready signal (R) throughout the fifth clock cycle. Figure C.2 shows that the next state is 28 (i.e., 011100) if the memory read will not complete in the current clock cycle and state 30 (i.e., 011110) if it will. As we have seen, it is the job of the microsequencer (Figure C.5) to produce the next state address.

The ten microsequencer control signals for state 28 are:

```
IRD/0       ; NO
COND/001    ; Memory Ready
J/011100
```

With these control signals, what next state address is generated by the microsequencer? For each of the first four executions of state 28, since R = 0, the next state address is 011100. This causes state 28 to be executed again in the next clock cycle. In the fifth clock cycle, since R = 1, the next state address is 011110, and the LC-3 moves on to state 30. Note that in order for the ready signal (R) from memory to be part of the next state address, COND had to be set to 001, which allowed R to pass through its four-input AND gate.

C.5 The TRAP Instruction

As we have said, each LC-3 instruction follows its own path from state 32 to its final state in its instruction cycle, after which it returns to state 18 to start processing the next instruction. As an example, we will follow the instruction cycle of the TRAP instruction, shown in Figure C.7.

Recall that the TRAP instruction pushes the PSR and PC onto the system stack, loads the PC with the starting address of the trap service routine, and executes the service routine from privileged memory.

From state 32, the next state after DECODE is state 15, consistent with the TRAP instruction opcode 1111. In state 15, the Table register, which will be used to form MAR[15:8] of the trap vector table entry, is loaded with x00, the PC is incremented (we will see why momentarily), and the MDR is loaded with the PSR in preparation for pushing it onto the system stack. Control passes to state 47.

In state 47, the trap vector (IR[7:0]) is loaded into the eight-bit register Vector, PSR[15] is set to Supervisor mode since the trap service routine executes in privileged memory, and the state machine branches to state 37 or 45, depending on whether the program that executed the TRAP instruction was in User mode or Supervisor mode. If in User mode, state 45 saves the User Stack Pointer in Saved_USP, loads the stack pointer from Saved_SSP, and continues on to state 37, where the processor starts pushing PSR and PC onto the stack. If the program executing the TRAP instruction is already in Privileged mode, state 45 is not necessary.

In states 37 and 41, the PSR is pushed onto the system stack. In states 43, 46, and 52, the PC is pushed onto the system stack. Note that in state 43, the PC is decremented before being pushed onto the stack. This is necessary in the case of dealing with interrupts and exceptions, which will be explained in Section C.7. This is not necessary for processing the TRAP instruction, which is why PC is incremented in state 15.

The only thing remaining is to load PC with the starting address of the trap service routine. This is done by loading MAR with the address of the proper entry in the trap vector table, obtained by concatenating Table and Vector (in state 54), loading the starting address from memory into MDR (in state 53), and loading the PC (in state 55). This completes the execution of the TRAP instruction, and control returns to state 18 to begin processing the next instruction – in this case, the first instruction of the trap service routine.

The last instruction in every trap service routine is RTI (return from trap or interrupt). From DECODE in state 32, the next state of RTI is state 8, consistent with its eight-bit opcode 1000. In states 8, 36, and 38, the PC is popped off the system stack and loaded into PC. In states 39, 40, 42, and 34, the PSR is popped off the system stack and loaded into PSR. This returns the PC and PSR to the values it had before the trap service routine was executed. Finally, if the program that invoked the TRAP instruction was in User mode, PSR[15] must be returned to 1, the Supervisor Stack Pointer saved, and the User Stack Pointer loaded into SP. This is done in state 59, completing the instruction cycle for RTI.

C.6 Memory-Mapped I/O

As you know from Chapter 9, the LC-3 ISA performs input and output via memory-mapped I/O, that is, with the same data movement instructions that it uses to read from and write to memory. The LC-3 does this by assigning an address to each device register. Input is accomplished by a load instruction whose effective address is the address of an input device register. Output is accomplished by a store instruction whose effective address is the address of an output device register. For example, in state 25 of Figure C.2, if the address in MAR is xFE02, MDR is supplied by the KBDR, and the data input will be the last keyboard character typed. On the other hand, if the address in MAR is a legitimate memory address, MDR is supplied by the memory.

Table C.3			Truth Table for Address Control Logic				
MAR	MIO.EN	R.W	MEM.EN	IN.MUX	LD.KBSR	LD.DSR	LD.DDR
xFE00	0	R	0	x	0	0	0
xFE00	0	W	0	x	0	0	0
xFE00	1	R	0	KBSR	0	0	0
xFE00	1	W	0	x	1	0	0
xFE02	0	R	0	x	0	0	0
xFE02	0	W	0	x	0	0	0
xFE02	1	R	0	KBDR	0	0	0
xFE02	1	W	0	x	0	0	0
xFE04	0	R	0	x	0	0	0
xFE04	0	W	0	x	0	0	0
xFE04	1	R	0	DSR	0	0	0
xFE04	1	W	0	x	0	1	0
xFE06	0	R	0	x	0	0	0
xFE06	0	W	0	x	0	0	0
xFE06	1	R	0	x	0	0	0
xFE06	1	W	0	x	0	0	1
other	0	R	0	x	0	0	0
other	0	W	0	x	0	0	0
other	1	R	1	mem	0	0	0
other	1	W	1	x	0	0	0

The state machine of Figure C.2 does not have to be altered to accommodate memory-mapped I/O. However, something has to determine when memory should be accessed and when I/O device registers should be accessed. This is the job of the address control logic (ADDR.CTL.LOGIC) shown in Figure C.3.

Table C.3 is a truth table for the address control logic, showing what control signals are generated, based on (1) the contents of MAR, (2) whether or not memory or I/O is accessed this cycle (MIO.EN/NO, YES), and (3) whether a load (R.W/Read) or store (R.W/Write) is requested. Note that, for a memory-mapped load, data can be supplied to MDR from one of four sources: memory, KBDR, KBSR, or DSR. The address control logic provides the appropriate select signals to the INMUX. For a memory-mapped store, the data supplied by MDR can be written to memory, KBSR, DDR, or DSR. The address control logic supplies the appropriate enable signal to the corresponding structure.

C.7 Interrupt and Exception Control

The final piece of the state machine needed to complete the LC-3 story are those states that control the initiation of an interrupt, those states that control the return from an interrupt (the RTI instruction), and those states that control the initiation of one of the three exceptions specified by the ISA.

Interrupts and exceptions are very similar. Both stop the program that is currently executing. Both push the PSR and PC of the interrupted program onto the system stack, obtain the starting address of the interrupt or exception service routine from the interrupt vector table, and load that starting address into the Program Counter. The main difference between interrupts and exceptions is the nature of the event that causes the program that is executing to stop. Interrupts are events that usually have nothing to do with the program that is executing. Exceptions are events that are the direct result of something going awry in the program that is executing. The LC-3 specifies three exceptions: a privilege mode violation, an illegal opcode, and an ACV exception. Figure C.7 shows the state machine that carries these out. Figure C.8 shows the data path, after adding the additional structures to Figure C.3 that are needed to make interrupt and exception processing work.

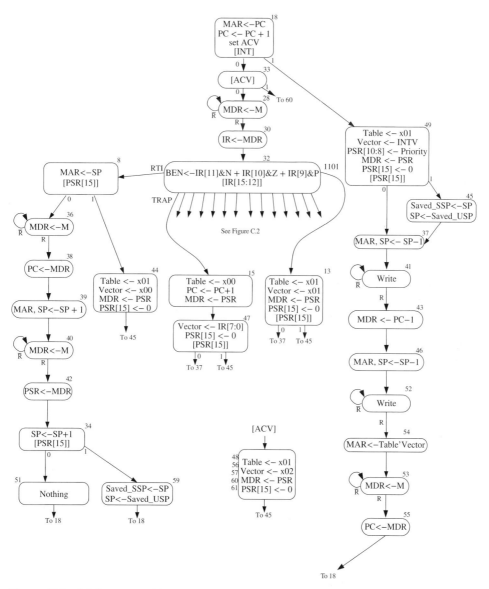

Figure C.7   LC-3 state machine showing interrupt control.

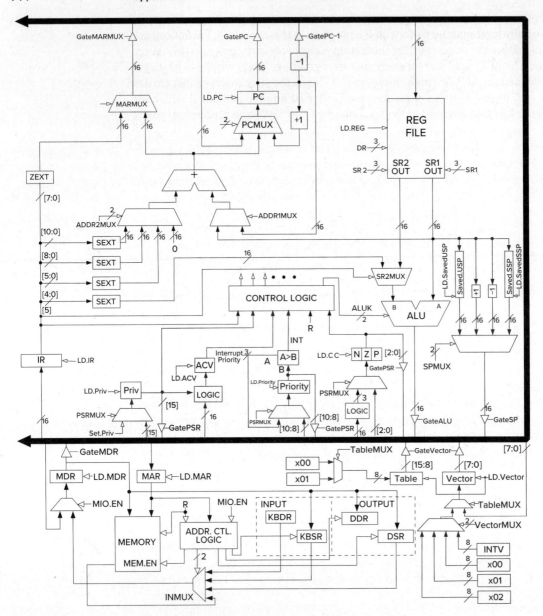

Figure C.8   LC-3 data path, including additional structures for interrupt control.

Section C.7.1 describes the flow of processing required to initiate an interrupt.
Section C.7.3 describes the flow of processing required to initiate an exception.

C.7.1 Initiating an Interrupt

While a program is executing, an interrupt can be requested by some external
event so that the normal processing of instructions can be preempted and the control can turn its attention to processing the interrupt. The external event requests

an interrupt by asserting its interrupt request signal. Recall from Chapter 9 that if the priority level of the device asserting its interrupt request signal is higher than both the priority level of the currently executing program and any other external interrupt request asserted at the same time, INT is asserted and INTV is loaded with the interrupt vector corresponding to that external event. The microprocessor responds to INT by initiating the interrupt. That is, the processor puts itself into Supervisor mode if it isn't in Supervisor mode, pushes the PSR and PC of the interrupted process onto the supervisor stack, and loads the PC with the starting address of the interrupt service routine. The PSR contains the privilege mode PSR[15], priority level PSR[10:8], and condition codes PSR[2:0] of a program. It is important that when the processor resumes execution of the interrupted program, the privilege mode, priority level, and condition codes are restored to what they were when the interrupt occurred.

The microarchitecture of the LC-3 initiates an interrupt as follows: Recall from Figure C.2 that in state 18, while MAR is loaded with the contents of PC and PC is incremented, INT is tested.

State 18 is the only state in which the processor checks for interrupts. The reason for only testing in state 18 is straightforward: Once an LC-3 instruction starts processing, it is easier to let it finish its complete instruction cycle (FETCH, DECODE, etc.) than to interrupt it in the middle and have to keep track of how far along it was when the external device requested an interrupt (i.e., asserted INT). If INT is only tested in state 18, the current instruction cycle can be aborted early (even before the instruction has been fetched), and control directed to initiating the interrupt.

The test is enabled by the control signals that make up COND5, which are 101 only in state 18, allowing the value of INT to pass through its four-input AND gate, shown in Figure C.5, to contribute to the address of the next state. Since the COND signals are not 101 in any other state, INT has no effect in any other state.

In state 18, the ten microsequencer control bits are as follows:

```
IRD/0       ; NO
COND/101    ; Test for interrupts
J/100001
```

If INT = 1, a 1 is produced at the output of the AND gate, which in turn makes the next state address not 100001, corresponding to state 33, but rather 110001, corresponding to state 49. This starts the initiation of the interrupt (see Figure C.7).

Several functions are performed in state 49. The PSR, which contains the privilege mode, priority level, and condition codes of the interrupted program, are loaded into MDR, in preparation for pushing it onto the supervisor stack. PSR[15] is cleared, reflecting the change to Supervisor mode, since all interrupt service routines execute in Supervisor mode. The three-bit priority level and eight-bit interrupt vector (INTV) provided by the interrupting device are recorded. PSR[10:8] is loaded with the priority level of the interrupting device. The internal register Vector is loaded with INTV and the eight-bit register Table is loaded with x01 in preparation for accessing the interrupt vector table to obtain the starting address of the interrupt service routine. Finally, the processor tests the old PSR[15] to determine whether the stack pointers must be adjusted before pushing PSR and PC.

If the old PSR[15] = 0, the processor is already operating in Supervisor mode. R6 is the Supervisor Stack Pointer (SSP), so the processor proceeds immediately to states 37 and 41 to push the PSR of the interrupted program onto the supervisor stack. If PSR[15] = 1, the interrupted program was in User mode. In that case, the User Stack Pointer (USP) must be saved in Saved_USP and R6 must be loaded with the contents of Saved_SSP before moving to state 37. This is done in state 45.

The control flow from state 49 to either 37 or 45 is enabled by the ten microsequencer control bits, as follows:

```
IRD/0      ; NO
COND/100   ; Test PSR[15], privilege mode
J/100101
```

If PSR[15] = 0, control goes to state 37 (100101); if PSR[15] = 1, control goes to state 45 (101101).

In state 37, R6 (the SSP) is decremented (preparing for the push), and MAR is loaded with the address of the new top of the stack.

In state 41, the memory is enabled to WRITE (MIO.EN/YES, R.W/WR). When the write completes, signaled by R = 1, PSR has been pushed onto the supervisor stack, and the flow moves on to state 43.

In state 43, the PC is loaded into MDR. Note that state 43 says MDR is loaded with PC-1. Recall that in state 18, at the beginning of the instruction cycle for the interrupted instruction, PC was incremented. Loading MDR with PC-1 adjusts PC to the correct address of the interrupted program.

In states 46 and 52, the same sequence as in states 37 and 41 occurs, only this time the PC of the interrupted program is pushed onto the supervisor stack.

The final task to complete the initiation of the interrupt is to load the PC with the starting address of the interrupt service routine. This is carried out by states 54, 53, and 55. It is accomplished in a manner similar to the loading of the PC with the starting address of a TRAP service routine. The event causing the INT request supplies the eight-bit interrupt vector INTV associated with the interrupt, similar to the eight-bit trap vector contained in the TRAP instruction. This interrupt vector is stored in the eight-bit register INTV, shown on the data path in Figure C.8.

The interrupt vector table occupies memory locations x0100 to x01FF. In state 54, the interrupt vector that was loaded into Vector in state 49 is combined with the base address of the interrupt vector table (x0100) and loaded into MAR. In state 53, memory is READ. When R = 1, the read has completed, and MDR contains the starting address of the interrupt service routine. In state 55, the PC is loaded with that starting address, completing the initiation of the interrupt.

It is important to emphasize that the LC-3 supports two stacks, one for each privilege mode, and two stack pointers (USP and SSP), one for each stack. R6 is the stack pointer and is loaded from the Saved_SSP when privilege changes from User mode to Supervisor mode, and from Saved_USP when privilege changes from Supervisor mode to User mode. When the privilege mode changes, the current value in R6 must be stored in the appropriate "Saved" stack pointer in order to be available the next time the privilege mode changes back.

C.7.2 Returning from an Interrupt or Trap Service Routine, RTI

Interrupt service routines, like trap service routines already described, end with the execution of the RTI instruction. The job of the RTI instruction is to restore the computer to the state it was in before the interrupt or trap service routine was executed. This means restoring the PSR (i.e., the privilege mode, priority level, and the values of the condition codes N, Z, P) and restoring the PC. These values were pushed onto the stack during the initiation of the interrupt or execution of the TRAP instruction. They must, therefore, be popped off the stack in the reverse order.

The first state after DECODE is state 8. Here we load the MAR with the address of the top of the supervisor stack, which contains the last thing pushed (that has not been subsequently popped)—the state of the PC when the interrupt was initiated. At the same time, we test PSR[15] since RTI is a privileged instruction and can only execute in Supervisor mode. If PSR[15] = 0, we can continue to carry out the requirements of RTI.

States 36 and 38 restore PC to the value it had when the interrupt was initiated. In state 36, the memory is read. When the read is completed, MDR contains the address of the instruction that was to be processed next when the interrupt occurred. State 38 loads that address into the PC.

States 39, 40, 42, and 34 restore the privilege mode, priority level, and condition codes (N, Z, P) to their original values. In state 39, the Supervisor Stack Pointer is incremented so that it points to the top of the stack after the PC was popped. The MAR is loaded with the address of the new top of the stack. State 40 initiates the memory READ; when the READ is completed, MDR contains the interrupted PSR. State 42 loads the PSR from MDR, and state 34 increments the stack pointer.

The only thing left is to check the privilege mode of the interrupted program to see whether the stack pointers have to be switched. In state 34, the microsequencer control bits are as follows:

```
IRD/0       ; NO
COND/100    ; Test PSR[15], privilege mode
J/110011
```

If PSR[15] = 0, control flows to state 51 (110011) to do nothing for one cycle. If PSR[15] = 1, control flows to state 59, where R6 is saved in Saved_SSP and R6 is loaded from Saved_USP. In both cases, control returns to state 18 to begin processing the next instruction.

C.7.3 Initiating an Exception

The LC-3 identifies three cases where processing is not allowed to continue normally due to something going awry in the executing program. We refer to these cases as exceptions. They are initiated in the same way interrupts are initiated, by pushing the PSR and PC onto the system stack, obtaining the starting address of the exception service routine from the interrupt vector table, and loading that address into the PC to initiate the exception service routine.

The three exceptions identified in the LC-3 are (1) a privileged mode exception caused by the program attempting to execute the RTI instruction while in User mode, (2) the illegal opcode exception caused by the program trying to execute an instruction whose opcode is 1101, and (3) an access control violation (ACV) exception caused by the program trying to access a privileged memory location while in User mode.

C.7.3.1 Privilege Mode Exception

If the processor is in User mode ($PSR[15] = 1$) and is attempting to execute RTI, a privilege mode exception occurs. The processor pushes the PSR and the address of the RTI instruction onto the supervisor stack and loads the PC with the starting address of the service routine that handles privilege mode violations. Figure C.7 shows the flow, starting with a branch from state 8 to state 44 if $PSR[15] = 1$.

In state 44, the eight-bit Table register is loaded with x01, indicating the address of an entry in the interrupt vector table, and the eight-bit Vector register is loaded with x00, indicating the first entry in the interrupt vector table. The contents of x0100 is the starting address of the service routine that handles privilege mode exceptions. The MDR is loaded with the PSR of the program that caused the exception in preparation for pushing it onto the system stack. Finally, $PSR[15]$ is set to 0, since the service routine will execute with supervisor privileges. Then the processor moves to state 45, where it follows the same flow as the initiation of interrupts.

The main difference between this flow and that for the initiation of interrupts is in state 54, where MAR is loaded with x01'Vector. In the case of interrupts, Vector is loaded in state 49 with INTV, which is supplied by the interrupting device. In the case of the privilege mode violation, Vector is loaded in state 44 with x00.

There are two additional functions performed in state 49 that are not performed in state 44. First, the priority level is changed, based on the priority of the interrupting device. We do not change the priority in handling a privilege mode violation. The service routine executes at the same priority as the program that caused the violation. Second, a test to determine the privilege mode is performed for an interrupt. This is unnecessary for a privilege mode violation since the processor already knows it is executing in User mode.

C.7.3.2 Illegal Opcode Exception

Although it would be a rare situation, it is possible, we suppose, that a programmer writing a program in machine language could mistakenly include an instruction having opcode = 1101. Since there is no such opcode in the LC-3 ISA, the computer cannot process that instruction. State 32 performs the DECODE, and the next state is state 13.

The action the processor takes is very similar to that of a privilege mode exception. The PSR and PC of the program are pushed onto the supervisor stack, and the PC is loaded with the starting address of the Illegal Opcode exception service routine.

State 13 is very similar to state 44, which starts the initiation of a privilege mode exception. There are two differences: (1) Vector is loaded with x01, since the starting address of the service routine for the illegal opcode exception is in x0101. (2) In the case of the privilege mode exception, we know the program is in User mode when the processor attempts to execute the RTI instruction. In the case of an illegal opcode, the processor can be in either mode, so from state 13 the processor goes to state 37 or state 45, depending on whether the program is executing in Supervisor mode or User mode when the illegal opcode instruction is encountered.

Like state 44, the priority of the running program is not changed, since the urgency of handling the exception is the same as the urgency of executing the program that contains it. Like state 49, state 13 tests the privilege mode of the program that contains the illegal opcode, since if the currently executing program is in User mode, the stack pointers need to be switched as described in Section C.7.1. Like state 49, the processor then microbranches either to state 37 if the stack pointer is already pointing to the supervisor stack, or to state 45 if the stack pointers have to be switched. From there, the initiating sequence continues in states 37, 41, 43, etc., identical to what happens when an interrupt is initiated (Section C.7.1) or a privilege mode exception is initiated (Section C.7.3.1). The PSR and PC are pushed onto the supervisor stack and the starting address of the service routine is loaded into the PC, completing the initiation of the exception.

C.7.3.3 Access Control Violation (ACV) Exception

An Access Control Violation (ACV) exception occurs if the processor attempts to access privileged memory while operating in User mode. The state machine checks for this in every case where the processor accesses memory, that is, in states 17, 19, 23, 33, and 35. If an ACV violation occurs, the next state is respectively states 56, 61, 48, 60, or 57 (see Figure C.2). In all five states, the processor loads Table with x01, Vector with x02, MDR with the PSR, sets PSR[15] to 0, exactly like state 44, with one exception. Vector is set to x02 since the starting address of the ACV exception service routine is in memory location x0102. Processing continues exactly like in state 44, moving first to state 45 to switch to the system stack, and then pushing PSR and PC onto the stack and loading the PC with the starting address of the service routine.

C.8 Control Store

Figure C.9 completes our microprogrammed implementation of the LC-3. It shows the contents of each location of the control store, corresponding to the 52 control signals required by each state of the state machine. We have left the exact entries blank to allow you, the reader, the joy of filling in the required signals yourself. The solution is available from your instructor.

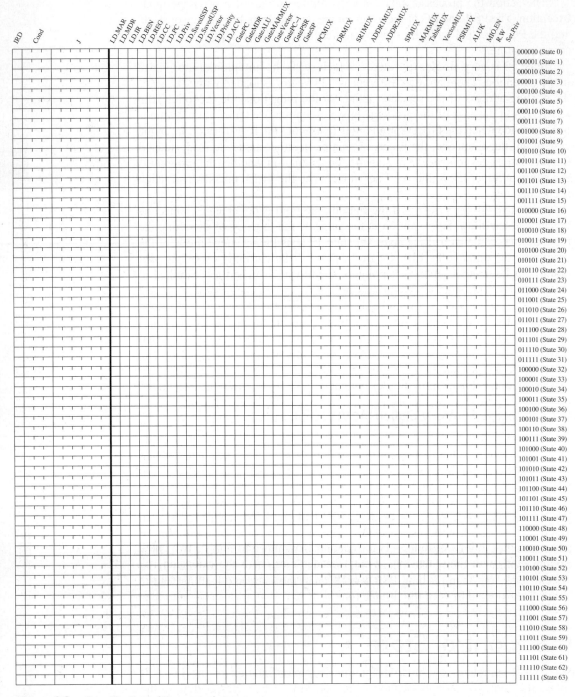

Figure C.9   Specification of the control store.

The C Programming Language

D.1 Overview

This appendix is an ANSI C (C18) reference manual oriented toward the novice C programmer. It covers a significant portion of the language, including material not covered in the main text of this book. The intent of this appendix is to provide a quick reference to various features of the language for use during programming for courses based on this textbook. Each item covered within the following sections contains a brief summary of a particular C feature and an illustrative example, when appropriate.

D.2 C Conventions

We start our coverage of the C programming language by describing the lexical elements of a C program and some of the conventions used by C programmers for writing C programs.

D.2.1 Source Files

The C programming convention is to separate programs into files of two types: source files (with the extension .c) and header files (with the extension .h). Source files, sometimes called .c or dot-c files, contain the C code for a group of related functions. For example, functions related to managing a stack data structure might be placed in a file named stack.c. Each .c file is compiled into an object file, and these objects are linked together into an executable image by the linker.

D.2.2 Header Files

Header files typically do not contain C statements but rather contain function, variable, structure, and type declarations, as well as preprocessor macros. The programming convention is to couple a header file with the source file in which the declared items are *defined*. For example, if the source file stdio.c contains the definitions for the functions printf, scanf, getchar, and putchar, then the header file stdio.h contains the declarations for these functions. If one of these functions is called from another .c file, then the stdio.h header file should be #included to get the proper function declarations.

D.2.3 Comments

In C, comments begin with the two-character delimiter //. Comments within comments are not legal and will generate a syntax error on most compilers. Comments within strings or character literals are not recognized as comments and will be treated as part of the character string. The ANSI C standard also allows for /* and */ as comment delimiters, which was the only comment delimiter in older versions of C.

D.2.4 Literals

C programs can contain literal constant values that are integers, floating point values, characters, character strings, or enumeration constants. These literals can be used as initializers for variables, or within expressions. Some examples are provided in the following subsections.

D.2.4.1 Integer

Integer literals can be expressed either in decimal, octal, or hexadecimal notation. If the literal is prefixed by a 0 (zero), it will be interpreted as an octal number. If the literal begins with a 0x, it will be interpreted as hexadecimal. Thus, it can consist of the digits 0 through 9 and the characters *a* through *f*. Uppercase *A* through *F* can be used as well. An unprefixed literal (i.e., it doesn't begin with a 0 or 0x) indicates it is in decimal notation and consists of a sequence of digits. Regardless of its base, an integer literal can be preceded by a minus sign, −, to indicate a negative value.

An integer literal can be suffixed with the letter *l* or *L* to indicate that it is of type long int. An integer literal suffixed with the letter *u* or *U* indicates an unsigned value. Refer to Section D.3.2 for a discussion of long and unsigned types.

The first three examples that follow express the same number, 87. The two last versions express it as an unsigned int value and as a long int value.

```
87      //  87 in decimal
0x57    //  87 in hexadecimal
0127    //  87 in octal
-24     // -24 in decimal
-024    // -20 in octal
-0x24   // -36 in hexadecimal
87U
87L
```

D.2.4.2 Floating Point

Floating point constants consist of three parts: an integer part, a decimal point, and a fractional part. The fractional part and integer part are optional, but one of the two must be present. The number preceded by a minus sign indicates a negative value. Several examples follow:

```
1.613123
.613123
1. // expresses the number 1.0
-.613123
```

Floating point literals can also be expressed in exponential notation. With this form, a floating point constant (such as 1.613123) is followed by an *e* or *E*. The *e* or *E* signals the beginning of the integer exponent, which is the power of ten by which the part preceding the exponent is multiplied. The exponent can be a negative value. The exponent is obviously optional, and if used, then the decimal point is optional. Examples follow:

```
6.023e23     // 6.023 * 10^23
454.323e-22  // 454.323 * 10^(-22)
5E13         // 5.0 * 10^13
```

By default, a floating point type is a `double` or double-precision floating point number. This can be modified with the optional suffix *f* or *F*, which indicates a `float` or single-precision floating point number. The suffix *l* or *L* indicates a `long double` (see Section D.3.2).

D.2.4.3 Character

A character literal can be expressed by surrounding a particular character by single quotes, for example, `'c'`. This converts the character into the internal character code used by the computer, which for most computers today, including the LC-3, is ASCII.

Table D.1 lists some special characters that typically cannot be expressed with a single keystroke. The C programming language provides a means to state them via a special sequence of characters. The last two forms, octal and hexadecimal, specify ways of stating an arbitrary character by using its code value, stated

Table D.1	Special Characters in C
Character	**Sequence**
newline	\n
horizontal tab	\t
vertical tab	\v
backspace	\b
carriage return	\r
formfeed	\f
audible alert	\a
backslash \	\\
question mark ?	\?
single quote '	\'
double quote "	\"
octal number	\0nnn
hexadecimal number	\xnnn

as either octal or hex. For example, the character 'S', which has the ASCII value of 83 (decimal), can be stated as '\0123' or '\x53'.

D.2.4.4 String Literals

A string literal within a C program must be enclosed within double quote characters, ". String literals have the type `char  *` and space for them is allocated in a special section of the memory address space reserved for literal constants. The termination character '\0' is automatically added to the character string. The following are two examples of string literals:

```
char greeting[10] = "bon jour!";
printf("This is a string literal");
```

String literals can be used to initialize character strings, or they can be used wherever an object of type `char  *` is expected, for example, as an argument to a function expecting a parameter of type `char  *`. String literals, however, cannot be used for the assignment of arrays. For example, the following code is **not** legal in C.

```
char greeting [10];

greeting = "bon jour!";
```

D.2.4.5 Enumeration Constants

Associated with an enumerated type (see Section D.3.1) are enumerators, or enumeration constants. These constants are of type `int`, and their precise value is defined by the enumerator list of an enumeration declaration. In essence, an enumeration constant is a symbolic, integral value.

D.2.5 Formatting

C is a freely formatted language. The programmer is free to add spaces, tabs, carriage returns, new lines between and within statements and declarations. C programmers often adopt a style helpful for making the code more readable, which includes adequate indenting of control constructs, consistent alignment of open and close braces, and adequate commenting that does not obstruct someone trying to read the code. See the numerous examples in the C programming chapters of the book for a typical style of formatting C code.

D.2.6 Keywords

The following list is a set of reserved words, or keywords, that have special meaning within the C language. They are the names of the primitive types, type modifiers, control constructs, and other features natively supported by the language. These names cannot be used by the programmer as names of variables, functions, or any other object that the programmer might provide a name for.

auto	extern	short	while
break	float	signed	_Alignas
case	for	sizeof	_Alignof
char	goto	static	_Atomic
const	if	struct	_Bool
continue	inline	switch	_Complex
default	int	typedef	_Generic
do	long	union	_Imaginary
double	register	unsigned	_Noreturn
else	restrict	void	_Static_assert
enum	return	volatile	_Thread_local

D.3 Types

In C, expressions, functions, and objects have types associated with them. The type of a variable, for example, indicates something about the actual value the variable represents. For instance, if the variable kappa is of type int, then the value (which is essentially just a bit pattern) referred to by kappa will be interpreted as a signed integer. In C, there are the *basic data types*, which are types natively supported by the programming language, and *derived types*, which are types based on basic types and which include programmer-defined types.

D.3.1 Basic Data Types

There are several predefined basic types within the C language: int, float, double, char, _Bool, _Complex, _Imaginary. They exist automatically within all implementations of C, although their sizes and range of values depend upon the computer system being used.

D.3.1.1 int

The binary value of something of int type will be interpreted as a signed whole number. Typical computers use 32 bits to represent signed integers, expressed in 2's complement form. Such integers can take on values between (and including) $-2,147,483,648$ and $+2,147,483,647$.

D.3.1.2 float

Objects declared of type float represent single-precision floating point numbers. These numbers typically, but not always, follow the representations defined by the IEEE standard for single-precision floating point numbers, which means that the type is a 32-bit type, where 1 bit is used for sign, 8 bits for exponent (expressed in bias-127 code), and 23 bits for fraction. See Section 2.7.1.

D.3.1.3 `double`

Objects declared of type `double` deal with double-precision floating point numbers. Like objects of type `float`, objects of type `double` are also typically represented using the IEEE standard. The precise difference between objects of type `float` and of type `double` depends on the system being used; however, the ANSI C standard specifies that the precision of a `double` should never be less than that of a `float`. On most machines a `double` is 64 bits.

D.3.1.4 `char`

Objects of character type contain a single character, expressed in the character code used by the computer system. Typical computer systems use the ASCII character code (see Appendix E). The size of a `char` is large enough to store a character from the character set. C also imposes that the size of a `short int` must be at least the size of a `char`.

Collectively, the `int` and `char` types (and enumerated types) are referred to as *integral* types, whereas `float` and `double` are floating types.

D.3.1.5 Enumerated Types

C provides a way for the programmer to specify objects that take on symbolic values. For example, we may want to create a type that takes on one of four values: `Penguin`, `Riddler`, `CatWoman`, `Joker`. We can do so by using an *enumerated* type, as follows:

```
// Specifier
enum villains { Penguin, Riddler, CatWoman, Joker };

// Declaration
enum villains badGuy;
```

The variable `badGuy` is of the enumerated type `villains`. It can take on one of the four symbolic values defined by enumerator list in the specifier. The four symbolic values are called *enumeration constants* (see Section D.2.4.5) and are actually integer values.

In an enumerator list, the value of the first enumeration constant will be 0, the next will be 1, and so forth. In the type `villains`, the value of `Penguin` will be 0, `Riddler` will be 1, `CatWoman` will be 2, `Joker` will be 3. The value of an enumerator can be explicitly set by the programmer by using the assignment operator, `=`. For example,

```
// Specifier
enum villains { Penguin = 3, Riddler, CatWoman, Joker };
```

causes `Penguin` to be 3, `Riddler` to be 4, and so forth.

D.3.2 Type Qualifiers

The basic types can be modified with the use of a type qualifier. These modifiers alter the basic type in some small fashion or change its default size.

D.3.2.1 `signed, unsigned`

The types `int` and `char` can be modified with the use of the `signed` and `unsigned` qualifiers. By default, integers are signed; the default on characters depends on the computer system.

For example, if a computer uses 32-bit 2's complement signed integers, then a `signed int` can have any value in the range $-2,147,483,648$ to $+2,147,483,647$. On the same machine, an `unsigned int` can have a value in the range 0 to $+4,294,967,295$.

```
signed int c;      // the signed modifier is redundant
unsigned int d;

signed char j;     // forces the char to be interpreted
                   // as a signed value

unsigned char k;   // the char will be interpreted as an
                   // unsigned value
```

D.3.2.2 `long, short`

The qualifiers `long` and `short` allow the programmer to manipulate the physical size of a basic type. For example, the qualifiers can be used with an integer to create `short int` and `long int`.

It is important to note that there is no strict definition of how much larger one type of integer is than another. The C language states only that the size of a `short int` is less than or equal to the size of an `int`, which is less than or equal to the size of a `long int`. Stated more completely and precisely:

```
sizeof(char) <= sizeof(short int) <= sizeof(int) <= sizeof(long int)
```

New computers that support 64-bit data types make a distinction on the `long` qualifier. On these machines, a `long int` might be a 64-bit integer, whereas an `int` might be a 32-bit integer. The range of values of types on a particular computer can be found in the standard header file `<limits.h>`. On most UNIX systems, it will be in the `/usr/include` directory.

The following are several examples of type modifiers on the integral data types.

```
short int q;
long int p;
unsigned long int r;
```

The `long` and `short` qualifiers can also be used with the floating type `double` to create a floating point number with higher precision or larger range (if such a type is available on the computer) than a `double`. As stated by the ANSI C specification, the size of a `float` is less than or equal to the size of a `double`, which is less than or equal to the size of a `long double`.

```
double x;
long double y;
```

D.3.2.3 `const`

A value that does not change through the course of execution can be qualified with the `const` qualifier. For example,

```
const double pi = 3.14159;
```

By using this qualifier, the programmer is providing information that might enable an optimizing compiler to perform more powerful optimizations on the resulting code. All variables with a `const` qualifier must be explicitly initialized.

D.3.3 Storage Class

Memory objects in C can be of the *static* or *automatic* storage class. Objects of the automatic class are local to a block (such as a function) and lose their value once their block is completed. By default, local variables within a function are of the automatic class and are allocated on the run-time stack (see Section 14.3.1).

Objects of the *static* class retain their values throughout program execution. Global variables and other objects declared outside of all blocks are of the static class. Objects declared within a function can be qualified with the `static` qualifier to indicate that they are to be allocated with other static objects, allowing their value to persist across invocations of the function in which they are declared. For example,

```
int Count(int x)
{
  static int y;

  y++;
  printf("This function has been called %d times.", y);
}
```

The value of *y* will not be lost when the activation record of `Count` is popped off the stack. To enable this, the compiler will allocate a static local variable in the global data section. Every call of the function `count` updates the value of *y*.

Unlike typical local variables of the automatic class, variables of the static class are initialized to zero. Variables of the automatic class must be initialized by the programmer.

There is a special qualifier called `register` that can be applied to objects in the automatic class. This qualifier provides a hint to the compiler that the value is frequently accessed within the code and should be allocated in a register to potentially enhance performance. The compiler, however, treats this only as a suggestion and can override or ignore this specifier based on its own analysis.

Functions, as well as variables, can be qualified with the qualifier `extern`. This qualifier indicates that the function's or variable's storage is defined in another object module that will be linked together with the current module when the executable is constructed.

D.3.4 Derived Types

The derived types are extensions of the basic types provided by C. The derived types include pointers, arrays, structures, and unions. Structures and unions enable the programmer to create new types that are aggregations of other types.

D.3.4.1 Arrays

An array is a sequence of objects of a particular type that is allocated sequentially in memory. That is, if the first element of the array of type T is at memory location X, the next element will be at memory location X + sizeof(T), and so forth. Each element of the array is accessible using an integer index, starting with the index 0. That is, the first element of array list is list[0], numbered starting at 0. The size of the array must be stated as a constant integral expression (it is not required to be a literal) when the array is declared.

```
char string[100]; // Declares array of 100 characters
int  data[20];    // Declares array of 20 integers
```

To access a particular element within an array, an index is formed using an integral expression within square brackets, [ ].

```
data[0]        // Accesses first element of array data
data[i + 3]    // The variable i must be an integer
string[x + y]  // x and y must be integers
```

The compiler is not required to check (nor is it required to generate code to check) whether the value of the index falls within the bounds of the array. The responsibility of ensuring proper access to the array is upon the programmer. For example, based on the previous declarations and array expressions, the reference string[x + y], the value of x + y should be 100 or less; otherwise, the reference exceeds the bounds of the array string.

D.3.4.2 Pointers

Pointers are objects that are addresses of other objects. Pointer types are declared by prefixing an identifier with an asterisk, *. The type of a pointer indicates the type of the object that the pointer points to. For example,

```
int *v;   // v points to an integer
```

C allows a restricted set of operations to be used on pointer variables. Pointers can be manipulated in expressions, thus allowing "pointer arithmetic" to be performed. C allows assignment between pointers of the same type, or assignment, of a pointer to 0. Assignment of a pointer to the constant value 0 causes the generation of a null pointer. Integer values can be added to or subtracted from a pointer value. Also, pointers of the same type can be compared (using the relational operators) or subtracted from one another, but this is meaningful only if the pointers involved point to elements of the same array. All other pointer manipulations are not explicitly allowed in C but can be done with the appropriate casting.

D.3.4.3 Structures

Structures enable the programmer to specify an aggregate type. That is, a structure consists of member elements, each of which has its own type. The programmer can specify a structure using the following syntax. Notice that each member element has its own type.

```
struct tag_id {
  type1 member1;
  type2 member2;
  :
  :
  typeN memberN;
};
```

This structure has member elements named `member1` of type `type1`, `member2` of type2, up to `memberN` of `typeN`. Member elements can take on any basic or derived type, including other programmer-defined types.

The programmer can specify an optional tag, which in this case is `tag_id`. Using the tag, the programmer can declare structure variables, such as the variable x in the following declaration:

```
struct tag_id x;
```

A structure is defined by its tag. Multiple structures can be declared in a program with the same member elements and member element identifiers; they are different if they have different tags.

Alternatively, variables can be declared along with the structure declaration, as shown in the following example. In this example, the variable firstPoint is declared along with the structure. The array image is declared using the structure tag point.

```
struct point {
  int x;
  int y;
} firstPoint;

// declares an array of structure type variables
struct point image[100];
```

See Section 19.2 for more information on structures.

D.3.4.4 Unions

Structures are containers that hold multiple objects of various types. Unions, on the other hand, are containers that hold a single object that can take on different predetermined types at various points in a program. For example, the following is the declaration of a union variable joined:

```
union u_tag {
  int    ival;
  double fval;
  char   cval;
} joined;
```

The variable joined ultimately contains bits. These bits can be an integer, double, or character data type, depending on what the programmer decides to put there. For example, the variable will be treated as an integer with the expression joined.ival, or as a double-precision floating point value with joined.fval, or as a character with joined.cval. The compiler will allocate enough space for union variables as required for the largest data type.

D.3.5 `typedef`

In C, a programmer can use typedef to create a synonym for an existing type. This is particularly useful for providing names for programmer-defined types. The general form for a typedef follows:

```
typedef type name;
```

Here, type can be any basic type, enumerated type, or derived type. The identifier name can be any legal identifier. The result of this typedef is that name is a synonym for type. The typedef declaration is an important feature for enhancing code readability; a well-chosen type name conveys additional information about the object declared of that type. Following are some examples.

```
typedef enum {coffee, tea, water, soda} Beverage;
Beverage drink;    // Declaration uses previous typedef
typedef struct {
    int xCoord;
    int yCoord;
    int color;
} Pixel;

Pixel bitmap[1024*820]; // Declares an array of pixels
```

D.4 Declarations

An *object* is a named section of memory, such as a variable. In C, an object must be declared with a declaration before it can be used. Declarations inform the compiler of characteristics, such as its type, name, and storage class, so that correct machine code can be generated whenever the object is manipulated within the body of the program.

In C, functions are also declared before they are used. A function declaration informs the compiler about the return value, function name, and types and order of input parameters.

D.4.1 Variable Declarations

The format for a variable declaration is as follows:

```
[storage-class] [type-qualifier] {type} {identifier} [ = initializer] ;
```

The curly braces, { }, indicate items that are required and the square brackets, [ ], indicate optional items.

The optional *storage-class* can be any storage class modifier listed in Section D.3.3, such as `static`.

The optional *type-qualifier* can be any legal type qualifiers, such as the qualifiers provided in Section D.3.2.

The *type* of a variable can be any of the basic types (`int`, `char`, `float`, `double`), enumerated types, or derived types (array, pointer, structure, or union).

An *identifier* can be any sequence of letters, digits, and the underscore character, _. The first character must be a letter or the underscore character. Identifiers can have any length, but for most variables you will use, at least 31 characters will be significant. That is, variables that differ only after the 31st character might be treated as the same variable by an ANSI C compiler. Uppercase letters are different from lowercase, so the identifier `sum` is different from `Sum`. Identifiers must be different from any of the C keywords (see Section D.2.6). Several examples of legal identifiers follow. Each is a distinct identifier.

```
blue
Blue1
Blue2
_blue_
bluE
primary_colors
primaryColors
```

The *initializer* for variables of automatic storage (see Section D.3.3) can be any expression that uses previously defined values. For variables of the static class (such as global values) or external variables, the initializer must be a constant expression.

Also, multiple identifiers (and initializers) can be placed on the same line, creating multiple variables of the same type, having the same storage class and type characteristics.

```
static long unsigned int k = 10UL;
register char 1 = 'Q';
int list[100];
struct node_type n;  // Declares a structure variable
```

Declarations can be placed at the beginning of any *block* (see Section D.6.2), before any statements. Such declarations are visible only within the block in which they appear. Declarations can also appear at the outermost level of the program, outside of all functions. Such declarations are *global variables*. They are visible from all parts of the program. See Section 12.2.3 for more information on variable declarations.

D.4.2 Function Declarations

A function's declaration informs the compiler about the type of value returned by the function and the type, number, and order of parameters the function expects to receive from its caller. The format for a function declaration is as follows:

```
{type} {function-id}([type1] [, type2], ... [, typeN]);
```

The curly braces, { }, indicate items that are required and the square brackets, [ ], indicate items that are optional.

The *type* indicates the type of the value returned by the function and can be of any basic type, enumerated type, a structure, a union, a pointer, or void (note: it cannot be an array). If a function does not return a value, then its type must be declared as void.

The *function-id* can be any legal identifier that has not already been defined.

Enclosed within parentheses following the *function-id* are the types of each of the input parameters expected by the function, indicated by *type1*, *type2*, *typeN*, each separated by a comma. Optionally, an identifier can be supplied for each argument, indicating what the particular argument will be called within the function's definition. For example, the following might be a declaration for a function that returns the average of an array of integers:

```
int Average(int numbers[], int howMany);
```

D.5 Operators

In this section, we describe the C operators. The operators are grouped by the operations they perform.

D.5.1 Assignment Operators

C supports multiple assignment operators, the most basic of which is the simple assignment operator =. All assignment operators associate from right to left.

A standard form for a simple assignment expression is as follows:

```
{left-expression} = {right-expression}
```

The *left-expression* must be a modifiable object. It cannot, for example, be a function, an object with a type qualifier const, or an array (it can, however, be an element of an array). The *left-expression* is often referred to as an *lvalue*. The *left-expression* can be an object of a structure or union type.

After the assignment expression is evaluated, the value of the object referred to by the *left-expression* will take on the value of the *right-expression*. In most usages of the assignment operator, the types of the two expressions will be the same. If they are different, and both are basic types, then the right operand is converted to the type of the left operand.

The other assignment operators include:

```
+=   -=   *=   /=   %=   &=   |=   ^=   <<=   >>=
```

All of these assignment operators combine an operation with an assignment. In general, A op= B is equivalent to A = A op (B). For example, x += y is equivalent to x = x + y.

Examples of the various assignment operators can be found in Sections 12.3.2 and 12.6.3.

D.5.2 Arithmetic Operators

C supports basic arithmetic operations via the following binary operators:

```
+    -    *    /    %
```

These operators perform addition, subtraction, multiplication, division, and modulus. These operators are most commonly used with operands of the basic types (int, double, float, and char). If the operands have different types (such as a floating point value plus an integer), then the resulting expression is converted according to the conversion rules (see Section D.5.11). There is one restriction, however: the operands of the modulus operator % must be of the integral type (e.g., int, char, or enumerated).

The addition and subtraction operators can also be used with pointers that point to values within arrays. The use of these operators in this context is referred to as pointer arithmetic. For example, the expression ptr + 1 where ptr is of type type *, is equivalent to ptr + sizeof(type). The expression ptr + 1 generates the address of the next element in the array.

C also supports the two unary operators + and -. The negation operator, -, generates the negative of its operand. The unary plus operator, +, generates its operand. This operator is included in the C language primarily for symmetry with the negation operator.

For more examples involving the arithmetic operators, see Section 12.3.3.

D.5.3 Bit-Wise Operators

The following operators:

```
&    |    ^    ~    <<    >>
```

are C's bit-wise operators. They perform bit-wise operation only on integral values. That is, they cannot be used with floating point values.

The left shift operator, <<, and right shift operator, >>, evaluate to the value of the left operand shifted by the number of bit positions indicated by the right operand. In ANSI C, if the right operand is greater than the number of bits in the representation (say, for example, 33 for a 32-bit integer) or negative, then the result is undefined.

Table D.2 provides some additional details on these operators. It provides an example usage and evaluation of each with an integer operand x equal to 186 and the integer operand y equal to 6.

Table D.2	Bit-Wise Operators in C		
Operator Symbol	Operation	Example Usage	x=186 y=6
&	bit-wise AND	x & y	2
|	bit-wise OR	x | y	190
~	bit-wise NOT	~ x	−187
^	bit-wise XOR	x ^ y	188
<<	left shift	x << y	11904
>>	right shift	x >> y	2

D.5.4 Logical Operators

The logical operators in C are particularly useful for constructing logical expressions with multiple clauses. For example, if we want to test whether both condition A and condition B are true, then we might want to use the logical AND operator.

The logical AND operator takes two operands (which do not need to be of the same type). The operator evaluates to a 1 if both operands are nonzero. It evaluates to 0 otherwise.

The logical OR operator takes two operands and evaluates to 1 if either is nonzero. If both are zero, the operator evaluates to 0.

The logical NOT operator is a unary operator that evaluates to the logical inverse of its operand: it evaluates to 1 if the operand is zero, 0 otherwise.

The logical AND and logical OR operators are *short-circuit* operators. That is, if in evaluating the left operand, the value of the operation becomes known, then the right operand is not evaluated. For example, in evaluating $(x \mid\mid y{+}{+})$, if x is nonzero, then y++ will not be evaluated, meaning that the side effect of the increment will not occur.

Table D.3 provides some additional details on the logical operators and provides an example usage and evaluation of each with an integer operand x equal to 186 and the integer operand y equal to 6.

Table D.3	Logical Operators in C		
Operator Symbol	Operation	Example Usage	x=186 y=6
&&	logical AND	x && y	1
||	logical OR	x || y	1
!	logical NOT	!x	0

D.5.5 Relational Operators

The following operators:

```
==   !=   >   >=   <   <=
```

are the relational operators in C. They perform a relational comparison between the left and right operands, such as equal to, not equal to, and greater than. The typical use of these operators is to compare expressions of the basic types. If the relationship is true, then the result is the integer value 1; otherwise, it is 0. Expressions of mixed type undergo the standard type conversions described in Section D.5.11. C also allows the relational operators to be used on pointers. However, such pointer expressions only have meaning if both pointers point to the same object, such as the same array.

D.5.6 Increment/Decrement Operators

The increment/decrement operators in C are ++ and --. They increment or decrement the operand by 1. Both operators can be used in *prefix* and *postfix* forms.

In the prefix form, for example ++x, the value of the object is incremented (or decremented). The value of the expression is then the value of the result. For example, after the following executes:

```
int x = 4;
int y;

y = ++x;
```

both x and y equal 5.

In the postfix form, for example x++, the value of the expression is the value of the operand prior to the increment (or decrement). Once the value is recorded, the operand is incremented (or decremented) by 1. For example, the result of the following code:

```
int x = 4;
int y;

y = x++;
```

is that x equals 5 and y equals 4.

Like the addition and subtraction operators, the increment and decrement operators can be used with pointer types. See Section D.5.2.

D.5.7 Conditional Expression Operators

The conditional expression operator in C has the following form:

```
(expressionA) ? (expressionB) : (expressionC)
```

Here, if *expressionA* is logically true, that is, it evaluates to a nonzero value, then the value of the entire expression is the value of *expressionB*. If *expressionA* is logically false, that is, it evaluates to zero, then the value of the entire expression is the value of *expressionC*. For example, in the following code segment:

```
w = x ? y : z;
```

the value of the conditional expression x ? y : z will depend on the value of x. If x is nonzero, then w will be assigned the value of y. Otherwise w will be assigned the value of z.

Like the logical AND and logical OR operators, the conditional expression short-circuits the evaluation of *expressionB* or *expressionC*, depending on the state of *expressionA*. See Section D.5.4.

D.5.8 Pointer, Array, and Structure Operators

This final batch of operators performs address-related operations for use with the derived data types.

D.5.8.1 Address Operator

The address operator is the &. It takes the address of its operand. The operand must be a memory object, such as a variable, array element, or structure member.

D.5.8.2 Dereference Operator

The complement of the address operator is the dereference operator. It returns the object to which the operand is pointing. For example, given the following code:

```
int *p;
int x = 5;

p = &x;
*p = *p + 1;
```

the expression *p returns x. When *p appears on the left-hand side of an assignment operator, it is treated as an lvalue (see Section D.5.1). Otherwise *p evaluates to the value of x.

D.5.8.3 Array Reference

In C, an integral expression within square brackets, [ ], designates a subscripted array reference. The typical use of this operator is with an object declared as an array. The following code contains an example of an array reference on the array list.

```
int x;
int list [100];

x = list[x + 10];
```

D.5.8.4 Structure and Union References

C contains two operators for referring to member elements within a structure or union. The first is the dot, or period, which directly accesses the member element of a structure or union variable. The following is an example:

```
struct pointType {
    int x;
    int y;
};
typedef pointType Point;

Point pixel;

pixel.x = 3;
pixel.y = pixel.x + 10;
```

The variable `pixel` is a structure variable, and its member elements are accessed using the dot operator.

The second means of accessing member elements of a structure is the arrow, or `->` operator. Here, a pointer to a structure or union can be dereferenced and a member element selected with a single operator. The following code demonstrates:

```
Point pixel;
Point *ptr;

ptr = &pixel;
ptr->x = ptr->x + 1;
```

Here, the pointer variable `ptr` points to the structure variable `pixel`.

D.5.9 `sizeof`

The `sizeof` operator returns the number of bytes required to store an object of the type specified. For example, `sizeof(int)` will return the number of bytes occupied by an integer. If the operand is an array, then `sizeof` will return the size of the array. The following is an example:

```
int list [45];

struct example_type {
   int    valueA;
   int    valueB;
   double valueC;
};
typedef struct example_type Example;

...

sizeA = sizeof(list);      /* 45 * sizeof(int)  */
sizeB = sizeof(Example);   /* Size of structure */
```

D.5.10 Order of Evaluation

The order of evaluation of an expression starts at the subexpression in the innermost parentheses, with the operator with the highest *precedence*, moving to the operator with the lowest precedence within the same subexpression. If two operators have the same precedence (e.g., two of the same operators, as in the expression $2 + 3 + 4$), then the *associativity* of the operators determines the order of evaluation, either from left to right or from right to left. The evaluation of the expression continues recursively from there.

Table D.4 provides the *precedence* and *associativity* of the C operators. The operators of highest precedence are listed at the top of the table, in lower numbered precedence groups.

Table D.4		Operator Precedence, from Highest to Lowest. Descriptions of Some Operators Are Provided in Parentheses

Precedence Group	Associativity	Operators
1 (highest)	l to r	( ) (function call) [ ] (array index) . ->
2	r to l	++ -- (postfix versions)
3	r to l	++ -- (prefix versions)
4	r to l	* (indirection) & (address of) + (unary) - (unary) ~ ! sizeof
5	r to l	(type) (type cast)
6	l to r	* (multiplication) / %
7	l to r	+ (addition) - (subtraction)
8	l to r	« »
9	l to r	< > <= >=
10	l to r	== !=
11	l to r	&
12	l to r	^
13	l to r		
14	l to r	&&
15	l to r	||
16	l to r	?:
17 (lowest)	r to l	= += -= *= etc.

D.5.11 Type Conversions

Consider the following expression involving the operator *op*.

```
A op B
```

The resulting value of this expression will have a particular type associated with it. This resulting type depends on (1) the types of the operands *A* and *B*, and (2) the nature of the operator *op*.

If the types of *A* and *B* are the same and the operator can operate on that type, the result is the type defined by the operator.

When an expression contains variables that are a mixture of the basic types, C performs a set of standard arithmetic conversions of the operand values. In general, smaller types are converted into larger types, and integral types are converted into floating types. For example, if *A* is of type double and *B* is of type int, the result is of type double. Integral values, such as char, int, or an enumerated type, are converted to int (or unsigned int, depending on the implementation). The following are examples.

```
char   i;
int    j;
float  x;
double y;

i * j     // This expression is an integer
j + 1     // This expression is an integer
j + 1.0   // This expression is a float
i + 1.0   // This expression is a float
x + y     // This expression is a double
i + j + x + y      // This is a double
```

As in case (2) above, some operators require operands of a particular type or generate results of a particular type. For example, the modulus operator % only operates on integral values. Here integral type conversions are performed on the operands (e.g., `char` is converted to `int`). Floating point values are not allowed and will generate compilation errors.

If a floating point type is converted to an integral type (which does not happen with the usual type conversion, but can happen with casting as described in the next subsection), the fractional portion is discarded. If the resulting integer cannot be represented by the integral type, the result is undefined.

D.5.11.1 Casting

The programmer can explicitly control the type conversion process by *type casting*. A cast has the general form:

```
(new-type) expression
```

Here the expression is converted into the *new-type* using the usual conversion rules described in the preceding paragraphs. Continuing with the previous example code:

```
j = (int) x + y; // This results in conversion of
                 // double into an integer
```

D.6 Expressions and Statements

In C, the work performed by a program is described by the expressions and statements within the bodies of functions.

D.6.1 Expressions

An expression is any legal combination of constants, variables, operators, and function calls that evaluates to a value of a particular type. The order of evaluation is based on the precedence and associativity rules described in Section D.5.10. The type of an expression is based on the individual elements of the expression, according to the C type promotion rules (see Section D.5.11). If all the elements of an expression are `int` types, then the expression is of `int` type. Following are several examples of expressions:

```
a * a + b * b
a++ - c / 3
a <= 4
q || integrate(x)
```

D.6.2 Statements

In C, simple statements are expressions terminated by a semicolon, ;. Typically, statements modify a variable or have some other side effect when the expression is evaluated. Once a statement has completed execution, the next statement in sequential order is executed. If the statement is the last statement in its function, then the function terminates.

```
c = a * a + b * b;  // Two simple statements
b = a++ - c / 3;
```

Related statements can be grouped together into a compound statement, or *block*, by surrounding them with curly braces, { }. Syntactically, the compound statement is the same as a simple statement, and they can be used interchangeably.

```
{                    // One compound statement
  c = a * a + b * b;
  b = a++ - c / 3;
}
```

D.7 Control

The control constructs in C enable the programmer to alter the sequential execution of statements with statements that execute conditionally or iteratively.

D.7.1 If

An if statement has the format

```
if  (expression)
    statement
```

If the *expression*, which can be of any basic, enumerated, or pointer types, evaluates to a nonzero value, then the *statement*, which can be a simple or compound statement, is executed.

```
if (x < 0)
    a = b + c; // Executes if x is less than zero
```

See Section 13.2.1 for more examples of if statements.

D.7.2 If-else

An if-else statement has the format

```
if (expression)
    statement1
else
    statement2
```

If the *expression*, which can be of any basic, enumerated, or pointer type, evaluates to a nonzero value, then *statement1* is executed. Otherwise, *statement2* is executed. Both *statement1* and *statement2* can be simple or compound statements.

```
if (x < 0)
    a = b + c; // Executes if x is less than zero
else
    a = b - c; // Otherwise, this is executed.
```

See Section 13.2.2 for more examples of if-else statements.

D.7.3 Switch

A switch statement has the following format:

```
switch(expression)  {
case const-expr1:
        statement1A
        statement1B
        :

case const-expr2:
        statement2A
        statement2B
        :


        :
        :


case const-exprN:
        statementNA
        statementNB
        :

}
```

A switch statement is composed of an *expression*, which must be of integral type (see Section D.3.1), followed by a compound statement (although it is not required to be compound, it almost always is). Within the compound statement exist one or more case labels, each with an associated constant integral expression, called *const-expr1, const-expr2, const-exprN* in the preceding example. Within a switch, each case label must be different.

When a switch is encountered, the controlling *expression* is evaluated. If one of the case labels matches the value of *expression*, then control jumps to the statement that follows and proceeds from there.

The special case label default can be used to catch the situation where none of the other case labels match. If the default case is not present and none of the labels match the value of the controlling expression, then no statements within the switch are executed.

The following is an example of a code segment that uses a switch statement. The use of the break statement causes control to leave the switch. See Section D.7.7 for more information on break.

```
char k;

k = getchar();
switch (k) {
case '+':
  a = b + c;
  break;        // break causes control to leave switch

case '-':
  a = b - c;
  break;

case '*':
  a = b * c;
  break;

case '/':
  a = b / c;
  break;
}
```

See Section 13.5.1 for more examples of `switch` statements.

D.7.4 While

A `while` statement has the following format:

```
while (expression)
  statement
```

The `while` statement is an iteration construct. If the value of *expression* evaluates to nonzero, then the *statement* is executed. Control does not pass to the subsequent statement, but rather the *expression* is evaluated again and the process is repeated. This continues until *expression* evaluates to 0, in which case control passes to the next statement. The *statement* can be a simple or compound statement.

In the following example, the `while` loop will iterate 100 times.

```
x = 0;
while  (x < 100)  {
   printf("x = %d\n", x);
   x = x + 1;
}
```

See Section 13.3.1 for more examples of `while` statements.

D.7.5 For

A `for` statement has the following format:

```
for (initializer;  term-expr;  reinitializer)
  statement
```

The `for` statement is an iteration construct. The *initializer*, which is an expression, is evaluated only once, before the loop begins. The *term-expr* is an expression that is evaluated before each iteration of the loop. If the *term-expr* evaluates to nonzero, the loop progresses; otherwise, the loop terminates and control passes to the statement following the loop. Each iteration of the loop consists of the execution of the *statement*, which makes up the body of the loop, and the evaluation of the *reinitializer* expression.

The following example is a `for` loop that iterates 100 times.

```
for (x = 0; x < 100; X++)  {
    printf("x = %d\n", x);
}
```

See Section 13.3.2 for more examples of `for` statements.

D.7.6 `Do-while`

A `do-while` statement has the format

```
do
    statement
while (expression);
```

The `do-while` statement is an iteration construct similar to the `while` statement. When a `do-while` is first encountered, the *statement* that makes up the loop body is executed first, then the *expression* is evaluated to determine whether to execute another iteration. If it is nonzero, then another iteration is executed (in other words, *statement* is executed again). In this manner, a `do-while` always executes its loop body at least once.

The following `do-while` loop iterates 100 times.

```
x = 0;
do {
    printf("x = %d\n", x);
    x = x + 1;
}
while (x < 100);
```

See Section 13.3.3 for more examples of `do-while` statements.

D.7.7 `Break`

A `break` statement has the format:

```
break;
```

The `break` statement can only be used in an iteration statement or in a `switch` statement. It passes control out of the smallest statement containing it to the statement immediately following. Typically, break is used to exit a loop before the terminating condition is encountered.

In the following example, the execution of the break statement causes control to pass out of the for loop.

```
for (x = 0; x < 100; x++)  {
    :
    :
    if (error)
        break;
    :
    :
}
```

See Section 13.5.2 for more examples of break statements.

D.7.8 continue

A continue statement has the following format:

```
continue;
```

The continue statement can be used only in an iteration statement. It prematurely terminates the execution of the loop body. That is, it terminates the current iteration of the loop. The looping expression is evaluated to determine whether another iteration should be performed. In a for loop, the *reinitializer* is also evaluated.

If the continue statement is executed, then x is incremented, and the *reinitializer* executed, and the loop expression evaluated to determine if another iteration should be executed.

```
for (x = 0; x < 100; x++)  {
    :
    :
    if (skip)
        continue;
    :
    :
}
```

See Section 13.5.2 for more examples of continue statements.

D.7.9 return

A return statement has the format

```
return expression;
```

The return statement causes control to return to the current caller function, that is, the function that called the function that contains the return statement. Also, after the last statement of a function is executed, an implicit return is made to the caller.

The expression that follows the return is the return value generated by the function. It is converted to the return type of the function. If a function returns a value, and yet no `return` statement within the function explicitly generates a return value, then the return value is undefined.

```
return x + y;
```

D.8 The C Preprocessor

The C programming language includes a preprocessing step that modifies, in a programmer-controlled manner, the source code presented to the compiler. The most frequently used features of the C preprocessor are its macro substitution facility (#define), which replaces a sequence of source text with another sequence, and the file inclusion facility (#include), which includes the contents of a file into the source text. Both of these are described in the following subsections.

None of the preprocessor directives are required to end with a semicolon. Since #define and #include are preprocessor directives and not C statements, they are not required to be terminated by semicolons.

D.8.1 Macro Substitution

The #define preprocessor directive instructs the C preprocessor to replace occurrences of one character sequence with another. Consider the following example:

```
#define A B
```

Here, any token that matches A will be replaced by B. That is, the *macro* A gets *substituted* with B. The character A must appear as an individual sequence; that is, the A in APPLE will not be substituted, nor will an A that appears in quoted strings, that is, "A".

The replacement text spans until the end of the line. If a longer sequence is required, the backslash character, \, can be used to continue to the next line.

Macros can also take arguments. They are specified in parentheses immediately after the text to be replaced. For example:

```
#define REMAINDER(X, Y)    ((X) % (Y))
```

Here, every occurrence of the macro COPY in the source code will be accompanied by two values, as in the following example.

```
valueC = REMAINDER(valueA, valueB + 15);
```

The macro REMAINDER will be replaced by the preprocessor with the replacement text provided in the #define, and the two arguments A and B will be substituted with the two arguments that appear in the source code. The previous code will be modified to the following after preprocessing:

```
valueC = ((valueA) % (valueB + 15));
```

Notice that the parentheses surrounding X and Y in the macro definition were required. Without them, the macro REMAINDER would have calculated the wrong value.

While the REMAINDER macro appears to be similar to a function call, notice that it incurs none of the function call overhead associated with regular functions.

D.8.2 File Inclusion

The #include directive instructs the preprocessor to insert the contents of a file into the source file. Typically, the #include directive is used to attach header files to C source files. *C header files* typically contain #defines and declarations that are useful among multiple source files.

There are two variations of the #include directive:

```
#include <stdio.h>
#include "program.h"
```

The first variation uses angle brackets, $<$ $>$, around the filename. This tells the preprocessor that the header file can be found in a predefined directory, usually determined by the configuration of the system and which contains many system-related and library-related header files, such as stdio.h. The second variation, using double quotes, " ", around the filename, instructs the preprocessor that the header file can be found in the same directory as the C source file.

D.9 Some Standard Library Functions

The ANSI C standard library contains over 150 functions that perform a variety of useful tasks (e.g., I/O and dynamic memory allocation) on behalf of your program. Every installation of ANSI C will have these functions available, so even if you make use of these functions, your program will still be portable from one ANSI C platform to another. In this section, we will describe some useful standard library functions.

D.9.1 I/O Functions

The <stdio.h> header file must be included in any source file that contains calls to the standard I/O functions. Following is a small sample of these functions.

D.9.1.1 getchar

This function has the following declaration:

```
int getchar(void);
```

The function getchar reads the next character from the standard input device, or stdin. The value of this character is returned (as an integer) as the return value.

The behavior of getchar is very similar to the LC-3 input TRAP (except no input banner is displayed on the screen).

Most computer systems will implement `getchar` using buffered I/O. This means that keystrokes (assuming standard input is coming from the keyboard) will be buffered by the operating system until the Enter key is pressed. Once Enter is pressed, the entire line of characters is added to the standard input stream.

D.9.1.2 `putchar`

This function has the following declaration:

```
void putchar(int c);
```

The function `putchar` takes an integer value representing an ASCII character and puts the character to the standard output stream. This is similar to the LC-3 TRAP OUT.

If the standard output stream is the monitor, the character will appear on the screen. However, since many systems buffer the output stream, the character may not appear until the system's output buffer is *flushed*, which is usually done once a newline appears in the output stream.

D.9.1.3 `scanf`

This function has the following declaration:

```
int scanf(const char *formatstring, *ptr1, ...);
```

The function `scanf` is passed a format string (which is passed as pointer to the initial character) and a list of pointers. The format string contains format specifications that control how `scanf` will interpret fields in the input stream. For example, the specification %d causes `scanf` to interpret the next sequence of non–white space characters as a decimal number. This decimal is converted from ASCII into an integer value and assigned to the variable pointed to by the next pointer in the parameter list. Table D.5 contains a listing of the possible specifications for use with `scanf`. The number of pointers that follow the format string in the parameter list should correspond to the number of format specifications in the format string. The value returned by `scanf` corresponds to the number of variables that were successfully assigned.

Table D.5	`scanf` Conversion Specifications
`scanf` Conversions	Parameter Type
%d	signed decimal
%i	decimal, octal (leading 0), hex (leading 0x or 0X)
%o	octal
%x	hexadecimal
%u	unsigned decimal
%c	char
%s	string of non–white space characters, \0 added
%f, %e	floating point number
%lf	double precision floating point number

D.9.1.4 `printf`

This function has the following declaration:

```
int printf(const char *formatString, ...);
```

The function `printf` writes the format string (passed as a pointer to the initial character) to the standard output stream. If the format string contains a format specification, then `printf` will interpret the next parameter in the parameter list as indicated by the specification and will embed the interpreted value into the output stream. For example, the format specification %d will cause `printf` to interpret the next parameter as a decimal value. `printf` will write the resulting digits into the output stream. Table D.6 contains a listing of the format specifications for use with `printf`. In general, the number of values following the format string on the parameter list should correspond to the number of format specifications in the format string. `printf` returns the number of characters written to the output stream. However, if an error occurs, a negative value is returned.

Table D.6	`printf` Conversion Specifications
`printf` Conversions	Printed as
%d, %i	signed decimal
%o	octal
%x, %X	hexadecimal (a–f or A–F)
%u	unsigned decimal
%c	single char
%s	string, terminated by \0
%f	floating point in decimal notation
%e, %E	floating point in exponential notation
%p	pointer

D.9.2 String Functions

The C standard library contains around 15 functions that perform operations on strings (i.e., null-terminated arrays of characters). To use the string functions from within a program, include the `<string.h>` header file in each source file that contains a call to a library string function. In this section, we describe two examples of C string functions.

D.9.2.1 `strcmp`

This function has the following declaration:

```
int strcmp(char *stringA, char *stringB);
```

This function compares `stringA` with `stringB`. It returns a 0 if they are equal. It returns a value greater than 0 if `stringA` is lexicographically greater than `stringB` (lexicographically greater means that `stringA` occurs later in a dictionary than `stringB`). It returns a value less than 0 if `stringA` is lexicographically less than `stringB`.

D.9.2.2 `strcpy`

This function has the following declaration:

```
char *strcpy(char *stringA, char *stringB);
```

This function copies `stringB` to `stringA`. It copies every character in `stringB` up to and including the null character. The function returns a pointer to `stringA` if no errors occurred.

D.9.3 Math Functions

The C standard math functions perform commonly used mathematical operations. Using them requires including the `<math.h>` header file. In this section, we list a small sample of C math functions. Each of the listed functions takes as parameters values of type `double`, and each returns a value of type `double`.

```
double sin(double x);    // sine of x, expressed in radians
double cos(double x);    // cosine of x, expressed in radians
double tan(double x);    // tan of x, expressed in radians
double exp(double x);    // exponential function, e^x
double log(double x);    // natural log of x
double sqrt(double x);   // square root of x
double pow(double x, double y)   // x^y -- x to the y power
```

D.9.4 Utility Functions

The C library contains a set of functions that perform useful tasks such as memory allocation, data conversion, sorting, and other miscellaneous things. The common header file for these functions is `<stdlib.h>`.

D.9.4.1 `malloc`

As described in Section 19.4, the function `malloc` allocates a fixed-sized chunk from memory.

This function has the following declaration:

```
void *malloc(size_t size);
```

The input parameter is the number of bytes to be allocated. The parameter is of type `size_t`, which is the same type returned by the `sizeof` operator (very often, this type is `typedef`ed as an unsigned integer). If the memory allocation goes successfully, a pointer to the allocated region of memory is returned. If the request cannot be satisfied, the value `NULL` is returned.

D.9.4.2 `free`

This function has the following declaration:

```
void free(void *ptr);
```

This function returns to the heap a previously allocated chunk of memory pointed to by the parameter. In other words, `free` deallocates memory pointed to by `ptr`. The value passed to `free` must be a pointer to a previously allocated region of memory, otherwise errors could occur.

D.9.4.3 `rand` and `srand`

The C standard utility functions contain a function to generate a sequence of random numbers. The function is called `rand`. It does not generate a truly random sequence, however. Instead, it generates the same sequence of varying values based on an initial *seed* value. When the seed is changed, a different sequence is generated. For example, when seeded with the value 10, the generator will always generate the same sequence of numbers. However, this sequence will be different than the sequence generated by another seed value.

The function `rand` has the following declaration:

```
int rand(void)
```

It returns a pseudo-random integer in the range 0 to `RAND_MAX`, which is at least 32,767.

To seed the pseudo-random number generator, use the function `srand`. This function has the following declaration:

```
void srand(unsigned int seed);
```

APPENDIX

E

Useful Tables

E.1 Commonly Used Numerical Prefixes

Table E.1	Numerical Prefixes			
Amount	Commonly Used Base-2 Approx.	Prefix	Abbreviation	Derived From
10^{24}	2^{80}	yotta	Y	Greek for eight: okto
10^{21}	2^{70}	zetta	Z	Greek for seven: hepta
10^{18}	2^{60}	exa	E	Greek for six: hexa
10^{15}	2^{50}	peta	P	Greek for five: pente
10^{12}	2^{40}	tera	T	Greek for monster: teras
10^{9}	2^{30}	giga	G	Greek for giant: gigas
10^{6}	2^{20}	mega	M	Greek for large: megas
10^{3}	2^{10}	kilo	k	Greek for thousand: chilioi
10^{-3}		milli	m	Latin for thousand: milli
10^{-6}		micro	μ	Greek for small: mikros
10^{-9}		nano	n	Greek for dwarf: nanos
10^{-12}		pico	p	Spanish for a little: pico
10^{-15}		femto	f	Danish and Norwegian for 15: femten
10^{-18}		atto	a	Danish and Norwegian for 18: atten
10^{-21}		zepto	z	Greek for seven: hepta
10^{-24}		yocto	y	Greek for eight: okto

E.2 Standard ASCII codes

Table E.2			The Standard ASCII Table								
ASCII			ASCII			ASCII			ASCII		
Character	Dec	Hex	Character	Dec	Hex	Character	Dec	Hex	Character	Dec	Hex
nul	0	00	sp	32	20	@	64	40	`	96	60
soh	1	01	!	33	21	A	65	41	a	97	61
stx	2	02	"	34	22	B	66	42	b	98	62
etx	3	03	#	35	23	C	67	43	c	99	63
eot	4	04	$	36	24	D	68	44	d	100	64
enq	5	05	%	37	25	E	69	45	e	101	65
ack	6	06	&	38	26	F	70	46	f	102	66
bel	7	07	'	39	27	G	71	47	g	103	67
bs	8	08	(	40	28	H	72	48	h	104	68
ht	9	09	)	41	29	I	73	49	i	105	69
lf	10	0A	*	42	2A	J	74	4A	j	106	6A
vt	11	0B	+	43	2B	K	75	4B	k	107	6B
ff	12	0C	'	44	2C	L	76	4C	l	108	6C
cr	13	0D	-	45	2D	M	77	4D	m	109	6D
so	14	0E	.	46	2E	N	78	4E	n	110	6E
si	15	0F	/	47	2F	O	79	4F	o	111	6F
dle	16	10	0	48	30	P	80	50	p	112	70
dc1	17	11	1	49	31	Q	81	51	q	113	71
dc2	18	12	2	50	32	R	82	52	r	114	72
dc3	19	13	3	51	33	S	83	53	s	115	73
dc4	20	14	4	52	34	T	84	54	t	116	74
nak	21	15	5	53	35	U	85	55	u	117	75
syn	22	16	6	54	36	V	86	56	v	118	76
etb	23	17	7	55	37	W	87	57	w	119	77
can	24	18	8	56	38	X	88	58	x	120	78
em	25	19	9	57	39	Y	89	59	y	121	79
sub	26	1A	:	58	3A	Z	90	5A	z	122	7A
esc	27	1B	;	59	3B	[	91	5B	{	123	7B
fs	28	1C	<	60	3C	\	92	5C	|	124	7C
gs	29	1D	=	61	3D	]	93	5D	}	125	7D
rs	30	1E	>	62	3E	^	94	5E	~	126	7E
us	31	1F	?	63	3F	_	95	5F	del	127	7F

E.3 Powers of 2

Table E.3	Powers of 2	
Amount	Decimal Conversion	Common Abbreviation
2^1	2	—
2^2	4	—
2^3	8	—
2^4	16	—
2^5	32	—
2^6	64	—
2^7	128	—
2^8	256	—
2^9	512	—
2^{10}	1,024	1K
2^{11}	2,048	2K
2^{12}	4,096	4K
2^{13}	8,192	8K
2^{14}	16,384	16K
2^{15}	32,768	32K
2^{16}	65,536	64K
2^{17}	131,072	128K
2^{18}	262,144	256K
2^{19}	544,288	512K
2^{20}	1,048,576	1M
2^{30}	1,073,741,824	1G
2^{32}	4,294,967,296	4G

Solutions to Selected Exercises

Solutions to selected exercises can be found on our website:
http://www.mhhe.com/patt3

APPENDIX

Solutions to Selected
Exercises

Index

m